THIRD EDITION

International
Trade & Investment

THEORY
POLICY
ENTERPRISE

Franklin R. Root
Associate Professor of Multinational Enterprise
The Wharton School
University of Pennsylvania

Published by

S77 **SOUTH-WESTERN PUBLISHING CO.**

CINCINNATI   WEST CHICAGO, ILL.   DALLAS   PELHAM MANOR, N.Y.
BURLINGAME, CALIF.   BRIGHTON, ENGLAND

Printed in the United States of America

PREFACE

International Trade and Investment offers the reader an integrated treatment of theory, policy, and enterprise in international trade and investment. A knowledge and understanding of these interdependent subjects is vital for all those who plan to enter an international business career or work for governments and international organizations in activities that relate to international economic relations. Apart from career interests, anyone who wants to improve his understanding of the world in which he lives is seriously handicapped without an awareness, if not comprehension, of the economic dynamics and policy issues of trade and investment flows among nations.

Theory refers to the body of knowledge that seeks to explain the causal factors which determine the size, composition, and direction of international economic transactions. A grasp of theory enables us to analyze events occurring in the world economy and to evaluate the wisdom of national policies.

Policy encompasses the role of governments in their efforts to regulate, restrict, promote, or otherwise influence the conduct of international trade and investment. A study of national policies brings us to an intersection of international economics and international politics, an amalgam traditionally designated as political economy. This book carries the description and analysis of national policies to a much greater depth than is customary in a basic text, with emphasis on the problems and issues of the 1970's.

Enterprise designates the multinational enterprise, which undertakes production in many countries in pursuit of a global business strategy transcending national jurisdictions. Study of the multinational enterprise brings us face to face with the business firms that are responsible for much of the trade and most of the direct foreign investment in the world economy today.

International economists have traditionally maintained a *macroscopic* perspective of international economic relations by considering trade and investment only at the national level. This macroscopic approach is necessary

iii

but no longer sufficient to explain the behavior of the world economy. Possessing vast resources, multinational companies enjoy a market power that makes them independent actors in the international economic system, forcing changes in national economies and provoking policy responses by governments. Hence, to understand the contemporary world economy we must combine the traditional, macroscopic perspective with a *microscopic* perspective of the multinational enterprise. This text breaks new ground with a systematic presentation of the multinational enterprise as the dominant private institution in international trade and investment.

International Trade and Investment constitutes a major revision of the previous edition. The five chapters in Part Three and Chapter 14 are entirely new; the treatment of monetary reform and the U.S. balance of payments has been expanded from one to two chapters, as is also true of the material concerning the developing countries; and other chapters have been reconstructed with substantial additions of new material. Chapter 1 introduces the reader to the international political, economic, and multinational enterprise systems, examines the distinctive features of international trade and investment, and then considers the national interest in international trade. Chapter 2 takes the reader through many empirical dimensions of world trade to give him a background for later chapters. Part One, which embraces Chapters 3 through 10, covers the theory of trade, the transfer of international payments, foreign exchange rates, the balance of international payments, and the theory of adjustment. Chapters 11 through 20 make up Part Two, which is primarily concerned with government policies in international trade and investment. The instruments and goals of foreign economic policy, trade restrictions, protectionism, exchange control, U.S. commercial policy and GATT, economic integration in Western Europe, the developing countries, the U.S. balance of payments problem, and international monetary reform are taken up in order. Part Three, comprising Chapters 21 through 25, explores the multinational enterprise, which in many ways is the most formidable and controversial institution in contemporary international trade and investment. Each of the principal aspects of the multinational enterprise is described and analyzed: the nature and scope of the multinational enterprise, its empirical dimensions, its role in the world economy, U.S. policy toward the multinational enterprise, and the challenge to national sovereignty posed by the multinational enterprise.

The authorship of a book of this size and coverage carries a long sentence of solitary confinement. Let me take this opportunity, therefore, to thank my wife and children for their amused tolerance of my antisocial behavior over many months. Let me also pay my respects to Roland L. Kramer and Maurice Y. d'Arlin, my colleagues for many years at Wharton, who collaborated with me on two earlier editions of this work.

Franklin R. Root

CONTENTS

INTRODUCTION

What is the international political system? What is the international economic system? What is the multinational enterprise system? What are the distinctive features of international trade and investment? What is the national interest in international trade? What are the empirical dimensions of world trade? What are the empirical dimensions of U.S. trade? These are the principal questions taken up in the first two chapters. Their consideration will prepare us for a more intensive study of the theory, policy, and enterprise of international trade and investment in the remainder of the text.

CHAPTER 1

THE INTERNATIONAL ECONOMY AND THE NATIONAL INTEREST

No nation inhabits an economic vacuum. Its industries, its commerce, its technology, its standard of living, and all the other facets of its economy are related to the economies of foreign nations by complex flows of goods, capital, technology, and enterprise. Every nation must come to terms with this interdependence, and every nation can enlarge the benefits and lessen the costs of interdependence through rational policies. But to do so, nations—individually and collectively—must base their policies on the objective analysis of international economic relations. It is the social function of international economists to develop the concepts and theories that make objective analysis possible.

From a broader perspective, every nation inhabits a global political and social environment as well as a global economic environment.[1] At the immediate, sensational level of perception, the international environment appears as a bewildering sequence of seemingly random events: a coup d'etat occurs in country A, prices rise in country B, the government of country C devalues its exchange rate, the government of country D expropriates a foreign-owned company, and so on. When each event is perceived as a unique, isolated phenomenon unrelated to other phenomena, then it is impossible to understand *why* the event has occurred. To comprehend the international environment, therefore, we must simplify by classifying individual events into groups or categories of events and by tracing out the relationships among these aggregates. In other words, we must construct a *system* that is characterized by defined elements (variables) and their interrelationships that together determine the behavior of the system. We are then able to interpret an event in terms of its place in the system. If the system is a good approximation of the fundamental conditions

---

[1] Ecologists dramatically remind us that every nation also inhabits a global physical environment.

3

and forces actually at work in the world, then we can also predict the consequences of an event with a reasonable degree of confidence. What we have done is to build a model that enables us to comprehend a reality that defies comprehension in the raw.

In our exploration of international economic relations we shall make use of many concepts (such as the nation-state, gross national product, the balance of payments, and multinational enterprise) that bring together diverse phenomena and order them in ways that facilitate analysis. We shall also employ theories that seek to explain *why* the international economy behaves as it does, or how it *should* behave to maximize certain values. However, before proceeding with our study of the international economy, some preliminary remarks are in order about the *international political system*.

THE INTERNATIONAL POLITICAL SYSTEM

Mankind is organized in a society of nation-states. The elemental constituents of a nation-state are a people, a territory, an economy, and a sovereign government. The necessary constituent of statehood is *national sovereignty*.

NATIONAL SOVEREIGNTY

International law recognizes the national government as having exclusive jurisdiction over the territory of the state and as being the only legal representative of the state vis-à-vis other states. The state is not subordinate to any legal authority, and it has the right to abrogate any agreements with other states or with their citizens. Furthermore, national states have a legal monopoly on physical force both at home and abroad. Since states control the entire land surface of the earth, every individual and organization is a legal resident of a particular state and is subject to its authority.[2] Among its other consequences, the principle of national sovereignty raises many problems for international economic cooperation and for multinational enterprises, which operate on the territory of more than one nation.

Although *legally* a state can do as it pleases, its actual conduct in international affairs is constrained by the power of other states. For a very weak state national sovereignty may become a legal fiction even within its own territory.

EXTERNAL RELATIONS OF STATES

Each state seeks to have relations with other states that will sustain or promote its own national interests as they are conceived by government

---

[2] This system of sovereign territorial states was formally established by the Peace Treaty of Westphalia in 1648. At first limited to Europe, it has since spread to encompass the globe. See Joseph Frankel, *International Relations* (New York: Oxford University Press, 1964), p. 7.

leaders. Foremost among these interests is the continuing survival of the state itself; economic growth and development are also prominent interests of contemporary states.

To carry out its foreign policies a state must be able to influence the behavior of other states. In this sense, *power* is the essence of international political relations. The elements of state power include the armed forces, the economy, population, geography, the government, morale, ideology, and other intangible factors. Because of the latter, precise measures of national power are illusory. Moreover, national power is a *relationship* between two or more states that depends, in part, on how each state perceives its own power vis-à-vis others. History affords us many examples of misjudgements by states of their relative power positions.

To say that international political relations are essentially power relations is not to say that they always involve conflict. National governments understand that the achievement of many, if not all, of their foreign policy goals depends on *cooperation* with other governments. States are willing, therefore, to take actions that benefit other states if the latter reciprocate in some measure. Cooperative arrangements among states are highly developed in economic and functional areas, such as trade, finance, communications, and transportation.

Antagonistic relations express a clash of interests between two or more states. When these interests are considered vital, they may limit or destroy other cooperative arrangements. Because of the "cold war," for instance, trade between the United States and the Soviet Union has been restricted to very low levels.

Many international relations are *competitive* rather than cooperative or antagonistic. States exhibit various forms of rivalry that fall short of direct opposition to each other. They compete in economic performance, technological innovation, ideology, cultural achievements, and so on.

To conclude, the external relations of states are essentially power relations that are expressed in changing mixes of cooperation, competition, and antagonism. When account is taken of the existence of some 150 heterogeneous sovereign states, the pattern of international political relations becomes intricate indeed.

NATIONALISM

In the contemporary world, states are also nations. While the state is a political entity, the nation is an ethnic or social entity. When these two entities combine they form a *nation-state*.

The citizens of a nation share a sense of common identity stemming from a common community, history, language, religion, race, or ideology. *Nationalism* is the emotional cement which binds a people together to make a nationality; it is marked by loyalty and devotion to a nation which exalt it above all other nations. At least since the French Revolution in the late eighteenth century, nationalism has been the driving force in the creation of new states. Born in Europe, nationalism was the prime mover in the transformation of European colonies into independent states following World War II and is now being experienced by practically all the world.

In the twentieth century it became a widely accepted principle that each national community merits its own government and political independence. Self-determination, however, has its practical limits. In recent years, several very small states have entered the United Nations although their political and economic viability is highly questionable. At a time when sizeable European states have begun a process of integration to overcome the liabilities of "smallness," the emergence of so many mini-states in the past quarter century is a gross anomaly. The basic principle of self-determination also threatens the stability of older states which contain two or more ethnic groups, as witnessed by the separatist movements in Canada and Belgium. Ironically, many new states in Africa which owe their birth to the principle of national self-determination may eventually founder on divisive tribal loyalties that take precedence over national loyalties. The tragic civil war in Nigeria has emphasized the formidable obstacles to nation building in a multiethnic state.

However, for the most part the states of the world command the loyalties of their peoples and may be accurately depicted as nation-states, namely, "a form of political organization under which a relatively homogeneous people inhabits a sovereign state." [3] Because the citizens of a modern state share a common national society and culture, national boundaries carry a sociocultural significance as well as a political one.

Nationalism injects an emotional energy into international relations, bedeviling cross-national communication and inciting governments to behavior that can undermine the achievement of their own political and economic goals. Encompassing a personal identification with, and a loyalty to, a particular state, nationalism often expresses negative attitudes toward other states. But nationalism is also a cultural phenomenon. Even before the emergence of nation-states, ethnic and tribal groups held attitudes toward other groups, ranging from xenophobia (a hatred and fear of all foreigners) to, at times, cosmopolitanism (a sophisticated, open view of foreigners). Today, nationalistic attitudes toward economic relations with foreigners animate many government policies that restrict international trade and investment. When, for example, a business enterprise starts operations in a foreign country, its reception by the government and people will depend in substantial measure on the blend of nationalism which predominates there.

INTERNATIONAL ORGANIZATIONS

Cooperation among nation-states has led to the creation of many international organizations for both political and economic purposes. Although

---

[3] *Webster's Seventh New Collegiate Dictionary* (Springfield, Mass.: G. and C. Merriam Company, 1969).

these organizations seldom have any explicit supranational powers, they may gain an institutional strength over time that enables them to influence the behavior of individual states to a significant degree. Hence, they may assume an autonomous international role which makes them "actors" in the international political and economic systems along with the nation-states. For example, the policies of the International Monetary Fund (IMF) and the International Bank for Reconstruction and Development (IBRD) are more than a simple consensus of the national policies of their member states. Even more impressive in this regard is the European Economic Community.

Summing up, the international political system comprises some 150 sovereign nation-states and their mutual power relations, which may be characterized as cooperative, competitive, or antagonistic. Nationalism, which generally carries an antiforeign bias, adds an emotional tone to the foreign policies of nation-states, making them less cooperative than would otherwise be the case. On the other hand, some international organizations have emerged as autonomous (or quasi-autonomous) actors in the international political system along with the nation-states.

THE INTERNATIONAL ECONOMIC SYSTEM

Every nation-state has an economy, and the mutual relations among national economies constitute the *international economic system*. Just as the distinguishing feature of the political relations among states is power, the distinguishing feature of their economic relations is *market transactions*. With the rather modest exception of unilateral transfers ("gifts"), international economic relations result from the exchange of assets having market value. The sum of a nation's economic transactions with the rest of the world over a period of time is recorded in its balance of payments. Transactions give rise to flows of merchandise, services, money, capital, technology, and enterprise, thereby creating patterns of interdependence among national economies. Shifts in the size and direction of these flows which are initiated in one national economy will affect, directly or indirectly, the behavior of other national economies. The economic theory that explains *why* these flows occur and *how* national economies as a whole interact with the world economy is the subject of Part One.

Contemporary nation-states, however, are not willing to allow their international economic relations to be determined *only* by the market forces we shall analyze in Part One. All national governments have foreign economic policies which are intended to regulate, restrict, promote, or otherwise influence international trade and investment. The description and evaluation of these policies is taken up in Part Two.

The relative importance of noneconomic or political factors in the determination of foreign economic policies varies from one nation-state to another. However, we can loosely classify countries into two groups in that regard. International transactions of the *industrial countries* (mainly North America, Western Europe, and Japan) and of the *developing countries* (mainly Africa, Asia, and Latin America) are predominantly undertaken by *private business firms,* most notably in the form of multinational enterprises. Because the motivation behind these transactions is economic gain, the trade and investment flows among these countries are mainly explicable in economic terms. Nonetheless, government policies in these countries both constrain and stimulate international economic transactions so as to bring about a divergence from the pattern of interdependence which would result from purely market forces.

The second group comprises the *centrally planned countries* (mainly Eastern Europe, the Soviet Union, and Mainland China), which, in accordance with Communist ideology, outlaw private enterprise. All foreign economic transactions are conducted by *state enterprises,* whose decisions are guided by national economic plans and foreign policy. Hence, the international economic relations of the Communist countries are highly "politicized." Although state-trading organizations may choose to maximize economic values (behaving like private firms), they can also choose to behave as purely political organizations, ignoring economic gain.

It is fruitless to speculate in the abstract on whether international economic relations determine international political relations (as the Marxists contend) or whether international political relations determine international economic relations. International economic and political relations are interdependent; both the international economic and political systems are best regarded as subsystems of the same nation-state system. In some circumstances, political forces may dominate economic forces, while in other circumstances the converse may hold. One thing, however, is certain: whenever a government considers the behavior of some or all of its country's international economic transactions as vital to national interests, it will try to make that behavior conform to those interests.

THE MULTINATIONAL ENTERPRISE SYSTEM

International economists have traditionally maintained a *macroscopic perspective* on international economic relations. By considering trade and investment only on the national level they have implicitly regarded national economies to be the *agents* of international transactions. Although we shall rely on the macroscopic (or national) perspective in Parts One and Two, we must recognize that this perspective is necessary but no longer sufficient to explain the behavior of the international economy. Multinational enterprises have become responsible for a sizeable (and increasing) share of world trade and for most international investment. As big, oligopolistic companies, multinational enterprises possess a market power that makes them independent actors in the international economic system. Unlike firms in purely competitive markets, multinational enterprises enjoy managerial discretion in their decisions; they do not simply respond to market conditions and public policies in a predetermined way. Indeed, their actions force changes in national economies and compel governments to respond to them. Thus, to understand the contemporary international economy we must supplement a macroscopic perspective with a *microscopic* perspective which considers the role of the multinational enterprise. This is the task of Part Three, and here we make only a few additional comments on this subject.

A firm becomes a multinational enterprise when it extends its production and organization into foreign countries.[4] The *multinational enterprise system,* therefore, consists of a parent company, its producing and marketing affiliates in foreign countries, and the flows of products, services, capital, technology, management, and funds among them. These *intraenterprise transfers* (flows) cross national boundaries and therefore enter the balance of payments of nations in the same way as international transactions between independent buyers and sellers.

Although it has roots in the past, the multinational enterprise has become a dominant institution only in the last decade. Since the late 1950's, the political and economic systems of the industrial West (primarily the North Atlantic region) have favored the spread of international production by corporations in search of market opportunity. As a consequence, the traditional *international* economy of traders is giving way to a *world* economy of international producers. Our comprehension of this world economy is modest indeed; economists have yet to develop a satisfactory theory of the multinational enterprise. Part Three, therefore, will be an exploration of new terrain in international economic relations.

DISTINCTIVE FEATURES OF INTERNATIONAL TRADE AND INVESTMENT

The distinctive features of international trade and investment are traceable to the environment in which they occur—the nation-state system and its political, sociocultural, and economic subsystems. In particular, national sovereignty is the ultimate source of most of the differences that distinguish international trade and investment from their domestic counterparts. As we have already indicated some of the implications of these environmental systems for international trade and investment, this section is partly a recapitulation of our earlier discussion.

DIFFERENT LANGUAGES AND CUSTOMS

Most nations have a distinctive linguistic and cultural identity in addition to a basic political identity. This is not always true; we can all call to mind nations that have more than one official language and more than one cultural group in their populations. Moreover, several nations may share a common language and a common cultural heritage. Nevertheless, it is true that people tend to be like each other in more ways when they belong

---

[4] For a fuller definition, see Chapter 21.

to the same nation than when they belong to different nations. Hence, international trade and investment, unlike most interregional trade and investment within nations, involve persons of different languages, customs, attitudes, values, and other cultural traits. Although such differences do not affect the basic economic similarity between interregional and international trade and investment, they do complicate relations between governments and introduce many new elements into the conduct of international business enterprise. As noted earlier, nationalism intensifies the sociocultural differences among the world's peoples.

SEPARATE NATIONAL ECONOMIC POLICIES

National economic policies may be compatible with the free flow of merchandise, services, and enterprise between nations or they may be responsible for the regulation and suppression of that flow. As we shall discover, national economic policies that are apparently wholly domestic in nature may have profound effects on international trade and investment. To maintain an equilibrium in its international payments without resort to controls, a nation must keep its economy adjusted to the world economy. This means, for example, that it must pursue fiscal and monetary policies which keep its prices and costs competitive with those of other nations. It also means that there is sometimes a conflict between the aims of domestic policy and international adjustment. Because of political pressures this conflict is often resolved in favor of the former, while international maladjustment is frozen by the imposition of controls over foreign trade and payments.

When certain nations adopt domestic policies that are detrimental to their external stability, all trading nations suffer the consequences. For the international economy to function in an atmosphere of freedom there must be agreement among nations as to the criteria of sound domestic and international economic policies. It too often happens, however, that nations follow policies that are conceived in purely domestic terms, and the resulting welter of policies causes international maladjustments that are met by a rash of restrictive measures. Unlike domestic trade and investment, therefore, international trade and investment is subject to the influence of many separate national economic policies that are often in disharmony with each other.

One consequence of separate national policies is jurisdictional overlap. Thus, for instance, a multinational enterprise may be taxed on the same income by two governments (double taxation). More generally, the enterprise may be subjected to the conflicting demands of both home and host governments in any number of policy areas.

NATIONAL MONETARY SYSTEMS

Unlike their domestic counterparts, international trade and investment take place between economies that have different monetary systems. This gives rise to the need to exchange one currency for another at an agreed ratio. The purchase and sale of foreign currency is conducted in the foreign exchange market, and the exchange ratio between currencies is known as the *exchange rate*. Dealings in foreign exchange often appear mysterious to the layman, and perhaps more than anything else, except nationalism, they have convinced him that international trade and investment are entirely distinct from the familiar domestic trade and investment. Even some domestic producers have been daunted by the prospect of dealings in foreign exchange until relieved by the calm advice and aid of bankers.

Actually the presence of different monetary systems need not alter the character of international trade and investment from that of their domestic counterparts. When exchange rates are stable and currencies are freely convertible into each other, international payments are just as easily made as are domestic payments. In these circumstances the national monetary systems comprise one international monetary system, and for all practical purposes they are one and the same. Before World War I such an international monetary system did in fact exist. National currencies were linked to gold and were freely transferable into each other; an international payment was no different from a domestic payment except that the former involved residents of different countries.

Today the situation is far different, and international trade and investment are sharply set off from domestic trade and investment by the restrictions imposed by many governments on transactions in foreign exchange and by variations in foreign exchange rates. Although the currencies of the industrial countries (mainly North America, Western Europe, and Japan) are for the most part freely convertible at stable rates, the currencies of most nonindustrial countries and of all Communist countries are inconvertible in one way or another and the exchange rates of the former are also frequently unstable. Currency inconvertibility can have profound effects on the conduct of international trade and investment. An importer may not be able to buy merchandise from the country of his choice because he cannot buy the necessary foreign exchange from his government. He may be compelled, therefore, to import inferior or higher priced goods from a country to which he is permitted to make payments. When currencies are freely convertible but unstable, foreign traders and investors may suffer exchange losses unless they can hedge against them. We should remember, however, that it is more the exercise of national sovereignty to restrict international payments or vary exchange rates than the mere presence of national monetary systems that is a distinctive feature of international trade and investment.

GOVERNMENT REGULATION OF INTERNATIONAL TRADE AND INVESTMENT

Governments have interfered with international trade and investment ever since the beginnings of the nation-state system some five hundred years ago. Even during the last half of the nineteenth century, when the majority of governments followed a policy of laissez-faire with respect to domestic economic activities, the use of tariff protection was commonplace. Great Britain and the Netherlands were the only important trading nations that rid themselves of protective tariffs and adopted free trade in that period of liberal economic policies. Since World War I all nations without exception have regulated their foreign trade and investment and have done so with many new control devices in addition to the traditional tariff.

As noted previously, many contemporary governments restrict the convertibility of their currencies. This is known as *exchange control* and allows a comprehensive regulation of the international movement not only of merchandise but of services and capital as well. Commodity trade is also regulated through quotas, licenses, tariffs, bilateral trading arrangements, commodity agreements, and other techniques. Restrictions are generally applied against imports, while exports may be stimulated by subsidies, exchange depreciation, bilateral agreements, and other methods. Mention should also be made of the fact that government regulation involves a great deal of red tape and bureaucratic delay that are often a potent deterrent to trade and to the entry of foreign firms.

THE INTERNATIONAL MOBILITY
OF FACTORS OF PRODUCTION

In the nineteenth century, classical economists distinguished international trade from domestic trade by the criterion of factor mobility. It was assumed that the factors of production—natural resources, capital, management, and labor—moved freely within a country but did not move between countries. For this reason international trade obeyed laws of economic behavior that differed from those of domestic trade.

As the nineteenth century progressed, these twin assumptions of perfect factor *mobility* within countries and perfect factor *immobility* between countries came more and more into conflict with the facts of economic life. Neoclassical economists observed that factors of production often do not move freely from one place to another inside the same country and, on the other hand, that a substantial migration of capital was proceeding from Europe to the other continents. Economists came to agree, therefore, that a sharp distinction between domestic interregional trade and international trade could not be drawn in terms of factor mobility. Rather, *both* kinds of trade were based on factor immobilities; that is, trade was a substitute for investment and other factor movements.

In the absence of political restrictions on the international movement of capital, enterprise, and persons, it is likely that factor mobility between countries would still be somewhat less than factor mobility within countries. International differences in customs and languages, distance, and the like would work in this direction. Under these circumstances no one would argue that factor movements between countries were essentially different from factor movements within countries. In actuality, as we all know, they *are* different; for nations throughout the world restrict immigration (and sometimes emigration) as well as the movement of capital and enterprise. Thus, the exercise of national sovereignty has greatly limited the international mobility of productive factors, and in so doing it has altered the scope and character of international trade and investment. At the same time, the multinational enterprise has remarkably accelerated the flow of factor services among countries in the last decade.

To conclude, although the international mobility of factors tends to be less (and in the case of ordinary labor, much less) than their domestic mobility, the degree of factor mobility does not provide a *fundamental* distinction between domestic and international trade. It follows that international economic theory must encompass both trade flows and factor flows (mainly *via* the multinational enterprise) if it is to explain the behavior of the contemporary world economy.

THE NATIONAL INTEREST IN INTERNATIONAL TRADE

What is the national interest in international trade? This question has colored many debates down through the ages, and it will undoubtedly continue to do so in the future. In closing this introductory chapter we offer some preliminary remarks on the gains from trade at the levels of the nation, consumer, international business enterprise, and domestic import-competing enterprise.[5] We shall leave to Part Three a consideration of the national interest in international investment and the national interest as it relates to the multinational enterprise.

THE NATIONAL GAINS FROM INTERNATIONAL TRADE

Although conceivably a nation might have a sufficient variety of productive factors to produce every kind of good and service, it would not be able to produce each good and service with equal facility. The United States *could* produce hand-woven rugs, but only at a high cost since the production of such rugs requires great quantities of labor, which is expensive in this country. The production of hand-woven rugs, however, would afford a reasonable employment for the large supply of cheap labor in a country like India. It would be advantageous for the United States, therefore, to specialize in a commodity such as trucks, whose production makes use of the abundant supply of capital in this country, and to export trucks in exchange for hand-woven rugs from India.

This example illustrates in a very simple way the gains that result from international specialization—each nation is able to utilize its productive

---

[5] The discussion of the basis and gains of international trade in the following subsections is introductory to the detailed analysis of Chapters 3, 4, and 5.

factors in their most productive combinations. By raising the productivity of national economies, international specialization increases the output of goods and services. This is its economic justification and the justification of the international trade that makes possible such specialization.

The contribution of international trade is so immense that few countries could become self-sufficient even with the greatest effort. Contemporary economies have been shaped by the international trade and specialization of the past, and their continued viability is closely dependent on the world economy. For example, it is physically impossible for the United Kingdom and Japan to feed, clothe, and house their present populations without imports from other countries. Economic self-sufficiency for these two nations would mean mass starvation and poverty standards of living unless emigration proved possible on a very large scale. The survival of these countries depends essentially on the export of manufactures that require little space to produce in exchange for foodstuffs and raw materials which require great space to produce or are found in only certain areas of the earth.

The United Kingdom and Japan are examples of high dependence on international trade. But even countries that are able to supply their own peoples with the basic necessities of life out of domestic production would be faced with an unbearable decline in living standards if they were cut off from international trade.[6] New Zealand produces far more foodstuffs than are needed to nourish its sparse population, and it is able to trade this surplus for manufactures with industrial countries like the United Kingdom and Japan. Hence, for New Zealand economic self-sufficiency would not mean starvation but rather the deprivation of manufactured goods that are necessary to sustain its current standard of living. Of course, New Zealand could produce some manufactures to take the place of imports, but its efforts in that direction would be limited by its scarce supplies of labor, capital, and industrial raw materials. The New Zealand economy is itself the product of international specialization and trade, and a far different and poorer economy would have evolved in the absence of world markets.

The United States, with its continental sweep and immense resources, could afford economic self-sufficiency with the least cost of any nation, with the possible exception of the Soviet Union. Perhaps this explains why, far more than other peoples, Americans are inclined to underestimate the importance of international trade.

But even for this country, the cost of self-sufficiency would be formidable. American consumers would experience an immediate pinch in their standards of living. An entire range of foodstuffs would no longer be available or would be available only at exorbitant prices. That American institution—the cup of coffee—would become a luxury to all but a few, and most of us would be forced to do without our daily stimulant or to use

---

[6] Much of the decline in living standards during a war is due to the cessation of international trade, as illustrated by the experience of neutral countries such as Sweden and Switzerland in World War II.

inferior substitutes. Even then, the sugar for our beverage would be an expensive item.

As regards basic foodstuffs, we should, of course, have a plentiful supply. In fact, we would become embarrassed by growing stockpiles of agricultural products as farmers lost export outlets for one-fourth of their wheat crop, one-third of their cotton crop, and large fractions of many other crops. Eventually many farmers would be ruined, and the agricultural sector of our economy would become less important.

Manufacturing industries would also face many difficulties. Without imports, many raw materials would no longer be available and inferior substitutes would replace them. Domestic supplies of other raw materials would no longer be supplemented by imports and their prices would rise to increase costs of production all along the line. The loss of export markets would also cause severe dislocations in many manufacturing industries.

Thus, the outcome of economic self-sufficiency for the United States would be a noticeable decline in the American standard of living. Only those producers in direct competition with imports would benefit from self-sufficiency, but the improvement in their fortunes would be purchased at the cost of a general deterioration in the economic well-being of most Americans. Because of the rising dependence on imports of raw materials (particularly petroleum), the national interest of the United States in foreign trade will grow in the future: more than at any time in the past our economic prosperity in the years ahead must rest upon an expanding world economy.

DOMESTIC SPECIALIZATION AND
INTERREGIONAL TRADE

The gains from specialization that are possible through international trade are fundamentally of the same nature as the gains from specialization achieved by interregional trade *within* a country. The distinctive features of international trade originate, for the most part, in the political fact of national sovereignty—not in economic conditions. Basically, trade within a country is identical with trade between countries. Both derive from the fact that individual regions and countries can gain through trade by specializing in the production of those goods and services that utilize the most productive combinations of their natural resources, labor, capital, management, and technology.

At the present time over half of the foreign trade of Western European countries is with each other. If these countries should one day federate and become one nation, this trade would become interregional rather than international, but its virtues would be neither greater nor less by reason of that change alone.[7] International trade and interregional trade are

---

[7] Undoubtedly trade between European countries would expand greatly if these nations merged into one political unit, since the restraints now imposed on this trade by individual governments would disappear. But this would not make interregional trade any "better" than international trade. See Chapter 16.

substitutes for each other. Thus, the explanation of the *relatively* small foreign trade of the United States is found in the vast interregional trade within its borders.

We readily comprehend the great advantages of regional specialization within the domestic economy. Nationalism may blind us to the gains from international trade, but it does not stand in the way of our appreciation of domestic trade. It is true that local producers and merchants may seek to turn consumers away from products "imported" from other domestic regions, but these efforts are largely wasted since localities and regions do not have the authority to impose restrictions on interregional trade.[8] Moreover, almost all of us consider the national economy to be a single economy rather than an agglomeration of regional economies, and we oppose any interference with trade in the domestic market.

To illustrate, we should view as absurd a petition by New England textile producers requesting the federal government to impose restrictions on the sale of textiles produced in the South. We might sympathize with the plight of several New England communities as their chief industry shut its doors and headed south, but we should feel that such a situation is bound to occur now and then in a competitive economy and that in the long run everyone benefits by having goods and services produced in those places where costs are at a minimum. When, however, those same producers demand protection against imports of textiles from Japan, their appeal sounds reasonable to many of us despite the fact that the economic issue is the same; namely, whether domestic consumers are to have the right to purchase lower-cost textiles made in the South or in Japan.

To conclude, recognition of the basic similarity of interregional and international trade is essential to a proper understanding of the latter. That recognition will keep us from reaching the erroneous conclusion that, because of the many characteristics which distinguish international trade, it is a unique sort of trade and must be treated differently from domestic trade. Widespread awareness that the gains from international trade rest upon the same economic conditions as do the gains from domestic trade would eradicate much of the confusion and downright falsity that envelop public discussions of matters pertaining to our trade with other nations.

THE INTEREST OF CONSUMERS

As consumers all of us have an interest in international trade, although we are usually unaware of the influence of international trade on the prices, quality, and availability of goods. Goods are imported only because they are less expensive than domestic goods or are differentiated from them in

---

[8] Interstate trade barriers are forbidden by the United States Constitution. Despite this fact, individual states do restrain interstate trade in certain products (mostly agricultural) through a variety of devices ostensibly employed for other purposes, such as pest control and public safety. Arrangements between domestic producers to restrain interstate trade are forbidden by the antitrust laws.

one way or another. U.S. imports of textiles from Hong Kong and television sets from Japan are examples of the first type of imports, while imports of bananas from Guatemala, perfumes from France, beer from Denmark, and automobiles from West Germany are examples of the second type of imports. Without such imports the American consumer would pay a higher price for textiles and television sets and would not have the opportunity to enjoy bananas, Chanel perfumes, Carlsberg beer, and the Volkswagen "beetle."

Imports of raw materials and other industrial goods likewise benefit the consumer by lowering domestic costs of production and in some instances enabling the production of goods that depend exclusively on foreign sources of supply. The consumer also has an interest in domestic exports since they provide the means to pay for imports. Hence, as consumers we all benefit from the greater abundance and variety of goods and the lower prices that international trade makes possible.

The contribution of international trade to the welfare of domestic consumers is the most basic of all. The end of economic activity is consumption; production is only a means to that end. A policy of production for the sake of production or of employment for the sake of employment ignores the fundamental reason for economic activity. For this reason economists have usually identified the national economic interest with the economic well-being of a nation's people. It follows that a policy or economic activity that adds to the supply of goods and services that people wish to consume is a policy or activity in the national interest. Contrariwise, a policy or economic activity that brings about a level of national consumption that is below the level attainable by an alternative policy or activity is not in the national interest. This criterion of national interest may be modified to take account of illegal production, consumption harmful to health, the need to refrain from current domestic consumption in order to promote economic growth, and the like, but it differs from other criteria of national interest in its emphasis on consumer welfare. Of course, when a nation is at war the aim of national survival takes precedence over consumer welfare or any other objective.

When we employ the criterion of consumer welfare to decide whether international trade is in the national interest, we find that it benefits the nation by increasing the supply of goods and services available for domestic consumption. Moreover, all trading nations gain from international trade. This gain rests squarely on the specialization that arises from the opportunity to buy and sell in foreign markets.

THE INTEREST OF INTERNATIONAL BUSINESS ENTERPRISES

The value of international trade to the manufacturers, extractive producers, middlemen, transportation agencies, financial institutions, and other enterprises that engage in international trade is easily understood. Simply stated, international trade is a source of income and profits.

Domestic producers gain from international trade in many ways. They depend upon imports to meet their industrial needs of raw materials and productive equipment at a lower cost than the same items can be acquired from domestic sources of supply. Exports afford domestic producers a profit on sales and they often make possible a larger scale of production with lower unit costs. Imports and exports, moreover, tend to moderate fluctuations in the supply, demand, and prices of individual goods. Sudden shifts in the availability of domestic raw materials may be offset by opposing shifts in raw material imports, and producers with substantial sales abroad are less sensitive to purely domestic economic conditions compared to producers in the same industries who dispose of their entire output at home.

A domestic concern may further find in export markets a means of additional growth that enables it to compete more effectively in the home market. Often the knowledge and experience gained from selling in foreign markets can be used to improve the efficiency and success of domestic marketing operations. In short, international trade allows domestic producers to escape the confines of the domestic market through imports that lower costs of production or improve the quality of the product, and through exports that enhance sales and profits. For the multinational enterprise, international trade offers opportunities to link multicountry production bases with markets throughout the world.

International trade cannot be carried on by producers alone. Many specialized middlemen and agencies are needed to conduct and facilitate its operations. This is particularly true of merchandise trade: the merchandise must be bought and sold; transportation services must be provided by railroads, ships, trucks, airplanes, and other agencies; international shipments must be insured, financed, and paid for; customs and other government requirements must be met; exports must be stimulated through advertising and other promotion devices; and so on. Specialized middlemen and agencies are also needed in the field of international investment, in the tourist trade, and in other nonmerchandise transactions of an international character. All of the many business concerns involved in carrying out these functions have a direct stake in international trade. When international trade is booming, they experience expansion and profits. Conversely, when international trade enters a slump, these concerns are the first to suffer losses.

THE INTEREST OF IMPORT-COMPETING ENTERPRISES

The contribution of international trade to the many business enterprises involved cannot automatically be identified with the national interest since other groups are also part of the national economy. Domestic producers who face close competition from imports may be injured by an expansion of international trade. Moreover, the labor used by such producers may suffer from unemployment or lower wages as a consequence of import competition. The adverse effects of import competition are particularly noticeable when import-competing industries are concentrated in specific localities. In measuring the national gain from international trade, therefore, the losses experienced by these groups must be set against the benefits received by other groups.

It must not be supposed, however, that the losses experienced by domestic producers and others hurt by import competition are permanent. In an expanding economy, labor, capital, and management are able to shift out of stagnant lines of production into more productive lines. Indeed, one of the virtues of a competitive economy lies in its flexibility in adjusting production to meet new technologies, new demands, and new competition—domestic or foreign.

SOME ARGUMENTS AGAINST INTERNATIONAL TRADE

In spite of the economic gain for the nation, many arguments have been voiced against international trade, some of which are stated below.

1. A nation dependent on foreign sources of supply is in a particularly vulnerable position during a war.
2. International trade is a source of instability and interferes with economic planning.
3. International trade creates losses for those domestic industries whose products are displaced by imports.

International specialization brings to a nation a higher standard of living, but it also implies dependence on foreign markets as sources of supply and as outlets for domestic production. Some persons contemplate this dependence with marked distaste and argue that the national interest demands that it be lessened to one degree or another. The aversion toward international specialization is rationalized in many ways, and it often camouflages the interests of private groups that stand to gain from the removal of import competition. The most important ally of attacks against international specialization and trade is nationalism—the ideology that holds the nation-state to be the *only* source of political and economic security.

National Defense. It is argued that a nation dependent on foreign sources of supply is in a particularly vulnerable position during a war. The harrowing experience of the United Kingdom in both World Wars is cited as proof of this assertion—twice the German submarine blockade almost brought that country to her knees by cutting off imports of food and raw materials. This is, of course, a political or military argument rather than an economic one, but it has many economic implications. Its proper evaluation requires not only a careful forecast of the probable nature of a future war but a searching study of the relationships between economic strength and military capacity as well. For example, if another world war promises destruction of everyone's productive facilities within a few hours, then it is military strength in being that counts and the military argument for economic self-sufficiency falls by the wayside.

In conclusion, there is no assurance that greater economic self-sufficiency will enhance a nation's military power, and by the same token there is no justification to deny out of hand the compatibility of international specialization and a nation's ability to defend itself against armed aggression.

Instability and Economic Planning. International trade is also condemned as a source of economic instability. This attitude gained prominence in the 1930's when depression spread from one country to another by disrupting the international flow of goods, services, and capital. In particular, foreign observers were wont to protest the folly of close dependence on such a volatile economy as that of the United States. In our own day this argument against international trade has been reinforced by government policies directed toward full employment and economic development. To many economic planners, foreign trade is a nuisance unless carefully controlled to fit the master economic plan. This is not the place to evaluate the bearing of international trade and investment on domestic stability, employment, and economic development, but it may be pointed out that most nations are unable to achieve the objectives of full employment and economic development except as members of a world trading system.

Protectionism. Traditionally, the attacks against foreign trade have been leveled against imports. Several arguments in addition to those already mentioned have been used to justify the protection of domestic industry against foreign competition. These arguments are described and analyzed in Chapter 13, and we shall say nothing about them here except to indicate that insofar as protectionism lowers a nation's imports, it also eventually lowers a nation's exports (unless the protectionist country loans or gives away its exports) since other nations must finance their imports through their exports.

The roll call of arguments against international specialization and trade is indeed a formidable one—national security, economic stability, full employment, economic development, economic planning, protectionism, and others of lesser note. All of these arguments pack a powerful emotional appeal to the man on the street. Nevertheless, international trade exhibits a vitality and growth that is difficult to reconcile with its alleged disadvantages. It would appear that the supreme economic advantages of international specialization and trade, when weighed against the supreme economic costs of national self-sufficiency, cannot be denied by nationalistic fervor or the special pleading of private vested interests.

SUMMARY

1. Every nation inhabits a global political and social environment, as well as a global economic environment. To comprehend this international environment,

we must simplify by classifying individual events into groups or categories of events and by tracing out the relationships among these aggregates. In other words, we must construct analytical systems.

2. Mankind is organized in a society of nation-states. The elemental constituents of a nation-state are a people, a territory, an economy, and a sovereign government. The principle of national sovereignty gives each national government exclusive jurisdiction over the national territory and makes it the only legal representative of the nation vis-à-vis other nations. The external *political* relations of nation-states are essentially power relations which are expressed in changing mixes of cooperation, competition, and antagonism. The *international political system* comprises some 150 sovereign nation-states and their mutual power relations. Nationalism makes nation-states less cooperative than would otherwise be the case.

3. Every nation-state has an economy, and the mutual relations among national economies constitute the *international economic system.* With the modest exception of gifts, international economic relations result from *transactions,* the exchange of assets having market value. The sum of a nation's economic transactions with the rest of the world over a period of time is recorded in its balance of payments.

4. It is fruitless to speculate in the abstract on whether international economic relations determine international political relations, or vice versa. International economic and political relations are interdependent; both the international economic and political systems are best regarded as subsystems of the same nation-state system.

5. Although we shall rely on the macroscopic (or national) perspective in Parts One and Two, we must recognize that this perspective is necessary but no longer sufficient to explain the behavior of the international economy. Multinational enterprises have become responsible for a sizeable (and increasing) share of world trade and for most international investment. The *multinational enterprise system* consists of a parent company, its producing and marketing affiliates in foreign countries, and the flows of products, services, capital, technology, management, and funds among them. Hence, *intra-enterprise transfers* characterize this system.

6. The distinctive features of international trade and investment—different languages and customs, separate national economic policies, national monetary systems, government regulations, and the lower mobility of the factors of production—are traceable to the nation-state system and its subsystems.

7. The contribution of international trade is so immense that few countries could become self-sufficient even with the greatest effort. Even the United States would find the costs of self-sufficiency formidable. The gains from international specialization are fundamentally of the same nature as the gains from domestic interregional specialization. Thus, international trade and interregional trade are basically the same, and the distinctive features of international trade are largely owing to the political fact of national sovereignty.

8. The interest of domestic consumers is benefited by international trade because it lowers the prices of goods and makes available goods that

cannot be produced at home. If we agree that the proper end of economic activity is consumption, then we should agree that the interest of consumers in international trade is identical with the national interest. National welfare is enhanced by international trade because the latter permits international specialization that leads to a more productive use of the natural resources, capital, and labor of nations.

9. It is easy to understand the contribution of international trade to the business enterprises that are engaged in the export and import of merchandise, services, and capital. They are interested in international trade as a source of income and profits. On the other hand, the interest of management, labor, and capital employed in domestic industries in close competition with imports from abroad may be injured by an expansion of international trade. It must be noted, however, that such injury is one of the costs of a competitive economic system.

10. There are several arguments against international specialization and trade —national security, economic stability, full employment, economic development, protection of domestic industries, and so on. Nevertheless, the advantages of international trade are so great that it exhibits vitality and growth.

QUESTIONS AND APPLICATIONS

1. What is a nation-state? What is the nation-state system? Compare the United States and four other nation-states of your own choosing in terms of territory, population, and gross national product.

2. Define the international political system. What is intended by the statement: "International political relations are essentially power relations"?

3. What is nationalism? Cite five cases of nationalism which have appeared in recent issues of *The New York Times* or other newspapers.

4. Define the international economic system. What is an economic transaction?

5. Why is a macroscopic or national perspective necessary but no longer sufficient to explain the behavior of the international economy? What is the multinational enterprise system?

6. What are the distinctive features of international trade and investment? Why are they distinctive?

7. What is the national interest in international trade? Why do we assert that the interest of consumers is identical with the national interest?

8. Which of the arguments against international trade presented in Chapter 1 do you consider the most formidable? Why?

SELECTED READINGS

Haberler, Gottfried. "Integration and Growth of the World Economy in Historical Perspective." *American Economic Review* (March, 1964).

Polk, Judd. "The New World Economy." *Columbia Journal of World Business* (January-February, 1968).

CHAPTER 2

THE DIMENSIONS OF WORLD TRADE

In its broadest sense international trade covers not only trade in merchandise but in services as well. The value of merchandise exports and imports, however, far exceeds the value of international service transactions. In this chapter we offer a statistical overview of merchandise trade in the world economy, leaving until Chapter 22 a similar overview of direct foreign investment which encompasses the international transfer of *factor* services, namely, capital, management, and technology. The reader will become acquainted with the full range of international transactions in Chapter 8 when we describe the balance of international payments.

As indicated, the approach of Chapter 2 is mainly statistical. We offer quantitative measures of different aspects of world trade with particular emphasis on the position of the United States. In so doing, our intent is to disclose important economic relationships that have a far greater significance than individual economic aggregates considered in isolation. These relationships are often the consequence of developments working slowly over decades, and they exhibit a degree of stability that contrasts with the ever-changing levels of international trade and its components.

VALUE AND VOLUME OF WORLD TRADE

World trade is enormous even by American standards. In 1970 world merchandise exports (excluding exports of the nonmarket Communist countries) were almost $280 billion—an amount equal to approximately three-tenths the U.S. gross national product and nearly three times the British gross national product. The vast size of world trade is also suggested by a comparison with the personal consumption of durable and nondurable goods in the United States, which was $353 billion in 1970.

Table 2-1 shows the dollar values of world exports for selected years since 1913. These dollar values, however, cannot be used to measure the growth of world trade, particularly over a long period of years, because of changes in price levels. Between 1913 and 1970 the general price level of merchandise entering international trade more than doubled—mainly the consequence of inflation bred by two world wars only partially offset by the deflation of the 1930's. To trace changes in the *volume* of world trade since 1913, therefore, we must remove the effects of price level changes. This is done by calculating an index of quantum (volume) of world exports. The export quantum index in Table 2-1, based on 1963, indicates that the volume of world exports (and thus imports) rose from 32 in 1913 to 182 in 1970, or somewhat less than fivefold. This contrasts with the thirteenfold increase in dollar values from $19.8 billion to $277.9 billion over the same period.

Table 2-1

WORLD TRADE OF MARKET ECONOMIES: DOLLAR EXPORTS, QUANTUM EXPORTS, AND WORLD INDUSTRIAL PRODUCTION

Year	Exports (Billions of Dollars)	Index of Quantum of Exports (1963 = 100)	Index of World Industrial Production * (1963 = 100)
1913	19.8	32	23
1928	32.7	41	33**
1938	20.6	38	31
1948	52.7	39	44
1958	94.4	71	70
1964	151.3	110	103
1970	277.9	182	159

Sources: W. S. Woytinsky and E. S. Woytinsky, *World Commerce and Governments* (New York: Twentieth Century Fund, 1955). United Nations, *Monthly Bulletin of Statistics* (New York: United Nations, various issues).
Note: Data from 1948 to the present do not include the centrally planned economies of the Communist countries (U.S.S.R., East Germany, Bulgaria, Rumania, Albania, Czechoslovakia, Hungary, Poland, Mainland China, North Korea, and North Vietnam). However, these data do include Cuba.
* Mining, manufacturing, electricity, gas, and water.
** 1929.

The growth in world trade since 1913 has not been steady. Both the value and volume of trade fell greatly in the early 1930's—the volume of world exports in 1932 was only four-fifths the volume of 1928. Even in 1938 the volume of world trade was less than in 1928 and was not notably higher than in 1913. Since World War II, however, there has occurred a remarkable upsurge of world trade, and in 1970 the volume of exports was far above the level of 1938.

INTERNATIONAL TRADE AND INDUSTRIAL PRODUCTION

Table 2-1 also suggests a relationship between the volume of world trade and world industrial production. Between 1913 and 1970 the volume of industrial production rose by almost 600 percent while the volume of trade rose by almost 500 percent. The higher growth rate for industrial production is mostly traceable to the years during and preceding World War

II. Since 1948 the increase in the volume of world trade has outpaced that of industrial production—367 percent compared to 261 percent.

The relationship between industrial production and international trade is not fortuitous. As we shall observe later in the chapter, most of the world's trade is generated by the industrial countries. When the economies of these countries experience a rapid growth, international trade is stimulated and also expanded; conversely, recession in the industrial countries depresses world trade as well as domestic economic activity. Although industrial production is the dominant partner in this relationship, changes in world trade also cause changes in industrial production. This is particularly true of countries highly dependent on international trade, and in many instances domestic economic growth is limited by the growth of a country's exports.

In viewing the relationship between industrial production and international trade, we must also remember that nations have promoted industrialization and at the same time have restricted foreign trade. There is no way of knowing how greatly tariffs, quotas, exchange controls, and other restrictions have dampened the growth of world trade since 1913, but there is little question that its volume would be higher in their absence.

PRINCIPAL TRADING COUNTRIES

The ten leading countries in world trade in 1971 are shown in Table 2-2.[1]

Table 2-2

PRINCIPAL TRADING COUNTRIES OF THE WORLD'S MARKET ECONOMIES IN 1971
(Billions of Dollars)

Exports		Imports	
United States	43.5	United States	45.5
West Germany	39.0	West Germany	34.3
Japan	24.1	United Kingdom	23.9
United Kingdom	22.4	France	21.0
France	20.3	Japan	19.7
Canada	17.5	Italy	16.0
Italy	15.1	Canada	15.5
Netherlands	14.0	Netherlands	15.5
Belgium-Luxembourg	12.0	Belgium-Luxembourg	12.3
Sweden	7.5	Switzerland	7.2

Source: United Nations, *Monthly Bulletin of Statistics* (New York: United Nations, May, 1972).

Note: The value of world exports is somewhat less than the value of world imports due to the fact that most nations value exports f.o.b. (free on board) at the point of exportation and imports c.i.f. (cost, insurance, freight) at the point of importation. Thus, the value of world imports exceeds the value of world exports by the amount of transportation and other costs incurred in the physical movement of merchandise between countries. The United States, Canada, and a few other countries value imports as well as exports at their f.o.b. values. In 1971, total exports of the market economies were $309.2 billion while their imports were $325.4 billion.

[1] If the nonmarket Communist countries were included, only the Soviet Union would place in the first ten traders, with a ranking of ninth in both exports and imports.

Several points may be drawn from an examination of these data.

1. Seven of the ten major exporting and importing countries are located in Western Europe, indicating the key importance of that region in the world economy.

2. The order of countries is not always the same for both exports and imports. Japan ranks third in exports but fifth in imports; the United Kingdom ranks fourth in exports but third in imports. These and other shifts result from the fact that some countries have net import balances, others have net export balances, and net balances, whether import or export, vary greatly in size. Although the precise ordering may change from one year to the next, the ten principal trading countries were the same in 1964 as in 1971 with the exception of Switzerland, which took the place of Sweden on the import side. Japan experienced the most dramatic change in position, rising from sixth place in both exports and imports to third place in exports and fifth place in imports in 1971.[2]

3. The United States ranks first in both exports and imports, but is trailed closely by West Germany in exports. In 1971, for the first time in the twentieth century, the United States showed an import balance.

4. Total exports of the ten countries were $215.4 billion, accounting for almost 70 percent of the exports of all market economies and for over 60 percent of world exports *including* the Communist countries. Imports of the ten countries totaled $210.9 billion, or nearly 65 percent of the imports of all market economies.[3]

Table 2-3 reveals the changes that have occurred in the relative *export* positions of the major trading areas since 1913.

Table 2-3

EXPORTS OF MARKET ECONOMIES: UNITED STATES, UNITED KINGDOM. WESTERN EUROPE, JAPAN, AND REST OF WORLD
(Billions of Dollars)

Year	United States	United Kingdom	Western Europe *	Japan	Rest of World	Total World**
1913	2.5	3.1	7.9	0.3	6.0	19.8
1928	5.1	3.5	9.9	0.9	13.3	32.7
1938	3.1	2.7	6.3	1.1	7.4	20.6
1948	12.7	6.4	11.0	0.3	22.3	52.7
1958	17.9	9.0	31.5	2.9	33.1	94.4
1964	26.2	11.9	58.6	6.7	47.9	151.3
1971	43.5	22.4	131.3	24.1	87.9	309.2

Sources: U.S. Department of Commerce. League of Nations, *Industrialization and Foreign Trade* (Geneva: League of Nations, 1949). W. S. Woytinsky and E. S. Woytinsky, *World Commerce and Governments* (New York: Twentieth Century Fund, 1955). United Nations, *Monthly Bulletin of Statistics* (New York: United Nations, various issues).
* Austria, Belgium-Luxembourg, Denmark, Finland, France, West Germany, Greece, Italy, Netherlands, Norway, Portugal, Spain, Sweden, Switzerland, and Yugoslavia.
** Excludes nonmarket Communist countries after 1948.

[2] United Nations, *Monthly Bulletin of Statistics* (New York: United Nations, June, 1965).
[3] *Ibid.* (May, 1972).

Before World War I, the United Kingdom was the premier exporting country, but in the 1920's its export leadership passed to the United States. Given the trends of the 1960's, it is quite possible (and even probable) that West Germany or Japan will become the world's leading exporter sometime in the 1970's, pushing the United States into second or third place.

Western Europe (excluding the United Kingdom and Ireland) is by far the most important trading *region* in the world economy. In 1971 its exports were more than three times the size of U.S. exports. Because of very rapid growth, Western Europe's share of world exports is now substantially higher than in 1938.

The most eminent trading country outside North America and Europe is Japan. In the 1960's, Japan achieved an astounding export growth; in 1971, its exports surpassed those of the United Kingdom. In 1958, Japan's share of world exports was only 3.1 percent, but by 1971 it had more than doubled to reach 7.8 percent.

In contrast to Western Europe and Japan, the U.S. share of world exports fell drastically in the 1960's, from 19.0 percent in 1958 to 14.0 percent in 1971. Clearly the United States has lost much of its former dominance in world exports as did the United Kingdom in the 1920's.

Another area of slow export growth is the rest of the world, mainly comprising the nonindustrial, developing countries. The share of this area in world exports in 1971 was substantially less than its share in 1938 and earlier years because of the far more rapid growth in the exports of the industrial areas, notably Western Europe and Japan.

THE TRADE OF INDUSTRIAL AND NONINDUSTRIAL AREAS

It is a common misconception that most international trade consists in the exchange of foodstuffs and raw materials for manufactures between nonindustrial and industrial countries. The error of this view becomes apparent when we analyze the data in Table 2-4 (page 28) on trade between industrial and nonindustrial areas.

The dominance of the industrial areas in international trade is clearly evident. In 1970 these areas originated 78.0 percent and absorbed 76.9 percent of the trade among the market economies.[4] Trade *between* countries of the industrial areas accounted for 60.1 percent of the total world trade of the market economies. In other words, *over three-fourths of the international trade of the industrial countries is with other industrial countries.*

The nonindustrial areas originated 22.0 percent and absorbed 23.1 percent of the trade among the market economies. However, only 5.2 percent

---

[4] If Australia, New Zealand, and South Africa are included in the industrial areas, then the industrial countries originated 80.8 percent and absorbed 80.2 percent of the total exports of the market economies. General Agreement on Tariffs and Trade, *International Trade 1970* (Geneva: 1971), Appendix, Table E.

Table 2-4

TRADE WITHIN AND BETWEEN INDUSTRIAL AND NONINDUSTRIAL AREAS AS A PERCENTAGE OF WORLD TRADE OF MARKET ECONOMIES

Exports from / Exports to	Industrial Areas (%)	Nonindustrial Areas (%)	All Market Economies (%)
Industrial areas*			
1938	38.6	28.2	66.8
1957	41.4	26.9	68.3
1963	53.2	19.9	73.1
1970	60.1	17.9	78.0
Nonindustrial areas**			
1938	25.0	8.2	33.2
1957	21.7	10.0	31.6
1963	20.3	6.5	26.9
1970	16.8	5.2	22.0
All market economies***			
1938	63.6	36.4	100.0
1957	63.1	36.9	100.0
1963	73.5	26.5	100.0
1970	76.9	23.1	100.0

Sources: General Agreement on Tariffs and Trade, *Trends in International Trade* (Geneva: 1958), Appendix, Table A. General Agreement on Tariffs and Trade, *International Trade 1970* (Geneva: 1971), Appendix, Table E.
* Industrial areas comprise North America (United States and Canada), Western Europe, and Japan.
** Nonindustrial areas comprise Latin America, Asia (excluding Communist countries), the Middle East, Africa, and Oceania. Australia, New Zealand, and South Africa are included in non-industrial areas to insure comparability between 1938 and later years, although today they are properly classifiable as industrial areas.
*** Excludes centrally planned, Communist economies.

of this trade arose out of trade *between* the nonindustrial areas. That is to say, *less than one-fourth of the exports of the nonindustrial countries went to other nonindustrial countries*. This fact underscores the dependence of the nonindustrial areas on the industrial areas for export markets.

In 1970 exports of the industrial areas to the nonindustrial areas amounted to 17.9 percent of world trade while exports of the nonindustrial areas to the industrial areas amounted to 16.8 percent. Hence, the non-industrial areas experienced a net import balance in their trade with the industrial areas in 1970.

Summing up, in 1970, 60.1 percent of the world trade of the market economies was between countries of the industrial areas, 5.2 percent between countries of the nonindustrial areas, and only 34.7 percent was between the industrial and nonindustrial areas. Furthermore, the exchange of merchandise between industrial and nonindustrial areas has become a progressively smaller share of world trade since the early 1950's. This decline reflects the high positive correlation between international trade and economic growth. The most dynamic sector of world trade is trade among the rapidly growing, developed countries; the most stagnant sector is trade among the slowly growing, developing countries. The trade problems of the developing countries are taken up in Chapters 17 and 18.

Trade between the industrial and developing areas (the nonindustrial areas excluding Australia, New Zealand, and South Africa) is mainly the traditional exchange of manufactures for primary products (food, raw materials, minerals, and fuels). In 1970, 83.0 percent of the exports of the industrial areas to the developing areas was in manufactures while 77.1 percent of the exports of the developing areas to the industrial areas consisted of primary products, of which almost one-half were fuels (mostly petroleum). It may surprise us to learn that in 1970 primary products made up 25.4 percent of the trade among the industrial countries. In fact, in 1970 the industrial countries exported more primary products to other industrial countries ($37.6 billion) than the developing countries exported to the industrial countries ($30.7 billion). In that same year, manufactures accounted for 29.1 percent of the trade among the developing countries. The composition of the exports of the industrial and developing areas in 1970 is shown in Table 2-5.

Table 2-5

GROSS COMPOSITION OF EXPORTS OF THE INDUSTRIAL AND DEVELOPING AREAS IN 1970
(Billions of Dollars)

Exports from / Exports to	Industrial Areas	Developing Areas
Industrial areas		
Primary products	37.6	6.6
Manufactures	110.4	32.2
Developing areas		
Primary products	30.7	7.3
Manufactures	9.1	3.0

Source: General Agreement on Tariffs and Trade, *International Trade 1970* (Geneva: 1971), Table 10, p. 22.

EAST-WEST TRADE

Up to this point we have looked only at trade among the market economies of the West and the South.[5] What of the international trade of the centrally planned economies of the East, the Communist countries comprising the Eastern Trading Area? Table 2-6 (page 30) indicates the role of this area in world trade.

---

[5] The "West" designates the industrial market economies and the "South," the developing market economies. They correspond only loosely with geographical location.

Table 2-6

TRADE WITHIN AND BETWEEN THE MARKET ECONOMIES OF THE WEST AND SOUTH AND THE CENTRALLY PLANNED ECONOMIES OF THE EAST IN 1970
(Billions of Dollars of Exports)

Exports from \ Exports to	Industrial Areas	Developing Areas	Total Market Economies	Eastern Trading Area*	Total World***
Industrial areas** ..	172.7	41.8	214.5	8.4	224.7
Developing areas ...	40.3	10.6	50.9	3.1	55.0
Total market economies	213.0	52.4	265.4	11.5	279.7
Eastern Trading area	7.8	4.5	12.3	19.8	32.8
Total world	220.8	56.9	277.7	31.3	312.5

Source: General Agreements on Tariffs and Trade, *International Trade 1970* (Geneva: 1971), Appendix, Table E.
* Comprises Albania, Bulgaria, Czechoslovakia, East Germany, Hungary, Poland, Rumania, U.S.S.R., Mainland China, Mongolia, North Korea, and North Vietnam.
** Includes Australia, New Zealand, and South Africa.
*** Includes some unspecified trade.

The most striking feature of Table 2-6 is the comparatively small amount of exports originating in the Eastern Trading Area. Communist planners are generally biased in favor of the development of self-sufficient national economies, avoiding international specialization of production. They restrict imports to goods that are deemed vital to the fulfillment of the current national plan and consider exports as the means to pay for imports. As a consequence, the foreign trade of the Communist countries is a smaller fraction of their domestic output than is true of the market economies. In 1970 the countries comprising the Eastern Trading Area exported $32.8 billion, only 10.5 percent of total world exports ($312.5 billion). Furthermore, over three-fifths of these exports were between countries of the Area.

It follows that East-West trade is comparatively modest.[6] In 1970 the Eastern Trading Area exported $7.8 billion to the industrial areas and $4.5 billion to the developing areas, a total of $12.3 billion to the market economies. Conversely, the market economies of the West and South exported $11.5 billion to the Eastern Trading Area. Hence, total exports generated by East-West trade totaled $23.8 billion, only 7.6 percent of total world trade. About 4 percent of the exports of the industrial areas and about 6 percent of the exports of the developing areas went to the Eastern Trading Area in 1970.

---

[6] Trade between market and Communist countries is conventionally designated as "East-West" trade although it includes trade with the developing countries of the South as well as the industrial countries of the West.

Although the size of East-West trade in 1970 was about equal to the combined exports and imports of Belgium-Luxembourg (see Table 2-2), this trade has been growing rapidly and has become important to some market economies. The year 1953 marked the end of the Stalin era of dogmatic self-sufficiency and discouragement of Soviet trade relations with the West. Under Khrushchev, the Soviet leadership began to promote trade with the West, publicizing attractive opportunities for Western industrialists and pushing an aid-trade program with nonindustrial countries. At the same time, the West—notably Western Europe—eased its restrictions on trade with Communist countries and increasingly sought to expand exports to them. As a result of this reciprocal shift in policy, East-West trade trebled in the 1950's and trebled once again in the 1960's. Table 2-7 indicates the trade of individual industrial countries with the Eastern Trading Area in 1971.

Table 2-7

TRADE OF INDIVIDUAL INDUSTRIAL COUNTRIES WITH THE EASTERN TRADING AREA IN 1971
(Millions of Dollars)

Country	Exports to East	Imports from East
West Germany	1,673.4	1,373.3
Japan	1,147.1	953.3
France	848.3	660.7
Italy	810.2	966.7
United Kingdom	685.8	930.1
United States	384.0	228.0
Canada	379.2	102.4

Source: Organization for Economic Cooperation and Development, Department of the Treasury, *Overall Trade by Countries* (Paris: April, 1972).

The United States remains a very small trader with the East for a number of reasons. First, this country maintains very strict controls over exports to the Soviet bloc and until 1971 prohibited *any* trade with Communist Asia. Second, the United States refuses to extend most-favored-nation (MFN) treatment to Communist countries so that imports from the East must pay the very high 1930 tariff rates.[7] The United States also has other import restrictions that discriminate against imports from the East, such as an embargo on certain furs. Third, the United States forbids private residents to grant credit to any Communist country beyond short-term commercial credit (normally six months). This stultifies trade because the Communist countries want to buy much more from the United States than this country wants to buy from them.

[7] In the Eastern Trading Area only Poland receives MFN treatment.

The prospects are good for a substantial liberalization of U.S. restrictions on trade with Communist countries in the 1970's. But even with a significant liberalization, U.S. trade with the East will remain modest unless this country also grants long-term credits to finance exports. Although we can reasonably expect a continuing expansion of East-West trade, it will likely remain a small percentage of total world trade throughout the 1970's.

COMPOSITION OF WORLD TRADE

Table 2-8 indicates the comparative importance of manufactures, food, and raw materials in world trade for the years 1937, 1953, 1960, and 1970. In 1970 manufactures comprised almost two-thirds of world trade; food, about one-seventh; and raw materials, a little over one-sixth.

Table 2-8

COMPOSITION (PERCENTAGE) OF WORLD TRADE

	1937	1953	1960	1970
Manufactures	39.5	45.5	54.3	64.4
Food	22.4	22.1	19.6	14.8
Raw materials*	38.1	30.0	25.1	18.4
Residual	——	2.4	1.0	2.4
Total world trade**	100.0	100.0	100.0	100.0

Sources: W. S. Woytinsky and E. S. Woytinsky, *World Commerce and Governments* (New York: Twentieth Century Fund, 1955). General Agreement on Tariffs and Trade, *International Trade 1963* (Geneva: 1964), Table 8, p. 20; and *International Trade 1970* (Geneva: 1971), Table 10, p. 22.
* Includes ores, minerals, fuels, and agricultural raw materials.
** Includes countries of the Eastern Trading Area.

The most dramatic change in the composition of world trade is the secular growth in the importance of manufactures. The basic explanation of this shift is the rapid expansion of industrial output compared to primary production throughout the world. The world's physical production has become progressively dominated by manufactures, and this evolution has been reflected in the changing character of international trade.

Other developments, however, have also caused a shift in favor of manufactures. During the 1930's many countries, especially in Europe, adopted government measures to increase self-sufficiency in foodstuffs by subsidizing domestic agriculture and restricting agricultural imports. Most countries have strengthened such programs since that time. Also, certain technological advances have created substitutes for raw materials or have lowered the input of raw materials per unit of output. Artificial fibers and synthetic rubber are among the most outstanding examples of this technological displacement. These developments have tended to lower international trade in raw materials because many of the new products may be manufactured by the use of domestic raw materials.

Contrary influences are also operative. Most noteworthy is the rising dependence of the industrial countries on imports of minerals and fuels. In the 1960's, world exports of these commodities nearly maintained their percentage shares of total trade, and they may well increase in the 1970's.

When all the forces acting on the composition of world trade are taken into account, however, it would appear that the share of manufactures will continue to rise in the future as it has in the past few decades.

MULTILATERAL PATTERN OF INTERNATIONAL TRADE

Earlier we discussed the direction of world trade among the industrial areas, the developing areas, and the Eastern Trading Area. Table 2-9 (page 34) carries the analysis a step further by indicating the net trade balances among the regional members of the industrial trade areas and the other trading areas. Observe that each area has export balances with some areas and import balances with others; instead of a *bilateral* balance of trade (an equality of exports and imports between any two areas), the pattern of trade is *multilateral*. The same is true of the individual countries comprising the trading areas.

International trade develops a multilateral pattern because of fundamental economic conditions. There is no economic reason why the exports of one country or region to another country or region should equal its imports from the latter, either over the short or long run. Such an equality would exist only under conditions of barter or when forced by government restrictions.[8] Simply put, the basis of international trade is specialization and thus the exports of a particular product ordinarily come from a comparatively small number of countries.[9] To illustrate this fact, the following list indicates the major country sources of some representative commodity exports:

Coffee	Brazil, Colombia, Ivory Coast
Wheat	United States, Canada, Australia, France
Rubber	Malaya, Indonesia, Thailand
Cocoa	Ghana, Nigeria, Ivory Coast
Cotton	United States, Brazil, Egypt, Mexico
Iron Ore	Canada, Australia, Sweden, Venezuela, India
Copper	Chile, Zambia, Zaire, Peru
Petroleum	Saudi Arabia, Libya, Iran, Kuwait, Algeria, Iraq, Abu Dhabi, Qatar, Nigeria, Indonesia, Venezuela

---

[8] The Communist countries do seek a bilateral balance of trade with other countries (including Communist countries) but they do not always succeed, particularly in trade with the developing countries.

[9] International specialization in commodities (food, minerals, fuels, etc.) depends primarily on the availability of natural resources; international specialization in manufacturing depends primarily on the availability of capital, human skills, enterprise, and technology.

Table 2-9

NET BALANCES IN INTERNATIONAL TRADE IN 1970
(Millions of Dollars)

	North America	Western Europe	Japan	Australia-New Zealand-South Africa	Developing Areas	Eastern Trading Area	World Total*
North America	—	+4,510	−1,180	+850	+3,000	+320	+7,500
Western Europe	−4,510	—	−1,210	+1,890	−2,690	−120	−6,640
Japan	+1,180	+1,210	—	−550	+860	+290	+2,990
Australia, New Zealand, and South Africa area	−850	−1,890	+550	—	+370	+210	−1,610
Developing areas	−3,000	+2,690	−860	−370	—	−1,350	−2,890
Eastern Trading Area	−320	+120	−290	−210	+1,350	—	+650

Source: General Agreement on Tariffs and Trade, *International Trade 1970* (Geneva: 1971), Appendix, Table E.
* Does not include small amounts of unspecified trade.

Note: This table should be read from left to right. A "+" indicates a net *export* balance; "−," a net *import* balance. The table indicates, for example, that North America had a net *export* balance of $4,510 million with Western Europe in 1970.

/ Introduction

The explanation of international specialization is taken up in Chapters 3, 4, and 5; at this point we may merely observe that natural resources, to say nothing of human skills, capital, technology, and enterprise, are not spread evenly over the earth.

At the same time that nations specialize in their exports, they tend to generalize in their imports; that is, they desire a broad variety of goods that can usually be obtained only from a great number of countries. There is no conflict between export specialization on the one hand, and import generalization on the other, when nations can buy and sell in world markets without the necessity of bilaterally balancing their trade with every other nation. The essence of multilateral *settlement* is the use of a net export balance in one direction to offset a net import balance in another direction. Multilateral settlement involves a "closed circuit" of net balances between the respective trading areas. To take a hypothetical example, multilateral settlement is possible between areas A, B, and C when, let us say, A has a net export balance with B; B has a net export balance with C; and C has a net export balance with A. Settlement will be complete, however, only when the net export balances of the three areas are equal.[10]

It is evident that the pattern of world trade in 1970 was not well adapted to multilateral settlement on a global level. This has been true since the early 1930's, when the international trading system that emerged in the last quarter of the nineteenth century came to an end. How, then, is settlement achieved in contemporary world trade? First, we must recognize that trade in services (notably transportation, travel, and income on foreign investments) also enters the trade balances (or more precisely, the current account balances) of nations. Although service trade alters these balances, it is not likely to establish multilateral circuits on a *global* basis in present circumstances. Its most important effects are to increase the import balance of the developing areas (which are large importers of transportation and investment services), increase the net export balance of North America, and decrease the net import balance of Western Europe. For the most part, therefore, the settlement of net balances in the contemporary international trading system relies on net outflows of capital (loans, investments, and foreign assistance grants) from trade surplus areas to trade deficit areas. As a consequence, the pattern of world trade today is very sensitive to changes

---

[10] Perhaps the most famous historical example of multilateral settlement is the triangular trade developed by New England merchants in the colonial period. New England had a large import balance with Great Britain because the mother country wanted few things other than ships from that region. This difficulty was overcome by New England's exporting to areas that had a positive balance in their trade with Great Britain. One triangular trade route involved the export of rum (made from molasses imported from the West Indies) to Africa in exchange for slaves, which were then exchanged for molasses and pounds sterling in the West Indies. The pounds sterling were used to finance New England's import balance with Great Britain.

in the pattern of capital flows, much more sensitive than the pattern of trade before World War I. Until very recently, the United States has been the primary source of such equilibrating capital flows.

In later chapters we shall trace the steps that have been taken to construct a multilateral world trading system in which the individual trader is free to buy and sell in international markets in accordance with his own business judgment. In more significant terms, international trade can bring the highest gains to its participants only when it is allowed to develop a multilateral structure that fully reflects the comparative advantages of national economies.

THE UNITED STATES IN WORLD TRADE

Although its preeminence in world trade is declining, the United States remains a giant in the world economy. With 6 percent of the world's population and less than 7 percent of its land area, the United States produces and consumes about 30 percent of the world's goods and services.[11] In 1971 its overall exports were 14.1 percent of total world exports, and its share of world exports of manufactured goods was 19.9 percent.

In view of its tremendous strength, it is understandable that the economic fortunes of other nations should depend, directly or indirectly, upon events within the United States economy. This country dominates the markets of the Western Hemisphere both as a buyer and supplier. Canada and many Latin American countries depend on the United States for more than half their exports and imports. Japan gets more than one-fourth of its imports from, and sends almost one-third of its exports to, the United States market. Most European countries depend on this country for about 10 percent of their imports and a smaller percentage of their exports. But many of Europe's export markets, in turn, are highly dependent on the U.S. market, and this relationship indirectly intensifies Europe's dependence. Hence, the network of world trade remains centered on the United States, although to a lesser degree than in the past.

A serious depression in the United States would be a catastrophe not only for the American people, but for other free peoples as well. Although the statement "when the American economy sneezes, the rest of the world catches a cold" has been invalidated by the resurgence of Western Europe and Japan, there is small doubt that a bad case of economic pneumonia in this country would eventually spread to other nations. The sensitivity of foreign governments to American policy in the field of tariffs, import quotas, export subsidies, private foreign investment, and other policy areas often surprises Americans, but it is based on an acute awareness of the deep impact of that policy on foreign economies. It follows that the future behavior of the United States in the world economy will determine in large measure the growth and pattern of international trade.

---

[11] In 1950, the U.S. share of world production was 40 percent.

VALUE AND VOLUME OF U.S. TRADE

Table 2-10 shows the value of U.S. merchandise exports and imports from 1871 to 1971. As was true of world trade, values are misleading when they are used to measure changes in the volume of exports and imports. Accordingly, this table also includes the quantity indexes of exports and imports; quantity indexes are not available for the years preceding 1913, or for the years 1916-1920, 1966-1970, and 1971.

Table 2-10

VALUE AND VOLUME OF U.S. EXPORTS AND IMPORTS
(Millions of Dollars)

Yearly Average or Year*	Exports**	Imports	Excess of Exports over Imports	Quantity Index of Exports (1967 = 100)	Quantity Index of Imports (1967 = 100)
1871-1900	793	663	130	————****	————****
1901-1915	1,868	1,337	531	18.8***	15.8***
1916-1920	6,521	3,358	3,163	————****	————****
1921-1930	4,587	3,741	846	24.4	25.0
1931-1940	2,622	2,097	525	20.6	25.0
1941-1945	10,051	3,514	6,537	51.3	28.3
1946-1955	13,581	8,745	4,836	50.7	37.0
1956-1960	19,292	14,025	5,267	64.5	53.9
1961-1965	24,002	17,656	6,346	81.0	69.6
1966-1970	36,014	32,295	3,719	————****	————****
1970	43,226	39,963	3,263	123.9	132.9
1971	43,498	45,648	−2,150	————****	————****

Sources: U.S. Department of Commerce, *Statistical Abstract of the United States* (Washington: U.S. Government Printing Office, various editions). *Federal Reserve Bulletin* (Washington: U.S. Government Printing Office, May, 1972), Table 1, p. A74.
* Fiscal years 1871-1915; calendar years thereafter.
** Includes transfers under military grant programs.
*** 1913.
**** Data not available.

Since 1913 neither export nor import volume has experienced a steady upward movement. During the 1930's the volume of exports sank below that of the 1920's and the volume of imports stayed the same. The explanation of this movement is, of course, the global depression of the 1930's. During those years the value of exports and imports fell more than their volumes because of falling price levels, but even by 1939 the volume of exports and imports had not regained the levels of 1929. This stagnation was ended by World War II. With the opening of war in the fall of 1939, American exports began a rapid climb that extended through the 1960's. The volume of exports in 1970 was almost twice the level of the 1956-1960 period.

Starting from very low levels in the 1940's, U.S. imports grew at a rapid rate during the next two decades—so rapid, in fact, that imports finally surpassed the value of exports in 1971. This appearance of a net import balance in U.S. trade may well mark a turning point in the international economic relations of this country.

Before 1876 U.S. merchandise imports were usually in excess of merchandise exports. From that year until 1971, however, this country experienced a negative balance of trade only in 1888, 1889, and 1893, and then for only small amounts. The explanation of this shift from a chronic import balance to a chronic export balance lies in the evolution of the United States from a net international debtor to a net international creditor.

The excess of merchandise imports over exports before 1876 was used to transfer the capital that came to the young American economy from Europe, especially from Great Britain. As the United States developed, the *net* inflow of investment capital slackened and in the last half of the 1870's an export balance arose to transfer the earnings from the earlier European investment. Later, at the turn of the century, the United States began to invest abroad and this investment further sustained the export balance. In the twentieth century America became the principal international lender and a net merchandise export balance continued to transfer capital to foreign countries. During the two world wars massive government loans and grants to Europe and elsewhere pushed the export balance to extraordinarily high levels, levels that were substantially maintained up to the mid-1960's by postwar foreign aid and private foreign investment. In the second half of the 1960's, however, the export balance deteriorated, culminating in the import balance of 1971.

Before we consider the reversal of the U.S. international trading position somewhat later, a few comments are in order about the fallacies of maintaining an export balance for its own sake. First, a historical note—Great Britain maintained a chronic merchandise import balance all during the period of her economic supremacy in the nineteenth and early twentieth centuries. Second, when a nation has an export balance it is sending more goods abroad than it is receiving from abroad. Temporarily, at least, it is lowering its standard of living. When we consider that the fundamental end of economic activity is the consumption of goods and services, then exports make sense only as a means of obtaining imports either immediately or at some time in the future. Third, when a country insists upon maintaining a chronic merchandise export balance, it raises obstacles to the eventual repayment of its international loans unless an import balance on services more than offsets the merchandise export balance. A merchandise export balance may be desirable at some stage in a country's development, but it is never desirable *per se*. Finally, a merchandise export balance cannot be evaluated without reference to all the other items that comprise a nation's balance of international payments.[12]

---

[12] The items that comprise a nation's balance of international payments are enumerated and described in Chapter 8.

COMPOSITION OF U.S. TRADE

Tables 2-11 and 2-12 indicate the percentage composition of U.S. exports and imports respectively by principal end-use categories since 1925. Both tables reveal a secular shift toward finished products and away from industrial supplies and materials in the structure of exports and imports.

Before World War II, finished products accounted for somewhat less than 30 percent of total U.S. exports, but after the war their share rose steadily to reach 51.2 percent in 1970. This shift was dominated by capital equipment, which became one-third of total exports in 1970. The sharp jump in exports of automotive products in the 1966-1970 period is entirely owing to the U.S.-Canadian Automotive Products Trade Act of 1965, which established free trade between the two countries in motor vehicles and original parts.[13] In 1970 the percentage share of automotive exports was almost the same as the share before World War II. The share of nonfood consumer goods in 1970 was also about the same as before World War II.

Table 2-11

COMPOSITION OF U.S. EXPORTS BY PRINCIPAL END-USE CATEGORIES
(Percent)

End-Use Category	Average 1925-29	Average 1930-39	Average 1946-58	Average 1959-65	Average 1966-70	1970
Finished (final) products	24.8	29.3	43.5	45.6	51.2	51.2
Capital equipment	10.2	13.7	23.8	28.1	31.8	33.2
Automotive *	8.4	8.3	7.0	6.3	9.1	8.4
Nonfood consumer goods	6.1	6.6	7.5	6.8	6.6	6.4
Military goods **	0.1	0.7	5.2	4.3	3.6	3.2
Industrial supplies and materials	56.2	56.7	38.3	34.6	31.5	31.8
Foods, feeds, beverages	16.5	11.7	15.6	17.2	14.5	13.5
All other ***	2.5	2.3	2.6	2.6	2.8	3.5
Total exports	100.0	100.0	100.0	100.0	100.0	100.0

Source: "OBE's End-Use Classification of Foreign Trade: The Changing Pattern of U.S. Exports and Imports Since the Mid-1920's," *Survey of Current Business* (Washington: U.S. Government Printing Office, March, 1971), p. 22.
* Automotive vehicles, parts, and engines.
** Sales and transfers under military programs.
*** Reexports, low-value shipments, and miscellaneous special transactions.

The expanding share of finished products in U.S. exports has been accompanied by a diminishing share of industrial supplies and materials,

---

[13] In the 1959-1965 period, automotive exports to Canada were 2.3 percent of total exports; in the period 1966-1970, they were 6.0 percent of total exports. "OBE's End-Use Classification of Foreign Trade: The Changing Pattern of U.S. Exports and Imports Since the Mid-1920's," *Survey of Current Business* (Washington: U.S. Government Printing Office, March, 1971).

which dropped from 56.7 percent before World War II to 31.8 percent in 1970. The share of foods, feeds, and beverages has fluctuated between 12 and 17 percent since the 1920's with no definite trend.

Table 2-12

COMPOSITION OF U.S. IMPORTS BY PRINCIPAL END-USE CATEGORIES
(Percent)

End-Use Category	Average 1925-29	Average 1930-39	Average 1946-58	Average 1959-65	Average 1966-70	1970
Finished (final) products	11.1	10.4	10.7	22.4	38.4	43.3
Capital equipment .	*0.6*	*0.7*	*2.1*	*5.0*	*8.8*	*9.5*
Automotive *	**	**	*1.1*	*3.9*	*12.4*	*14.9*
Nonfood consumer goods	*10.5*	*9.6*	*7.5*	*13.5*	*17.1*	*18.9*
Industrial supplies and materials	65.7	59.8	58.9	51.9	41.7	37.8
Foods, feeds, beverages	22.1	27.5	27.8	21.1	15.9	15.4
All other***	1.0	2.3	2.6	4.6	4.0	3.5
Total imports	100.0	100.0	100.0	100.0	100.0	100.0

Source: "OBE's End-Use Classification of Foreign Trade: The Changing Pattern of U.S. Exports and Imports Since the Mid-1920's," *Survey of Current Business* (Washington: U.S. Government Printing Office, March, 1971), p. 22.
* Automotive vehicles, parts, and engines.
** Less than 0.05 percent.
*** Low-value shipments, U.S. goods returned, and miscellaneous special transactions.

As shown in Table 2-12, U.S. imports have also shifted toward finished products, which rose from 10.4 percent of total imports in the period 1930-1939 to 43.3 percent in 1970. Although this shift started later than the similar shift in exports, it proceeded very rapidly in the 1960's, when the share of finished products in total imports nearly doubled. Unlike exports, this shift has occurred in all three major categories of finished products: capital equipment, automotive products, and nonfood consumer goods. As was also true of exports, the jump in the automotive share of imports in the period 1966-1970 was mostly due to higher imports from Canada under the Automotive Products Trade Act.[14] This growth in the import share of finished products has been accompanied by a decline in the shares of both industrial supplies and materials and in foodstuffs. Much of the food and beverage imports comprise commodities not produced in the United States (such as coffee and cocoa) or not produced in sufficient quantity (such as sugar).

___

[14] Automotive imports from Canada in the period 1959-1965 averaged only 0.4 percent of total imports, but in the period 1966-1970 they averaged 7.5 percent. *Survey of Current Business* (Washington: U.S. Government Printing Office, March, 1971).

A comparatively small number of individual products (or product types) accounts for large amounts of U.S. exports and imports, as is shown in Tables 2-13 and 2-14, respectively.

Table 2-13

THE TEN LEADING EXPORT PRODUCTS
OF THE UNITED STATES IN 1970
(Millions of Dollars)

Product or Product Type	Value
1. Road motor vehicles and parts	3,244
2. Aircraft and parts	2,658
3. Chemical elements and compounds	1,642
4. Power-generating machinery	1,395
5. Soybeans	1,216
6. Iron and steelmill products	1,190
7. Wheat and wheat flour	1,112
8. Electronic computers	1,104
9. Coarse grains	1,073
10. Coal	961
All ten products	15,595
All exports	42,593*

Source: U.S. Department of Commerce, *Statistical Abstract of the United States* (Washington: U.S. Government Printing Office, 1971), Table 1242, pp. 772-773.
* Figure does not include "transfers under military grants."

Table 2-14

THE TEN LEADING IMPORT PRODUCTS
OF THE UNITED STATES IN 1970
(Millions of Dollars)

Product or Product Type	Value
1. Automobiles and parts	5,067
2. Petroleum and products	2,770
3. Iron and steelmill products	1,954
4. Clothing	1,267
5. Coffee, green	1,160
6. Telecommunications apparatus	1,103
7. Paper and manufactures	1,087
8. Meat and preparations	1,014
9. Fish	794
10. Engines and parts	782
All ten products	16,998
All imports	39,963

Source: U.S. Department of Commerce, *Statistical Abstract of the United States* (Washington: U.S. Government Printing Office, 1971), Table 1247, pp. 777-778.

In 1970 the ten leading export products accounted for 36.6 percent of all exports while the ten leading import products accounted for 42.5 percent of all imports. Two products appear in both the export and import lists: motor vehicles rank first in both categories, and iron and steelmill products rank sixth in exports and third in imports. This apparent duplication reflects the growing *similarity* in the basic structures of U.S. exports and imports, as both have shifted toward finished products. (See Tables 2-11 and 2-12.) A decade ago exports and imports were much less similar in their composition. Because finished goods may differ in quality, design, innovation, specifications, and in many other ways, international specialization and trade in finished products can attain high degrees of refinement. Every American knows, for instance, that the automobiles imported by the United States are different in many ways from those produced and exported by this country. The same observation also applies to American buyers of chemicals, machinery, and other manufactured products.

DIRECTION OF U.S. TRADE

The destination of U.S. exports and the origin of U.S. imports by geographical areas since 1871 are indicated in Tables 2-15 and 2-16.

Table 2-15

DISTRIBUTION OF U.S. EXPORTS BY GEOGRAPHICAL AREAS
(Percent)

Yearly Average or Year	Canada	Latin America	Europe	Asia*	Africa
1871-1880	5.6	9.8	81.8	2.4	0.5
1921-1925	14.3	16.9	52.7	14.5	1.6
1936-1940	16.2	18.9	41.4	19.3	4.2
1951-1955	22.6	26.9	28.0	18.2	4.4
1956-1960	21.9	24.0	30.9	19.3	4.0
1965	20.5	15.6	34.0	25.4	4.7
1970	21.0	15.1	34.3	25.9	3.7

Source: U.S. Department of Commerce, *Statistical Abstract of the United States* (Washington: U.S. Government Printing Office, various editions).
Note: Percentages may not add to 100.0 because of rounding.
* Includes Australia and Oceania.

In the nineteenth century most U.S. exports were directed to Europe. From 1871-1880, 81.8 percent of total exports by value went to that continent. In the twentieth century, however, Europe lost this imposing position, although it still takes a greater share of exports than any other single area. At the same time other areas became more important as export markets. In the 1950's Canada took over one-fifth of U.S. exports, a share it has maintained up to the present. However, Latin America's share has steadily declined since the early 1950's, falling to the level of the 1920's by 1970.

In the 1960's the most dynamic markets for U.S. exports were Western Europe and Japan. Because of Japan, Asia has emerged as the second most important market for U.S. exports. We have already seen that trade among the industrial areas is growing more rapidly than trade between the industrial and developing areas, and now we see that the United States is part of that trend. More specifically, the share of U.S. exports going to other industrial countries has risen from 64.4 percent in 1960 to 69.1 percent in 1970.

Table 2-16

DISTRIBUTION OF U.S. IMPORTS BY GEOGRAPHICAL AREAS
(Percent)

Yearly Average or Year	Canada	Latin America	Europe	Asia *	Africa
1871-1880	5.7	29.4	53.1	11.2	0.6
1921-1925	11.5	27.1	30.4	28.9	2.1
1936-1940	14.8	23.5	25.3	33.1	3.3
1951-1955	22.4	33.3	20.2	18.9	5.5
1956-1960	21.2	29.7	26.6	18.4	4.1
1965	22.6	20.5	29.5	23.3	4.1
1970	27.8	14.6	28.5	26.3	2.8

Source: U.S. Department of Commerce, *Statistical Abstract of the United States* (Washington: U.S. Government Printing Office, various editions).
Note: Percentages may not add to 100.0 because of rounding.
* Includes Australia and Oceania.

During the nineteenth century over half of all U.S. imports came from Europe, although that area was less important as a source of supply than as an export market. In the late 1930's, Asia supplied about one-third of U.S. imports while Europe and Latin America each supplied about one-fourth. In the early 1950's, Latin America's share rose to one-third, but in the late 1950's and into the 1960's that area rapidly lost ground to Asia, Canada, and Europe. The jump in Europe's share reflects, of course, the growth in its industrial capacity; the upward surge in Asia's share is mainly attributable to the emergence of Japan as a formidable international competitor in electronic, automotive, steel, and other manufactures; the rise in Canada's share is traceable to the Automotive Products Trade Act of 1965. In 1970 these three areas were closely matched as suppliers to the United States, each contributing somewhat over one-fourth of total U.S. imports.

As was true of exports, these shifts in import sources show an increasing U.S. dependence on the industrial countries and, at the same time, a decreasing dependence on the developing countries. In 1960 the United States obtained 58.7 percent of its imports from other industrial countries; in 1970, it obtained 73.2 percent from them.

DEPENDENCE OF THE UNITED STATES ON INTERNATIONAL TRADE

In a previous section we pointed out the vital importance of the United States to the world economy. But what of the importance of the world economy to the United States?

More than most peoples, Americans are likely to underestimate the significance of exports and imports to the functioning of the domestic economy and to their own standard of living. To be sure, U.S. trade looks very small when set against the total activity of the U.S. economy, and it is easy to demonstrate the self-sufficiency of that economy relative to the economies of most other countries. One method is to compare the ratio of U.S. trade (merchandise exports *plus* imports) to U.S. gross national product with similar ratios of other countries, as is done in Table 2-17 for the industrial countries.[15]

Table 2-17

INTERNATIONAL TRADE (EXPORTS PLUS IMPORTS) OF THE INDUSTRIAL COUNTRIES AS A PERCENTAGE OF THEIR GROSS NATIONAL PRODUCTS IN 1970

Country	Percent
Belgium-Luxembourg	89.4
Netherlands	80.4
Switzerland	57.1
Norway	52.7*
Denmark	48.8*
Austria	44.8
Sweden	44.1
Canada	36.4
West Germany	34.6
United Kingdom	34.1
Italy	29.4*
France	23.1*
Japan	19.5
United States	8.9

Source: International Monetary Fund, *International Financial Statistics* (Washington: International Monetary Fund, February, 1972), country tables.
* 1969.

It would seem that the United States could dispense with its international trade with only minor consequences to its economy. Aggregate relationships, however, are often deceiving and especially so in this instance.

When we investigate the dependence of the American economy on *specific* imports as sources of supply and *specific* exports as outlets for domestic production, we come to closer grips with the question of the essentiality of international trade. The picture that we find does not agree with the image of United States self-sufficiency that is suggested by the comparison of international trade with gross national product.

Today there are only two metals—magnesium and molybdenum—for which American industry is not partially or wholly dependent on foreign supplies. One hundred percent of our consumption of natural rubber and

---

[15] The gross national product is defined in Chapter 9, p. 212.

tin; 90 percent or more of our consumption of nickel, bauxite, beryllium, cobalt, chromite, asbestos, and manganese; over 50 percent of our consumption of tungsten; and 25 percent or more of our consumption of lead, copper, and zinc ores must be met through imports.[16] We are similarly dependent on imports of certain foodstuffs such as coffee, cocoa, and tea, which come entirely from foreign sources of supply. All studies point to an even greater dependence on imports of industrial raw materials in the future. Further examples of import dependence are offered in Table 2-18.

Table 2-18

U.S. IMPORTS ACCOUNTING FOR 20 PERCENT OR MORE OF NEW SUPPLY AND AMOUNTING TO MORE THAN $50 MILLION IN 1968

Product	Percent of New Supply
Coffee	100
Cocoa beans	100
Tea	100
Crude rubber and allied gums	100
Bananas and plantains	100
Copra	100
Bauxite and other aluminum ores	86
Cut diamonds and other lapidary work	72
Wool, except mohair	53
Finfish	52
Shellfish	52
Sewing machines and parts*	42
Scouring and combing mill products	40
Iron ores and concentrates*	35
Motorcycles, bicycles, and parts	35
Pulp mill products*	31
Tree nuts, edible	31
Copper smelting and refining products*	30
Bottled liquors, except brandy	28
Potash, soda, and borate minerals	27
Lead and zinc ores	27
Rubber footwear	23
Steel nails and spikes	22
Sugar and by-products	22
Sulfur	20
Canned and cured seafood	20
Wines and brandy	20

Source: U.S. Department of Commerce, *U.S. Commodity Exports and Imports as Related to Output, 1967 and 1968* (Washington: U.S. Government Printing Office).
Note: *New supply* is defined as U.S. production *plus* imports. Thus, the percentage measures the ratio: imports/domestic production plus imports. Import values are values in the foreign country and do not include U.S. import duties, transportation costs, etc.
    * Substantial amounts also exported.

---

[16] Your automobile probably has thirty-one materials imported from thirty-two countries; your telephone has forty-eight materials imported from eighteen countries; and your newspaper is most likely printed on imported newsprint. See National Foreign Trade Council, Inc., *Memorandum No. 300* (May, 1972).

Table 2-19 shows how important export markets are to American farmers and many American manufacturers. Farmers, in particular, are dependent on foreign markets for their livelihood. This country exports the crops of one out of every four harvested acres, providing employment to one out of eight farm workers. More than one-third of U.S. wheat, rice, soybeans, cotton, and tobacco go to foreign markets. Not all of these exports are cash sales; many farm exports to developing countries are financed under U.S. foreign assistance programs. Clearly the prosperity of American agriculture hinges on exports. The agricultural slump in the 1920's and the difficulties of farmers in the middle 1950's are traceable to the loss of foreign markets. Whatever protectionist groups may tell them, farmers have everything to gain from liberal government policies that foster an expanding world trade.

Table 2-19

U.S. EXPORTS ACCOUNTING FOR 15 PERCENT OR MORE OF DOMESTIC OUTPUT AND AMOUNTING TO MORE THAN $100 MILLION IN 1968

Product	Percent of Domestic Output
Milled rice and by-products	62
Leaf tobacco	43
Phosphate rock	42
Electronic computers, calculating and accounting machines	37
Medicinals and botanicals, including pharmaceuticals	35
Cotton farm products	32
Oil-filled machinery and equipment	30
Construction machinery and equipment	29
Pulp mill products	28
Cash grain farm products	24
Mining machinery and equipment	24
Copper smelting and refining products	23
Special industry machinery	22
Animal and marine fats and oils	21
Soybean oil mill products	20
Bituminous coal and lignite	19
Food products machinery	18
Textile machinery and parts	18
Pumps and compressors	17
Aircraft	17
Mechanical measuring and controlling instruments	16
Electric measuring instruments	16
Printing trades machinery and parts	15

Source: U.S. Department of Commerce, *U.S. Commodity Exports and Imports as Related to Output, 1967 and 1968* (Washington: U.S. Government Printing Office).

Foreign markets also represent the difference between profit and loss for many U.S. manufacturers. Actually the importance of foreign markets is minimized when measured as a percentage of domestic production.

The break-even point of many producers is so high that 5 or 10 percent of sales may be responsible for a disproportionate share of profits.

Many jobs also depend on exports. The U.S. Department of Labor estimates that each $1 billion of exports requires 91,000 workers. In 1969 more than 2.65 million jobs in the United States were associated with merchandise exports, about 3.8 percent of total private employment.[17]

In conclusion, our dependence on both imports and exports is much greater than is suggested by the relationship between international trade and national income. Inability to obtain many imports would mean higher costs of production and in many instances the use of inferior substitutes. Exports are a necessity for farmers, and a large number of manufacturers would be forced into bankruptcy or seriously injured by the loss of foreign markets. Finally, millions of workers gain their livelihoods directly or indirectly from international trade.

THE DETERIORATION OF THE U.S. TRADE BALANCE

We observed earlier that the U.S. merchandise export balance started to deteriorate in the mid-1960's, and in 1971 it became negative for the first time since 1893. Between 1960 and 1964 U.S. exports grew at an average annual rate of 7.1 percent and U.S. imports at a rate of 5.6 percent, thus generating the substantial trade surpluses of that period. But between 1964 and 1970 U.S. imports rose precipitously at an average annual rate of 13.5 percent while exports grew only at a rate of 8.8 percent. Is this deterioration attributable to short-run, *cyclical* factors, or does it represent a long-run, *structural* shift in the U.S. trade balance? The most appropriate answer to this question appears to be that both sets of factors are at work, but structural factors are by far the most important.

Let us turn first to imports. The upward surge in imports in the second half of the 1960's is due largely to inflation in the United States. Between 1965 and 1970 the share of imports in the U.S. gross national product (the *average* propensity to import) rose from 3 percent to 4 percent, a remarkable increase in such a short period of time. As inflation is curbed we can expect a considerable slowing of the *rate* of import growth in the 1970's.

However, cyclical factors cannot explain the marked shift in the composition of U.S. imports toward finished manufactured products. (See Table 2-12.) One special factor is the Automotive Products Trade Agreement with Canada: in 1964, U.S. net exports of automotive products to Canada were +$588 million; in 1970, they were −$170 million.[18] This trade shift, therefore, amounted to a deterioration of $758 million in the U.S. trade balance between those years. More generally, other industrial countries

---

[17] *Ibid.* However, the author's calculations indicate that more than 3.9 million jobs in the United States were associated with merchandise exports, or about 6.7 percent of total private employment in 1969.

[18] See General Agreement on Tariffs and Trade, *International Trade 1970* (Geneva: 1971), Table 42, p. 97.

have gained strong positions in U.S. markets over a broad range of manufactures in the consumer, automotive, and capital equipment sectors. In many manufactured products foreign producers have achieved levels of technology equal or superior to those in the United States, as well as having achieved the economies that go with large-scale production. Furthermore, they have learned how to distribute and promote their products in the U.S. marketplace. This shift toward finished manufactured products is expected to continue in the 1970's, providing a persistent upward thrust to imports.

On the export side, structural factors appear to be working to slow the growth rate of U.S. exports of manufactures. Table 2-20 demonstrates that the United States has experienced a steady erosion of its foreign-market shares in manufactured products for over a decade. For manufactures as a whole, the U.S. market share dropped from 27.7 percent in 1958 to only 19.9 percent in 1971. In that year West Germany surpassed the United States as the principal supplier of manufactures to all markets outside the United States.[19]

Table 2-20

U.S. PERCENTAGE SHARES IN WORLD EXPORTS OF MANUFACTURES

Product	Percent of World Exports to Foreign Markets*		
	1958	1965	1971
Chemicals	29.6	24.7	19.9
Nonelectric machinery	35.0	30.9	25.5
Electric machinery	32.8	24.0	21.0
Transport equipment	35.3	28.4	29.5
Other manufactures	19.7	15.8	12.2
Total manufactures	27.7	22.8	19.9

Source: U.S. Department of Commerce, "Manufactures Market: U.S. Share Slips to New Low," *Commerce Today* (Washington: U.S. Government Printing Office, June 12, 1972), pp. 39-40.
Note: The term "manufactures" excludes mineral fuel products, processed foods, fats, oils, firearms of war, and ammunition.
* World exports are exports from fourteen industrial countries which account for four-fifths of world exports of manufactures to foreign markets (excluding exports to the United States).

As we noted earlier, the most dynamic U.S. exports are capital goods which incorporate high levels of technology. Table 2-21 indicates that the United States has maintained a substantial net export balance in technologically intensive products, such as computers, jet aircraft, and control instruments. Moreover, the United States is expected to increase that balance by 1973. The strength (or comparative advantage) of the U.S. in capital goods is based on a steady stream of highly sophisticated innovations

---

[19] West Germany became the top exporter of manufactures to all markets (including the United States) in 1970. U.S. Department of Commerce, "Manufactures Market: U.S. Share Slips to New Low," *Commerce Today* (Washington: U.S. Government Printing Office, June 12, 1972), pp. 39-40.

which are initially developed for the U.S. market, coupled with the economies of scale of large production units. This lead in new products gives the United States a quasi monopoly in foreign markets which lasts until foreign producers (including U.S. multinational enterprises) learn to duplicate them at lower costs of production.

Table 2-21

U.S. FOREIGN TRADE BY LEVEL OF TECHNOLOGY, 1965-1967 AND PROJECTED 1973
(Billions of Dollars)

	Science-Industry Products*	Materials and Supplies**	Other Manu- factured Products
Exports			
1965	5.4	2.2	6.9
1966	5.9	2.4	7.7
1967	6.9	2.4	8.3
Projected 1973	10.9	2.9	12.2
Imports			
1965	1.6	3.8	2.7
1966	2.2	4.3	4.1
1967	2.3	4.1	5.0
Projected 1973	4.8	5.2	9.5
Trade balance			
1965-1967 average	4.0	−1.8	3.7
Projected 1973	6.1	−2.3	2.7

Source: U.S. Department of Commerce, *U.S. Foreign Trade, A Five-Year Outlook with Recommendations for Action* (Washington: U.S. Government Printing Office, 1969), Table 7, p. 59.
* Industries which support research and development expenditures in excess of 4 percent of sales. Chemicals, aircraft, business machines, electronics, photographic products, instruments, and heavy electrical equipment are included.
** Alloys, scrap, ores, textiles, lumber, paper, glass, metals, etc.

What, then, is the outlook for the U.S. trade balance in the 1970's? In a study addressed to this question, the U.S. Department of Commerce concluded:

> Relief of the domestic economy from inflationary pressures would greatly reduce the current excessive import demand and bring an improvement in the trade surplus. Nonetheless, other factors indicate a probable long-term downward trend toward small surpluses or deficits. These factors include the probable persistence of forces conducive to strong import growth, existing independently of inflation; a moderate decline in overall export competitiveness; and the prevalence of a variety of trade conditions which place the United States at a disadvantage.[20]

[20] U.S. Department of Commerce, *U.S. Foreign Trade, A Five-Year Outlook with Recommendations for Action* (Washington: U.S. Government Printing Office, 1969), p. 8.

In brief, the United States is becoming increasingly an exporter of new, sophisticated capital goods and an importer of older, more standardized manufactured goods, encompassing both consumer products and capital equipment.[21] At the same time, the United States is also becoming a specialist in the export of *factor services* (capital, technology, and management) *via* the multinational enterprise, which is the subject of Part Three. More and more, large U.S. manufacturers are exploiting foreign markets by establishing production affiliates abroad.[22]

The role of the United States in the world economy, therefore, would appear to be in transition from leading exporter to leading investor (international producer) as American multinational enterprises continue to build new production facilities throughout the world.[23] In other words, the United States is becoming a *mature, creditor* country much like Great Britain before World War I. Such a country uses its large net income on foreign investments to pay for a chronic import balance in merchandise trade. Like all fundamental changes, however, this transition will require major adjustments, which are often painful, on the part of United States industry and labor. Whether the United States attempts to maintain its traditional export balance by restricting imports or turns positively toward a new role as a mature, creditor country exporting factor services in exchange for merchandise imports is the single most vital issue confronting the world economy in the 1970's.

SUMMARY

1. For the most part, Chapter 2 consists of statistical presentations of different aspects of world trade and the foreign trade of the United States. We are more interested in the relationships that are disclosed by the statistical data than in the data themselves.

2. Changes in the volume of world trade must be measured by a quantum index that removes the effects of changing price levels over time. The export quantum index indicates a rapid growth in the volume of world trade since World War II.

3. World trade and world industrial production are closely related since a large part of world trade is generated by the industrial countries. Trade has risen faster than industrial production in recent years.

---

[21] The United States remains a strong exporter of agricultural products because of its natural land endowment and the use of advanced technology.

[22] Interestingly enough, the same companies account for the lion's share of U.S. manufactured exports, particularly in technologically intensive sectors. See Chapter 22, p. 538.

[23] This transition is in line with the transition of the U.S. economy toward a postindustrial, services economy. Between 1947 and 1969, services employment grew 81 percent in the U.S. economy while employment in goods-producing industries grew by only 31 percent. See Lawrence B. Krause, "Trade Policy for the Seventies," *Columbia Journal of World Business* (January-February, 1971), p. 7.

4. The United States, West Germany, Japan, and the United Kingdom are leaders in world trade. Of the ten major exporting and importing countries, seven are located in Western Europe.

5. In 1970 about one-third of the world's trade was between industrial and nonindustrial areas, while most of the remainder was among industrial areas. Trade among the nonindustrial areas, which is a falling share of world trade, was only 5.2 percent of world trade in 1970.

6. Trade between the market economies of the West and South and the centrally planned, Communist economies of the East (East-West trade) has increased rapidly since 1953, but it was still less than 8 percent of total world trade in 1970. Owing to restrictions, U.S. trade with the Communist countries remains very small.

7. The share of manufactures in world trade has grown at the expense of the share of foodstuffs and raw materials. In 1970 manufactures constituted almost two-thirds of world trade.

8. The pattern of international trade is multilateral. Today's pattern of trade differs considerably from the pre-World War I pattern, and it is highly dependent on capital flows from the trade surplus to the trade deficit areas.

9. Although its preeminence in world trade is declining, the United States remains a giant in the world economy. In 1971 its exports were 14.1 percent of total world exports, and its share of world exports of manufactures was 19.9 percent.

10. From 1893 to 1971 the United States sustained a chronic net export balance in its foreign trade. Such a balance may or may not be desirable, depending on the other items in the balance of payments.

11. Since at least the 1930's, the composition of both U.S. exports and imports has been shifting toward finished products and away from industrial supplies and materials. In 1970 finished products made up 51.2 percent of U.S. exports and 43.3 percent of U.S. imports. A comparatively small number of individual products accounts for large amounts of U.S. exports and imports.

12. The geographical destination of U.S. exports and the geographical origin of U.S. imports have shifted several times over the last century. In the 1960's the most dynamic markets for U.S. exports were Western Europe and Japan, while the most dynamic import sources were Western Europe, Japan, and Canada.

13. The United States is far more dependent on its international trade than is suggested by overall measures, such as the relationship between international trade and gross national product. This is brought out by an examination of individual imports and exports.

14. The U.S. merchandise export balance started to deteriorate in the mid-1960's, and in 1971 it became negative for the first time since 1893. The United States is becoming increasingly an exporter of new, sophisticated capital goods and an importer of older, more standardized manufactured goods.

15. The role of the United States in the world economy would appear to be in transition from leading exporter to leading investor (international producer) as American multinational enterprises continue to build new production facilities throughout the world.

QUESTIONS AND APPLICATIONS

1. Since 1913 the *value* of world trade has grown thirteenfold while the *volume* of world trade has grown somewhat less than fivefold. How do you explain this apparent discrepancy?

2. "The connection between industrial production and world trade is not fortuitous." Explain.

3. (a) Which are the principal trading countries?
   (b) How do you explain the rise of the United States to the position of first exporter and first importer?

4. "It is a common misconception that most international trade comprises the exchange of foodstuffs and raw materials for manufactures between non-industrial and industrial countries." Discuss.

5. What have been the principal changes in the composition of world trade since 1937?

6. (a) What is multilateral trade? Multilateral settlement?
   (b) What is the basis of multilateral trade?

7. "The most striking feature of East-West trade is its comparatively small size." Why is this so?

8. "A merchandise export balance is favorable to a nation and hence always desirable." Discuss.

9. What have been the main shifts in the composition of U.S. exports and imports since the 1920's?

10. "The United States could easily dispense with international trade because it is only a small fraction of the U.S. gross national product." Discuss the validity of this statement.

11. "The deterioration of the U.S. balance of trade in the second half of the 1960's is owing to both cyclical and structural factors." Discuss.

SELECTED READINGS

(The following publications are the principal sources of statistics on international trade.)

General Agreement on Tariffs and Trade (GATT). *International Trade*. Geneva: Annual.

Organization for Economic Cooperation and Development (OECD). *General Statistics*, monthly; *Overall Trade by Countries*, monthly.

United Nations:
> *Commodity Trade Statistics*, quarterly.
> *Direction of International Trade*.
> *Monthly Bulletin of Statistics*.
> *Yearbook of International Trade Statistics*.

United States Department of Commerce:
> *Historical Statistics of the United States*.
> *Statistical Abstract*, annual.
> *Survey of Current Business*, monthly.

PART ONE   THEORY

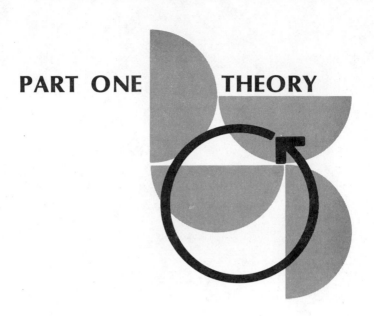

To grasp the significance of everyday events occurring in the vast field of activity that we call international trade and investment, we must first gain an
understanding of fundamental causal relationships,
institutions, and unifying concepts. The eight chapters
of Part One deal with the foundation stones of
international trade and investment, which are
the indispensable prerequisites of our later study of
international economic policies and the multinational
business enterprise.

CHAPTER **3**

THE THEORY OF INTERNATIONAL TRADE: COMPARATIVE ADVANTAGE AND THE GAINS FROM TRADE

In this chapter we seek the answers to two key questions: (1) Why does international trade take place? (2) What are the gains from international trade?

WHY NATIONS TRADE—COMPARATIVE ADVANTAGE

Economists explain international trade with the theory of comparative advantage.[1] Because this theory is complex and easily misunderstood, we shall develop it in a series of steps. We begin with the proximate cause of international trade—absolute international differences in prices.

ABSOLUTE INTERNATIONAL DIFFERENCES IN PRICES

Absolute differences between the prices of foreign goods and the prices of similar goods produced at home are the immediate basis of international trade. When these differences are greater than the costs of transferring goods from one country to another, it becomes profitable to import goods from the lower-price country to the higher-price country. An extreme case arises when a country *must* obtain a good from abroad (or else go without it) because of the physical impossibility of producing it at home. Thus, a country totally lacking coking coal has no choice but to import that commodity if it wishes to produce steel. In many instances, however, a country is physically able to produce the goods that it imports, but—and this is the important point—only at prices higher than it pays for imports. The United States *could* produce coffee and bananas but only at prices so high that few consumers could afford them.

---

[1] We refer to the modern version of this theory based on the mutual interdependence theory of prices rather than the older classical version based on the labor theory of value.

Absolute international differences in prices come to light when there is an exchange rate that equates domestic and foreign currencies. For example, without an exchange rate between the dollar and the pound sterling it would not be possible to compare the prices of goods in the United States with the prices of similar goods in the United Kingdom. But when we know, say, that £1 equals $2, then direct price comparisons are possible and we can ascertain any absolute differences in the prices of specific goods.

Although absolute price differences are the immediate basis of international trade, they do not provide a final explanation. We want to know *why* such differences exist and whether they are fortuitous or systematic.

ABSOLUTE INTERNATIONAL DIFFERENCES IN COST

Our first step is to note that absolute international differences in prices imply absolute international differences in costs. Prices are lower in one country than in another because costs are lower. When markets are purely competitive, prices and costs are identical.[2] Prices also equal costs of production when markets are monopolistically competitive; that is, when producers are able to differentiate their products but are unable to make long-run monopoly profits because of competition. Under oligopoly (few sellers) and monopoly (one seller), however, prices may be higher than costs of production due to the opportunity for long-run monopoly profits. In all instances prices must cover costs of production in the long run if a firm is to stay in business. With the exception of oligopoly and monopoly prices, then, prices equal costs of production in the long run although they may be greater or less than costs in periods of short-run adjustment to changes in demand.

DISSIMILAR COST RATIOS

We have found that absolute international differences in prices are based on absolute international differences in costs. But what causes such cost differences? The answer to this question is most unexpected: absolute international differences in costs arise when pretrade cost ratios *within* each country are dissimilar. This assertion is the core of the theory of comparative advantage and may be demonstrated by a simple arithmetical example.

Suppose there are only two countries (the United States and the United Kingdom); and, in isolation, each country produces two commodities (wheat and textiles). Assume further that the cost ratios between wheat and textiles *differ* between the two countries as shown in Table 3-1.

---

[2] Pure or perfect competition exists for a product when (a) the number of buyers and sellers is so large that no one buyer or seller can influence its price, and (b) the product is homogeneous—it cannot be differentiated by sellers or buyers. Under pure competition, equilibrium costs of production include normal profits but not monopoly profits.

Table 3-1

	United States (Dollars)	United Kingdom (Pounds Sterling)
Unit cost (price) of wheat	1.00	3.00
Unit cost (price) of textiles	2.00	1.00

In the United States the cost ratio of wheat to textiles is 1:2 whereas in the United Kingdom the same ratio is 3:1. These ratios indicate that the United States has a *comparative cost advantage* in the production of wheat and a *comparative cost disadvantage* in the production of textiles. The converse situation exists in the United Kingdom. Gainful trade occurs when the United States exports wheat and imports textiles while the United Kingdom exports textiles and imports wheat.

We know this last statement to be true even though we have assumed no exchange rate that permits a direct comparison of absolute costs (prices) between the two countries. With the same cost the United States can produce either one unit of wheat or one-half unit of textiles. Since costs are determined by the inputs and prices of the productive factors (land, labor, management, and capital) required to carry on production, this means that the same quantity of factors can produce one unit of wheat or one-half unit of textiles in the United States. Factors devoted to wheat production cannot at the same time be used to produce textiles; consequently, the *real* cost of one unit of wheat in the United States is one-half unit of textiles. This is the *opportunity cost* of producing wheat in the United States.

In the United Kingdom, on the other hand, the opportunity cost of producing one unit of wheat is three units of textiles. Clearly, the United States has a lower opportunity cost of producing wheat; that is, it has a comparative advantage in that commodity, and, in the event of trade, it will be exported. Similarly, the opportunity cost of producing a unit of textiles in the United States is two units of wheat—resources used to produce one unit of textiles could have produced two units of wheat. In the United Kingdom, however, the opportunity cost of producing one unit of textiles is only one-third unit of wheat. Thus, the United Kingdom will export textiles and the United States will import them. The United States has a comparative *dis*advantage in the production of textiles.[3]

---

[3] The role of dissimilar cost ratios may be expressed in general terms as follows: Let a_1 be the unit cost of product a in country 1 and b_1 the unit cost of product b in country 1. Let a_2 be the unit cost of product a and b_2 the unit cost of product b in country 2. Then trade is gainful when $a_1/b_1 \neq a_2/b_2$. If $a_1/b_1 > a_2/b_2$, then country 1 will import a and export b, while country 2 will export a and import b. If $a_1/b_1 < a_2/b_2$ (as in our example above) then country 1 will export a and import b, and conversely for country 2.

To make this clearer, suppose that the exchange rate is £1 equals $1. Then the dollar price of wheat in the United Kingdom is $3 compared to $1 in the United States, and the dollar price of textiles is $1 in the United Kingdom compared to $2 in the United States. Trade is distinctly profitable with the United States exporting wheat and the United Kingdom exporting textiles.

Actually, when cost ratios are dissimilar, there is a *range* of exchange rates that will permit the United States to export wheat and the United Kingdom to export textiles. One limit of this range is that exchange rate which makes the price of wheat the same in both countries. In our example this rate is £1 equals one-third of a dollar ($1 equals £3) whereby the price of wheat becomes equivalent to $1 in both countries. The other limit is that exchange rate which makes the price of textiles the same in both countries. This rate is £1 equals $2 ($1 equals one-half of a pound). The pound price of textiles in the United Kingdom then has a dollar equivalent of $2, the price of textiles in the United States. Trade is possible at either limit or at any exchange rate lying between them.

If trade occurs at an exchange rate marking one of the limits, then one country will neither gain nor lose from trade because the ratio of exchange between its exports and imports will equal its domestic ratio of exchange (the opportunity cost ratio) between the same products. To illustrate, when the exchange rate is £1 equals one-third of a dollar, the United Kingdom must export three units of textiles (equivalent to $1) to obtain one unit of wheat from the United States. But the United Kingdom could do just as well by producing wheat at home where its opportunity cost is also three units of textiles. At this rate of exchange, trade is possible although it makes no difference to the United Kingdom whether it trades or not since the entire gain goes to the United States.

If, however, the pound were to equal anything less than one-third of a dollar, the United Kingdom would be able to obtain its wheat more cheaply from domestic production and would refuse to trade. Hence, the opportunity cost ratio in the United Kingdom determines one limit of the range of exchange rates that permit trade between the two countries. The other limit is set by the opportunity cost ratio in the United States. When the dollar equals anything less than one-half of a pound (the pound equals anything *more* than two dollars) the United States will not trade because it can obtain its textiles more cheaply from domestic production. At any exchange rate lying between the two limits both countries will gain from trade with each other.

To sum up, when cost ratios are dissimilar in two countries, there is a range of exchange rates between their respective currencies that will permit gainful trade between them. One limit of this range is determined by the opportunity cost ratio in one country; the other limit, by the opportunity cost ratio in the second country.

IDENTICAL COST RATIOS

The role of dissimilar cost ratios in providing the basis for international trade is further clarified by considering the effect of *identical* cost ratios. The following example differs from our first example only in the assumption of identical cost ratios:

Table 3-2

	United States (Dollars)	United Kingdom (Pounds Sterling)
Unit cost (price) of wheat	1.00	2.00
Unit cost (price) of textiles	2.00	4.00

In the United States the ratio of the dollar cost of a unit of wheat to the dollar cost of a unit of textiles is 1:2. In the United Kingdom the same ratio (expressed in pounds sterling) is identical—2:4 or 1:2. *Under these conditions no gainful trade is possible. Any* rate of exchange between the dollar and the pound will make the dollar (or sterling) prices of wheat and textiles either (1) the same in both countries, (2) higher in the United States, or (3) lower in the United States. The first possibility—the identity of dollar prices in both countries—clearly rules out international trade. If the second or third possibility exists, the United States will either import or export *both* commodities. But this is impossible since exports must equal imports in the absence of loans or gifts—exports must pay for imports.

To illustrate, suppose that the exchange rate is £1 equals $1. At this rate the dollar price of wheat in the United Kingdom is $2 and the dollar price of textiles is $4—both higher than their respective prices in the United States. Since prices are lower at home, Americans will not buy either commodity from the United Kingdom; and the British, unable to export, will be unable to import. In short, no trade is possible. Again, suppose that the exchange rate is £1 equals 40 cents. Then the dollar price of wheat in the United Kingdom is 80 cents and the dollar price of textiles, $1.60. Prices of both commodities are now lower in the United Kingdom and again no trade is possible. Finally, suppose that the exchange rate is £1 equals 50 cents. At this rate the dollar prices of wheat and textiles are the same—there are no absolute price differences of any kind and trade is obviously out of the question.

In conclusion, trade between two countries is not possible when cost (price) ratios within each country are identical. In such circumstances neither country can gain from trading with the other.

DISSIMILAR FACTOR PRICE RATIOS

In our search for the underlying basis of international trade we have traced absolute international *price* differences to absolute international *cost* differences, and absolute international cost differences to dissimilar *cost ratios* within the trading countries. Once again, however, we are faced with a question: why do countries have dissimilar cost ratios?

The immediate explanation is that the marginal cost of production (which is equal to price under pure competition) is determined by the prices paid to the marginal inputs of the factors of production—land, labor, capital, and management; and the ratio of factor prices within each country may be dissimilar. Different commodities are made with different combinations of factor inputs. Consequently, the commodity cost ratio in each country reflects its factor price ratios—the ratios between rent, wages and salaries, interest, and normal profits. In one country wages may be low relative to rent, while in another country wages may be high relative to rent. Thus, the first country will be able to produce goods that will require a great deal of labor and not much land more cheaply than goods that will require a great deal of land but not much labor. In the second country the opposite will be true.

To summarize, it is because factors of production are not perfect substitutes for each other and must be used in different combinations to produce different goods that dissimilar factor price ratios in two countries give rise to dissimilar cost ratios in the same countries.

The role of factor price ratios in the determination of cost ratios may be clarified by a simple illustration. We assume that in the United States the price of a unit of land is $1 and the price of a unit of labor is $2, and that in the United Kingdom, the price of a unit of land is £4 and the price of a unit of labor is £1. Thus land is relatively cheap in the United States and relatively expensive in the United Kingdom, while the converse is true of labor. We assume further that to produce a unit of wheat in either country requires five units of land and one unit of labor, and to produce a unit of textiles in either country requires one unit of land and ten units of labor. These inputs of land and labor per unit of output are the *technical coefficients of production.*[4] The table on the following page results from these assumptions.

---

[4] We are assuming that the coefficients do not vary between countries and that they do not change with the level of output. At a given level of technology there is usually a fairly narrow range of possible factor combinations that may be used to produce a specific commodity, known as the *production function.* Which combination will be used within this range will depend on relative factor prices; that is, each producer will attempt to produce with the combination of factors that will involve the lowest cost. To make our example more realistic we might have assumed that somewhat higher land inputs and somewhat lower labor inputs are used in the production of wheat and textiles in the United States compared to production in the United Kingdom. The added realism, however, would not change our conclusions since the range of permissible variation is normally small; factors of production are only *partial* substitutes for each other. The existence of dissimilar production functions among nations is treated in detail in Chapter 5.

Table 3-3

	United States (Dollars)	United Kingdom (Pounds Sterling)
Unit price of land	1.00	4.00
Unit price of labor	2.00	1.00
Unit cost of wheat	7.00	21.00
Unit cost of textiles	21.00	14.00

The United States has a comparative advantage in the production of wheat (3:1), while the United Kingdom has a comparative advantage in the production of textiles (3:2). This follows from the fact that wheat production is *land-intensive* and the United States is able to use its relatively cheap factor (land) to greatest advantage in that production. On the other hand, the United States has a comparative *dis*advantage in textile production, which is *labor-intensive,* requiring comparatively large amounts of its relatively expensive factor (labor). The converse situation holds in the United Kingdom.

We conclude that when the ratios of factor prices in two countries are dissimilar, each country will have a comparative advantage in those goods whose production requires comparatively large amounts of its relatively cheap factor(s) and comparatively small amounts of its relatively expensive factor(s). It will have a comparable *dis*advantage in those goods whose production depends on comparatively large amounts of its relatively expensive factor(s) and comparatively small amounts of its relatively cheap factor(s).

The price of each factor is determined by its supply and the demand for its use in production. The demand for a factor is derived from the demand for the products that the factor helps to produce. Thus, if the demand for automobiles goes up, the demand for workers, raw materials, capital, etc., that are required to increase the production of automobiles will also rise.[5] Since factor prices are determined by supply and demand, the existence of dissimilar factor price ratios in two countries implies dissimilar factor supply and/or factor demand ratios in the same countries.

DISSIMILAR FACTOR SUPPLY RATIOS

Countries differ greatly in their relative supplies of factors of production. A country like Canada has an abundant supply of natural resources relative to its supply of labor and capital. The Netherlands, on the other hand, has a relatively scarce supply of natural resources but a relatively abundant

---

[5] Raw materials are not an original factor of production, but the demand for raw materials stimulates a demand for the labor, land, etc., that produce them.

supply of labor and capital. Such differences multiply when we take into account the fact that the four factors of production are not homogeneous. Actually there are several kinds of land and many varieties of labor, management, and capital.[6] Thus, one country has a temperate climate, another has a tropical climate; one country has coal but lacks iron ore, another has iron ore but lacks coal; one country has large supplies of educated skilled workers, another has a predominantly illiterate, unskilled labor force; one country has steel plants, another has none; and so on. The number of specific factors of production is so large that any one country is certain to have factor supply ratios that diverge in some respect from the ratios of other countries.

Disregarding factor demand for the time being, a factor in relatively abundant supply commands a price that is comparatively lower than the price of a factor in relatively scarce supply. We should expect, for example, that land rent relative to wages is low in Australia compared to land rent relative to wages in Belgium, since the former country has a density of population that is only a fraction of its density in the latter country. Again, the long-term interest rate relative to wages is lower in the United States than in Brazil because there is much more capital per worker in the former country than in the latter.

Common observation reveals that there are numerous dissimilarities in the factor supply ratios of different countries. Unless offset by relative factor demand, the prices of factors in relatively abundant supply are low compared to the prices of factors in relatively scarce supply. From this it follows that a country will have a comparative advantage in the production of those goods that require comparatively large amounts of its factors of production in relatively abundant supply, and a comparative *dis*advantage in the production of goods that use comparatively large amounts of factors in relatively scarce supply. Indirectly, therefore, a country exports the services of abundant factors of production and imports the services of scarce factors of production.

DISSIMILAR FACTOR DEMAND RATIOS

Even if the relative supplies of land, labor, management, and capital were indentical in two countries (a most unlikely condition), dissimilar demands for the use of these factors in production would create dissimilar factor price ratios and would thereby provide a basis for international trade. This influence of demand on factor price *ratios* is likely to be weak, however, and it will seldom offset the influence of factor supplies. Per capita demand for wheat will not necessarily be high in a country that has relatively

---

[6] Management is often considered a subtype of labor. We have distinguished it from labor, however, because of its key role in the organization and direction of production.

abundant land resources, and people must have food in order to live even though the land resources of their country are relatively scarce.

It is true that patterns of *consumption* differ considerably between countries that have dissimilar standards of living. But the differences are due more to income than to consumer tastes; and, as poor countries develop their economies, they tend to match the consumption patterns of the more-developed countries. Moreover, what appears as a difference in consumer tastes may often be traced to a difference in relative factor supplies. For example, the demand for shelter and clothing is usually less in a tropical climate than in a temperate climate. Although the ratio of factor demands may be a causative agent in the determination of relative factor prices, it is much less important than the ratio of factor supplies. In any event, the former is not likely to counteract the influence of the latter.

THE BASIS OF INTERNATIONAL TRADE

In our investigation of the basis of international trade we have moved from absolute international price differences to absolute international cost differences, from absolute international cost differences to dissimilar cost ratios within each country, from dissimilar cost ratios to dissimilar factor price ratios, and from dissimilar factor price ratios to dissimilar factor supply and factor demand ratios. Dissimilar factor supply ratios are the most fundamental links in this chain of causation. There is, however, no single *ultimate* basis of international trade—all of the market conditions that combine to determine prices in each country together constitute the basis of trade. These market conditions are mutually interdependent; each is both a cause and an effect. This interdependence is illustrated in Figure 3-1, which depicts the principal relationships that determine prices in a "closed economy" with no international trade.

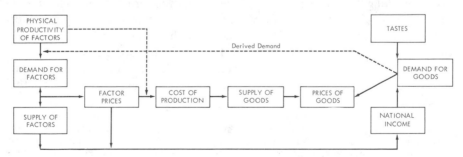

Figure 3-1

PRICE DETERMINATION IN A CLOSED ECONOMY

Since consumption is the ultimate end of economic activity we start our analysis of Figure 3-1 with the demand for goods. The demand for goods is dependent on consumer tastes and the level and distribution of national income.[7] National income, in turn, derives from the prices and amounts of productive factors used to produce the national product, that is, the sum total of wages and salaries, interest, rent, and profits.[8] The demand for goods interacts with the supply of goods to determine prices. The supply of goods is itself determined by the cost of production and, as we have noted, when markets are purely competitive the price of a good equals its marginal cost of production. Because the production of goods requires the use of factors of production, the demand for goods creates a derived demand for factors of production. The demand for factors is also influenced by their physical productivity or physical input-output relationship (production function). If, for example, there is a demand for ten units of good A and each labor input contributes two units to the output of good A in accordance with the production function for good A, then there will be a demand for five inputs or units of labor. Other factors of production experience similar derived demands. Factor productivity depends on physical laws and the level of technology. Factor demand interacts with factor supply to determine factor prices, and factor prices multiplied by the factor quantities needed to produce a unit of output of each good make up its unit cost of production. Looked at the other way, the payments to factors for their productive services constitute the national income. And so, our analysis has come full circle as we have traced the major links in the mutual interdependence theory of prices.[9]

When a closed economy is opened up to international trade, its system of prices interacts with foreign price systems. The immediate impact of international trade is felt in the demand for goods—goods with a comparative advantage experience a new foreign demand, while goods with a comparative *dis*advantage lose their domestic markets to imports. These changes in demand then feed back to affect eventually the prices of productive factors. Over the long run, international trade may even bring about changes in factor supplies as they respond to shifts in factor prices. Given time, international trade may so transform the economy that it bears little resemblance to the sort of economy that would be feasible in the absence of trade.

The theory of comparative advantage provides us with an understanding of the basis of international trade. Loosely speaking, we may say that

---

[7] The *pattern* of consumption is dependent not only on the average per capita level of national income, but on its distribution as well, which is determined by the conditions of factor ownership. Two countries with the same per capita income and the same tastes may have contrasting patterns of consumption if in one country there are a very few rich consumers and a large number of poor consumers while in the other country most people are in the middle class with few very rich or very poor consumers.

[8] See Chapter 9 for a discussion of national income and product.

[9] Figure 3-1 greatly simplifies the mutual interdependence theory of prices. More correctly, it is the *marginal* supply and demand of factors and goods that determine prices, not the total supply and demand. However, consideration of marginalities would not change the basic relationships.

dissimilar factor supply ratios in different countries are the basis of international trade. We must not forget, however, that the influence of factor endowments may be tempered by factor demands. Dissimilar factor endowments (relative to demand) give rise to dissimilar cost ratios that are transformed into absolute international cost differences upon the establishment of an exchange rate. These absolute differences in costs (and prices) are the immediate stimuli of international trade, but failure to understand their dependence on the cost ratios within each trading country leads to mistaken conceptions of trade and unwise government policies.

THE GAINS FROM INTERNATIONAL TRADE

Through international trade a nation is able to obtain more goods with which to satisfy the needs and desires of its people (the ultimate end of economic activity) than if it were to produce all goods at home. This is the true gain from international trade; it is the fruit of international specialization in accordance with comparative cost advantages. International trade is indirect production. It enables each country to combine its factors of production more effectively by specializing in the production of those goods that are best produced by using large amounts of its relatively abundant factors and small amounts of its relatively scarce factors. In this way a country may produce for export those goods in which it has a comparative advantage and import those goods in which it has a comparative disadvantage.

THE DIVISION OF GAINS

Both countries will gain from international specialization and trade, but the exact division of gains between them will depend upon the rate of exchange between their two currencies. The rate of exchange itself is determined by the demand of each country for the other's goods.[10]

To illustrate the determination of the rate of exchange and the role that it plays in the distribution of the gains from trade we return to our earlier example of dissimilar cost ratios:

Table 3-4

	United States (Dollars)	United Kingdom (Pounds Sterling)
Unit cost (price) of wheat	1.00	3.00
Unit cost (price) of textiles	2.00	1.00

With these cost ratios the range of exchange rates that allow gainful trade runs from £1 equals $2 to £1 equals one-third dollar. Over this

---

[10] The determination of exchange rates is analyzed at length in Chapter 7.

range (including the two extremes) the exchange rate will be determined by the *reciprocal demand* of two countries. The exchange rate must be such that the exports and imports of each country are equal; this is the *equilibrium rate of exchange.*[11]

To show how reciprocal demand determines the equilibrium rate of exchange, let us assume an initial equilibrium rate of £1 equals $1, and that at this rate the United States imports 1,000 units of textiles while the United Kingdom imports 1,000 units of wheat. Then the *dollar* prices of wheat and textiles in both countries are as follows:

Table 3-5

	United States (Dollars)	United Kingdom (Dollars)
Unit cost (price) of wheat	1.00	3.00
Unit cost (price) of textiles	2.00	1.00

At this exchange rate the United States is able to import one unit of textiles (worth $1) from the United Kingdom for the export of each unit of wheat (worth $1). *Without* international trade the United States could acquire only one-half unit of textiles for each unit of wheat—the domestic opportunity cost ratio. Its gain from trade, therefore, is one-half unit of textiles for each unit of wheat.

Similarly, for the export of each unit of textiles (worth $1) the United Kingdom is able to import one unit of wheat (worth $1). *Without* trade the United Kingdom could obtain only one-third unit of wheat for each unit of textiles—the domestic opportunity cost ratio. Thus, the United Kingdom gains two-thirds unit of wheat from the export of each unit of textiles. The *total* gain from trade for the United States is 500 units of textiles (1,000 times 0.5 units of textiles), which at the domestic cost equal $1,000. The *total* gain for the United Kingdom is 666.6 units of wheat, which at the domestic cost equal $2,000. Although the gain of the United Kingdom is twice that of the United States, both countries gain from trade and both would be worse off without trade.

Now suppose that the demand for textiles in the United States rises to 1,200 units at the current exchange rate while the demand for wheat remains the same in the United Kingdom. At the exchange rate of £1 equals $1, United States imports would be $1,200 and its exports $1,000. But this is not possible since exports must pay for imports. Therefore, the dollar price of pounds will now rise (the pound price of dollars will fall) until a new equilibrium rate of exchange is attained that brings about an equality between the exports and imports of both countries. The new equilibrium rate might

---

[11] We are continuing to assume the absence of any international lending that would finance a gap between exports and imports.

be £1 equals $1.50 with the amount of textiles demanded by the United States, say 1,100 units, and the amount of wheat demanded by the United Kingdom, 1,650 units. The effect of the new exchange rate upon the *dollar* prices of wheat and textiles in the United Kingdom (the dollar prices in the United States and the pound prices in the United Kingdom remaining unchanged) is as follows:

Table 3-6

	United States (Dollars)	United Kingdom (Dollars)
Unit cost (price) of wheat	1.00	4.50
Unit cost (price) of textiles	2.00	1.50

At this new rate of exchange the total value of imports equals the total value of exports in both countries—$1,650. But it is obvious without detailed calculations that the United States gain from trade is now less (and the United Kingdom gain greater) than in the previous example when the exchange rate was £1 equals $1. The *commodity terms of trade* have worsened for the United States: it must now pay more for its imports (textiles) while the price of its exports (wheat) has remained constant.[12] Conversely, the terms of trade have bettered for the United Kingdom since the dollar price of its exports has risen while the dollar price of its imports has remained the same. Both countries, however, continue to gain from trade.

The lesson we draw from these two examples is that the country with the more intense demand for the other country's goods will gain less from trade than the country with the less intense demand.[13] In the extreme case, the exchange rate is identical with the cost ratio in one country and that country neither gains nor loses from trade while the second country reaps all of the gain. This possibility, however, is exceedingly remote in the real world

---

[12] The *commodity terms of trade* refer to the exchange ratio between exports and imports; that is, between wheat and textiles in our illustration. Arithmetically, the commodity terms of trade are expressed by a ratio of the *change* in the export price level over the *change* in the import price level, both changes being measured from a base year. An increase in the value of the ratio indicates an improvement in the commodity terms of trade (more imports per unit of exports). We should remember that a nation's gains from international trade are determined not only by its commodity terms of trade but also by the comparative cost ratios of the trading countries and the volume of trade. In our illustration, the terms of trade were altered by a movement of the exchange rate (a depreciation of the dollar vis-à-vis the pound) that was caused by a rise in the United States demand for textiles. If exchange rates were fixed, as under the gold standard, then adjustment to that shift in demand would involve an alteration in the terms of trade through changes in the domestic prices of the United States and the United Kingdom—a fall in the prices of the former country and a rise in the prices of the latter. See Chapters 9 and 10 for a fuller analysis of adjustments to restore equilibrium.

[13] The sensitivity (elasticity) of the amount demanded to changes in the exchange rate will also decide the equilibrium rate of exchange and therefore the division of gains from trade. See Chapter 7.

where international trade involves many commodities rather than only two. To conclude, the *division* of gains from international trade is determined by the relative intensities (and elasticities) of the demands of each country for the other's goods—reciprocal demand.

A BROADER INTERPRETATION OF GAINS

The preceding analysis provides us with a precise explanation of the gains from international trade and their division among the trading countries. This analysis, however, does not consider the enormous changes that international trade may bring to the economy of a country over time.

The contemporary economies of most countries would be radically different if they had not developed during a period of widespread trade. For example, the British economy produces only a small fraction of its food and raw material requirements—the cessation of all foreign trade would mean starvation for millions and a drastic reduction in the living standards of those fortunate enough to survive. To a lesser extent the same is true of Western Europe. In short, the basic structure of most national economies would be far different if nations were unable to specialize and trade with each other. Today's economies are largely a product of past international trade. Thus, the gains from trade are commensurate with the whole economy, and they are evidenced by its long-run development in the direction of greater international specialization.

MANY COUNTRIES AND MANY GOODS

For simplicity we have assumed only two countries and two goods. How do the many countries and many goods of the actual world affect the theory of comparative advantage?

The role of reciprocal demand in determining exports and imports is enhanced by the existence of several countries and several goods. We can show this most simply by first looking at an example of three countries and two commodities, and then looking at an example of two countries and several commodities.

THREE COUNTRIES AND TWO COMMODITIES

Let us suppose that the following prices for the same two commodities exist in the United States, the United Kingdom, and France:

Table 3-7

	United States (Dollars)	United Kingdom (Pounds Sterling)	France (Francs)
Unit (price) of wheat ..	1.00	2.00	1.00
Unit (price) of textiles .	3.00	2.00	2.00

Before the opening of trade the prices of wheat and textiles in each country are such that one unit of wheat exchanges for one-third unit of textiles in the United States, one unit of wheat exchanges for one unit of textiles in the United Kingdom, and one unit of wheat exchanges for one-half unit of textiles in France. It is clear that the United States has a comparative advantage in the production of wheat, since the opportunity cost of its wheat is the lowest (one-third unit of textiles) among the three countries. Similarly, the United Kingdom has a comparative advantage in the production of textiles since the opportunity cost of its textiles is the lowest (one unit of wheat) among the three countries. But what of France? Its comparative advantage will be determined by the terms of exchange between wheat and textiles once international trade begins, and the terms of trade will be determined by reciprocal demand—the demand of each country for the exports of the other two countries.

Since the opportunity cost of a unit of wheat is one-half unit of textiles in France, it is apparent that France will export wheat whenever it can get for each unit of wheat more than (or at least as much as) one-half unit of textiles in exchange. If, for example, one unit of wheat exchanges for two-thirds unit of textiles, both the United States and France will export wheat to the United Kingdom in exchange for textiles. On the other hand, France will export textiles whenever it can get for each unit of textiles more than (or at least as much as) two units of wheat. Thus, if one unit of textiles exchanges for two and one-half units of wheat, both the United Kingdom and France will export textiles to the United States in exchange for wheat. There is a third possibility that France will not trade in either commodity. This will happen if the terms of trade between wheat and textiles are identical with the ratio of exchange within France in the absence of trade; that is, one unit of wheat for one-half unit of textiles. In that event, the United States will export wheat to the United Kingdom in exchange for imports of textiles.

The peculiar position of France is due to the fact that its domestic price ratio between wheat and textiles (1:2) lies between the price ratio in the United States (1:3) and in the United Kingdom (1:1). As we learned earlier, trade is profitable between the United States and the United Kingdom over the range of exchange ratios marked off by their respective domestic price ratios, that is, from ⅓ to 1. We also learned that upon the opening of trade the exact exchange ratio is determined by reciprocal demand through its influence on the exchange rate. We now see in our present example that reciprocal demand determines whether France will trade or not and, if she does, the commodity that she will export and the commodity that she will import.[14] This substantiates our previous statement that the existence of many countries enhances the role of reciprocal demand.

---

[14] The possibility that a country will cease entirely to trade because of a shift in reciprocal demand is remote when we drop our assumption of two commodities.

TWO COUNTRIES AND SEVERAL COMMODITIES

Let us suppose we have the domestic prices, shown in the following table, for a number of commodities in the United States and the United Kingdom.

It is obvious that the United States will export commodity A and the United Kingdom will export commodity G if there is trade between the two countries. Beyond that we can say nothing definite until a rate of exchange is established between the dollar and the pound, and the precise rate of exchange will depend upon reciprocal demand. Any shift in demand that increases the number of pounds exchanged for a dollar (a slackening in demand for imports in the United States or a rise in demand for imports

Table 3-8

Commodity	United States (Dollars)	United Kingdom (Pounds Sterling)
A	1.00	15.00
B	2.00	13.00
C	4.00	11.00
D	7.00	11.00
E	9.00	12.00
F	10.00	6.00
G	12.00	1.00

in the United Kingdom) will extend the number of commodities exported by the United Kingdom and lessen the number of commodities exported by the United States. Conversely, any shift in demand that decreases the number of pounds exchanged for one dollar will cause the United States to export a greater number of commodities and the United Kingdom to export a smaller number.

To conclude, reciprocal demand is of much greater importance in determining the nature of a country's trade than is suggested by our simple two-country, two-commodity model.

INCREASING COSTS

Up to this point we have assumed that unit costs were independent of the level of production.[15] Actually, the unit cost of producing any good will start to rise at *some* level of output, although that level may be high or low, depending on the specific production process. Until the point of increasing unit costs is reached, unit costs may decrease slowly or rapidly; that is to say, the U-shaped cost curve of a firm may be shallow or deep.

---

[15] Alternatively, we have assumed constant opportunity costs. See the next section.

THE PRINCIPLE OF DIMINISHING MARGINAL PRODUCTIVITY

The basic cause of increasing unit costs is found in the *principle of diminishing marginal productivity*. This principle states that when inputs of one factor (or factors) are added one at a time to a fixed input of another factor (or factors), production at first will increase at an increasing rate, then level off, and eventually decrease. Accordingly, unit costs of production will first decrease, then level off, and finally increase.[16]

An example drawn from agriculture will clarify this principle. Suppose a farmer has twenty acres of land and he decides to produce wheat by combining labor with his land. (To simplify matters we assume the necessary seed and tools are provided without cost.) The production of wheat might respond to additional inputs of labor as follows:

Table 3-9

Inputs of Labor (man-days)	Output of Wheat— Total Product (bushels)	Change in Output of Wheat—Marginal Product (bushels)
0	0	0
1	100	100
2	250	150
3	450	200
4	550	100
5	600	50
6	600	0
7	550	—50

With no labor inputs, the production of wheat is zero. When one labor input is added to the twenty acres of land, production rises to 100 bushels. This change in production brought about by the last input of labor (the input first hired in this case) is the *marginal product* of labor. As more inputs of labor are added to the fixed supply of land, the marginal product rises until the fourth labor input is hired. At this point the marginal product falls. The sixth input contributes nothing to production, and the seventh input actually lowers production because its marginal product is negative.

The principle of diminishing marginal productivity is applicable to all kinds of production because there are always certain factors of production that are relatively fixed in supply.[17] Together with transportation costs, the

---

[16] Unit costs will not vary precisely with the addition of factor inputs because of the cost of the fixed factor inputs.

[17] It follows that *constant costs* imply that factors are either perfect substitutes of each other and can be treated as a single factor or, what amounts to the same thing, factors are required in the same fixed proportions at all levels of production. Both of these conditions are absent in the real world.

principle explains why all the world's wheat is not produced on one acre of land or all the world's textiles are not turned out by one factory. In manufacturing, the fixed factors are usually buildings, capital equipment, and technical and managerial personnel.

When a large firm or industry expands production, it may be able to obtain additional labor or other factors only at progressively higher prices. Higher factor prices, then, may be a second source of increasing unit costs.

THE EFFECTS OF INCREASING COSTS ON INTERNATIONAL TRADE

The effects of increasing costs on international trade are two: (1) increasing costs generally rule out complete specialization of production between countries; and, (2) increasing costs as compared to constant costs narrow the opportunity for gainful trade. These effects are succinctly shown

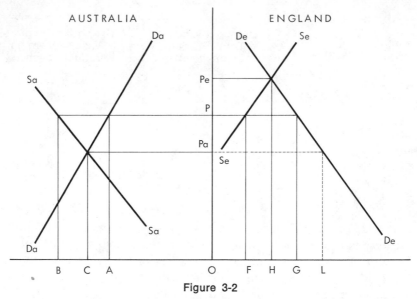

Figure 3-2

PARTIAL SPECIALIZATION UNDER INCREASING COSTS: TWO COUNTRIES

in Figure 3-2. The left half of Figure 3-2 shows the supply and demand schedules for wool in Australia: *Sa* and *Da,* respectively. With no international trade these schedules intersect to determine price, *O-Pa*; and at this price, *O-C* of wool is both supplied and demanded. Similarly, the supply and demand schedules for wool in England are indicated in the right half of Figure 3-2 as *Se* and *De*. In isolation, the price of wool in England is *O-Pe*, and the amount demanded and supplied at this price is *O-H*. The price of wool is much lower in Australia because the production of wool requires comparatively large supplies of land, which are relatively abundant in Australia and relatively scarce in England. Both countries will gain if Australia exports wool to England and imports a commodity in which it has a comparative disadvantage.

If costs were constant, Australia would be able to supply unlimited units of wool at price $O\text{-}Pa$, whereas England could supply no units of wool at a price below $O\text{-}Pe$. Upon the opening of trade, therefore, constant costs would bring about a complete specialization of wool production in Australia. England would produce no wool and would import $O\text{-}L$ wool from Australia at price $O\text{-}Pa$.

Wool production, however, faces increasing costs in both countries. When trade begins, Australia will encounter higher unit costs as it expands wool production to meet the new English demand. At the same time, the unit cost of producing wool in England will fall as domestic production is cut back in the face of imports from Australia. This process of adjustment comes to an end when the marginal cost of wool in Australia—the cost of producing the last unit—has risen to $O\text{-}P$, and the marginal cost of wool in England has fallen to $O\text{-}P$. At this marginal cost, which is equal to price under pure competition, Australia will consume $O\text{-}A$ wool, produce $O\text{-}B$ wool, and export $A\text{-}B$ wool. England will consume $O\text{-}G$ wool, producing $O\text{-}F$ wool at home and importing $F\text{-}G$ wool. The price of wool is now the same in both countries ($O\text{-}P$), and exports ($A\text{-}B$) are equal to imports ($F\text{-}G$). Because of increasing costs, England continues to produce $O\text{-}F$ wool, and the volume of trade ($F\text{-}G$) is clearly smaller than it would be if costs were constant ($O\text{-}L$).

Despite the existence of increasing costs, there are many examples of complete international specialization in the world economy. At times a nation is physically unable to produce a specific commodity or cannot produce even a small amount except at a cost higher than foreign cost.[18] A large fraction of the international trade in minerals and food products falls into this category. Full international specialization also occurs when a domestic industry is able to meet the demand for its product over a range of *decreasing* unit costs, a subject treated in the next chapter.

A RESTATEMENT OF THE THEORY OF TRADE— PRODUCTION POSSIBILITIES AND INDIFFERENCE CURVES

In presenting the theory of trade in the foregoing pages, we chose to start with absolute international price differences in order to proceed from the immediate (and familiar) basis of trade to a more fundamental (and

---

[18] In terms of Figure 3-2 this means that the domestic supply schedule of the importing country, despite an upward slope from left to right, lies entirely above the price of imports.

obscure) basis; namely, dissimilar factor endowments. We now employ an opposite approach that begins with national production capabilities deriving from dissimilar factor endowments and then proceeds towards absolute international cost and price differences. Although more abstract, this second analysis is intended to reinforce the reader's understanding of comparative advantage and the gains from trade.

PRODUCTION POSSIBILITIES: CONSTANT OPPORTUNITY COSTS

Assume there are only two countries in the world, the United States and France, and each produces only two commodities, beef and wine. Assume further that if each country uses *all* of its productive factors (land, labor, management and capital), it can produce the following alternative outputs of beef and wine:

Table 3-10

	Units of Beef	Units of Wine
United States	100	50
France	50	150

Translating this output data into graphical form gives us the production possibilities curves of the two countries, shown in Figures 3-3 and 3-4.

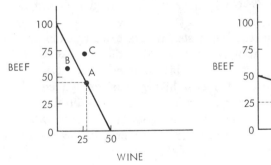

Figure 3-3

U.S. PRODUCTION POSSIBILITIES: CONSTANT OPPORTUNITY COSTS

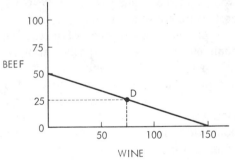

Figure 3-4

FRENCH PRODUCTION POSSIBILITIES: CONSTANT OPPORTUNITY COSTS

The U.S. production possibilities curve indicates the various combinations of beef and wine that the U.S. productive factors can produce when they are fully employed and used efficiently. For example, one possible output combination shown by point *A* on the curve represents 45 units of beef and 27.5 units of wine. Point *B*, on the other hand, represents a beef-wine combination that is smaller than possible production because of factor

Part One / Theory

unemployment and/or inefficient use. Point C to the right of the curve denotes a beef-wine combination that is beyond the physical production capacity of the United States. Similar remarks can be made about the French production possibilities curve.

Both curves depict constant opportunity costs for beef and wine.[19] To increase the output of wine by one unit in the United States, factors must be taken away from the production of beef in such amount as to lower the output of beef by two units. Hence, the opportunity cost of one wine unit is two beef units and this cost is not affected by the output levels of beef and wine. In France the opportunity cost of one wine unit is always a one-third beef unit. These constant opportunity costs are shown by the constant slopes of the respective curves, -2 for the United States and $-\frac{1}{3}$ for France. The rate at which the output of one product must be reduced in order to increase the output of the other product is the *marginal rate of substitution in production* (MRS_p). In the case of the United States, the MRS_p of beef into wine is 2, which (disregarding sign) equals the slope of the production possibilities curve. When opportunity costs are constant, the MRS_p is also constant. Under conditions of pure competition, the domestic barter rate of exchange of beef for wine (the *marginal rate of substitution in trade,* or MRS_t) equals the MRS_p or slope of the production possibilities curve. In the United States two units of beef will exchange for one unit of wine while in France one unit of beef will exchange for three units of wine.

In the absence of trade, each country can elect to consume only a beef-wine combination that lies somewhere on its production possibilities curve, such as A in Figure 3-3 (45 beef units and 27.5 wine units) and D in Figure 3-4 (25 beef units and 75 wine units). The existence of different marginal rates of substitution in production, however, offers both countries an opportunity to gain from mutual trade and consume a beef-wine combination that lies beyond their production possibilities frontiers. This pleasant outcome will occur when beef and wine are traded at any barter rate of exchange that falls between the domestic barter rates which, in turn, are equal to the respective marginal rates of substitution in production.

The gains from trade are depicted in Figures 3-5 and 3-6. Reciprocal demand determines an international barter rate of exchange (commodity terms of trade) that is shown by the slope of the dashed lines, which is identical in both figures. At this rate of exchange (one beef unit = one wine unit), the United States will specialize completely in beef production because it can obtain from France more wine for each unit of beef than it can at home. Conversely, France will specialize entirely in wine production, obtaining all its beef from the United States. At the international rate, the United States chooses to consume 40 units of wine, importing them from

---

[19] Constant opportunity costs imply that (1) the factors of production are perfect substitutes or are used in the same fixed proportions to produce both goods and (2) returns to scale are constant for both goods, that is to say, a doubling of all factor inputs will double output.

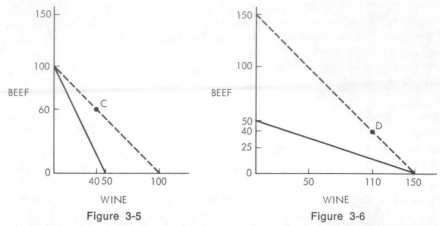

Figure 3-5

U.S. GAINS FROM TRADE: CONSTANT OPPORTUNITY COSTS

Figure 3-6

FRENCH GAINS FROM TRADE: CONSTANT OPPORTUNITY COSTS

France in exchange for 40 units of beef.[20] The converse is true for France. As a result of trade, then, the United States is able to consume a beef-wine combination, indicated by C on the international barter exchange line, that is bigger than any combination the United States can produce in isolation. For France, D represents a beef-wine combination that is superior to any combination producible at home. Both countries gain from trade: because of specialization their combined output of beef and wine is higher than before and the production increment is shared by consumers in both countries.

An arithmetic recapitulation of the before- and after-trade situations is instructive:

Table 3-11

Before Trade

	Production Beef	Wine	Consumption Beef	Wine	Gains from Trade Beef	Wine
United States ..	45	27.5	45	27.5	0	0
France	25	75	25	75	0	0
Combined	70	102.5	70	102.5	0	0

After Trade

	Production Beef	Wine	Consumption Beef	Wine	Gains from Trade Beef	Wine
United States ..	100	0	60	40	15	12.5
France	0	150	40	110	15	35
Combined	100	150	100	150	30	47.5

[20] An explanation of consumption choices is offered in the next section.

The international barter rate of exchange of one beef unit for one wine unit is an *equilibrium* rate because it clears the market; that is, exports equal imports. Any change in reciprocal demand, however, would establish a new equilibrium rate and thereby alter the division of gains. Gainful trade for both countries will occur at any barter rate of exchange that falls between the two domestic barter rates; at any rate beyond the range set by the two domestic barter rates, only one country will gain, and trade will not occur because the other country will be better off without trade. When the international barter rate is the same as the domestic barter rate of one country, then that country will neither gain nor lose from trade and all the gain will go to the second country. This will happen when the trading economies differ so much in size that the bigger country cannot completely satisfy its demand for the product in which it has a comparative disadvantage through imports, but must also rely on some domestic production. In that event, the bigger country will trade at its domestic barter rate and all the gain will go to the smaller country. Sometimes it pays to be small!

So far we have talked only in terms of *barter* rates of exchange between two goods. When money is introduced, it is a simple matter to convert barter rates into prices and foreign exchange rates. For example, if two beef exchange for one wine in the United States before trade, then it follows that the price of beef is one-half the price of wine, say, $1.00 and $2.00, respectively. The price ratio between two goods is the reciprocal of the barter ratio. Similarly, the exchange rate between the dollar and the franc can be derived from the international barter rate, given the domestic money prices of beef and wine. Hence, the statement on p. 58 (". . . when cost ratios are dissimilar in two countries, there is a range of exchange rates between their respective currencies that will permit gainful trade between them") is precisely analogous to the statement: when domestic barter rates are dissimilar in two countries, there is a range of international barter rates of exchange for the same goods that will permit gainful trade between those countries.

PRODUCTION POSSIBILITIES: INCREASING OPPORTUNITY COSTS

The assumptions behind constant opportunity costs are highly unrealistic. In actuality, the factors of production are only partial substitutes for each other, and each good is produced with different factor combinations or intensities. With a given technology, good A will be generally more labor (and less capital) intensive in production than good B.[21] The existence of

---

[21] However, good A may not have the same labor intensity at (1) different prices of labor relative to other factor prices, or (2) at different scales of output. It is even conceivable that good A will switch from a labor intensive to a capital intensive good at some factor price relationship or scale of output, a phenomenon known as *factor reversibility*.

different factor intensities for two goods will make a country's production possibilities curve concave to the origin, indicating increasing opportunity costs.[22]

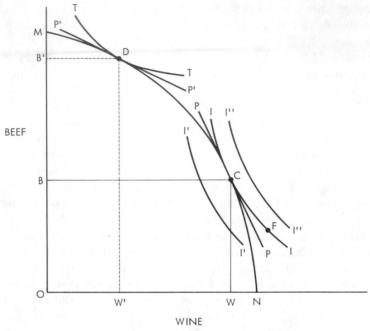

Figure 3-7

U.S. PRODUCTION POSSIBILITIES: INCREASING OPPORTUNITY COSTS

Such a curve is shown for the United States in Figure 3-7. Note that the marginal rate of substitution in production (the slope of curve MN) is no longer constant. The meaning of increasing opportunity costs may be described as follows. Suppose the United States is producing only wine at N. Now it decides to produce one unit of beef. To do so, it must draw factors of production from wine, forcing a drop in wine output. Note, however, that this drop is small (the slope of the production possibilities curve is steep near N) because the withdrawn factors of production are actually better suited to beef production than to wine production. But as the production of beef is progressively increased, greater and greater amounts of wine must be sacrificed to obtain one more unit of beef (the slope of the curve gets flatter and flatter). Why should the opportunity cost of beef increase? Because the factors of production drawn from wine production (such as land) are less and less suited to the production of beef. As the latter

---

[22] Even if factor intensities were the same, decreasing returns to scale (a doubling of all factor inputs causes less than a doubling of output) for one good would create increasing opportunity costs for both goods. However, factor intensities are the principal explanation of increasing opportunity costs.

approaches *M*, very large quantities of wine must be given up to get one more unit of beef. Similarly, if the United States starts at *M* and then progressively transfers resources from beef to wine production, it will eventually encounter increasing opportunity costs.[23]

What determines the domestic barter rate of exchange between beef and wine under conditions of increasing opportunity costs? The answer is the demand preferences or tastes of consumers, the combination of beef and wine that a nation's people want to consume. We can portray the demand preferences of U.S. consumers by an *indifference map* that consists of an infinite number of *indifference curves*. In Figure 3-7, *I'*, *I*, and *I''* represent indifference curves belonging to the same indifference map. *Each* indifference curve indicates all possible combinations of beef and wine that yield the same level of satisfaction: the nation's consumers are "indifferent" to any combination lying on the indifference curve. Thus, the combination of beef and wine indicated by point *F* on indifference curve *I-I* provides the same satisfaction to consumers as the combination at *C*. The slope of an indifference curve at any point is the *marginal rate of substitution in consumption* (MRS_c); in this instance, the amount of beef consumers are willing to give up to obtain another unit of wine. The shape of each indifference curve is determined by consumer tastes; a change in tastes will generate a new family of indifference curves.[24]

It follows from the definition of an indifference curve that different indifference curves offer different levels of satisfaction. Graphically, the further an indifference curve is from the origin, the higher its level of satisfaction. Thus, in Figure 3-7, *I''-I''* represents a higher level of satisfaction than *I-I*, which in turn represents a higher level of satisfaction than *I'-I'*. Consumers, therefore, will maximize their satisfaction by consuming a combination of beef and wine that lies on the *highest* indifference curve attainable with their income. This occurs at point *C*, where the U.S. production possibilities curve is tangent to *I-I*. At that point consumers obtain the combination of beef and wine that gives them the most satisfaction of any combination the nation is able to produce. Indifference curve *I'-I''* is not attainable in the absence of international trade because it lies beyond the production possibilities curve. At point *C* the marginal rate of substitution

---

[23] The principle of diminishing marginal productivity (p. 71) is related to increasing opportunity costs because it also derives from imperfect factor substitutability. However, this principle applies to the physical output of one product only.

[24] Indifference curves were devised to analyze the preferences of the *individual* consumer who presumably is able to determine the different combinations of two goods that would give him the same satisfaction. Can we add up the indifference curves of individuals to get a *community* indifference curve for the entire nation? Strictly speaking, the answer is no. Different consumers have dissimilar indifference maps that are literally incomparable. One man may want a lot of beef and only a little wine; another man may want the converse. Although it is not possible to make interpersonal comparisons of welfare (satisfaction), the community indifference curve is most useful in demonstrating the influence of demand preferences on international trade. In so using it, however, we must bear in mind that its welfare implications are ambiguous. For a discussion of trade and welfare, see pages 16-17.

in production equals the marginal rate of substitution in consumption—any movement away from this equality would lower welfare. The slope of their common tangent, indicated by P-P, is the domestic barter rate of exchange between beef and wine. Hence, at point C, $MRS_p = MRS_c = MRS_t$.

Suppose there occurs a change in taste that generates a new indifference map. What happens? T-T is the new indifference curve that is tangent to the production possibilities curve at point D. Compared to point C, consumers now want more beef and less wine. Their demand, therefore, will push up the price of beef relative to the price of wine (in barter terms, *decrease* the marginal rate of substitution in trade of beef for wine). Producers will respond by shifting out of wine into beef production until the marginal rate of substitution in production once again equals the marginal rate of substitution in consumption at point D. Here their common tangent, P'-P', becomes the new barter rate of exchange.

Let us now consider the gains from trade under increasing opportunity costs of production. Figures 3-8 and 3-9 depict the production possibilities and indifference curves for the United States and France. Before trade the United States produces at C on its production possibilities curve, producing (and consuming) O-B beef and O-W wine. The U.S. barter exchange line (P_s-P_s) is tangent to both the production possibilities curve and an indifference curve I-I at point C. Hence, C is an equilibrium position. Similarly, France produces and consumes at K (O-G beef and O-F wine) where its barter exchange line (P_f-P_f) is tangent to its production possibilities curve and an indifference curve T-T. Since the slopes of the two barter price lines differ, the two countries have different marginal rates of substitution in trade. Hence, there is a basis for gainful trade.

When trade opens up, reciprocal demand determines an international barter exchange line (P-P) that is the same for both countries. Since the international barter price of beef is higher than its U.S. domestic price, U.S. producers will shift out of wine into beef until the MRS_p is equal to the new MRS_t at A. Here the United States specializes in beef (O-B') but continues to produce some wine (O-W'). At the new barter price, U.S. consumers choose to consume a beef-wine combination denoted by C', the point of tangency between P-P and indifference curve I-I'. The United States exports D-C' beef in exchange for A-D wine from France. After trade, U.S. beef consumption is domestic beef production (O-B') *minus* beef exports (D-C') and U.S. wine consumption is domestic production (O-W') plus wine imports (A-D), a combination indicated by C'. The United States clearly gains from trade because it is able to reach a higher indifference curve. It has chosen to consume more beef (O-C' > O-B) and more wine (O-C' > O-W) than before trade.[25]

---

[25] Instead of more of both goods, the gains from trade might be a combination that has more of one good and less of another than the pretrade combination, but the former would lie outside the production possibilities curve. The precise combination will depend on demand preferences.

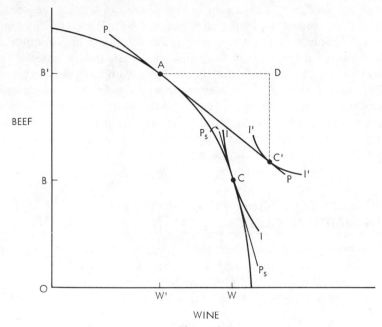

Figure 3-8

U.S. GAINS FROM TRADE: INCREASING OPPORTUNITY COSTS

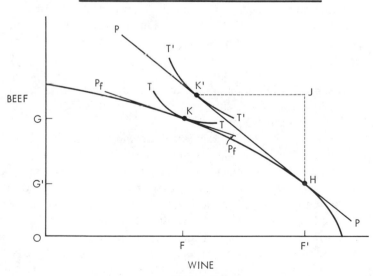

Figure 3-9

FRENCH GAINS FROM TRADE: INCREASING OPPORTUNITY COSTS

In France, producers respond to *P-P* by shifting from beef to wine production until at *H* the MRS$_p$ equals the MRS$_t$. France exports *K'-J* wine in exchange for *J-H* beef, consuming a beef-wine combination denoted by *K'* where *P-P* is tangent to indifference curve *T'-T'*. This combination is superior to *K* because it lies on a higher indifference curve. France has chosen to consume more of both beef and wine than before trade.

Since U.S. exports of beef must equal French imports and vice versa, *D-C'* = *J-H* and *A-D* = *K'-J*. In after-trade equilibrium, the U.S. marginal rate of substitution in production is equal to the marginal rate of substitution in international trade which, in turn, equals the marginal rate of substitution in consumption, and these rates are equal to the same marginal rates in France. Because of increasing opportunity costs, both countries continue to produce beef and wine.[26]

IDENTICAL PRODUCTION POSSIBILITIES WITH DISSIMILAR TASTES

We have seen how dissimilar production possibilities curves of two countries afford a basis for gainful trade between them. But under conditions of increasing opportunity costs, dissimilar tastes in two countries can also provide a basis for gainful trade even when their production possibilities are the same.

Assume the United States and France have the same production possibilities curve *F-F* in Figure 3-10.[27] However, the Americans strongly prefer beef over wine while French tastes run in the opposite direction, as is shown by the indifference curves *I-I* and *T-T,* respectively. Consequently, before trade the United States chooses to produce and consume combination *C* of beef and wine with a domestic price line *P_s-P_s*. On the other hand, France chooses to produce and consume a great deal of wine and only a little beef as shown by combination *K* where its domestic price line *P_f-P_f* is tangent to its production possibilities curve and indifference curve *T-T*. Since the marginal rates of substitution in trade are different at *C* and *K,* there is a basis for gainful trade.

With the opening of trade, reciprocal demand establishes an international price line *P-P*. U.S. producers adjust to *P-P* by moving from *C* to *G* (cutting down on beef production, increasing wine production), while French producers do the opposite, moving from *K* to *G*. U.S. consumers adjust to *P-P* by consuming *C'* of beef and wine, where *P-P* is tangent to the indifference curve *I'-I'*. Hence, the United States exports *C'-B* of wine in exchange for *B-G* beef imports. French consumers choose combination *K'* where *P-P* is tangent to indifference curve *T'-T'*. France exports *H-K'* (= *B-G*) beef in exchange for *G-H* (= *C'-B*) wine imports. Both countries gain from trade because their consumption now lies on higher indifference curves. The United States now consumes more beef and the same amount

---

[26] Figure 3-2 on p. 72 shows incomplete specialization under conditions of increasing opportunity costs when those costs are translated into rising supply schedules.

[27] Only the *shape* of the two curves has to be identical, not the absolute size.

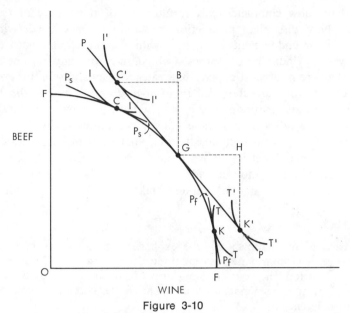

Figure 3-10

U.S. AND FRENCH GAINS FROM TRADE: DISSIMILAR
TASTES WITH SAME PRODUCTION POSSIBILITIES

of wine as before trade and France consumes more wine and slightly more beef. Where does this gain come from? Before trade the United States was highly specialized in beef production, using some factors of production that were much better suited to wine production. The converse was true for France. Trade permitted the United States to shift factors from beef to wine production and France to shift factors from wine to beef production. The gains from trade come from a lesser degree of specialization in production but a higher degree of specialization in consumption.

The assumption of similar production possibilities curves for two countries is, of course, unlikely to be matched in the real world. But can dissimilar tastes ever overwhelm dissimilar production possibilities so that a nation exports the product in which it has a comparative *cost* disadvantage while importing the product in which it has a comparative cost advantage? Yes, theoretically. But the probability of such a situation may be regarded as very low.[28] Actually, consumer tastes appear to be converging rather than diverging as "demonstration effects" penetrate all countries.[29] However, demand preferences must be taken into account in any full statement of the theory of comparative advantage because they undoubtedly influence domestic marginal rates of substitution in trade (price ratios).

---

[28] The same opinion is expressed in other language on p. 62: "This influence of demand on factor price *ratios* . . . will seldom offset the influence of factor supplies."

[29] Demonstration effects are transmitted via communication of all kinds (including travel) as well as via trade and investment. But see the discussion of income gaps on p. 129 ff.

We have now completed this restatement of the theory of trade. We have seen how dissimilar production possibilities curves (deriving from dissimilar factor endowments) together with demand preferences or tastes as portrayed by indifference curves (which may or may not be similar) determine different domestic marginal rates of substitution in trade, and thereby a basis for gainful trade. In after-trade equilibrium, the marginal rates of substitution in production in both countries equal the marginal rate of substitution in international trade (under conditions of increasing opportunity cost) which, in turn, equals the marginal rates of substitution in consumption in the two countries. When money is introduced, dissimilar domestic marginal rates of substitution in trade become dissimilar price ratios which, as stated at the beginning of the chapter, make gainful trade possible.

SUMMARY

1. The basis of international trade is explained by the theory of comparative advantage. The immediate basis of trade lies in absolute differences between the prices of foreign goods and the prices of similar goods produced at home. Under perfect and monopolistic competition these price differences reduce to cost differences.

2. Absolute international differences in costs (prices) arise upon the establishment of an exchange rate when the cost ratios within each country are dissimilar, for then the opportunity costs of producing similar goods will differ between countries and each country will have a comparative cost advantage in producing some goods and a comparative cost *dis*advantage in producing other goods. When cost ratios are identical between countries, opportunity costs are also identical and there is no basis for gainful international trade.

3. When cost ratios are dissimilar, there is a range of exchange rates that permits gainful international trade. The two extremes of this range are determined by the cost ratios within each country. At rates beyond these extremes, trade is unprofitable for one or the other countries and, therefore, will not occur.

4. Dissimilar cost ratios derive from dissimilar factor price ratios. This is because the factors of production (land, labor, capital, and management) are not perfect substitutes for each other and must be used in different combinations to produce different goods. Factor price ratios, in turn, are determined by the relative supply and demand of the factors of production.

5. Countries differ greatly in their relative supplies of factors of production. Since a factor in relatively abundant supply has a comparatively low price while a factor in relatively scarce supply has a comparatively high price, dissimilar national factor supplies give rise to dissimilar national factor prices. Dissimilar national factor demands may also cause dissimilar national factor prices. Although there is no single basis of international trade, we may say in a loose sense that the fundamental basis of international trade lies in dissimilar national factor endowments.

6. The gains from international trade stem from the greater production that is possible when nations specialize in accordance with their comparative advantages. The division of these gains between the trading nations will depend upon reciprocal demand.

7. The presence of many countries and many goods enhances the role of reciprocal demand in determining the character of a country's foreign trade.

8. In the real world constant unit costs rarely hold in production. Because of the principle of diminishing marginal productivity, the unit cost of producing any good will start to rise at some level of output. Increasing unit costs of production generally rule out complete international specialization, and thereby narrow the opportunity for gainful international trade.

9. An alternative approach to the theory of comparative advantage uses production possibilities and indifference curves. The slope of a country's production possibilities curve at any point is the marginal rate of substitution in production (MRS_p) at that point. The slope of a country's indifference curve at any point is the marginal rate of substitution in consumption (MRS_c) at that point. In the absence of international trade, equilibrium is achieved in both production and consumption at the point of tangency between the production possibilities curve and an indifference curve. This common tangency is the marginal rate of substitution in trade (domestic barter rate of exchange). In equilibrium, therefore, $MRS_p = MRS_c = MRS_t$.

10. When the production possibilities curves of two countries have dissimilar shapes but their indifference curves have the same shape, then their pretrade domestic marginal rates of substitution in trade will differ, providing a basis for gainful trade. Under conditions of increasing opportunity cost, post-trade equilibrium is achieved when the marginal rates of substitution in production and consumption of each country equal the marginal rate of substitution in international trade. This is the optimal welfare position.

11. Although dissimilar tastes (indifference curves) afford a separate basis for gainful trade, they are not likely to overwhelm the influence of dissimilar opportunity costs in production on the direction of trade.

12. The production possibilities and indifference curve approach to the theory of trade leads to the same conclusion as our first approach: dissimilar price ratios between countries make gainful trade possible.

QUESTIONS AND APPLICATIONS

1. Why are absolute international differences in prices not the *final* explanation of international trade?

2. Assume that two countries (United States and France) each produce the same two commodities (wine and electric toasters) with the following costs:

	United States (Dollars)	France (Francs)
Unit cost of wine	2.00	3.00
Unit cost of electric toasters	4.00	12.00

(a) What are the opportunity costs of producing wine and electric toasters in both countries?

(b) Is gainful trade possible between the two countries? If so, what will be its nature?

(c) Is there a range of exchange rates between the dollar and the franc that will permit gainful trade? If so, what is it?

3. "Loosely speaking, we may say that dissimilar factor supply ratios in different countries are the basis of international trade." Explain.

4. Referring to Question 2 above, what are the gains per unit of exports for each country when the exchange rate is one franc equals 0.5 dollars? Assuming that U.S. exports total 30 units at that rate of exchange, what is the number of units of U.S. imports? Why?

5. Explain how reciprocal demand determines the equilibrium rate of exchange and thus the division of gains from trade.

6. How does the existence of many countries and many goods affect the theory of comparative advantage?

7. (a) What is meant by "increasing costs"?
   (b) What are the effects of increasing costs on international trade? Why?

8. Draw production possibilities curves for two countries that have the same shapes under conditions of increasing opportunity costs.
   (a) Assuming similar tastes (indifference curves), demonstrate graphically that no gainful trade is possible.
   (b) Assuming dissimilar tastes, demonstrate graphically that gainful trade is possible.

SELECTED READINGS

See the list of readings given at the end of Chapter 5.

CHAPTER **4**

QUALIFICATIONS OF THE SIMPLE THEORY OF INTERNATIONAL TRADE (1)

In the preceding chapter, variable factor proportions (endowments) and, to a lesser degree, different tastes were shown to cause dissimilar domestic price ratios that provided a basis for gainful trade among nations. We shall refer to this factor-endowments model as the "simple" theory of trade because it rests on many assumptions that are not representative either in whole or in part of the actual world economy. These assumptions are: (1) the absence of transportation or other transfer costs in the international movement of physical goods; (2) perfect competition; (3) full employment of all factors of production; (4) fixed supplies of homogeneous factors of production; (5) the absence of technological innovation and the sameness of production functions in different countries; and (6) perfect immobility of the factors of production among countries.

How is the simple theory of trade affected by the abandonment of these assumptions? Hopefully, an answer to this question will advance our understanding of the forces that determine the actual volume, composition, and direction of international trade. It will become quickly apparent, however, that in making the simple theory more relevant to the real world, we unavoidably add to its complexity.

TRANSPORTATION AND OTHER TRANSFER COSTS

The movement of merchandise from one country to another involves a number of transfer costs. They may be classified as (1) costs of physical transfer and (2) transfer costs associated with the government regulation of international trade. Costs of physical transfer include the costs incurred in packing, transporting, and handling merchandise. Such costs are omnipresent, and they affect the movement of goods both within and between nations. Transfer costs also arise out of the government regulation of foreign trade such as import duties, quotas, and exchange restrictions.[1] These transfer costs differ from physical transfer costs in that they pertain only to international trade. Their nature and individual effects on trade are described in later chapters; for the present we shall restrict our discussion to the significance of physical transfer costs.

Physical transfer costs influence international trade in two ways. First, transfer costs increase the prices of imports and thereby restrict the opportunity for gainful trade. Second, transfer costs affect international trade by their bearing on the location of industry and the geographical pattern of production.

THE EFFECTS OF TRANSPORTATION COSTS ON INTERNATIONAL TRADE

Transportation is the main source of physical transfer costs; handling and packing facilitate transportation and are subsidiary to it. To simplify matters, we shall confine our analysis to the effects of transportation costs on international trade. The effects of handling and packing costs are the same, but usually of lesser importance.

The restrictive effects of transportation costs on the volume of international trade may be seen by comparing Figures 3-2 (page 72) and 4-1, which are drawn to the same scale. Figure 3-2 shows that Australia's wool exports (A-B) to England are equal to England's wool imports (F-G) from Australia at price O-P. Now let us introduce transportation costs. Instead of a single price ruling in both countries (O-P in Figure 3-2), there will be two prices that differ by the cost of transporting a unit of wool from Australia to England. We indicate this effect in Figure 4-1 by raising Australia's supply and demand schedules a distance O-O' higher than England's schedules. By so doing we recognize that the cost of Australian wool to English importers is the Australian price *plus* unit transportation costs represented by O-O'. The two equilibrium prices in Figure 4-1 are O'-P in Australia and O-P in England. At these prices Australia will export A-B wool and England will import F-G wool. Observe that the volume of trade in Figure 4-1 is less than the volume in Figure 3-2. Because of transportation costs the English now produce somewhat more wool at home (compare O-F in the two figures). Observe also that the English now pay a higher price for wool (O-P in Figure 4-1 is greater than O-P in Figure 3-2) but that the increase is somewhat less than transportation costs (O-O') because the price in Australia has fallen in response to a smaller export demand (O'-P in Figure 4-1 is less than O-P in Figure 3-2). In this illustration Australia continues to export wool in spite of transportation

---

[1] Trade restrictions that prohibit trade either entirely or beyond specified amounts, such as import quotas, have the same economic effects as infinite transfer costs.

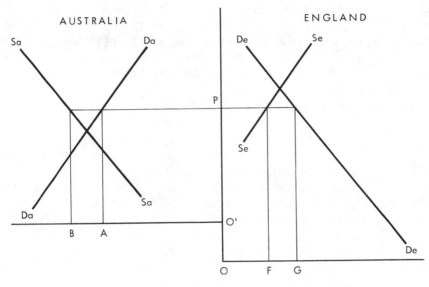

Figure 4-1

EFFECTS OF TRANSPORTATION COSTS ON INTERNATIONAL TRADE

costs. If transportation costs rose to equal *Pa-Pe* in Figure 3-2, however, Australia would cease to export any wool because transportation costs would entirely offset its pretrade price advantage.

Actually, commodities vary greatly in their capacity to absorb transportation costs. Commodities that are heavy, bulky, and hard to handle cannot absorb their transportation costs unless they command a high unit price. Bricks and sand are examples of this sort of commodity—to move them more than a short distance involves such high transportation costs that they cease to be competitive in price. On the other hand, commodities that take up little space or are easily handled may be economically transported over great distances even when their unit prices are low. The traditional staples of international trade, such as grains, wheat, cotton, and wool, fit the latter category of easy handling.

Transportation costs are not simply dependent on distance and the physical character of commodities. Transportation agencies, especially ocean shipping and railroad, have a very heavy investment in fixed capital and correspondingly high fixed costs. For this reason, steamship and railroad companies have a strong incentive to utilize the full capacity of their ships and freight cars at all times. To do so, they tend to "charge what the traffic will bear." This means that freight rates vary among commodities far more than can be justified by differences in weight, bulk, ease of handling, or other physical factors. Commodities that can easily absorb freight costs because of high unit values, such as electronic equipment, are charged high rates. By the same token, bulky commodities of low unit value, such as wheat, are charged low rates. Generally speaking, manufactured goods pay much higher rates than primary goods.

This tendency to charge what the traffic will bear also helps account for freight rates that vary with the *direction* of physical movement. Frequently, the volume of trade between two ports, or geographical regions, is less in one direction than the other. To get full cargoes at ports where the volume of outgoing freight is low, steamship companies will charge shippers only low "backhaul" rates. In the nineteenth century, ships left Great Britain loaded down with coal and carried cargoes back to Britain at very low backhaul rates. These favorable rates undoubtedly stimulated British imports and the development of London as a reexport center for primary products.

The role of direction as a discriminatory factor in transportation rates is revealed in an investigation of ocean freight rates in United States trade by the Joint Economic Committee.[2] The Committee found that the international ocean freight rate structure was "weighted against" United States exports. In trade between the United States Pacific Coast and the Far East, freight rates on American exports exceeded rates on corresponding imports on 80 percent of the sampled items. Rate discrimination against American exports also occurred on 70 percent of the products traded between United States Atlantic and Gulf ports and the Far East, and on 60 percent of the goods shipped from the Atlantic Coast to Western Europe. For example, it cost $61.25 to ship radios from New York to Japan but only $40 to ship them from Japan to New York. The Committee also uncovered third country discrimination. A sample of rates on 40 export commodities showed that the average rate from the United States to ports in South America, South Africa, and India was $9.85 per 1,000 miles, whereas the average rate from Japan and from London to these same ports was $4.14 and $5.30, respectively. An American paid $39 to ship an automobile to Rio de Janeiro, Brazil, while an Englishman paid only $15.05, although New York is 500 miles closer to Rio de Janeiro than Liverpool.

In answer to the Committee's findings, ocean shipping spokesmen pointed out that United States liner exports were 1½ times greater in weight tons than imports, and rather than send vessels to the United States in ballast, shipowners charged only out-of-pocket, or variable, costs on shipments to the United States. The Committee rejected this explanation,

---

[2] Congress of the United States, Joint Economic Committee, *Discriminatory Ocean Freight Rates and the Balance of Payments* (Washington: U.S. Government Printing Office, 1965). The data in this and the next paragraph are taken from this document.

asserting that even when the quantity and value of United States imports were roughly equal to United States exports it found discrimination. Furthermore, this argument did not apply to third country discrimination. The Committee felt that the monopolistic determination of ocean freight rates was more to the point. Most ocean freight rates are set by associations, or conferences, of steamship companies, and United States flag lines are outnumbered in all but seven of the more than 100 active steamship conferences involved in United States trade. The Committee obtained some evidence that foreign lines, regardless of flag, voted as a bloc against United States lines. The question of ocean freight rate discrimination in United States trade is a very complex subject, and we have merely touched on it here. Its importance, however, should not be underestimated. In 1962 ocean freight rates represented 12 percent of the value of United States exports and 10 percent of the value of United States imports.

We may generalize this discussion of transportation costs in international trade by stating that the existence of transportation costs separates goods into two classes—*domestic* goods and *international* goods. Domestic goods do not enter international trade because transportation costs make it impossible to sell them at competitive prices in foreign markets.[3] International goods, however, are able to absorb transportation costs and still meet foreign competition.

The existence of transportation costs, like increasing costs of production, means that international specialization will not be complete. When transportation costs are taken into account, there will be a number of goods that can be acquired more cheaply from domestic industries despite the fact that foreign industries can produce the same goods at a lower cost. Low-cost housing construction in one country will not benefit home buyers in another country. There is, however, no sharp dividing line between domestic and international goods. A higher foreign demand may make it economically feasible to export a good that has not entered foreign trade in the past. An improvement in transportation that greatly lowers cost will convert many domestic goods into international goods.

This last observation suggests the tremendous effects upon international trade of the "transportation revolution" that occurred in the nineteenth century, particularly in its last quarter. Before this revolution, the vast hinterlands of North and South America and the productive resources of such countries as Australia and New Zealand were unable to supply the world market, centered in Europe, because of prohibitive costs of transportation. Argentine beef was left to rot in the sun because only skins and horns

---

[3] Perishable goods are likely to be domestic goods unless techniques of preservation or very rapid means of transportation permit their sale at competitive prices in foreign markets. This is also true of interregional trade as is testified by the local character of milk and bread production.

could be exported to Europe. Australia was able to export wool but not mutton. North American wheat could not compete in European markets. Hence, the railroad, the steamship, refrigeration, and many other improvements in transportation that came thick and fast after 1870 completely altered the character of world trade. A worldwide system of multilateral trade evolved to bring an ever-widening exchange of goods, illustrating in reverse the restrictive effects of transportation costs.

THE EFFECTS OF TRANSPORTATION COSTS ON THE LOCATION OF INDUSTRY

Transportation costs also influence international trade by affecting the *location* of production. In seeking to minimize costs of production, business firms must take full account of the transportation costs incurred in acquiring raw materials and in marketing final products. The best location for a firm is that location which minimizes total costs of production, including all transportation costs. This location may be near raw materials (*resource-oriented*), near the market or markets of the final product (*market-oriented*), or somewhere in between (*footloose*), depending upon the character of production processes.

When the cost of transporting raw materials used by an industry is substantially higher than the cost of shipping its finished products to markets, then the industry will usually locate closer to its raw material sources than to its markets. This situation exists when the industrial processes characterizing an industry use large quantities of bulky, low-value raw materials and fuels which do not enter into the final product. Such processes are described as "weight-losing" because the final product is so much less bulky or weighty than the materials and fuels necessary for its production. Steel, basic chemicals, aluminum, and lumber are among the products that utilize weight-losing industrial processes for their manufacture.

In the nineteenth century, steel production was an outstanding example of a resource-oriented industry. Loss of weight in production was very high; all of the coking coal and a big share of the iron ore were consumed in the smelting process. Thus, a steel industry usually located between deposits of coking coal and deposits of iron ore with a tendency to locate somewhat closer to coal deposits because of the greater weight loss. In the United States the bulk of the steel industry stretched from Buffalo and Pittsburgh westward to Detroit and Chicago, getting its coal from Pennsylvania and West Virginia and its iron ore from the Lake Superior region of Minnesota. This locational pattern of steel mills had a profound influence on the creation of the American industrial heartland because so many industries are dependent on steel as a basic industrial commodity. Today the traditional locational forces are changing in the steel industry as the Mesabi ores become depleted and the United States becomes increasingly dependent on iron ore imports from Canada and South America.[4] Both the Bethlehem mill at Sparrow's Point near Baltimore and the Fairless Works at Morrisville near Philadelphia obtain iron ore by ship and are also favorably placed with respect to domestic coal, as well as markets.

Frequently, transportation costs are minimized for weight-losing industries at river or ocean ports where advantage can be taken of low freight rates for the water transportation of bulky products (sometimes made even more attractive by backhaul rate discrimination) and the avoidance of trans-shipping raw materials from one mode of transportation to another, such as from ship to railroad car. This explains, at least in part, why weight-losing industries are often found at ocean or river ports in the United States and Europe, and why Sparrow's Point and the Fairless Works are favorably located, even though their iron ore comes from mines thousands of miles away.

When the cost of transporting finished products is substantially higher than the cost of transporting the raw materials and fuels that are used in their manufacture, industries locate close to their markets. This relationship develops when industrial processes add bulk or weight in production; that is, they are *weight-gaining*. Then industries try to postpone manufacture of the final product until it is physically close to its market. Although United States automobile companies have concentrated basic manufacture in the Detroit area, they have established regional assembly centers within the United States and assembly centers in many foreign countries because it is much cheaper to ship unassembled auto parts than the whole vehicle.[5] Many other manufactured goods are shipped as parts to assembly plants located near markets for the same reason. A prominent example of weight-gaining occurs in the construction of buildings, where the final product is so much bulkier than its components. Thus, building construction is mainly an assembly job at the construction site. Beverage manufacture offers another example of how weight-gaining processes push final manufacture towards the market. Coca Cola and Pepsi Cola ship syrup concentrate to plants all over the world which, in turn, add water to the concentrate and bottle the mixture. Recently, Scotch whiskey has started coming to the United States in concentrated form. Finally, mention should be made of the extreme

---

[4] Technological changes such as beneficiation of iron ore at the mine, the oxygen converter process, and others are also affecting location economics in the United States steel industry. The lesser degree of resource-orientation in the U.S. steel industry today as compared with the past is also demonstrated by the emergence of the Japanese steel industry (third largest in the world), despite the lack of iron ore and coking coal resources in Japan. Generally, improvements in transportation and production technology are making more industries market-oriented or even footloose both within and among nations.

[5] Many countries also impose high duties on whole vehicles, while imposing low or zero duties on vehicle parts in order to encourage assembly operations in their own territory.

market orientation shown by service industries such as wholesaling and retailing firms and transportation agencies.

When transportation costs are not an important factor on either the resource or market side, or when they tend to neutralize each other, and when location close to the market is not particularly advantageous, then industries are highly mobile or footloose, locating where the availability and cost of labor and other factors of production give them the lowest manufacturing cost. Companies producing electronic components, shoes, garments, containers, and small housewares offer examples of high locational mobility. U.S. electronics manufacturers are now shipping their components to foreign countries, such as Taiwan and South Korea, for assembly by low-cost, semi-skilled workers. The assemblies are then brought back to the United States where they are "packaged" for the domestic market.

The economics of location is extremely complex.[6] The fact that a firm may use several raw materials (including water, fuel, and power) drawn from different geographical areas and sell many products in several geographical markets can make it very difficult to determine the optimal location that minimizes transportation costs.[7] This difficulty is compounded by the need to also consider the availability and cost of factors of production (land, labor, and capital) at different locations.[8] The availability of unskilled and semiskilled labor is often decisive in location decisions, especially in market-oriented and footloose industries. In the simple two-country model we used in Chapter 3, the costs and availability (supply) of factors of production provided the basis (along with reciprocal demand) for international specialization. Now we see that the influence of transportation costs on the location of industry adds another variable to the theory of comparative advantage.

In effect, transportation inputs must be viewed, along with the traditional factors of production, as a determinant of a nation's opportunity cost and comparative advantage.[9] International specialization is dependent not

---

[6] Readers interested in location theory should look into Edgar M. Hoover, *The Location of Economic Activity* (New York: McGraw-Hill Book Company, 1948); and Walter Isard, *Location and Space-Economy* (New York: The Technology Press and John Wiley and Sons, Inc., 1956).

[7] Linear programming can sometimes be used to solve this problem.

[8] Local taxes are also a factor in location. Many governments seek to attract industry to less-developed regions within their countries by offering preferential tax treatment to domestic and foreign investors. As part of its Mezzogiorno program, for example, Italy gives a 10-year tax holiday to manufacturing plants that locate in regions south of Rome.

[9] In Chapter 9 of his book, *Location and Space-Economy*, Isard constructs an international trade model that utilizes "transport inputs." He states: "From the standpoint of trade theory we have introduced explicitly the distance factor (in the concept of transport inputs) and shown how the opportunity cost formulation can be easily extended to embrace industries which are typically transport-oriented intranationally." (page 215). However, Isard's model is highly simplified, and the integration of international trade and location theory to form a single theoretical system has not been accomplished as yet.

only on the relative endowments of land, labor, and capital among the trading nations, but also on the cost of overcoming geographical distance, which for a given product may vary from one place to another both within and among nations, because of the location of raw materials or markets. In resource-oriented industries, transportation inputs may be a stronger influence on location and international specialization than relative supplies of productive factors. They will also be significant in determining international specialization in many market-oriented industries. Only in the case of footloose industries can we safely ignore the independent effects of transportation costs on location and international specialization. In broader terms, the influence of transportation costs on location suggests that countries which are distant from world markets for finished goods and have no substantial domestic markets will tend to have a comparative disadvantage in market-oriented industries, while countries close to world markets or with large domestic markets will attract market-oriented industries. Thus, the location of a country may give it an advantage in export markets, even though its factor costs of producing some export goods are no lower (or are even higher) than the factor costs of producing similar goods in a country distant from those markets.

IMPERFECT COMPETITION

The simple theory of trade rests on the assumptions of perfect competition, which are: (1) many independent firms produce a homogeneous product (hence, the individual firm cannot influence price); (2) there are no legal, financial, technical or other obstacles to entry into the industry; (3) there are many independent *buyers*, none of whom can influence price; and (4) each firm has full knowledge of cost and demand data for both the present and the future (economic risk and uncertainty are nonexistent and pure profits are zero in equilibrium).[10]

The first three assumptions are fairly representative of trade in basic foodstuffs and agricultural raw materials, although national farm programs and international commodity agreements have steadily introduced noncompetitive factors. However, international trade in minerals and manufactured goods departs in one way or another from the conditions of perfect competition. Although minerals are homogeneous commodities, their production and trade are usually dominated by a relatively small number of producers who can influence the market price and other conditions of sale. Much trade in manufactured goods also occurs under conditions of oligopoly (few sellers), and even when it does not, product differentiation is common.

---

[10] Perfect competition in product markets implies perfect competition in factor markets. Perfect competition is associated with the conditions of a *static* economy: constant tastes, constant factor supplies, and unchanging technology. The last two conditions are examined in the next chapter.

In brief, perfect competition is the exception rather than the rule in international trade.

The effects of this imperfect competition on international trade may be restrictive, neutral, or expansive, depending on the particular variety of imperfect competition in question and the policies of individual firms. In this section we shall briefly sketch the principal types of imperfect competition and their most likely influence on the course of international trade. In particular, we wish to know whether international trade differs significantly from what it would be if all markets were perfectly competitive.

TYPES OF IMPERFECT COMPETITION

Imperfect competition in international trade may arise from monopoly, oligopoly, monopolistic competition, cartels, international commodity agreements, and state trading.

Briefly, monopoly refers to a single seller; oligopoly to a small number of sellers who produce the same or a differentiated product; and monopolistic competition to a large numbers of sellers, each of whom produces a differentiated product with close substitutes.

Cartels and commodity agreements involve restrictive arrangements among producers in various countries or among national governments.[11] State trading occurs when part or all of the foreign trade of a country is in the hands of its government. Today, the Communist countries exhibit the most extreme form of state trading; Communist government agencies are the sole buyers of all imports (monopsony) and the sole sellers of all exports (monopoly).

Monopoly and oligopoly may affect international trade via *monopoly profits, economies of scale,* and/or *technological innovation.* Monopolistic competition (and some oligopoly) may also influence international trade via *nonprice competition,* which is its principal feature.

MONOPOLY PROFITS

Traditionally, economists have extolled perfect competition and, at the same time, have depored imperfect competition. This attitude is based on the theoretical finding that the allocation of factors of production under imperfect competition does not maximize production and consumer satisfaction as under perfect competition. Under perfect competition the price of a good tends to equal its lowest unit cost of production, and the cost of production includes only the profits necessary to attract and keep the management factor plus the other factor payments. Furthermore, payments to an individual factor in any employment are equal to its marginal product in all employments. Thus, it is *not* possible to increase national output by

---

[11] Various restrictive business practices, as well as East-West business arrangements, are treated in Chapter 24, and international commodity agreements, in Chapter 18.

reallocating factor supplies among different lines of production. As observed in the preceding chapter, this means that national price and cost ratios are the same, and cost ratios reflect relative factor supplies and demands. Under the equilibrium conditions of perfect competition, therefore, comparative cost advantages and disadvantages are fully expressed in absolute international price differences.

Under monopoly and oligopoly, however, excess profits—profits not required to retain the management factor in production—may occur, although not necessarily. The existence of excess or *monopoly profits* makes the price of a good (or service) higher than its marginal cost of production, and for the nation as a whole the price ratios between goods differ from their cost ratios. In this way, the international allocation of production (international specialization) is not fully adjusted to opportunity costs; in other words, the gains from trade are less.

MONOPOLY AND OLIGOPOLY PRICES

Although the presence of excess profits distorts the price system and tends to restrict the volume of international trade, it does not follow that monopoly and oligopoly prices are necessarily higher than perfectly competitive prices or that the volume of trade is necessarily less under monopoly and oligopoly than under perfect competition. A monopolistic or oligopolistic industry may be able to achieve economies of scale and a rate of technological discovery and capital investment that would not be possible if the same industry were perfectly competitive. Perfect competition may require that an industry be made up of small firms unable to achieve economies of scale or engage in research on new products and processes.[12] When there are significant economies of scale, therefore, monopoly or oligopoly prices may be less than perfectly competitive prices, even though the former include excess profits and the latter do not. When this happens, the volume of international trade is greater under monopoly or oligopoly than under perfect competition. Of course, trade would be even greater if there were no excess profits. The effect of economies of scale on international trade deserves further attention.

ECONOMIES OF SCALE

Although all production will experience increasing unit costs sooner or later, many manufactured goods may be produced at *decreasing* unit costs over a broad range of output. Decreasing unit costs are mostly found

---

[12] Until recently, this sort of situation has characterized the United States cotton textile industry. Now bigger companies are being formed through mergers and acquisitions, and these companies are benefiting from economies of scale and more research. Many industries have started with a large number of small firms, but subsequently, economies of scale have transformed them into oligopolies. The history of the United States automobile and steel industries offers instructive examples.

in those manufacturing industries that use great quantities of capital to implement the technology of mass production, such as the chemical, petroleum refining, steel, and automobile industries. The sources of *internal* economies of scale lie in the indivisibility of specific factors of production and the advantages of specialization within the firm. Giant machines, the assembly-line organization of production, high levels of labor and managerial specialization, much research and development, and mass marketing are economical only for firms that have reached a substantial size. Productivity increases at higher levels of output because indivisible factors of production can be more fully utilized along with more specialized labor and management.

Technological innovations may enhance economies of scale over the long run. Ten years ago an ammonia plant produced 150 tons a day; now several plants each produce 1500 tons a day and designers are heading toward 3000 tons. In the 1940's tanker ships reached 28,000 deadweight tons; by 1973, they will achieve 477,000 deadweight tons.[13] Innovations that promote scale economies are not confined to physical production. New information systems based on the computer are making it possible for managers to direct and control bigger, more complex organizations. Global communications systems are creating economies of scale for research, production, marketing, and financial activities that are undertaken simultaneously in many countries by a single firm.

Another source of decreasing unit costs may be found in *external* economies of scale that arise outside the firm or industry. The individual firm or industry functions within a broad economic environment and its costs of production are dependent upon the efficiency of the economy as a whole. As an economy develops, transportation and communication facilities, raw materials, capital equipment, supplies and parts, skilled labor, financing, etc., may become progressively more available and cheaper to the firm. The firm may also benefit from an expansion of its own industry. External economies— unlike internal economies—operate over the long run and are compatible with perfect competition.

Unlike increasing costs, decreasing costs enhance the opportunity for gainful trade. Unless their effects are blocked by tariffs or other restrictions, decreasing costs lead to complete international specialization. Thus, economies of scale provide a basis for international trade, along with differences in factor endowments and tastes.

Assume, for example, that two countries (A and B) have the same factor proportions, the same tastes, and the same level of technology. In terms of the simple model used in Chapter 3, no gainful trade is possible under these conditions because cost and price ratios are identical. But now

---

[13] "In Industry, Sheer Size Really Pays," *Business Week* (October 17, 1970), p. 172.

let us suppose that country A has a big domestic market that allows it to achieve economies of scale in producing a manufactured good (say, automobiles) while country B has only a small domestic market that limits it to a high-cost, small-scale production of automobiles. This is shown in Figure 4-2. Although the long-run average cost curve (LRAC) is the

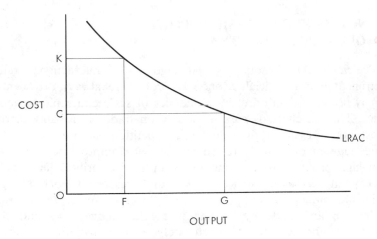

Figure 4-2

LONG-RUN AVERAGE COSTS WITH ECONOMIES OF SCALE

same in both countries, the representative producer in country A is producing O-G automobiles at a unit cost of O-C while the representative producer in country B is producing O-F automobiles on a smaller scale at a unit cost of O-K. Thus, country A has a comparative advantage in automobiles based on economies of scale. When trade opens up, country A will export automobiles to country B and, in return, import a good from country B in which country A now has a comparative disadvantage because of the shift in opportunity cost ratios resulting from economies of scale. To eliminate country A's comparative advantage in automobiles, producers in country B would have to invest in new plant and equipment that would achieve the economies of scale enjoyed by producers in country A. But this would require both massive capital investment and time. And even if this investment were forthcoming, producers in country B would have to absorb losses until the new plants were actually in operation. Without government assistance, these obstacles might prove insurmountable even over the long run.

Many American producers are able to compete effectively in the world market because their unit costs of production have been lowered through the economies of scale they have achieved in satisfying the vast domestic demand. On the other hand, countries with relatively abundant supplies of capital but only small domestic markets are seldom able to secure these economies of scale and therefore have a comparative disadvantage in goods that lend themselves to mass production.[14] Since advances in technology are usually biased in favor of mass production, comparative advantages based on factor indivisibilities and domestic mass consumption are likely to grow with the passage of time.

THE NET EFFECT OF MONOPOLY
AND OLIGOPOLY ON TRADE

The *net* effect of monopoly and oligopoly on international trade may be detrimental or beneficial. Monopoly profits are always detrimental, but they may be more than offset by economies of scale and rapid technological advance. The net effect of *pure* monopoly on trade is probably detrimental in most cases. Lacking the spur of competition, a monopoly firm may become stagnant or actually retard technological improvements in order to sustain high profits. Nor is a monopoly firm necessarily a large-scale producer enjoying decreasing unit costs. For these reasons a monopoly, particularly an old monopoly, is apt to restrict the opportunity for international specialization and trade by holding prices far above costs and charging "what the traffic will bear." Fortunately pure monopoly is exceedingly rare in international trade. Its effects on trade, however, may be closely matched by cartels and state trading.

Oligopolies are very common in the mass-production industries where a few firms can supply the entire market. Oligopoly differs from monopoly in that there may be effective competition among oligopolists unless they organize a cartel or reach a less formal agreement not to compete, both forbidden by American law but often permitted in foreign countries.[15] The possibility that the relatively small number of producers will "gang up" on buyers by agreeing to hold up prices, allocate markets, freeze technology, and the like is the greatest danger of oligopoly. When competition does exist in an oligopolistic industry, it will usually be *nonprice* competition in quality, style, or services, rather than in prices. The heavy burden of fixed costs in the mass-production industries creates such a great risk of price wars that the firms within those industries tend to raise and lower prices together. We are all familiar with this sort of price behavior in cigarettes, automobiles, and gasoline—all products of oligopolistic industries.

---

[14] If international trade is free of official restrictions, then a small country may obtain the advantages of large-scale production by producing for the world market. But this is difficult and risky in the real world where external markets may be suddenly closed off by foreign government action. One of the purposes of the European Economic Community is to overcome this obstacle to large-scale production by creating free trade among its members. See Chapter 16.

[15] The Webb-Pomerene Act, however, does allow American producers to organize an export cartel.

When there is effective competition among oligopolistic firms, international trade will generally benefit from economies of scale and rapid improvements in technology. After all, the most dynamic industries are likely to be the mass-production industries in which oligopoly is the usual market arrangement.[16] The aggressive competition of oligopolies in this country and their willingness and ability to exploit foreign sources of supply and foreign market opportunities are responsible in considerable measure for the expansion of United States trade.

NONPRICE COMPETITION AND ITS EFFECT ON TRADE

Most of the manufactured goods that enter international trade are sold in either oligopolistically or monopolistically competitive markets. In the latter variety of market, each good is produced by a large number of producers, but each producer has succeeded in differentiating his product from competitive products in some way. This differentiation is achieved by the technique of nonprice competition, which is the hallmark of monopolistic competition. Although price competition is close and competitors' prices can never be disregarded, it is nonprice competition in quality, style, and services that makes up the aggressive front of monopolistic competition.

American consumers encounter nonprice competition at every turn. Television, radio, and other advertising media daily assault our eyes and ears with clever appeals to buy this or that product. Price appeals are relatively rare, and they are usually drowned out by the host of selling points centered on nonprice factors. We are warned, cajoled, sweet-talked, entertained, and implored—all with the intent to make us rush out to buy brand X. American advertising has a pervasiveness and vigor that is not matched in other countries, but the use of advertising is rising sharply in all countries of the free world, much of it sponsored by American companies that market abroad.

Nonprice competition often employs appeals based on style factors. Not only is the style cycle of traditional style goods speeded up by this competition, but style is also created in goods that were formerly standardized. The evolution of the American automobile from the Model T to the contemporary stylized product is a case in point. Style introduces a rapid obsolescence of merchandise as the style has its day and then passes on; this raises problems of inventory, timing, and market information that are largely absent in the marketing of standardized merchandise. There is,

---

[16] In 1969 the twenty largest industrial corporations in the United States were all members of oligopolistic industries—automotive, petroleum, steel, electrical, communications, chemical, business machines, rubber, and aerospace. See *The Fortune Directory* (May, 1970).

however, another side of the coin—style obsolescence periodically renews demand by making buyers dissatisfied with their earlier acquisitions.

A great variety of services is also used to distinguish a product from its competitors—quick delivery, return guarantees, warranties, right of inspection before acceptance of merchandise, the availability of repair parts, servicing of the product and instruction in its use, etc. One reason behind the establishment of overseas branches and subsidiaries by domestic concerns is to facilitate service competition.

The effect of nonprice competition on international trade is expansive. Nonprice competition stimulates demand by acquainting buyers with goods, by transforming latent demand into active demand, by introducing new products and new uses for old products, by heightening the availability of products, and in other ways. The dynamism of nonprice competition in creating new demand contrasts with the passivity of price competition—accepting demand but doing nothing to change it.

It is sometimes argued that nonprice competition restricts international trade because selling costs make prices higher than they would be under perfect competition. This accusation fails to note, however, that many goods do not sell themselves and that nonprice competition enlarges the sales of such goods beyond the levels attainable through perfect competition. Economies of scale may be possible only when production is bolstered through mass consumption induced by nonprice competition. The charge that nonprice competition is wasteful and costly is valid only when it does not enhance the demand for a product. This criticism is often leveled against cigarette advertising, which, it is alleged, does not raise the consumption of cigarettes but simply redistributes the existing demand among the individual producers.[17]

In the long run (the time needed to change productive capacity) monopolistic competition forces an identity between costs and prices. This absence of monopoly profits means that cost and price ratios are the same, and hence international trade moves in accordance with the principle of comparative advantage. We may conclude, therefore, that nonprice competition brings a dynamic, expansive element to international trade without the distortion of chronic monopoly profits. This is not to deny the importance of price competition; nonprice competition does not take the place of price competition but rather supplements it. It does mean, however, that the theory

---

[17] Criticism of nonprice competition ultimately derives from welfare propositions; namely, that some things are better for society than others. The case for or against cigarette advertising is now complicated by the health issue. As for international advertising, a further point needs mention. International markets may differ greatly in their consumption levels and saturation percentages for the same product. Thus, the promotional elasticity of the same advertising may, and often does, vary widely among national markets. Finally, much criticism of nonprice competition either ignores product innovations or denies their usefulness.

of comparative advantage must take account of nonprice competition as well as price competition if it is to explain the full scope of international trade.

IGNORANCE, UNCERTAINTY, AND RISK
IN INTERNATIONAL TRADE

Ignorance and uncertainty are important sources of market imperfection in international trade that are assumed away in the simple model of Chapter 3.

Ignorance refers to a trader's incomplete knowledge about markets and costs in the present. This ignorance gap exists because information is not a free good; it is acquired only at a cost in time and money. For most business firms the acquisition of information about foreign markets is constrained by factors of distance, scarce or unreliable data, language and other cultural factors, and cost to a higher degree than the acquisition of market information at home. Because of ignorance, traders do not fully utilize comparative advantage and the gains from trade are correspondingly less. Thus, ignorance limits trade in much the same way as transfer costs. Conversely, improvements in market information widen the perceived opportunities for gainful trade among nations.

Uncertainty refers to a trader's incomplete knowledge about markets and costs in the future. Although the present is conceptually fully knowable (zero ignorance), only seers and astrologers claim to know the future with finality. For the rest of us (including the trader) the future offers an array of possible but uncertain events. In forecasting the future, therefore, the most that any trader can do is to make probability judgments of possible future events and then relate those judgments to his trading decisions. Although there are many forecasting techniques that may help the trader improve his judgments about the future, he must inevitably assume risks because his knowledge is never certain. Because of the greater number and variety of possible events in the world economy as compared to the domestic economy, firms tend to perceive risks in international trade (and investment) as higher than at home. Like ignorance, therefore, uncertainty also narrows the scope of international trade.

Another consequence of uncertainty is the appearance of *windfall* profits and losses and what may be called *entrepreneurial* profits and losses. Windfall profits accrue to the international trader when he benefits from unexpected changes in his trading environment, such as an increase in market demand or a reduction in import duties. Windfall losses also come from unexpected events such as the imposition of import barriers or emergence of a strong competitor. Entrepreneurial profits are a reward for the *deliberate* assumption of risks by the trader. When, for example, a trader introduces a new product or enters a new market, he knowingly assumes risks in the expectation of a profit reward. Of course, he may be mistaken and end up with losses, but that is the meaning of risk. The presence of profits in international trade, therefore, is not necessarily a sign of monopoly; more commonly, profits arise from unexpected events and from the deliberate assumption of risk by the trader. Entrepreneurial profits play a key role in the dynamics of international trade. We shall have more to say about risk and uncertainty in Part Three.

UNEMPLOYMENT AND COMPARATIVE ADVANTAGE

In Chapter 3 we assumed that a nation's factors of production were fully employed at all times. Hence, the production of one good could only be increased by decreasing the production of one or more other goods; that is, the opportunity cost of every good was positive. When, however, a nation's factors of production are not fully employed, it is possible to increase the production of one or more goods without lowering production elsewhere by using idle supplies of land, labor, management, and capital. In this event, the new production is a net addition to the national income, and its opportunity cost is zero.[18]

Does the existence of unemployed factors of production invalidate the theory of comparative advantage? We shall examine this question in some detail in Chapter 13 when we look at the employment argument for protection. Suffice it to say at this point that full employment can be achieved without sacrificing the gains from international trade. A nation can have both full employment and unrestricted trade; it is not a question of choosing one over the other. Hence, the theory of comparative advantage is not invalidated by unemployment.

SUMMARY

1. In Chapter 3, several assumptions were made in order to simplify our presentation of the theory of comparative advantage. In this and the next chapter we modify or withdraw these assumptions to make the theory more relevant to the actual course of international trade. In so doing, we unavoidably add to its complexity.

2. Transfer costs may be divided into costs of physical transfer and the transfer costs associated with government regulation of foreign trade. Costs of physical transfer are mainly attributable to transportation. Transportation costs separate goods into two classes—domestic goods and international goods. Domestic goods do not enter international trade because transportation costs make it impossible to sell them at competitive prices in foreign markets. Hence, the

---

[18] In other words, a nation can move from a point *inside* its production possibilities curve to a point on the curve with zero opportunity costs.

existence of transportation costs narrows the opportunity for international trade.

3. Transportation costs also influence the location of industry and, thereby, the international specialization of production. Location may be near raw materials (resource-oriented), near the market or markets of the final product (market-oriented), or somewhere in between (footloose), depending upon the character of production processes. In effect, transportation inputs must be viewed, along with the traditional factors of production, as a determinant of a nation's opportunity cost and comparative advantage.

4. International trade, especially in minerals and manufactured goods, departs in one way or another from the conditions of perfect competition. The monopoly profits of monopolies and oligopolies lower the gains from trade by introducing a discrepancy between national cost ratios and national price ratios. However, monopoly and oligopoly prices may be lower than perfectly competitive prices because of economies of scale and technological innovation.

5. Economies of scale may achieve decreasing unit costs over a broad range of output. Internal economies of scale are not compatible with perfect competition because they make possible the domination of markets by a small number of firms (oligopoly). But unlike increasing costs, economies of scale enhance the opportunities for gainful international trade and constitute a basis for trade along with differences in factor endowments and tastes. Hence, the net effects of oligopoly on trade may be detrimental (monopoly profits) or beneficial (economies of scale and technological innovation).

6. Nonprice competition deriving from product differentiation brings a dynamic, expansive element to international trade; and, in the case of monopolistic competition, it does so without the distortion of monopoly profits.

7. Ignorance and uncertainty are important sources of market imperfection in international trade that are assumed away in the simple theory. One consequence of uncertainty is the appearance of windfall and entrepreneurial profits and losses. Entrepreneurial profits are a reward for the deliberate assumption of risk, and they play a key role in the dynamics of international trade. Hence, the presence of profits in international trade is not necessarily a sign of monopoly power.

8. Full employment may be achieved without the sacrifice of gains from international trade.

QUESTIONS AND APPLICATIONS

1. How do transportation costs directly affect the volume of international trade?

2. "Transportation costs are not simply dependent on distance and the physical character of commodities." Explain.

3. What is meant by "weight-losing" and "weight-gaining" industrial processes? How do these processes influence location?

4. Why is the "economics of location" so complex?

5. What are the types of imperfect competition?

6. (a) What are the sources of economies of scale?

   (b) Why do decreasing costs lead inevitably to complete international specialization unless their effects are blocked by restrictions on trade?

7. Why may the *net* effect of monopoly and oligopoly on international trade be detrimental or beneficial?

8. (a) What is nonprice competition?

   (b) Why is its effect on international trade likely to be expansive?

9. (a) Do you consider ignorance and uncertainty to be greater in international trade than in domestic trade? Explain your answer.

   (b) Do ignorance and uncertainty constrain international trade? Why or why not?

SELECTED READINGS

See the list of readings given at the end of Chapter 5.

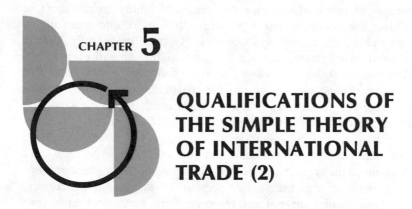

CHAPTER 5

QUALIFICATIONS OF THE SIMPLE THEORY OF INTERNATIONAL TRADE (2)

This chapter concludes our examination of the assumptions behind the simple theory of international trade. We now investigate the theoretical implications of heterogeneity and change in factor endowments, technological innovation and dissimilar production functions, international factor mobility, and differences in per capita income levels.

HETEROGENEITY AND CHANGE IN FACTOR ENDOWMENTS

The simple factor-endowments theory of trade in Chapter 3 assumes that the individual factors of production are homogeneous and fixed in supply. Actually, there are many subvarieties of land, human factors, and capital. Furthermore, factor endowments (however defined) are continually changing over time through the effects of technical advance, population growth, and investment. This section considers the implications of factor heterogeneity and change (mostly growth) for international trade.[1]

LAND FACTORS

Land factors, or natural resources, comprise the many elements of the natural environment which contribute to the production of goods and services useful to man. Whether a natural element can and does contribute to production at any given time depends upon man's capacity and willingness to utilize it.

Contrary to popular understanding, natural resources are dynamic rather than fixed in supply. Elements of the natural environment *become*

---

[1] Technological innovation is treated as a separate source of economic growth in the following section.

natural resources as mankind develops the need and ability to use them in production. Over the centuries man has transformed more and more of his natural environment into natural resources. Early man made only modest use of his natural environment, as does the Australian bushman even today. The availability of coal had no effect on the economy of the American Indian because he had no productive use for coal and, consequently, it was not a natural resource to him. A generation ago much the same could be said of uranium for our own contemporary economy. One authority believes that the basic raw materials for industries of the future will be seawater, air, ordinary rock, sedimentary deposits of limestone and phosphate rock, and sunlight.[2] It is most likely that the oceans will become a much more important natural resource than they are at present. Fundamentally, therefore, what we call land factors, or natural resources, are dependent upon our technical knowledge and how we choose to use that knowledge. Man must be aware of the existence of natural elements, must recognize their usefulness to him, and must want and know how to exploit them before they can become natural resources possessing an economic significance.

Natural resources are conventionally classified as agricultural land, forests, fisheries, and mineral deposits. Viewed broadly, natural resources also include topographical land features, solar radiation, water, winds, and any other natural elements that contribute directly or indirectly to economic activities. Each of these natural resource types has many variations. Agricultural lands differ in natural fertility, insolation, rainfall, latitude, height, and in many other ways. Mineral deposits are even more diverse. Not only are there hundreds of different minerals, but deposits of one mineral will vary in size, accessibility, and quality. The many kinds of natural resources and the wide variations in their quality and other attributes preclude any precise measurement of the *totality* of national resource endowments or their comparison. Even international comparisons of one resource type, such as agricultural land, can be approximate only. Because of this complexity, sweeping statements about a country's resource endowment can be misleading. For example, although Switzerland is often described as "resource-poor," its topographical features (especially the Alps) are a prime tourist attraction and also provide an abundant supply of waterpower for electricity generation.

Even though broad international comparisons of natural resources are only approximate, it is most evident that *specific* natural resources are distributed unevenly over the earth. Zimmerman classifies the frequency of resource occurrence as follows: (1) *ubiquities,* which occur everywhere, such as oxygen in the air; (2) *commonalities,* which occur in many places, such as tillable soil; (3) *rarities,* which occur in only a few places, such as tin; and

---

[2] Harrison Brown, *The Challenge of Man's Future* (New York: The Viking Press, 1956), p. 218.

(4) *uniquities,* which occur in one place, such as commercial cryolite.[3] He also points out that production processes generally involve a *combination* of materials so that usable combinations of, say, coal and iron may be quite rarely found in the same place even though both occur frequently alone. As we observed in Chapter 3, the uneven distribution of natural resources is an important cause of different factor proportions among nations.

So intimate is the relation between man and natural resources, the latter are sometimes indistinguishable from other factors of production, especially capital. We all know that much of Holland's land (about two-fifths) has been reclaimed from the sea and is therefore as much capital as a natural resource. Less well known is how extensively the centuries of man's habitation in Western Europe have changed its physical nature:

> Sweat has flowed freely to bring European landscapes to their present shape. The climate and topography of the continent did not determine its present aspect. Once dense forests covered areas in France, Germany and Russia that are now almost treeless and completely under the plow. Where brush once predominated, pine woods grow. Where played the waves of the sea, rich harvests of wheat sway in the wind. Where desert marshes stretched, now great cities stand.[4]

The settlement of North America has likewise altered the landscape, soil conditions, and other aspects of the original natural environment. In more general terms, natural resources must first be discovered and then exploited, and this requires the complementary use of labor and capital.

It should be evident by now that national resource endowments are dynamic. Technological innovations develop new natural resources from materials that had no previous economic use, and they also improve the accessibility of existing resources. New discoveries (also aided by technological advances) add to the known supply of resources. Offsetting this expansion is the exhaustion of natural resources through use and misuse. Oil wells run dry, iron mines peter out, forests sometimes disappear, fertile grasslands can become dust bowls, water tables sink, and so on. Because of this exhaustion process (as well as higher usage), the United States must now import many minerals, such as iron ore and copper, that were formerly supplied entirely from domestic sources or even exported in large quantities.

HUMAN FACTORS

International variations in human factor endowments are both quantitative and qualitative. Aside from variations in overall size which derive

---

[3] Henry L. Hunker, *Erich W. Zimmermann's Introduction to World Resources* (New York: Harper and Row, Inc., 1964), p. 120.

[4] Jean Gottmann, *A Geography of Europe* (New York: Holt, Rinehart, and Winston, 1962), p. 52.

mainly, although not exclusively, from variations in population, the *composition* of labor and management often differs markedly among nations. In poor, underdeveloped economies the bulk of the labor force is unskilled, occupied in traditional forms of agriculture, while only a small fraction is skilled in industrial pursuits, and an even smaller fraction has technical and management training. In contrast, the labor force in highly developed economies, such as the United States or Western Europe, is mainly composed of semiskilled and skilled workers in industry, white collar workers engaged in service occupations, and a significant proportion of technical and management people.

International differences in the quality of human factors are difficult to measure, but nonetheless important. Again, they are most striking between poorly developed and highly developed economies. Qualitative variations arise because humans are shaped by an economic, political, social, and cultural milieu that is not everywhere the same nor is ever likely to be. Thus, there is a diversity among peoples in ways that influence economic performance, such as physical vigor, motivations and attitudes towards work, technical skills, organizational and management capacities, and many other attributes. In addition to disparities among individuals living in different cultures, there are also dissimilarities in social conditions which bear directly on economic performance. Some societies are rigid, offering little opportunity for lower-class individuals; other societies are open, allowing individuals to move upward to higher social levels (or fall to lower levels). In a rigid society, movement from one labor group to another is a slow, painful process which limits the capacity of the economy to make positive adaptations to change.[5]

Qualitative disparities among the human factors of different countries are so pervasive that skilled workers (or any other subtype of labor) in one country are never quite the same as in another country and may, in fact, be very dissimilar. Such qualitative disparities influence comparative costs in the same way as quantitative disparities. If workers in one country are generally twice as productive as workers in a second country because of quality differences (as distinguished from differences arising from the use of complementary factors, especially capital), then the effect on comparative costs is equivalent to doubling the size of the first country's labor force.

The gist of this discussion is that *at any point of time* the human factor endowment of a nation will be heterogeneous and will differ both in

---

[5] Even in the mobile societies of advanced economies, the subtypes of labor tend to form "noncompeting" groups with little movement of people among them over the short run. The persistence of unemployment in the United States is a case in point. Many of the American unemployed are workers whose services are no longer in demand because of the implementing of technological innovations which require more education and new skills.

composition and quality from the human factor endowments of other nations. This, as we know, is a basis for profitable international trade. But this is not all. Each nation's human factor endowment changes *through time,* injecting a dynamic element into its comparative cost structure.

First, the overall supply of labor is strongly affected by the rate of growth and the age distribution of population. Second, the many subtypes of labor—unskilled, semiskilled, technical, etc.—are subject to different rates of change. The radical expansion in the number of white collar workers and the simultaneous decline in the number of unskilled workers in the United States since the turn of the century are illustrative. Third, the quality of labor alters with changes in education, technology, and economic opportunity. An upgrading of labor has been particularly pronounced in this country— jobs once staffed by high school graduates are now staffed by college graduates. Conversely, the quality of certain subtypes of labor may worsen. It is said that the productivity of coal miners in Europe is now less than before World War II after full account is taken of relevant circumstances. Again, certain subtypes of labor may disappear along with their jobs due to technological displacement. These transformations in the level, composition, and quality of the labor force introduce continuing changes in the relative factor endowments of a nation and hence in its foreign trade.

What we have said concerning labor is substantially true of the other human agent of production—management. Changes in the size and the quality of management are largely determined by the freedom of economic opportunity, the rate of growth of the economy, and the rate of technological advance. When economic opportunity is impaired by a social caste system or by monopoly organization of the economy, when the economy is stagnant, and when the techniques of production are static, the management factor will initiate few changes in its supply relative to the supplies of other factors of production.

In an economy like the United States, however, management is a most dynamic factor of production. In this country, management adapted to the operation of large-scale business has grown at a faster pace than other types of management; and the rapid rise of business schools suggests the qualitative changes that have occurred, and are occurring, in this factor.

CAPITAL

Capital is the most dynamic factor of production, and it exhibits most strongly the influence of changing technology. An economy becomes more productive by increasing the supply of its capital relative to other factor supplies and by improving the quality of its capital. Today, the American factory worker produces more in less time than did his grandfather, primarily because he has more (and better) machines and more horsepower to help him.

Growth in the quantity and quality of capital is spurred by technological improvements. An advancing economy produces not only more factories, utilities, machines, and other varieties of capital, but also more productive factories, utilities, etc., to take the place of the old. The growth of capital may markedly alter the relative factor endowment of a country within a few generations. The outstanding contemporary example is the Soviet Union, which has been transformed from a predominantly agricultural economy into the world's second industrial power within a period of approximately forty years.

Drastic changes in a nation's capital supply usually cause substantial shifts in the nature of its foreign trade. In Chapter 2 we observed that the United States was once primarily an exporter of agricultural products and raw materials, and an importer of manufactures. Now, with an abundant supply of capital, this country is a major exporter of manufactures and a heavy importer of raw materials.

Nations differ widely both in their stocks of capital goods and in their capacity to add to capital stocks through investment. Capital stocks constitute *real* capital which includes many varieties of equipment, buildings, and other instruments of production, as well as "social capital" such as transportation, communications, and educational facilities. Basically, however, real capital must be financed out of savings representing the surplus of current production over current consumption. Unlike real capital, investment funds (*financial* capital) may be viewed as a homogeneous factor of production commanding a single price which is the long-term interest rate adjusted for variations in risk.

Consumption exhausts most of the production of poor economies unless heroic austerity measures are undertaken by government authorities. Hence, the rates of investment of these poor economies tend to be low, perpetuating international differences in capital endowments. Because the supply of investment funds is low, long-term interest rates are high. Unless they are impaired by government restrictions, political unrest, or other disturbances, investment funds will flow from the more advanced economies which have high rates of saving to underdeveloped economies in order to earn higher returns. But even under the best of circumstances, international investment can do no more than to supplement domestic investment, which must carry the main responsibility of financing additions to a country's capital stock.[6] As a result of persisting disparities in existing capital stocks and the rate of new capital investment among nations, capital endowments will continue to be an important factor in the determination of international differences in comparative costs.

---

[6] Chapters 17 and 18 examine these and other aspects of underdeveloped economies.

EFFECTS ON TRADE: FACTOR HETEROGENEITY

The heterogeneity of factors of production raises the possibility that a given subfactor may be *unique* to a nation with no counterparts in other nations. We can visualize this possibility most easily in the case of a mineral exploitable in only one country, but it could also happen with a labor or capital subfactor, at least in the short run. The possibility of sub-factor uniqueness is heightened for labor and management when we take into account the many qualitative differences arising out of dissimilar socio-cultural environments.

Unlike comparative advantage arising from dissimilar proportions of the *same* factors, a country's possession of a unique factor gives it an *absolute* advantage in those goods requiring that factor in production. However, absolute advantage based on a unique factor is probably not too important: few subfactors are perfectly unique (without any substitutes), and even so, they are not likely to remain unique indefinitely in a world of rapid technological change. In this regard we can call to mind how Chile lost its sodium nitrate monopoly during World War I when chemists discovered an economical process for making nitrates out of nitrogen drawn from the air. As we shall see in the next section, however, a nation may gain an absolute advantage in trade through product innovations that are not matched (at least for a time) in the rest of the world.

More important, the existence of numerous subfactors indicates that national comparative cost structures are highly complex, and that a broad similarity in the cost structures of two countries in terms of the three traditional factors most probably masks a rich diversity in their relative supplies of subfactors. For this reason, the possibility of identical comparative costs among nations is only theoretical. Nations can always find a basis to trade profitably with each other.

EFFECTS ON TRADE: FACTOR CHANGE

The effects of changes in a nation's factor endowments may be anti-trade, neutral, or protrade. Figure 5-1 (page 114) depicts these three possible outcomes.

Country X starts out with the production possibilities curve *A-B*. At the given terms of trade, it produces combination *C* of both goods and has a comparative advantage in the labor-intensive good which it exports in exchange for imports of the capital-intensive good. Now suppose that its supplies of labor and capital grow in the same degree so that factor proportions remain the same. As a result, the *A-B* curve shifts outward to make a new production possibilities curve *F-D*. Since the terms of trade are constant, country X now produces combination *K* which represents more of both goods but in the same proportion as combination *C*. (Both *C* and *K* lie on the same straight line drawn from the origin.) The effect of these factor changes on trade is *neutral* because they do not alter the comparative cost advantage (or disadvantage) of the country: the *shape* of the production possibilities curve stays the same.

What happens if only the supply of capital grows with no change in the labor supply? This is shown by a shift of *A-B* to *A-B'*. Assuming once again that the relative prices of the two goods are constant, then country X uses the new capital to produce more of the capital-intensive (import-competing) good, at the same time drawing some labor away from the production of the labor-intensive good. The resulting production mix at *M* has more of the import-competing good and less of the export good than the earlier mix at *C*. This increase in the country's relatively scarce factor (capital) is, therefore, *antitrade;* it has lessened the country's comparative advantage in the labor-intensive export good.[7]

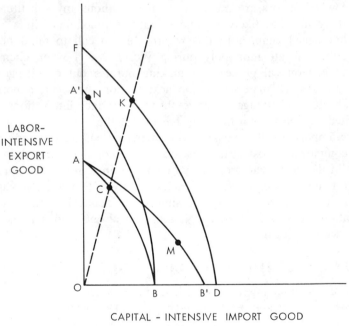

LABOR-
INTENSIVE
EXPORT
GOOD

CAPITAL - INTENSIVE IMPORT GOOD

Figure 5-1

PRODUCTION EFFECTS OF FACTOR GROWTH WITH CONSTANT TERMS OF TRADE

Now take the converse situation: a growth in the labor endowment with no change in the capital endowment. *A-B* shifts to *A'-B*, with the

---

[7] If this capital growth continues, at some point country X will develop a comparative advantage in the capital-intensive good and start exporting it in exchange for labor-intensive imports.

country producing combination *N,* which has more of the labor-intensive export good and less of the capital-intensive, import-competing good. Country X's comparative advantage in the labor-intensive good is now stronger than before and so, correspondingly, is its degree of specialization in that good. Hence, this increase in the country's relatively abundant factor is *protrade.*

Suppose both factors are growing, but at different rates. In that event the output of both goods will increase, but the resulting production mix will differ from the pregrowth mix. The effect will be antitrade if the scarce factor grows more than the abundant factor, and protrade if the abundant factor grows more than the scarce factor.

These *supply* effects of factor growth on trade may be intensified or weakened by the *consumption* effects of the higher real income (higher production) by country X. The consumption effect of a greater increase in the home demand for the import good than in the home demand for the export good is protrade, and vice versa. The *net* effects of factor growth on trade will depend, therefore, on both the production and consumption effects. A full analysis of factor growth effects on trade must also take account of any accompanying shifts in the terms of trade which were assumed to remain constant in the preceding analysis. Antitrade factor growth will tend to *improve* the terms of trade for country X because its import demand will fall relative to the foreign export demand from combined production and consumption effects. On the other hand, protrade factor growth will tend to *harm* country X's terms of trade. If the production effects of growth strongly increase the supply of the export good while its consumption (income) effects strongly increase the demand for the import good, then the terms of trade may become so adverse as to lower country X's *pregrowth* gains from trade, a situation designated as *immiserizing growth.*[8]

This short appraisal of factor endowments has shown that each of the factors of production is subjected to many influences which alter its supply within a nation over time. Factor changes are a continuing phenomenon within nations, causing shifts in factor proportions and in comparative cost structures. Hence, a nation's trade is not stereotyped or static, but frequently changing in magnitude, composition, and direction at a rate which varies from time to time and from country to country. It follows that nations must adjust continuously to shifts in comparative advantage because they cannot reasonably expect their future trade to be a mere repetition of their present trade. In this dynamic world, nations that quickly adapt their trade and economies to change (regardless of its origin) have an obvious advantage over nations with sluggish responses.

---

[8] The question of immiserizing growth in the developing countries is raised in Chapter 17.

TECHNOLOGICAL INNOVATION: FACTOR PRODUCTIVITY, DISSIMILAR PRODUCTION FUNCTIONS, AND NEW PRODUCTS

The role that technology plays in shaping economic activities must be included in a modern theory of trade. In the preceding section we spoke of technological innovation as an agent of change in factor endowments. In this section we take a closer look at the implications of technological innovation for theory of comparative advantage.

Technology is the accumulated knowledge, skills, and techniques that are applied to the production of goods and services. Inventions and discoveries are the source of technology, but they must be used in production to become innovations. Today, inventions and discoveries come mainly out of systematic research programs oriented toward technical innovations. The immense resources now devoted to research, along with the drive by management to apply its results to enterprise, have created an environment of explosive technological change, especially in advanced industrial economies. Technological innovations affect not only production and domestic and international trade, but also the living styles of countless millions of people around the globe. One innovation alone—the automobile—has transformed American society and is doing the same in Europe and elsewhere.

Technological innovations assume two basic forms: (1) new and more economical ways of producing existing products (new production functions), by innovations in producing specific products (such as a new way of making a chemical) or by general innovations affecting a broad range of production (such as automation); and (2) the production of wholly new products, industrial and consumer, such as computers, television, plastics, and synthetic fibers (to name only a few of the more prominent products introduced since the end of World War II), and improvements in existing products. These two forms are closely related; many new products, for example, are capital goods which make possible new production functions.

Because the influence of technological innovation on economic behavior is so pervasive, it has manifold effects on the volume, direction, and composition of international trade. Changing technology not only creates dissimilar production functions among countries at any given point of time, but also transforms the trade of nations over time. We have already observed that technology determines what natural elements become land factors, making these factors dynamic rather than passive. Technology also vitally affects the training and education of labor, giving rise to qualitative differences among nations. Capital is directly influenced by technology because so much technology takes the form of capital equipment and, more basically, because technology contributes importantly to a nation's investment capacity by raising per capita productivity and real income.

The bearing of technology on international trade is not limited to the changes it provokes in the size and the quality of factor endowments.

Technology also creates new production functions that raise the productivity of existing factors of production, profoundly affecting the scope of international trade through innovations in transportation and communication. By fostering new products, technology has a direct impact on the composition and growth of international trade. The competitive strength of United States exports owes much to product innovations in capital and consumer goods— as older products, such as automobiles, are displaced by foreign competition, they are replaced by new products, such as commercial jet aircraft, that for a time have no foreign counterparts. For this reason alone, a rapid rate of technological progress is a vital weapon in world markets.

The simple comparative cost model in Chapter 3 made two implicit assumptions about technology: (1) the existence of a given state of technology, and (2) the same access to technology everywhere; that is, all countries use the same production functions. These assumptions do not hold in the real world. When we drop them, what happens to the factor proportions theory of trade?

HIGHER FACTOR PRODUCTIVITY VIA INNOVATION: EFFECTS ON TRADE

When technological innovation takes the form of new ways to produce existing products, it pushes out a nation's production possibilities frontier. With new production functions, the nation can now produce a greater output with the same endowments of productive factors.[9] Indeed, technical advances in production are a major source of growth in contemporary economies. In effect, a new production function "saves" some or all the factors of production needed to produce a given level of output as compared with the old production function.

The effects of this "saving" may be neutral, protrade, or antitrade. Analytically, the situation is similar to the effects of factor growth on trade which was treated in the previous section. A technological innovation that causes a rise in the productivity of, say, labor has a production effect similar to an increase in the supply of labor. When an innovation saves all factors to the same degree, its effect on trade is neutral, as in the case when all factors grow to the same degree. However, when an innovation saves a country's relatively abundant factor but does not save its relatively scarce factors (or saves them to a lesser extent), then the effect will be protrade. The country will now have a greater comparative advantage than before in the production of goods that require relatively large amounts of its abundant factor. Conversely, when an innovation saves a country's relatively scarce factor more than it saves the relatively abundant factors, the effect will be antitrade as production shifts towards goods that replace imports.

---

[9] A production function is the relationship between the output of a good and the necessary factor inputs. It may be most simply expressed as follows: $P = f\ (a,\ b,\ c \ldots)$ where P is output and $a, b, c \ldots$ are factor inputs.

INTERNATIONAL TECHNOLOGY GAPS:
DISSIMILAR PRODUCTION FUNCTIONS

Technical discoveries do not occur in all countries at the same pace; nor are discoveries spread instantaneously from one country to another; nor are they applied to production at the same rate in different countries. Advanced industrial countries generate most of the new technology which then spreads to other countries after varying time lags. The most prominent example of this diffusion process is the Industrial Revolution (a combination of technical innovations involving the steam engine, new kinds of machinery, the factory system of organization, and other developments adding up to a transformation of the entire economy) which started in England in the eighteenth century, then spread to Western Europe and North America during the following century, to Japan and Russia early in this century, and is still spreading to many parts of South America, Africa, and Asia. Because this process is not instantaneous, we can distinguish between nations that are technological leaders and those that are technological followers.

At any given time, therefore, countries may be using different technologies to produce the same products; that is to say, dissimilar production functions exist. Since most technological innovations in production take the form of capital, a technological leader usually employs a capital-intensive method to produce a good which is traditionally labor- or land-intensive. Dissimilar production functions are strikingly evident in agriculture. Over the past generation, a technical revolution has transformed U.S. agriculture, encompassing a high level of mechanization, improved soil care, pest control, new varieties of seed, etc., and a large-scale organization of production, resembling a factory more than traditional farming. U.S. agriculture has become capital-intensive (there are only four million farmers and half of them produce almost all the commercial agricultural output) while in many countries it has remained labor-intensive. The employment of capital-intensive production functions (made possible by new technology) explains how the United States has retained, and probably increased, its comparative advantage in agriculture despite rising wage and land costs.

The significance of this discussion is that *a good cannot be uniquely defined as capital-intensive or labor-(land) intensive because it may be produced in both ways in countries using different production functions.*[10]

---

[10] The "Leontieff paradox" is pertinent to this statement. Using input-output tables and 1947 foreign trade figures, Wassily Leontieff found that United States exports were less capital-intensive and more labor-intensive than United States imports. This finding provoked a fierce controversy in the economic literature (which we cannot discuss here) because it seemed to contradict the factor proportions theory of trade. According to that theory, United States exports should be more, not less, capital-intensive than United States imports. Leontieff himself tried to explain the paradox by suggesting that United States labor is three times as productive as labor elsewhere. A more satisfactory explanation, however, would appear to be the existence of dissimilar production functions among nations. It may be, for example, that import-competing industries in the United States are comparatively capital-intensive because United States capital is a

Hence, the link between factor endowments and the *specific* kinds of products a country will export and import is now broken.[11] We can still say a nation will export those goods that use relatively large inputs of its abundant factors and import those goods that use relatively large inputs of its scarce factors, but we cannot say what those goods will be without knowing the production functions in question. In brief, by creating dissimilar production functions among nations, technological innovation can serve as a basis of international trade, along with dissimilar factor endowments, economies of scale, and location.

We can show this by means of a simple two-country (A and B), two-product (wheat and textiles), two-factor (labor and capital) model in which both countries have the same factor proportions (providing no basis for trade) but use different production functions to produce wheat. Specifically, both countries produce textiles with the same production function which requires 3 units of labor and 2 units of capital to produce one unit of textiles. However, in producing one unit of wheat, country A uses one unit of labor and 4 units of capital (a capital-intensive process) while country B uses 5 units of labor and one unit of capital to produce wheat in the traditional labor-intensive way. Under these conditions, the two countries have different comparative costs: country A has a comparative advantage in wheat and country B, a comparative advantage in textiles, and both will gain from trade.

Table 5-1

	Country A (dollars)	Country B (pesos)
Unit price of labor	2	4
Unit price of capital	1	2
Unit cost of textiles	8	16
Unit cost of wheat	6	22

better substitute than United States labor for foreign natural resources and labor. See W. W. Leontieff, "Factor Proportions and the Structure of American Foreign Trade: Further Theoretical and Empirical Analysis," *Review of Economics and Statistics* (November, 1956); and his original article "Domestic Production and Foreign Trade: The American Capital Position Re-examined," which has been reprinted in *Economia Internazionale* (February, 1954). Gottfried Haberler gives a succinct treatment of the Leontieff paradox in *A Survey of International Trade Theory*, Special Papers in International Economics, Princeton University, No. 1 (July, 1961), pp. 21-22.

[11] This may also be true even when countries use the *same* production function for a specific good if there is a high degree of factor substitutability (that is, the technical coefficients of production can assume a broad range of values) such that at one set of factor prices a product is, say, capital-intensive while at another set of factor prices it becomes labor-intensive. (See Footnote 4 on page 60 for an early comment on coefficients of production.) Technically, this situation is called *factor reversal;* its frequency is a matter of dispute among economists. Part of the problem lies in the difficulty of distinguishing the use of the *same* production function with different coefficients of production, on the one hand, from the use of *different* production functions, on the other, in concrete situations where both differences may be operative.

International technology gaps in production functions have a dynamic impact on trade among nations as innovations open up new gaps and technological diffusion closes old gaps. There is ample evidence that both the opening and closing of technology gaps now occurs much more rapidly than at any time in the past. Diffusion occurs in several ways. Technical and other news media transmit knowledge of new discoveries from one country to another, as does trade in new products. Companies in advanced countries like the United States license technical know-how and assistance to foreign companies in return for royalty payments and fees, or set up their own operations abroad using new technology.[12] Diffusion is especially swift among the industrial countries because they have the capacity to use the new technical knowledge immediately. An outstanding example of this rapidity is the transistor. Developed by the United States, it was Japan that first used the transistor to make small radios, which then found a big market in the United States. Technological leadership is constantly threatened, therefore, by innovations elsewhere. Technologically speaking, nations must run hard to avoid falling behind. In the nineteenth century, comparative advantages changed slowly over a generation or more; in our own time, a country may enjoy a comparative advantage in a product for only a few years before technical diffusion and imitation or new technical discoveries wipe it out. The life cycle of new products offers the most dramatic evidence of this process.

INTERNATIONAL TECHNOLOGY GAPS: NEW PRODUCTS

Commonly, technological innovations assume the form of new products or product improvements rather than new production functions for old products. Such innovations may create entirely new industries. In 1945, television, jet travel, and the digital computer industries were commercially nonexistent in the United States; in 1965, they contributed $13 billion to the U.S. gross national product and provided 900,000 jobs.[13] American manufacturers place thousands of new products on the home market every year, and sooner or later many of these products are exported to foreign markets. The technological leaders in American manufacturing are aerospace, electrical machinery (including communication), transportation equipment (including automobiles), chemicals (including pharmaceuticals), and nonelectrical machinery. These industries accounted for 80 percent of the total research and development expenditures ($16.8 billion) in the United States in 1967.[14] It is hardly coincidental that these same industries are also the most aggressive competitors in world markets via direct exports and investment in foreign production.

---

[12] The role of international enterprise as a transfer agent for technology and technological innovation is examined in Chapter 23.

[13] U.S. Department of Commerce, *Technological Innovation: Its Environment and Management* (Washington: U.S. Government Printing Office, 1967), p. 4.

[14] "The Cash Pours Out For R and D," *Business Week* (May 18, 1968), p. 72.

Accumulating evidence demonstrates that the United States has a comparative advantage in new products designed and developed for high-income markets. The share of U.S. companies in world exports of research-intensive product groups (aircraft, electrical, and chemical) is about 30 percent, or twice the share of U.S. companies in all industrial exports.[15] Keesing has discovered a high correlation by industry between R and D expenditures (as a percentage of sales) and the U.S. share of exports by the OECD (Organization for Economic Cooperation and Development) countries.[16] Also, this country enjoys a strong positive balance on "technological" payments for technical know-how, licenses, and patents. For example, in 1964 the United States paid out $88 million for imports of technology from the other industrial countries but received $550 million for its own technology exports to the same countries.[17]

Although the significance of product innovations has been largely ignored by economic theorists, marketing scholars have developed the concept of the *product life cycle*. One version of this concept involves three successive stages: specialty, standard product, and commodity. Briefly, the life cycle starts when a company introduces a product that is entirely or partially differentiated from old products. (The introduction of the stainless steel razor blade by Wilkinson Sword in the early 1960's is a case in point.) In this first stage the product is a specialty and, for the time being, the manufacturer has a monopoly. However, most new products are soon imitated (or even improved upon) by competitors.[18] Hence, the original product loses its specialty status to become a standardized product that is manufactured and sold by several companies. In this second stage, some product differentiation is maintained by individual manufacturers through promotion, packaging, and services (nonprice competition), but as more companies enter the market and the different brands become more and more alike to consumers, the product may slip into the third stage as a commodity. Brand competition now gives way to price competition.

Vernon and others have used this concept of a product life cycle to explain the behavior of U.S. exports of manufactures.[19] A four-stage model is postulated: (1) U.S. export monopoly in a new product; (2) start

---

[15] "The Impact of Science and Technology on Social Economic Development," *The OECD Observer* (Paris: April, 1968), p. 21.

[16] Donald B. Keesing, "The Impact of Research and Development on United States Trade," *Journal of Political Economy* (February, 1967). The OECD countries include Western Europe, Japan, Canada, and the United States.

[17] *The OECD Observer, op. cit.,* p. 26.

[18] Patent protection may inhibit imitation (as in the case of the Polaroid Land camera), but it is seldom complete. Furthermore, many new products are not patentable.

[19] Raymond Vernon, "International Investment and International Trade in the Product Cycle," *The Quarterly Journal of Economics* (May, 1966), pp. 190-207. Louis T. Wells, Jr., "A Product Life Cycle for International Trade?" *Journal of Marketing* (July, 1968), pp. 1-6. For an application of the product life cycle to export marketing at the enterprise level, see Franklin R. Root, *Strategic Planning for Export Marketing* (Scranton, Pa.: International Textbook Company, 1964), pp. 66-68.

of foreign production; (3) foreign production becomes competitive in export markets; and (4) U.S. imports of the no-longer-new product. Vernon asserts that U.S. producers are likely to be the first to exploit market opportunities for high-income and labor-saving new products because such opportunities first appear in the affluent United States. Furthermore, they will first produce these new products in the United States because close proximity to customers and suppliers is imperative for design and marketing flexibility. In this first stage, U.S. producers have a monopoly in export markets and they proceed to build up sales with no concern for local competition. However, during the second stage, producers in one or more industrial countries start to manufacture the product whose design and production is now standardized.[20] Consequently, the overall rate of growth of U.S. exports declines while exports to the countries of foreign production become minimal. In the third stage, foreign producers displace U.S. exports in the remaining export markets. Finally, foreign producers achieve sufficient competitive strength (due to economies of scale and lower labor costs) to export to the United States itself. In short, the export effects of product innovation are undermined by technological diffusion and lower costs abroad.

The time period for completion of the trade cycle is determined by the income elasticity of demand, economies of scale, transfer costs, and the capacity to imitate abroad. Wells has found that American exports of consumer durables for the period 1952-63 are consistent with predictions of the cycle model.[21] More generally, this model appears to be a useful explanation of the behavior of many product innovations in international trade. Factual observations support its twin assumptions: (1) the United States is the leader in high-income product innovations, and (2) sooner or later these innovations are imitated in foreign production at a lower cost. There is also evidence that the trade cycle is speeding up. For example, in 1970 Japan made about half of all the calculators sold in the United States and about 70 percent of those sold in the world. The striking point is that Japan did not start to mass produce calculators until 1967 and used to import them from the United States.[22]

New products do not always expand the volume of world trade; they may simply displace older *export* products or actually contract the volume of trade as substitutes for *import* products. Nylon has largely eliminated

---

[20] Some of these foreign producers may be subsidiaries of American companies who anticipate later stages in the export life cycle. See Chapter 21.

[21] Louis T. Wells, Jr., "Test of a Product Cycle Model of International Trade: U.S. Exports of Consumer Durables," *The Quarterly Journal of Economics* (February, 1969), pp. 152-162.

[22] "A Yen for Business Machines," *Forbes* (December 15, 1970), p. 19. This calls to mind the wisecrack: "In January, an American invents a new product; in February, Tass announces that a Russian had invented it thirty years ago; and by March, Japan is exporting the product to the United States!"

the raw silk trade, synthetic rubber casts a pall over the long-run future of natural rubber, plastics have cut into the international trade of some traditional products, and coal, displaced by petroleum, has a relatively minor role in world commerce compared to the past. On balance, however, technological innovations in all their many forms have been, and continue to be, a positive force in world trade.

THE INTERNATIONAL MOBILITY OF FACTORS

The simple theory of international trade presented in Chapter 3 assumes the absence of *any* factor movements among nations. Given this assumption, national factor endowments are determined only by internal conditions that perpetuate international dissimilarities in endowment structures and thereby afford a basis for gainful trade. The significance of this assumption for the simple theory of trade may be understood by tracing the implications of the contrary assumption; namely, perfect international factor mobility.

If labor, capital, and other factors moved freely among nations in response to opportunities for economic gain, they would move until the supply of each factor was everywhere fully adapted to demand and the price of each factor was the same in every country and in every use. Under the assumptions of the simple theory, therefore, perfect international factor mobility would destroy the basis for gainful trade; given identical production functions, the shapes of all national production possibilities curves would be similar and the opportunity cost of any good would be the same in all countries. In the simple theory, therefore, factor mobility acts as a perfect substitute for goods mobility (trade).[23]

However useful they may be for economic analysis, the assumptions of perfect international factor mobility or immobility are fictions; neither is found to exist in the real world. Instead we find different degrees of factor mobility that vary among factors, among nations, and over time. Even within a country, noncompeting labor groups and other conditions constrain the free movement of factors and thereby provide an opportunity for interregional trade. Although factor mobility among countries is usually (but not always) lower than domestic mobility because of physical, social, and political obstacles, it is by no means small. Indeed, a key development in the world economy in recent years has been an extraordinary growth in international flows of management, capital, and technology, particularly among the advanced industrial countries. The principal agent in this factor transfer is the international enterprise (especially its most advanced form, the multinational corporation), which is the subject of Part Three. The

---

[23] When we drop the assumptions of the simple theory, this statement is no longer valid. Even with perfect factor mobility, opportunities for gainful trade would continue to be generated by economies of scale, product differentiation, and technology gaps.

emergence of customs unions and free trade areas, notably the European Economic Community, has also encouraged the international movement of factors.

THE MOBILITY OF LAND FACTORS

Natural resources are completely immobile. It is not physically possible to move land area, climate, soil, forests, mines, landforms, and other "gifts of nature" from one place to another. Since the international distribution of natural resources is most haphazard, their immobility assures a permanent dissimilarity in the supplies of national land factors. This immobility is not a distinctive feature of international trade, however, because the land factor is also immobile among regions of the same country.

THE MOBILITY OF LABOR

The human agents of production (ordinary workers, professional workers, and managers) are physically able to move from one country to another. In practice, however, this potential mobility is constrained by motivations, opportunities, and ignorance, especially in the case of ordinary workers.

Ordinary workers will not emigrate to a foreign country unless they are attracted by favorable prospects abroad or pressed by unhappy circumstances at home. Social inertia tends to keep people in their native countries. This inertia is the sum total of attachments to one's place of birth, one's family, and one's friends; of adaptation to the language, customs, and way of life of the native country; and of many similar conditions. Reluctance to move is fortified by the strange and unknown risks of emigration. Generally, the emigrant must face a new language, new customs, new laws, and an ignorance of specific economic opportunities. Despite these obstacles, however, large masses of people have moved from one country to another, particularly during periods of widespread unrest brought on by natural disasters, revolution, or war at home.[24]

In our own day the absence of motivations to emigrate has been much less important than limited opportunities to emigrate in explaining the low international mobility of labor. All contemporary governments restrict immigration and some, such as the Soviet government, also restrict emigration. With few exceptions, then, the international migrant must pass through a careful screening before admittance to a foreign country.[25] Actually, the

---

[24] Many waves of migration to the United States have been associated with unrest in Europe and elsewhere. The latest example is the influx of Cubans.

[25] One exception deserves mention. Labor shortages in some western European countries have encouraged a substantial migration of workers, especially from southern Europe. West Germany has more than one million foreign workers, and in Switzerland about one-third of the labor force is foreign. Higher labor mobility is an important objective of the European Economic Community (see Chapter 16). This increase in international labor mobility *within* Western Europe has not been matched elsewhere in the world.

international mobility of ordinary labor is so low that international differences in relative labor supplies are probably growing wider due to disparate rates of population growth and of capital accumulation.

The international mobility of professional workers, such as engineers and scientists, is much higher than that of ordinary workers for several reasons. Mainly, these workers possess highly-valued skills that meet international standards. A German physicist can perform the same activities in the United States that he performs at home; a Chilean engineer can build bridges abroad as well as in Chile. Secondly, professional workers have a superior knowledge of job opportunities in foreign countries because they belong to a profession that is international in scope. Many students from the developing countries obtain advance degrees from universities in North America and Western Europe and learn about professional opportunities there. Thirdly, professional workers have a greater capacity to adapt to foreign cultures, such as languages, because of their higher education. Furthermore, they are likely to be interested in professional advancement whether at home or abroad. At times, the mobility of professional workers may be so high that national governments become concerned about "brain drains." The developing countries annually lose hundreds of their brightest professionals to North America and Europe, many of them being recent graduates who decided not to return home. Undoubtedly, this mobility would be far higher if governments did not impose entry restrictions and if professional organizations (such as the medical societies in the United States) did not lay down rigorous qualifications that frequently have nothing to do with professional competence.

THE MOBILITY OF MANAGEMENT

The international mobility of managers is probably higher today than at any time in the past. The international company with production and marketing affiliates in several countries has become a powerful vehicle for the transfer of managerial skills such as innovating, planning, directing, organizing, and controlling. A new type of professional, international executive is now coming to the fore, an individual who is able to move quickly from a management post in one country to a new post in another country. Sophisticated, cosmopolitan, and highly educated, this new breed of international manager has the capacity to manage business operations effectively in a broad variety of national milieux. The movement of these managers has been enormously facilitated by the jet airplane.

THE MOBILITY OF CAPITAL

The international mobility of capital goods (construction, capital equipment, and inventories) varies with the nature of the good. Construction is largely tied to specific sites and is highly immobile while the mobility of capital equipment and inventories is limited only by transfer costs and government trade controls, like other goods. It is important to realize, however, that a nation does not necessarily transfer capital to another nation by exporting capital goods to the latter. Instead, capital is transferred by international loans and investments (and occasionally by gifts) that provide the purchasing power needed to finance either the construction of capital goods in the borrowing country or the import of capital goods from abroad. Therefore, the criterion of the international mobility of capital is the ease of foreign investment.

Viewed in this way, the international mobility of capital may be very high. During the nineteenth century and up to the 1930's, most international investment took the form of private lending via subscriptions to foreign bond issues. Although in the 1960's private lending of this sort once again became substantial, the bulk of private foreign investment today is undertaken by international companies that make direct equity investments in foreign affiliates. The rapid expansion of direct foreign investment by U.S. and European (and lately Japanese) companies is a dominant force in the evolution of the contemporary world economy.[26] Much capital also moves from rich to poor nations through international institutions, such as the World Bank, and through bilateral government aid programs.[27]

The international mobility of capital is constrained by political and economic instability, exchange controls, exchange devaluation, expropriation, and other factors that may be found in recipient countries. It is also constrained by restrictions in capital-exporting countries, such as the foreign investment controls the United States government has imposed since 1965.

INTERNATIONAL TRADE AND FACTOR MOVEMENTS AS SUBSTITUTES

Both trade and factor movements act to bring about a superior allocation of production among nations. As we have seen, trade achieves this result according to the simple theory through an international specialization that allows nations to export products that require relatively abundant factors in their production in exchange for products that require relatively scarce factors. More generally, trade enables a country to export products with low opportunity costs and import products with high opportunity costs.

Factor movements achieve a superior allocation of productive agents directly. Relatively abundant factors in country A (such as management and capital) move to country B where the same factors are relatively scarce, and they are then combined in production with country B's relatively abundant factors. In terms of price theory, factors move from country A where their marginal productivities are low (because they are relatively abundant) to country B where their marginal productivities are higher

---

[26] Chapter 22 explores the nature of private direct foreign investment.
[27] See Chapter 18 for a discussion of foreign aid.

(because they are relatively scarce). Under conditions of perfect competition, the flow of factors continues until their marginal productivities (and prices) are the same in all countries. When this occurs, the international allocation of factors is perfect because any further factor movement would lower production and consumer satisfactions for the world as a whole. Because of many obstacles and continuous economic change, this ideal allocation can never be achieved even among regions of the same country; it can only be approached in varying degrees. Thus, the higher the mobility of factors among countries, the better the global allocation of factors and production. At the same time, factor mobility will tend to equalize factor prices among countries.

Does international trade also tend to equalize factor prices? To answer that question let us turn to the example in Chapter 3, in which the United States has a comparative advantage in wheat production and a comparative *dis*advantage in textile production while the converse holds in the United Kingdom. The production of wheat is land-intensive and the United States has a relatively abundant supply of land that commands a relatively low rent. The production of textiles is labor-intensive and the United States has a relatively scarce supply of labor that commands a relatively high wage. The opposite is true in the United Kingdom.

When trade begins, the demand facing United States wheat rises as foreign demand is added to domestic demand. With increasing unit costs, this higher demand leads to higher wheat prices and feeds back to create a higher demand and higher prices for the factors of production—especially land—used to produce wheat. At the same time, imports of textiles from the United Kingdom are displacing United States production of textiles. The falling demand for the latter initiates a falling demand and falling prices for the factors of production—especially labor—used to produce textiles. As a consequence, land rent rises relative to wages in the United States. Simultaneously, wages rise relative to land rent in the United Kingdom. Thus, the abundant factors (land in the United States, labor in the United Kingdom) become relatively more expensive while the scarce factors (labor in the United States, land in the United Kingdom) become relatively less expensive. It follows that the gap between the factor prices of the two countries becomes narrower.

Will international trade ever achieve a full equalization of factor prices between the trading countries? Only under certain limiting assumptions could it ever happen. They are: national factor endowments are not too unequal, there are no transfer costs, technology is the same in all countries, and there is only partial specialization—each country continues to produce some import-type goods. But only the last assumption holds in the real world.

The foregoing analysis points to a *substitutive* relation between trade and factor movements. In the preceding example, a flow of labor from the United Kingdom to the United States would increase the opportunity cost of textiles in the first country and lower it in the second country, thereby narrowing the gainful opportunity for trade. The question of a substitutive relation between foreign investment (capital outflow) and trade is now a matter of controversy in the United States. Do restrictions on U.S. investment abroad raise or lower U.S. exports? What about U.S. imports? Increasingly, labor union spokesmen assert that foreign investment causes a loss of jobs to American workers as U.S. companies transfer production to foreign locations. Although we shall examine the relation (or rather, the relations) between factor flows and trade at some length in Chapter 24, some observations are made in the following section to indicate that factor movements and trade may also be complementary.

INTERNATIONAL TRADE AND FACTOR MOVEMENTS AS COMPLEMENTS: ECONOMIC INTEGRATION

The conclusion that trade and factor movements are substitutes derives from the factor-endowments theory that is concerned only with allocational efficiency under static conditions (perfect competition, fixed factor endowments, and no technology gaps). When these assumptions are dropped to allow for dynamic elements, it is no longer evident that international factor movements cause a general decrease in international trade. What the static analysis ignores are the effects of factor movements on economic growth and, particularly, economic integration.

As stated earlier, international factor flows are mainly initiated by international companies that transfer a mix of management, capital, and technology from one country to another. These factors are combined with local factors to manufacture products that, for the most part, are new to the host economy.[28] This process contributes both directly and indirectly to the growth of the economy.[29] By promoting economic growth, factor movements increase the capacity of nations to trade with one another; expansion occurs in both the size and diversity of production and markets. Although factor movements have displaced trade in some products, statistical data suggests that their growth effects on trade have been more powerful than their substitution effects. In the past decade, trade and factor flows have expanded together for the world as a whole; in the European Economic Community, factor transfers among the member countries have been accompanied by a growth in mutual trade that has exceeded the growth in trade with outside countries. At the enterprise level, it is also noteworthy that the principal exporters of manufactures from the United States are also the principal investors in production abroad.

Generally, we are witnessing a process of economic integration on a global scale (particularly among the industrial countries) that is being

---

[28] The term "host economy" refers to the country that receives the factor transfers.
[29] This is intended only as a general statement: some factor transfers are more growth-generating than others. For this and other qualifications, see Chapter 25.

carried forward by a complex mix of trade and factor flows. Economists generally agree that factor movements constitute a more powerful instrument for factor-price equalization than trade in products. Consequently, factor transfers can be expected to attain a higher degree of integration of national economies than goods transfers alone. As local and regional markets earlier gave way to national markets, so national markets are now giving way to world markets. In the past, trade created an international economy; today, factor flows are creating a world economy.

A MARKETING THEORY OF TRADE: INCOME GAPS

According to the factor-endowments theory, international trade is based on dissimilar cost structures that mainly derive from differences in factor endowments: the greater the differences, the broader the opportunity for gainful trade. One would expect, therefore, that the greatest share of trade occurs between industrial (capital-abundant) countries, on the one hand, and nonindustrial (land- and labor-abundant) countries, on the other; and that this trade involves the exchange of manufactured goods for primary goods. However, the factual evidence points to a contrary state of affairs. Statistical data in Chapter 2 revealed that (1) the industrial countries generate about three-fourths of total world exports; (2) over 75 percent of these exports go to the industrial countries themselves, and this trade is primarily (although not exclusively) an exchange of manufactures for manufactures; (3) trade between the industrial and nonindustrial countries is only about one-third of world trade, mainly consisting of an exchange of manufactures for primary products; and (4) the economic structures of the industrial countries are becoming more, not less, similar. At the same time, income gaps are widening between the industrial group of countries and the nonindustrial group.

Clearly the facts do not agree with the factor-endowments theory. Either the theory is wrong or it is only a partial explanation that overlooks the powerful effects of other factors. Dissatisfaction with this version of comparative advantage, especially with regard to trade in manufactures, has stimulated new approaches. The most comprehensive revision of trade theory has been elaborated by Linder.[30]

Linder asserts that differences in factor endowments explain trade in natural resource-intensive products, but not in manufactures. His basic proposition is that the range of a country's manufactured exports is determined by *internal* demand. Thus, it is necessary (but not sufficient) that a product be consumed or invested at home before it can become a potential export product. Comparative advantage in manufactures requires an earlier production for the domestic market. Linder supports this proposition

---

[30] Staffan Burenstam Linder, *An Essay on Trade and Transformation* (New York: John Wiley and Sons, Inc., 1961). Discussion in the text is drawn from Chapters 2 and 3 of Linder's book.

by reference to the ignorance of entrepreneurs with regard to foreign markets as compared with domestic markets. He argues that an entrepreneur is not likely to think about satisfying a need that does not exist at home; even if he did, he might not conceive the product that would fill that need; and even if he conceived and developed the right product, it is still improbable that the product could be finally adapted to strange market conditions without prohibitive costs. Since internal demand also determines which products a country may import, the range of its potential exports is the same as, or included in, the range of its potential imports.

It follows that the more *similar* the demand structures for manufactured goods in two countries, the more *intensive* is the potential trade in manufactures between them.[31] If two countries have the same demand structures, then their consumers and investors will demand the same goods with the same degrees of quality and sophistication. But what determines the structure of demand?

The most important influence, says Linder, is average or per capita income.[32] Countries with high per capita incomes will demand high-quality, "luxury" consumer goods and sophisticated capital goods, while low per capita income countries will demand lower-quality, "necessity" consumer goods and less sophisticated capital goods. Consequently, differences in per capita incomes are a potential obstacle to trade: a rich country that has a comparative advantage in the production of high-quality, advanced manufactures will find its big export markets in other rich countries where people demand such products, not in poor countries where the demand is small. By the same token, manufactured exports of the poor countries should find their best markets in other poor countries with similar demand structures. Linder does not rule out all trade in manufactures between rich and poor countries because there will always be some overlapping of demand structures due to an unequal distribution of income: some of the people in rich countries are poor while some of the people in poor countries are rich. But when the degree of overlap in demand structures is small, the potential trade in manufactures will also be small.

The situation is different for primary products. Because they are land-intensive, relative factor proportions are the main determinant of their prices. Linder arrives, therefore, at two explanations for trade, one for manufactures, the other for primary products. Trade in the former is caused by the same forces that cause domestic trade: economies of scale, product

---

[31] By "intensive" Linder does not mean the *absolute* size of trade between two countries which is influenced by the absolute size of the trading economies, but rather the size of trade after adjustment for the size of the economies.

[32] The factor-endowments theory ignores the effects of per capita income differences on trade. It recognizes the influence of tastes (assumed to be marginal because of a similarity of tastes among countries), but tastes alone do not determine the structure of demand—they must be supported by purchasing power (income).

differentiation, and technology gaps. Linder concludes that the effect of per capita income levels on trade in manufactures may be constrained or distorted by entrepreneurial ignorance, cultural and political differences, transportation costs, and man-made obstacles such as tariffs.

Linder's model is consistent with the observed pattern of trade in manufactured products. Furthermore, it is in agreement with studies of international marketing at the enterprise level and with the hypothesis of a product life cycle. In Chapter 21 we shall trace the evolution of the typical international enterprise as it emerges from a purely domestic company. Only with rare exceptions do manufacturers enter into exports (or foreign investment) before establishing firm market positions at home. Once they do venture into exports, manufacturers usually find their most attractive markets in other industrial countries where incomes, tastes, and demand patterns most closely resemble those at home. In estimating sales potentials for their products in foreign markets, entrepreneurs give more weight to per capita income (and related phenomena) than they do to any other single economic factor.

Aside from the question of market size, there is the question of marketing costs that must be incurred to exploit the market opportunity. These costs are associated with the activities that the firm must undertake to overcome a variety of "market separations" that isolate the foreign market from the firm's production base in the home country.[33] The more a foreign economy resembles the home economy, the smaller these separations tend to be and the lower the cost of marketing.[34] Product adaptation illustrates this relationship. To export successfully, the manufacturer must adapt his product to fit the characteristics of the foreign market. The need to make substantial modifications (at times, wholly new designs) to meet the specific demands of non-Western markets frequently discourages American companies from taking a serious interest in those markets.[35] To reach markets in poor countries, some U.S. manufacturers have "invented backwards," such as the hand-cranked cash register built by the National Cash Register Company. In addition to product adaptation, manufacturers ordinarily encounter far greater obstacles to the distribution and promotion of their products in low-income countries than in high-income countries. Finally, entrepreneurs are usually more aware of market opportunities in other industrial countries than in nonindustrial countries.

---

[33] Market separations derive from space, time, seller-buyer perceptions, value and ownership, as well as government restrictions. For a discussion of separations in international marketing see Franklin R. Root, "Towards an Enterprise Theory of International Marketing" in *New Essays in Marketing Theory* (Boston: Allyn and Bacon, 1971).

[34] Social and cultural similarities also make for smaller separations.

[35] Richard D. Robinson, "The Challenge of the Underdeveloped National Market," *Journal of Marketing* (October, 1961), pp. 19-25.

To conclude this point, the smaller market separations that are associated with similar per capita incomes (as well as similar social and cultural conditions) go far in explaining why so much trade in manufactures takes place among the industrial countries.

Two further observations about Linder's model can be made. Although Linder distinguishes between manufactures and primary products, a finer distinction exists between differentiated products and nondifferentiated commodities. As we observed earlier in our discussion of the product life cycle, when manufactured products become commodities they compete on the basis of price and cost. Unless economies of scale are significant, therefore, the factor endowments underlying costs are the principal explanation of trade in commodities, whether they are manufactures or primary products. Thus, poor countries have a comparative advantage in labor-intensive commodity manufactures such as basic textiles.

A second observation concerns the bearing of factor mobility, particularly management, on Linder's major proposition that countries only export manufactures that are first produced for the home market. Although this proposition appears to be generally true today, it will probably be less true in the future. International companies are now starting to establish manufacturing subsidiaries in poor countries as sources for products (mostly components rather than final products) that are exported to their operations in other countries. Because these arrangements are between a subsidiary and its parent, market separation is very low. Thus, the mobility of international companies may enable nonindustrial countries to export manufactured products that are not sold in their domestic markets.

A SHORT RECAPITULATION OF THE THEORY OF COMPARATIVE ADVANTAGE

After the many qualifications of the simple trade model presented in Chapter 3, what can we say about the theory of comparative advantage?

The simple model attributes a country's comparative cost structure to its relative factor endowments. Although this theory recognizes the influence of demand on factor prices, it relegates factor demand to a minor role in the determination of comparative costs by assuming a similarity in national patterns of taste. Since countries differ in their relative factor endowments, they develop dissimilar comparative cost structures that serve as a basis for gainful trade. Specifically, a country will export those goods whose production requires large inputs of its relatively abundant (cheap) factors and import those goods whose production requires large inputs of its relatively scarce (expensive) factors.

This model is simple because it uses several restrictive assumptions. Some of these assumptions may be modified to make them more "realistic" without endangering the theory's fundamental proposition; namely, the dependence of comparative costs on factor endowments. Thus, increasing costs, dissimilar tastes, changes in factor endowments, and unemployment may be absorbed into the theory without difficulty, although they undoubtedly complicate the explanation of trade. When we modify certain other assumptions, however, we call into question the essence of the theory or, at the very least, introduce additional explanations of trade.

We have uncovered many economic conditions that can generate opportunities for gainful trade *even in the absence of differences in factor endowments*: dissimilar tastes, transportation costs, economies of scale, product differentiation, dissimilar production functions, new products, and similar per capita incomes. A nation may gain (or lose) a comparative advantage through the effects of any of these conditions. Is the factor-endowments theory, then, no longer useful?

This theory would appear to have a declining relevance to trade among industrial countries. Through high levels of capital investment and technological innovation, these countries have the capacity to manufacture products independently of their natural resource endowments. In other words, their production possibilities are no longer (or only marginally) constrained by the absence of land factors. The comparative advantages of the industrial countries are man-made, arising from economies of scale, product differentiation, and technology gaps. The Linder model offers an explanation of trade among the industrial countries that is not only consistent with its actual pattern, but also in agreement with the concept of "market separation" drawn from international marketing studies.

The factor-endowments theory, however, continues to be relevant to the trade of the nonindustrial, developing countries. The production possibilities of these countries are closely linked to their natural resource endowments.

Regretfully, there is no simple theory that is adequate to explain the actual structure of world trade and changes in that structure over time. Instead, we have several partial explanations that nevertheless can be highly useful in the analysis of trade in specific products. Moreover, it is doubtful that any trade models as such will be adequate to explain the dynamics of a world economy in which factors move as well as goods. What is needed is a theory of *international economic integration* that will encompass both trade and factor flows in a systematic way. Economic relations among nation-states are becoming so intimate as to resemble more and more the economic relations among regions of the same nation-state. The process of integration is furthest advanced among member countries of the European Economic Community, somewhat advanced among members of the Organization for Economic Cooperation and Development, and least advanced for the nonindustrial and socialist countries.

A theory of international economic integration will have to pay far more attention to the international business enterprise than does traditional trade theory. By concentrating on trade only at the national level, economists have left to marketing and management scholars the task of explaining the behavior of the international firm. As long as international trade was largely carried on by middlemen while producers remained at home, this neglect was not serious. But today, international firms have burst the confines of the individual nation-state to carry on their operations throughout the world. It has become meaningful to talk about the comparative advantages of such firms as they bring to bear on world markets a mix of productive factors, technological innovation, and entrepreneurial drive. It is no longer possible to understand the trade of the industrial countries (notably the United States) unless full account is taken of the behavior of international firms. The theory of international enterprise must become part of a broader theory of international economic integration if we are to understand the forces now shaping the world economy.

SUMMARY

1. Although the simple theory assumes that the individual factors of production are homogeneous and fixed in supply, there are actually many subvarieties of land, human factors, and capital that are continually changing in supply over time through the effects of technical advance, population growth, and capital investment. The existence of numerous subfactors means that national comparative cost structures are highly complex, and the possibility of identical factor endowments among nations is only theoretical. The effects of changes in a nation's factor endowments may be antitrade, neutral, or protrade.

2. Technological innovation influences trade through higher factor productivity, production functions, and new products. A new production function "saves" some or all of the factors of production needed to produce a given level of output as compared with the old production function. The effects of this "saving" may be neutral, protrade, or antitrade. At any given time, countries may be using different technologies to produce the same products; that is to say, they have dissimilar production functions (technology gap). Hence, there is no fixed relationship between factor endowments and the *specific* kinds of products a country will export and import. Technological innovation also creates technology gaps in new products, giving rise to international trade cycles.

3. However useful they may be for economic analysis, the assumptions of perfect international factor mobility or immobility are fictions; neither is found to exist in the real world. Instead we find different degrees of factor mobility that vary among factors, among nations, and over time. A key development in the world economy in recent years has been an extraordinary growth in international flows of management, capital, and technology under the aegis of the international business enterprise. Both international trade and factor mobility tend to equalize factor prices among nations, pointing to a substitutive relationship between the two. But factor movements may also generate trade by stimulating economic growth. Today we are witnessing a process of economic integration on a global scale that is being carried forward by a complex mix of trade and factor flows.

4. Although the simple theory suggests that the greatest share of trade should occur between the industrial and nonindustrial countries, the factual evidence is otherwise. Linder asserts that differences in factor endowments explain trade in natural resource-intensive products, but not in manufactures. The range of a country's manufactured exports is determined by internal demand; and the more *similar* the demand structures for manufactured goods in two countries, the more intensive is the potential trade in manufactures between them. Linder's model is consistent with the observed pattern of trade in manufactures and with studies of international marketing at the enterprise level (including the product life cycle).

5. We have uncovered many economic conditions that can generate opportunities for gainful trade among nations even in the absence of differences in factor endowments: dissimilar tastes, transportation costs, economies of scale, product differentiation, dissimilar production functions, new products, and similar per capita incomes. The simple factor-endowments theory would appear to have a declining relevance to trade among the industrial countries, but continues to be relevant to trade of the nonindustrial countries. What is needed is a theory of international economic integration that will encompass both trade and factor flows in a systematic way. Such a theory will have to pay far more attention to the international business enterprise than does traditional trade theory.

QUESTIONS AND APPLICATIONS

1. What are the effects on international trade of factor heterogeneity? Of factor change?

2. Although the terms are frequently used interchangeably, can you draw a meaningful distinction between technology as such and technological innovation? Illustrate your answer with examples.

3. What has happened to U.S. exports and imports of automobiles since the Second World War? Is the product life cycle a useful explanation? (Justify your answer by reference to U.S. trade statistics.)

4. Explain how both trade and factor movements tend to equalize factor prices among nations. What conditions will prevent a full equalization of factor prices?

5. "The conclusion that trade and factor movements are substitutes derives from the factor-endowments theory that is concerned only with allocational efficiency under static conditions." Explain this statement.

6. How does the Linder model explain trade in manufactures among the industrial countries? Does the composition of trade in manufactures between the United States and Western Europe support this model? What are the implications of the model for the nonindustrial countries?

SELECTED READINGS

Caves, R. E., and H. G. Johnson (eds.). *Readings in International Economics.* Homewood, Ill.: Richard D. Irwin, Inc., 1968. Parts I and II.

Corden, W. M. *Recent Developments in the Theory of International Trade.* Special Papers in International Economics No. 7. Princeton: Princeton University Press, 1965. Chapters II, III, and IV.

Haberler, G. *A Survey of International Trade Theory.* Special Papers in International Economics No. 1. Princeton: Princeton University Press, 1961. Chapters II and III.

Heller, H. Robert. *International Trade.* Englewood Cliffs, N. J.: Prentice-Hall, Inc., 1968.

Hoover, E. M. *The Location of Economic Activity.* New York: McGraw-Hill Book Company, 1948.

Kenen, P. B. *International Economics.* Foundations of Modern Economics Series. Englewood Cliffs, N. J.: Prentice-Hall, Inc., 1964. Chapter 2.

Kindleberger, C. P. *Foreign Trade and the National Economy.* New Haven: Yale University Press, 1962.

Ohlin, B. G. *Interregional and International Trade.* Cambridge: Harvard University Press, 1935. Part II.

Ricardo, D. *Principles of Political Economy and Taxation.* Everyman's Library. New York: E. P. Dutton and Co., Inc., 1912. Chapter 7.

CHAPTER **6**

THE TRANSFER OF INTERNATIONAL PAYMENTS

In presenting the theory of trade in the preceding chapters, we sought to explain the physical or *real* flows of goods and factor services among nations. Now we turn our attention in the remaining chapters of Part One to the money or *payments* side of international transactions. In so doing, we shall seek answers to several questions: How are international payments made? What determines foreign exchange rates? What is the balance of payments and when is it in disequilibrium? How do nations adjust to payments disequilibrium in a stable-rate system? How do nations adjust to payments disequilibrium in a variable-rate system?

How are international payments made? If one has money, making *domestic* payments presents no problem—dollars are acceptable throughout the United States, pounds sterling serve equally well in the United Kingdom, and the French need only francs in their dealings with each other. But suppose an American resident must make payment to a British resident, or a British resident must make payment to a French resident. What then? The American has only dollars, the Britisher desires payment in pounds sterling, and the French creditor asks for payment in francs. This problem of making payments internationally is solved by the mechanism of the foreign exchange market. The purpose of this chapter is to elucidate the fundamental principles that underlie the functioning of this market, to explain the role of commercial banks and international financial centers, and to trace the effects of international payments upon the money supply of the nation.

TRANSFER THROUGH PRIVATE COMPENSATION

One way to make international payments is by the method of private compensation. Say an American resident *owes* a British resident 20 pounds sterling, which at the current rate of exchange is equivalent to $60. Suppose further that a second American resident is *owed* $60 by a second British resident. Then the following steps may be taken to solve the payments problem for all four parties. (1) The first American resident, a debtor, hands over $60 to the second American resident, a creditor. In this way the former is able to liquidate his debt in dollars while the latter receives in dollars what is owed him by the second British resident. (2) Simultaneously, the second British resident, a debtor, gives 20 pounds sterling to the first British resident, a creditor. Again, the debtor is able to pay in domestic currency and the creditor is paid in domestic currency. Thus, by two simultaneous transactions, both of which are purely domestic, all four parties obtain satisfaction.

Private compensation demands considerable patience and a streak of luck on the part of the participants. Not only must the American debtor find an American creditor (or vice versa) and the corresponding British parties be brought together, but the amounts owing and owed must also be equal if there is to be a full cancellation of all obligations. This cumbersomeness rules out private compensation as a mode of international payment unless, for one reason or another, payments are not possible through the foreign exchange market.[1] The real importance of private compensation lies in the fact that it illustrates in a clear-cut fashion the basic principle of all methods of international payment—*the clearance or offsetting of one international debt against another*. In our example, the debt owed by the first American resident was offset against the debt owed by the second British resident, and since both debts were equal the clearance was perfect.

THE FOREIGN EXCHANGE MARKET

The overwhelming majority of international payments is made through the medium of foreign exchange traded in foreign exchange markets. We shall first examine the nature of foreign exchange and then the functions of the foreign exchange market.

FOREIGN EXCHANGE

Foreign exchange is a financial asset involving a cash claim held by a resident of one country against a resident of another country. Foreign exchange is represented by a wide variety of credit instruments. Thus, an American resident may hold foreign exchange in the form of foreign currencies, bank balances in foreign countries, bills of exchange drawn on foreign residents, or other highly liquid claims on foreigners. Despite this proliferation of forms, however, foreign exchange used to effect international payments may be described as either *transfers* or *bills of exchange*.

A *transfer* is an order sent by cable or mail to a foreign bank directing that bank to debit the deposit account of the orderer and credit the account of a named person or institution. Ordinarily, the transfer takes one or two

---

[1] An important exception to this statement is private compensation *within* the same international enterprise. For example, if the British and German subsidiaries of an American company hold cash claims against each other, then headquarters may instruct them to clear their mutual indebtedness and transfer only the uncleared balance through the foreign exchange market.

days, although same-day transfers are possible. In the age of the jet, mail transfers are about as fast as cable transfers, and often the rate is the same for both. Transfers account for most transactions in the foreign exchange market; usually they involve a domestic and a foreign bank. Suppose, for example, an American needs to make payment of a specified sum in francs to a French resident. He buys from his bank a cable transfer for the required amount of francs, paying dollars at the prevailing rate of exchange. The American bank then cables its correspondent bank in France to debit the American bank's account and credit the account of the French resident who is receiving payment.[2] However, banks are not the only sellers of cable transfers. Multinational companies that maintain balances abroad are able to shift funds back home by selling cable drafts to their domestic banks.

A *bill of exchange* is an unconditional order in writing addressed by one person (the drawer) to another (the drawee) requiring the latter to pay on demand or at a fixed and determinable future time a specified sum in money to order or to bearer (the payee). When the drawer and drawee are residents of different countries, the bill of exchange becomes a bill of foreign exchange. Most bills of exchange originate in the financing of merchandise exports and imports.[3] The bill of exchange is a negotiable instrument that may be transferred from one holder to another by endorsement. An example of a bill of exchange used in making international payments is illustrated below.

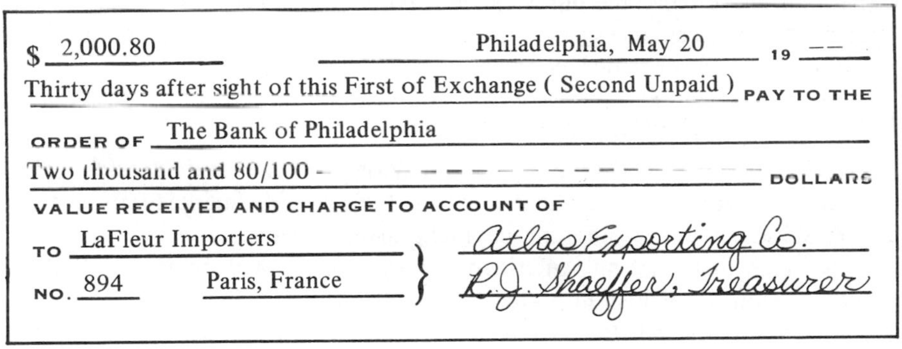

$ 2,000.80	Philadelphia, May 20	19 __

Thirty days after sight of this First of Exchange (Second Unpaid) PAY TO THE

ORDER OF The Bank of Philadelphia

Two thousand and 80/100 - - - - - - - - - - - - - DOLLARS

VALUE RECEIVED AND CHARGE TO ACCOUNT OF

TO LaFleur Importers   } *Atlas Exporting Co.*

NO. 894   Paris, France   } *R.J. Shaeffer, Treasurer*

Figure 6-1

A BILL OF EXCHANGE

---

[2] The French bank informs the French resident of this payment. If the American wanted to pay the Frenchman directly without going through a foreign bank, he would buy a *bank draft* from the American bank and then mail it to the Frenchman, who could cash it at his own bank. A bank draft is simply a written order by a domestic bank to a foreign bank holding its account to make a specified payment to a designated person or institution upon presentation of the draft.

[3] Broadly conceived, transfers are also bills of exchange and they are sometimes called *banker's bills* or *banker's drafts* because both the drawer and drawee are banks. However, the term "bill of exchange" ordinarily refers to a bill of exchange drawn by an exporter, and we have followed this practice. To confuse matters even more, bills of exchange are also called drafts.

Bills of exchange may be distinguished in several ways. A *commercial* bill of exchange is drawn by an exporter against a foreign importer while a *bank* bill of exchange is drawn by an exporter on the importer's bank or its correspondent bank. A bill of exchange that is payable immediately on presentation to the drawee is known as a *sight* bill; a bill that is payable at some later date (usually expressed as so many days after sight, such as a thirty-day sight bill) is a *time* bill. The use of time bills enables importers to obtain credit through the foreign exchange market.

Another distinction is between *clean* and *documentary* bills. A documentary bill is accompanied by a bill of lading and other documents such as an insurance certificate. The importer can only obtain the bill of lading which is needed to take physical possession of the imported goods upon payment (if the bill of exchange is sight) or upon "acceptance" (if the bill is payable so many days after sight). Because a documentary bill thereby lowers the risk of nonpayment, it is commonly used to finance international trade. As its name implies, a clean bill is not accompanied by documents of any sort.

When a time bill of exchange is presented to the drawee, he signifies his willingness to abide by its terms by writing "accepted" on the bill's face, followed by the date and his signature. The bill of exchange then becomes an *acceptance* which is legally a promise to pay with a definite maturity. If the drawee is an importer, the accepted bill is called a *trade acceptance*; if the drawee is a bank, the bill is called a *bank* acceptance. Bank acceptances (but not trade acceptances) may be easily discounted in acceptance markets that are active in all major financial centers.

FINANCING EXPORT SHIPMENTS

To further our understanding of bills of exchange and transfers used in making international payments, let us look at the financing of a U.S. export shipment under different payment arrangements.

Assume, first, that an American exporter draws a documentary bill of exchange against a British importer, payable in *dollars* thirty days after sight, and then sends the bill to his bank.[4] The bank, in turn, mails it (together with the bill of lading and other documents) to its correspondent bank in Britain, which presents the bill to the British importer for acceptance. Upon acceptance, the importer obtains the bill of lading that gives him a legal right to the imported goods. The exporter's bill of exchange has now become a dollar trade acceptance that may be held by the exporter until maturity or

---

[4] Because the dollar is the major trading currency, American exporters are able to ask for payment in dollars and American importers are able to pay in dollars most of the time. Thus, a large part of the foreign exchange transactions involved in U.S. foreign trade occur in foreign exchange markets abroad rather than in New York, and the risk of adverse fluctuations in the exchange rate is assumed by foreign importers and exporters. This traditional practice was disrupted by the international currency crisis that began in August, 1971, (discussed in Chapter 20) but it will almost certainly be resumed with the restoration of exchange stability.

sold to his bank at a discount. If the acceptance is discounted, the bank assumes a financing function. Thirty days after the date of acceptance, the correspondent bank presents the bill to the importer for payment. The importer then goes into the London foreign exchange market and purchases a dollar cable (mail) transfer (or possibly a dollar bank draft) payable to the holder of the acceptance (either the exporter or his bank). Note that the foreign exchange transaction has taken place in the London market.

Let us now assume that an American exporter draws a documentary bill of exchange against a British importer payable in pounds sterling. The initial steps are the same as in our first example, but now the exporter (or his bank) holds a *sterling* trade acceptance. Upon maturity, the importer writes a check on his British bank payable to, say, the exporter's bank. The latter now owns a sterling bank balance which it may sell in the foreign exchange market at the prevailing rate of exchange. In this instance, the foreign exchange transaction occurs in New York.

In the event of default on the part of the drawee of a commercial bill of exchange, the holder of the bill has recourse to the drawer (the exporter in our examples). Under commercial bill of exchange financing, therefore, the exporter must assume the risk of nonpayment. At times, the risk of nonpayment may be heightened by the presence of exchange controls abroad that may suddenly deny the importer access to foreign exchange. In such circumstances, the exporter may insist that the importer arrange financing under a *commercial letter of credit.*

A commercial letter of credit is a document issued to the importer by his own bank covering a specific shipment of merchandise and in favor of a named beneficiary (the exporter). The issuing bank notifies the exporter through its correspondent bank in the exporter's country that it has issued a letter of credit in his favor. The letter of credit permits the exporter to draw a bill of exchange without recourse against the foreign issuing bank rather than the importer. When accepted by the issuing bank, the bill of exchange becomes a *bank* acceptance that is easily discounted by the holder in the acceptance market. Thus, the exporter can receive his payment quickly and no longer bears the risk of nonpayment by the importer. However, the exporter still bears the risk of nonpayment that may result from new exchange restrictions or from revocation of the letter of credit by the issuing bank.[5]

To eliminate this risk, the exporter may insist upon a *confirmed, irrevocable* letter of credit. A letter of credit is confirmed when a correspondent bank in the exporter's country allows the exporter to draw a bill of exchange against it without recourse.[6] In this way the exporter avoids all risk of nonpayment if he meets the stipulations of the letter of credit regarding the

---

[5] There is also the risk of bank failure, but ordinarily this is a remote contingency.

[6] The correspondent bank will not confirm the letter of credit unless it is also irrevocable. With an irrevocable, *unconfirmed* letter of credit, the exporter is still exposed to the risk of nonpayment by the issuing bank because of exchange control.

nature of the merchandise, time of shipment, payment terms, and accompanying documents and the like. The exporter simply draws a bill of exchange on the domestic confirming bank for a sum payable in domestic currency. If it is a sight bill, he is paid immediately; if it is a time bill, he receives a *bank* acceptance which is easily discounted in the acceptance market. When the confirming bank makes final payment, it debits the account of the foreign issuing bank.

Although letter of credit financing is the safest from the standpoint of the exporter, it can be onerous for the importer because it amounts to cash payment on his part.[7] In the decade following World War II, American exporters were able to insist on letters of credit, but the return of international competition, the slackening of exchange controls in many parts of the world, and other changes have led to an increasing use of time bills of exchange or even more liberal financing arrangements. Exporters now sell on open account or even consignment when they believe the risk of nonpayment is low, and the competitive advantage of such terms is strong. In particular, multinational companies are likely to ship merchandise to their overseas branches and subsidiaries on open account. Shipments to countries with stable, convertible currencies such as Canada, Mexico, Germany, and Switzerland are also frequently sold on open account. Under this arrangement the importer pays the exporter at the end of the account period (30 or 60 days ordinarily) with a cable (mail) transfer or a bank draft.

FUNCTIONS OF THE MARKET

Foreign exchange markets perform three major functions: (1) the transfer of international payments; (2) the provision of credit; and (3) payment at a distance.

Transfer of International Payments. Foreign exchange markets relieve the individual and business concern of the problem of making or receiving foreign payments by using the same principle of debt clearance that was exemplified in private compensation. But the wholesale volume of clearance, the developed skills and facilities of the foreign exchange dealers, and the competitive nature of the market (barring exchange control by government) make for a far greater degree of efficiency and convenience.

Provision of Credit. Although the primary function of the foreign exchange market is the transfer of international payments, the market also acts as a source of credit. Most importers are neither willing nor prepared to pay cash for their purchases; they much prefer to delay payment until funds

---

[7] The issuing bank usually requires prepayment from the importer. Complete protection against nonpayment is also afforded by cash payments before shipment of the merchandise. In addition to the nonpayment risk, exporters face an exchange risk due to fluctuations in the exchange rate. This risk is passed on to the importer when the exporter can arrange for payment in his own currency.

have been received from the resale of the merchandise. On the other hand, many exporters have little capacity or desire to extend credit to foreign buyers and thereby tie up their working capital. The fact that foreign buyers are residents of another country, conduct business in a different legal and political environment, and are usually quite distant as well, also makes exporters wary of affording them direct commercial credit. The absence of a source of external credit, therefore, would sharply curtail the volume of international trade. By providing such credit, the foreign exchange dealer helps his own business by helping the business of the foreign trader.

Payment at a Distance. The ease with which the foreign exchange market carries out the transfer and credit functions is due, in large measure, to the means of instant communication that link exchange dealers in one country with dealers throughout the world. The cable, telegraph, and telephone enable payments to be made between distant points literally at the speed of light. Postal services offer a less expensive but relatively slower means of communication. The intimate contact of one foreign exchange dealer with another, regardless of physical distance, is exploited to the fullest degree through reciprocal and cooperative arrangements. Since all of the services that result from these facilities are available to any who deal in the foreign exchange market, we may consider them as representing a third function of the market.[8]

THE ROLE OF COMMERCIAL BANKS AS FOREIGN EXCHANGE DEALERS

Most foreign exchange dealers are large commercial banks located in major financial centers. In the United States the foreign exchange market is mainly in New York, where approximately twelve American banks and some agencies of foreign banks engage in the bulk of foreign exchange transactions. Commercial banks throughout the United States maintain correspondent relations with these New York banks so that it is possible to buy or sell foreign exchange almost anywhere in the country. Foreign countries possess similar arrangements.

Dealers make up the foreign exchange market by standing ready at all times to buy and sell foreign exchange against domestic money. Bills of exchange are bought from domestic exporters and others who have demand claims against foreign residents. Bank drafts drawn by dealers on their balances abroad are sold to domestic importers and others who must make payment to foreign residents. Exchange brokers, acting as intermediaries between the exchange dealers, serve to unify the foreign exchange market and keep it competitive.

---

[8] By permitting hedging against exchange risks, the forward exchange market performs a fourth function. See Chapter 7.

Transactions in the New York foreign exchange market occur on three levels: (1) transactions between dealer banks and their customers; (2) transactions among the dealer banks through brokers; and (3) transactions between the New York dealer banks and banks abroad. To handle these transactions, each bank has several traders who operate in a trading room with elaborate communications equipment. The big New York banks each have hundreds of correspondent banks in foreign countries.

Commercial banks that deal in foreign exchange maintain demand deposits in foreign correspondent banks or in their own foreign branches. To transfer funds to a foreign resident, the bank needs simply to write a draft against its deposit in the resident's country. If individuals or business firms were in the habit of maintaining balances in foreign banks, they could make international payments by personal drafts sent to foreign creditors. Actually large corporations with overseas branches sometimes follow this practice, and thereby circumvent the banker's draft. The considerable risks associated with variations in the exchange rate, however, and the imposition of exchange controls by government, as well as inconvenience, are sufficient to limit this practice. Most individuals and business concerns prefer to rely on the banker's draft (transfer) to effect foreign payments.

Today, American banks maintain only minimum working balances in many foreign countries. This practice results from the prevalence of exchange control and the risk of variations in exchange rates. Exchange control often limits the availability and use of foreign balances owned by domestic banks while alterations in the exchange rate bring shifts in the value of foreign balances in terms of domestic money. Before World War I and for a short period in the 1920's most countries were on the international gold standard, and there was no risk of blocked funds or of wide swings in the exchange rate. Accordingly, exchange dealers were often willing to maintain substantial foreign deposits although, even then, they did not permit them to rise beyond a certain level. The foreign exchange dealer is able to get along with only a small inventory of foreign exchange by matching his sales and purchases of foreign exchange during each trading day. In this way he minimizes the risks of exchange rate variations and of exchange control. Dealers may, however, deliberately assume open foreign exchange positions in convertible currencies in the expectation of making a speculative gain on rate variations, especially in forward exchange.[9] Indeed, such speculation is the major source of their profits (and losses).

To conclude, commercial banks located in the principal financial centers are the dominant dealers in foreign exchange, and the actual transfer of payment from one country to another is usually made through a draft drawn by a domestic bank against a foreign bank. Commercial banks also provide most of the credit in foreign trade by purchasing time bills of exchange

---

[9] See Chapter 7 for a discussion of forward exchange.

from exporters. As a consequence, international payments consist of interbank transfers; that is, of changes in the ownership of demand deposits which domestic and foreign banks maintain with each other.

THE CLEARANCE OF INTERBANK DEBT

This chapter opened with a discussion of private compensation, pointing out that international payments are made through the offsetting or clearance of debt. We then asserted that private compensation is unnecessary when foreign exchange markets are in operation, but that clearance of debt remains the basic principle of international payments. We now inquire further into the nature of the debt clearance performed by the foreign exchange market.

We have remarked that the foreign exchange market effects international payments through the clearance of bank debt rather than private debt as was true in private compensation. To illustrate, let us return to our earlier example of private compensation. There, an American resident owed 20 pounds sterling (equivalent to $60) to a British resident while a second American resident was owed $60 by a second British resident. We saw how payment was made through the clearance of one private debt against the other, but we now suppose that this clearance occurs in the foreign exchange market. We further assume that the American creditor is an exporter and the American debtor, an importer; and that initiative for payment is taken by the Americans.

First, the American exporter draws, say, a bill of exchange payable in pounds sterling at sight against the British importer, and discounts this bill at his bank for dollars at the bank's buying rate for sterling.[10] The American bank now sends the bill to its correspondent bank in the United Kingdom, which, in turn, presents it to the British importer for immediate payment.[11] The British importer pays by drawing a sterling check for 20 pounds against his bank in favor of the American bank. In this way the latter acquires a sterling demand deposit of 20 pounds, which is held in its correspondent bank in the United Kingdom. At this stage the American bank has exchanged dollars, paid to the American exporter, for a sterling balance that makes it a creditor of its correspondent bank. Thus, the original debt between the American exporter and the British importer has been transformed into an interbank debt.

The American bank is now able to draw a banker's draft against its foreign balance and thereby sell sterling exchange. The opportunity to do

---

[10] The exporter will not receive the full face value of his bill of exchange because it will take a few days before the bill can be presented to the British importer for payment. The longer the maturity of the bill, the greater the discount. The exporter has used the bank's buying rate for sterling in calculating the price of his export shipment.

[11] If the bill of exchange were a time bill, then the importer would "accept" the bill but would not pay it until the bill matured.

this occurs when an American importer comes to the American bank to buy 20 pounds sterling in order to pay a British exporter. The bank now draws a draft against its sterling deposit and sells it to the American importer at the bank's selling rate for sterling.[12] The importer then remits the draft to the British exporter, who cashes it at his own bank. In selling this banker's bill for 20 pounds sterling, the American bank fully utilized the sterling deposit that arose from its previous purchase of a sterling bill of exchange from the American exporter—both payments offset each other and the clearance was perfect. The debt owed by the British importer to the American exporter was converted into a debt (demand deposit) owed by the British correspondent bank to the American bank. This interbank debt was then canceled when the American bank assumed the sterling debt of the American importer.

But suppose the American bank had no sterling to sell. In that event the American importer would not have been able to pay his sterling debt. The foreign exchange dealer must be able to buy and sell an equal amount of foreign exchange if he is to effect international payments; otherwise there is no basis, or only a partial basis, for clearance. Of course, this example is highly simplified. A single dealer need not clear his exchange transactions as long as the dealers making up the foreign exchange market are able to do so as a group. Moreover, dealers in one country may extend credit to dealers in another in order to permit the full clearance of foreign exchange transactions.[13] Further, the supply of bills of exchange originates not only in the export of merchandise but also in all the credit items comprising the balance of payments. Similarly, the demand for bills of exchange arises out of all debit items in the balance of payments. Nevertheless, there are times when the available supply of foreign exchange falls short of demand.

When the amount of foreign exchange in demand is equal to the amount of foreign exchange in supply, then foreign exchange dealers, taken as a group, are able to bring about a perfect clearance of international payments and the foreign exchange market is said to be in *equilibrium*. When, however, the amounts of foreign exchange demanded and supplied do not coincide, the market is in *disequilibrium*. In that event some sort of adjustment to achieve a balance is required whose nature will depend upon the institutional structure of the foreign exchange market and the character of the disequilibrium: gold and short-term capital movements may replenish a deficient supply of exchange, the rate of exchange may vary and remove the deficiency, or the government may ration the available supply of exchange

---

[12] Since the bank's selling rate is higher than its buying rate, a draft for 20 pounds sterling will cost something more than $60. This was taken into account by the importer in making his decision to buy from the British exporter.

[13] There is an almost continuous flow of buy and sell orders among banks in the important financial centers (New York, London, Paris, Amsterdam, Frankfurt, and Zurich) via telephone, cable, and teletype.

by a regime of exchange control. These matters are more fully discussed in Chapters 8, 9, and 10.

THE MONETARY EFFECTS OF INTERNATIONAL PAYMENTS

It should now be clear that international payments are made through the clearance of debt between domestic and foreign banks. But this clearance of interbank debt also involves the increase or decrease of privately held demand deposits when bank debt is substituted for private debt; and because demand deposits are part of the national money supply, the result is a rise or fall in the supply of money.[14] Such changes in the supply of money constitute the *monetary effects* of international payments.

INTERNATIONAL PAYMENTS AS BANK DEBITS AND CREDITS

Since international payments cause changes in the assets and/or deposit liabilities of the respective national banking systems, we can trace the monetary effects of international payments by entering payments transactions in a simple T account drawn up for each banking system. The T account has two sides, one showing changes in assets, the other showing changes in liabilities. Using T accounts, we now evaluate the monetary effects of a purchase and sale of sterling exchange by the American banking system. To simplify our presentation, we shall assume that the American banking system comprises only one bank and that the same is true of the British banking system.

PURCHASE OF STERLING EXCHANGE BY AN AMERICAN BANK

When an American exporter sells a sterling bill of exchange to his bank, he gets paid in the form of a demand deposit at the bank. This transaction appears as follows in the T account of the American bank:

Assets	Liabilities
+ Sterling bill	+ Demand deposit (exporter)

---

[14] Banking systems are able to increase or decrease the money supply because they need maintain only fractional reserves behind their demand deposits. When a banking system acquires assets, they are paid for by the creation of demand deposits; and when assets are sold, demand deposits are liquidated. The reader who is unfamiliar with the monetary role of the banking system is referred to any modern text in basic economics.

The exporter can spend his demand deposit as he sees fit; the money supply of the United States (the creditor country) has *increased*.

Next, the American bank sends the sterling bill to its British correspondent bank, which, after payment by the British importer, adds the proceeds to the demand deposit maintained with it by the American bank. The effect of this transaction upon the American bank is to convert one asset (sterling bill) into another asset (sterling deposit):

Assets	Liabilities
− Sterling bill + Sterling deposit	

At the same time the T account of the British correspondent bank is as follows:

Assets	Liabilities
	− Demand deposit (importer) + Demand deposit (American bank)

The purchase of a sterling bill by the American bank thus causes an *increase* in the money supply of the United States (the creditor country) and a *decrease* in the supply of money owned by domestic residents in the United Kingdom (the debtor country). In the latter country a demand deposit has been transferred from the ownership of the British importer to the ownership of the American bank.

SALE OF STERLING EXCHANGE BY AN AMERICAN BANK

When the American bank sells a sterling draft to a domestic importer, the following changes occur in its assets and liabilities:

Assets	Liabilities
− Sterling deposit	− Demand deposit (importer)

That is to say, the supply of money in the United States *decreases* as the demand deposit of the American importer is extinguished when he purchases sterling from the bank.

At the same time, the payment of the sterling draft by the British correspondent bank against which it was drawn involves a shift in the ownership of a sterling demand deposit from a foreign resident (the American bank) to a domestic resident (the British exporter who received the sterling draft from the American importer). This change appears as follows in the T account of the British bank:

Assets	Liabilities
	− Demand deposit (American bank)
	+ Demand deposit (British exporter)

NET MONETARY EFFECTS

In the previous sections we examined the monetary effects of a purchase and sale of sterling exchange by the American banking system. We might have chosen other examples of international payments, such as transactions in bills of exchange payable in dollars or in bills of a third currency rather than in sterling, but in every instance we should have found that the supply of money owned by domestic residents of the creditor or exporting country increased while the supply of money owned by domestic residents of the debtor country decreased. Over a period, therefore, the *net* effects of international payments upon the money supply of the nation will depend upon the net discrepancy between receipts and payments of foreign exchange.[15] If receipts exceed payments, the country will experience a rise in the money supply held by domestic residents; if receipts are less than payments, the opposite change in the money supply will occur. When receipts and payments are equal, there is no net change in the money supply and, consequently, no net monetary effects; this is true when the foreign exchange market is in equilibrium.

The presence of net monetary effects is, therefore, a sign of disequilibrium in the foreign exchange market and in the balance of payments. Adjustment toward a balance between the receipts and the payments of foreign exchange is in order, and this adjustment will be facilitated by the influence exerted by the net monetary effects on the economic activity of the domestic and other countries unless this influence is counteracted by government measures. The role of net monetary effects in the removal of disequilibrium in the balance of payments is treated in Chapter 9.

INTERNATIONAL FINANCIAL CENTERS

Domestic and foreign banks are able to act as dealers in foreign exchange because they are willing to hold balances in other countries. The mechanism of international payments, therefore, is based upon a pattern of

---

[15] More precisely, the net effects of international payments will depend on the net discrepancy between receipts and payments of foreign exchange arising out of *autonomous* transactions in the balance of payments. See Chapter 8.

interbank debt that covers the entire world. This pattern may be decentralized, centralized, or somewhere between these two extremes.

DECENTRALIZED AND CENTRALIZED SYSTEMS OF INTERNATIONAL PAYMENT

When the banking system in one country is linked to the banking systems in all other countries by a series of bilateral debt arrangements, the number of arrangements equal to the number of other countries, and when all international payments are cleared bilaterally, the system of international payment is fully decentralized. Figure 6-2 shows a fully decentralized payments system for a world of six countries.

When, on the other hand, banks in one country are linked to banks in other countries through balances maintained at *one* financial center, and when all international payments are cleared through this center, then the system of international payments is fully centralized. Figure 6-3 illustrates the fully centralized system of international payments for a world of six countries.

THE LONDON FINANCIAL CENTER

During the half century that preceded World War I, the system of international payments was highly centralized. The focus of this system was London. Banks throughout the world maintained sterling balances in London and transferred funds from one country to another by drawing sterling bills. A Brazilian exporting coffee to the United States would draw a sterling bill on the American importer, who, when the time came to buy, would remit a sterling draft. In this way international payments occurred through shifts in the ownership of sterling balances located in London. Although most countries were on the gold standard at this time, it was the pound sterling that made up most of the world's payments.

The prominence of London was due to many factors. First, the United Kingdom was the world's greatest importer, and its policy of free trade permitted foreign suppliers an easy access to its domestic market. Second, the London money market was unparalleled in its efficiency and resources—banks, acceptance houses, discount houses, dealers, etc., made up a market in which sterling funds could be invested or borrowed on short term in any amount and at any time. Third, London was by far the paramount source of long-term investment capital; its highly evolved securities markets dealt in the securities of the entire world. First trader, first financier, and first investor of the world during a period when trade and finance were unrestricted by government policies, it was inevitable that most international payments should flow to, from, and through the London financial center.

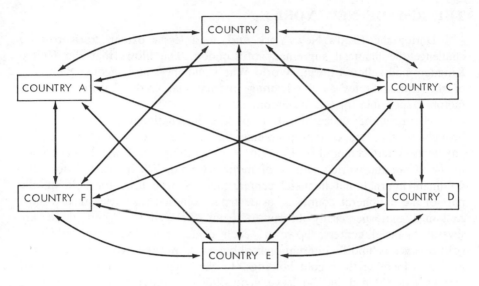

Arrows indicate reciprocal bank balances of foreign exchange dealers.

Figure 6-2

**PERFECTLY DECENTRALIZED SYSTEM OF
INTERNATIONAL PAYMENTS: SIX COUNTRIES**

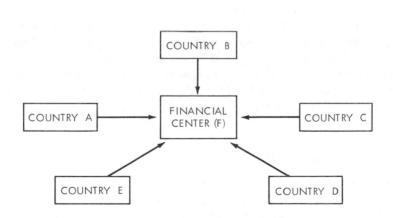

Direction of arrows indicates the location of foreign bank balances
maintained by foreign exchange dealers.

Figure 6-3

**PERFECTLY CENTRALIZED SYSTEM OF
INTERNATIONAL PAYMENTS: SIX COUNTRIES**

THE RISE OF NEW YORK

During the 1920's New York and, to a lesser extent, Paris rose to challenge the financial supremacy of London. The blows that the United Kingdom had suffered during World War I and the simultaneous emergence of the United States as the leading international creditor were the main factors responsible for this development.

The resulting decentralization of the international payments system brought to the fore certain problems that had not existed in the earlier payments system centered on London. For one thing, there was less economy in the use of the world's supply of monetary gold. When there is only one dominant international financial center, there is little need for gold on the part of the peripheral countries, aside from domestic reserves, since foreign exchange may be easily borrowed from the center. When there are several financial centers, however, each center must maintain individual gold reserves behind its international obligations, and the peripheral countries may also increase their gold holdings. In the twenties the shortage of gold was also heightened by the large acquisitions of the United States during the war.[16]

Another problem that arose in the twenties was the movement of speculative capital between London and New York, stemming from the general uncertainty regarding the future course of exchange rates and from lack of faith in the ability of certain countries to maintain their newly restored gold standard. The movement of this capital was made easier by the decentralization of the international payments system; when there is only one financial center, there is less likelihood of a sudden flight of capital since it can move only to a peripheral country. In the twenties the volatility of short-term capital movements also heightened the gold shortage since each financial center was compelled to maintain greater reserves behind its foreign obligations. Despite these drawbacks, the decentralized system of the twenties, based on the London-New York axis, would probably have developed into a more workable arrangement in time. It was destroyed, however, by the onset of world depression in the early thirties.

THE CONTEMPORARY PAYMENTS SYSTEM

After World War II, the international monetary system came to rest on the dollar and New York emerged as the dominant financial center. Foreign governments (central banks) maintained balances in New York which, together with gold, constituted their official international reserves.

---

[16] United States gold reserves rose from $1.7 billion in December, 1914, to $2.7 billion in December, 1918. Reserves continued to rise until December, 1924, when they reached $4.1 billion. Board of Governors of the Federal Reserve System, *Banking and Monetary Statistics* (Washington: U.S. Government Printing Office, 1943), p. 544.

Private foreign banks also maintained sizeable dollar balances to finance their foreign exchange transactions throughout the world. However, in the 1960's the persistent deficit in the U.S. balance of payments placed this system under severe strain. Finally, in 1971 the United States itself forced a reform of the system by halting the gold convertibility of the dollar. The postwar system, the difficulties that beset it, and the prospects for a new international payments system are examined in Chapters 19 and 20.

SUMMARY

1. International payments involve the exchange of one country's money for the money of another country. This transfer function, along with the functions of credit and payment at a distance, is performed by the foreign exchange market. Dealers in foreign exchange are mainly commercial banks located in major financial centers, such as New York and London. The basic principle of the system of international payments is the clearance of debt, whether private debt as in private compensation, or bank debt as in the foreign exchange market.

2. Foreign exchange is a money claim held by a resident of one country against a resident of another. Foreign exchange appears in tangible form as a wide variety of credit instruments, all of which, however, are either money itself or other highly liquid claims. Despite the great number of forms of foreign exchange, most foreign exchange that is used to effect international payments consists of bank transfers and bills of exchange of some sort. Bills of exchange vary according to the nature of the drawer and the drawee, the maturity, and the existence of accompanying documents.

3. Dealers in foreign exchange transform private debt into interbank debt, and it is the clearance of this debt through transfers that provides the basis of the system of international payments. Since foreign exchange dealers are exposed to the risks of variations in the exchange rate and of exchange control, they seek to carry only a minimum inventory of foreign exchange by balancing sales against purchases during each trading day.

4. International payments cause a decrease in the domestic money supply of the debtor or importing country, and an increase in the domestic money supply of the creditor or exporting country. When payments and receipts do not coincide, there is a net monetary effect; the foreign exchange market and the balance of payments are also in disequilibrium. Adjustment to bring about a balance between payments and receipts of foreign exchange is then in order.

5. The system of international payments may be decentralized, centralized, or somewhere between these two extremes. Before World War I the London financial center was supreme, and the system of payments was highly centralized. During the twenties, however, New York rose to challenge London and the payments system became decentralized with certain resulting difficulties. Today New York is the dominant international financial center, but there are widespread demands for a reform of the world's monetary system.

QUESTIONS AND APPLICATIONS

1. How is international payment achieved through private compensation?
2. (a) What is foreign exchange?
   (b) What forms of foreign exchange are used to effect international payments?
3. What are the functions of the foreign exchange market?
4. Explain how the foreign exchange market effects international payments through the clearance of interbank debt.
5. What is the exchange risk?
6. Using T accounts, trace the monetary effects of an international payment resulting from a sight draft drawn by an American exporter against a French importer.
7. What is the meaning of decentralized and centralized systems of international payment?

SELECTED READINGS

Crump, Norman. *The ABC of the Foreign Exchanges.* London: Macmillan & Co., 1951. Chapters 1-7.

Holmes, Alan R. and Francis H. Schott. *The New York Foreign Exchange Market.* New York: Federal Reserve Bank of New York, 1965.

CHAPTER 7

FOREIGN EXCHANGE RATES AND THEIR DETERMINATION

Foreign exchange rates are of key significance in directing the flow of merchandise, services, and capital between nations. This chapter explores the different kinds of exchange rate behavior and the relationship between exchange rates in the many financial centers.

THE RATE OF EXCHANGE

Foreign exchange is bought and sold in the foreign exchange market at a price that is called the *rate of exchange*. More specifically, the exchange rate is the *domestic* money price of foreign money, establishing an equivalence between dollars and British pounds sterling, dollars and French francs, dollars and Argentine pesos, and so on. The daily quotations of foreign exchange are based on the domestic price of cable transfers, which are the quickest means of international payment. Table 7-1 (page 156) indicates the selling rates for cable transfers in New York on November 4, 1971.

Although there is an exchange rate between the domestic currency and every other currency, most foreign exchange transactions involve only a small number of "international" currencies. Probably half the trading in the New York market is in pounds sterling and another third in Canadian dollars. The remaining transactions are almost entirely in continental European currencies, particularly the German mark and the Swiss franc. For most currencies only a "spot" rate is quoted. Spot exchange is foreign exchange for immediate delivery (ordinarily within one or two days) that is used in making international payments. For international currencies, however, the New York market also quotes "forward" rates for foreign exchange that is promised for delivery at a time in the future—30, 60, or 90 days. Unless

Table 7-1

SELLING RATES FOR CABLE TRANSFERS IN NEW YORK ON THURSDAY, NOVEMBER 4, 1971

(U.S. Dollars and Dollar Decimals)

Country	Thursday	Prev. Day
Canada (Dollar)	.9965	.9969
Great Britain (Pound)	2.4933	2.4927
30-Day Futures	2.4944	2.4935
90-Day Futures	2.4945	2.4937
Australia (Dollar)	1.1640	1.1640
New Zealand (Dollar)	1.1675	1.1675
South Africa (Rand)	1.4100	1.4100
Austria (Schilling)	.0420	.0420
Belgium (Franc)	.021575	.021550
Denmark (Krone)	.1375	.1375
France (Franc)		
Commercial rate	.18085	.1807
Financial rate	.1848	.1840
Holland (Guilder)	.2991	.2990
Italy (Lira)	.001640	.0016335
Norway (Krone)	.1459	.1459
Portugal (Escudo)	.0370	.0370
Spain (Peseta)	.0147	.0147
Sweden (Krona)	.1993	.1993
Switzerland (Franc)	.2507	.2506
West Germany (Deutschmark)	.2996	.2998

LATIN AMERICA:

Argentina (Hard Peso)	b.1340	b.1330
Brazil (Cruzeiro)	.1850	.1850
Chile (Escudo)	.0370	.0370
Colombia (Peso)	.0490	.0490
Ecuador (Sucre)	.0415	.0415
Mexico (Peso)	.0801	.0801
Peru (Sol)	.0235	.0235
Uruguay (Peso)	.002710	.002710
Venezuela (Bolivar)	.2230	.2230

NEAR EAST:

Iraq (Dinar)	2.95	2.95
Israel (Pound)	z	z
Lebanon (Pound)	.3160	.3160

FAR EAST:

Hong Kong (H.K. Dollar)	.1720	.1720
India (Rupee)	.1350	.1350
Japan (Yen)	.003050	.003050
Pakistan (Rupee)	.2195	.2195
Philippines (Peso)	.1580	.1580
Singapore (Dollar)	.3390	.3390

Source: *The Wall Street Journal*, November 5, 1971.
b Financial rate.
z Not available.

otherwise noted, our analysis of exchange rate behavior relates to the spot rate.

Actually, there are several spot rates of exchange for a given currency. The domestic price of cable transfers is the *base* rate of exchange, and other means of international payment—sight and time bills—usually sell at a discount from this base rate. These discounts reflect varying delays or risks of payment compared to the cable transfer. Even payment by a bank draft sent airmail requires two or three days between New York and London, and during that time the foreign exchange dealer has the use of both the domestic money paid for the draft and the foreign balance against which the draft is drawn. Time drafts postpone payment for a much longer period. The discount on a given kind of foreign exchange, say a 30-day bill, will depend upon the current rate of interest since, in effect, the buyer of the bill is lending money to the seller of the bill until its maturity date. Discounts from the base rate of exchange stem also from differences in the risk of payment. For that reason trade bills are quoted below bank bills of similar maturity.

The rates of different kinds of foreign exchange are, then, linked to the base rate of exchange by discounts that take into account liquidity and risk factors. Although these discounts will vary with the two aforementioned factors, the resulting pattern of exchange rates will rise and fall with the base rate. In our analysis of the determination of foreign exchange rates, therefore, we shall consider the pattern of spot rates as one rate, namely, the base rate of exchange for cable transfers.

The behavior of exchange rates will depend upon the nature of the foreign exchange market. When there are no restrictions on private trading in the market and official agencies do not stand ready to stabilize the rate of exchange, the exchange rate will fluctuate from day to day in response to changes in the supply and demand of foreign exchange. When, however, government authorities follow a policy of stabilization but do not interfere with private market transactions in foreign exchange, the exchange rate will move only within narrow limits, although these limits may be substantially altered from time to time by official action. Finally, the government may restrict private transactions by becoming the sole buyer and seller of foreign exchange; the rate of exchange is then no longer determined by supply and demand but instead is the end product of bureaucratic decisions. We now examine more closely the determination of these three types of exchange rate behavior—freely fluctuating rates, stable rates, and controlled rates.

FREELY FLUCTUATING EXCHANGE RATES

When the rate of exchange is not stabilized or controlled by government authorities, the foreign exchange market very closely approaches the theoretical model of pure competition. Except for the liquidity and risk differentials that are allowed for by discounts, the foreign exchange of any given country is one homogeneous product. Moreover, the number of buyers and sellers of foreign exchange is so large that no one buyer or seller can measurably influence the rate of exchange, but must accept it as given. In a free, unstabilized market, therefore, the rate of exchange is determined by the many individual acts of buying and selling, none of which individually is able to affect it, but all of which interact to set its level.

THE DEMAND FOR FOREIGN EXCHANGE

In a free market the rate of exchange, like any other price, is determined by the interplay of supply and demand. The foreign exchange that is demanded at any time will depend upon the volume of international transactions that requires payments to foreign residents. That is to say, the demand for foreign exchange originates in the *debit* items of the balance of payments.[1]

As is true of most goods, the amount of foreign exchange in demand varies inversely with its price—the amount demanded at a high rate is less than the amount demanded at a low rate, provided other conditions remain the same. A high exchange rate makes imports expensive to domestic buyers because they must offer more domestic money to obtain a unit of foreign money. As a result, a high rate of exchange reduces the volume of imports and thus lessens the amount of foreign exchange demanded by domestic residents. Conversely, a low rate of exchange, by stimulating imports, increases the amount of foreign exchange demanded.

This explanation points to the dependence of the demand for foreign exchange on debit transactions in merchandise, services, and capital items; but it also suggests the influence that the exchange rate itself exerts over the volume of those same transactions. The demand relationship of foreign exchange is indicated in Figure 7-1 by the familiar downward-sloping demand schedule *D-D*. In this instance the schedule shows the quantity of sterling exchange demanded at each rate of exchange in the New York market; thus, it is an aggregate of all the individual demand schedules of those who wish to transfer funds abroad.

In analyzing the determination of the exchange rate, it is important to distinguish between a movement along a given demand schedule (change in the amount demanded) and a shift in the entire schedule (change in demand). We have noted that a movement along the demand schedule is downward from left to right because the exchange rate determines the

---

[1] This is not strictly true because the balance of payments may record transactions that do not involve the foreign exchange market, such as direct barter, gifts in kind, and settlement by private compensation. See Chapter 8.

domestic price of imports and thereby affects their volume and the amount of foreign exchange demanded to pay for them. Changes in income,

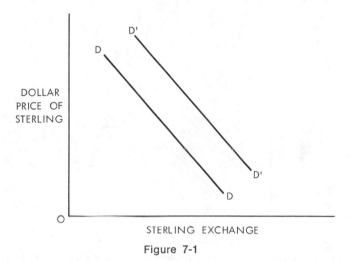

Figure 7-1

DEMAND FOR STERLING EXCHANGE IN NEW YORK

costs, prices, tastes, and other factors may, however, cause shifts in the debit items of the balance of payments independent of the exchange rate. When this happens, the entire demand schedule shifts either left or right, depending on whether there has been a decrease or an increase in the volume of debit transactions. For example, a rise in the national income of the United States will cause a rise in imports, and this will shift the demand schedule for foreign exchange to the right as more foreign exchange is demanded at each rate of exchange. Such a development is shown in Figure 7-1 by *D'-D'*.

THE SUPPLY OF FOREIGN EXCHANGE

The supply of foreign exchange in the foreign exchange market derives from international transactions that require money receipts from foreign residents; that is, from *credit* items in the balance of payments. Unlike the amount demanded, the amount of foreign exchange supplied to the market varies *directly* with the rate of exchange. When the rate of exchange is high, domestic prices appear low to foreigners since they are able to acquire a unit of domestic money with a small expenditure of their own money. This cheapness stimulates domestic exports and thereby brings a larger supply of foreign exchange into the market. Conversely, a low exchange rate restricts exports and lowers the amount of foreign exchange offered to the market.

Figure 7-2 shows the supply relationship of foreign exchange by a schedule that slopes upward from left to right. A shift of the entire supply schedule either to the left or right occurs with a change in the credit items

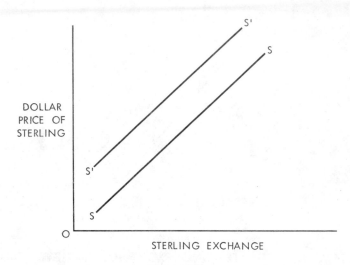

Figure 7-2

SUPPLY OF STERLING EXCHANGE IN NEW YORK

of the balance of payments brought about by factors other than the exchange rate. For example, a shift to the left would occur if deflation abroad caused a decrease in American exports. This would decrease the amount of foreign exchange supplied to the market at each exchange rate. A decrease in the supply of sterling exchange in the New York market is shown in Figure 7-2 by S'-S'.

DETERMINATION OF THE RATE OF EXCHANGE

The rate of exchange is determined by the intersection of the demand and the supply schedules. At this rate of exchange, and at no other rate, the market is cleared; the rate will remain stable until a shift occurs in either one or both schedules. It is unlikely that this equilibrium rate of exchange will last very long, or even be attained, in a free, unstabilized foreign exchange market, since continuing shifts in demand and supply will force continuing adjustments toward new equilibrium positions. Thus, the exchange rate will fluctuate continuously, just as the prices of securities traded in the security market. To simplify our analysis, however, we shall assume that there is time for the exchange rate to adjust fully to a change in demand or supply.

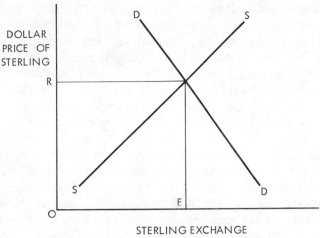

Figure 7-3

**DETERMINATION OF EQUILIBRIUM STERLING
EXCHANGE RATE IN NEW YORK**

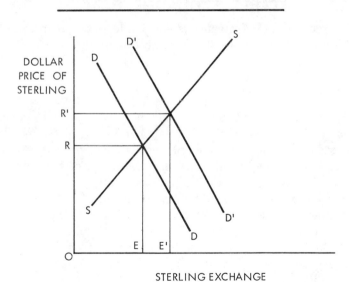

Figure 7-4

**DETERMINATION OF A NEW EQUILIBRIUM
STERLING EXCHANGE RATE IN NEW YORK**

In Figure 7-3 the equilibrium rate of exchange is *O-R*; at this rate the amount supplied is equal to the amount demanded, and both suppliers and buyers of foreign exchange are satisfied. Suppose now that the demand for sterling increases from *D-D* to *D'-D'* as in Figure 7-4. In response to this increase, the equilibrium rate rises from *O-R* to *O-R'*, where once again the amounts of sterling exchange supplied and demanded are equal. This higher rate calls forth an increase in the amount supplied of *E-E'*, since it stimulates more American exports. Similarly, a shift of the demand schedule to the left (fall in demand) will bring about a decline in the rate of exchange. On the other hand, a shift in the supply schedule to the left (fall in supply) will raise the exchange rate while a shift to the right (rise in supply) will lower it.

In summary, the exchange rate in a free, unstabilized market is determined by the supply of and the demand for foreign exchange, which derive from the credit and debit items of the balance of payments, respectively. The exchange rate itself also influences the balance of payments, and this influence is shown by the shape of the demand and the supply schedules of foreign exchange.[2] There is, therefore, a mutual relationship between the foreign exchange rate and the balance of payments; each is both determined by, and a determinant of, the other.

STABLE EXCHANGE RATES

In this section several arguments for stable rates are presented, after which specific techniques of stabilization are discussed.

ARGUMENTS FOR STABLE RATES

Exchange rates have seldom been left free to vary with supply and demand. Even before World War I when there was general agreement on the benefits of flexible market prices in merchandise, services, and securities, fluctuating exchange rates were viewed with marked distaste. At this time all of the leading trading nations were firm adherents of the gold standard, which provided fixed rates of exchange. Fluctuating exchange rates, therefore, were considered a mark of failure to remain on the gold standard. Apart from the gold standard, however, there are strong arguments for stable exchange rates.

It is forcibly argued that the exchange rate is unlike the price of an ordinary commodity, and that it is illogical to view the two in the same light. When the exchange rate varies, the prices of *all* exports are changed for foreign buyers; and, simultaneously, the prices of *all* imports are changed for domestic buyers. These widespread price effects unloose a series of repercussions that extend throughout the domestic and foreign economies. This critical nature of the exchange rate, the argument runs, rules out the unlicensed freedom of the unstabilized foreign exchange market. It

---

[2] The influence of the exchange rate on the balance of payments is an important means of adjustment to disequilibrium that is taken up in Chapter 10.

is also contested that fluctuating rates invite foreign exchange speculation that may intensify balance of payments difficulties. Less fundamental arguments for stable rates spring from considerations of trade and finance. Fluctuating rates provoke uncertainty in foreign payments and investments. The exporter is unable to make a sound calculation of his profit margin since the domestic value of his foreign exchange receipts depends upon an unstable rate of exchange. Lenders and borrowers are also subject to this exchange risk.[3]

TECHNIQUES OF STABILIZATION

Unlike the controlled exchange market, the stabilized market imposes no restraints on private transactions in foreign exchange; the factors of supply and demand are fully operative. How, then, is it possible to prevent fluctuations in the rate of exchange? The answer lies in the open-market operations of government authorities that compensate for movements in the ordinary demand and supply of foreign exchange. Successful stabilization of the rate of exchange requires that the stabilization agency be able to offset movements in market supply and demand to any desired degree. To do so, the agency must possess adequate supplies of domestic and foreign exchange.[4] Under the gold standard, stabilization is assured by the willingness of the monetary authorities to buy or sell gold without limit at a fixed price. This *passive* stabilization contrasts with the *active* stabilization practices of today whereby government agencies buy and sell foreign exchange in the market to offset any undesired movements in exchange rates.

Passive Stabilization: The Gold Standard. A country is on the gold standard when its basic monetary unit (dollar, pound sterling, franc, etc.) is defined in terms of a specified weight of gold and when its monetary authorities stand ready at all times to buy and sell gold in unlimited quantities at the rate fixed by the legal gold content of the monetary unit. As long as this second condition of unrestricted convertibility is observed, the gold value of the monetary unit cannot vary and the price of gold remains constant. In actual practice there are several varieties of the gold

---

[3] The case for fluctuating rates (also referred to as flexible or floating rates) is presented in Chapter 10.

[4] This may be illustrated by the price stabilization of wheat in the United States. To keep the price of wheat from falling below a minimum level, the stabilization authority (Commodity Credit Corporation) must have enough dollars to buy all the wheat offered at that level; to keep the price of wheat from rising above a maximum level, the authority must have enough wheat to satisfy demand at that level. In practice, the Commodity Credit Corporation has acted to restrain a decline in the price of wheat rather than a rise; that is to say, it has followed a policy of one-sided stabilization.

standard; these include gold-coin, gold-bullion, qualified gold-bullion, and gold-exchange standards, all of which have existed at one time or another.

The minimum conditions for a true *international* gold standard are two: (1) two or more countries must adopt monetary units with a designated gold content, and (2) the monetary authorities of each country must permit the free, unlimited export and import of gold at a rate fixed by the gold content of the respective monetary unit. Since the gold standard creates fixed exchange rates only between countries on the gold standard, however, it makes its greatest contribution to exchange rate stability when several currencies, particularly key currencies such as the dollar and the pound sterling, are tied to gold.

Gold standard currencies hold a fixed relationship to each other because they all hold a fixed relationship to gold. Before World War I and during the last half of the twenties, the British pound sterling was defined as 113 grains of gold and the United States dollar as 23.22 grains. The gold content of the pound, therefore, was 4.8665 times greater than the gold content of the dollar. This latter relationship was the *mint parity* of the pound and the dollar at that time—one pound sterling was equivalent to $4.8665. Any holder of 113 grains of gold could obtain one pound sterling from the British monetary authorities, or, alternately, $4.8665 from the American authorities.

Under the gold standard, the mint parity and the exchange rate between two currencies need not be identical. Because of the costs of shipping gold from one country to another (freight, insurance, handling, and interest), the exchange rate is free to vary within narrow limits known as *gold points*. The higher the costs of shipping gold, the greater the spread between mint parity and the gold points. The costs of shipment, when added to mint parity, establish the *gold export point;* the costs of shipment, when subtracted from mint parity, establish the *gold import point*. When the exchange rate rises to the gold export point, gold begins to flow out of the country; on the other hand, when the exchange rate falls to the gold import point, gold begins to flow into the country. These flows of gold provide the compensatory changes in the supply of and the demand for foreign exchange that are necessary to keep the foreign exchange rate from moving beyond the gold points.

This stabilizing function of gold flows under the international gold standard may be illustrated by an example. Let us assume that the mint parity of the pound sterling is $4.8665, and that shipping costs make the gold export point in New York $4.8865 and the gold import point, $4.8465. Now suppose that the rate of exchange in New York rises to the gold export point of $4.8865. The rate will not rise further because foreign exchange dealers can acquire all the pounds sterling they desire at a rate of $4.8865 by purchasing gold for dollars from the American monetary authorities, shipping the gold to London, and then selling the gold for pounds to the British monetary authorities. Thus, the supply of foreign exchange becomes perfectly elastic at the gold export point, and the rate of exchange cannot rise beyond it.[5]

Similarly, the gold import point sets a floor below which the rate of exchange cannot fall: exchange dealers will not sell pounds at a rate below $4.8465 because they can obtain that many dollars for each pound sterling by converting pounds into gold in London, shipping the gold to New York, and then converting the gold into dollars. In other words, the demand for foreign exchange becomes perfectly elastic at the gold import point.[6]

When the rate of exchange is between the gold points, there is no longer an option on the part of dealers to acquire foreign exchange by gold exports or to dispose of foreign exchange by gold imports, since to do so would involve losses. If, in our example, the sterling exchange rate were $4.8665 (the mint parity), then to acquire or dispose of sterling by gold shipments would mean a loss of two American cents per pound sterling for each transaction (the costs of shipment). Between the gold points, therefore, the rate of exchange is determined as in a free, unstabilized market. The spread between the gold points, however, is so narrow that we may regard exchange rates under the gold standard as fixed.

It will be noted that this stabilization is achieved without any intervention in the foreign exchange market on the part of the monetary authorities who behave simply as residual buyers and sellers of gold. Gold moves "automatically" from one country to another in response to the supply of and demand for foreign exchange.

Active Stabilization by Monetary Authorities. A true international gold standard has not functioned since the first half of the 1930's, and since that time exchange rates, unless controlled outright, have been stabilized by official compensatory transactions in the foreign exchange market.[7]

The policy objectives of active stabilization, however, differ considerably from the policy objectives of passive stabilization under the gold standard. Under the old gold standard, the fundamental aim of international

---

[5] All the foreign exchange that is demanded at the gold export point will be supplied.

[6] All the foreign exchange that is supplied at the gold import point will be demanded.

[7] The first stabilization agency was the British Exchange Equalization Account, which was established in 1932 after the United Kingdom abandoned the gold standard. Upon the devaluation of the dollar in 1934, the United States also established a stabilization agency; and, by the end of the thirties, most countries had adopted a policy of exchange stabilization whether implemented by special agencies, central banks, or treasuries.

monetary policy was to remain on the gold standard and to avoid any change in the gold content of the monetary unit. The almost incidental result of this policy was a fixed exchange rate. As a matter of fact, the exchange rates of the major trading countries were fixed at the same level for several decades preceding World War I. In contrast, active stabilization seeks to achieve stability in the exchange rate, but allows for occasional adjustments in the rate in order to correct disequilibrium in the balance of payments. This policy of "stable, yet flexible" rates attempts to secure the advantages of stability and, at the same time, to use the exchange rate as an instrument of international adjustment.

We have already briefly described the basic mechanism of exchange rate stabilization; we now look more closely into its actual operation. In order to stabilize the dollar price of sterling between, say, $2.38 and $2.42, the United States monetary authorities (Treasury and Federal Reserve System) require two assets: (1) dollars, and (2) sterling exchange, or other foreign exchange freely convertible into sterling, or gold. The dollars are needed so that the authorities are able to buy all the sterling that may be offered in New York at $2.38; that is, so they can make the demand for sterling perfectly elastic at that rate. Foreign exchange or gold is needed so that the authorities can satisfy any demand for sterling at $2.42, thereby providing the ability to make the supply of sterling perfectly elastic at that rate.

As part of the government, the monetary authorities have no difficulty in obtaining sufficient dollars for their operations, but the supply of foreign exchange and gold presents a different problem since the government cannot create foreign exchange, and domestic gold production is limited. In the 1950's this country had nothing to worry about on that score—the balance of payments was strong and gold reserves were at a level adequate to meet any foreseeable pressures on the rate of exchange. Today the situation is far different. The persistent deficit in the United States balance of payments has cut into gold reserves to such an extent that some observers believe that U.S. gold reserves are insufficient to insure the stability of the dollar.[8] When stabilization activities are inhibited by inadequate reserves of foreign exchange and gold, governments frequently resort to exchange control.[9]

There is another reason why American monetary authorities need not be concerned over their holdings of dollars. As we have noted, domestic currency is necessary to put a floor under the dollar price of sterling, that is, to avert a depreciation of sterling and a simultaneous appreciation of the dollar. Ordinarily, however, domestic authorities do not support the exchange

---

[8] See Chapters 19 and 20.

[9] An explanation of the role of international reserves in international adjustment is offered in Chapter 9.

value of a foreign currency; they are usually interested only in one-sided stabilization, the avoidance of depreciation of the domestic currency. In practice, therefore, the United States authorities impose a ceiling over the dollar price of sterling, while at the same time the British authorities place a floor below the dollar price of sterling.[10] This division of labor also occurs under gold standard stabilization: gold flows out of a country to maintain an upper price limit (gold export point) on foreign exchange and flows into a country to maintain a lower price limit (gold import point).

CONTROLLED EXCHANGE RATES

Neither the fluctuating rate market nor the stabilized market imposes restrictions on private transactions in foreign exchange. A wide gulf separates these two markets from the controlled foreign exchange market that prohibits private transactions not authorized by the control authority. The controlled exchange rate does not directly respond to shifts in supply and demand; government rationing supersedes the allocating function of the exchange rate and the currency becomes inconvertible. When exchange controls are relaxed, the job of maintaining stable exchange rates is passed on to stabilization agencies or their counterparts.

We shall examine the nature and the effects of exchange control in Chapter 14. At present we are interested only in the essential mechanism of exchange control—how it works in the foreign exchange market. To simplify our analysis, we assume a completely controlled market in which the control authority is the exclusive buyer (monopsonist) and exclusive seller (monopolist) of foreign exchange. All foreign exchange must be sold to the authority at its stipulated rate, and all foreign exchange must be bought from the authority at its stipulated rate. We further assume that there is only one rate of exchange, although in practice the control agency may charge a much higher rate than it pays for foreign exchange in order to earn a monopoly profit, and/or it may adopt several discriminatory rates.

The supply of foreign exchange is derived from the credit items of the balance of payments, and the control authorities have only a limited influence over it. To raise the supply of foreign exchange, steps must be taken to expand exports, encourage foreign loans, and the like; many of these steps lie beyond the jurisdiction of the control agency. The agency, therefore, considers the supply of foreign exchange as relatively fixed with respect to its own powers, and its main task is the allocation of this fixed supply among those who demand it. This is usually done by an exchange or trade-licensing system—unless a domestic resident can obtain a license he cannot secure

---

[10] In other words, the British authorities impose a ceiling over the pound price of dollars in London.

foreign exchange. This rationing brings about a "suppressed disequilibrium" between supply and demand by forcibly choking off all excess demand.

The determination of the controlled rate of exchange is shown in Figure 7-5. If the market were free, the equilibrium rate of exchange would

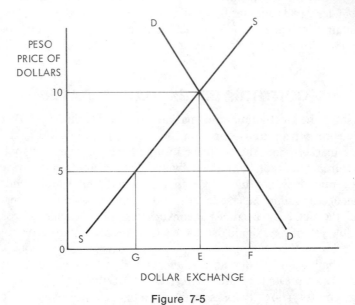

Figure 7-5

THE CONTROLLED RATE OF EXCHANGE: PESO COUNTRY

be ten pesos for one dollar where the supply and demand schedules intersect. At this equilibrium rate both the amount demanded and the amount supplied would be *O-E* dollars. At the controlled rate of five pesos, however, the amount demanded (*O-F*) exceeds the amount supplied (*O-G*) by an amount of dollars (*G-F*); that is to say, the market is not cleared at the controlled rate. It follows that the control authority must suppress the excess demand (*G-F*) by issuing licenses only for the purchase of *O-G* dollars; otherwise the authority will be unable to maintain the controlled rate.

We can draw the following conclusions from our analysis of the controlled rate of exchange: (1) the controlled rate is less than the equilibrium rate—the controlled rate overvalues the peso in terms of dollars; (2) the amount of dollars supplied to the market at the controlled rate is less than the amount supplied at the equilibrium rate (*O-G* compared to *O-E*)—the controlled rate discourages exports by making them more expensive to foreign buyers; (3) the market is not truly cleared—the excess demand (*G-F*) is not satisfied; and (4) the purchase of dollars at the controlled rate is smaller than the purchase at the equilibrium rate (*O-G* compared to *O-E*)—the controlled market cuts imports below the level permitted by the free market.

EXCHANGE ARBITRAGE

We have learned that the rate of exchange is determined by supply and demand in the foreign exchange market or else controlled by monetary authorities. Most of our discussion has focused on the New York market, and we have said nothing about the relationship between rates in that market and rates in the markets of other trading countries. We now explore this topic.

Since it is to be expected that each foreign exchange market will have its own particular supply and demand conditions, does not the rate of exchange, say the price of dollars, differ between markets? The answer is no. Actually, in the absence of exchange control, the price of dollars is identical in all markets no matter where they are located. It is identical because exchange arbitrage conducted by private traders will quickly close any gap existing between markets in the price of dollars or of any other currency.

DEFINITION

Exchange arbitrage involves the simultaneous purchase and sale of a currency in different foreign exchange markets. For example, arbitrage occurs when dollars are bought in New York and simultaneously sold in the same amount in London. Arbitrage becomes profitable whenever the price of a currency in one market differs even slightly from its price in another market. Then, through its effect on the supply of and demand for that currency, arbitrage rapidly erases the discrepancy. Thus, exchange arbitrage provides the link between exchange rates in the market of one country and exchange rates in the markets of other countries. In this way arbitrage creates one global foreign exchange market with one rate for each currency.

Arbitrage may require operations in two currencies (bilateral), three currencies (trilateral), or more than three (multilateral). Regardless of the number of currencies, the basic principle of arbitrage must be observed: a sale in one market is offset by a simultaneous purchase in another market. Because of the need for simultaneity, arbitrage is effected through the cooperation of exchange dealers located in separate markets. Bilateral arbitrage in dollars and pounds sterling, for example, is carried out by a dealer in New York and his partner in London. Successful arbitrage rests upon continuous market information, substantial resources, rapid means of communication between markets, and trained minds that are quick to perceive and act upon any discrepancies in rates. For this reason, most arbitrage is done by the large commercial banks that serve as dealers in foreign exchange.

BILATERAL OR TWO-POINT ARBITRAGE

Suppose that sterling is quoted in New York at $4 but is quoted in London at $4.01. Sterling is therefore relatively cheap in New York and relatively expensive in London. Arbitragers will profit by buying sterling in the cheap market and simultaneously selling it in the expensive market. The arbitrager in New York and his partner in London will take the following steps: (1) buy, say, 10,000 pounds sterling in New York for $40,000; (2) simultaneously sell 10,000 pounds sterling in London for $40,100. The pounds purchased in New York will cover the pounds sold in London, while the dollars spent in New York will be covered by the dollars received in London. The profit on these transactions is $100 (minus cable costs), which is split between the two partners.[11]

The effect of these and similar transactions is to wipe out the spread in rates between New York and London. By increasing the amount demanded, the purchase of sterling in New York pushes up its price, and the sale of sterling in London, by increasing the amount supplied, pushes down its dollar price.[12] When the rising price of sterling in New York and the falling price of sterling in London come together, say at $4.005, arbitrage is no longer profitable and it ceases.

TRILATERAL OR THREE-POINT ARBITRAGE

Arbitrage in three currencies is more complex than in two, but the principle is the same. Assume that the price of sterling is $4 and the price of francs, $0.02 in New York. In New York, therefore, one pound sterling exchanges for 200 francs via their respective dollar rates; this is the franc-sterling *cross rate*. But now suppose that at the same time it is possible to buy sterling in Paris at a rate of 198 francs while the dollar price of francs in Paris and the dollar price of sterling in London are identical with their prices in New York. Thus, in terms of francs, sterling is more expensive in New York than it is in Paris. Bilateral arbitrage is not profitable in this instance but trilateral arbitrage can take advantage of the discrepancy between

---

[11] This illustration of bilateral arbitrage has been somewhat simplified. In practice, the New York dealer will buy a sterling cable (draft) while, at the same time, the London dealer will buy a dollar cable (draft). The sterling bought in New York will cover the sterling spent in London, and the dollars bought in London will cover the dollars spent in New York. If the situation is reversed—sterling is cheaper in London than it is in New York—then the New York dealer will sell a sterling cable, while the London dealer will sell a dollar cable.

[12] To the London market the increase in the amount of sterling supplied will appear as an increase in the amount of dollars demanded.

the franc-sterling cross rate in New York and the franc price of sterling in Paris; the former, 200 francs, and the latter, 198 francs.[13] The arbitrager in New York and his partner in Paris will (1) buy, say, 500,000 francs for $10,000 in New York; (2) simultaneously sell 500,000 francs for 2,525.2 pounds sterling in Paris; (3) simultaneously sell 2,525.2 pounds for $10,-100.80 in New York. The francs acquired in New York cover the francs sold in Paris, while the sterling sold in New York is covered by the sterling purchased in Paris. The resulting profit of $100.80 (minus cable costs) is split between the partners.

The purchase of francs in New York will raise their dollar price, the sale of francs in Paris will raise the franc price of sterling, and the sale of sterling in New York will lower its dollar price. Arbitrage will cease when the franc-sterling cross rate in New York is identical with the franc price of sterling in Paris.[14]

EXCHANGE SPECULATION AND CAPITAL FLIGHT

In the previous pages we have covered many of the factors that determine exchange rates: the ordinary supply of and demand for foreign exchange, gold movements, the compensatory transactions of monetary authorities, exchange controls, and arbitrage. We now turn to a brief description and analysis of exchange speculation and capital flight that may provoke violent disturbances in the rate of exchange.

SPECULATION PROPER

The speculator purposely assumes an open position in the foreign exchange market with the intent of making a windfall profit from fluctuations in the rate of exchange. When the speculator expects the exchange rate of a specific currency to rise in the near future, he goes *long* on that currency by buying it. Conversely, when he expects the exchange rate of a currency to fall in the near future, he goes *short* either by selling the currency in the forward market for future delivery or by borrowing the currency on short term and then exchanging it for a currency he considers stable. When the expectations of speculators are not borne out, they suffer windfall losses. Curiously enough, however, if speculation in a currency is strong and one-sided, it may itself force the exchange rate to move in the anticipated direction.

---

[13] If the franc price of sterling is identical in Paris and London, the London rate on francs is also out of line with the New York franc-sterling cross rate. If, on the other hand, the franc price of sterling is *not* identical between Paris and London, then bilateral arbitrage in those two currencies is profitable until an identity is achieved.

[14] As in the case of bilateral arbitrage, the actual transactions consist of cable transfers, namely, the purchase of a franc cable in New York, the purchase of a sterling cable in Paris, and the sale of a sterling cable in New York.

By going long on a currency, speculators sustain its exchange rate—they increase demand and thus help ward off depreciation or even bring about appreciation. For this reason, monetary authorities, anxious to avert depreciation but not concerned about appreciation, tend to view long speculators with less distaste than short speculators. Interwar and postwar currency experiences, however, have made speculators pessimistic, and today they are more apt to undermine a currency by going short than to support it by going long.

Speculation may be *stabilizing* or *destabilizing*. Stabilizing speculation goes *against* the market. When the demand for a currency is falling (or its supply increasing), speculation helps to stabilize the exchange rate by going long and buying the currency. Conversely, when the exchange rate is rising, stabilizing speculation will retard the rise by going short and selling the currency. Stabilizing speculation was common under the gold standard before World War I, when everyone felt certain that the gold points would limit any movements in the exchange rate. Today, however, there is no such assurance, and speculation, by going *with* the market, is predominantly destabilizing.

At times in the past, destabilizing speculation, coupled with capital flight, has swamped the ordinary transactions of the foreign exchange market and has plunged the exchange rate into a dizzy spiral of depreciation. When general confidence in the exchange rate of a currency is shaky, destabilizing speculation may become cumulative: speculation provokes depreciation and this, in turn, provokes further speculation. As was true of the German mark in the early twenties and the Chinese yuan after World War II, this interaction may attain a truly fantastic velocity and bring about a rate of exchange that is below its true value though domestic inflation may be running rampant.

CAPITAL FLIGHT

Unlike speculation proper, *capital flight* is initiated not by the hope of gain but the fear of loss. When a country faces the prospect of exchange depreciation, the imposition of exchange controls, political instability, or war, domestic and foreign residents who own assets in that country seek safety by transferring funds to a country that is considered stable. The consequence may be a mass flight of capital that seriously weakens the currencies of some countries and brings unneeded foreign exchange and gold to other countries.

Speculative and flight capital movements inevitably occur when there is fear of exchange devaluation, exchange restrictions, or political instability. During the 1960's flows of speculative capital repeatedly threatened the stability of the pound sterling and the dollar. A massive flow of speculative capital out of the dollar in 1971 finally led to the abandonment of the gold convertibility of the dollar and a wholesale realignment of exchange rates, a subject which is taken up in Chapter 20.

THE FORWARD RATE OF EXCHANGE

The markets that we have analyzed deal in foreign exchange bought and sold for immediate delivery. Closely allied to these spot exchange markets are the forward exchange markets that deal not in foreign exchange, but in promises to buy or sell foreign exchange at a specified rate and at a specified time in the future with payment to be made upon delivery. These promises are known as *forward exchange,* and the price at which they are traded is the *forward rate of exchange.*[15]

The forward exchange market resembles the futures markets found in organized commodity exchanges, such as those for wheat and coffee. The primary function of any futures or forward market is to afford protection against the risk of price fluctuations. Forward exchange markets, therefore, are most useful when the rate of exchange is freely fluctuating, and when there are significant exchange risks for those who are committed to make or receive international payments. When the rate of exchange is stabilized, forward exchange is most useful when there is a strong possibility that the exchange rate will be allowed to depreciate in the near future. Since the forward exchange market must be free, it cannot function under exchange control.

Foreign exchange dealers commonly seek to balance their sales and purchases of forward exchange in a given currency in order to avoid the exchange risk, and they may refuse to enter forward contracts of long maturity because they cannot find an offsetting contract of equal maturity. At times, dealers may offset an open position in forward exchange with an opposing open position in spot exchange, a practice known as "swapping." At other times, dealers may function as professional risk bearers by deliberately assuming an open forward position in the expectation of making a speculative gain. Because of their own role as speculators, foreign exchange dealers are usually reluctant to enter forward contracts with individuals who want to speculate rather than protect themselves against an exchange risk.

HEDGING

The forward exchange market offers protection against the exchange risk by permitting hedging. *Hedging* is the procedure of balancing sales and purchases of an asset so there is no net open position on the market.

---

[15] The 30- and 90-day forward rates for sterling are shown in Table 7-1. One-year forward contracts are common in Canadian dollars and sterling and three-year contracts are arranged from time to time.

Hedging is practiced by the foreign exchange dealer when he covers his exchange risk by balancing sales and purchases of foreign exchange over the trading day. In this instance hedging is done solely in spot exchange, but there are times when hedging is possible only by offsetting spot transactions in foreign exchange with forward transactions.

To illustrate, suppose that an American importer must pay a specified sum in francs to a French exporter two months hence. During those two months the importer is short on the exchange market and he will be hurt by a rise in the dollar price of francs. Of course, he might buy his francs immediately, but this would mean immobilizing his funds for two months and, in effect, he would be paying cash for his imports despite the two-month credit arrangement. He can avoid this difficulty and still protect himself by purchasing the necessary francs on a two-month forward contract, which specifies the dollar price he will pay when the francs are delivered to him. The importer has now offset his short position on spot francs with an equivalent long position on forward francs; regardless of what happens to the spot rate of exchange, he will obtain the francs he needs at the rate stipulated in the forward contract. When the time comes for payment, the importer will secure the francs on the forward contract and remit them to the French exporter. In this illustration hedging has replaced an indefinite dollar payment with a definite one.

Hedging, however, is not limited to an importer or someone else who is obligated to make a foreign currency payment sometime in the future. Anyone who is to receive payment in a foreign currency at a future time is also exposed to the exchange risk, and he can hedge by selling forward exchange. In this way an American exporter can substitute a definite dollar receipt for an indefinite one.

Hedging provides complete protection against both speculative gains and losses only when the spot and forward rates of exchange are either equal or move together over the life of the forward contract. The two rates are, however, rarely equal. Forward exchange will usually sell at a discount under, or a premium over, the spot rate of exchange. Normally the forward rate is closely tied to the spread between the short-term interest rates of the relevant financial centers because of interest arbitrage; and, when this is true, hedging will offer a successful, although not necessarily perfect, protection against exchange risks. When, however, forward exchange is used to speculate on the future of the spot rate of exchange, then the forward rate may behave erratically with respect to the spot rate. In such circumstances, hedging in the forward market may offer little or no protection.

THE DETERMINATION OF THE FORWARD RATE: INTEREST ARBITRAGE

The forward rate of a currency is determined by the forces of supply and demand that derive from hedging transactions, interest arbitrage, and speculation. In the absence of destabilizing speculation and capital flight, *interest arbitrage* establishes a relationship between the spot and forward rates of a currency that reflects the interest differential between the domestic and the foreign-currency money markets.

For example, if the interest rate on 91-day British Treasury bills is higher than the rate on U.S. Treasury bills, then investors will shift funds from New York to London if they can cover the exchange risk in the forward market at a cost that is less than the interest differential. Suppose the interest spread in favor of London is 2 percent per annum while the discount on 90-day forward sterling is only 1 percent.[16] Then investors in the United States will buy spot sterling for investment in British Treasury bills, thereby earning 2 percent more interest than an investment in U.S. Treasury bills. But they are now exposed to an exchange risk. To cover this risk they will sell 90-day forward sterling in an amount that fully offsets their purchase of spot sterling. Ninety days later when the British Treasury bills mature, the U.S. investors will be able to convert their sterling into dollars at the forward rate. Since the cost of forward cover is 1 percent, the net gain to investors is 1 percent (the interest spread *minus* the cost of cover). However, this opportunity for a sure gain of 1 percent will not endure because the purchase of spot sterling will raise the spot rate while the sale of forward sterling will lower the forward rate. Thus, the forward sterling discount (the gap between the spot and forward rates) will widen until it reaches 2 percent and interest arbitrage ceases because it is no longer profitable.[17] When the forward discount (or premium) exactly offsets the interest rate differential, then the forward rate is said to be at *interest parity*.

Table 7-2 (page 176) shows the interest rate spread on Treasury bills between the United States and the United Kingdom and the premium or discount on forward sterling on Fridays of the period July, 1970, through November, 1970.

As noted above, the net incentive (effective yield) equals the interest rate spread minus the cost of covering the exchange risk in the forward market. On July 10, for example, the London rate was .16 percent higher than the New York rate while the cost of covering against the sterling exchange risk was .30 (the discount on forward sterling). Since the cost exceeded the gain, there was no incentive to move funds from New York

---

[16] Forward exchange rates are frequently quoted at an annual rate of discount or premium from spot rates. If 90-day sterling is quoted at $2.39 while spot sterling is quoted at $2.40, then the forward *discount* on an annual basis is [(2.39–2.40) × 100/2.40] × 4, or − 1.66 percent.

[17] This assumes that the interest differential remains at 2 percent. However, the flow of funds from New York to London may narrow the differential by raising the rate in New York and lowering it in London, in which case interest arbitrage will end somewhat sooner. Interest rate differentials are likely to be insensitive to interest arbitrage since they respond primarily to domestic factors.

Table 7-2

ARBITRAGE ON TREASURY BILLS
(Percent Per Annum)

Date	United States and United Kingdom				
	Treasury bill rates			Premium (+) or discount (−) on forward pound	Net incentive (favor of London)
	United Kingdom (adj. to U.S. quotation basis)	United States	Spread (favor of London)		
1970					
July 2............	6.72	6.40	.32	.11	.43
10............	6.69	6.53	.16	− .30	− .14
17............	6.75	6.37	.38	− .53	− .15
24............	6.66	6.23	.43	− .39	.04
31............	6.70	6.31	.39	− .16	.23
Aug. 7............	6.69	6.42	.27	− .18	.09
14............	6.70	6.48	.22	− .31	− .09
21............	6.69	6.27	.42	− .53	− .11
28............	6.69	6.22	.47	− .85	− .38
Sept. 4............	6.69	6.37	.32	− 1.38	− 1.06
11............	6.69	6.35	.34	− 2.54	− 2.20
18............	6.69	6.08	.61	− 1.38	− .77
25............	6.69	5.74	.95	− 1.02	− .07
Oct. 2............	6.69	5.80	.89	− .92	− .03
9............	6.69	6.01	.68	− 1.27	− .59
16............	6.69	5.86	.83	− 1.14	− .31
23............	6.69	5.71	.98	− .96	.02
30............	6.69	5.79	.90	− .83	.07
Nov. 6............	6.69	5.44	1.25	− .89	.36
13............	6.69	5.46	1.23	− 1.18	.05
20............	6.69	5.10	1.59	− .86	.73
27............	6.69	5.00	1.69	− .98	.71

Source: *Federal Reserve Bulletin* (Washington: U.S. Government Printing Office, December, 1970).
Note: *Treasury bills*: All rates are on the latest issue of 91-day bills. U.S. rates are market offer rates 11 a.m. Friday; U.K. rates are Friday opening market offer rates in London.

to London. Indeed, since the forward *premium* on dollars (reflecting the forward discount on sterling) exceeded the London interest rate advantage, there was an incentive to move funds from London to New York. Observe how quickly interest arbitrage reduces the net incentive to transfer funds between the two financial centers. On September 11, the heavy discount on forward sterling (heavy premium on forward dollars) created a very strong incentive to move funds from London to New York. One week later, however, the incentive was much lower as interest arbitrage reduced the discount on forward sterling while the bill rate in New York also fell. Finally, by September 25, the net incentive was almost eliminated by a continued decline in the discount on forward sterling and in the New York bill rate.

Table 7-2 shows the generally inverse relationship between the interest spread and the price of forward sterling. During this period interest rates were higher in London than in New York and, as we would expect, forward sterling sold at a discount (with the exception of July 2). Although interest arbitrage pushes the forward rate toward interest parity, the discount or premium on forward exchange will seldom equal the differential in short-term yields on a given day. For one thing, autonomous changes in the interest rate differential do not elicit an immediate response from investors that is sufficient to wipe out the investment incentive. Also, investors may make uncovered transfers of funds that do not influence the forward rate. Generally, anything that restricts the flow of funds between international financial centers, ranging from simple ignorance to exchange control, weakens the operation of the interest arbitrage mechanism and may even bring it to a halt. Finally, one-way speculation in a currency can snap the links between the forward rate, the spot rate, and the interest rate spread.

SPECULATION IN FORWARD EXCHANGE

Monetary authorities are not obligated under the rules of the International Monetary Fund to stabilize forward exchange rates, although they may decide to influence them from time to time. Hence, speculative pressures on a currency usually show up very quickly in forward rate discounts. When speculators believe that a country will devalue its currency in the near future, they rush to sell that currency forward in the expectation of fulfilling their forward contracts with cheaper spot exchange after the devaluation. This pushes the forward rate below the stabilized spot rate (which is also under attack) and if the speculative pressure is intense, the discount may become very wide, far exceeding the interest parity. On March 14, 1968, for example, the price of 90-day sterling was only $2.3343, far below the spot rate of $2.3918.[18] A lack of confidence in the ability of the British authorities to maintain a par value of $2.40 for the pound sterling created this wide discount. In this case the speculators were wrong and, as a result, they lost money.

---

[18] In contrast, when there is confidence in a currency, the forward rate will stay within the support range of the spot rate, which at that time was $2.38-$2.42.

When there is a heavy forward discount on a country's currency due to speculation, even high interest rates may fail to attract funds. On December 22, 1967, the Treasury bill rate was 2.34 percent higher in London than in New York. In normal circumstances this would have induced a flow of funds from New York to London until the forward sterling rate reached interest parity with a discount of 2.34 percent. Actually, the discount on forward sterling was 4.67 percent, thereby providing a net incentive of 2.33 percent for investors to move funds from London to New York. This perverse situation continued until speculative pressures on the pound gave way to confidence.

SUMMARY

1. The exchange rate is the domestic money price of foreign money. The domestic price of cable transfers is the base rate of exchange, and all other means of international payment usually sell at a discount from the base rate. Unless otherwise specified, we assume the exchange rate to be one rate, namely, the base rate. The behavior of the exchange rate will depend upon the nature of the foreign exchange market. We can distinguish three sorts of behavior: freely fluctuating rates, stable rates, and controlled rates.

2. Freely fluctuating rates result when the rate of exchange is free to respond to the movements of supply and demand. The rate of exchange is then determined by the intersection of the supply and demand schedules which, in turn, are determined by the credit and debit items of the balance of payments respectively. The rate of exchange, however, also affects the balance of payments, and there is, therefore, a mutual interdependence between them.

3. There are several arguments in favor of stable exchange rates. Under the gold standard, international gold movements prevent any variation in the exchange rate outside the narrow limits of the gold points. Exchange rates may also be stabilized by compensatory purchases and sales of foreign exchange on the part of government agencies.

4. Controlled rates result from the monopoly purchase and sale of foreign exchange by a government agency. The available foreign exchange is distributed by a rationing system; and, because the controlled rate is maintained below the equilibrium rate, there is an excess demand that is not satisfied. The exchange rate is determined by bureaucratic decision rather than supply and demand.

5. Exchange arbitrage involves the simultaneous purchase and sale of foreign exchange in different foreign exchange markets. When arbitrage is permitted, the price of a currency inevitably becomes the same in all foreign exchange markets. Arbitrage may operate in two, three, or more currencies.

6. Exchange speculation and capital flight also influence exchange rates. Because these short-term capital movements usually undermine the exchange rate and weaken the balance of payments, monetary authorities view them with marked distaste.

7. Forward exchange consists of promises to buy or sell foreign exchange at a specified price and at a specified time in the future. Forward exchange permits hedging to protect against fluctuations in the exchange rate. Except in periods of intense speculation, interest arbitrage will tend to bring about an equality between interest rate differentials and the premium or discount on forward exchange. When this happens the forward rate is at interest parity.

QUESTIONS AND APPLICATIONS

1. What is the base rate of exchange?
2. What are the three kinds of exchange rate behavior?
3. (a) How is the exchange rate determined when it is freely fluctuating?
   (b) What is the mutual relationship between the exchange rate and the balance of payments?
4. Using graphs, show the effects on the exchange rate of the following shifts:
   (a) Decrease in demand.
   (b) Increase in supply.
5. (a) What are the minimum conditions of an international gold standard?
   (b) Explain how the international gold standard prevents fluctuations of the exchange rate beyond the gold points.
6. What is the function of a stabilization agency? How does it perform this function?
7. Using a graph, show how exchange control determines the rate of exchange. Why is the market not cleared under exchange control?
8. Suppose the price of pounds sterling in New York is $4 while the price of dollars in London is £0.26. Is exchange arbitrage feasible? If so, how? What is the effect of arbitrage on exchange rates?
9. (a) Distinguish between stabilizing and destabilizing speculations.
   (b) What is capital flight?
10. (a) How does forward exchange differ from spot exchange?
    (b) Explain how forward exchange makes hedging possible.
11. Suppose the U.K. Treasury bill rate stays at 7 percent while the U.S. rate stays at 6 percent. What is the interest parity rate for 90-day forward sterling? How would interest parity be achieved?

SELECTED READINGS

Einzig, Paul. *A Dynamic Theory of Forward Exchange.* London: Macmillan & Co., 1961.

Glahe, Fred R. *An Empirical Study of the Foreign-Exchange Market: Test of a Theory.* Princeton Studies in International Finance No. 20. Princeton: Department of Economics in Princeton University, 1967.

Hawtrey, R. G. *The Gold Standard in Theory and Practice,* 4th ed. London: Longmans, Green & Company, 1939. Chapter 2.

Machlup, Fritz. "The Theory of Foreign Exchanges." *Economica,* Vol. VI (New Series) (November, 1939), pp. 375-397, and (February, 1940), pp. 23-49. Reprinted in Ellis, Howard S., and Lloyd D. Metzler (eds.). *Readings In The Theory of International Trade.* Philadelphia: The Blakiston Co., 1949.

Stein, Jerome L. *The Nature and Efficiency of the Foreign Exchange Market.* Essays in International Finance No. 40. Princeton: Department of Economics in Princeton University, 1962.

Ward, Richard. *International Finance.* Englewood Cliffs, N. J.: Prentice-Hall, Inc., 1965. Chapter 7.

CHAPTER **8**

THE BALANCE OF INTERNATIONAL PAYMENTS

During the course of a year the residents of one country engage in a vast number and variety of transactions with residents of other countries—exports and imports of merchandise and services, cash payments and receipts, gold flows, gifts, loans and investments, and other transactions. These transactions are interrelated in many ways, and together they comprise the international trade and payments of the national economy. Before we can analyze and evaluate a nation's international transactions, however, they must be classified and aggregated to make a balance of payments.

As a statistical classification and summary of all economic transactions between domestic and foreign residents over a stipulated period (ordinarily one year), the *balance of payments* of a nation affords an overall view of its international economic position. For this reason, the balance of payments is particularly helpful to government authorities—treasuries, central banks, and stabilization agencies—who are directly charged with the responsibility of maintaining external economic stability. Moreover, international trade is so important to many countries that the balance of payments must be carefully considered in the formulation of domestic economic policies, such as employment, wages, and investment.

The balance of payments of a country may also influence the decisions of businessmen. The experienced international trader or investor does not overlook the intimate bearing of the balance of payments upon the foreign exchange market and the course of government policy. A domestic exporter may hesitate to deal with an importer if he suspects that the authorities of the importer's country will shortly impose or tighten exchange controls in the face of an adverse balance of payments. Dealers in foreign exchange also pay close attention to the balance of payments of countries whose currencies they handle in daily transactions. Failure to realize the close dependence of international business upon the balance of payments of the domestic and foreign countries has often led to losses or even outright business failures.

THE COMPILATION OF THE BALANCE OF PAYMENTS

Three principles underlying the compilation of the balance of payments of a nation are worth special emphasis. First, only economic transactions between domestic and foreign *residents* are entered in the balance of payments. Second, a distinction is made between *debit* and *credit* transactions. Third, the balance of payments is a *double-entry* accounting statement.

THE CONCEPT OF RESIDENCE

The balance of payments summarizes all economic transactions between domestic and foreign residents. Residence should not be confused with the legal notions of citizenship or nationality.

Individuals who represent their government in foreign countries, including members of the armed forces, are always considered residents of their own country. Thus, when an American serviceman buys a glass of wine in France, an international transaction occurs that enters the balance of payments of both the United States and France.

Individuals who do not represent a government are considered to be residents of that country in which they have a permanent residence and/or in which they find their "center of interest." In some instances an individual's center of interest may be in doubt, but ordinarily such criteria as customary place of work, residence of employer, or principal source of income are sufficient to determine it. In the event of conflict, the permanent place of habitation takes precedence over center of interest. For example, an individual working at the United Nations in New York who does not represent a foreign government, but who resides here permanently, is treated as a resident of the United States despite his foreign center of interest.

In preparing a balance of payments, the question of individual residence is much less important than the question of business residence. A corporation is a resident of the country in which it is incorporated, but its foreign branches and subsidiaries are viewed as foreign residents. Hence, shipments between an American concern and its overseas branch are international transactions and, as such, are entered in the United States balance of payments. At times the residence of a business may be difficult to decide. For example, a company may be incorporated in the domestic country, owned by residents of a second country, and conduct all of its business in a third country. In most instances, however, the residence of a business enterprise is readily apparent.

Government residence is the clearest of all: all government agencies are residents of their own country regardless of location.

INTERNATIONAL TRANSACTIONS AS DEBITS AND CREDITS

Transactions between domestic and foreign residents are entered in the balance of payments either as debits or credits. *Debit transactions* are all transactions that involve payments by domestic residents to foreign residents. *Credit transactions* are all transactions that involve receipts by domestic residents from foreign residents.[1]

This distinction is most clearly seen when we examine transactions between American and foreign residents and assume that all payments and receipts are made in dollars.[2] Then debit transactions involve dollar payments by Americans to foreigners, and credit transactions involve dollar receipts by Americans from foreigners.

What transactions involve dollar payments to foreign residents? They may be listed as follows:

1. Imports of merchandise.
2. Transportation services bought from foreign residents.
3. Purchases of American residents traveling abroad.
4. Services provided by foreign-owned capital in American production.
5. Miscellaneous services bought from foreign residents.
6. Gifts to foreign residents.
7. Investment abroad by American residents.
8. Imports of monetary gold.

Each of these transactions implies dollar payments by American residents to foreign residents. This is most apparent in the case of imports of merchandise and services. Americans must pay for the merchandise, transportation, travel accommodations, and miscellaneous services that they buy from foreign residents. Americans must also pay interest and dividends for the use of foreign-owned capital in the United States. Similarly, American residents make dollar payments when they give to foreign residents or invest in foreign countries. Finally, Americans must pay for the gold that they import from abroad.

Conversely, the following transactions involve dollar receipts from foreign residents and are entered in the balance of payments as credits:

1. Exports of merchandise.
2. Transportation services sold to foreign residents.
3. Purchases of foreign residents traveling in the United States.
4. Services provided by American-owned capital in foreign production.
5. Miscellaneous services sold to foreign residents.
6. Gifts received from foreign residents.
7. Investments in the United States by foreign residents.
8. Exports of monetary gold.

---

[1] More precisely, *debit* transactions in the balance of payments involve either an increase in a country's assets (acquired from foreign residents) or a decrease in its liabilities (owing to foreign residents), and *credit* transactions involve either a decrease in a country's assets or an increase in its liabilities.

[2] The balance of payments is usually drawn up in the currency of the domestic country. Regardless of the currency in which they are made, international payments and receipts may be expressed in the domestic currency by the use of appropriate exchange rates for conversion from foreign to domestic currencies.

Exports of merchandise and services are financed by dollar payments of foreign residents, which are, of course, dollar receipts for American residents. The services of American-owned capital abroad provide American investors with receipts of interest and dividends from foreign residents. Americans also receive dollars from the gifts of foreign residents and from investments made by foreign residents in the United States. Exports of gold, like merchandise exports, must be paid for by foreign residents and thereby create dollar receipts for Americans.

DOUBLE-ENTRY ACCOUNTING

Although it is convenient to speak of "debit transactions" and "credit transactions," each international transaction is an exchange of assets and therefore has both a debit and a credit side. Conceptually, therefore, the balance of payments is a double-entry accounting statement in which total debits and credits are always equal. We can demonstrate this double-entry approach with some hypothetical examples. (The entry designations are fully explained in the next section.)

Merchandise and Services. Suppose, for example, a U.S. exporter sells $100 of merchandise to a French importer and is paid with a French bank balance. The merchandise side of this transaction is entered in the U.S. balance of payments as a credit item because it represents the transfer of a real asset from domestic to foreign ownership. The exporter's receipt of payment, involving the transfer of a monetary asset (the franc bank balance) from foreign to domestic ownership, is entered in the U.S. balance of payments as a *short-term capital export*. This debit entry is made because the franc receipts represent an increase in U.S. liquid financial claims against a foreign resident (the French bank). The entire transaction appears like this in the U.S. balance of payments:

	Debit	Credit
Merchandise export		$100
Short-term capital export	$100	

Again, suppose an American tourist spends $500 while traveling abroad. The *service* side of this transaction (hotel accommodations, transportation, etc.) represents the transfer of real assets from foreign to domestic ownership requiring payment by a U.S. resident. Thus, it is entered in the U.S. balance of payments as a debit. Conversely, the payment for tourist services involves the transfer of financial assets (money) from domestic to foreign ownership. It is therefore entered in the U.S. balance of payments as a credit, a *short-term capital import* that indicates an increase in U.S. liquid liabilities owed to foreigners or, alternatively, a decrease in U.S. liquid claims on foreigners.

	Debit	Credit
Import of tourist services	$500	
Short-term capital import		$500

Gifts (Unilateral Transfers). Ordinary economic transactions are two-sided, but gifts and other unilateral transactions are only one-sided since there is no offsetting payment. It would appear, therefore, that the inclusion of unilateral transfers would upset the formal equality of debits and credits in the balance of payments. This problem is solved by a "unilateral transfers" entry, which fully offsets the actual unilateral transfer. To illustrate, assume that the U.S. Government gives a $1000 U.S. bank balance to a foreign government. This unilateral transaction is entered in the U.S. balance of payments:

	Debit	Credit
Unilateral transfer	$1000	
Short-term capital import		$1000

The $1000 given to the foreign government represents a U.S. short-term capital import because it increases foreign-held liquid claims against a U.S. resident (the bank) or, to say the same thing, it increases U.S. liabilities owed to a foreign resident (the recipient government). The debit entry of $1000 in the unilateral transfer account is the offsetting entry that makes this gift transaction two-sided in an accounting sense. If the U.S. government gives merchandise to a foreign country, then the debit entry in the unilateral transfer account offsets a merchandise export.

International Investments. Suppose a U.S. company invests $200 in a foreign company. On the one hand, the U.S. company receives $200 in securities (equity shares or bonds) while, on the other hand, the foreign company receives a $200 balance in an American bank. Both sides of the transaction, therefore, are financial. The acquisition of securities is entered in the U.S. balance of payments as a debit, a *long-term capital export* that shows an increase in long-term financial claims held by a U.S. resident against a foreign resident. At the same time, the transfer of the bank balance to the foreign company is entered as a credit, a *short-term capital import* that shows an increase in liquid liabilities owed to a foreigner.

	Debit	Credit
Long-term capital export	$200	
Short-term capital import		$200

Monetary Gold Transactions. Monetary gold serves as an international means of payment among central banks. Suppose the Bank of England sells $300 of gold to the Federal Reserve Bank of New York, which, in payment, credits the Bank of England with a $300 demand deposit. The import of gold is entered in the U.S. balance of payments as a debit because it increases U.S. financial claims against foreigners. The transfer of the demand deposit to the Bank of England is entered as a credit, a short-term capital import that increases U.S. liquid liabilities to foreigners.

	Debit	Credit
Gold import	$300	
Short-term capital import		$300

The Balance of Payments as a Whole. We have now demonstrated how international transactions involving merchandise, services, unilateral transfers, investments, and monetary gold are entered in the balance of payments. Assuming that these transactions make up the whole of U.S. international transactions during the accounting period, then the entire balance of payments is as follows:

	Debit	Credit
Merchandise		$ 100
Tourist services	$ 500	
Unilateral transfers	$1000	
Long-term capital	$ 200	
Short-term capital		$1900
Gold	$ 300	
Total debits and credits	$2000	$2000

Note that we have consolidated short-term capital exports and imports into a single net entry. As we shall observe in the following section, the balance of payments is actually compiled by recording the different items separately rather than by entering explicitly two offsetting entries for each transaction. Nonetheless, the equality of debits and credits is maintained with a "net errors and omissions" entry.

BALANCE OF PAYMENTS PRESENTATION

International transactions are always entered in the balance of payments as debits or credits, but they may be grouped in several ways. Three distinctions have a major analytical significance: (1) The distinction between *real* or current transactions (goods and services) and *financial* or capital transactions; (2) the distinction between long-term (nonliquid) and short-term (liquid) financial transactions; and (3) the distinction between transactions of the national monetary authorities (central bank and Treasury), on the one hand, and all other transactions, on the other. To be most useful, a balance of payments presentation should make these distinctions in one way or another. Another desirable feature of such a presentation is its comparability among nations. The Standard Presentation developed by the International Monetary Fund (IMF) scores well on both of these points. The IMF publishes this statement on a continuing basis for some seventy-five member countries, all expressed in U.S. dollars.[3] Table 8-1 shows the Standard Presentation for the United States in 1969.

---

[3] See International Monetary Fund, *Balance of Payments Yearbook* (Washington: International Monetary Fund, monthly issues). The Fund also offers an Analytic Presentation that places private short-term capital movements and official monetary movements in separate categories. The Fund further provides a Standard Presentation by Regions that shows international transactions with selected groups of countries.

Table 8-1

THE IMF STANDARD PRESENTATION OF THE U.S. BALANCE OF PAYMENTS IN 1969
(Millions of U.S. Dollars)

	Debit	Credit
A. *GOODS AND SERVICES*	*53,864*	*58,046*
1. Merchandise (f.o.b.)	35,619	36,471
2. Nonmonetary gold	216	2
3. Freight	1,503	907
4. Other transportation	2,105	2,224
5. Travel	3,390	2,058
6. Investment income	4,894	11,370
6.1 On direct investment	848	8,171
6.2 Other private	3,269	2,267
6.3 Government interest	777	932
7. Other government	5,429	2,319
8. Other private	709	2,694
NET GOODS AND SERVICES	——	*4,182*
B. *UNREQUITED (UNILATERAL) TRANSFERS*	*3,280*	*315*
9. Private	1,097	313
10. Government	2,183	2
NET UNILATERAL TRANSFERS	*2,965*	——
NET GOODS, SERVICES, AND TRANSFERS	——	*1,217*
C. *CAPITAL FLOWS (EXCLUDING GROUP D)*	——	*4,325*
Nonmonetary Sectors	*4,007*	——
11. Direct investment	4,339	——
11.1 In United States	——	1,263
11.2 Abroad	5,602	——
12. Other private long-term	——	1,885
12.1 Liabilities	——	3,803
12.2 Assets	1,910	——
13. Other private short-term	——	372
13.1 Liabilities	——	76
13.2 Assets	——	296
14. Local government	——	——
15. Central government	1,925	——
Monetary Sectors	——	*8,333*
16. Private institutions	——	8,333
16.1 Liabilities	——	8,874
16.2 Assets	541	——
17. Central institutions	——	——
D. *OFFICIAL RESERVES*	*2,700*	——
18. Liabilities	1,513	——
18.1 Use of Fund credit	——	——
18.2 Gold deposit liabilities to IMF	11	——
18.3 Liquid liabilities to foreign official sectors..	506	——
18.4 Other liabilities to foreign official sectors..	996	——
19. Assets	1,187	——
19.1 Monetary gold	967	——
19.2 Reserve position in the Fund	1,034	——
19.3 Convertible currencies	——	814
NET ERRORS AND OMISSIONS	*2,841*	——

Source: Adapted from International Monetary Fund, *Balance of Payments Yearbook*, Vol. 22, September, 1971.

The Standard Presentation groups all transactions into four major accounts: goods and services, transfer payments, capital flows, and official reserves.

GOODS AND SERVICES ACCOUNT

This account includes all the real (as opposed to financial) international transactions that enter the nation's gross national product. The net balance on goods and services is identical to the net foreign investment sector of the gross national product. It is for this reason that the goods and services account is commonly called the *current account* or the *income account* of the balance of payments.[4] On the credit side, this account shows the domestic output of current and past production plus the original services of domestic factors of production (mainly capital) that are exported to foreigners. On the debit side, it shows the foreign output of current and past production plus the original services of foreign factors (again mainly capital) that are imported from foreigners.

For most countries, the merchandise entries (item A.1) are by far the biggest in the goods and services account (item A). They cover all international changes in the ownership of goods crossing the customs frontiers of the domestic country, with some exceptions. The principal kinds of merchandise transactions not included in the merchandise account are nonmonetary gold (item A.2), ship's stores (part of item A.4), purchases by travelers (part of item A.5), and goods bought and used abroad by diplomatic and military agencies, including their personnel (part of item A.7).

The nonmonetary gold account includes: (1) the purchase and sale of gold between the country's nonmonetary residents (all residents except commercial banks and official monetary authorities) and foreigners, and (2) gold transactions between domestic nonmonetary residents and domestic monetary residents.[5] When, for example, a domestic mining company sells gold to nonresidents, there is a credit entry in item A.2 because a private gold export is treated like an ordinary merchandise export. When that same company sells gold to its own monetary authorities, item A.2 is credited while item D.19.1 is debited to show an increase in official gold reserves.

Item A.3 covers all sales and purchases of transportation and insurance services between residents and foreigners that are associated with international trade (mainly item A.1). Item A.4 comprises all transportation services other than freight, such as ship repairs, harbor fees, passenger fares, and shipboard expenses.

---

[4] At times, the current account may be defined to include transfer payments.

[5] In its presentation of the balance of payments, the U.S. Department of Commerce does not show nonmonetary gold as a separate item, putting it instead in the merchandise account.

The travel account (item A.5) includes all goods and services bought by residents while visiting a foreign country (debit entry) and the sale of goods and services to foreigners traveling in the domestic country (credit entry). The purchase and sale of transportation services to and from foreign countries is placed in item A.4.

The credit entry in the investment income account (item A.6) covers all income (interest, dividends, profits) earned by residents (both private and government) on their investments in foreign countries. Conversely, the debit entry shows the income earned by foreigners on their investments in the domestic country.

Foreign investment is classified into *direct* and *portfolio*. Direct investment is defined as investment in enterprises located in one country but "effectively controlled" by residents in another country. Direct investment is a distinctive feature of international business because it usually involves the ownership of branches and subsidiaries abroad by domestic parent companies.[6] For balance of payments purposes, the IMF assumes effective control exists when: (1) the residents of one country own 50 percent or more of the stock of a company located in another country, or (2) a single resident or an organized group of residents of one country owns 25 percent or more of the voting stock of a company located in another country. Since foreign branches (unlike subsidiaries, which are foreign companies) are an integral part of the parent company, all branch investment is direct. Investment in commercial real estate (but not government military installations) is also considered direct.

The IMF records direct investment income (item A.6.1) to include interest and dividends received from foreign subsidiaries, the undistributed net profits of subsidiaries, and the total net profits of branches.[7] Nondirect investment income covers interest and dividends on portfolio securities, partnership income, and interest and charges on official loans by governments and international agencies (items A.6.2 and A.6.3).

Item A.7 covers all transactions of the domestic government in goods and services not included in items A.1 through A.6, and the personal expenditures of government employees who work in foreign countries. Similar transactions of foreign governments and their employees in the domestic country are also placed in this account. For many countries today, military transactions make up the bulk of this account. The large debit entry results from the stationing of U.S. troops abroad.

---

[6] See Chapter 22.

[7] Undistributed net profits are offset by entries in the Capital Flows Account as reinvested earnings (item C.11). The U.S. Department of Commerce does not include undistributed profits but only income actually repatriated to the United States in the investment income accounts, and therefore does not include reinvested earnings in the capital account.

Item A.8 is a catchall. Some of the transactions that comprise this account are management fees, royalties, agents' fees, film rentals, communications, and construction activities.

When all the items in the Goods and Services Account are added up, there is a net credit or debit entry. For the United States in 1969, the net balance on goods and services (current account) was a credit of $4,182 million, indicating that exports exceeded imports by that amount. There is no necessity or even desirability for the net balance on current account to approach zero. What is significant is how *any* net balance is financed in the rest of the balance of payments.

UNREQUITED (UNILATERAL) TRANSFERS ACCOUNT

Transfer payments are unilateral transactions that have no quid pro quo. Most unilateral transfers are gifts of one sort or another. For the most part, private transfers (item B.9) consist of institutional expenditures for missionary, charitable, educational, and like purposes, and personal remittances arising out of gifts by migrants to their families back home, legacies, bequests, and the transfer of capital by individuals migrating from one country to another. Government transfers (item B.10) include pensions, tax receipts from nonresidents, compulsory or contractual transfers, and nonmilitary grants. Large-scale government aid directed toward the developing nations makes grants the chief element of government transfers in most nations' balance of payments.

When transfer payments take the form of goods and services (transfer payments in *kind*), they show up as goods and services exports of the donor country and imports of the receiving country. When they are made in money or another liquid financial claim (transfer payments in *cash*), they alter the international financial assets and/or liabilities of both the donor and receiving countries. Thus, a cash gift appears as a credit entry somewhere in the Capital Flows Account of the donor country and as a debit entry in the same account of the receiving country. The transfer payments entries, therefore, are the "fictitious" counterparts of unilateral transactions recorded in other accounts that are made to preserve the double-entry accounting that underlies the balance of payments.

It is to be expected that the United States, as a major industrial nation, should show a debit entry for net transfer payments because of its economic assistance to poor nations.

A net debit in transfer payments increases the nation's international payments in the same way as its commercial imports of goods and services. Similarly, a net transfer credit adds to the nation's international receipts. Often it is useful to calculate a nation's net balance on goods, services, *and* unilateral transfers. For the United States in 1969, this combined balance was a credit of $1,217 million. Thus, the United States sold or received gratis

$1,217 million more in goods, services, and financial assets (cash gifts) than it bought or gave away. How did foreigners pay for their net purchases from the United States in 1969? The answer to this question is found in the Capital Flows Account and the Official Reserves Account.

CAPITAL FLOWS ACCOUNT

This account records the net changes in the nation's international financial assets and liabilities (excluding changes in official reserves) over the balance of payments period. The IMF breaks the account into nonmonetary and monetary sectors. The nonmonetary sector shows net capital transactions of both a short- and long-term nature in which the domestic creditor or debtor is neither a bank nor an official monetary institution. The monetary sectors cover primarily money transactions of commercial banks with nonresidents.

Capital transactions, whether long- or short-term, are customarily designated as *capital inflows* or *capital imports,* and *capital outflows* or *capital exports.* A capital inflow (import) occurs either: (1) when the international financial assets of residents (claims on foreigners) *decrease,* or (2) when resident international financial liabilities (indebtedness to foreigners) *increase.* Thus, a capital inflow or import is a *credit* entry in the balance of payments. When, for example, residents sell bonds to foreigners, this transaction is entered as a credit in item C.12.1 because it is a long-term capital inflow that adds to the long-term international liabilities of residents.[8]

Conversely, a capital outflow or export takes place when resident financial claims on foreigners (international assets) *increase* or liabilities owed to foreigners *decrease.* It follows that a capital outflow is a *debit* entry in the balance of payments. Suppose residents buy bonds from foreigners. This is a long-term capital export because it increases the long-term claims of residents against foreigners. Like other debit transactions, it also generates payments, in this instance to the foreigners selling the bonds.

The terminology used for monetary gold flows (item D.19.1) is identical with that used for merchandise. A monetary gold export is a credit; a monetary gold import, a debit. Since monetary gold is an international financial asset (a claim on foreigners), a gold export is equivalent to a capital inflow, while a gold import is a capital outflow. Ordinarily, however, gold movements are designated as such rather than as capital flows.

Let us now turn to the individual items comprising the Capital Flows Account. Item C.11 records the net flow of direct investment (including

---

[8] The residents, of course, obtain money from foreigners in exchange for the bonds. This receipt of money is a short-term capital outflow or debit that is entered in items C.16.1 or C.16.2, depending on whether payment is made in domestic or foreign money (foreign exchange). Thus, a capital inflow (sale of bonds in this instance) generates money receipts for residents. That is why it is called an inflow or import.

reinvestment of undistributed profits) resulting from the direct investment in the United States by foreign business firms (item C.11.1) and the direct investment abroad by U.S. business firms (item C.11.2). The net debit of $4,339 million represents a capital outflow that involves payments to foreigners. More concretely, direct investment abroad reflects the establishment by American companies of production and marketing affiliates in foreign countries, an activity that will occupy our attention in Part Three.

Other private long-term capital (item C.12) covers all international transactions in assets or liabilities (other than direct investment) with an original maturity of more than one year in which domestic, private, nonmonetary residents are creditors or debtors. (Direct investment is always treated as long-term capital but is separately classified in item C.11.) These transactions involve mainly loans and securities: new issues of both domestic and foreign bonds, and the sale and purchase of outstanding securities. Long-term commercial credits to finance trade are also included in this item. In 1969, the United States was a net long-term borrower (capital inflow) of $1,885 million.

Item C.13—other private short-term capital—records the net change in international assets and liabilities with an original maturity of one year or less in which private, nonmonetary residents are creditors or debtors. For the most part, liabilities comprise commercial short-term obligations and short-term borrowings from foreign banks. Assets comprise foreign notes and coins, deposits in foreign banks, holdings of foreign government and corporate short-term obligations, and commercial claims. Commercial obligations and claims consist of trade bills, acceptances, and other short-term claims arising from the financing of international trade.[9]

Because of their variety, intangibility, and private character, estimates of private short-term capital movements are the least reliable of the balance of payments items. During times of uncertainty about exchange rates or political conditions, short-term capital may shift erratically from one country to another. This speculative and flight capital may force devaluations or the imposition of controls, and in general disrupt the functioning of the international monetary system.

Item C.14 covers all capital transactions (loans and securities) of all government entities (cities, states, provinces) except the central government. If, for example, a city in the United States issued construction bonds that were purchased by foreigners, a credit entry (capital inflow) would be made in this item. For most countries this item is of little significance.

Item C.15 includes all international transactions in financial assets and liabilities of the central government except those of (1) public enterprises resembling private firms (such as a nationalized steel company) and are placed in the private accounts, and (2) monetary institutions. The principal

---

[9] See Chapter 6.

transactions embrace official lending and borrowing, repayments of official loans, and transactions with international nonmonetary institutions such as the International Bank for Reconstruction and Development (IBRD). Government foreign aid *loans* are placed in this item.

The international transactions of monetary institutions fall into two sectors: commercial banks (item C.16), and monetary authorities (item C.17).

As we saw in Chapter 6, the normal, everyday payments and receipts arising out of international trade and finance occur mainly through shifts in the ownership of demand deposits and other liquid deposits in banks at home and abroad. These appear in the balance of payments on a *net* basis as changes in the international assets and liabilities of resident banks that, for the most part, are commercial banks. However, item C.16 also covers the international transactions of other private financial institutions (such as savings banks) whose liabilities closely resemble the time deposits of commercial banks.

Item C.17 represents transactions by the central monetary authorities that do not involve changes in official reserves.

OFFICIAL RESERVES ACCOUNT

Items D.18 and D.19 show the net foreign transactions of the central bank (the Federal Reserve System in the United States), the central government Treasury, and (possibly) an exchange stabilization agency, that collectively constitute the monetary authorities of the nation. These authorities hold the nation's official international reserves of gold and foreign exchange, and they intervene in the foreign exchange market in order to stabilize the rate of exchange.[10] As we shall see, the foreign transactions of the monetary authorities provide the residual compensation required to finance any net balance on the other items in the balance of payments.

THE BALANCE OF PAYMENTS ALWAYS BALANCES: NET ERRORS AND OMISSIONS

Because the balance of payments uses a double-entry system of accounting, *total* credits and debits must always equal each other. However, two offsetting entries are not made explicitly for each transaction; instead, the different items are recorded separately on the basis of statistical or aggregate data drawn from a variety of sources. Since at least some of these sources are incomplete or inaccurate, an item called "errors and omissions" is needed to bring total debits and credits into an arithmetic equality.

---

[10] These same authorities also issue currency and create the domestic reserves for commercial banks. Their responsibility for monetary policy (the cost and availability of credit) gives them a powerful role in external payments adjustment in addition to compensatory financing.

In light of this explanation, it is only superficially correct to say that the balance of payments always balances because of the errors and omissions entry. Actually, this entry is necessary only because the balance of payments *must* balance like any double-entry accounting statement.

Much of the errors and omissions entry derives from the comparatively poor record of private short-term capital movements (item C.13). A radical shift in the size or sign of this entry from one payments period to the next is usually interpreted as a symptom of speculative or flight capital. Short-term capital may enter or leave a country outside the normal payments mechanism, especially when there is an intent to evade exchange controls and other official restrictions. In any event, short-term capital movements may either lead or lag the transactions they finance and thus show up in another payments period. For example, payment for a merchandise export shipped in December may not be recorded by a bank until January of the following year, or even later if the importer has received credit. Cash pre-payment may cause the opposite situation.

The necessary existence of an arithmetic balance in the balance of payments has no economic significance. What is significant is whether or not the balance of payments is in surplus or deficit *disequilibrium*. This can be discovered only by analyzing the internal structure of debits and credits; that is, by analyzing the relationships among the balance of payments items.

BALANCE OF PAYMENTS ANALYSIS: EQUILIBRIUM AND DISEQUILIBRIUM

A balance of payments is always in accounting balance, but it is not always in *equilibrium*. The essential meaning of equilibrium is a sustainable relationship between two or more economic variables, such as the supply, demand, and price of an individual good. A balance of payments is in equilibrium when the nation's economy is in "fundamental adjustment" to the world economy. Conversely, when the balance of payments is in disequilibrium, the national economy must undergo changes in its price level, income, exchange rate, and/or other economic variables in order to restore a sustainable relationship with the rest of the world. The concept of balance of payments equilibrium is a market adjustment concept. Thus, official measures to control international transactions do not eliminate a deficit, but merely suppress it.

Under what conditions are a nation's external economic relations sustainable over a period of time? If we take a very long time measured in decades, the answer is plain. In the very long run, a nation *must* pay for its imports of goods and services through its exports of goods and services. That is to say, in the very long run a nation cannot depend on international credit (whether short- or long-term) to finance a net import balance on current account. Nor can it hope to sustain a net export balance. Long-run equilibrium demands, therefore, that the net current account balance out to zero over the secular time period.

Ordinarily, our time frame of reference in balance of payments analysis is much shorter than decades; it seldom exceeds three to five years, or about long enough to encompass short-run cyclical variations in national income. What are the conditions of balance of payments equilibrium over this time period? It is no longer necessary for the nation to balance imports against exports: it can sustain an import balance if *long-term* credits are available to finance it. Similarly, the nation can sustain an export balance on current account if it is willing to lend (or give) an equal amount on long-term to the rest of the world. In such circumstances, there are no pressures for immediate adjustment of the balance of payments. Eventually, of course, a long-term borrower must repay the lender, but this is a future contingency that can be met or prepared for over a lengthy period of time.[11]

Suppose, however, a current account debit balance is financed by gold and short-term capital movements. What then? The balance of payments is now in disequilibrium because the current account deficit is being financed by short-term credit and monetary gold that is limited in supply. If the deficit persists beyond a few years, the availability of short-term credit will run out along with gold reserves.[12] The nation is compelled, therefore, to eliminate the current account deficit either by increasing exports, decreasing imports, or both.

Equilibrium in external payments implies equilibrium in the foreign exchange market over the relevant time period. The amounts of foreign exchange in supply and demand are equal, and thus, there is no need for compensatory movements of gold and short-term capital or for adjustments in the exchange rate. Equilibrium further implies the absence of government measures to adjust international payments by restricting imports or by artificially promoting exports.[13]

When equilibrium conditions are no longer present, the result is disequilibrium in international payments. The symptoms of disequilibrium, however, do not always appear in the same way. When exchange rates are held stable either through adherence to the gold standard or through the actions of a stabilization authority, disequilibrium usually appears as a one-way movement of gold and/or short-term capital. When, on the other hand, the exchange rate is free to respond to fluctuations in supply and demand, disequilibrium shows up as a one-way movement of the exchange

---

[11] A family that finances a home on a twenty-five-year mortgage offers a crude analogy. As long as the family is able to service the mortgage, it is not forced to make adjustments in income, expenditures, or savings. The situation is sustainable.

[12] This statement is true for most nations, assuming the deficit is of significant size. The exceptional immunity of the United States in this regard in the 1960's is treated in Chapter 19.

[13] Many economists would also add that equilibrium in international payments is inconsistent with the presence of widespread unemployment. The latter is hardly an element of stability.

rate. In that event net movements of gold and short-term capital are absent or minor and, consequently, disequilibrium does not appear in the balance of payments. At times disequilibrium may be "suppressed" by exchange control and other restrictive devices, so that it appears neither in the balance of payments nor in the foreign exchange market.

The most comprehensive definition of disequilibrium in the balance of payments is based on the distinction between *compensatory* and *autonomous* items. Compensatory items are called into existence to finance autonomous items which, in contrast, are independent of other items in the balance of payments.[14] To illustrate, the export of merchandise is autonomous because it depends on factors such as prices, quality, and other market conditions, rather than on the presence or absence of other items in the balance of payments. The export of merchandise, however, requires payment by foreign residents that appears in the balance of payments as a short-term capital outflow. Thus, the short-term capital outflow in this instance is compensatory because it has been induced by another item in the balance of payments.

Most international movements of short-term capital are compensatory, occurring in response to the need to finance autonomous transactions between countries. Capital flight and many speculative capital movements, however, are autonomous: they do not finance other items in the balance of payments, but rather create the need for compensatory financing.

Disequilibrium prevails in a nation's balance of payments when a net balance of compensatory items is needed to finance an opposing net balance of autonomous items. In these circumstances, the balance of payments is unstable because the supply of compensatory financing is limited and cannot continue indefinitely. Net compensatory financing is temporary "stopgap" financing. No nation has unlimited supplies of monetary gold and foreign exchange nor unlimited access to compensatory unilateral transfers or compensatory loans. If disequilibrium persists in the balance of payments, then sooner or later the sources of compensatory financing will become depleted. The net balance of compensatory items must then be eliminated through long-run adjustment in the current account, involving a decrease in imports and/or an increase in exports, together with suitable changes in other autonomous items such as long-term capital. When autonomous items fully offset each other, long-run adjustment is complete, and the balance of payments is in equilibrium.

This last statement needs qualification. Capital flight and destabilizing speculative capital movements are autonomous in that they provoke or

---

[14] In practice, the distinction between compensatory and autonomous items depends on the purpose of one's analysis. For this reason there is more than one measure of surplus or deficit in the balance of payments, as we shall discover in Chapter 19. Here, however, we are interested only in the concept of *fundamental* equilibrium and disequilibrium in which the current and long-term capital accounts constitute the principal autonomous items.

worsen disequilibrium in the balance of payments rather than supply compensatory financing. Because of their inherent volatility and the fact that they reflect disturbances in the international economy, it is best to consider any large-scale movements of flight and destabilizing speculative capital as symptoms of disequilibrium.

We are now in a position to restate the concept of balance of payments equilibrium. A balance of payments is in *fundamental* equilibrium when autonomous items fully offset each other over a period of time long enough to encompass self-corrective seasonal, random, and cyclical disturbances (say, three to five years), and there are no substantial movements of flight and speculative capital of the destabilizing variety. It follows that *temporary* disequilibrium which is self-corrective within this span of time is consistent with fundamental equilibrium.

MAJOR SOURCES OF DISEQUILIBRIUM

As a consolidated account of a nation's international transactions, the balance of payments is related to the domestic and foreign economies by a complex pattern of interdependence. Similarly, the supply and demand of foreign exchange is dependent on all the credit and debit transactions of the balance of payments, respectively. Fundamentally, then, equilibrium in the balance of payments and the foreign exchange market demands a stable, mutual adjustment among national incomes, prices, interest rates, money supplies, wages, and other economic variables at home and abroad, as mediated by the rate of exchange. Payments equilibrium does not rule out a change in any one of these variables as long as its effects are neutralized by a change or changes in one or more other variables. Thus, for example, equilibrium will be sustained if a rise in exports, stimulated, say, by higher incomes abroad, is matched by an equal rise in net long-term capital outflows, attracted, say, by higher interest rates abroad. That is to say, equilibrium can be dynamic; indeed, it must be so in a world of continuing movement. When, however, changes in economic variables at home or abroad are not neutralized by changes in other variables, they will cause disequilibrium in the balance of payments mainly by altering the size and direction of money expenditures, by altering prices (including the exchange rate), or by altering both expenditures and prices.

Despite the large number of potential sources of disequilibrium, however, it is possible to classify them into the following relatively few broad categories:

1. Seasonal and random disequilibrium.
2. Cyclical disequilibrium.
3. Structural disequilibrium.
4. Destabilizing speculation and capital flight.
5. Other sources of disequilibrium.

We shall discuss these categories as sources of *deficit* disequilibrium, but since a deficit disequilibrium in one country implies a surplus disequilibrium in one or more other countries, it should be clear that they are also sources of surplus disequilibrium.

Seasonal and Random Disequilibrium. A nation's exports and imports vary seasonally due to seasonal changes in production and consumption, but usually this seasonal variation is not the same for both. The result is seasonal disequilibrium in the balance of payments. Seasonal disequilibrium is ordinarily of little consequence since it is short-lived and self-reversible—a deficit in one season offsetting a surplus in another.

Seasonal disequilibrium is likely to be most visible in the balance of payments of less-developed countries that depend on agricultural products for the bulk of their exports. Seasonal import variations may also be substantial for these countries when the agricultural sector depends on imports of fertilizers, mechanical equipment, and fuels for its seasonal requirements, or when food must be imported to meet consumption needs in the period preceding domestic harvests. Seasonal variations in trade are less prominent in the balance of payments of industrial countries, although they are never entirely absent.

Irregular, nonsystematic, short-lived disturbances may also cause disequilibrium in the balance of payments. The traditional example of this kind of disequilibrium is a crop failure that curtails exports or forces a nation to import foodstuffs. Labor strikes that tie up transportation or immobilize industries can also affect exports or imports and thus the balance of payments. The long steel strike in the United States in 1959 not only cut back steel exports but also brought about a sharp increase in steel imports. Other sources of random disequilibrium include natural disasters such as floods and earthquakes. The foregoing random disturbances have a once-for-all impact on the balance of payments; they cause only a *temporary* disequilibrium. When disturbances are of such a magnitude as to have pervasive and lasting effects on the economy and trade of a nation (war, revolution, civil strife, etc.), then they are not random in the sense that we are using the term.

Although seasonal disequilibrium is largely predictable and random disequilibrium is not, both are short-lived and do not call for equilibrating adjustments in incomes, prices, or exchange rates. Seasonal deficits should be financed out of seasonal surpluses; random deficits should be financed out of international reserves that are maintained in part for this very purpose.

Cyclical Disequilibrium. Variations in the national incomes of trading countries, whether involving changes in price levels, changes in the levels of production and employment, or both, may lead to cyclical disequilibrium in the balance of payments.

In the early 1930's massive deflations in real income and production (accompanied by widespread unemployment) occurred in the industrial countries of North America and Western Europe. In the nonindustrial countries where the agricultural sector accounted for the bulk of national income, deflation mainly took the form of a catastrophic fall in prices, wages, and terms of trade, rather than in production and employment. This global deflation caused enormous payments disequilibria, wrecked the international monetary system, and forced nations into competitive depreciations and the wholesale use of trade and payments restrictions.

Since the end of World War II the industrial countries have avoided deflation; by and large they have been able to achieve steady growth at full-employment levels. But they have been far less successful in avoiding inflation generated by an effective demand running ahead of production. The situation in many developing countries has been far worse: "runaway" inflation of 50 percent or more in a single year is not uncommon. Brazil and Indonesia may be cited as examples. We can fairly say that inflation has been the single most important source of payments disequilibrium in the postwar years.[15]

Cyclical disequilibrium may be a misnomer to denote payments disequilibrium caused by deflationary and inflationary movements in national income and price levels, because at most it is only roughly periodic. It can be regarded as temporary or persistent depending on whether the responsible change in national income is self-corrective or can be corrected by monetary and fiscal measures within, say, two years or so.

Structural Disequilibrium. Shifts in the demand for *specific* export goods, whether brought about by changing tastes, a new distribution of income in export markets, or by changes in the availability or prices of competitive products offered by foreign suppliers, are common events in foreign trade. Shifts in the demand for import goods also occur for similar reasons. When a national economy is slow to adapt to these shifts, persistent structural disequilibrium appears in its balance of payments. We were referring to this kind of disequilibrium in earlier chapters dealing with comparative costs when we observed that in a dynamic world a nation cannot reasonably expect its comparative cost advantages to last indefinitely. On the contrary, continuing movements (large and small) in the direction and composition of a nation's exports and imports are a normal condition of world trade.

What is needed to remedy structural disequilibrium is a reallocation of production to conform to new patterns of demand and supply. Persistent structural disequilibrium may be viewed as a failure of the price system, which is supposed to guide and encourage reallocation in a market economy.

---

[15] Whether the United States balance of payments deficit should be attributed to domestic inflation is touched on in Chapter 19.

Reallocation is sluggish when prices respond only slowly, if at all, to shifting market conditions because of monopoly, administrative pricing, price agreements, or other arrangements that limit price competition.

Adjustments in production usually demand a reallocation in the use of factors of production. In the export sector, for example, labor and other factors must move out of lines of production no longer in demand in foreign markets and into lines that enjoy a comparative advantage. When wages and the prices of other factors employed in declining export industries are hard to lower (sticky downwards), the reallocating function of factor prices is crippled and must depend on the attraction of higher factor rewards in growing industries in the export sector or elsewhere in the economy. A more serious deterrent to a prompt reallocation of factors is low factor mobility, especially labor. This creates the problem of structural unemployment.

To conclude, a wide variety of forces operating at home and abroad, such as technological and product innovations, new competition, changes in tastes, improvements in productivity, growing populations, and so on, may cause shifts in the supply and demand of individual exports and imports that result in a structural disequilibrium in the balance of payments.

Destabilizing Speculation and Capital Flight. These two phenomena (described in Chapter 7) constitute another source of payments disequilibrium. Although conceptually distinct, these autonomous short-term capital movements tend to occur together. Both intensify an existing disequilibrium, and capital flight may actually create one since it is motivated by fears of safety which sometimes originate in conditions unrelated to the balance of payments, notably the prospect of war or revolution.

In recent years the primary stimulus of destabilizing speculation and capital flight has been the expectation of devaluation in a major currency already weakened by a balance of payments deficit.

Other Sources of Disequilibrium. The preceding four categories cover the main sources of disequilibrium, but they are not exhaustive. As we shall discover later, the United States payments deficit does not fit neatly into any one of these categories. In particular, we should recognize that a huge, sustained outflow of long-term investment capital can also create a payments deficit that calls for adjustment.[16] Disequilibrium may also originate in an unrealistic exchange rate, not uncommon when there is exchange control. Some economists also speak of *secular* disequilibrium that arises from technological and other changes that occur slowly as an economy moves from one stage of growth to another over a period of decades.

---

[16] This is the foreign investment transfer problem. See Chapter 23.

SURPLUS AND DEFICIT DISEQUILIBRIUM

Disequilibrium in the balance of payments may be *surplus* or *deficit*.[17] Surplus disequilibrium usually appears in a country's balance of payments when its exports exceed imports on current account (merchandise and services), and this net credit balance is not offset by an autonomous export of long-term capital or by autonomous unilateral transfers. Instead, the net autonomous balance is financed by a compensatory export of capital, a compensatory import of gold, or by compensatory unilateral transfers to foreign countries. However, an export balance on current account is not a necessary condition of surplus disequilibrium. When an *import* balance on current account is less than an autonomous inflow of long-term capital, then the balance of payments is also in surplus disequilibrium. In recent years Switzerland, and at times other European countries, has exhibited this sort of surplus disequilibrium.[18]

Surplus disequilibrium adds to the international reserves of the surplus country unless that country is willing to finance the surplus in its balance of payments by furnishing compensatory aid to deficit countries.

Conversely, deficit disequilibrium occurs when a country's autonomous debit transactions are greater than its autonomous credit transactions. The resulting net balance is financed in whole or in part by a compensatory import of short-term capital, a compensatory export of gold, or, less commonly, a receipt of compensatory unilateral transfers. In most cases, a deficit disequilibrium originates in the current account where imports are running ahead of exports and the resulting net debit balance is greater than any net autonomous long-term capital inflow. But deficit disequilibrium may also originate in the long-term capital account or, less likely, in the unilateral transfer account. During the first half of the 1960's the United States achieved a very strong surplus on current account, but its balance of payments nevertheless stayed in deficit disequilibrium because this surplus was exceeded by net debit balances on other autonomous items.

Deficit disequilibrium causes a nation to lose reserves of gold and foreign exchange unless the deficit is financed by a net inflow of foreign short-term capital or compensatory aid from abroad.

Surplus disequilibrium, accompanied by rising international reserves, seldom causes concern in the surplus country. An exception occurs, as

---

[17] A balance of payments in surplus disequilibrium is often called "favorable," and one in deficit disequilibrium, "unfavorable."

[18] At times, Switzerland has also received substantial amounts of flight and speculative capital which, as noted, are symptoms of disequilibrium. Although adding to Switzerland's monetary reserves, these kinds of capital can leave as suddenly as they arrive, posing a potential threat to the Swiss balance of payments. For this reason and to combat domestic inflation, the Swiss monetary authorities sometimes restrain short-term capital imports.

observed in the case of Switzerland, when reserves are swollen by large-scale inflows of speculative and flight capital that threaten future payments stability and (possibly) intensify domestic inflation. Deficit disequilibrium is another matter. Falling reserves must be checked if the exchange rate is to be held at its current level without the imposition of controls. Autonomous debit transactions must be contracted; autonomous credit transactions expanded. This involves income and price adjustments and/or direct government action to curtail imports, raise exports, discourage long-term capital outflows, stop capital flight or speculative capital outflows, and so on. In short, deficit disequilibrium compels adjustment—one way or another.

Surplus disequilibrium in one country's balance of payments is only possible if there is deficit disequilibrium in the balance of payments of one or more other countries. Even though a country may seek to preserve a surplus in its balance of payments, therefore, the surplus cannot endure any longer than the deficits that are its counterparts in the balance of payments of foreign countries. Actually, the surplus country has everything to gain by facilitating adjustments toward equilibrium in its balance of payments. Otherwise, one day its exports may face a barrier of discriminatory restrictions imposed by deficit nations.

THE NEED FOR ADJUSTMENT

In Chapter 3 two fundamental questions were raised: (1) Why does international trade take place? (2) What are the gains from international trade? We now raise a third important question: How do nations adjust to disequilibrium in foreign trade or, more broadly, in the balance of payments and foreign exchange market?

The achievement and maintenance of equilibrium in international payments is a key objective of national economic policy. No country is immune to changes that can upset its external payments equilibrium. During the late forties and most of the fifties, Americans grew accustomed to a strong balance of payments at home and weak balances of payments abroad. The conventional wisdom of the times implied that balance of payments troubles happened only to others, not to Americans. But the sharp deterioration of the United States balance of payments in 1958 marked the end of this era. Since then, the restoration of external payments equilibrium has been the most pressing and bothersome international economic problem confronting the United States government. In a later chapter we shall describe and evaluate the steps taken by the United States to improve its balance of payments. First, however, we must fully understand the theory of international payments adjustment, which will give us the concepts and other intellectual tools needed to intelligently assess balance of payments policy in the world economy.

No nation can continue indefinitely to experience an excess of autonomous imports over autonomous exports or, for that matter, an excess of autonomous exports over autonomous imports. Foreign exchange required to pay for imports cannot be manufactured at home; over the long run it must be earned by exports of merchandise and services or obtained through an inflow of long-term investment capital. In the end, adjustment to a persistent deficit in the balance of payments involves a reorientation of domestic production and consumption—more resources must be devoted to exports and/or there must be a lower consumption of imports.

MARKET VERSUS NONMARKET ADJUSTMENT

Basically, a nation may adjust to a *persistent* or fundamental deficit in its balance of payments in one of three ways: (1) through an internal deflation of prices and incomes relative to foreign prices and incomes, (2) through a depreciation of its rate of exchange, or (3) through an imposition of exchange and trade controls.

The first two methods of adjustment work through market processes involving changes in income, prices, exchange rates, money supplies, interest rates, and other economic phenomena. Market adjustment, however, does not imply the absence of governmental action. Indeed, successful market adjustment to an external deficit depends upon government fiscal and monetary policies directed toward reinforcing equilibrating market forces. Otherwise, government monetary and fiscal policies, while not controlling or supplanting market adjustment, may counteract its equilibrating effects on the balance of payments by introducing disequilibrating changes in income, prices, and the like. Generally, exchange depreciation involves a government decision because most nations seek to stabilize their exchange rates.

Nonmarket adjustment stands in sharp contrast to market adjustment. Government controls and regulatory devices replace the market in order to suppress an external deficit. Controlled adjustment is not true adjustment. Although the symptoms of disequilibrium (net compensatory items in the balance of payments or depreciation of the exchange rate) are removed by direct controls, the causes of disequilibrium (cyclical, structural, etc.) are left untouched. The result is *suppressed disequilibrium.* Suppressed disequilibrium generally results from the widespread use of import quotas and exchange restrictions. But restrictive measures and direct controls may take any number of particular forms: tied loans and grants, ceilings on direct investment outflows, generalized tariff surcharges, domestic buying preferences, restrictions on the purchase of foreign bonds and on bank loans to foreigners, to name only the more prominent. As we shall see, many of these restrictions have been imposed by the United States government in an effort to eliminate the United States payments deficit.

VARIETIES OF MARKET ADJUSTMENT

Market adjustment to persistent disequilibrium takes two different paths depending upon whether exchange rates are stable or free to vary. When exchange rates are held stable, either through adherence to the gold standard or through official stabilization agencies, adjustment occurs mainly via changes in incomes and prices *within* the domestic and foreign economies. On the other hand, when exchange rates are free to vary, adjustment mainly occurs within the foreign exchange market (with repercussions on domestic and foreign income and prices) where the exchange rate moves until an equality is established between the amounts of foreign exchange supplied and demanded as a result of autonomous transactions.

It follows that in a stable-rate system the domestic economy is closely linked to foreign economies, whereas in a fluctuating-rate system the domestic economy is insulated to some extent from foreign economic influences (and vice versa) by the foreign exchange market. The contemporary international monetary system is often termed an "adjustable-peg" system because, although exchange rates are normally held stable, adjustment to balance of payments disequilibrium is made at times by varying the exchange rate. When this happens adjustment substantially agrees with that in a fluctuating-rate system.

In the next chapter we trace the path of adjustment in a stable-rate system and in Chapter 10 look at adjustment in a variable-rate system. Although differences between these two systems are often stressed (and debated) by economists, we shall find that adjustment to deficit disequilibrium in both systems involves a shift of resources to the export sector and a drop in expenditures on imports, brought about by income and price changes.

SUMMARY

1. The balance of payments is a statistical classification and summary of all economic transactions between residents of one country and residents of other countries over a stipulated period of time, ordinarily one year. Residence is primarily determined by permanent location, and secondarily by "center of interest."

2. The balance of payments classifies international transactions as debits or credits. Debit transactions involve payments by domestic residents to foreign residents; credit transactions involve receipts by domestic residents from foreign residents.

3. The Standard Presentation of the balance of payments developed by the International Monetary Fund groups all transactions into four major accounts: (a) goods and services, (b) transfer payments, (c) capital flows, and (d) official reserves.

4. When Americans invest abroad, whether on a long- or short-term basis, the United States is said to experience a capital outflow or export. A capital outflow is a debit in the balance of payments because it involves payments to foreign residents. Conversely, when foreign residents invest in the United States, this country experiences a capital inflow or import, which is a

credit in the balance of payments because it involves receipts from foreign residents.

5. An examination of the U.S. balance of payments for 1969 reveals how these principles and concepts are followed in practice, and it tells us much about the international economic position of this country in that year.

6. The balance of payments is always in accounting balance, that is, total debits equal total credits. The balance of payments records the total international receipts of the nation and their complete disposition as international payments.

7. The most comprehensive definition of disequilibrium in the balance of payments is based on the distinction between *compensatory* and *autonomous* items. Compensatory items are called into existence to finance autonomous items which, in contrast, are independent of other items in the balance of payments. Disequilibrium prevails in a nation's balance of payments when a net balance of compensatory items is needed to finance an opposing net balance of autonomous items. Another, but less satisfactory, measure of disequilibrium is the net change that occurs in a country's reserves of gold and foreign exchange over a period. *Deficit* disequilibrium arises when a net autonomous import or debit balance is financed by a net compensatory export or credit balance. Conversely, a net autonomous export or credit balance financed by a net compensatory import or debit balance indicates a *surplus* equilibrium.

8. The presence of substantial movements of flight and speculative capital of the destabilizing variety is always a sign of disequilibrium, even in the unlikely event they are fully offset by other autonomous items.

9. Despite the large number of potential sources of disequilibrium, it is possible to classify them into a relatively few broad categories: seasonal and random, cyclical, structural, destabilizing speculation and capital flight, and other. The most important distinction is between temporary and persistent disequilibrium.

10. Adjustment to international payments disequilibrium is necessary because no nation can continue indefinitely to import more than it exports in autonomous items, or vice versa. Adjustments may occur through market processes (income, prices, exchange rate, etc.) or be suppressed by government controls. When exchange rates are stable, market adjustment to a persistent disequilibrium is effected mainly through income and price changes within the domestic and foreign economies. Otherwise, it occurs mainly through variations in the exchange rate.

QUESTIONS AND APPLICATIONS

1. What is the balance of international payments?
2. What determines whether a transaction is entered as a debit or a credit in the balance of payments?
3. What is the distinction between current transactions, unilateral transfers, capital transactions, and official reserve transactions?

4. Draw up a balance of payments for the United States and enter the following transactions as debits or credits in the appropriate accounts:

   (a) Export of merchandise.
   (b) Services sold to foreign travelers in the United States.
   (c) Gifts to foreign residents.
   (d) Import of gold.
   (e) Investments by foreign residents in the United States.

5. Why is the balance of payments always in an accounting balance?
6. Define balance of payments equilibrium and disequilibrium in terms of compensatory and autonomous items.
7. Distinguish between surplus and deficit disequilibrium.
8. Describe the major sources of disequilibrium.
9. Why does disequilibrium, especially deficit disequilibrium, call for adjustment?
10. Explain the difference between market and nonmarket adjustments.

SELECTED READINGS

Badger, Donald G. "The Balance of Payments: A Tool of Economic Analysis." *International Monetary Fund Staff Papers,* Vol. II, No. 1 (Washington: International Monetary Fund, September, 1951), pp. 86-197.

Host-Madsen. *Balance of Payments: Its Meaning and Uses.* Washington: International Monetary Fund, 1967.

International Monetary Fund. *Balance of Payments Concepts and Definitions.* Washington: International Monetary Fund, 1968.

International Monetary Fund. *Balance of Payments Yearbook.* Washington: International Monetary Fund, annual.

CHAPTER 9

INTERNATIONAL PAYMENTS ADJUSTMENT IN A STABLE-RATE SYSTEM

In this chapter we are interested in market adjustment to *persistent* disequilibrium occurring in a stable-rate system. First, however, we need to say something about the *initial* response to disequilibrium in the balance of payments when exchange rates are fixed or stable.

SHORT-RUN ADJUSTMENT

In a stable-rate system such as the international gold standard, the initial response to disequilibrium in the balance of payments takes the form of compensatory movements of short-term capital and gold. This *short-run* adjustment may be adequate when the disequilibrium is *temporary* (seasonal, random, some cyclical).

COMPENSATORY FINANCING

Compensatory movements of short-term capital and gold are symptoms of disequilibrium in the balance of payments, but they also serve as the instruments of short-run adjustment to disequilibrium in a stable-rate system by performing two functions. First, compensatory items are the means of financing the net autonomous debit or credit in the balance of payments. Second, compensatory items transfer purchasing power from the deficit to the surplus country and thereby initiate changes in income and prices that eventually lead to adjustment when disequilibrium is persistent.

Short-run adjustment occurs quickly in the capital account of the balance of payments, whereas income and price adjustments work slowly in the current account. Hence, short-run adjustment affords the necessary time as well as the stimulus for long-run adjustment—equilibrating changes in exports and imports of merchandise and services that eliminate the net balance (debit or credit) on autonomous items.

The compensatory items that finance a net autonomous balance in the balance of payments may come from a number of sources, which are listed below:

1. The deficit country experiences an inflow of short-term capital when its foreign exchange dealers draw down their foreign balances to finance the excess of imports.

2. Short-term capital may move from the surplus to the deficit country because short-term interest rates rise in the latter country and fall in the former.

These opposing shifts in interest rates are brought about by the net monetary effects of international payments. The greater supply of money in the surplus country tends to lower its short-term interest rate, while the smaller supply of money in the deficit country tends to raise its short-term interest rate. To gain a higher rate of return, therefore, funds move from the surplus to the deficit country.

3. Stabilizing speculation may supply compensatory short-term capital to the deficit country. When the rate of exchange of the deficit country's currency rises toward its gold export point or toward the ceiling maintained by a stabilization authority, speculators may buy that currency in anticipation of a subsequent decline in its rate. Such speculation supplies foreign exchange (short-term capital) to the deficit country.

4. Compensatory short-term capital may also come from the deficit country's central bank or stabilization agency when it uses foreign exchange reserves to restrain a rise in the rate of exchange.

5. Compensatory short-term capital may be provided by unilateral transfers and stabilization loans from a surplus to the deficit country.

6. Finally, compensatory financing may come from gold exports of the deficit country.

IMPORTANCE OF SHORT-TERM
CAPITAL MOVEMENTS

The viability of a stable-rate system depends upon large equilibrating flows of short-term capital because most countries have only a small supply of gold. Otherwise, short-run adjustment is unable to provide the financing that may be needed to ride out a temporary disequilibrium or to afford the time required for long-run adjustment in income and prices if the disequilibrium is persistent. When the supply of short-term capital is meager, most countries are forced to adjust through exchange depreciation unless they decide to suppress the disequilibrium with controls.

Before World War I, compensatory movements of short-term capital were encouraged by the adherence of countries to the gold standard "rules of the game." In conformity with these informal rules, the central bank of a deficit country raised its rediscount rate while the central bank of a surplus country lowered its rate. These actions reinforced the interest rate changes brought about by the net monetary effects of international payments.[1] Another unspoken gold-standard rule made it mandatory that a country alter the gold content of its currency only as a last extremity. Stabilizing speculation was thereby encouraged by a well-founded belief in the fixity of exchange rates.

In the 1920's the gold standard rules were less influential over the conduct of monetary authorities. The rediscount rate was increasingly regarded as an instrument of domestic stabilization rather than international adjustment.[2] Moreover, the general abandonment of the gold standard during the war and the subsequent difficulties encountered in returning to it during the twenties caused a loss of faith in the ability of countries to maintain fixed exchange rates. As a consequence, movements of short-term capital and gold in the twenties were often disequilibrating rather than equilibrating.

Today the bulk of compensatory movements of short-term capital and gold is initiated by governments and their central banks. In the postwar period compensatory financing has come mainly from intergovernment stabilization loans and unilateral transfers, official gold and foreign exchange reserves, the International Monetary Fund, and credit arrangements negotiated by central banks. In general, therefore, national governments now decide on the nature and degree of short-run adjustment.

When compensatory financing is not forthcoming, short-run adjustment with stable rates is not possible, and the deficit nation must either impose or tighten controls over its international trade and payments, depreciate its exchange rate, or (if there is time) bring about equilibrating changes in its national income and price level.

TRANSFER OF PURCHASING POWER

In addition to financing a temporary disequilibrium in the balance of payments, gold and short-term capital movements also act to transfer purchasing power from the deficit to the surplus country. This transfer initiates price and income changes in both countries that bring about equilibrating changes in the exports and imports of merchandise and services. In this way

---

[1] During this period the rediscount rate of the Bank of England was of primary importance. The power of the interest rate to attract funds from abroad is attested by the saying, common in London at the time, that "8 percent would bring gold from the moon."

[2] After studying the period 1880-1914, Bloomfield concluded that the differences between the pre-1914 gold standard and after World War I were essentially "differences of degree rather than of kind." Before 1914 central banks were not indifferent to the effects of discount policy on domestic economic activity, and did not respond automatically to payments disequilibrium. However, in the period studied, convertibility was the dominant objective of central banks and they "invariably acted decisively in one way or another when the standard was threatened." See Arthur I. Bloomfield, *Monetary Policy under the International Gold Standard: 1880-1914* (New York: Federal Reserve Bank of New York, 1959).

short-run adjustment prepares the ground for long-run adjustment to persistent disequilibrium, to which we now turn.

THE CLASSICAL THEORY OF ADJUSTMENT

The first coherent theory of international payments adjustment was devised by David Hume (1711-76), British philosopher and economist extraordinary.[3] In opposition to the dominant mercantilist thought of the age, Hume asserted the impossibility of maintaining a chronic "favorable balance of trade" in order to acquire gold and silver (specie) from foreign countries.

THE PRICE-SPECIE FLOW MECHANISM

Hume's theory of adjustment has come down to us as the *price-specie flow mechanism*. It asserts that an inflow of specie resulting from an excess of exports over imports increases the nation's money supply, and that the latter, in turn, increases domestic prices. These higher prices then curtail exports. At the same time there occurs a fall in the money supply and prices of foreign countries experiencing an outflow of specie. This decline in prices stimulates the exports of those countries, including exports to the country receiving specie. In this way international specie movements eliminate any disequilibrium in the balance of payments—higher prices in the surplus country cause its exports to fall and its imports to rise while lower prices in the deficit country or countries cause exports to rise and imports to fall. International specie movements are, therefore, symptoms of payments disequilibrium, and they will continue until the money supplies and price levels of the trading nations achieve an equality between the exports and imports of each country.

CRITIQUE OF PRICE-SPECIE FLOW MECHANISM

Succeeding generations of classical and neoclassical economists (Ricardo, Mill, Marshall, Taussig, and others) added refinements to Hume's price-specie flow mechanism, but made no basic changes in it. The theory was modified to take account of service or "invisible" items in the balance of payments; short-term capital movements; the fractional reserve system of banking; and the differential price behavior of export goods, import-competing goods, and domestic goods. However, the underlying assumptions of the theory—the quantity theory of money and the effect of price changes on exports and imports—were not effectively challenged until the Keynesian revolution in economic thinking of the late 1930's.

---

[3] This theory appeared in Hume's *Political Discourses* published in Edinburgh in 1752.

The price-specie flow mechanism is open to all the criticisms that have been leveled against the quantity theory of money. This theory assumes that a change in the quantity of money will bring about a proportionate change in the price level. A change in the quantity of money will, however, affect prices only if it affects spending, and the change in spending induced by a given change in the money supply may be relatively large or small depending on the latter's velocity of turnover. Moreover, the influence of a given change in spending on prices will vary according to the general level of employment and output and the degree of price flexibility in the economy. Hence, there is no direct or certain price response to a change in the money supply, and, under conditions of excess productive capacity and unemployment or of imperfect competition, there may be little or no response.

The main criticism of the price-specie flow mechanism, however, is its emphasis upon price adjustment to the almost complete neglect of income adjustment. Classical and neoclassical economists realized that the deficit country underwent a decline in its purchasing power relative to the surplus country, and that this decline, along with the adverse shift in its terms of trade, brought about adjustment by raising its exports and lowering its imports. But this purchasing power or income effect was viewed as the incidental accompaniment of price changes, which were the main instruments of international adjustment. There was no conception of an *autonomous* change in income unrelated to a change in prices. In the classical world of full employment and purely competitive markets, this oversight was almost inevitable, for under such conditions a change in spending will cause a change in prices and there are no income effects unaccompanied by price changes.

Writing in 1928, Taussig, the foremost neoclassical economist in America, felt that something was missing in the price-specie flow explanation of international payments adjustment, although he was unable to lay his finger on it. In speaking of adjustment to a movement of long-term investment capital, he wrote as follows:

> What is puzzling is the rapidity, almost simultaneity, of the commodity movements. The presumable intermediate state of gold flow and price changes is hard to discern, and certainly extremely short.[4]

At another point he remarked:

> It must be confessed that here we have phenomena not fully understood. In part our information is insufficient; in part our understanding of other connected topics is also inadequate.[5]

---

[4] Frank W. Taussig, *International Trade* (New York: Macmillan Co., 1928), p. 260.

[5] *Ibid.*, p. 239.

Income adjustment is the key to this puzzle. Along with price adjustment it makes up the modern theory of long-run adjustment to balance of payments disequilibrium.

NATIONAL INCOME AND FOREIGN TRADE

When exchange rates are held stable, either through adherence to the gold standard or through official stabilization agencies, short-run adjustment to a balance of payments disequilibrium occurs through the movement of compensatory items in the balance of payments, principally gold and short-term capital. Long-run adjustment to a persistent disequilibrium involves an internal deflation of income and prices in the deficit country and, simultaneously, an internal inflation of income and prices in the surplus country.

The modern theory of long-run adjustment places great emphasis on the role of income changes, both in the deficit and the surplus countries, in effecting adjustment to balance of payments disequilibrium. It does not neglect, however, the equilibrating price movements that may accompany the changes in income.

The modern theory states that a persistent disequilibrium in the balance of payments will cause a cumulative deflation of income in the deficit country and, simultaneously, a cumulative inflation of income in the surplus country. Declining income in the deficit country will lessen the external deficit by inducing a decline in imports and by releasing goods from domestic consumption for export. Rising income in the surplus country will lessen the external surplus by inducing a rise in imports and by drawing export goods into domestic consumption.

Falling prices in the deficit country and rising prices in the surplus country will also aid adjustment. In the deficit country, imports will become less attractive to buyers, while in the surplus country, imports will become more attractive.

In this section we examine the relationships between national income and foreign trade, and in the next section, the mechanism of income adjustment to a balance of payments disequilibrium. Price adjustment is described in the final section of the chapter.

THE GROSS NATIONAL PRODUCT
AND INCOME EQUATIONS

The *gross national product* (GNP) of a nation is the market value of all goods and services produced by the national economy over a period of time which is usually a year. In practice, the GNP is estimated by aggregating the total expenditures on goods and services of individuals, business, government, and foreigners in the markets of the nation over the year. Since these are final expenditures, no single good or service is ever counted more than once.

In a *closed* economy with no foreign trade all expenditures are domestic and GNP may be expressed as follows:

$$GNP = C + I + G$$

where C represents expenditures by individuals for consumption; I, expenditures by business for gross investment (capital equipment, construction, and net additions to inventories); and G, expenditures by government for both consumption and investment.

In an *open* economy, however, GNP is affected by the exports and imports of goods and services that make up the current account of the nation's balance of payments. Exports measure the expenditures by foreigners in domestic markets and therefore are part of GNP. Imports, on the other hand, measure expenditures by domestic individuals, business, and government for goods and services produced by *other* nations, and must be *deducted* from total expenditures to get the *domestic* gross national product.

Hence, in an open economy GNP assumes this form:

$$(1) \quad GNP = C + I + G + X - M$$

where X represents expenditures on exports and M, expenditures on imports. The expression $X - M$ links gross national product to the balance of payments because this expression is the net balance on current account which is also the net foreign investment of the nation.

To show this, we can rewrite (1) as follows:

$$(2) \quad GNP = C + I_d + G + (X - M)$$

where I_d represents *domestic* gross investment and $(X - M)$, net foreign investment.

The production of the goods and services making up the gross national product generates an equal flow of income to the factors which contribute their productive services. Some of this income is spent by individuals on consumption and some is saved by them, some is saved by business as depreciation and "retained corporate profits," and the rest is taxed away by government. Thus we can define *gross national income* (GNI) as follows:

$$(3) \quad GNI = C + S_p + S_b + T$$

where C represents income spent on consumption; S_p and S_b, personal and business saving, respectively; and T, income taxed away by government.

Since GNP is equal to GNI, we now have this identity:

$$(4) \quad C + I_d + G + (X - M) = C + S_p + S_b + T.$$

Simplifying and transposing we get:

$$(5) \quad I_d + G + (X - M) = S_p + S_b + T.$$
$$(6) \quad S_p + S_b + (T - G) - I_d = X - M.$$

Since $(T - G)$ is the excess of tax revenue over government expenditure, or *government saving*, $S_p + S_b + (T - G) = S$, where S represents *total* domestic saving. Thus:

$$(7) \quad S - I_d = X - M.$$

This is a basic equation relating gross national income (or product) to foreign trade. It states that any excess of exports over imports (current account surplus) is matched by an excess of domestic saving over domestic investment. Conversely, an excess of imports over exports (current account deficit) is matched by an excess of domestic investment over domestic saving. If domestic saving equals domestic investment, then exports also equal imports.

This discussion of gross national income and product may take on more meaning for readers if we end it with a presentation of those two accounts for the United States in 1970. This presentation is given below in Table 9-1.

Table 9-1

GROSS NATIONAL PRODUCT AND INCOME OF THE UNITED STATES IN 1970

(Billions of Dollars)

GNP		GNI	
C	616.7	C	616.7
I_d	135.7	S_p	50.2
G	220.5	S_b	98.1
X	62.2	T	212.5*
M	—58.6	Statistical Discrepancy	—1.0
GNP	976.5	GNI	976.5

Source: Adapted from *Federal Reserve Bulletin* (Washington: U.S. Government Printing Office, May, 1971), pp. A68-69.
* Net of government transfer payments, contributions to social insurance, net interest paid by the government, and subsidies less current surplus of government enterprises.

Readers may find it instructive to insert these figures into the gross national product and income equations. In so doing, do not forget the statistical discrepancy on the income side!

DETERMINATION OF NATIONAL INCOME

How do *changes* in gross national income (product) affect the balance of payments? How do *changes* in foreign trade affect gross national income?

To answer these questions, we must understand how national income is determined.[6]

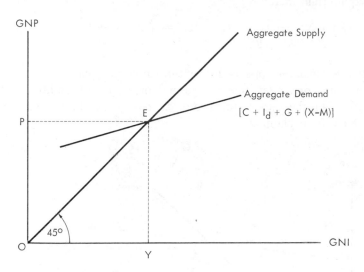

Figure 9-1

THE DETERMINATION OF ACTUAL GROSS NATIONAL PRODUCT (INCOME) BY AGGREGATE DEMAND

Although the *potential* size of the real gross national product (the production possibilities frontier) depends on the supply and productivity of the nation's factors of production, its *actual* size is determined by the level of aggregate demand—the planned expenditures of domestic consumers, investors, and government agencies *plus* the net planned expenditures of foreigners $[C + I + G + (X - M)]$. In Figure 9-1, GNP is determined by the intersection of the aggregate demand schedule with the aggregate (real) supply schedule at E. The equilibrium level of GNP is O-P, which generates an equal level of GNI; that is to say, O-$P = O$-Y.[7] Only at E is the level of national output equal to the level of planned expenditures. At any income level below O-Y, aggregate demand exceeds real output. This excess demand will stimulate producers to expand their output until the excess demand is eliminated at E. On the other hand, at any income level higher than O-Y, aggregate demand falls short of aggregate supply. In this instance producers will respond by contracting output until the

---

[6] We can offer here only a very condensed version of the theory of income determination. For a fuller treatment see any introductory text on economics.

[7] Since the aggregate supply line is drawn at 45° to the origin, GNP = GNI at every point on the line. As noted above, GNP and GNI are always equal.

demand deficiency is eliminated at E. Hence, the only stable level of GNI is O-Y, as determined by E.

In equilibrium therefore:

$$(8)\ GNP = C + I_d + G + (X - M) = GNI = C + S_p + S_b + T.$$

Although this equation appears to be the same as equation (4), it is not. The expenditures on the left side are planned or *ex ante* expenditures, whereas in equation (4) the expenditures are *ex post* expenditures that may or may not have been planned.

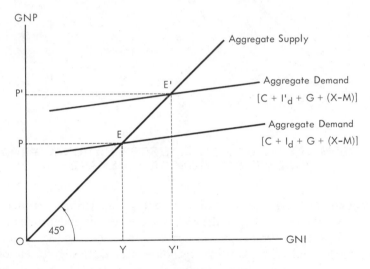

Figure 9-2

THE DETERMINATION OF A NEW EQUILIBRIUM LEVEL OF GROSS NATIONAL PRODUCT (INCOME) BY AN UPWARD SHIFT IN AGGREGATE DEMAND

Any increase in planned expenditures will cause an increase in GNP and GNI, subject to the constraint of the production possibilities frontier. In Figure 9-2, the initial equilibrium position is E where aggregate demand and aggregate supply are equal. But now an increase in planned domestic investment pushes up the aggregate demand schedule, creating excess demand at the existing level of GNI. Producers respond to this excess demand by expanding output to E', where planned expenditure once again equals aggregate supply. At this new equilibrium GNP is O-P' and GNI is O-Y'. In similar fashion, a *decrease* in the planned expenditure causes a contraction in GNP and GNI.

Part One / Theory

Equation (8) can be rewritten as follows:

$$(9)\quad C + I_d + G + X = C + S_p + S_b + T + M.$$

| Income Injections | Income Leakages |

Simply put, all increases (decreases) in expenditures on domestic goods and services will increase (decrease) national income. The different expenditures, however, do not play the same role in *initiating* changes in national income. Basically, changes in domestic investment and government and export expenditures are *autonomous* with respect to national income. That is to say, they are not dependent on any prior change in income, but rather cause changes in income. On the other hand, changes in consumption expenditure are *induced* by prior changes in national income and do not *initiate* changes in it. In other words, consumption expenditures do not determine national income, but instead are determined by national income. Henceforth, we shall refer to autonomous expenditures (domestic investment, government, and exports) as *income injections*.

In contrast to expenditures, domestic saving, taxes, and imports act to *depress* national income. Saving is a decision not to spend, taxes lower spendable income in the hands of individuals and business, and imports divert expenditures away from domestic goods and services to foreign output. For this reason we shall call them *income leakages*.

National income is in equilibrium when the expenditures that business, government, and foreigners want, or *intend*, to make in domestic markets are equal to saving, taxation, and imports. That is to say, when

$$(10)\quad G + I_d + X = S_p + S_b + T + M.$$

To simplify matters we can view $(T - G)$ as part of domestic saving (S) along with S_p and S_b, reducing (10) to

$$(11)\quad I_d + X = S + M.$$

This equation resembles (7), but it is not the same because in our present discussion we are speaking of *intended* expenditures, saving, and imports. Equation (7) always holds, but (11) holds *only* when national income is in equilibrium. If, for example, businessmen end up the year with unwanted, or unintended, additions to their inventories, then they will take steps to reduce them and thus lower income in the following year. Only when intended income injections are equal to income leakages is national income "determined," that is, stable. We can draw here an analogy with the balance of payments. As we have seen, the balance of payments

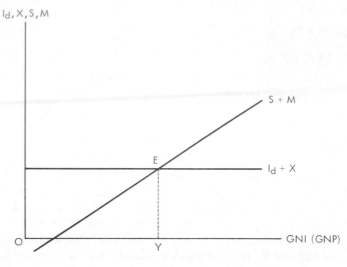

Figure 9-3

THE DETERMINATION OF GROSS NATIONAL INCOME:
INJECTION-LEAKAGE APPROACH

is always in accounting balance, but it is in equilibrium only when autonomous items cancel out to a zero balance.

Figure 9-3 indicates the determination of national income in terms of income injections and leakages, equation (11). The $S + M$ schedule shows how savings and imports vary with the level of national income; it is the sum of the savings schedule (S) and the import schedule (M), which are not shown separately. The $I_d + X$ schedule is the sum of the domestic investment schedule (I_d) and the export schedule (X). Since both the domestic schedule and the export schedule are autonomous with respect to national income, the composite $I_d + X$ schedule is drawn parallel to the abscissa. The equilibrium level of income $(O\text{-}Y)$ is determined by the intersection of the two composite schedules at E. An autonomous upward shift in the $I_d + X$ schedule will bring about a higher equilibrium level of national income while a downward shift will bring about a lower level. This injection-leakage approach to national income determination gives the same result as the total-expenditures approach used in Figure 9-1.

FUNCTIONAL RELATIONSHIP OF EXPENDITURES, SAVING, AND IMPORTS TO REAL DOMESTIC INCOME

In discussing the relationships between changes in expenditures, saving, and imports, on the one hand, and changes in national income, on the other, we shall be talking of *real* income changes, that is, income changes that are *not* accompanied by price changes. The assumptions underlying this condition are indicated later on in the chapter.

As discussed above, changes in domestic investment and exports are independent of changes in domestic national income.[8] Investment expenditure depends on the expected return on capital (marginal efficiency of capital) interacting with the cost of capital (interest rate). Changes in exports depend upon changes in tastes and real income in foreign countries. Consumption, saving, and imports, however, are all dependent on income.

The relation between consumption and income is known as the *marginal propensity to consume* (MPC), which is expressed as dC/dY, where dY is a change in national income and dC is the change in consumption induced by the change in income. If, for example, the MPC is 0.8, then a $100 change (increase or decrease) in national income will induce an $80 change in consumption. In brief, the marginal propensity to consume is the fraction or percentage of new income that is spent on consumption.

Some of the consumption expenditure goes to buy imports. Thus, the marginal propensity to consume *includes* the *marginal propensity to import* (MPM). The latter is expressed as dM/dY. The marginal propensity to import, then, is the percentage of new income that is spent on imports. If the MPM is 0.2, then a $100 change in national income will induce a $20 change in imports.

The expression dS/dY is the *marginal propensity to save* (MPS), which relates a change in national income to the change in saving induced by the former. Since income is either spent or saved, the MPC and MPS together always add up to one. If the MPC is 0.8, then the MPS must be 0.2.

The marginal propensities are not necessarily the same at different levels of national income. For example, as family incomes rise beyond a subsistence level, the marginal propensity to consume may decline or, to say the same thing, the marginal propensity to save may increase. For the sake of simplicity, however, we shall assume in this and later discussions that the marginal propensities are constant.

DOMESTIC AND FOREIGN TRADE INCOME MULTIPLIERS

Reverting to equation (11), an autonomous shift in domestic investment or in exports will cause a change in national income in the same direction. Increases in these expenditures will raise national income; decreases will lower it. Furthermore, the resulting change in national income will be a *multiple* of the autonomous change in investment or exports. This is because the income first generated by the autonomous expenditure will be respent by its recipients, which, in turn, will generate another change in income, and so on. This process of income change (expansion or

---

[8] This is generally true, but at times changes in investment may be induced by changes in consumption (accelerator principle), and changes in domestic income may alter the supply of export goods and services. Basically, however, investment and exports are autonomous.

contraction) will come to a stop when the income leakages induced by the income change become equal to the autonomous income injection. As we have noted, this is when $I_d + X = S + M$.

The relationship between an autonomous change in domestic investment and the subsequent change in national income that it induces is called the *domestic income multiplier,* or dY/dI_d. If the domestic multiplier is 2, then a $100 increase (decrease) in domestic investment will cause a $200 increase (decrease) in national income. We may derive the *domestic* income multiplier as follows:

(a) $I_d + X = S + M$.

Now introduce a change in domestic investment (dI) which will induce a change in domestic saving (dS) and imports (dM) via an induced change in national income. Since exports are not affected, we can rewrite (a):

(b) $dI_d = dS + dM$.

Dividing both sides of (b) into the induced change in national income (dY), we have

(c) $dY/dI_d = dY/dS + dY/dM$, or

(d) $dY/dI_d = \dfrac{1}{dS/dY} + \dfrac{1}{dM/dY} = \dfrac{1}{dS/dY + dM/dY} = \dfrac{1}{MPS + MPM}$.

This last equation tells us that the domestic income multiplier (dY/dI_d) equals the *reciprocal of the sum of the marginal propensities to save and import.* If MPS is 0.1 and MPM is 0.1, then the multiplier is 1/0.2, or 5. Thus, an autonomous change in domestic investment of (say) $50 would cause a change of $250 in national income. In mathematical terms:

(e) $dY = (dY/dI_d)\ dI_d$

which says that the change in income equals the multiplier $\left(\dfrac{dY}{dI_d}\right)$ *times the* autonomous change in domestic investment (dI_d).

The relationship between an autonomous change in exports (dX) and the induced change in national income (dY) is known as the *foreign trade multiplier.* We can derive the foreign trade multiplier in exactly the same way we derived the domestic multiplier, and it assumes the same form: $dY/dX = 1/MPS + MPM$. The induced change in national income will be the autonomous change in exports *times* the multiplier [$dX\ (dY/dX)$].

We may summarize this exposition by saying that changes in national income are induced by autonomous changes in domestic investment or exports. The resulting change in national income will be the product of the autonomous change in investment or exports *times* the income multiplier.

Both the domestic and foreign trade multipliers may be expressed as the reciprocal of the sum of the marginal propensities to save and import, or the reciprocal of the sum of the *income leakages*.[9] National income will reach a new equilibrium position (and cease to change) when intended expenditures (income injections) equal the income leakages, that is, $I_d + X = S + M$.

PAYMENTS ADJUSTMENT VIA THE FOREIGN TRADE MULTIPLIER

We are now prepared to see how the foreign trade multiplier helps to bring about adjustment to a persistent disequilibrium in the balance of payments. But first, some general remarks about the relationship between payments adjustment and national income.

ADJUSTMENT AND DOMESTIC EXPENDITURE

Let us rewrite (2) as follows:

(12) $X - M = GNP - C - I_d - G$, or

(13) $X - M = GNP - (C + I_d + G)$.

This tells us that when exports are greater than imports, GNP (GNI) is greater than *domestic* expenditures on goods and services $(C + I_d + G)$ by the same amount. Conversely, when imports are greater than exports, GNP is less than domestic expenditure by the same amount.

Let us now suppose that M is greater than X, and that this net import balance on current account is financed by a compensatory inflow of short-term capital and/or an export of gold. Clearly, the balance of payments is in deficit disequilibrium. We now see that a current account deficit disequilibrium in terms of national income means that domestic expenditure is greater than gross national product. Payments adjustment requires, therefore, either (1) an increase in GNP in real terms, that is, an increase in physical output, or (2) a decrease in domestic expenditure (whether in C, I_d, G, or all three) in real terms; that is, a decrease in the *domestic absorption* of goods and services.

The period of time allowed for adjustment to a persistent payments deficit is limited by the availability of compensatory financing, and for most countries it is probably not more than two or three years. When an economy is fully employed, further growth in gross national product must depend mainly upon an improvement in productivity which seldom goes beyond 5 percent a year and is often less. Under full-employment conditions, therefore,

---

[9] An alternative formulation of the multiplier uses the marginal propensity to consume which, as we have noted, is equal to $1 - MPS$. Thus, MPS is equal to $1 - MPC$. Substituting this expression for MPS in the multiplier, we have $1/1 - MPC + MPM$, or $1/1 - (MPC - MPM)$.

it is usually not possible to raise GNP to any significant degree during the period allowed for payments adjustment. Thus, adjustment under full-employment conditions calls for *a reduction in domestic expenditure (absorption) in real terms*, and thus, a smaller allocation of goods and services to domestic use. *This is true whether adjustment takes place in a staple-rate or in a variable-rate system.*

When the economy is functioning at less than full employment and has unused productive capacity, it may be possible to adjust to a payments deficit through a rise in GNP with no necessary contraction in domestic expenditure. But this would require that higher real domestic saving would *not* be fully matched by higher domestic investment (I < S), thereby releasing new output for export and/or import substitution. On the other hand, if we assume (as in the following section) that exports are autonomous and the MPS and MPM are constant, then adjustment to a payments deficit will require a reduction in domestic expenditure (absorption) even when the economy is at less than full employment.[10]

OPERATION OF THE FOREIGN TRADE MULTIPLIER

How does the foreign trade multiplier function to bring about an adjudgment to persistent deficit disequilibrium in the balance of payments?

We can indicate income adjustment most simply with a diagram. In Figure 9-4 the initial equilibrium income level is O-Y, as determined by the intersection of the $X + I_d$ schedule (income injection) and the $M + S$ schedule (income leakage). The M and X schedules also intersect at O-Y income: imports equal exports and hence, the balance of payments is in equilibrium.[11] The country is enjoying both internal and external balance.[12] Now, however, an autonomous drop in exports from X to X' creates a balance of payments deficit (dX) and also causes an equal drop in autonomous expenditure from $X + I_d$ to $X' + I_d$. This lower injection of spending forces a contraction of output that reduces national income to a new equilibrium level of O-Y'. At O-Y' no further changes occur in the level of income because income injection ($X' + I_d$) is once again equal to income leakage ($M + S$).

Note that the decrease in income (dY) is greater than the autonomous decrease in exports (dX) as a result of the foreign trade multiplier. The

---

[10] We are talking here of a deficit disequilibrium that originates in the current account of the balance of payments. Thus, this statement does not necessarily apply to a persistent deficit that originates in the unilateral transfer or long-term capital accounts. This unusual kind of deficit has characterized the United States balance of payments in some years. Chapter 24 discusses adjustment to a net long-term capital flow. For a further discussion of domestic absorption, see Chapter 10, p. 245.

[11] In order to focus on adjustment to a current account deficit, we are assuming the absence of any net autonomous movements of capital.

[12] Internal balance means that O-Y is accompanied by full employment. The problem of achieving internal and external balance at the same time is explored in Chapter 11. Observe that at O-Y' there is neither internal nor external balance.

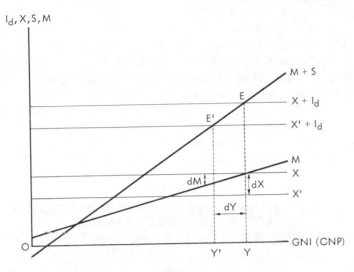

Figure 9-4

INCOME ADJUSTMENT TO AN AUTONOMOUS DECREASE IN EXPORTS

multiplier is *greater* than one because the combined marginal propensities to import and save (the slope of the $M + S$ schedule) are *less* than one. Income adjustment to the balance of payments deficit occurs through a fall in imports (dM) that is induced by the contraction in national income (dY) via the marginal propensity to import (the slope of the M schedule). In this instance, income adjustment is not sufficient to wipe out the entire deficit ($dM < dX$). As we shall observe shortly, adjustment through the foreign trade multiplier can be completed only when there is no savings leakage ($MPS = O$). Figure 9-4 shows only the *final* effect of the foreign trade multiplier on national income and the balance of payments (imports). To gain an insight into the *process* of income adjustment we now turn to arithmetic examples.

Let us suppose that exports of the domestic country fall $100 because of lower foreign demand and that this fall is permanent. Assuming a prior equilibrium, the balance of payments now has a persistent deficit, and long-run adjustment is necessary. We further assume the following marginal propensities in the deficit country: MPC = 1, MPM = 0.4, and MPS = 0. Thus, all new income is spent on consumption—0.4 on imports and 0.6 on domestic output. In the same way, a drop in income induces an equal decrease in consumption spread over imports and domestic output. There is no domestic savings leakage.

We now trace the equilibrating income effects of this permanent fall in exports as they occur over income periods. An income period is the time necessary to spend the income earned in the preceding income period and to earn the income that will be spent in the next income period. (It has been estimated that an income period in the United States economy has a duration of about three months.) Turning now to Table 9-2, we observe that there is no change in the level of exports in Income Period 0, and consequently, there are no induced changes in imports, domestic consumption, or domestic income. In Income Period 1, however, exports drop $100 to a new level that is sustained throughout our example. This causes a decline of $100 in the income received by those domestic residents who produce and sell the merchandise and services comprising the $100 drop in exports.

Table 9-2

INCOME ADJUSTMENT TO A PAYMENTS DEFICIT
WITH NO SAVINGS LEAKAGE

Income Period	Export Income Injection (dX)	Import Income Leakage (dM)	Decrease in Domestic Consumption (dC)	Decrease in Domestic Income (dY)
0	$ 0	$ 0	$ 0	$ 0
1	− 100	0	0	− 100
2	− 100	− 40	− 60	− 160
3	− 100	− 64	− 96	− 196
n	− 100	− 100	− 150	− 250

In Income Period 2, these residents cut their spending on imports by $40 (0.4 *times* $100) and their spending on domestic output by $60 (0.6 *times* $100). As a result, a second group of residents which produces and sells domestic goods going to the first group of residents now suffers an income loss of $60. (What is spending to the buyer is income to the seller.) The $40 drop in imports reduces foreign income, but not domestic income. Thus, in Income Period 2 domestic income falls by $160—an induced decline in domestic consumption ($60) plus the continuing negative export injection ($100). This process of income deflation continues into Income Period 3, and domestic income falls $196 below its level in Period 0.

As we know, the overall contraction in domestic income is determined by the foreign trade multiplier. In this case the multiplier is the reciprocal of the marginal propensity to import because the marginal propensity to save is zero. Thus, the multiplier is 2.5 and domestic income will fall by 2.5 *times* $100, or $250, in Income Period n after all the multiplier effects have taken place. This decline in domestic income induces a $100 fall in imports which exactly matches the autonomous fall in exports, thereby restoring equilibrium in the balance of payments. The process of income contraction comes to a halt in Income Period n because the autonomous fall in export expenditure is fully offset by an induced decline in the import leakage, that is, $dM = dX$.

The Savings Leakage. When spending on imports is the only income leakage, then adjustment to a balance of payments deficit (surplus) is complete—imports fall (rise) until they exactly offset the autonomous decrease (increase) in exports. Income, however, is rarely spent entirely on consumption; part of it is generally saved and this saving, as we have observed, constitutes a second income leakage. Because of the savings leakage the foreign trade multiplier is too small to effect a full adjustment in the balance of payments—the induced change in imports is less than the autonomous change in exports.

Table 9-3 demonstrates this incomplete adjustment by assuming MPC = 0.9, MPM = 0.4, and MPS = 0.1.

Because the combined marginal leakage propensities (marginal import propensity plus marginal savings propensity) are 0.5, the multiplier is only 2 (1/0.5), and domestic income does not contract sufficiently to induce a fall in imports equal to the autonomous fall in exports. Actually, imports fall only $80 and thus there remains a $20 deficit (equal to the savings leakage) in the balance of payments. It is apparent, then, that the foreign trade multiplier will not effect full adjustment to disequilibrium when there is a domestic savings leakage.

Table 9-3

INCOME ADJUSTMENT TO A PAYMENTS DEFICIT
WITH SAVINGS LEAKAGE

Income Period	Export Income Injection (dX)	Import Income Leakage (dM)	Savings Leakage (dS)	Decrease in Domestic Consumption (dC)	Decrease in Domestic Income (dY)
0	$ 0	$ 0	$ 0	$ 0	$ 0
1	− 100	0	0	0	− 100
2	− 100	− 40	− 10	− 50	− 150
3	− 100	− 60	− 15	− 75	− 175
n	− 100	− 80	− 20	− 100	− 200

The Foreign Repercussion Effect. The conclusion reached in the last paragraph is true, but incomplete. To get a complete picture of income adjustment to payments disequilibrium we must take note not only of domestic income changes induced by the balance of payments but also of income changes induced in foreign countries.

The autonomous fall in domestic exports appears to the rest of the world as a $100 fall in its imports which creates a *surplus* disequilibrium in its balance of payments. Now the foreign trade multiplier functions as soon as there is disequilibrium in the balance of payments regardless of whether the disequilibrium results from a change in exports or a change in imports. Thus, the surplus disequilibrium in the rest of the world starts a cumulative expansive movement in foreign incomes which, in turn, induces an increase in imports from the deficit country via the foreign marginal propensity to import. This complicated interaction between the foreign trade multipliers of different countries restrains the decline in income in the deficit country and the rise in income in the surplus country.

The foreign repercussion effect depends on foreign propensities to import and save. Returning to our previous example, let us now assume that the foreign propensity to import is 0.3 and the foreign propensity to save is 0.1. Then the foreign trade multiplier for the domestic country would be 1.25 rather than 2 and domestic income would fall only $125.[13] Because in this instance we are assuming that the domestic and foreign propensities to save are both 0.1, foreign income would rise $125. Thus, the rest of the world would increase its imports from the domestic country by $37.5 (0.3 *times* $125) or, to say the same thing, the domestic country's *exports* would increase by $37.5. At the same time, the domestic country would reduce its imports by $50 (0.4 *times* $125). The end result of these income adjustments would be to decrease the domestic country's deficit from $100 to $12.5 because of a foreign repercussion effect of $37.5 and an induced import leakage of $50. Note that the deficit would be less than in our previous example ($12.5 compared to $20) but that adjustment would remain incomplete. This will always be the case unless the domestic savings leakage is offset by a change in domestic investment expenditure *induced* by the change in domestic income.

The foreign repercussion effect will be insignificant for a country whose exports and imports are only a small part of world trade. However, for major trading countries like the United States and Great Britain, the foreign repercussion effect must be taken into account in estimating the foreign trade multiplier.

The Domestic Income Multiplier. We have now examined long-run adjustment via the foreign trade multiplier, noting how income changes originating in the balance of payments work toward the establishment of a new equilibrium. But all changes in income do not proceed from disequilibrium in the balance of payments. New income may also be created (or old income extinguished) by independent shifts in domestic investment

---

[13] The foreign trade multiplier that takes account of this interaction, or foreign repercussion effect, is $1/MPSd + MPMd + MPMf (MPSd/MPSf)$, where $MPSd$ and $MPMd$ are the marginal propensities to save and import, respectively, of the domestic country, and $MPSf$ and $MPMf$ are the marginal propensities to save and import, respectively, of the rest of the world.

(construction, capital equipment, inventories) or domestic government expenditures. These shifts in domestic expenditure cause a multiple expansion (or contraction) of domestic income via the *domestic* income multiplier. The change in domestic income then affects the level of imports through the marginal propensity to import, and the result, assuming a prior equilibrium, is a cyclical disequilibrium in the balance of payments.

The fact that income changes originating within the domestic economy will induce changes in domestic imports and thereby provoke disequilibrium in the balance of payments explains why inflation has been the leading cause of deficit disequilibrium in the balance of payments of many nations during the postwar period. It also explains the rapid spread of deflation from one country to another during the early thirties. Because of the domestic income multiplier, government fiscal and monetary policies become key instruments of balance of payments adjustment. By the same token, however, these policies may delay international adjustment by bringing about changes in domestic income that counteract the equilibrating income changes of the foreign trade multiplier. This situation often occurs since nations usually place the objectives of domestic full employment and rapid economic development above that of balance of payments equilibrium.

THE ROLE OF PRICE ADJUSTMENT

In our treatment of the foreign trade multiplier, we concluded that income adjustment to a payments deficit (or surplus) is incomplete when there is a domestic savings leakage. Since a positive marginal propensity to save is a normal condition, what, then, acts to complete adjustment? The answer is changes in price levels and in relative prices within the deficit and surplus countries.[14]

The relative importance of income and price adjustment in a particular instance will depend upon the degree of unemployment and excess capacity, the degree of flexibility in wages and prices, and the price elasticities of supply and demand in the economies of trading nations. When (1) prices and wages are inflexible downwards and (2) unemployment and excess capacity prevail throughout an economy, then an autonomous change in expenditure (domestic investment or exports) will cause changes in *real* income with only modest, or no, changes in wages and prices. That is to say, a fall in expenditure will initiate a decrease in production and employment rather than a decrease in prices and wages, and a rise in expenditure will initiate an increase in production and employment rather than an

---

[14] This assumes, of course, that the exchange rate is not altered. When income adjustment is incomplete and, for one reason or another, domestic price adjustment is not possible or desirable, then depreciation is necessary to complete the process of *market* adjustment to a deficit disequilibrium.

increase in prices and wages. We assumed the existence of these two conditions in our presentation of income adjustment because we wanted to focus on income changes alone, unaccompanied by price changes.

It is unlikely that these conditions would ever exist in the actual world to such a degree as to rule out *all* equilibrating price adjustments. Nor can we accept the empirical validity of another set of conditions that would rule out all equilibrating *income* adjustments: (1) full employment, (2) highly flexible wages and prices both downwards and upwards, and (3) high price elasticities of supply and demand.[15] To conclude, neither the assumptions behind the income adjustment model nor those behind the classical model ever fully match actual conditions. In periods of massive unemployment, the income-adjustment model becomes a more valid explanation of the actual adjustment process; in periods of full employment and inflation, the classical model gains in relevance. In both situations, however, income and price changes interact to bring about adjustment to payments disequilibrium.

Let us now trace through the price adjustments that will accompany, to a small or large degree, income adjustment to a deficit in the balance of payments. Again we start with an autonomous fall in exports. This will induce a decline in money income and spending in the deficit country that will cause a general fall in prices, although the fall may be spotty and somewhat retarded because of market imperfections. In addition to this fall in the price level, there will also occur changes in the *relative* prices of export, import, and domestic (nontraded) goods. Since the impact of the autonomous fall in export demand is concentrated on specific export goods, they are likely to suffer the greatest price declines. On the other hand, as domestic residents switch from imports (whose prices are rising) to domestic import-competitive goods, the latter experience a rise in demand that will moderate (or even reverse) any price declines. Price declines in other goods will be somewhere between these two extremes: smaller than the decline in specific export prices, greater than the decline in import-competitive prices.

The effect of the general price deflation in the deficit country is to encourage exports by making them cheaper to foreign buyers and to discourage imports by making them more expensive to domestic buyers relative to domestic substitutes. The effect of the relative price changes is to encourage a reallocation of production more in conformity with the new conditions of export demand. Relatively low wages and prices in the specific export sector experiencing an autonomous fall in demand stimulate a movement of labor and capital to other export sectors and to the domestic sector, including import-competing industries where wages and prices are now relatively high. Factors may also move from other domestic industries to the import-competing industries. Both price deflation and shifts in relative prices, therefore, help eliminate the deficit in the balance of payments.

---

[15] These are the implicit assumptions of the classical theory of adjustment.

Simultaneously, surplus countries will experience an expansion of money income and spending. This will cause a general rise in the price level (unless there is widespread unemployment and excess capacity) and shifts in relative prices that will encourage imports and discourage exports.

In effect, general price adjustment works through a shift in the terms of trade of both the surplus and deficit countries. The surplus country enjoys an improvement in its terms of trade as its import prices fall and its export prices rise, while the deficit country suffers a deterioration in its terms of trade as its import prices rise and its export prices fall.[16]

PRICE ELASTICITIES

The degree to which the terms of trade must shift in favor of the surplus country in order to remove disequilibrium in the balance of payments will depend upon the price elasticities of supply and demand of both exports and imports.[17] When elasticities are high, a relatively small change in prices calls forth a relatively large response in the quantity of exports and imports, and the terms of trade need change little to effect adjustment. With low elasticities, however, relatively large price changes will stimulate only relatively small changes in the quantity of exports and imports, and there must be a wide swing in the terms of trade to effect adjustment.

The price elasticities of export and import supply will depend upon the mobility of productive factors within both the surplus and deficit countries. When labor and other resources are induced by only slight variations in relative wages and other factor prices to move from one industry to another, the supply of goods is elastic—the amount supplied can be adjusted to changing demand with relatively small changes in the supply price. When, however, productive resources are relatively immobile, supply elasticities are low; and any adjustment to balance of payments disequilibrium is impeded. In a many-nation world the price elasticity of import supply for a specific country will also depend on whether foreign suppliers have alternative markets. When the domestic demand for import goods is small compared to the world demand, it will have little or no influence over import prices and import supply will appear highly elastic to the domestic country.

---

[16] Hence, the surplus country obtains a greater share of the gains from trade as a result of price adjustment. See Chapter 3.

[17] Price elasticities measure the response in the amount demanded or supplied to a given change in price. The price elasticity of demand assumes this expression: $\dfrac{dD/D}{dP/P}$, where D is the original amount demanded, P is the original price, and dD and dP are the changes in the amount demanded and price, respectively. This may be more simply expressed as the ratio: percentage change in amount demanded/percentage change in price. Similarly, the price elasticity of supply is $\dfrac{dS/S}{dP/P}$, where S and dS are the original amount supplied and the change in amount supplied, respectively. Or more simply: percentage change in amount supplied/percentage change in price.

The price elasticities of export and import demand will depend on the nature of the export and import goods and the availability of domestic substitutes. Thus, the demand for luxury imports is more elastic than the demand for essential imports and, other things being equal, the demand for imports with close domestic substitutes is more elastic than the demand for imports with only distant or no domestic substitutes. In a many-nation world substitutes for imports from a given country may also be found in imports from other countries. Hence, the demand facing the exports of a country is apt to be less elastic than otherwise when that country supplies most of the world market, that is, when foreign customers have little opportunity to obtain similar goods elsewhere. Conversely, export demand is likely to be more elastic than otherwise when the exporting country supplies only a small portion of the world market.

OBSTACLES TO PRICE ADJUSTMENT

Fundamentally, international adjustment requires shifts in the level and composition of both supply and demand in the surplus and deficit countries. Equilibrating changes in prices are effective in bringing about such shifts when the price elasticities of supply and demand are high. Anything that lowers price elasticities, therefore, hinders price adjustment to balance of payments disequilibrium.

Price adjustment is undoubtedly less effective today than before World War I. As we observed in Chapter 4, few contemporary markets are close to pure competition. Markets for agricultural staples, such as wheat, cotton, and coffee, are usually subject to price stabilization by government agencies, while the majority of markets for manufactured goods have monopolistic elements that allow the seller (or, in the case of monopsony, the buyer) some control over price. Administered pricing by large-scale oligopolistic industries and the enforcement of wage floors by powerful labor unions are common examples of price inflexibility in today's economies. Of special importance is the international cartel that outlaws price competition and fixes the pattern of foreign trade in its products. The widespread abandonment of price competition in favor of nonprice competition in quality, style, and services; government schemes to control production and marketing; and the innumerable devices used by governments to insulate the domestic economy from foreign economic influences have all diminished the importance of price adjustment.

Despite these developments, however, equilibrating changes in prices remain a significant instrument of international adjustment. The prices of many raw materials and foodstuffs in international trade remain uncontrolled and respond quickly to changes in supply and demand. Moreover, all international goods show plenty of price flexibility upward, as postwar inflation has demonstrated time and again. We can conclude that price adjustment, when permitted, is an effective ally of income adjustment and that both are required in a stable exchange rate system if exchange depreciation or suppressed disequilibrium is to be avoided.

SUMMARY

1. When exchange rates are held stable, short-run adjustment to balance of payments disequilibrium comprises international movements of gold and short-term capital, which are also the symptoms of disequilibrium. These movements provide compensatory financing of the autonomous deficit in the balance of payments; and, in doing so they also transfer purchasing power from the deficit to the surplus country. The latter initiates changes in income and prices that lead to long-run adjustment. Short-run adjustment is adequate to meet temporary disequilibrium. When disequilibrium persists from one period to the next, however, long-run adjustment is necessary—the equilibration of exports and imports of merchandise and services.

2. The viability of a stable-rate system depends upon large equilibrating movements of short-term capital since most countries have only a small supply of gold. When compensatory financing is not forthcoming, short-run adjustment is not possible. Then the deficit nation must either impose or tighten controls over its international trade and payments, depreciate its exchange rate, or (if there is time) bring about equilibrating changes in its national income and price level.

3. The classical theory of adjustment in a stable exchange rate system (the gold standard) is the price-specie flow mechanism, which stresses the equilibrating role of price changes but ignores changes in income.

4. The gross national product (GNP) is the market value of all goods and services produced by the national economy over the year; it is equal to gross national income (GNI). $S - I_d = X - M$ is a basic equation relating gross national income (or product) to foreign trade.

5. National income is in equilibrium when intended expenditures are equal to the income leakages, that is, $I_d + X = S + M$. The foreign trade multiplier equals the reciprocal of the marginal propensities to save and import, or $dY/dX = 1/MPS + MPM$.

6. Under full-employment conditions, adjustment calls for a contraction of expenditure in real terms. When there is a savings leakage, adjustment to a payments disequilibrium via the foreign trade multiplier is incomplete even when allowance is made for the foreign repercussion effect.

7. The actual process of adjustment in a stable-rate system involves equilibrating changes in both income and prices. In effect, price adjustment works through a shift in the terms of trade of both the surplus and deficit countries.

QUESTIONS AND APPLICATIONS

1. (a) How is short-run adjustment accomplished with stable exchange rates?
   (b) What is the major limitation of short-run adjustment?

2. (a) When is long-run adjustment necessary?

(b) Describe and evaluate the price-specie flow mechanism.

3. (a) What are the components of gross national product and gross national income?

(b) Why is GNP equal to GNI?

(c) Derive the equation $I_d + X = S + M$ from the gross national product and income equations.

4. (a) What are the equilibrium conditions of national income?

(b) Derive both the domestic and foreign trade multipliers from the equation $I_d + X = S + M$.

5. (a) How does the foreign trade multiplier explain income adjustment to a disequilibrium in the balance of payments?

(b) When is income adjustment complete? Incomplete?

6. (a) What determines the effectiveness of a shift in the terms of trade in bringing about adjustment in the balance of payments?

(b) What are the obstacles to price adjustment?

7. Under what conditions is income adjustment likely to dominate adjustment in a stable-rate system? Under what conditions is price adjustment likely to dominate?

SELECTED READINGS

See the list of readings given at the end of Chapter 10.

CHAPTER **10**

INTERNATIONAL PAYMENTS ADJUSTMENT IN A VARIABLE-RATE SYSTEM

In a variable-rate system adjustment to a payments disequilibrium occurs through an alteration in the rate of exchange.

There are many possible kinds of variable-rate systems. At one extreme is the system of fluctuating rates in which the rate of exchange is determined solely by supply and demand in the foreign exchange market with no attempt by government authorities to limit or moderate fluctuations.[1] At the other extreme is the "adjustable-peg" system in which rates are stabilized by government authorities in the short run and then adjusted once-for-all to a new stabilized level.[2] In between these two extremes there are any number of variant systems which have more rate variability than the adjustable-peg system but less variability than the fluctuating-rate system. We shall call these middle variants "floating-rate" systems because the rate of exchange may vary beyond the limits imposed on stable rates, but is constrained within wider limits decided by monetary authorities which may or may not change in line with market trends. In all of these systems, however, the rate of exchange continuously or occasionally varies and, in so doing, influences the balance of payments. This variability distinguishes them from a stable-rate system.

ADJUSTMENT THROUGH VARIABLE RATES

We now examine payments adjustment in the fluctuating-rate and adjustable-peg systems. Later we shall analyze the effects of depreciation in *any* variable-rate system.

---

[1] The determination of freely fluctuating rates was examined in Chapter 7.

[2] Since the adjustable-peg system involves both stable and variable exchange rates, it may be considered as a variant of either the stable-rate or variable-rate systems. In Chapter 7 we described briefly the adjustable-peg system in our treatment of active stabilization. In this chapter our interest lies in the variable-rate element of the adjustable-peg system.

ADJUSTMENT THROUGH FLUCTUATING RATES

When exchange rates are stable, compensatory movements of short-term capital and gold provide a short-run adjustment to balance of payments disequilibrium. Such movements, however, are small or nonexistent when exchange rates are freely fluctuating—international flows of short-term capital and gold are then exposed to the exchange risk. Under these circumstances, foreign exchange dealers are unwilling to maintain large foreign balances, and any possible gain from higher interest rates in the deficit country is outweighed by the prospect of an exchange loss. There is no reason why speculation should be preponderantly stabilizing when there are no limits to variations in the exchange rate. Furthermore, when the exchange rate is freely fluctuating there is no official stabilization agency to supply compensatory short-term capital, and gold has lost its fixed value and is just another commodity. Hence, movements of short-term capital and gold can be expected to afford little or no short-run adjustment to disequilibrium when exchange rates are freely fluctuating.

Short-run adjustment (as well as long-run adjustment) must, then, occur through variations in the rate of exchange. When exporters supply bills of exchange, they must be sold immediately to importers who wish to make foreign payments since dealers are unwilling to hold them. An increase in the supply of bills (foreign exchange) will force down the rate of exchange until the bills are taken up by those who wish to buy from abroad. In this way exports are offset by imports and there is no net compensatory movement of short-term capital. Similarly, a higher demand for bills will push up the exchange rate until sufficient bills are supplied to the market and imports are financed by concurrent exports. This absence of any net movement of compensatory short-term capital or gold in a fluctuating-rate system also means that there is no net transfer of purchasing power from one country to another. In consequence, income and price adjustments do not occur.

In a fluctuating-rate system, therefore, movements in the exchange rate achieve a continuing equilibrium in the balance of payments. At the equilibrium rate of exchange the amounts of foreign exchange in supply and demand that derive from autonomous items in the balance of payments (excluding disequilibrating movements of speculative and flight capital) are equal and the foreign exchange market is fully cleared. Disequilibrium does not show up in the balance of payments because there are no compensatory items to finance a deficit or surplus. The equilibrium rate of exchange is shown as $O\text{-}E'$ in Figure 10-1 on page 238.

ADJUSTMENT THROUGH OCCASIONAL
DEPRECIATION (DEVALUATION)

What we have just said applies to a system in which exchange rates are *always* free to respond to changes in supply and demand. It does not apply to a payments system in which exchange rates are *occasionally* varied from one stable level to another stable level. In this system, short-run adjustment occurs as under a stable-rate system, while a planned and limited variation in the exchange rate effects a long-run adjustment. Under these conditions a variation in the exchange rate will have income and price effects since it is closing a gap in the balance of payments—a gap that could not exist in a fluctuating-rate system due to the lack of any compensatory financing. In this adjustable-peg system, adjustment to persistent deficit disequilibrium takes the form of *exchange devaluation*—a limited increase in the domestic price of foreign money.

In a freely fluctuating-rate system, the equilibrium rate is determined by the impersonal tug and pull of supply and demand. When, however, a nation that normally stabilizes its exchange rate decides to devalue in order to correct a deficit disequilibrium, the equilibrium rate of exchange is not known in advance, even though successful devaluation requires depreciation to the equilibrium rate. The exchange rate will, otherwise, continue to be too low, with domestic currency overvalued; or too high, with domestic currency undervalued.[3]

One solution to this difficulty is to set loose the exchange rate to find its equilibrium rate in the market and then, when equilibrium is restored, to stabilize the rate at the new level.

When exchange controls are in existence, either the illegal black market rate or the official "free" rate is sometimes taken to be the equilibrium rate of exchange. Although these rates will usually reveal whether the domestic currency is overvalued or not, they are apt to be unreliable indicators of the equilibrium rate, since the forces of supply and demand acting to determine them often diverge widely from the forces that would exist in a freely fluctuating-rate market.

The Purchasing-Power Parity Doctrine. During World War I and in the early twenties, when most countries were off the gold standard, there was widespread discussion as to the exchange rates at which they should return to the gold standard. Gustav Cassel, a Swedish economist, argued that the new rates of exchange should reflect the relative purchasing powers of the different currencies. This proposition is the well-known *purchasing-power parity doctrine*. This doctrine states that the equilibrium rate of exchange between two currencies is the ratio of their respective domestic purchasing powers. Therefore, if the general price level in the United States is double that in the United Kingdom, then the purchasing power of the dollar is one-half that of the pound and the equilibrium exchange rate of the pound is $2.

---

[3] At times a nation may deliberately seek to overvalue or undervalue its currency, but even this policy presumes a knowledge of the equilibrium rate. See p. 237.

When this absolute version of the doctrine proved inconsistent with the facts, it was replaced by an explanation of the role of the purchasing-power parity in determining the exchange rate with respect to a base period when the exchange rate was in equilibrium. Suppose that the equilibrium rate of the pound was $4.86 (the gold mint parity) in 1913, but that during the period 1913-20 the price level rose four times in the United Kingdom and two times in the United States. Then, according to the relative version of the purchasing-power parity doctrine, the equilibrium rate of exchange for the pound in 1920 was $2.43, since the decline in its purchasing power relative to 1913 had been twice the decline in the purchasing power of the dollar during the same period.

We do not have the space for a full critique of the purchasing-power parity doctrine and shall only mention its main inadequacies. The principal drawback of the doctrine lies in its inadequate coverage of the transactions that determine the rate of exchange. Only the commodity price level is used to determine the purchasing-power parities, whereas the exchange rate is determined by service and capital transactions in addition to merchandise transactions. Furthermore, the doctrine does not distinguish between domestic and international goods and does not account for the demand and supply elasticities of exports and imports. Nor does it take cognizance of the fact that a shift in buyers' preferences or in income may affect the exchange rate independently of any change in price levels and thus the purchasing-power parity.

For these reasons, the purchasing-power parity between two currencies cannot serve as an indication of the equilibrium rate of exchange. The purchasing-power parity doctrine does, however, make a contribution by stressing the influence that may be exerted on exchange rates by divergent movements of the price levels in different countries, and its greatest usefulness is during periods of inflation when such movements may be extremely large.

Deciding on the Equilibrium Rate. If the purchasing-power parity doctrine, black market rates, and official free rates are not reliable indications of the equilibrium rate of exchange, how, then, may a government—intent on devaluation but unwilling to set free the exchange rate—discover the equilibrium rate of exchange? The best that the government can do is to evaluate the many factors that determine the rate of exchange, including the likely responses of those same factors to a variation in the exchange rate itself.

We learned in Chapter 7 that there is a mutual interdependence between the exchange rate and the balance of payments. When changes in the balance of payments place it in deficit disequilibrium, exchange devaluation is successful only if it reverses those changes or induces new compensating changes. An intelligent policy of devaluation, therefore, depends upon a careful appraisal of the sources of disequilibrium in the balance of payments and of the conditions (supply and demand elasticities, income and price effects, etc.) that will determine the efficacy of a given devaluation in overcoming a specific disequilibrium. Even then, the dynamic nature of economic phenomena makes impossible any certain discovery of the equilibrium rate of exchange and any firm guarantee of successful devaluation. Deciding upon the equilibrium rate of exchange, then, is partly economic analysis and partly hunch.

Competitive Depreciation and Overvaluation. Depreciation stimulates exports and simultaneously deters imports. During the 1930's many countries took advantage of this fact by depreciating their currencies beyond the equilibrium rate of exchange. Their purpose was to create a surplus in the balance of payments and thereby foster greater income and employment in the domestic economy. Since this policy required a deficit disequilibrium in the balance of payments of other countries that also faced depression, it amounted to exporting unemployment. For this reason, the attempt to depreciate more than other countries—*competitive depreciation*—has received the uncomplimentary designation of "beggar-my-neighbor policy." Competitive depreciation is not likely to be effective in the long run since other countries will also depreciate in retaliation, and the end result for a country is usually a disruption of its foreign trade rather than any improvement in the domestic economy.

Competitive depreciation developed out of the rigors of international depression. In our own day widespread inflation has led to *overvaluation* of the exchange rate through exchange control, especially in developing countries. Depreciation is feared for its inflationary impact on the domestic economy, and it is avoided even when overvaluation of the currency perpetuates a deficit in the balance of payments.

THE EFFECTS OF EXCHANGE DEPRECIATION

The primary effect of depreciation upon the balance of payments depends upon the responses made by the supply and demand of foreign exchange to the new higher price of foreign exchange. When supply and demand are sensitive to depreciation, or highly elastic, then depreciation is very effective in removing a deficit disequilibrium; but when elasticities are low, depreciation must be severe to wipe out even a small deficit.

This effect of exchange depreciation is shown in Figures 10-1 and 10-2 (page 238). Suppose the French government decides to depreciate the franc to remove a deficit in the balance of payments. If, as in Figure 10-1, the elasticities of the demand and supply of foreign exchange (dollars) are high, then the depreciation will be very effective and will not need to be great. In Figure 10-1, the exchange rate before depreciation is O-E and the deficit

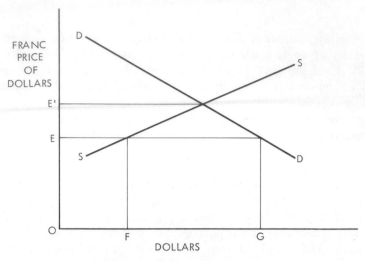

Figure 10-1

**EXCHANGE DEPRECIATION WITH HIGH DEMAND
AND SUPPLY ELASTICITIES**

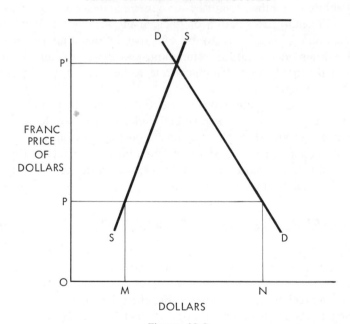

Figure 10-2

**EXCHANGE DEPRECIATION WITH LOW DEMAND
AND SUPPLY ELASTICITIES**

is *F-G*. This deficit is closed by a relatively slight depreciation from *O-E* to *O-E'*. On the other hand, when elasticities are low, a considerable depreciation is needed to bring about adjustment. In Figure 10-2, the exchange rate before depreciation is *O-P* and the deficit, *M-N*. To wipe out this deficit, the franc must be depreciated from *O-P* to *O-P'*. It will be noted that, despite the fact that the deficit in Figure 10-2 is equal to the deficit in Figure 10-1, the exchange depreciation is much larger in the former case.

THE ELASTICITY OF FOREIGN EXCHANGE SUPPLY

The elasticity of the supply of foreign exchange is mainly dependent on the elasticity of foreign demand for domestic exports. Upon depreciation the foreign exchange price of exports falls. When foreign demand is elastic, this decline in export prices will stimulate an expansion in the quantity exported that will be sufficient to enlarge total receipts of foreign exchange despite the lower prices in terms of foreign exchange. On the other hand, when the elasticity of foreign demand is low, total receipts of foreign exchange may even be smaller after depreciation. In this unlikely event, depreciation will widen the deficit insofar as the supply of foreign exchange is concerned.

We can distinguish three cases that describe the influence of the elasticity of export demand on the elasticity of foreign exchange supply. (When *domestic* export prices do not change after depreciation because export *supply* is perfectly elastic, then the export demand elasticity *fully* determines the supply elasticity of foreign exchange.)

1. When the elasticity of export demand has a value of *one* (unit elastic), then a 10 percent depreciation causes a 10 percent increase in the quantity of exports.[4] Hence, the receipts of foreign exchange are the same before and after depreciation. The elasticity of *foreign exchange supply*, therefore, is zero—foreign exchange receipts do not respond to a variation in the exchange rate—and the effect of depreciation on the supply of foreign exchange is neutral.

2. When the elasticity of export demand is greater than one, then a 10 percent depreciation causes a greater than 10 percent increase in the quantity of exports. Receipts of foreign exchange, therefore, increase and help close the deficit in the balance of payments. In this case the elasticity

---

[4] We earlier defined the price elasticity of demand as the ratio: percentage change in amount demanded/percentage change in price. (Algebraically speaking, this ratio carries a minus sign since the amount demanded and price are inversely related. However, following common practice, we shall ignore the sign.) When demand elasticity is one, then the percentage changes in amount demanded and price are the same, and the amount spent on the product in question stays the same after a price change. When elasticity is greater than one, total expenditure increases (decreases) with a fall (rise) in price. When elasticity lies between one and zero, then total expenditure decreases with a fall in price. When elasticity is zero, then total expenditure decreases the same percentage as the fall in price. Similarly, the quantity supplied changes the same, a greater, or lesser percentage than the percentage change in price, depending on whether the elasticity of supply is one, greater than one, or less than one. It should be noted that the amount supplied and price are positively related: they change in the same direction. The use of percentages to define elasticities is a crude simplification and an approximation only. Mathematically, elasticity is $(dQ/dP)\,(P/Q)$ where dQ/dP is the rate of change (derivative) of Q with respect to P.

of foreign exchange supply is greater than zero—foreign exchange receipts respond positively to a higher domestic price of foreign money.

3. When the elasticity of export demand is zero, then a 10 percent depreciation causes no increase in the quantity of exports and foreign exchange receipts fall by 10 percent. When the elasticity lies between zero and one, then the percentage increase in the quantity of exports is less than the percentage depreciation. In both instances depreciation causes a fall in the receipts of foreign exchange that worsens the deficit. Thus, the elasticity of foreign exchange supply is less than zero, or negative—on a graph the supply schedule slopes *downward* from left to right, unlike the normal supply schedule.

In summary, when the elasticity of export demand is greater than one (elastic), then depreciation causes an increase in the receipts of foreign exchange and helps close the deficit. When, on the other hand, the elasticity of export demand is less than one, or zero (inelastic), then depreciation lowers foreign exchange receipts and insofar as the supply of foreign exchange is concerned, worsens the deficit. The elasticities of foreign exchange supply that we have discussed are shown in Figure 10-3, where e_s is the appropriate elasticity.

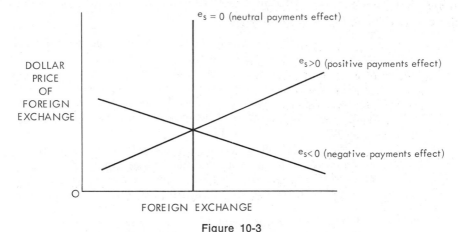

Figure 10-3

ELASTICITIES OF FOREIGN EXCHANGE SUPPLY

Under what conditions is export demand likely to be elastic? We can make only a few pertinent comments relating to the composition of exports, the relative importance of a nation's exports in world trade, and the presence of trade restrictions.[5] Generally speaking, the demand for manufactured products (especially "luxury-type" products) is more elastic than the demand for agricultural and other primary products, which is often inelastic. Many primary products satisfy basic needs and their consumption is relatively

---

[5] See also pp. 229-230 in Chapter 9.

insensitive to price changes. The same is true of intermediate goods that are purchased as raw materials, semimanufactures, and the like when these goods contribute only a small share to total costs of production. Such products face a derived demand that tends to be inelastic.

The demand facing a product with many substitutes is likely to be more elastic than a product with few or no substitutes. That is why a country whose exports are only a small fraction of world exports experiences a more elastic demand (other things equal) than a country like the United States whose exports bulk large in world trade. There is a greater opportunity for substitution between a country's exports and the competitive exports of other countries when the former holds only a modest share of foreign markets.

One final point. Tariffs, quotas, cartels, and other restrictions that inhibit the free play of competition in world markets act to lower effective demand elasticities by limiting the role of price in buying decisions. Trade in agricultural products is particularly restricted in the contemporary world economy.

THE ELASTICITY OF FOREIGN EXCHANGE DEMAND

The elasticity of the demand for foreign exchange depends mainly on the elasticity of the domestic demand for imports. When higher import prices in domestic currency cause a fall in the quantity of imports, then depreciation improves the balance of payments on the demand side. At the very worst, when the quantity of imports stays the same, depreciation has no effect on the balance of payments as far as foreign exchange demand is concerned.

When the *foreign exchange* price of imports does not change after depreciation (import *supply* is perfectly elastic), then the elasticity of import demand *fully* determines the demand elasticity of foreign exchange. We can distinguish two important cases.

1. When the import demand elasticity is *greater than zero*, then the quantity of imports decreases after depreciation and, therefore, (given an unchanged foreign exchange price of imports) the quantity of foreign exchange demanded also decreases. The higher the import elasticity, the greater the decline in the amount of foreign exchange in demand. In this case depreciation improves the balance of payments on the demand side.

2. When the elasticity of import demand is *zero*, then the quantity of imports does not change after depreciation and the *foreign exchange* value of imports is constant. In this case the demand for foreign exchange is perfectly inelastic (zero), and depreciation neither helps nor worsens the balance of payments on the demand side.

Figure 10-4 (page 242) illustrates these two cases.

The elasticity of import demand will tend to be high when the composition of imports is heavily weighted with luxury-type consumer goods (such as automobiles and household equipment) and expensive capital goods

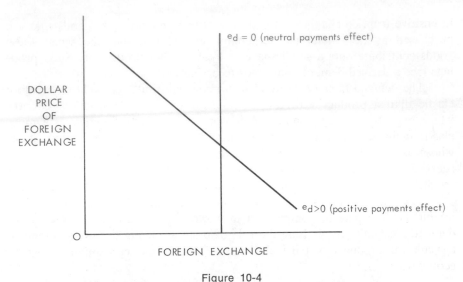

Figure 10-4

ELASTICITIES OF FOREIGN EXCHANGE DEMAND

(such as heavy machinery and transport equipment). Conversely, elasticity will tend to be low when most imports are raw materials, foodstuffs, and semimanufactures. Another factor is the degree of substitutability between import goods and domestic goods. When domestic substitutes are widely available at reasonable prices, then higher domestic prices for imports after depreciation will cause a switch to domestic sources of supply, thereby increasing the elasticity of import demand.

ELASTICITIES OF EXPORT AND IMPORT SUPPLY

In our analysis of the demand elasticities of exports and imports, we assumed that export and import *supply* elasticities were infinite or perfectly elastic. Thus, the domestic price of exports and the foreign exchange price of imports did not respond to depreciation. This is an unrealistic assumption and we must now take account of less-than-perfect elasticities of export and import supply.

The significance of supply elasticities may be understood if we make another unrealistic assumption, namely, perfectly inelastic (zero) export and import supplies. In that event depreciation has *no effect* on the balance of payments *regardless* of the demand elasticities. An export supply of zero elasticity means that the quantity of exports cannot be increased. Hence, a depreciation of 10 percent is promptly offset by a 10 percent *increase* in the domestic export price as foreign buyers bid for the same quantity of export goods. Thus, the *foreign exchange* price of exports remains the same and there is no change in foreign exchange receipts. Similarly, an import supply of zero elasticity means that a 10 percent depreciation is promptly matched by a 10 percent cut in the foreign exchange price of imports as foreign suppliers strive to maintain sales in the depreciating country. Thus, the domestic price of imports stays the same after depreciation and there is no effect on foreign exchange expenditures.

It would be tedious to recount the many combinations of demand and supply elasticities and their effects on the balance of payments. Suffice it to say that when demand elasticities are high, the effects of depreciation are most beneficial if supply elasticities are also high. Then lower foreign exchange export prices can expand exports and higher domestic import prices can contract imports. On the other hand, when demand elasticities are low, depreciation is most beneficial (or least harmful) if supply elasticities are low, for then foreign exchange export prices fall less and domestic import prices rise less than otherwise.

WHEN IS EXCHANGE DEPRECIATION SUCCESSFUL?

If the foreign exchange market is in stable equilibrium, then depreciation lessens or eliminates a deficit in the balance of payments as shown in Figures 10-1 and 10-2. But if the foreign exchange market is in *unstable* equilibrium, then depreciation hurts rather than helps the balance of payments in deficit. Figure 10-5 shows that unstable equilibrium occurs when the supply schedule cuts the demand schedule from *above*.[6]

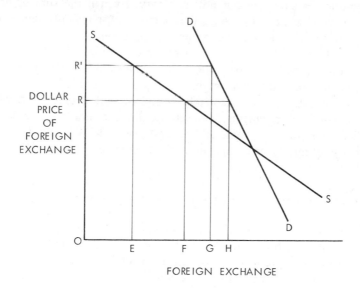

Figure 10-5

UNSTABLE EQUILIBRIUM IN THE FOREIGN EXCHANGE MARKET

---

[6] In that event the sum of the supply and demand elasticities is negative. See Figures 10-3 and 10-4.

At the exchange rate O-R, foreign exchange demanded exceeds foreign exchange supplied by F-H. In the attempt to wipe out this deficit the exchange rate is depreciated to O-R'. But this only makes matters worse as the deficit increases in size to E-G.

What, then, is the requirement for stable equilibrium in terms of export and import elasticities? Depreciation *always* helps to lessen a deficit in the balance of payments if the sum of the export and import demand elasticities is greater than one, that is, $e_x + e_m > 1$. This is known as the Marshall-Lerner condition and we may demonstrate its validity by citing two extreme examples. (The Marshall-Lerner condition assumes perfect elasticities of export and import *supply*.) Suppose the elasticity of export demand is zero and there is a 10 percent depreciation. Then foreign exchange receipts drop 10 percent, but if import demand elasticity is greater than one, foreign exchange expenditures decrease by more than 10 percent. Thus, the deficit becomes less. Again, suppose the elasticity of import demand is zero. Then foreign exchange expenditures do not change after depreciation, but if export demand elasticity is greater than one, a 10 percent depreciation leads to a greater than 10 percent increase in the quantity of exports and consequently an increase in foreign exchange receipts. Once again, the balance of payments improves.

When we introduce supply elasticities we discover that the Marshall-Lerner condition is sufficient but not necessary. Even if the sum of demand elasticities is somewhat below one, the balance of payments can improve provided that the supply elasticities are small enough.

What is the probability that the demand elasticities of exports and imports of a country will add to a sum greater than one? Today most economists believe the probability is high. As far as elasticities are concerned, therefore, a country can be reasonably confident that depreciation will improve its balance of payments. But elasticities are not the whole story. Depreciation also induces income and general price effects in the depreciating country that may nullify or compromise its effectiveness in remedying a payments deficit.

INCOME AND PRICE EFFECTS OF DEPRECIATION

In Chapter 9 we stated that adjustment to a payments deficit under full-employment conditions calls for a reduction in *real* domestic expenditure regardless of whether adjustment occurs in a stable-rate or a variable-rate system. Recall equation (13) in Chapter 9:

$$X - M = GNP - (C + I_d + G).$$

This can be simplified by letting $X - M = B$ (balance on current account), $Y = GNP$, and $C + I_d + G = A$ (domestic absorption). Then:

$$B = Y - A.$$

When B is in deficit (negative), then A exceeds Y. Adjustment to a deficit demands, therefore, either (1) an increase in real Y, or (2) a decrease in real A. Since physical output cannot be expanded in the short run with full employment, adjustment to a deficit in such a situation requires a reduction in the real absorption of goods and services (an *increase* in real saving) to allow for higher exports and lower imports.

As we have seen in Chapter 9, income adjustment to a deficit involves a fall in the level of aggregate demand. Thus, income adjustment via the foreign trade multiplier or via restrictive monetary and fiscal policies (the domestic multiplier) is *expenditure-reducing*. In contrast, exchange depreciation is *expenditure-switching*: it shifts domestic expenditures from imports to import-substitutes and shifts foreign expenditures to the country's exports via import and export elasticities. Where does the real output come from to support this expenditure switch? With full employment it can come only from a reduction in domestic absorption (A) that releases resources for the production of export and import-competing goods. Putting the matter somewhat differently, depreciation with full employment can only be successful if it is accompanied by an increase in domestic saving that matches the improvement in the balance of payments.[7] Can depreciation be expected to bring about the requisite increase in saving? The general answer is negative because depreciation exerts no direct influence on saving.

In failing to increase saving and thereby decrease domestic absorption, depreciation with full employment will cause an inflationary rise in the price level that will partly or fully offset its initial effects on exports and imports. When depreciation raises exports and lowers imports, it injects income into the domestic economy and starts a cumulative expansion of money income through the operation of the foreign trade multiplier. This higher money income stimulates higher expenditures on domestic goods whose supply cannot be expanded under full employment. The consequence, therefore, is inflation. If this general price rise is of the same order as the depreciation (say 10 percent), then the initial effects of depreciation are completely vitiated and the payments deficit remains the same. Depreciation may also stimulate a general price rise on the cost side. Higher domestic prices paid for imports of raw materials, capital equipment, and the like may impose an upward pressure on domestic costs of production and the price level. The higher prices of imported consumer goods may encourage labor unions to ask for higher wages; and, in countries where the wages of most workers are linked to a consumer price index, higher wages inevitably result when there is a substantial dependence upon such imports.[8]

---

[7] Recall that $X - M = S - I_d$. Assuming that I_d is autonomous, then a change in $X - M$ requires an equal change in S in the same direction, or $d(X - M) = dS$.

[8] In addition to general price effects, depreciation causes shifts in *relative* prices such as occur in a stable-rate system. Briefly, the domestic prices of exports and imports rise relative to the prices of domestic goods. This stimulates a movement of resources into the export and import-competing sectors of the economy. Unlike the general price effects, these relative price effects are part of the adjustment process.

Under full employment conditions, therefore, the income and price effects of depreciation limit its effectiveness, and in some instances they may nullify it entirely. Exchange-rate adjustment provides an initial impulse for a switch in a country's resources from domestic to external use, but it does not guarantee that such a switch will actually take place. Hence, expenditure-switching policies must be supported by expenditure-reducing policies. Unless the domestic government contracts real absorption through monetary, fiscal, and (possibly) wage-price policies, depreciation can only lead to inflation and a perpetuation of the balance of payments deficit.

Because of its price and income effects, depreciation is likely to be more effective in removing a payments deficit when the domestic economy has substantial unemployment and excess capacity. Then the rise in money income and expenditure provoked by the depreciation will cause an expansion of real gross national product (Y). As noted earlier, governments tried to utilize the "employment effect" of depreciation by overdepreciating their currencies in the 1930's. In this situation it may be possible to have one's cake and eat it too; that is, to achieve an improvement in the balance of payments and an increase in real domestic expenditure at the same time. But this does not necessarily happen, because some of the increase in real expenditure induces higher imports via the marginal propensity to import. Even under conditions of widespread unemployment and excess capacity, therefore, the effectiveness of depreciation may be constrained by its income effects, although these are unlikely to fully offset its elasticity effects.

To conclude, depreciation under full employment conditions can effect adjustment in the balance of payments only when it is accompanied by expenditure-reducing policies that contract real domestic absorption. In the absence of such policies, depreciation will simply cause inflation that will nullify its initial balance of payments effects. Successful depreciation demands, therefore, more than a manipulation of the exchange rate; it must be part of a broader policy of international adjustment.

THE EFFECT OF DEPRECIATION ON THE TERMS OF TRADE

Exchange depreciation improves the balance of payments if its direct effects are not neutralized by income and price effects that prevent a decline in domestic real expenditure. However, the effects of depreciation on the commodity terms of trade are uncertain.[9]

It may seem obvious that depreciation *worsens* the terms of trade of the depreciating country: the foreign exchange price of its exports drops while the foreign exchange price of its imports usually stays the same. But this price behavior is by no means certain. We can see why if we understand that an exchange depreciation of, say, 10 percent is equivalent to a *duty* of 10 percent on all imports and a *subsidy* of 10 percent on all exports. An

---

[9] For a definition of the commodity terms of trade, see Footnote 12 in Chapter 3.

import tariff tends to *improve* the terms of trade by lowering the foreign exchange price of imports, but an export subsidy tends to *worsen* the terms of trade by lowering the foreign exchange price of exports. The *net* effect of *both* duty and subsidy on the terms of trade depends on the interaction of the supply and demand elasticities of both imports and exports.

The general rule states that a depreciation worsens the terms of trade if the product of the two supply elasticities is *greater* than the product of the two demand elasticities, or $(e_{sx})(e_{sm}) > (e_{dx})(e_{dm})$. Otherwise, the terms of trade remain unchanged (the two products are equal) or improve (the product of the two supply elasticities is *less* than the product of the two demand elasticities).

THE ARGUMENT FOR FLEXIBLE EXCHANGE RATES

In Chapter 7 we noted some of the arguments for stable exchange rates. We now turn the tables and present the argument for variable or flexible exchange rates.

There is a strong theoretical case for fluctuating exchange rates. In highly simplified terms, it assumes this form. In a stable-rate system, adjustment to a deficit is carried out by deflationary movements in domestic income and prices that contract real expenditure. All goes well if wages and prices are flexible downward, for then employment and output are sustained at their previous levels. But if wages and prices are *inflexible downward,* then a contraction in real expenditure involves a fall in employment and output. There is abundant evidence indicating that the second course of events is the more likely to happen in contemporary national economies. Unions set floors under wages that are supplemented by official minimum wage policies; oligopolistic industries set administered prices that do not respond to a decline in effective demand that is met instead by a cutback in production. Under these conditions long-run adjustment in a stable-rate system will cause a downward spiral in employment and output. On the other hand, governments are pledged to the maintenance of a fully employed economy. Hence, they will act to frustrate any deflation induced by a deficit in the balance of payments by making use of expansionary fiscal and monetary policies that sustain the level of real expenditure necessary to full employment.

Given contemporary government policies with respect to employment and economic stability, then, long-run adjustment in a stable-rate system is not likely to be effective. There are two ways out of this impasse: (1) impose controls on trade and payments, or (2) devalue the rate of exchange. Controls, however, are incompatible with a market economy, and they provoke hostility and retaliation in foreign countries. We are left, then, with depreciation or, more comprehensively, variable exchange rates as the only mode of payments adjustment that is compatible both with domestic full-employment policies and the principle of free competition in world markets. Free exchange rates respond to disequilibrating forces and achieve a continuous adjustment in the balance of payments. This gives governments the freedom to follow domestic policies of full employment and growth without worrying about payments deficits.

The theoretical argument for an adjustable-peg system is less strong because adjustment in the exchange rate is apt to be delayed, and the degree of rate variation is determined by a government under circumstances that make the choice of the correct equilibrium rate a very difficult one. Delay in depreciating the exchange rate to correct a deficit is likely to occur in an adjustable-peg system for several reasons. The government often demonstrates a "stable-rate complex" and makes the mistake of identifying its prestige with the maintenance of the existing rate. Or the government may repeatedly postpone rate adjustment in the renewed expectation that the disequilibrium will prove to be "temporary" after all. Or, having decided in principle on depreciation, the government may take a long time to reach a political consensus on the appropriate amount of depreciation. All this adds up to the fact that there is a strong probability that a government will put off depreciation until it is forced to act because its reserves of gold and foreign exchange are running out and its international credit is exhausted. By that time it is clear to everyone that depreciation (or controls) is imminent, and this will stimulate a massive capital flight and destabilizing speculation that will intensify the drain on reserves. In these circumstances a government may feel compelled to undertake a very large depreciation in order to put a stop to speculative activity. In the end the government depreciates the exchange rate and blames the speculators for its troubles.

To sum up, in an adjustable-peg system depreciation to eliminate a deficit is likely to come too late and be too big. Moreover, the deficit country must do most of the adjusting because there is little or no incentive for surplus countries to *appreciate* their exchange rates. These drawbacks do not appear in a fluctuating-rate system shared by several countries: the exchange rates of all countries respond quickly to disturbances, and these prompt adjustments sustain a continuing equilibrium in international payments.

Despite the strong theoretical case for flexible exchange rates, governments and central bankers have been traditionally hostile to a fluctuating-rate system.[10] Unfortunately, the reputation of fluctuating rates has suffered from bad company in the past. In this century fluctuating rates involving several major currencies have appeared two times, but only by default: in the period following World War I before European countries returned to the gold standard in the middle twenties, and in the 1930's when global depression forced the wholesale abandonment of the international gold standard. Grave instability in international trade and payments characterized both periods. Not surprisingly, speculation and capital flight were rife; exchange rates behaved erratically, making sharp and sudden movements.

---

[10] For a further discussion of this point, see Chapter 20.

Thus, fluctuating exchange rates came to be associated with instability, speculation, and generally bad times.

The rebuttal of this presumed association is that there is here a confusion of symptom and cause. When underlying conditions are very unstable, then exchange rates will mirror this instability. The same conditions will provoke capital flight and unwanted shifts in domestic income and prices in a stable-rate system. When underlying conditions are only moderately unstable, then fluctuations in exchange rates will also be moderate.

There is also a widespread belief that fluctuating rates introduce exchange risks that hinder international trade and investment. The rebuttal argument is that forward exchange markets quickly develop in a fluctuating-rate system, making possible the hedging of foreign exchange risks. Moreover, there are trading risks of another kind in a stable-rate system caused by income and price adjustments, to say nothing of trade restrictions stemming from a failure, or rather frustration, of the market adjustment process.

SUMMARY

1. There are many possible kinds of variable-rate systems, ranging from a fluctuating-rate system to an adjustable-peg system. In a fluctuating-rate system movements in the exchange rate achieve a continuing equilibrium in the balance of payments. In the adjustable-peg system exchange rates are occasionally varied by government action from one stable level to another, and the choice of a new equilibrium rate is difficult. In the latter, the purchasing-power parity doctrine is of limited usefulness.

2. The initial effects of depreciation on the balance of payments depend on the elasticities of demand and supply of both exports and imports. Depreciation *always* improves the balance of payments when the sum of export and import demand elasticities is greater than one (Marshall-Lerner condition). Even if this sum is below one, depreciation improves the balance of payments provided supply elasticities are small enough.

3. Depreciation also has effects on domestic income and prices that tend to counteract its initial effects by sustaining the level of domestic real expenditure. Unless government policy firmly restrains inflation in a fully employed economy, depreciation only leads to further depreciation or to tighter controls. Even under conditions of widespread unemployment, depreciation must be buttressed by government action to restrain imports.

4. The effect of depreciation on the commodity terms of trade is uncertain. It depends on the size of the product of the two supply elasticities of exports and imports as compared with the product of their demand elasticities.

5. The basic argument for fluctuating exchange rates is that they are the most effective means of market adjustment to balance of payments disequilibrium in the kind of world in which we live. It is alleged by proponents of fluctuating rates that long-run adjustment in a stable-rate system is likely to be vitiated by domestic government policies of full employment and stability. The theoretical argument for an adjustable-peg system is less strong because exchange rate adjustment is apt to come too late and be too big.

QUESTIONS AND APPLICATIONS

1. (a) How do short- and long-run adjustments occur in a fluctuating-rate system?
   (b) How do they occur in an adjustable-peg system?

2. (a) Assuming infinite supply elasticities, construct a graph to show the effects of depreciation when the elasticity of export demand is zero and the elasticity of import demand is zero. Does depreciation improve the balance of payments?
   (b) Using graphs, show how the effectiveness of exchange depreciation is determined by the elasticities of the supply and demand of foreign exchange.
   (c) What is the Marshall-Lerner condition?

3. (a) Trace the effects of depreciation on domestic income and prices under both full-employment and less-than-full-employment conditions.
   (b) Why do these effects call for government action? What kind?

4. "The effect of depreciation on the commodity terms of trade is uncertain." Explain.

5. What is the basic argument for flexible exchange rates? Why have governments traditionally opposed flexible exchange rates?

SELECTED READINGS

Corden, W. M. *Recent Developments in the Theory of International Trade.* Special Papers in International Economics No. 7. Princeton: Princeton University Press, 1965. Chapter 1.

Friedman, Milton. "The Case for Flexible Exchange Rates." In *Essays in Positive Economics,* pp. 157-87. Chicago: The University of Chicago Press, 1953.

Haberler, Gottfried. *A Survey of International Trade Theory.* Special Papers in International Economics No. 1. Princeton: Princeton University Press, 1961. Chapter 5.

International Monetary Fund. *The Role of Exchange Rates in the Adjustment of International Payments.* A Report by the Executive Directors. Washington: International Monetary Fund, 1970.

Johnson, Harry G. "Towards a General Theory of the Balance of Payments." In *International Trade and Economic Growth: Studies in Pure Theory,* pp. 153-68. Cambridge: Harvard University Press, 1961. Reprinted in Caves, Richard E., and Harry G. Johnson (eds.). *Readings in International Economics.* Homewood, Ill.: Richard D. Irwin, Inc., 1968.

Nurkse, Ragnar. *Conditions of International Monetary Equilibrium.* Essays in International Finance No. 4. Princeton: Princeton University Press, 1945. Reprinted in Ellis, Howard S., and Lloyd D. Metzler (eds.). *Readings in the Theory of International Trade.* Philadelphia: The Blakiston Co., 1949.

Snider, Delbert A. *Optimum Adjustment Processes and Currency Areas.* Essays in International Finance No. 62. Princeton: Princeton University Press, 1967.

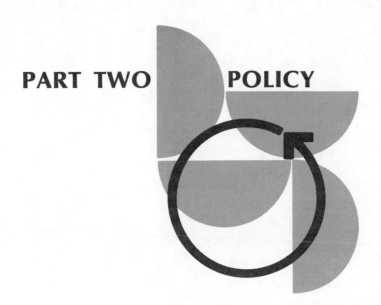

PART TWO POLICY

The theory of comparative advantage demonstrates the gains from international specialization through free trade. Nonetheless, governments are inclined to treat their international economic relations from the perspective of narrowly conceived national interests that commonly ignore the interests of the community of nations. Unfortunately, this approach to economic policy creates more problems than it pretends to solve. In Part Two we explore the causes of this reluctance to adjust policy to theory, and appraise the consequences of trade and exchange restrictions. We also evaluate efforts to liberalize and strengthen international trade and payments through many forms of international cooperation. Special attention is paid to the policies of the United States, the European Economic Community, and the developing countries. Part Two concludes with an examination of international monetary and payments policies which have overshadowed trade and foreign assistance policies in recent years.

CHAPTER 11

THE GOALS AND INSTRUMENTS OF FOREIGN ECONOMIC POLICY

The rationale of government economic policies throughout the world is that national economies, if left alone, would fail to achieve goals which are deemed to be in the national interest, such as full employment, a "satisfactory" rate of growth, an equitable distribution of income, and a "strong" balance of payments. Basically, therefore, national economic policies may be viewed as a rejection in whole or in part of the social virtues of an atomistic, laissez-faire economy, in which levels of economic activity and resource allocation are determined by impersonal market forces with only a minimal government presence.

Although governments have sought to influence the internal and external behavior of national economies since the birth of the nation-state in the sixteenth century, the goals and instruments of their policies have frequently shifted over time. Up to the middle of the nineteenth century, the major countries for the most part followed mercantilistic policies that aimed to advance power-political interests through a variety of controls on international trade and factor movements. The subsequent period that ended in World War I was marked by the ascendancy of a belief in the blessings of free, unfettered markets. Governments relied on monetary policy to smooth the operation of the international gold standard and generally relaxed or abandoned restrictions on external trade while at home they accepted with equanimity the ups and downs of the business cycle. The global depression of the 1930's ended this laissez-faire posture as governments everywhere undertook a variety of policy measures to stimulate economic recovery at home and to insulate the domestic economy from external influences. In the 1930's economic nationalism ran rampant, international cooperation almost disappeared, and international trade was throttled by tariffs, quotas, exchange control, and other devices. In our own day, national governments are committed to a broad range of economic goals that they try to achieve in a world of growing economic interdependence.

WHAT IS FOREIGN ECONOMIC POLICY?

Because there is no clear-cut distinction between a government's foreign and domestic policies, we may conceive foreign economic policy either broadly or narrowly, depending on our purposes.

A BROAD DEFINITION

Broadly conceived, foreign economic policy embraces all of the varied activities of national governments that bear, directly or indirectly, upon the composition, direction, and magnitude of international trade and factor flows. This conception of foreign economic policy covers not only such obvious examples as tariff policy, but also domestic governmental measures, such as monetary and fiscal policy, which have an impact upon foreign trade and investment. Since economic activity is characterized by a mutual interdependence, there are few, if any, economic policies of government that have only domestic effects.

Because of the signal importance of the American economy in the world, the economic policies of the United States government, whether ostensibly domestic or foreign, are of particular significance to the well-being of the world economy. Probably the greatest single contribution that our government can make toward the promotion and development of world trade and investment is the pursuit of policies at home that insure the stable growth of the American economy. In this sense the fiscal and monetary policies of the government are more basic to United States foreign economic policy than, for example, its much touted actions in the field of tariff negotiation.

Just as policies undertaken to achieve domestic goals (such as full employment) will have repercussions on a country's external economic relations, so will policies undertaken with respect to foreign trade, foreign aid, foreign investment, and the balance of payments have repercussions on the level, composition, and growth of national output and income, on employment, on prices, and on other aspects of the domestic economy.

In terms of effects, therefore, it is impossible to classify government policies as exclusively domestic or exclusively foreign. Instead, they may be regarded as occupying different positions along a continuum that stretches between an "internal effects" pole and an "external effects" pole. Policies that have only insignificant effects on foreign trade and investment (such as government subsidies for housing) are close to the "internal effects" pole while policies that have insignificant domestic effects (such as lowering a revenue duty on an imported good) are close to the "external effects" pole.

Most government policies, however, fall between these two poles, and growing international interdependence is pushing more and more policies toward the center.

A NARROWER DEFINITION

The interdependence of domestic and foreign economic policy (however defined) is a truth that must be kept in mind throughout our study of international trade and investment. Unfortunately for the peace of mind of those people who like to think in watertight compartments, the political boundary of a nation cannot serve to demarcate domestic and foreign interests. For reasons of space and analytical convenience, in Part Two we are compelled to limit foreign economic policy to the activities of government that are *intended* to regulate, restrict, promote, or otherwise influence the conduct of international trade and investment. While employing this narrower definition in our subsequent description and analysis of foreign economic policy, we do not propose to neglect its close relationship with domestic economic policy.

FOREIGN ECONOMIC POLICY AND PRIVATE INTERESTS

The foreign economic policy of governments is pervasive; it affects all of our lives in a number of ways—as consumers, as producers, and as citizens of a nation which itself is a member of the community of nations. Restrictive government policy forces us as consumers to pay a higher price for many imported goods and, at times, to do without them. On the other hand, liberal government policy enables us to reap the advantages of international specialization. As domestic producers we may be benefited or hurt by specific aspects of foreign economic policy depending upon our place in the economy. As international traders and producers we may be thwarted in our efforts to sell and produce in foreign countries by policies that keep us out or limit our opportunities. As international lenders or borrowers we may be encouraged or constrained by government policies at home or abroad. Finally, the foreign economic policy of our government may earn us the goodwill and support of other nations, or it may provoke mistrust and retaliation.

Although we cannot escape the impact of the foreign economic policy of our government and others upon our lives and fortunes, we are usually ignorant of its source. The bearing of this policy on our interests as consumers is ordinarily indirect and can be traced only by careful economic analysis. Certainly the man on the street is unaware of the relationship between foreign economic policy and the availability and prices of the goods and services that comprise his standard of living—particularly in the United

States. Consequently, most of us care little about the foreign economic policy of our own government and few of us seek to change it.

The situation is far different for business enterprises that are directly engaged in international trade and investment or that face competition from imports. They know well that government actions in the world economy may spell the difference between profit and loss. Hence, they take steps to influence foreign economic policy in the direction that best accords with their interests. Because of the apathy of the general public, the individuals and groups that have an obvious financial stake in the foreign economic policy of their governments have been able to exert an extraordinary influence on policy formation. The effectiveness of protectionist lobbies in Washington and elsewhere is a good example.

The excessive weight given to private vested interests in the formulation and execution of foreign economic policy is not only undemocratic but also represents a yielding of the national interest to the individual interest. Above our own individual welfare lies the welfare of the nation and the welfare of the community of nations, and, in the last analysis, they are inseparable. Enlightened self-interest demands, therefore, that we take full account of national and international interests in the formulation of foreign economic policy. To do so we must learn to evaluate foreign economic policy in the light of these broad perspectives.

THE GOALS OF FOREIGN ECONOMIC POLICY

There are several ways to classify the goals that nations may strive to achieve in their foreign economic policy, and few classifications are apt to be exhaustive or mutually exclusive. We do not intend to catalog the many ends of foreign economic policy; but, in order to illustrate their rich diversity, we have chosen for discussion seven of the most fundamental goals. At this time we are not interested in an analysis of these goals; our purpose is simply one of identification.

AUTARKY

At one extreme is the objective of *autarky* or national self-sufficiency. A full autarkic policy aims to rid the nation of all dependence on international trade and investment because this dependence is feared for economic, political, or military reasons. Autarky is clearly inconsistent with the continuance of economic relations with other countries; the political counterpart of autarky is isolationism.

Of course, most nations do not possess the domestic resources that are required to practice any significant degree of autarky. More common is a qualified autarkic policy that seeks self-sufficiency in only certain articles of trade, generally of a strategic military value.

ECONOMIC WELFARE

At the opposite extreme to autarky lies the goal of economic welfare that springs from a conception of international trade and investment as an opportunity to reap the gains of international specialization. In Part One we presented the cogent economic reasoning that underlies this conception of trade. Foreign economic policy in which the objective of economic welfare plays a leading role seeks to expand international trade and investment by lowering or eliminating tariffs and other barriers to promote the free exchange of goods, services, and factors. As noted above, this liberal philosophy of trade was dominant in the period preceding World War I, when the United Kingdom, the paramount trading nation at that time, espoused a policy of free trade and most other nations used only the tariff in controlling trade. Since World War II, economic welfare has emerged once again as a prominent goal in the foreign economic policies of the industrial countries of the West.

PROTECTIONISM

Between the two extremes—autarky, which would regulate foreign trade out of existence, and free trade, which would impose no restrictions whatsoever— there are many other goals that serve to motivate foreign economic policy. Chief among them is protectionism, the protection of domestic producers against the free competition of imports by regulating their volume through tariffs, quotas, and the like. Identification of a specific foreign economic policy as protectionist is sometimes difficult, since any policy that restricts imports has protectionist effects regardless of its objective. Protectionism, therefore, has many guises and it shows a remarkable ability to adjust to new circumstances by employing arguments and stratagems suited to the times.

FULL-EMPLOYMENT STABILITY
(INTERNAL BALANCE)

Since the 1930's, stability of the economy at full-employment levels has been among the most important objectives of national economic policy. Contemporary governments have committed themselves in many ways to chart safely the national economy between the Charybdis of inflation, on the one hand, and the Scylla of deflation and unemployment, on the other. When the aim of full-employment stability dominates the foreign economic policy of a nation, international trade and capital movements are viewed as both a source of disturbances to the domestic economy and a means of compensating for disturbances originating within the economy. Whether foreign trade and capital movements are restricted or encouraged depends mostly upon current levels of domestic economic activity.

BALANCE OF PAYMENTS EQUILIBRIUM (EXTERNAL BALANCE)

Sooner or later, all nations are compelled to remedy deficits in their balance of payments, whether through market adjustments or controls. When a nation's reserves are low and its balance of payments is weak, the objective of payments equilibrium may come to dominate other objectives of its foreign economic policy and even of its domestic policy. In the decade following World War II, the elimination of the dollar shortage occupied first place among the foreign economic policy objectives of Western European countries. In more recent years the United States balance of payments problem has come to overshadow the other foreign economic issues of this country. As we shall observe, balance of payments policy may conflict with domestic policies of full employment and growth.

ECONOMIC DEVELOPMENT

Today the nonindustrial countries of Asia, Africa, and Latin America are desperately striving to accelerate their economic growth and to raise the living standards of their peoples. The pressing concern of these nations with the mammoth problem of economic development has led their governments to regard international trade as an instrument to achieve such development to the exclusion of other ends. Thus, tariffs and other restrictive devices are employed to protect "infant industries" or to keep out "nonessential" consumer goods. On the other hand, capital goods and other "essential" imports are encouraged by subsidies or favorable exchange quotas. Exports may also be regulated in an attempt to promote economic development. Aside from these direct measures of control, economic development programs are likely to provoke disequilibrium in the balance of payments because of their inflationary impact on domestic income and price levels. Further controls may then be imposed to suppress the disequilibrium.

ECONOMIC WARFARE

During periods of actual warfare the international economic policies of nations are directed toward the overriding objective of winning the war. Even in the absence of armed conflict, however, economic warfare is often among the goals of international economic policy. We live in a time of political tensions between great powers, and it is to be expected that these powers should use foreign economic policy to further their own political and military advantages and to limit the advantages of those opposed to their vital interests. Thus, the United States and its allies impose strategic controls on trade with the Communist countries, and the latter follow a similar course of action against the United States. Foreign aid programs are also used to implement political objectives; indeed, the full range of foreign economic policy comes under the influence of this political contest among nations.

The injection of political and military considerations into international economic policy is nothing new. After all, foreign economic policy is part of the foreign policy of the nation and it is inevitably colored to some degree by national political aims. But the degree of coloring is important, and after the comparatively liberal international economic policy of the nineteenth century, the emergence of economic warfare in our own century appears as an abnormal state of affairs to many observers.

THE INSTRUMENTS OF FOREIGN ECONOMIC POLICY

Foreign economic policy involves instruments as well as goals. In accordance with our decision to use a narrower interpretation of the scope of foreign economic policy, we shall take policy instruments to signify the tools (market variables, such as exchange rates, and direct controls) that are employed by governments with the *intent* to influence the magnitude, composition, or direction of international trade and factor movements.

Much of the foreign economic policy of a nation is effected through agreements and treaties with other nations. For the most part, the legal rights that individuals and business enterprises enjoy in a foreign country are those spelled out in treaties and agreements previously negotiated by their own governments. Thus, international treaties and agreements determine the treatment to be accorded foreigners and foreign interests. Generally speaking, this treatment is either *national* or *most-favored-nation* treatment. Under national treatment, foreigners possess the same rights as nationals. National treatment extends chiefly to the protection of life and property; no Mexican policeman, for instance, would ask for a birth certificate before coming to the rescue of a person in trouble. Most-favored-nation treatment is based on a different concept of equity; it means that a nation treats a second nation as favorably as it treats any third nation. The main purpose of most-favored-nation treatment is to eliminate national discrimination. Its greatest application is in the field of tariffs and other measures of commercial policy.[1]

The instruments of foreign economic policy exhibit a broad variety, and it will prove helpful to examine them in terms of four broad policy areas, three of which deal with different segments of the balance of payments and one, with the balance of payments as a whole.

Figure 11-1 lists these policy areas together with the principal policy instruments that are available to governments of countries with market economies.[2] The dots indicate the policy instruments that are *primarily* associated with each policy area. However, it would be a mistake to identify

---

[1] See Chapter 15.

[2] The policy instruments available to governments in the centrally planned economies of Eastern Europe, the Soviet Union, and mainland China take the form of official edicts and administrative decisions with only a very limited reliance on market instruments, especially in foreign economic policy.

	Commercial Policy	Investment Policy	Foreign Aid Policy	Balance of Payments Policy
INSTRUMENTS / AREAS				
Tariffs	●			
Non-tariff trade barriers	●			
Export promotion	●			
Foreign investment restrictions		●		
Foreign investment inducements		●		
Official grants and loans			●	
Fiscal				●
Monetary				●
Exchange-rate adjustment				●
Exchange control				●

Figure 11-1

AREAS AND INSTRUMENTS OF FOREIGN ECONOMIC POLICY

a policy area with a particular set of policy instruments, for many of them may be used to achieve different policy goals depending on the circumstances. In particular, balance of payments policy may utilize *all* of the policy instruments shown in Figure 11-1. Actually, these policy instruments are more accurately defined as "policy instrument types" since each consists of several specific policy tools. For instance, nontariff trade barriers include quotas, border taxes, customs procedures, antidumping regulations, domestic subsidies, and others.

COMMERCIAL POLICY

Commercial policy refers to all government actions that seek to alter current account transactions, especially trade in merchandise. Historically, the main instrument of commercial policy has been the import tariff, but today nontariff barriers and export promotion are often of equal or of greater importance.

INVESTMENT POLICY

Investment policy covers government actions both with respect to international long-term lending and borrowing (portfolio investment) and with respect to the international movement of business enterprise, which involves not only capital, but management and technology as well (direct investment). Ordinarily, the governments of investing nations restrict investment outflows only for balance of payments reasons (as is true of the United States); more commonly, they promote direct investment outflows via inducements of one sort or another. On the other hand, although the governments of borrowing or host nations seldom deter inflows of portfolio investment, they frequently do so in the case of certain forms of direct investment while at the same time encouraging other forms. Because of the rapid development of multinational companies that produce and sell throughout the world, foreign investment policy has assumed a critical importance for both home and host countries.

FOREIGN AID POLICY

Foreign aid policy includes all of the activities involved in the field of governmental loans and grants that are intended to aid in the reconstruction, economic development, or military defense of the recipient country. Compared to the other policies, foreign aid policy is a newcomer; it was born out of the vicissitudes of the early postwar period when Europe lay economically prostrate. Later, a recognition of the obligation to help in the development of the economically backward countries of the world provided another stimulus to foreign aid policy. Simultaneously, the threat of the cold war gave rise to large-scale United States programs of military and economic aid that sought to buttress the free world against internal and external Communist aggression. Today, assistance for economic development is the most pervasive rationale for foreign aid. All of the industrial countries, many international organizations, and even the Communist countries now have aid programs that transfer resources to the developing countries.

Foreign aid involves a host of problems for both the donor and recipient nations. When foreign aid consists of grants, the donor nation must decide such issues as how much to give, to whom to give, and how to control the use of the gift. Recipient nations must, at the very least, decide whether to accept foreign aid and how far they should go in cooperating with the donor nation as to its use. Considerations of national prestige and international politics complicate these matters.

BALANCE OF PAYMENTS POLICY

Balance of payments policy embraces all of the actions of governments to maintain or restore equilibrium in their external accounts. In the short run, as discussed in Chapter 9, governments rely primarily on compensatory financing by drawing down their own international reserves and/or by borrowing from external sources in a variety of ways. In the face of an enduring, fundamental disequilibrium, however, governments must generally respond to a deficit (surplus) by (1) deflating (inflating) the domestic economy with monetary and fiscal instruments, or (2) devaluing (revaluing) the exchange rate, or (3) imposing exchange controls over some or all international transactions.[3] These basic instruments of adjustment may be used singly or in combination, and at times they may be rejected by governments in favor of policy instruments, such as tariffs and quantitative import restrictions, that are normally associated with other policy areas.

THE DIVERSITY AND CONFLICT OF GOALS

The goals of foreign economic policies are diverse on two counts: (1) each nation ordinarily pursues several goals simultaneously in its own foreign economic policy, and (2) the mix of goals pursued by one nation does not necessarily correspond to the goal mixes of other nations either over the short or long run. If these diverse goals could be successfully attained by each and every nation, there would be no need for our analysis of foreign economic policy. As is true of all human affairs, however, no single nation or group of nations can fully achieve the many objectives of its foreign economic policy. This failure stems from inconsistencies and conflicts among goals at both national and international levels and from inadequacies in policy instruments. Let us turn first to the question of goal conflict.

THE INTERNAL CONFLICT OF GOALS

Except possibly during a war, when the issue of national survival is paramount, no nation seeks to achieve a single objective in its foreign economic policy; rather, it has several objectives that reflect the complex needs and demands of the national society. A nation is made up of individuals and groups that occupy different positions in society, who do not equally benefit from the same economic events and government policies and who have, therefore, diverse economic views and interests. It is to be expected that individuals and groups will try to direct government policies toward goals that they deem beneficial. This conflict of interests is not easily resolved, and often a government resolves it in a way that satisfies one or another vested interest while the national interest is sacrificed on the altar of political expediency.

Two broad goal conflicts in particular are endemic in the foreign economic policy of nations: (1) internal versus external balance, and (2) protectionism versus free trade.

The goal of internal balance is a fully-employed economy with stable prices; the goal of external balance is equilibrium in the balance of payments. Inflation and recession are the two internal *im*balances while deficits

---

[3] Chapters 9 and 10 examined market adjustment to the balance of payments via changes in income, prices, and the exchange rate. Chapter 14 will look at exchange control.

and surpluses are the two external *im*balances. Conflict arises when the two goals become inconsistent so that an effort to achieve one goal renders more difficult or impossible the achievement of the other. Figure 11-2 depicts in summary fashion the incidence of conflict.

	BALANCE OF PAYMENTS →	Deficit	Surplus	Balance
DOMESTIC ECONOMY ↓	POLICY REQUIREMENT → Contraction	Expansion	None
Inflation	Contraction	No conflict 1.1	Conflict 1.2	Conflict 1.3
Recession	Expansion	Conflict 2.1	No conflict 2.2	Conflict 2.3
Balance	None	Conflict 3.1	Conflict 3.2	No conflict 3.3

Figure 11-2

THE INTERNAL CONFLICT OF GOALS: INTERNAL AND EXTERNAL BALANCE

The three conditions relating to internal balance (inflation, recession, and balance) combine with the three conditions relating to external balance (deficit, surplus, and balance) to make a 9 cell matrix whose entries indicate when the policy requirements for internal and external balance (contraction, expansion, or none) are consistent or in conflict. With generally inflationary situations in many countries, a common policy conflict is located in cell 1.2— inflation at home combined with a persistent balance of payments surplus. In 1969 West Germany tried to resolve this conflict by letting the mark appreciate in the foreign exchange market. In the late 1950's, early 1960's, and again in the early 1970's, the United States faced the policy conflict located in cell 2.1—unemployment at home with a persistent balance of payments deficit. This second policy dilemma is felt more keenly by governments than the first one because both unemployment and a balance of payments deficit are widely viewed as much more serious than inflation or a balance of payments surplus (which is often viewed as highly desirable).[4] We shall have more to say about policy conflicts between external and internal balance in Chapters 19 and 20.

Protectionism versus free trade is an age-old conflict in goals. Clearly, a nation cannot pursue a policy of free trade and at the same time protect

---

[4] Another critical policy conflict may arise out of slow economic growth and a weak balance of payments, an issue that has plagued Great Britain since World War II.

domestic industries against foreign competition. The justification of free trade is that it enables a nation to gain from international specialization while protectionism denies that proposition. And yet, nations are wont to subscribe to the principle of free trade and practice protectionism. The argument for free trade rests squarely on the theory of comparative advantage taken up in Part One; the instruments of, and arguments for, protection are examined in Chapter 13.

Many other instances of an internal conflict of goals will be encountered in subsequent chapters, such as the conflict in many developing countries between autarky (economic nationalism) and economic development.

THE EXTERNAL CONFLICT OF GOALS

Some countries are extremely dependent upon international trade for their economic livelihood; other countries approach varying degrees of self-sufficiency. Some countries are industrialized and enjoy a high standard of living; other countries are in the early stages of economic development and many of their people live close to starvation. Some national economies are organized on a private-enterprise basis; others have a feudalistic or socialistic basis of production. Some countries have strong balances of payments; others are hard pressed to meet their international obligations. These, and the many other differences that distinguish one nation from another, generate different attitudes and policies toward international trade and investment that are often in conflict. One nation may seek to take advantage of the gains from trade by lowering tariffs and other barriers, while other nations are raising barriers in order to protect domestic industry or to meet a drain on international reserves. Such conflicts of national interest abound in the historical and contemporary economic policies of nations.

It is important to understand that the external conflict of economic goals does not arise out of diversity as such but rather out of the interdependence of national economies. If all nations were to adopt a policy of full autarky, there could be no external conflict of economic goals because there would be no flows of goods and factors linking their economies. By the same token, any increase in the degree of international economic interdependence (such as is occurring today at a rapid pace) will heighten the probability of goal conflicts among economic policies that are determined at the national level. Interdependence calls into question the effectiveness of economic policies determined solely on the national level as opposed to the international level.

LESSENING THE CONFLICT OF GOALS

A great deal of international economic policy is made up of efforts to alleviate both the internal and external conflict of goals. Persuasion and compromise are the hallmarks of these efforts.

A nation must introduce order into its own foreign economic policy if it is to cooperate fruitfully with other nations. There must be a substantial measure of agreement by the government and the people (presumably the need for agreement by the people is not true of totalitarian governments) as to the relative importance of the competing objectives of foreign economic policy if effective action is to be taken. Otherwise an objective may be sacrificed willy-nilly in the attempt to attain a lesser one. This agreement, of course, is never complete; and even if it were, it would not guarantee a wise policy. Agreement must flow from the continuous processes of persuasion, education, and the spirit of compromise that lifts men out of the narrow vision of selfish interests.

Although the goals of foreign economic policy should be ordered into a hierarchy of priorities and degrees of importance in order to insure the minimum of coherence that is required of a successful program, there still remain the tasks of adjusting one goal to another, and the policy that results from this process is bound to displease the partisans of any specific goal. A successful foreign economic policy recognizes the principle that a number of half loaves is probably better, and certainly more attainable, than a single loaf.

The foreign economic policy of a nation must also be flexible in the mix of its goals if there is to be fruitful cooperation with other nations. Without this cooperation, the external conflict of goals will doom any foreign economic policy except one of outright self-sufficiency. Nations must be prepared to compromise a lesser end in order to achieve a greater end.

International agreements, like the General Agreement on Tariffs and Trade, are replete with exceptions that permit national behavior that is contradictory to the basic principles of the agreement. Without these compromises, international treaties and agreements would be impossible, and critics of such compromises must disavow any possibility of agreement if they honestly face the issues. Today, it is clear that the external conflict of goals will not be lessened except through understanding and compromise among nations, buttressed by formal treaties and agreements. If one accepts the belief that some lessening of this conflict is better than no lessening at all, he must also accept the spirit of compromise that is necessary to achieve it. As an ongoing process, cooperation can point the way toward *international* economic policies that will benefit all nations, not simply the few who are strong.

INADEQUACIES OF POLICY INSTRUMENTS: THE THEORY OF ECONOMIC POLICY

Even if the economic goals of a nation were both internally and externally consistent and each of the available policy instruments were effective, the government might fail to achieve those goals because its policy instruments were too few in number. To understand why this is so, let us turn to the theory of economic policy.[5]

The theory of economic policy postulates policy *instruments* and policy *targets*. An instrument is a variable that a government can manipulate to bring about a desired change in another variable that is the target of the policy action. To illustrate, a government may increase its spending (instrument variable) to raise employment levels (target variable) via the income multiplier. Or a government may devalue the exchange rate (instrument variable) to eliminate a balance of payments deficit (target variable). Instruments and targets are hierarchical; a target variable at one level may become an instrument variable at a higher level. A central bank may purchase securities in the open market (instrument variable) to lower interest rates (target variable). In turn, higher government authorities may consider lower interest rates as an instrument to attain a target level of private investment. Most target variables, therefore, are actually instruments to achieve the national policy goals discussed earlier in this chapter.

The fundamental proposition of the theory of economic policy is that for policy makers to achieve a given number of independent targets they must possess at least an equal number of effective instruments. If the number of effective instruments falls short of the number of targets, then some targets will not be reached; if the number of instruments exceeds the number of targets, then all targets may be reached in an infinite number of ways. Mathematically, a target variable is a function of one or more instrument variables.

To illustrate, suppose the government policy makers are trying to change one target variable (T) by manipulating two instrument variables (a,b). If the policy makers decide that the specific target level to aim for is T_1, then the policy will be successful when $T_1 = f(a,b)$. This function is plotted in Figure 11-3 (page 267).

Observe that an infinite number of combinations of a and b values may be used by the policy makers to achieve T_1, such as the a_1-b_2 combination or the a_2-b_1 combination. T_1, for instance, might be a desired import level of a specific good while a is an import duty variable and b an import quota variable. When the number of effective instruments exceeds the number of independent targets, government policy is very potent indeed!

But now suppose the policy makers are trying to reach two targets (T,S) with two instruments (a,b), and they set the specific target levels at T_1 and S_1. Then there are two equations in two unknowns with a determinate solution: $T_1 = f_1(a,b)$ and $S_1 = f_2(a,b)$. These two equations are plotted in Figure 11-4 (also on page 267).

In this situation, the policy makers must choose instrument values of a_1 and b_1 if they are to be able to achieve both targets. With any other set of

---

[5] For the classic exposition of this theory, see Jan Tinbergen, *On The Theory of Economic Policy* (Amsterdam: North Holland Publishing Co., 1952).

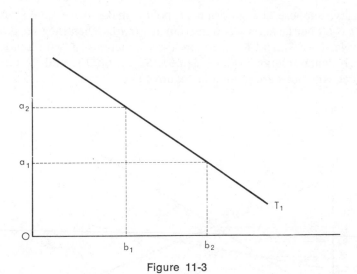

Figure 11-3

ECONOMIC POLICY: TWO INSTRUMENTS AND ONE TARGET

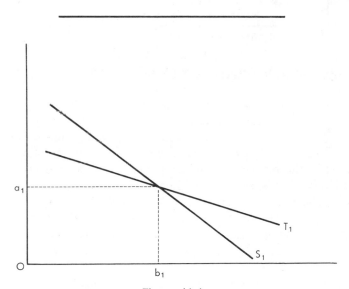

Figure 11-4

ECONOMIC POLICY: TWO INSTRUMENTS AND TWO TARGETS

instrument values, they will reach at most only one target. Only at the point of intersection are both targets satisfied. For example, T_1 might be a desired level of employment and S_1 a desired balance of payments level while a_1 is a specific value of the foreign exchange rate and b_1 a specific level of government expenditure.

Finally, suppose the government policy makers are aiming for three targets *(T,S,U)* but have only two instruments *(a,b)*. When they set the desired target levels at T_1, S_1, and U_1, there are three equations in two unknowns with an indeterminate solution: $T_1 = f_1(a,b)$; $S_1 = f_2(a,b)$; and $U_1 = f_3(a,b)$. These three equations are plotted in Figure 11-5.

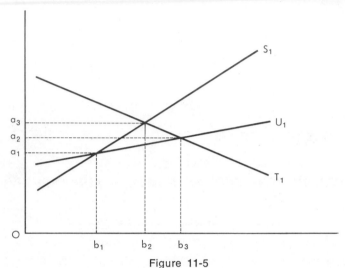

Figure 11-5

ECONOMIC POLICY: TWO INSTRUMENTS AND THREE TARGETS

Observe that at *none* of the three points of intersection are all three equations satisfied: instrument values a_1 and b_1 reach S_1 and U_1 but not T_1; values a_2 and b_3 reach T_1 and U_1 but not S_1; and values a_3 reach S_1 and T_1 but not U_1. T_1 is, say, a desired level of employment; S_1, a desired level in the balance of payments; and U_1, a desired rate of growth. Instrument variable *a* is, say, the exchange rate and *b* is government expenditure. Unless the policy makers can add a third effective policy instrument (say, the interest rate), they will have to abandon one target level or be satisfied with a compromise of some sort—somewhat less employment, a somewhat weaker balance of payments, and/or a somewhat slower growth rate.

The preceding analysis assumes that policy instruments are *effective* and policy targets are *consistent* with no internal and external conflicts. If neither of these assumptions hold, then an equal number of instrument and target variables becomes a *necessary* but not a *sufficient* condition for policy success. Policy instruments may be ineffective because of traditional, institutional, or political constraints. Policy makers ordinarily can vary, say, government spending, taxation, and interest rates only within fairly narrow limits before encountering formidable political opposition or other constraints. Policy instruments may also be rendered ineffective by lack of

Part Two / Policy

information and uncertainty: policy makers seldom know how a target variable will change over time in the absence of policy action, and they seldom know what the precise response of the target variable will be to a given policy action. In a world of uncertainty, therefore, policy makers may choose the wrong instrument, the right instrument but the wrong instrument value, or the right instrument value at the wrong time. When full account is taken of instrument constraints and uncertainty, one can reasonably conclude that government policy makers will need more policy instruments than the number of targets. Finally, *any* number of policy instruments will be insufficient when policy targets are inconsistent. All in all, then, we can expect to find frequent examples of failure in foreign economic policies either because of a shortage of effective policy instruments at the disposal of governments or because of inconsistencies (conflicts) among policy targets.

CONTEMPORARY ISSUES OF FOREIGN ECONOMIC POLICY

Five key issues dominate the foreign economic policies of governments today.

1. Further progress toward the liberalization of commercial policies, especially the policies of the advanced, industrial countries. Chapters 12, 13, and 15 deal with this issue.

2. The design and maintenance of an international monetary system that will allow governments to achieve domestic policy objectives and, at the same time, maintain open economies. Several aspects of this issue are taken up in Chapters 14, 19, and 20.

3. The emergence and consolidation of regional schemes of integration, particularly the European Economic Community, and their relations with nonmember countries. This is the subject of Chapter 16.

4. The acceleration of economic development in the nonindustrial countries and the strengthening of their role in the world economy. Chapters 17 and 18 investigate the special problems of the developing countries.

5. The explosive growth of the international enterprise, notably the multinational corporation whose business operations span the globe and whose business strategies run far beyond the interests of any one nation. This is the subject of Part Three.

SUMMARY

1. For reasons of space and analytical convenience, we define foreign economic policy to include the activities of government that are *intended* to regulate, restrict, promote, or otherwise influence the conduct of international trade and investment. However, we do not propose to neglect the interdependence between foreign and domestic economic policies.

2. Enlightened self-interest demands that governments take full account of national and international interests, as well as private interests, in the formulation of foreign economic policy.

3. Seven fundamental goals that nations may pursue in their foreign economic policies are: autarky, economic welfare, protectionism, full-employment stability (*internal balance*), balance of payments equilibrium (*external balance*), economic development, and economic warfare.

4. It is helpful to examine the instruments of foreign economic policy in terms of four broad policy areas: commercial policy, investment policy, foreign aid policy, and balance of payments policy.

5. The diversity of foreign economic policy goals engenders both internal and external conflicts. Two goal conflicts, in particular, are endemic in foreign economic policies: internal *versus* external balance and protectionism *versus* free trade. Interdependence among nations calls into question the effectiveness of economic policies determined solely on the national level as opposed to the international level. As an ongoing process, cooperation can point the way toward *international* economic policies that will benefit all nations, not simply the few who are strong.

6. When full account is taken of instrument constraints and uncertainty, one can reasonably conclude that government policy makers will need more policy instruments than the number of policy targets. Moreover, *any* number of policy instruments will be insufficient when policy targets are in conflict (inconsistent).

QUESTIONS AND APPLICATIONS

1. What are the implications of a broad definition of foreign economic policy?
2. What is the narrower definition of foreign economic policy that is to be used in Part Two?
3. What is meant by the *instruments* of foreign economic policy?
4. Identify and discuss the goals of foreign economic policy.
5. (a) Describe the four broad areas of foreign economic policy.
   (b) Evaluate the interdependence of these policy areas in terms of the balance of payments.
6. (a) Discuss the nature of the internal conflict of goals.
   (b) How does it differ from the external conflict of goals?
7. What steps may be taken to alleviate both the internal and external conflict of goals?
8. (a) Demonstrate theoretically why an equal number of instrument and target variables is a *necessary* condition for policy success.
   (b) Why is this necessary condition unlikely to be a *sufficient* condition?

SELECTED READINGS

Boulding, Kenneth E. *Principles of Economic Policy*. Englewood Cliffs, N. J.: Prentice-Hall, Inc., 1958. Chapters 6 and 11.

Cooper, Richard N. *The Economics of Interdependence: Economic Policy in the Atlantic Community*. New York: McGraw-Hill Book Company, 1968. Chapters 1 and 6.

Mundell, Robert A. *International Economics*. New York: Macmillan Co., 1968. Chapter 14.

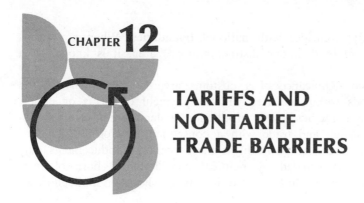

CHAPTER 12

TARIFFS AND NONTARIFF TRADE BARRIERS

Despite the theoretical support for free trade, governments, more often than not, have interfered with the movement of goods between nations by resorting to restrictive measures to achieve certain national objectives. These restrictive measures consist chiefly of (1) *tariffs,* which impose a tax or a customs duty on merchandise crossing the boundaries of a nation, and (2) *nontariff trade barriers,* which include quantitative restrictions, antidumping regulations, customs classifications and valuations, technical and health regulations, and other nontariff policies that hinder trade.

In addition to tariff and nontariff trade barriers, governments may restrain international trade through *exchange control,* the subject of Chapter 14. International commodity agreements, which also regulate or inhibit trade, are examined in Chapter 18.

TARIFFS AND TARIFF SYSTEMS

The systematic arrangement or schedule indicating the different customs duties to be levied is known as a tariff.

THE NATURE OF TARIFFS

The taxation of trade is probably as old as trade itself and it has been resorted to as a source of revenue under such different appellations as tolls, duties, dues, customs, and tariffs. The reference to such a tax as a tariff appeared only after the Crusades and has been in more or less constant use ever since. The Mercantilists of the eighteenth century were probably the first to make tariffs more an instrument of national control of international trade than a source of revenue. Tariffs have been used extensively ever since as a protective measure against foreign competition.

Customs Areas. A *customs area* is a geographical area within which goods may move freely without being subjected to customs duties. It generally, but not necessarily, coincides with national boundaries. When a customs area encompasses more than one distinct national area, it is known as a *customs union.*

The economic significance of a customs area lies essentially in the movement of goods within the area without payment of tariffs or duties, thus permitting greater efficiency in production under more favorable conditions of specialization and trade with a consequent rise of the standard of living within the area. As powerful as these economic inducements may be, they are often superseded by political considerations born of fear, suspicion, or ambition, feeding on the inevitable short-run difficulties of adjustment.

The most dramatic customs union development in history is undoubtedly the creation of the European Economic Community—also known as the European Common Market—by France, Italy, West Germany, Belgium, the Netherlands, and Luxembourg. While this experiment has contributed benefits to the entire area, it has also created new problems and difficulties for member as well as nonmember countries.[1]

Transit, Export, and Import Duties. There are three general classes of customs duties:

> 1. Transit duties, levied by a country on goods passing through its territories, but destined for another country.
> 2. Export duties, levied on goods destined for a foreign country.
> 3. Import duties, levied on goods coming from a foreign country.

Transit Duties. Duties imposed on goods originating in a foreign country and destined for another foreign country are called *transit duties.* They have practically disappeared from the international scene since the Barcelona Statute on Freedom of Transit in 1921. In earlier periods, however, they were used as a source of revenue by cities and states located along strategic trade routes.

Export Duties. This class of duty is levied on goods leaving a country for a foreign destination. Export duties, most popular in ancient times, have been applied down through the ages for revenue purposes. Today industrial countries have abandoned their use (the Constitution prohibits their use by the United States), but many developing countries impose duties on exports of primary commodities.

Import Duties. By far the most common form of customs duties is the import duty. Before World War I, import duties constituted the most formidable obstacle to international trade, and they continue to occupy a central

---

[1] See Chapter 16.

position in the commercial policies of nations. Although originally designed as a revenue measure, import duties are used mainly as protection against foreign competition, particularly in the developing countries of Asia, Africa, and Latin America.

Ad Valorem, Specific, and Compound Duties. There are two basic kinds of customs duties—ad valorem and specific. An *ad valorem* duty is stated in terms of a percentage of the value of an imported article, such as 10 or 20 percent ad valorem. A *specific duty,* on the other hand, is expressed in terms of an amount of money per quantity of goods, such as 20 cents per pound or per gallon. A combination of an ad valorem and a specific is called a *compound duty.*

Ad valorem duties generally lend themselves more satisfactorily to manufactured products, while specific duties are more adaptable to standardized and staple products. Ad valorem duties on higher priced manufactured goods are considered more effective than specific duties because a single ad valorem rate can usually maintain a more appropriate degree of protection, especially under conditions of rising prices. A specific rate, on the other hand, has the advantage of being more protective in a declining market or in a business recession when cheaper goods are favored. A specific rate will, moreover, discourage imports of the cheaper grade within a class of products as compared to the more expensive variety. For example, a specific rate of $2 per pair on shoes will discourage imports valued at $5 a pair to a greater extent than those valued at $10 a pair.

Compound duties frequently apply to manufactured goods containing raw materials that are on the dutiable list. In such cases the specific portion of the duty—known as a *compensatory duty*—is levied to offset the duty that grants protection to the raw material industry, while the ad valorem portion of the duty affords protection to the finished goods industry. In the United States, for example, the wool tariff provides for compound duties on worsteds to compensate domestic worsted producers for protection afforded the raw wool industry as well as to provide protection for their own woolen industry.

Sometimes a mixed ad valorem and specific duty is provided for a given product with the provision that the heavier of the two shall apply. This is not a true compound duty; it is an *alternative duty* since only one of the two duties is actually levied.

In recent decades, specific duties have given way to ad valorem duties in response to worldwide inflation and the growing importance of international trade in manufactures.

Tariff Classification of Products. There are countless articles of commerce that move in international trade and their number is constantly growing as newly developed products are added every day. For manageable tariff administration, some kind of comprehensive classification or "customs nomenclature" is necessary.

As a rule most countries have two major lists in their tariffs: (1) a dutiable list for goods subject to customs duties, and (2) a free list for goods permitted to enter free of duty. Classification in the dutiable list may be made according to: (1) an alphabetical arrangement, (2) the height of the duty, or (3) the attributes of the goods. Each of these methods has its advantages and its drawbacks. The alphabetical and the height-of-the-duty methods are simple in form, but they tend to make reference to any particular product or group of related products difficult. The attribute method of classification is more logical and more widely used in modern tariff systems. Under the attribute approach, classification may be made on the basis of the physical substance from which products are derived, the end-use of the products, or the degree of processing.

The advantages of a worldwide customs nomenclature are several. Such a nomenclature would facilitate the negotiation and administration of tariff agreements since all participating countries would classify products in the same way. It would also eliminate many of the trade obstructions and distortions that result from the administration of dissimilar nomenclatures. Further, it would give international traders the assurance of a uniform classification of their goods. Finally, the adoption of a common nomenclature is an essential step for countries that intend to enter into regional integration schemes. Much effort, therefore, has been devoted to the harmonization of product classifications in national tariff systems.

In 1950, several countries agreed to the Brussels Tariff Nomenclature (BTN), which classifies products according to their physical substance. Since that time, the BTN has been adopted by some 100 countries that account for two-thirds of total world trade. Among the industrial countries, only the United States and Canada continue to use their own tariff classifications. A second customs nomenclature, the Standard International Trade Classification (SITC), has been developed by the United Nations, but it is used by only a handful of countries. An item-by-item correspondence has been worked out between the SITC and the BTN so that it is easy to move from one to the other in making comparisons. The industrial and developing countries, therefore, have gone a long way toward harmonizing the product classifications of their tariffs. If the United States were to adopt the BTN, most of the world's trade would be classified in the same way for tariff purposes. A Customs Cooperation Council sitting in Brussels with a membership of some 60 countries actively encourages greater customs uniformity by preparing drafts for new conventions and by offering technical assistance in customs administration.[2]

---

[2] See "CCC: Oiling the Wheels of Trade," *International Trade Forum Supplement* (April, 1969), pp. 3-5.

TARIFF SYSTEMS

Tariff schedules may have one, two, or three different duties for each dutiable article. A nation is said to have a "single-column," a "double-column," or a "triple-column" tariff system, according to the number of different duties appearing on its schedules for each product. When customs duties are established by law they are called *autonomous,* but when they are the result of treaty agreements with other countries they are called *conventional.* Single-column schedules are, as a rule, autonomous, but multiple-column schedules may be either autonomous or partly autonomous and partly conventional.

Single-Column Tariff Schedule. A single-column schedule is essentially autonomous and nondiscriminatory since it provides only one duty for each product, whatever the country of origin.[3] It is not subject to change by negotiation unless legislative permission is afforded. A single-column schedule is best suited for a country whose purpose is either a tariff purely for revenue or purely for protection with no intention of bargaining.

Under present international commercial relations, the rigidity of a single-column tariff system is a handicap when dealing with other nations to resolve mutual trade problems, the supply of which is plentiful. Multiple-column systems, on the other hand, lend themselves more readily to the present needs of international bargaining.

Double-Column Tariff Schedule. This type of schedule has two levels of duties for each product. When both levels are established by law and are not subject to modification by international agreements, there is an autonomous tariff system of a "maximum-minimum form." When only the higher level of duties is established by law and the lower level is a composite of all the reduced duties granted to other nations by negotiation, it is partly autonomous and partly conventional, and is said to be of a "general and conventional form."

Usually under the maximum-minimum form, the maximum scale is used for normal duties, while the minimum scale is extended only to imports from nations that have signed reciprocal agreements to that effect. When the minimum scale is used for normal duties, however, the maximum scale becomes either a weapon resorted to in retaliation against the discriminatory practices of other nations or a threat that can be used to induce bargaining and concessions.

Under the general and conventional form, the autonomous higher scale is always used for normal duties; the lower scale is extended to imports from

---

[3] A single-column tariff schedule may, however, be conceived on the basis of discrimination if the duties therein are purposely chosen to affect imports from particular countries.

nations that have signed reciprocal agreements entitling them to their benefits. These reduced duties may, however, also be extended to third nations, either conditionally or unconditionally, under most-favored-nation treatment treaties or other expressed policies.

Triple-Column Tariff Schedule. A triple-column schedule is generally used by countries with colonial possessions or with close political affiliations with other countries. It is an extension of the double-column schedule by the addition of a third, lower scale that is reserved for intragroup application. This is known as a "preferential system" and it is designed to encourage trade between the different members of the system. The British Commonwealth falls into this category. A triple-column system is sometimes used by smaller countries seeking refinements in their discriminatory policies, generally for political reasons.

MITIGATION OF TARIFFS

The cost of a dutiable article to an importer is always higher than the foreign purchase price by at least the amount of the duty paid.[4] When dutiable raw materials and semifinished products are used in production by domestic industries, the final costs must reflect directly or indirectly the burden of this duty since it is an actual expenditure at some point in the channel of distribution. When goods so produced are reexported, the increased costs due to the tariff may become a serious handicap to trade without serving any protective purpose at home. Transit trade may be similarly affected by the imposition of a transit duty.

Under certain circumstances, tariff laws provide ways of mitigating this unwelcome effect in order to harmonize the conflicting aims of protection and the promotion of exports. This is achieved by either refunding the duty paid in the form of a drawback or by permitting imports to enter free of duty when they are destined for reexport.

Drawbacks. A *drawback* is a refund made by the government to the exporter, in whole or in part, of the tariff duties and taxes paid by the importer upon satisfactory proof of evidence of exportation. The United States refunds 99 percent of the original tariff duties as drawback. Occasionally a drawback is used in lieu of a compensatory duty by reimbursing a domestic manufacturer who uses the imported materials in the production of goods that are in competition with imports made of similar materials not otherwise dutiable. Canada had such a provision in 1935 for the silk that was used in the production of lining caps or other articles for domestic consumption.

---

[4] This statement is consistent with the fact that under some circumstances the imposition of a duty may induce a lower foreign purchase price.

Bonded Warehouses. Dutiable imports may be brought into a customs territory and left in *bonded warehouses* free of duty. Under strict governmental supervision, imported goods may be stored, repacked, manipulated, or further processed in bonded warehouses according to the laws of the particular country. The goods may be later reexported free of duty or withdrawn for domestic consumption upon payment of customs duties. When such goods have been processed in a bonded warehouse with additional domestic materials and later entered for consumption, only the import portion of the finished product is subject to duty.

The postponement of payment of the duty is an important consideration especially when large-scale operations are involved, since working capital need not be immobilized. This advantage, however, is often outweighed by the complex regulations and strict customs supervision of operations within a bonded warehouse.

Free Zones and Free Ports. A *free zone* is an isolated, enclosed area with no resident population (generally adjacent to a port) that offers extensive facilities for handling, storing, mixing, and manufacturing imported and domestic goods and materials without customs intervention or immediate disbursement of customs duties. The purpose of a free zone is to enlarge the benefits of a bonded warehouse by the elimination of the restrictive aspects of customs supervision and by offering more suitable manufacturing facilities.

Sometimes, a free zone is referred to as a *free port,* but a true free port is a whole city, or section of a city, isolated from the rest of the country for customs purposes. There are very few free ports left in the world where the population may enjoy the benefit of relatively free trade. Hong Kong and Gibraltar are among the most important of such ports. In medieval Europe, however, free ports abounded along the Mediterranean and northern seas. Venice, Genoa, Naples, Marseilles, Hamburg, and Bremen were prosperous free ports and leading centers of trade for a long period of time.

In the United States, free zones are commonly known as "foreign-trade zones" and are governed by an act of Congress passed in 1934, which provides for their establishment and operation. In 1937, the first foreign-trade zone was opened on Staten Island in New York, followed in 1947 by another in New Orleans, and later in other ports of the country. The history of foreign-trade zones in the United States tends to discourage their development; most of them have operated at a loss, mainly because the geographical position of the United States does not lend itself well to transit and reexport trade.[5]

---

[5] William A. Dymsza, *Foreign Trade Zones and International Trade* (Trenton, New Jersey: New Jersey Department of Conservation and Economic Development, 1964), p. 229 ff.

TARIFF MAKING AND TARIFF FUNCTIONS

When a country is faced with fiscal or other problems of maladjustment in its economy that are of either domestic or foreign origin or when it is in need of new or additional protection for domestic industries, it often resorts to tariff measures.

Depending upon the specific problems to be solved, decisions must be made about the kinds of goods to tax, the types of customs duties to levy, and the heights of the different rates of duties. It must also be decided whether to adopt a unilateral nondiscriminating single-column tariff or a multiple-column system that could be modified later by international agreements. Further, the possible use of more subtle, indirect means of protection, such as subsidies, prohibitions, or special extratariff measures may be explored.

Legislators who translate these decisions into law are seldom sufficiently conversant with the perplexities of the problems involved. Moreover, they are under great pressure from their constituents who are motivated by the immediate and the local aspects of national problems. As a group, legislators are pressured by highly organized lobbies representing entrenched interests that are seeking a more favorable outcome of such legislation for their own activities regardless of national interest. As a result of the combination of the conflicting influences faced by legislators, a tariff is seldom, if ever, a true picture of the overall needs of a country; it is rather the fruit of compromise and patchwork and the result of the forces at work behind the scene. It is not uncommon, therefore, to find in any tariff legislation a mixture of provisions sometimes incongruent and often incompatible with either logic or theory.

Taxation is a means by which different levels of government acquire the necessary income to finance their numerous activities. Taxation of international trade is generally reserved to the highest or national level, and it is put into effect through a variety of measures, of which tariffs are the most widespread.

National governments are also entrusted with the promotion and protection of the economic well-being of their countries. Thus, they use tariffs to regulate and control the flow of international commerce either for protection, for balance of payments adjustments, or for purposes extraneous to trade, such as the promotion of greater domestic employment, diversification of production, and a host of other national desiderata.

Irrespective of the merits of tariff-making procedures, tariffs, when adopted, perform certain functions that may or may not be fully as intended; but they do produce revenues and/or afford protection depending on their structure and the conditions under which they operate. Therefore, tariffs may be constructed to perform a revenue function or protection function as the case may be, or a combination of both depending upon the desired ultimate purposes. In addition, tariffs may be used to bring about an adjustment in the balance of international payments of a country or an improvement in its terms of trade.

REVENUE FUNCTION

In order to best perform their revenue function, tariff duties are applied to commodities of wide consumption; and the rates of these duties are kept low enough to maximize customs collections without unduly restricting trade. The same objective may also be attained by the imposition of a uniform low rate of duty on all merchandise crossing the border either as exports, imports, or in transit.

Because of the generally low rates of duties, tariffs for revenue do not substantially affect prices, production, or consumption. Whatever little influence they exert in these directions is reflected in a diminutive but similar fashion as that of protective tariffs which carry more substantial rates of duties.

The income accruing to the state is practically the only important economic effect of tariffs for revenue. Depending upon the number and kinds of products subjected to the tariff as well as upon the ultimate disposition of the customs revenues derived therefrom by the state, the ultimate effect will be reflected in the distribution of the national income. If the state diverts this income into additional or new expenditures of a civic or security character, additional employment may be effected in the domestic economy; but if this revenue is used to relieve other existing taxation, it will have only a diversionary effect because of the shifting of the tax burden to the consumers and/or the foreign suppliers of the products affected by the tariff.

The revenue function of a duty, therefore, is a relative concept. No matter how it is defined to perform its intended function, a duty is always characterized by an element of protection, however small or unimportant, except, of course, when the taxed product is not domestically produced, and the tariff serves a purely revenue function.

PROTECTION FUNCTION

A tariff designed for protection must provide rates of duties high enough to achieve one or more of the following three aims predetermined by national policies:

1. The encouragement of additional domestic production which could not take place without tariff duties because of prevailing cost disadvantages.
2. The reduction or elimination of domestic consumption of an imported commodity, thereby diverting expenditure to alternative goods of domestic or even foreign origin.

3. The development of new, or "infant" industries, which from the start could not compete with entrenched foreign producers without the benefit of protection.

The protection function of the tariff depends upon a partial or complete restriction of imports; this may be accomplished by the height of the relevant duties. When complete protection is desired, a given duty must be high enough to cover at least the difference in the marginal cost of production between domestic and all foreign producers, including transportation and incidental expenses of importing. If the tariff is to be only partially protective, however, the duty must remain below this difference. When partial protection is desired, goods will continue to be imported, but they will be imported in smaller quantities and the state will collect customs duties. The protection function, therefore—like the revenue function—will usually afford both protection and revenue, although its purpose is primarily one of protection.

The seeming incompatibility of the two functions in the same duty does not necessarily disqualify its adoption since most countries generally desire both protection and revenue. In the tariff schedules of nations, however, a tendency does exist to provide a certain number of generally low rates of duties designed essentially for revenue and other higher duty rates for protection.

BALANCE OF PAYMENTS FUNCTION

The adoption of a new tariff or changes in an existing one will tend to disturb the balance of trade of a country and, therefore, the equilibrium of its balance of international payments. The imposition of tariff duties will, moreover, start in motion economic forces of adjustment at home and abroad that will affect, among other things, prices, production, incomes, and employment.

Sometimes nations try to reverse the process and resort to tariffs in order to correct existing maladjustments in their balance of payments. When they do so, however, they are not attacking the fundamental causes of disequilibrium that may lie in other areas of their disturbed economies; nor are they likely to achieve their goals since other countries can, and often do, resort to similar action either in retaliation or self-defense. In any event, they forego some of the economic benefits of international specialization and trade, and they are more likely than not to end up with new problems of a more complex and intractable nature. When Great Britain in 1964 imposed a 15 percent surcharge on all imports (roughly doubling the existing tariff level) in response to a growing payments deficit, the opposition of other countries and international organizations forced the abandonment of this unorthodox corrective measure in the following year. Nevertheless, the use of tariffs for balance of payments purposes appears to be spreading: in 1971, both the United States and Denmark imposed a 10 percent surcharge on most dutiable imports.

ECONOMIC EFFECTS OF TARIFFS

The immediate effects of tariffs are those reflected in price changes and consequent adjustments in production and consumption. Because of the fact that tariffs for revenue have effects similar to those of protective tariffs, but to a lesser degree, we confine our discussion to protective tariffs, leaving it to the reader to make the appropriate application to revenue tariffs.

PRICE CHANGES INDUCED BY AN IMPORT DUTY

An import duty may affect the market price of the protected commodity in four different ways depending upon the condition of the market and the balance of elasticities of supply and demand at home and abroad of the protected product. This price effect may involve:

1. No price change at all.
2. A price rise of less than the amount of the duty.
3. A price rise equal to the amount of the duty.
4. A price rise greater than the amount of the duty.

No Price Change. When a country is an exporter of the protected product on balance, the imposition of a duty will be meaningless as far as the domestic price is concerned. If the domestic price rises above the world price behind the tariff wall, the entire supply will be offered in the home market and will tend to depress prices back to the world price level. This happened in the United States shortly after World War I, when the government attempted unsuccessfully to raise the domestic price of wheat above the world price to improve the farmers' purchasing power.

In a situation where the import supply is perfectly inelastic (most likely when the tariff country is an important market or even a monopsonist) the full amount of the duty will be absorbed by the foreign producer, leaving the cost to the domestic consumer unchanged.[6] When the foreign producer is a monopolist, he may try to maximize his total revenues by dumping into the protected market rather than maintaining a less-profitable uniform world price.

Price Rise of Less Than the Amount of Duty. When the price elasticities of import supply and import demand lie between zero and infinity, then a duty will cause a price rise by less than the duty. This is probably the most

---

[6] This statement assumes that import demand elasticity is greater than zero. See Chapter 10 for a discussion of price elasticities.

common price effect of the tariffs imposed by large trading countries such as the United States. This situation is depicted in Figure 12-1.

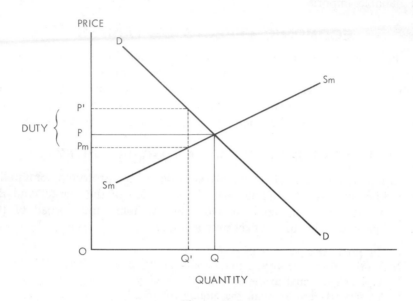

Figure 12-1

PRICE RISE LESS THAN AMOUNT OF DUTY

Before the duty is imposed, country A imports $O\text{-}Q$ of a given product at a price $O\text{-}P$, as determined by the intersection of its demand schedule, $D\text{-}D$, and the import supply schedule, $S_m\text{-}S_m$. To simplify the analysis, we assume that country A does not itself produce the imported product.

Now a duty equal to $P_m\text{-}P'$ is placed on imports. Observe that the postduty price rises from $O\text{-}P$ to $O\text{-}P'$, an amount less than the duty $(P\text{-}P' < P_m\text{-}P')$. Why? Because as their sales to country A begin to fall, foreign suppliers cut the supply price from $O\text{-}P$ to $O\text{-}P_m$. As indicated by their aggregate supply schedule, $S_m\text{-}S_m$, foreign suppliers are willing to sell $O\text{-}Q'$ to country A at price $O\text{-}P_m$. In turn, consumers in country A are willing to buy $O\text{-}Q'$ at the postduty price $O\text{-}P'$ (equal to $O\text{-}P_m$ plus the duty), as is shown by the demand schedule $D\text{-}D$. Hence, $O\text{-}P'$ is an equilibrium price that clears the market.

Price Rise Equal To the Amount of Duty. A tariff will tend to increase the price of the protected product by the full amount of the duty under conditions of perfect elasticity of import supply and less-than-perfect elasticity of import demand. The perfect elasticity of import supply may derive from constant costs of production or more commonly because the tariff country is too small to influence the world price of the product by the size of its demand.

Price Rise Greater Than the Amount of Duty. A tariff may raise the price to the consumer by more than the amount of the duty when the channel of distribution at home is lengthy and the different middlemen add their individual profit margins, or markups, at each step of the marketing process. The pyramiding of the multiple markups on the duty may force a rise in price substantially greater than the original duty.

The cumulative effect of markups would also occur under the prior assumptions of price increases of less than, or equal to, the amount of the duty whenever importers are not themselves the ultimate consumers, and whenever their goods must flow through extended domestic marketing channels.

THE NATURE OF TARIFF EFFECTS

In addition to the direct price effect of an import duty, multiple ulterior consequences that are far too intricate to trace here at length occur within the economy. Their nature may be suggested, however, by the mention of the fact that any alteration in the quantity demanded of an imported commodity will start a chain reaction involving a change in the demand for the factors of production. This resulting change will affect the relative costs of the factors of production and their reallocation to equalize marginal opportunity costs.

This, in turn, will alter the pattern of production, consumption, and international trade in a variety of products via price and income changes. These changes will disturb the pattern of international payments and set in motion monetary and foreign exchange mechanisms and possibly alter the rate of exchange between currencies. The effect of the changes could bring about a realignment of comparative cost conditions between different nations that could further affect the pattern of international trade. Finally, these changes may also be influenced by the way in which the additional customs revenues are expended by the tariff-imposing country.

Although an import duty may induce many changes in both the importing and exporting countries, its *direct* effects in the importing country may be classified as price, revenue, trade, protection, consumption, and income-redistribution effects. Figure 12-2 (page 284) shows these effects under the simplifying assumption of a perfectly elastic foreign supply.

At the prevailing price, $O\text{-}P$, the quantity demanded of a given product by country A is $O\text{-}Q$, determined by its domestic demand schedule, $D\text{-}D$, of which the portion $O\text{-}Q_1$ is domestically produced (determined by the intersection of price, $O\text{-}P$, and the domestic supply schedule, $S\text{-}S$), and the remaining part, $Q_1\text{-}Q$, is imported.

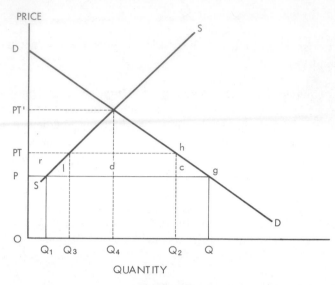

Figure 12-2

EFFECTS OF AN IMPORT DUTY WITH A
PERFECTLY ELASTIC FOREIGN SUPPLY

Upon the introduction of a tariff by country A, a customs duty of, say, *P-PT* is levied, raising the cost to domestic users from *O-P* to *O-PT*. At this higher cost, the quantities demanded of the protected product are reduced from *O-Q* to *O-Q₂*, of which *O-Q₃* is domestically supplied, and the remaining portion, *Q₃-Q₂*, is imported.

The *price* effect is the increase in price to domestic consumers because of the duty. In this instance, consumers bear the full incidence of the duty (price rises by the full amount of the duty, *P-PT*) because the foreign supply price remains the same (foreign supply is perfectly elastic). In other words, the duty does not alter the country's terms of trade and hence there is no redistribution of income from foreign countries to the tariff-levying country. If foreign supply were less than perfectly elastic, then some of the incidence of the duty would be borne by the foreign-supplying countries.

The *revenue* effect is the customs collections accruing to the government, represented by the rectangle *d*. It is the product of the quantity of imports *times* the duty *P-PT*.

The *trade* effect is the decline in imports resulting from the duty. At the preduty price *O-P*, imports were *Q₁-Q*; after the duty was imposed, they fell to *Q₃-Q₂*. The negative trade effect, therefore, is *Q₁-Q₃ + Q₂-Q*.

The *protection* effect is the increase in domestic production that is induced by the import duty, namely, *Q₁-Q₃*. This represents the substitution of domestic production for foreign production.

The *consumption* effect is the decrease in consumption resulting from the tariff. Because of a higher price, consumers cut their consumption of the product from $O\text{-}Q$ to $O\text{-}Q_2$. Hence, the consumption effect is $Q_2\text{-}Q$. (Note that the trade effect is the sum of the protection and consumption effects.)

The *income-redistribution* effect is the shift in income from domestic consumers to domestic producers. It is shown by quadrangle r, which measures the extra revenue, or pure rent, that is received by domestic producers above their supply price ($S\text{-}S$) as a result of the duty.

In a perfectly competitive economy, the net cost of the tariff to the domestic country is the sum of triangles 1 and c. The reasoning behind this conclusion is as follows. Some consumers enjoy an economic gain or surplus because they are willing to pay a higher price than the market price that they actually pay for some of the product. On the assumption that the prices consumers would be willing to pay for various quantities of the product measure the satisfactions they derive from the product, then the consumer surplus before the tariff is indicated by the area $D\text{-}g\text{-}P$ in Figure 12-2. The higher price caused by the tariff, however, reduces the consumer surplus to $D\text{-}h\text{-}PT$, resulting in a net loss of $PT\text{-}h\text{-}g\text{-}P$, which is equal to the sum of r, 1, d, and c. Since the net loss in consumer surplus is partly offset by the national gain of r and d, the net national loss is the sum of 1 and c. Specifically, 1 is the national loss attributable to the substitution of higher-priced domestic production for lower-priced foreign production and c is the national loss in consumption due to the higher postduty price, which causes the substitution of other goods providing less satisfaction than the foregone imports. When the tariff-levying country faces a perfectly elastic import supply, it always experiences a net national loss because domestic consumers bear the full incidence of the duty. When import supply is less than perfectly elastic, however, a country can improve its terms of trade by imposing a tariff and it may even enjoy a net national gain, a subject taken up in the next chapter.

If the duty is high enough to reach PT', there will be no imports—and the entire quantity demanded, $O\text{-}Q_4$, will be supplied by the domestic producers at price $O\text{-}PT'$.

The removal of our assumption of a constant foreign price, $O\text{-}P$, would complicate further the impact of a tariff without, however, invalidating our analysis. With less-than-infinite supply elasticity, the price effect would be somewhat less restrictive of imports and consumption since foreign prices would tend to drop, as established earlier in this chapter. This is especially likely if the importing country is a major consumer of the product.

MEASUREMENT OF TARIFF SYSTEMS

Several methods have been used to measure the trade and protection effect of national tariff systems.

Tariff Revenues. The most naive approach, favored by protectionists, is to divide a country's customs revenue either by the total value of its imports or by the total value of all *dutiable* imports. This method implicitly assumes that the protection effect of a tariff system is directly related to the duties collected on imports: the lower the ratio of customs revenue to imports, the lower the degree of protection. This assumption is demonstrably false. Suppose a country's duties are so high that no dutiable goods are imported—the trade effect is equal to the preduty import volume. In that event, no revenue would be collected—the ratio of revenue to imports would be zero! To conclude that the protection and trade effects are also zero would be patently absurd.

Height of Duties. Another approach is to add up all the duties in a tariff system and then calculate the unweighted average. A more sophisticated version of this method is to calculate an average of all duties weighted by the country's imports of each dutiable product. Thus, a product with imports of, say, $2 million is given twice the weight of a product with imports of $1 million.[7]

This approach assumes that trade and protection effects are proportional to the height of a duty and they are the same for all products and all countries. The unweighted average ignores the varying importance of different products in trade. On the other hand, an average that is weighted by the tariff-levying country's imports of each dutiable product has a downward bias: prohibitory duties are not counted (since they keep out all imports) and the more restrictive a duty, the less its weight. Despite this drawback, both the United States and the European Economic Community used such weighted averages to measure the heights of their own and the other's tariff system during the Kennedy Round negotiations.[8] The downward bias would be moderated, if not overcome, by using as weights the value of *world* trade in each product.[9]

Effective versus Nominal Rates. As we have seen, an import duty raises the domestic price of a good (unless the elasticity of its foreign supply is zero) and thereby encourages consumers to shift from the foreign good to a domestic substitute. Thus, the nominal duty, together with the relevant elasticities, determines the consumption effect.

---

[7] In mathematical form, the simple unweighted average is $\sum_{t=1}^{t=n} = d_t/n$, where d represents the individual duty expressed as a percentage and n, the number of duties. The weighted average is $\sum_{t=1}^{t=n} = (d_t) i_t$, where i is the weight defined as the fractional share of dutiable imports associated with the individual duty. The sum of all the weights is one.

[8] See Chapter 15.

[9] Due to lack of trade data, lack of comparability (different customs nomenclatures), and other statistical problems, weighting by world trade is generally considered impractical.

But for domestic producers the protection effect of a nominal duty on their final product is enhanced by the fact that their own production activity is responsible for only a part of the final product's value. At the same time, the protection effect of a nominal duty is *lowered* for domestic producers by any import duties on raw materials and other inputs that they use in manufacturing the final product. The tariff rate that is relevant to the protection effect, therefore, is the *effective* rate that takes into account both of these factors. The effective rate measures the degree of protection that is afforded the value added to the final product by domestic producers.

The formula for the calculation of the effective rate is $r = \dfrac{n - \Sigma pi}{1 - \Sigma p}$, where r is the effective rate, n is the nominal rate, p is the proportion of the final product represented by imported or importable inputs in the absence of any import restrictions, and i is the nominal rate of duty on raw materials and other intermediate goods. The expression $1 - \Sigma p$ is the value added to the final product by domestic producers as a proportion of the final value.

If no duties are imposed on imports of intermediate goods, then the formula becomes $r = \dfrac{n}{1 - \Sigma p}$. This gives the rate of protection against the value added by domestic producers (the final value of the product *minus* the value of importable inputs purchased from other producers who may be local or foreign).

Assume, for example, that a country places a 20 percent duty on imports of a final product but allows duty-free imports of intermediate goods that constitute one-half of the final product's value. Then the effective rate is $\dfrac{.20}{1 - \frac{1}{2}}$ or 40 percent. Assuming a price rise equal to the duty, this 20 percent duty enables domestic producers of the final product to increase their value added by 40 percent more than in a free trade situation with no duties.

Continuing with this example, let us now assume that a 10 percent rate is applied to imports of intermediate goods. (If more than one input is involved, then the rate is a weighted average.) The effective rate becomes $\dfrac{.20 - \frac{1}{2}(.10)}{1 - \frac{1}{2}}$ or 30 percent. Note that the tariff on intermediate goods has lowered the effective rate although it remains higher than the nominal rate. When the nominal rates applied to the final product and to intermediate goods are the same, then the effective rate is *equal* to the nominal rate for the final product. When the intermediate duty rate exceeds the final-product rate, then the effective rate becomes *less* than the nominal rate and may even be negative.

Because national governments generally admit raw materials and other intermediate goods either duty-free or at a lower rate than finished goods in order to encourage local manufacture, effective tariff rates are usually higher than nominal rates. Balassa has calculated that in 1962 the *effective* ad valorem equivalent (or weighted average) of the United States tariff system was 20.0 percent as compared to a *nominal* ad valorem equivalent of 11.6 percent. For the European Economic Community the figures were 18.6 percent and 11.9 percent, respectively.[10]

Elasticities and Market Share. Any method that pretends to measure the protection effect of a duty by its height (even when the effective rate is substituted for the nominal rate) implicitly ignores the foreign and domestic elasticities of supply and demand that vary from product to product and from country to country. A duty of any given height may or may not be restrictive depending on the relevant elasticities. But elasticities are difficult to determine empirically even for a single product. It is no wonder, then, that efforts to measure entire tariff systems comprising thousands of product classifications have relied on weighted averages of nominal or effective duties. Although such averages may be useful for intercountry and intertemporal comparisons, they should be interpreted only as crude indicators of the degree of tariff protection.

The elasticity of import demand is influenced by the share of imports in domestic consumption and domestic production, as well as by domestic supply and demand elasticities.[11] Other things equal, the smaller the import share, the greater the import elasticity. Given the domestic elasticities, therefore, a duty will restrict imports most when such imports are only marginal to domestic consumption and production, a situation that is probably more common in the United States than in other countries.

THE EFFECTS OF EXPORT DUTIES

Export duties are relatively easy to administer, and are commonly used as a revenue measure, especially by the raw-material producing countries. They are also used because of the prevalent belief that the burden of the duty falls upon the foreign consumer. In recent times export duties have been utilized to encourage domestic processing and industrial development in order to create additional employment opportunities.

The incidence of an export duty, if too high, may defeat its revenue purpose and may encourage technological developments abroad to provide substitutes for the taxed product. The classical example is Chile with its natural nitrate—at one time exercising a virtual monopoly. A high export duty, instituted in Chile in 1919, further encouraged the manufacture abroad of synthetic substitutes. As a result, Chile lost most of its markets; and in spite of its changed tariff policy, it never recovered its former dominant position.

---

[10] Bela Balassa, *Trade Liberalization Among Industrial Countries* (New York: McGraw-Hill Book Company, 1967), Table 3.2, p. 56.

[11] The formula is $e_m = e_d (C/M) + e_s (P/M)$, where e_m is the import demand elasticity; e_d and e_s, the domestic elasticities of demand and supply, respectively; C, domestic consumption; P, domestic production; and M, imports.

The price of an internationally traded commodity is determined by the world supply and demand conditions. Unless a given producer is a monopolist or a major supplier, he must meet the world price to dispose of his product. Hence, an export duty puts a competitive producer at a disadvantage and forces him to absorb the duty in order to remain in business. If the producer is a monopolist or a major supplier and, therefore, in a position to shift the burden of the export duty in some degree to the foreign consumer, the increased price of his product will reduce his total revenues unless foreign demand is inelastic. If the duty is too high, he may lose much of his market.

NONTARIFF TRADE BARRIERS: QUANTITATIVE RESTRICTIONS

Quantitative measures of restriction, like tariffs, are tools of national economic policy designed to regulate the international trade of a nation. Unlike tariffs, however, they impose absolute limitations upon foreign trade and inhibit market responses; this makes them extremely effective. Quantitative trade restrictions are used chiefly to regulate trade in commodities in order to afford protection to domestic producers and/or to bring about adjustment to a disturbed balance of payments. As a result, they affect the commercial and industrial activities of a country, as well as its international economic relations. Quantitative restrictions ordinarily take the form of import quotas that are administered by the issuance of import licenses to individual traders.

IMPORT QUOTAS

Three major types of import quota are in use throughout the world: unilateral quota, negotiated bilateral or multilateral quota, and tariff quota. All of them impose absolute limits in value or quantity on imports of a specific product or product group during a given period of time.

The *unilateral quota* is a fixed quota that is adopted without prior consultation or negotiation with other countries. It is imposed and administered solely by the importing country. Because of its unilateral aspect, this type of quota tends to create friction, antagonism, and retaliation abroad that undermine its ultimate success.

A unilateral quota may be *global* or *allocated* depending upon whether or not the fixed volume of imports is specifically assigned by shares to different exporting countries and/or to individual domestic importers or foreign exporters.

A *global quota* restricts the total volume without reference to countries of origin or to established importers and exporters engaged in the trade. In practice, the global quota becomes unwieldy because of the rush of both importers and exporters to secure as large a share as possible before the quota is exhausted. The result is frequently an excess of shipments over the quota, and charges of favoritism may be raised against traders fortunate enough to be the first to seize a lion's share of the business. To avoid the difficulties of a global quota system, a quota may be allocated by countries and by private traders on the basis of a prior representative period. This type of import quota is known as an *allocated quota*.

The period of time during which a given quota remains in effect has generally been short, frequently three months. No country has succeeded in placing its entire import trade under quota. A unilateral quota, whether global or allocated, lends itself to discrimination and mismanagement by the importing country and opens the door to abuse, corruption, and graft. A country may adopt an import quota to restrict imports in general rather than to discriminate between the different sources of such imports, to exact preferential treatment from other countries, or to retaliate against discrimination by other nations against its own exports.

The administration of quotas is fraught with difficulties. Foreign traders feel encouraged to misrepresent their products in order to exempt them from quota classification or to resort to methods ranging from simple persuasion to outright graft and corruption of government officials in charge of enforcement. To ease the administrative, as well as political, difficulties of unilateral quotas, many governments have turned to negotiated quotas.

Under the system of a *negotiated bilateral* or *multilateral quota,* the importing country negotiates with supplying countries, or with groups of exporters in those countries, before deciding the allotment of the quota by definite shares. Often the administration of licensing under a bilateral quota is left in the hands of the exporting countries.

A bilateral or multilateral quota tends to minimize pressure by domestic importers upon their own government and to increase cooperation by foreign exporters, thus enhancing the successful operation of the system. When licensing is entrusted to foreign private agencies, however, it often results in the bulk of trade falling into the hands of larger firms or of well-organized international cartels that are in a position to squeeze out most of the monopolylike profit induced by the restriction of supply relative to demand in the quota country. Hence, domestic importers are deprived of this source of income, and their government, of the opportunity to tax such income.

In recent years the United States has restricted certain imports through negotiated quotas administered by the governments of supplying countries, the so-called *voluntary export quotas*. In 1971, for example, Japan and other textile-exporting countries agreed to impose "voluntary" quotas on their exports of man-made textiles to the United States. Despite its name, a voluntary export quota is actually an import quota since the initiative for its establishment comes from the importing country and the motivation is protection of domestic industry.

Under a *tariff quota* a specified quantity of a product is permitted to enter the country at a given rate of duty—or even duty free. Any additional quantity that may be imported, however, must pay a higher duty. Thus, a tariff quota combines the features of both a tariff and a quota.

On the surface a tariff quota seems fair and reasonable. It is flexible enough to permit the importation, at a favorable rate of duty, of a limited quantity of a product that is necessary to meet the minimum requirements of the country without closing the gates to additional imports at a higher rate to satisfy those who are willing and able to afford the extra cost.

In practice, however, a tariff quota does not work out exactly that way. If the import needs of a country do not exceed the minimum quantities permitted to enter under the lower rates of duty, the quantities demanded and supplied are not materially affected by the quota and no quota profits are possible. The first rush to import in the early part of a quota period may, however, raise prices abroad and the benefits of the lower duty will then accrue largely to foreign exporters. On the other hand, if domestic needs exceed the quantities permitted by the quota under the lower rates of duty, the lure of a likely quota profit will encourage importers to acquire larger quantities to maximize their share before the exhaustion of the quota. Their action will tend to raise foreign supply prices as well as to glut the domestic market at the beginning of each quota period, thus depressing domestic prices to their own disadvantage. True, domestic prices after the first rush will tend to rise, but further imports that are subject to a higher rate of duty can only take place if the differential between domestic and external prices equals the amount of the duty. Even then, price instability is likely to minimize the possibility of a quota profit. Moreover, highly unstable prices are incompatible with orderly distribution and are hardly beneficial to importers and exporters in the long run.

Tariff quotas have been utilized for a long time to facilitate border-town trade between closely interdependent communities of adjacent countries. In recent decades, however, tariff quotas have been more frequently used as a vehicle for preferential treatment to encourage trade in particular commodities with certain countries.

EXPORT QUOTAS

Exports may also be subjected to quantitative restrictions by government action. Quantitative export controls are intended to accomplish one or more of the following objectives:

1. To prevent strategic goods from reaching the hands of unfriendly powers.
2. To assure all or a significant proportion of certain products in short supply for the home market.
3. To permit the control of surpluses on a national or an international basis in order to achieve production and price stability.

These objectives can be attained more positively and with greater ease by quotas than by tariffs. Like import quotas, export quotas may be unilateral when they are established without prior agreement with other nations, and bilateral or multilateral when they are the result of agreements. They are administered chiefly by licensing.

Export and production control measures have featured many schemes to improve the market and the price of certain raw materials. Such plans, pertaining to rubber, sugar, tin, wheat, and a number of other commodities, are of long standing. Export quotas are widely used for these commodities, usually under international supervision. The quotas are generally announced in advance with a fixed export price range for each quota period. These controls are identified with the international commodity agreements discussed in Chapter 18.

THE ECONOMIC EFFECTS OF QUOTAS

The economic effects of import quotas upon the domestic economy and the rest of the world are many and complex and vary between the short and the long run. This discussion is confined to the more salient effects of quotas upon prices and the balance of payments of the quota country and the relation of these effects to international trade.

Trade and Protection Effects. An import quota has price, trade, protection, consumption, and income-redistribution effects that are similar to those of an import duty. Instead of generating government revenue, however, an import quota ordinarily creates monopoly profits for the importers or exporters of the product in question.

Figure 12-3 illustrates the price and monopoly profit effects of an import quota under the simplifying assumptions of (1) a less-than-perfectly elastic foreign supply (increasing foreign costs of production), and (2) no domestic production.

The domestic demand schedule and the import supply schedule of country A are represented by Da-Da and Si-Si respectively, with quantity O-Q imported at the equilibrium price O-P. Upon the introduction of a quota, O-Q', by country A, foreign suppliers are willing to accept the price O-P' for the quantity O-Q' as indicated by the supply schedule Si-Si, while domestic users are willing to pay the price O-P'' for this same quantity on the basis of their demand schedule Da-Da. The price differential gives rise to quota profits P'-P''-L-K, that is, the excess of the selling price over the supply price (P'-P'') times the amount imported (O-Q').

What happens to the quota profits under our assumptions depends upon whether or not domestic importers and foreign exporters, as separate groups, are freely competing among themselves and with each other, or whether they are separately organized as monopsonists and monopolists. When importers and exporters as separate groups are freely competing in their respective markets with no licensing system in operation, then they will rush to supply the quota country before the quota becomes exhausted. Under such circumstances, quota profits will probably be shared by both importers and

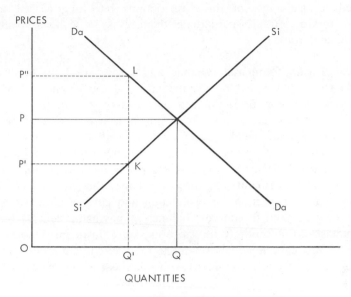

PRICES

Figure 12-3

PRICE EFFECTS OF A QUOTA

exporters depending on the competitive relations between them. If, however, these importers hold import licenses that put them in a monopoly position, they will reap the full benefits of the quota profits. Conversely, if the exporters rather than the importers are the holders of the licenses, or if they are organized and in full control of the market, they will reap the full benefits of the quota profits themselves. Finally, if the government auctions licenses, the quota profits are shared between the state and the licensees. The consumer, however, always pays the difference between the world price and the monopoly price charged him.

When the country is also a producer of the product in question, quota profits will be less than otherwise as a result of higher domestic output (protection effect). When the domestic supply of the import-competing good is highly elastic, then most of the quota profits will accrue to domestic producers as extra revenue (income-redistribution effect).

Finally, a tariff quota limits monopoly profits for importers or exporters because additional imports can always be obtained at a higher duty.

Import Quotas and the Balance of Payments. When a country experiences a trade deficit in its balance of international payments, it can quickly suppress such a deficit by the use of quotas. But the artificial reduction of imports disrupts trade patterns and trade relations, and other countries may be forced to adopt similar policies in self-protection.

Furthermore, once quantitative restrictions are adopted, they tend to create a new class of vested interests that will oppose changes even when the immediate usefulness of these restrictions has long ceased to exist. Quotas, therefore, tend to perpetuate themselves in artificial restraint of competition and trade.

Quotas and Tariffs Compared. Quotas and tariffs are both tools of protection. As such, they affect prices, income, and the balance of payments. Either may be used for discriminatory purposes in international trade.

Quotas, however, are absolute and inflexible irrespective of prices and elasticities. In contrast, the degree of protection afforded by tariffs is relative since it is subject to market responses. Quotas separate markets pricewise and raise domestic prices above world prices by freezing import supply relative to domestic demand. On the other hand, the price effect of tariffs depends on market conditions of production and consumption. Both quotas and tariffs may be used to suppress balance of payments deficits, but tariffs (unlike quotas) do not entirely foreclose market adjustment. Quotas are not conducive to meting out equal treatment to different countries; tariffs, on the other hand, are more amenable to such treatment under the most-favored-nation concept.

Several other differences between quotas and tariffs are noteworthy:

1. Quotas are better suited for quick emergency application by administrative action. Tariffs require statutory legislation, which is too slow for immediate action.

2. Quotas are a direct source of monopoly profits. Tariffs do not necessarily induce monopolistic practices, and they are ordinarily less burdensome to consumers.

3. Quotas invariably stifle competition. Tariffs usually allow some competition.

4. Quotas are simpler and easier to manage than tariffs, but they deprive the government of the revenues that accrue from customs duties (unless, of course, the state auctions import licenses).

5. Because quotas are a more effective tool of restriction than tariffs, they are also a more potent weapon for retaliation and bargaining.

In general, therefore, quotas are much more restrictive than tariffs. Although the industrial countries have abandoned import quotas on most trade in manufactures, they still use them extensively in agricultural trade. For the developing countries, quantitative trade restrictions continue to be a major instrument of commercial and balance of payments policies.

OTHER NONTARIFF TRADE BARRIERS

As the industrial countries progressively cut tariff rates and eliminate quotas under the auspices of the General Agreement on Tariffs and Trade, nontariff trade barriers are becoming more and more prominent.[12] The

---

[12] The General Agreement on Tariffs and Trade (GATT) is discussed in Chapter 15.

lowering of tariffs has been compared to the draining of a swamp: the lower water level has revealed all sorts of stumps and snags (nontariff barriers) that still make the swamp difficult to cross. Nontariff trade barriers form a heterogeneous collection of government policies and administrative practices that in one way or another either discriminate against imports or discriminate in favor of exports. Some nontariff measures are protectionist in both intent and effect, such as import quotas, discriminatory taxes, and customs valuations that do not reflect actual costs. But the majority of nontariff measures are protectionist in effect rather than in intent; for example, antidumping regulations, border tax adjustments, and health regulations, to mention only a few.

Their immense variety, their concealment in otherwise legitimate practices, their difficult-to-measure trade and protection effects, all combine to make any international efforts to eliminate nontariff trade barriers an exceedingly difficult enterprise as compared to tariffs and quantitative restrictions. The following sections simply identify the major kinds of nontariff trade barriers and their broad implications for international trade.

CUSTOMS CLASSIFICATION AND VALUATION

When a tariff is ad valorem, the duty imposed on a particular import good depends on how it is classified in the tariff schedule and how it is valued by the customs authorities. Complicated and obscure tariff nomenclatures coupled with ambiguous rules of classification give customs authorities plenty of opportunity for arbitrary classifications. The resulting uncertainty (and the higher duties in many instances) can act as a strong deterrent to trade.

Much more attention has been given to customs valuations that depart from the actual market value of the imported good. Foreigners commonly cite the "American Selling Price" or ASP as a prime example of a customs valuation that restricts imports. The United States values most import goods at their "foreign export value," the market value at the foreign point of export. For benzenoid chemicals and a few other products, however, the customs valuation is the selling price within the United States (ordinarily much higher than the foreign export value) whenever it is determined that the import is "competitive" with or "like or similar" to a domestic product. Clearly both the intent and effect of the ASP is to afford the U.S. chemical industry higher protection than it would receive with the standard valuation.

The protection effects now associated with customs classification and valuation would largely disappear if all countries were to adopt the Brussels Tariff Nomenclature and a uniform valuation system.

ANTIDUMPING REGULATIONS

The disparaging term "dumping" describes the practice of selling a product in one national market at a lower price than it is sold in another national market. Dumping, therefore, is price discrimination between national markets.

Economists distinguish between sporadic, predatory, and persistent dumping. Sporadic dumping occurs when producers dispose of unexpected surpluses abroad at lower prices than at home. Predatory dumping occurs when a producer uses low prices to weaken or drive out competitors in a foreign market; after competition is eliminated, the victorious producer is able to charge high, monopoly prices. Persistent dumping, as its name indicates, refers to the continuing sale of a product at lower prices abroad than at home. Such dumping may reflect the existence of a foreign demand that is more price-elastic than domestic demand. Persistent dumping may also arise when a producer prices his exports so as to cover only variable costs while absorbing his fixed costs in domestic sales.

Although persistent dumping benefits the importing country by improving its terms of sale, governments consider all forms of dumping by foreign producers to be bad. Consequently, many governments have antidumping regulations that usually involve a remedial or punitive antidumping duty. This duty is intended to nullify the "harmful" effects of the lower dumping price on domestic producers. Article 6 of the General Agreement on Tariffs and Trade stipulates that two criteria must be met for the legitimate application of antidumping duties by member states: "sales at less than fair value" (sales abroad at prices lower than in the country of origin) and "material injury" to a domestic industry.

Foreign governments have been critical of the way the United States administers its antidumping procedures, notably the sequential (rather than simultaneous) determination of "fair value" and "material injury" as well as the retroactive cessation of customs appraisal.[13] In turn, the U.S. Government has condemned the absence of specific, published, and open procedures in foreign antidumping investigations. Aside from these particular accusations, it is widely recognized that antidumping regulations can easily be used for protection against foreign competition.

In response to many complaints, a new antidumping code was negotiated during the Kennedy Round, entering into force on July 1, 1968.[14] The code requires the simultaneous determination of sales "at less than fair value" and "material injury," prohibits retroactive procedures, and gives assurance of open procedures to affected exporters and importers. The code also

---

[13] Under U.S. antidumping rules, the Secretary of the Treasury determines whether the sales of a good are being made at less than fair value. If he finds that sales are at less than fair value, then the case goes to the Tariff Commission for the determination of any injury to domestic industry. The Secretary of the Treasury is also authorized to suspend retroactively the customs appraisal of merchandise on any date after the 120th day before the question of dumping is presented to him. The new antidumping code (discussed below) would change these administrative procedures.

[14] The Kennedy Round is taken up in Chapter 15. The U.S. Congress has refused to amend the Antidumping Act to conform to the international code.

stipulates that the imports sold at less than fair value be the *principal* causal factor of any injury to a domestic industry producing "like products."

It is too early to say how effective the international code will be in eliminating protectionist abuses in the administration of antidumping regulations. Nevertheless, it represents a major step toward that end.

SUBSIDIES

Many national governments, anxious to see a greater development of certain domestic industries, frequently pay *subsidies* to domestic producers or exporters to stimulate the expansion of such industries. Subsidies may be extended in the form of outright cash disbursements, tax exemptions, preferential exchange rates, governmental contracts with special privileges, or some other favorable treatment. The granting of subsidies results in a cost advantage to the recipient, and for all intents and purposes, they are tantamount to an indirect form of protection.

Goods produced under a subsidy system that move in international trade tend to nullify the protective aspect of a tariff in the importing country. To reinstate the intended level of protection, the importing country may impose, in addition to the regular tariff duties, a special surtax or *countervailing* duty which is generally equal to the amount of the foreign subsidy.[15] In this manner, the landed cost to the domestic importer is raised by the amount of the subsidy granted to the foreign producer or exporter by his government.

Direct export subsidies for manufactured goods are prohibited by the General Agreement for Tariffs and Trade.[16] However, most of the industrial countries provide special financing and insurance arrangements that enable exporters to extend easier credit terms to foreign buyers. Commonly, exporters obtain credit at two or three percentage points below domestic market rates. This rate differential is a rough measure of the government subsidy. International efforts have been undertaken to harmonize national export credit policies, but many differences remain to distort the pattern of international trade.

Many domestic subsidies also influence imports and/or exports. Agricultural support programs are notorious in this regard, as are subsidies for shipbuilding. Although the trade and protection effects of individual production and consumption subsidies may be difficult to trace, their existence is seldom in question when they are applied to products that enter international trade. Since domestic subsidies are justified as desirable internal

---

[15] In illustration, in 1968 the United States imposed countervailing duties ranging up to 18 percent on imports of Italian and French canned tomatoes and tomato paste.

[16] Member states are also committed to "seek to avoid" export subsidies on primary (mainly agricultural) exports, and in no event to use subsidies to exceed their "equitable share" of export trade.

policy measures, international negotiations to remove trade-distorting subsidies are sure to be slow and only partly successful.

TAXES

Besides the basic customs duties prescribed in tariff schedules, certain imports may be subjected to excise taxes and processing taxes. *Excise taxes* are collectible upon the entry of the goods through customs, while *processing taxes* are payable upon the first domestic processing in the case of certain raw material and semifinished commodities.

The purpose of these special import taxes is generally to compensate for similar taxation of domestic goods. Very often, however, excise and processing taxes are levied exclusively on imports without corresponding levies on similar domestic products, or when similar or competing products are not produced in the domestic market. When excise and processing taxes are assessed exclusively on imports, they become protective measures concealed under less obvious identification, but no less a part of a protective tariff system.

Some internal taxes obviously discriminate against imports from some or all foreign countries, such as *road taxes* that are based on the cylinder capacity or horsepower of a vehicle rather than its value. For example, in Austria a Mercedes Benz 220 pays a road tax of about $30 a year while a similarly priced Ford Fairlane is taxed $275. Another illustration is the French practice of placing a surtax of $60 on a two-gallon container of grain spirits when all domestic liquors are distilled from fruits. To make matters worse, all advertising of grain liquors is prohibited in France. Actually, all governments are guilty of discriminatory taxation of one kind or another.

Border tax adjustments have received much attention in recent years because of their widespread use by the European Economic Community. Under GATT rules, a country that imposes a domestic *indirect* tax (a sales, turnover, excise, or value-added tax) on a good is permitted to give a tax rebate on exports of the same good and to levy an equivalent tax on imports of a similar good. In France, the border tax is about 20 percent of the duty-paid value of most industrial products. However, GATT prohibits any border adjustment for *direct* taxes, such as income, profits, payroll, social security, and property taxes. This system of border tax adjustment would be neutral in its effects on trade only if indirect taxes were fully shifted forward into prices while direct taxes were not shifted at all. Insofar as these conventional assumptions do not hold, border tax adjustments offer a trading advantage to countries relying primarily on indirect taxes for their revenue over other countries that depend mainly on direct taxes. The U.S. Government (which depends mostly on direct taxes) has argued that the new border taxes levied by the countries of the European Economic Community in the process of harmonizing their tax systems do, in fact, discriminate against American goods.

SOME ADDITIONAL NONTARIFF TRADE BARRIERS

The *procurement policies* of national and local governments afford a fertile soil for the discriminatory treatment of foreign products. The U.S. "Buy American" regulations of the Federal Government give domestic producers up to a 50 percent price spread advantage over foreign producers on Defense Department contracts and up to 12 percent on other government purchases. Several states have passed similar legislation. This discriminatory policy is matched by similar policies in other countries, whether by overt legislation or administrative practice.

Technical and health regulations refer to a variety of measures with respect to safety, health, marking, labelling, packaging, specifications, and standards. Although generally desirable on social grounds, such regulations may discriminate against imports by imposing greater hardships on foreign than on domestic producers. At present, there is only a modest degree of international agreement on technical and health regulations. Products that may freely enter one country may be banned in another country, especially in pharmaceuticals and foodstuffs. In illustration, American producers cannot export pickles to Norway because that country forbids the entry of food products containing alum, an ingredient of American pickle preservatives. In turn, the United States forbids the import of live animals or fresh meat products from a country that has hoof and mouth disease, even though the livestock in question may be grown in a region of the country that is free from that disease, a common situation in Argentina. In Canada, canned goods may be imported only in container sizes approved by the government.

Because of the increasing technical nature of products, rising living standards, and social pressures, we can expect a continuing proliferation of technical and health regulations. (Recently, foreign automobile producers have complained that the unilateral U.S. safety regulations do not consider the special problems of the small car and hence discriminate against imports.) Unless governments can agree to eliminate unnecessary regulations and to harmonize legitimate regulations, the outlook for any diminution of this class of nontariff trade barrier is a dim one.

Many countries have regulations that limit the proportion of foreign raw materials or other inputs that can be used in the production of specific domestic products. Known as *mixing quotas* or *linked-usage regulations*, they are similar in effect (and sometimes, intent) to ordinary import quotas. Australia, for example, requires its manufacturers of tobacco products to obtain 40 percent of their tobacco requirements from local growers. Governments may also promote import-substitution by imposing *local-content regulations* on certain industries, a practice especially favored in developing countries. In 1964, the Mexican government ordained that henceforth 60 percent of the production cost of each car made in Mexico must consist of Mexican-made parts.

From the foregoing discussion, it is evident that nontariff trade barriers are bewildering in their variety, frequently hidden in administrative practices, and, in many instances, exceedingly difficult to eliminate through international negotiations. Furthermore, new nontariff barriers are continually created as governments respond to changing circumstances. As a final illustration, it is likely that in the 1970's the U.S. Government will impose antipollution standards on a broad range of products, some of which may restrict imports. The U.S. Government may even go so far as to apply antipollution penalty duties on imports that have a cost advantage because they are produced in a country that lacks pollution controls.

SUMMARY

1. Despite the theoretical support for free trade, governments, more often than not, have interfered with the international movement of goods. These restrictive measures consist chiefly of (1) tariffs and (2) nontariff trade barriers.

2. There are three general classes of customs duties: transit, export, and import. Customs duties may be *ad valorem* or *specific*. All countries must develop a product classification or "customs nomenclature" to administer their tariff systems, and the advantages of a worldwide nomenclature are several. Most countries (but not the United States) now use the Brussels Tariff Nomenclature (BTN). Tariff schedules may have one, two, or three different duties for each dutiable article. Governments may mitigate the effects of their tariff rate systems through drawbacks, bonded warehouses, and free zones or ports.

3. Tariffs may be designed to serve a revenue function, a protection function, or a balance of payments function. The revenue and protection functions are contradictory: a tariff maximizes revenue when it does not restrict imports; it maximizes protection when it eliminates imports.

4. Depending upon the interplay of demand and supply elasticities, an import duty may raise the price of an import good (a) not at all, (b) less than the amount of the duty, or (c) equal to the amount of the duty. Because of pyramiding, a duty may even force a price rise greater than the amount of the duty.

5. In addition to price effects, an import duty has revenue, trade, protection, consumption, and income-redistribution effects.

6. Several methods have been used to measure the trade and protection effects of national tariff systems: (a) by tariff revenues, (b) by the height of duties (weighted or unweighted), (c) by effective rates rather than nominal rates, and (d) by elasticities and market share. Only the last method is fully justified by economic theory, but it is an enormous task to measure the elasticities of the thousands of products that make up a tariff system.

7. As the name implies, quantitative restrictions impose absolute limitations on foreign trade. Quantitative restrictions ordinarily take the form of import quotas administered by the issuance of import licenses to individual traders. Three major types of import quotas are in use throughout the world: unilateral quota, negotiated quota (bilateral or multilateral), and tariff quota. In recent years, the United States has restricted certain imports through negotiated quotas administered by the governments of supplying countries, the so-called voluntary export quotas.

8. The economic effects of an import quota are similar to those of an import duty. Instead of generating government revenue, however, an import quota usually creates monopoly profits for the importers or exporters of the product in question.

9. Whereas quotas are absolute and inflexible regardless of prices and elasticities, the trade and protection effects of tariffs are dependent on the market conditions of production and consumption. In general, therefore, quotas are more restrictive than tariffs.

10. Besides quotas, nontariff trade barriers include a bewildering variety of government measures that in one way or another either discriminate against imports or discriminate in favor of exports. The major kinds of nontariff trade barriers include customs classification and valuation, antidumping regulations, subsidies, and taxes. Other barriers that deserve mention are government procurement policies, technical and health regulations, and mixing quotas.

QUESTIONS AND APPLICATIONS

1. What is a tariff?

2. Distinguish between ad valorem, specific, and compound duties.

3. Differentiate between a bonded warehouse and a free zone.

4. "Tariffs provide revenue for the government and protection for domestic industries. Therefore, the higher the rate of duties, the greater the revenue and the greater the protection." Discuss the validity of this statement.

5. Utilizing a supply-demand diagram, indicate the various effects of an import duty. What happens to these effects when the foreign supply schedule becomes less elastic? When the domestic demand schedule becomes more elastic? When the domestic supply schedule becomes more elastic?

6. If the duty on a final product import is 15 percent while the weighted average of duties on importable inputs that contribute one-third of the value of the final product is 10 percent, what is the *effective* rate of duty on the final product?

7. Distinguish between unilateral, negotiated, and tariff quotas.

8. Why and how do import quotas create monopoly profits?

9. Compare quotas with tariffs, appraising their similarities and differences.

10. "Quotas are positive regulations of international trade while the results of tariffs are uncertain. Since a country must know where it is heading, the use of quotas is therefore preferable to the use of tariffs." Evaluate this statement.

11. Discuss the meaning of the following statement: "The majority of nontariff measures are protectionist in effect rather than in intent."

12. Why are direct export subsidies considered a nontariff trade barrier?

SELECTED READINGS

Balassa, Bela. *Trade Liberalization Among Industrial Countries.* New York: McGraw-Hill Book Company, 1967. Chapters 3 and 4.

Committee for Economic Development. *Nontariff Distortions of Trade.* New York: 1969.

Heck, Harold J. *The International Business Environment.* New York: American Management Association, Inc., 1969. Chapter 4.

Leighton, Richard I. *Economics of International Trade.* New York: McGraw-Hill Book Company, 1970. Chapter 4.

U.S. Department of the Treasury, Bureau of Customs. *Exporting to the United States.* Washington: U.S. Government Printing Office, 1969.

CHAPTER 13

ARGUMENTS FOR PROTECTION

International trade restrictions are man-made impediments to the free movement of goods and services among nations. They interfere with international specialization and the allocation of the natural, human, and capital resources of the world to their most productive uses. The extent, intensity, and directions of this interference vary with the conditions under which they operate.

The issue of "free trade" versus "protection" has been in dispute ever since the eighteenth century; the literature on this controversy is one of the most extensive in the annals of political economy. The arguments are often complex and subtle, although the controversy itself is rather simple.

THE CASE FOR FREE TRADE

The theory of international trade demonstrates that for the world as a whole free trade leads to a higher level of output and income than no trade (autarky). Free trade also enables each nation to obtain a higher level of production and consumption than can be obtained in isolation. Under perfect competition, free trade achieves a worldwide allocation of resources that meets the requirement of Pareto optimality: it is impossible to make anyone better off (through reallocation) without making someone else worse off. In the language of Chapter 3, free trade equalizes the marginal rate of substitution in production and the marginal rate of substitution in consumption for each product and for each nation.

However, most contemporary economists (unlike their predecessors) are reluctant to support free trade without some reservations. Their qualifications of the free trade doctrine spring from two basic concerns: (1) the departure of real-world markets from the conditions of perfect competition, and (2) the absence of any *necessary* correspondence between higher income and higher welfare at both national and international levels.

303

As we have discussed in Chapter 4, the (simple) theory of trade rests upon the assumptions of perfect competition—no monopoly or oligopoly, no product differentiation, no internal economies of scale, and no ignorance, uncertainty, or risk. Furthermore, the theory implicitly assumes that external economies and diseconomies do not cause a divergence between private and social benefits and costs, and that market prices truly indicate the full opportunity costs confronting a society.[1] Since these assumptions are only partially matched in actual markets, it follows that free trade will not achieve Pareto optimality and that more trade will not necessarily bring a higher allocative efficiency to the national and world economy.

However, to say that the allocative efficiency of free trade may not be optimal is a poor argument for protection. Rather, it is an argument for direct measures to improve the functioning of competitive markets through antitrust policies that eliminate or restrain monopoly and oligopoly, through improvements in the flow of information to consumers and producers (to reduce ignorance and risk), through taxes and subsidies to remove any divergences between private and social benefits and costs, and through other measures that promote competition.

Actually, protection is an ineffectual policy tool to overcome the defects of imperfect competition as compared to more direct tools. Furthermore, there is little assurance that the trade restrictions actually imposed by a government will add to economic efficiency. When account is taken of protectionist politics, the probability is high that restrictions will *lower* economic efficiency—a policy of throwing out the baby with the bath water. The existence of market imperfections, therefore, has not turned economists into protectionists, although they may argue the desirability of selective restrictions in carefully defined circumstances, the "theory of the second-best" described later in the chapter. And, because of the possible existence of internal economies of scale as well as external economies, economists have also traditionally recognized the legitimacy of the infant-industry argument for protection.

A second reason why most economists are reluctant to offer unqualified support of free trade is the question of economic welfare. Even if Pareto optimality were achieved in the allocation of national and world resources, it would not *necessarily* follow that free trade would also optimize national and world *welfare*. One problem is that competitive markets determine not only the prices of goods but also factor prices (incomes). By altering

---

[1] External economies exist when a firm (or industry) creates values for society that it cannot sell in a market (such as training workers who subsequently leave the firm for other employment). This situation makes the private value of the firm's output less than its social value. External diseconomies refer to social costs of production (such as pollution) that are not borne by the producer, making private costs less than social costs. In the case of external economies, the firm is producing too little to maximize social value; in the case of external diseconomies, too much.

relative prices, free trade also alters income distribution among individuals and groups both within and between nations. If the last (marginal) dollar of income earned by recipients in all countries provided the same satisfaction (welfare), then free trade under perfect competition would indeed maximize national and world welfare. Unfortunately, there is no objective way to make interpersonal comparisons of welfare. The presumption is strong, of course, that the marginal dollar received by a poor person contributes more welfare than the marginal dollar received by a rich person and, by extension, that poor countries benefit more than rich countries from the marginal income dollar. But in the final analysis this is an ethical judgment, not a scientific one.

The welfare question is hardly a general argument against free trade. A priori, there is no reason to believe that free trade worsens income distribution compared to no or restricted trade. In view of the motivations and political factors that actually determine protectionist policies, one can also be justifiably dubious that governments will select only those restrictions that improve national welfare, to say nothing of world welfare. Protection, therefore, is a singularly inappropriate policy to achieve higher levels of welfare for a group or nation.[2] Protection would sacrifice the gains from economic efficiency to an uncertain (and at times, perverse) welfare effect. More to the point, direct measures to redistribute income are available to all governments in the form of subsidies and taxation.[3]

To sum up, economic theory cannot demonstrate that under all circumstances free trade will improve economic efficiency or enhance economic welfare. In practice, however, economists remain firmly on the side of freer, if not free, trade. They remain skeptical of the capacity of governments to apply selective trade restrictions in such a way as to reach higher levels of economic efficiency or welfare. The history of protection is highly convincing on this score. At the same time, most economists would agree that free trade is not sufficient to achieve optimal world income and welfare, but must be coupled with government policies that improve the social efficiency of markets, achieve a better income distribution, and promote economic growth.

---

[2] What happens when governments seek to redistribute income by interfering with the market mechanism is clearly shown by agricultural programs that have promoted self-sufficiency at a cost of lower economic efficiency. A superior approach (granted the desirability of redistributing income to farmers) would be direct income subsidies financed out of general taxation, leaving markets free to allocate agricultural production both within and among nations.

[3] Mechanisms to redistribute income among countries are admittedly primitive compared to domestic mechanisms: there is no international authority to tax the rich and subsidize the poor. But attempts to achieve income redistribution between rich and poor countries via market restrictions (such as international commodity agreements) must reckon with the costs of lower economic efficiency. Direct income transfers avoid those costs.

Strictly speaking, the argument for free trade (like all arguments for economic policies) is a conditional one. It states that *if* a nation wants to attain a higher level of economic efficiency, then it can do so by trading with other nations. But a nation can choose to reject economic efficiency for noneconomic values (such as the preservation of a social group or a way of life against foreign influences) and, in so doing, reject free trade in part or in whole.

Economists have long recognized the legitimacy of the national defense argument for protection in a hostile world. Commonly, however, nations have chosen protection in ignorance of its economic costs. Only the mythical economic man would argue that economic efficiency should be the exclusive goal of society, but only a fool would argue that economic efficiency does not matter at all.

One last comment is in order. No one, including the most ardent protectionist, opposes specialization and trade among the different regions of his own country. And yet, the *economic* argument for free international trade is the same as the argument for unfettered interregional trade. The essential difference between external and internal trade is *political* only: one involves foreigners, the other does not. It is this difference that has nurtured protectionism through the ages; the principal ally of protectionism is economic nationalism.[4]

THE CASE FOR PROTECTION

Although in most circumstances the welfare of a country as a whole is reduced by import protection, the welfare of the specific factors of production associated with a protected industry will increase because of the income-redistribution effect.[5] In seeking protection, therefore, individual producers and labor unions are trying to improve their own well-being. Hence, any attempt to lower or eliminate existing protection is stubbornly resisted, and continuing pressure is applied to national governments to initiate new protection. Frank recognition of the fact that certain groups would lose with a free trade policy is essential to any understanding of the political strength of protectionism.

In presenting their case to the public and government, protectionists would not get far if they argued in terms of their own private gain. Thus, all their arguments assert that protection benefits the national interest. In so many words, protectionists maintain that what is good for my industry

---

[4] As we shall observe in Chapter 25, economic nationalism also nurtures resistance to foreign enterprise—another form of protectionism.

[5] See Figure 12-2 on p. 284. In the longer run, when there is time for factors to move into the protected industry, marginal factor returns in that industry will tend to equal marginal factor returns in other (unprotected) industries. The ultimate beneficiary of protection is the factor (or factors) used intensively in the protected industry; other factors suffer a loss in welfare.

is also good for my country.[6] In defending this proposition they are usually helped by the nationalistic attitudes of their fellow citizens.

The arguments against free trade try to show that (1) its advantages are outweighed by its shortcomings; (2) the interdependence of nations implicit in free trade subjects national economies to uncertainties inherent in sudden changes in the policies of other nations that often cause serious dislocations, if not losses, far greater than the benefits to be derived from a free-trade policy; and (3) the price system and perfect competition underlying the theory of free trade are, at best, only partially true in the real world where prices and production are subjected to controls and rigidities that contribute to what has been referred to as a *disequilibrium system* under which restrictions on consumers and/or producers are the tools of adjustment rather than price.

In the course of time many ingenious pleas have been advanced in direct support of protection. The pleas have been based on a variety of arguments, none of which possess unqualified economic validity. A few of these arguments rationalize short-term gains at the expense of long-term national benefits; others follow exactly the opposite approach; most of the remaining arguments have only partial economic validity or are completely fallacious, drawing their strength mainly from their engaging emotional mass appeal.

The long series of arguments for protection may be classified into four categories: (1) fallacious arguments, (2) questionable arguments, (3) qualified arguments, and (4) sophisticated arguments.

FALLACIOUS ARGUMENTS FOR PROTECTION

Fallacious arguments for protection rely on plausibility or mass emotional appeal rather than economic logic.

KEEP-MONEY-AT-HOME ARGUMENT

The proponents of this argument claim that when domestic residents buy imported goods, the country gets the goods and the foreigner gets the money. When, on the other hand, the residents buy domestic goods, it is argued that the country keeps both the goods and the money, and hence the country that prevents imports is richer for doing so.

The utter fallacy of this argument is rooted in the crudest form of mercantilistic theory, which maintained that money is wealth in itself. Money, as such, is a means of exchange. Money paid for imports must return sooner or later either in payment for exports or as investment, since it has no redemption value except in the country of its issue.

---

[6] For this reason, most protectionist arguments commit the *fallacy of composition*: what is true of the part is necessarily true of the whole.

HOME-MARKET ARGUMENT

This argument claims that the domestic producer has a right to the domestic market and that by reducing or eliminating imports, more goods will be produced at home, more jobs will be created, and increased domestic activity will be the result.

The fallacy of this argument stems from the fact that any shift from imports to domestic production is ultimately offset by a contraction of production for export. Unless a country is willing to give its goods away, it can only continue to export by continuing to import. Thus, the shift from foreign to domestic sources of supply does not in any way increase real purchasing power. In fact, the home market argument leads to a less efficient economy and a *decline* in real purchasing power.

EQUALIZATION-OF-COSTS-OF-PRODUCTION ARGUMENT

Some protectionists have favored the so-called "scientific method of tariff making" that is intended to equalize the costs of production between foreign and domestic producers and to neutralize any advantage the foreigner may have over the domestic producer in lower taxes, cheaper labor, or other costs. This argument allegedly implies a spirit of "fair competition," not the exclusion of imports. When, however, by reason of actual cost structure or artificial measures, costs of production become identical, the very basis of international trade disappears. The logical consequence of this pseudo-scientific method is the elimination of trade between nations. Thus, the equalization-of-costs-of-production argument for protection is utterly fallacious and is one of the most deceitful ever advanced in support of protection.

A close examination of the equalization-of-costs argument reveals the presence of many problems. Producers in any country have different and constantly changing costs for the same products. Whose costs are to serve as a frame of reference?

If we aim for protection of *all* domestic producers against *all* foreign producers, we must equalize the lowest foreign costs with the highest costs of the least efficient domestic producer. To accomplish this, a very high duty is required to overcome the extreme cost differential. Domestic prices to the consumer must rise to the high level of the domestic marginal producer's cost. The efficient domestic producer will reap an extra monopoly profit, and the domestic consumer will be forced to subsidize the highest form of inefficiency.

In addition, the literal enforcement of such a policy entails considerable administrative difficulties in the collection of the necessary cost information for duty adjustments. This seems to be hardly worthwhile when the result can only be the prevention of imports and the ultimate elimination of trade, as well as the impairment of the country's standard of living—surely a misconception of the scientific approach, to say the least.

Despite these objections, a tariff provision to equalize the costs of production was actually incorporated in the United States Tariff Acts of 1922 and 1930. This provision, however, has been enforced only in a few instances.

LOW-WAGE ARGUMENT

Some protectionists claim that a high-wage country cannot afford to trade with low-wage or "pauper-labor" countries without risking a reduction in its own wages through competition with the low foreign wage level, thereby jeopardizing its standard of living. They assert further that, to protect its workers from the competition of low-paid foreign workers, a high-wage country must impose a tariff duty on cheap goods that are imported from the low-wage countries.

More fundamentally, it is alleged that a country can only *lose* from trade with a low-wage country, since that country can undersell it. This argument has several weaknesses. First, it may be queried as to how any trade is possible if the domestic country is undersold in *all* products for, in that case, it could not export anything nor, therefore, import anything. If only *some* products are in question, then the argument is absurd since trade obviously requires that one country undersell the other country in some goods, and vice versa. Second, it must be pointed out that wages may be low and unit costs high when productivity is low. Thus, there is no necessary connection between low wages and low costs. Third, the low-wage argument must bow to the logic of the theory of comparative costs. As long as cost ratios are dissimilar, trade is profitable between countries regardless of absolute wage levels.

The low-wage argument is wrong when it infers that high prices necessarily result from high wages and low prices from low wages. High wages in the United States are a consequence of the high productivity of American labor, which is aided in its tasks by the availability of raw materials, massive capital equipment, advanced technology, sophisticated management, and an elaborate infrastructure of communication, transportation, power, and other facilities. This high productivity explains both the high American standard of living and the ability of American exporters to compete effectively with foreign producers who may pay far lower wages.[7] In light of the low-wage

---

[7] Because of high worker productivity, the highest wages in the United States are generally found in the export industries, such as aerospace, machinery, and chemicals. How, then, could anyone explain the existence of American exports if lower wages were the sole index of competitive advantage?

argument of U.S. protectionists, it is ironic that many producers in developing countries demand protection against U.S. products on the grounds that their (low-wage) industries cannot compete against the highly productive American industries!

It is true that domestic industries whose productivity is relatively low may find that high wages raise their costs above foreign costs. But such a situation is not a logical argument for protection. Rather, it is a signal for a reallocation of labor and capital to other lines of production that have a comparative advantage vis-à-vis foreign production. Such a reallocation occurs all the time as a result of domestic interregional competition, as witness, for example, the migration of the U.S. textile industry from New England to the South. It is the fear of a painful adjustment to import competition that really motivates the proponents of the low-wage argument rather than the unlikely danger of a general deterioration of the country's standard of living. Import restrictions, however, are neither the most desirable nor the only solution to this problem. What is needed is government assistance that will facilitate an orderly redeployment of capital and workers so as to minimize adjustment costs while, at the same time, preserving the benefits of international trade.

PREVENTION-OF-INJURY ARGUMENT

The prevention-of-injury argument is a relatively new argument designed to safeguard the vulnerability of an economy to increased imports subsequent to contemplated tariff concessions, or to concessions already granted under trade agreements. The advocates of this argument proclaim their willingness to reduce and maintain low tariffs, provided that in so doing no domestic industry or producer is threatened by excessive imports that result from such low rates of duties. Any contemplated concession must not reduce an existing rate to a preestimated low point, or *peril point*, that would jeopardize domestic producers. In addition, when previously reduced rates begin to threaten domestic producers, there should be an escape mechanism, or *escape clause*, to permit the restoration of higher rates or the tightening of quota controls.

On the surface, this argument sounds reasonable and implies an attitude of moderation. What this argument means in actual practice, however, is the elimination of international competition under comparative advantage when such competition threatens to divert a portion of the home market away from domestic producers, regardless of changed market conditions and technology at home and abroad.

The prevention-of-injury argument is closely related to the home-market and the equalization-of-costs-of-production arguments. It is an argument in denial of progress that is likely to encourage the perpetuation of static and regressive industries.

QUESTIONABLE ARGUMENTS FOR PROTECTION

Certain arguments for protection, although not entirely fallacious, represent an inferior policy or easily lend themselves to abuse.

EMPLOYMENT ARGUMENT

The basis for this argument is that the imposition of a tariff or other form of import restriction in periods of unemployment will reduce imports and generate home production. Increased domestic production in turn will increase employment and national income. Furthermore, since imports (like savings) cause a leakage in the domestic income stream, a reduction of imports will generate an even greater amount of domestic expenditure via the income multiplier.

Another version of the employment argument asserts that widespread unemployment justifies any sort of production regardless of comparative advantage since it will make a net addition to a country's national income. Thus, a country will benefit by restricting imports and using idle factors to produce similar goods at home—the opportunity cost of imports is the exports that must be exchanged for them, whereas the opportunity cost of new domestic production is zero. Hence, international specialization and trade must give way to self-sufficiency when unemployment arises in the domestic economy.

This argument was especially persuasive during the Depression of the thirties, but it rests upon several questionable assumptions: (1) full employment is the overriding national economic objective; (2) international trade must be sacrificed to attain full employment; and (3) the international consequences of a domestic full-employment policy can be safely ignored. We now turn to a brief evaluation of these assumptions.

First, employment for the sake of employment cannot be a sound national objective. Full employment is most productive when the factors of production are allocated in accordance with comparative advantage. In that way each factor is engaged in production in which its productivity is highest. Full employment is a means to the higher objective of national welfare, and this is maximized only when productivity cannot be raised by shifting factors of production from one economic activity to another. When imports are curtailed to afford opportunities for domestic employment, the losses occasioned by a lesser degree of international specialization must be set against any gains in national production.

Second, even though the gains in national production are greater than the losses brought about by the decline in international specialization, the policy of sacrificing international trade to increase domestic employment is not in the national interest, for there are other ways of stimulating employment that do not require the restriction of trade. An anticyclical employment policy should place main reliance on government fiscal and monetary policies that feed the inadequate stream of purchasing power in the economy. Not only will such policies alleviate unemployment in the domestic economy, but by sustaining or increasing imports they will also benefit foreign countries.

Third, the policy of curtailing imports to stimulate domestic employment is never in the interest of the community of nations. Actually that policy amounts to exporting unemployment to other nations since the decline in imports will depress foreign economies. Moreover, foreign countries can retaliate by restricting their own imports. As a consequence, international relations become embittered, international trade spirals downward, and few countries are better off in terms of employment while many are much worse off in terms of economic welfare. This sequence took place to an unfortunate extent in the early thirties.

While condemning the policy of exporting one's unemployment, we must also recognize the fact that few nations are capable of overcoming massive unemployment by the use of fiscal and monetary policies alone unless international economic cooperation is forthcoming. Such policies tend to increase imports while, at the same time, exports may be falling because of depression abroad, and few nations have the reserves to finance the resulting gap between their exports and imports until recovery sets in abroad. When, however, nations—particularly the major trading nations—cooperate with each other by extending credit and by harmonizing their domestic recovery measures, it may be possible for them to restore employment without seriously curtailing trade.

The foregoing remarks apply to *cyclical* unemployment that results from a deflationary gap in effective demand that cuts across all sectors of the economy. When protection is advocated as a remedy for *structural* unemployment, then the employment argument becomes even more questionable.

Structural unemployment occurs when the composition of a nation's output and/or the quality and supply of its factors of production fail to adapt to new patterns of demand and competition. That is to say, the *structure* of the economy is no longer suited to changing markets. Declining industries and regions make their appearance, and workers gradually lose their jobs while the rest of the economy is growing. The basic disturbance causing structural unemployment may originate at home, abroad as specific export markets dry up or foreign competitors enter domestic markets (import competition), or both at home and abroad.[8]

When import competition appears to be causing structural unemployment, workers and management in the affected industry are quick to demand

---

[8] Structural unemployment in the United States today mainly results from changes in the domestic economy: the automation of industry is cutting the demand for unskilled and semiskilled workers and mechanization of agriculture is forcing the family farm out of existence. The Appalachian region, in particular, has been badly hurt by both changes.

that government curtail imports by higher tariffs, quotas, or other means.[9] This protectionist solution attempts to preserve the status quo at the cost of losing the benefits of international specialization. If no other solution to the problem of structural unemployment were possible, protection would be justifiable as a way of utilizing labor and capital that would otherwise stand idle. But this is not the case. Basically, what is needed is a reallocation of productive factors, shifting them out of declining industries into expanding ones.

The capacity of an economy to adapt to change and thereby avoid or minimize structural imbalances is dependent primarily on the mobility of its factors of production and its overall rate of growth. When labor and capital move quickly out of declining industries into growing industries, then structural unemployment is transitional rather than prolonged. Mobility will be enhanced if the economy as a whole is growing, generating new opportunities for employment and capital investment. When, on the other hand, labor does not shift easily from one job to another or from one place to another, then structural unemployment may endure for a generation or more. Immobility is further intensified by a slowly growing economy.

All economies suffer from factor immobility, but it is most pervasive in underdeveloped countries, where economic, social, and cultural conditions favor stability over change. For such countries import protection may be necessary to give them time to transform their economies, but the ultimate solution is to develop a capacity to grow and adjust to change. For developed countries, however, protection is not a reasonable alternative to measures that are aimed directly at increasing labor and capital mobility. In the last analysis, the cause of structural unemployment lies in a failure to adapt to technological and other changes. As we have stressed earlier, the world economy is dynamic, and nations can obtain the full advantages of international specialization only by responding quickly to new market opportunities and competitive challenges.

ANTIDUMPING ARGUMENT

The dumping of goods in an importing country at prices below those prevailing in the exporting country may be beneficial or harmful, depending upon circumstances. If dumping is persistent, buyers in the importing country reap a continuous benefit that results from lower prices for foreign goods. If the importing country has no domestic industry competing with the dumped product, there is, of course, no argument for protection. If, on the other hand, such an industry exists, domestic producers are in no different position than if the dumping price resulted from a normal cost advantage in the exporting country. The fact that there is an element of unfairness to domestic producers in the situation is not a valid reason for protection since the nation as a whole is benefited.

---

[9] See Chapter 15.

When dumping is sporadic and is intended to harass or put a competing domestic industry out of business in order to raise prices afterwards, dumping becomes undesirable. To prevent such *predatory dumping*, action is necessary. High protection that precludes the possibility of predatory dumping, however, inflicts upon the domestic economy a permanent higher cost that is totally unjustified. By administrative action or by antidumping duties, predatory dumping can be prevented if and when it occurs by making its practice costly and ineffective. As observed in the preceding chapter, this limited use of antidumping measures is violated in practice: governments do not distinguish between persistent and predatory dumping and they frequently utilize devices in the name of antidumping that amount to sheer protection.

BARGAINING-AND-RETALIATION ARGUMENT

It has been argued that a country with a protective tariff is in a better position to bargain with other countries for concessions on its exports than is a country that has nothing to offer in return. It follows, therefore, that a free-trade (or low-tariff) country should adopt some form of protection in order to be in a bargaining position.

The logic of this argument is strong and such a policy may work out in actual practice. It does not, however, necessarily follow that the argument has economic validity. A free-trade country that resorts to protection for purposes of bargaining sacrifices the benefits of international specialization. Furthermore, once protection is introduced, domestic industries develop behind its shield and become entrenched, exerting pressures upon their government when the time comes to give up such protection. Experience proves that this kind of pressure is usually most successful in preventing the return to freer trade and, therefore, the country will, in all probability, become permanently committed to protection. Similarly, a country adopting a tariff for retaliation purposes is, so to speak, adding insult to injury by depriving itself of the benefits from unhindered imports. More to the point, retaliation can easily breed counterretaliation and a general worsening of trade relations rather than an abandonment of the measure that provoked the retaliation. To conclude, the bargaining-and-retaliation argument involves a certain loss and an uncertain gain together with ample opportunity for abuse.

QUALIFIED ARGUMENTS FOR PROTECTION

Some arguments for protection find their justification either in non-economic considerations, such as national defense, or in the expectation of long-term economic benefits that will more than compensate for the immediate costs of protection.

NATIONAL SECURITY ARGUMENT

It is argued that a nation dependent on foreign sources of supply is in a particularly vulnerable position during a war. The harrowing experience of the United Kingdom in both World Wars is cited as proof of this assertion—twice the German submarine blockade almost brought that country to her knees by cutting off imports of food and raw materials. This is, of course, a political or military argument rather than an economic one, but it has many economic implications. Its proper evaluation requires not only a careful forecast of the probable nature of a future war but a searching study of the relationships between economic strength and military capacity as well. For example, if another world war promises destruction of everyone's productive facilities within a few hours, then it is military strength in being that counts and the military argument for economic self-sufficiency falls by the wayside.

Few would disagree with the need to maintain an "adequate" national defense. Even Adam Smith, the venerable father of free trade, wrote in 1776 that "defense is much more important than opulence." [10] The problem lies in defining the specific requirements of national defense and the proper way to meet those requirements. Otherwise the national security argument may be used to justify complete self-sufficiency or the protection of *any* industry. Since most producers consider their activities essential to the defense of their country, the national security argument is particularly subject to abuse. In the United States, manufacturers of peanuts, candles, thumbtacks, umbrella frames, gloves, and many other products of ordinary consumption have all asked for protection on grounds of national security.

Today, military experts are inclined to view future wars in terms of "adequate strength in a constant state of readiness" to meet an all-out thermonuclear attack rather than in terms of "potential production capacity." If this is the true situation, then the protection of "strategic" domestic industries can make no contribution to national security. Apart from this consideration, direct subsidies are better policy tools than import restrictions to maintain defense industries: they are more precise in their effects, more subject to review, and less costly to the nation.[11]

In conclusion, there is no assurance that greater economic self-sufficiency will enhance a nation's military power, and by the same token there is no justification to deny out of hand the compatibility of free trade and a nation's ability to defend itself against armed aggression.

INFANT-INDUSTRY ARGUMENT

In its traditional form, the infant-industry argument asserts that a new industry having a potential comparative advantage may not get started in a country unless it is given temporary protection against foreign competition.

---

[10] Adam Smith, *The Wealth of Nations* (New York: Random House, Inc., 1937), p. 431.

[11] Because subsidies do not raise the price of the product in question, they avoid the consumption loss of tariffs or import quotas; they do, however, involve a production loss. (See page 285 for a discussion of consumption and production losses due to protection.) The United States subsidizes its merchant marine for reasons of national security.

Most often, the argument stresses the necessity of protected domestic markets that will offer an opportunity for economies of scale in production. In terms of Figure 4-2 on p. 99, it is argued that protection would enable local manufacturers to produce at least O-G automobiles at a unit cost of O-C, thereby making them competitive with foreign manufacturers who already enjoy economies of scale. Aside from economies of scale, protection would also afford local producers the time to improve their skills in management, production, marketing, and the application of technology. Once competitive strength was built up, protection would be abandoned for free trade.

The infant-industry argument is associated with Alexander Hamilton, the first Secretary of the Treasury of the United States, and Frederick List, a German economist who lived in this country as a political refugee. Alexander Hamilton published his famous *Report on Manufactures* in 1791, urging the use of tariffs to foster the growth of manufacturing and to strengthen the American economy that was then predominantly agricultural. He contended that the vast resources of the country could be advantageously developed to compete with foreign industries that held a vast lead due to a prior start; that even though time and ingenuity could ultimately bring about such a development, governmental aid and promotion would speed up the process; and that the need for governmental assistance would constitute only a temporary departure from the free-trade doctrine in order to bring about a more speedy, more secure, and more steady demand for the surplus produce of the soil.[12]

Frederick List's historical approach to the question of free trade versus protection led him to the general conclusion that free trade is a cosmopolitan concept that is not necessarily in the best interest of a country in an intermediate stage of economic development.[13] Such a developing country could not readily develop new industries without temporary protection.

Economists have long accepted the theoretical validity of the infant-industry argument, recognizing that the theory of trade is a static analysis that abstracts from economies of scale. On the other hand, they have raised many questions with regard to its practical application.

First, it is not at all self-evident that an infant industry requires protection to get started. After all, many new enterprises are able to compete with well-entrenched older enterprises *within* a country under conditions of free trade. Some of these new ventures may even displace the less-dynamic older ones through better management, product innovation, quick response to market opportunities, and the like. Why should international competition be any different? If the long-run outlook of a true infant industry is so good, why should domestic entrepreneurs start with protection? After all, they can

---

[12] Isaac Asher, *International Trade, Tariff and Commercial Policies* (Homewood, Ill.: Richard D. Irwin, Inc., 1948), Chapter 4.

[13] Frederick List, *The National System of Political Economy* (London: Longmans, Green & Company, 1922).

capitalize early losses as part of their initial investment, and as long as the eventual return will cover this investment at a satisfactory profit, they should go ahead. If the response to this line of reasoning is that a country lacks the necessary local entrepreneurs, then the remedy is not protection as such but rather state enterprise (assuming the government has the necessary entrepreneurial talents) or the attraction of foreign entrepreneurs.[14]

Second, it is most difficult for a government to identify an industry that deserves infant-industry protection. The search for an industry that has a potential comparative advantage requires, in the words of one writer, "the skill of the engineer, the brain of the economist, and the audacity of the entrepreneur."[15] In the light of historical experience, the probability of a mistake must be rated very high. One illustration is the U.S. woolen-worsted industry. Started in the early years of this country as an infant industry, it must still be protected against import competition and shows no signs of being able to overcome its comparative disadvantage.

This last example indicates that a mistake tends to become irreversible. Once a new industry is protected, the pressure of vested interests prevents the removal of protection even (or especially) when it becomes evident that the industry will not be competitive. *Temporary* protection usually turns into *permanent* protection. The result is a misallocation of resources that thwarts rather than promotes economic development.

Third, even if the proper choice of an infant industry is made by a government, it does not necessarily follow that import protection is the best way to promote that industry. In particular, direct subsidies have several advantages over tariffs. For one thing, subsidies are less likely to end up as permanent protection because they are dependent on annual appropriations. Protectionists oppose subsidies for this very reason, but manufacturers who honestly seek only infant-industry protection should have no objection to them.

Although internal economies of scale are most often cited as the rationale for infant-industry protection, a stronger case rests on *external* economies. Suppose the industry in question would powerfully stimulate the growth of other industries (and the economy in general) through its research and development activities, its training of managers and workers whose skills are transferable to other industries, its assistance to suppliers, and in other ways. Such an industry that generates many backward and forward linkages with other industries would have a social value greater than its private value. But since entrepreneurs could not retain this extra social value, they might never start the industry without protection of some sort. In this situation, protection would eliminate the disparity between private and social values and thereby improve the allocation of the country's resources. However, the practical application of protection to "strategic" industries encounters all of

---

[14] Protection may be used to attract foreign entrepreneurs. See Chapter 25.

[15] John P. Powelson, *Latin America: Today's Economic and Social Revolution* (New York: McGraw-Hill Book Company, 1964), p. 198.

the difficulties already mentioned plus the added difficulty of identifying and measuring external benefits. The mistakes made by several developing countries in granting infant-industry protection to supposedly strategic industries such as steel, chemicals, and automobiles testify to the perils of policy in this area.

To conclude, the infant-industry argument is theoretically sound, especially in regard to external economies. But the difficulties of practical application insure that infant-industry protection will often turn into permanent protection with all its attendant costs. It should also be evident that the infant-industry argument does not apply to industrial countries such as the United States.

DIVERSIFICATION ARGUMENT

The diversification argument for protection is actually two arguments that commonly masquerade as one. One argument urges import protection as a means to bring about a diversification of *exports* so as to lessen instability in export income. The second argument proposes import protection as a means to achieve *diversification in the domestic economy* and thereby promote economic growth. Both arguments are put forth mainly by spokesmen of the nonindustrial, developing nations.

The diversification-for-stability argument proceeds from the dependence of many developing countries on one or two agricultural or mineral products for most of their export income. This "overspecialization" makes such countries highly sensitive to supply and/or demand shifts in a single export product. Furthermore, it is widely accepted that primary commodities experience wide cyclical fluctuations in prices because of low price elasticities of supply and demand.[16] In this context, therefore, the stability argument becomes an argument for the substitution of manufactured exports for primary exports via import protection that fosters the development of domestic industry.

Theoretically, the diversification-for-stability argument derives its validity from a possible divergence of private and social values in a world of change and uncertainty. When private costs do not fully reflect social costs, then the gains from higher economic efficiency may be more than offset by long-run losses due to economic disruptions caused by dependence on foreign markets. The policy application of this argument, however, is fraught with difficulties in choosing the proper diversification mix and the means to achieve it. In particular, import protection may be an ineffective policy tool compared to export subsidies and other measures of direct export promotion. Indeed, protection has a qualified validity *only* when export diversification requires the prior development of new industries to produce goods that are presently being imported by the country in question. Thus, the diversification-for-

---

[16] The export problems of the developing countries are explored in Chapter 17.

stability argument for protection is really a version of the infant-industry argument that emphasizes export stability rather than economies of scale.

The diversification-for-growth argument rests upon the doctrine of "balanced" economic growth that asserts the necessity for a simultaneous or parallel development of all industries throughout the economy.[17] This argument, therefore, may be used to justify a policy of general import substitution that cuts across all categories of industrial products. Lacking the specific criteria of the traditional infant-industry argument, the diversification-for-growth argument lends itself to easy abuse by protectionists. At its extreme, it closely resembles the argument for autarky in its real consequences. Following World War II many developing countries, especially in Latin America, adopted indiscriminate policies of import substitution under the banner of economic growth. Although these policies did achieve varying degrees of industrial diversification, they did so only in the form of many high-cost industries that will require indefinite protection to survive. Furthermore, these noncompetitive industries can make no contribution to the expansion of industrial exports. By discarding all considerations of comparative advantage in headlong pursuit of industrialization, these countries have gratuitously forsaken the gains from international specialization. In practice, therefore, the diversification-for-growth argument represents a highly questionable extension of the infant-industry argument. Unless diversification is introduced with extreme care, the national loss in economic efficiency (to say nothing of the international loss) brought about by the sacrifice of international specialization may turn out to be greater than the realized gains of economic growth.

SOPHISTICATED ARGUMENTS FOR PROTECTION

This section looks at two arguments that may justify import restrictions under certain conditions: the terms-of-trade argument (optimum tariff) and the theory of the second-best. Strictly speaking, they are not arguments for protection. The first is an argument for the exploitation of a national monopsony (or monopoly) position; the second, for the imposition of a tariff as a second-best policy when the first-best policy (free trade) is not possible. We call these arguments "sophisticated" because they appear in the formidable literature of economic theory rather than in the mouths of protectionists.

TERMS-OF-TRADE ARGUMENT AND THE OPTIMUM TARIFF

The terms-of-trade argument rests upon the proposition that at least part of a duty is absorbed by foreign suppliers when the price elasticity

---

[17] In opposition, the doctrine of "unbalanced" economic growth emphasizes the need to concentrate on key or strategic industries that will stimulate general economic development. This doctrine is consistent with the traditional infant-industry argument.

of import supply is less than infinite and the price elasticity of import demand is greater than zero. Given these elasticity conditions, we showed in Figure 12-1, p. 282, that the imposition of a duty raises the domestic price of the import good by less than the amount of the duty as foreign suppliers lower their prices in an attempt to maintain sales in the tariff-levying country. Hence, that country experiences an improvement in its terms of trade: the price it pays foreigners for the import good falls while the price it charges foreigners for its export goods remains the same.

The national gain from an improvement in the terms of trade, however, must be set against the national loss resulting from the trade effect of the tariff. In terms of Figure 12-2, p. 284, the *net* national gain is the sum of the revenue effect (*d*, which includes the terms-of-trade gain) and the income-redistribution effect (*r*) *minus* the loss in consumers' surplus due to the negative trade effect (*l* and *c*). This analysis leads to the concept of the *optimum tariff* that maximizes the net national gain.

At one extreme, when the entire duty is absorbed by foreign suppliers (perfectly inelastic supply), the *net* national gain equals the revenue effect, which is fully traceable to an improvement in the terms of trade. Since the duty does not affect the price paid by domestic consumers, there is no change in consumers' surplus and the trade effect is zero. In this situation the optimal tariff rate is infinite; the tariff-levying country is a pure *monopsonist* that can continually improve its terms of trade by raising the duty while importing the same volume of the good in question.

At the other extreme, when import supply is perfectly elastic, the optimum tariff rate is zero. In this situation a country cannot improve its terms of trade by imposing a duty because the entire duty is absorbed by domestic consumers who pay a postduty price that is higher than the preduty price by the full amount of the duty. The outcome is depicted in Figure 12-2, p. 284. Between the two extremes, the optimum tariff rate will depend on the price elasticities of import demand and import supply. In general, the more elastic the import demand and the more inelastic the import supply, the higher the optimum duty rate. However, this rate will be less than the rate that maximizes an improvement in the terms of trade because of the negative trade effect.

The terms-of-trade argument is not really an argument for protection; nor has it been used by protectionists. We have seen that the optimal tariff is highest when there is no protection effect, hardly a comforting thought to domestic producers who are anxious to keep out imports. When applied to imports, the terms-of-trade argument is rather an argument for the exploitation of monopsonistic power. It can be applied equally well to exports to justify an export tariff that improves the terms of trade by exploiting *monopolistic* power. The optimal tariff provides a gain to the tariff-levying country by causing the rest of the world to suffer a loss, and insofar as the optimal tariff lowers trade it causes a net loss to the world economy.

Although the theoretical argument for an optimum tariff is valid (given its assumptions), its application in policy raises serious administrative, economic, and political questions. For one thing, the determination of the optimal tariff requires a knowledge of the relevant elasticities, which are likely to change over time. Their accurate measurement and the quick adjustment of the optimum rate to elasticity changes run far beyond the capabilities of economic analysts and tariff administrators. For another, an optimal tariff policy would transfer income from the poor to the rich countries that have monopsonistic power because of their huge markets.[18] This consequence would undercut the foreign aid programs of those same rich countries. Finally, an optimum tariff policy would probably effect its own failure by inciting retaliation by countries faced with a deterioration in their terms of trade. After a series of retaliations and counterretaliations all trading nations would end up on lower indifference curves.

THE THEORY OF THE SECOND-BEST

The theory of the second-best may be traced to the proposition that free trade will *not* necessarily achieve Pareto optimality in the worldwide allocation of production and consumption when private monopoly, government policies, and externalities create divergences between private and social costs and benefits. If policy makers cannot eliminate these divergences so as to pursue a first-best policy (free trade), then a second-best policy may require the introduction of new distortions (such as tariffs) that will neutralize or offset the existing distortions.[19]

The theory of the second-best is applicable to all economic policy, not only trade policy. It recognizes that at any given time policy makers may confront many constraints that run beyond the constraints assumed by the theory of trade (factor supplies, tastes, technology, and foreign supply/demand conditions). Given the existence of constraints such as subsidies and taxes, the optimum values of other variables in the economy will differ from their values in perfectly competitive markets. That is to say, there will be a second-best optimum. The theory of the second-best is pertinent to policy making whenever market prices that guide the actions of producers and consumers fail to indicate the real opportunity costs of the economy and thereby cause discrepancies between private and social values.

---

[18] A poor country, or organized group of poor countries, might have *monopoly* power in the export of some primary products, such as coffee and petroleum. An exploitation of this power by export tariffs or other means would transfer income from the rich to the poor countries. In recent years OPEC (Organization of Petroleum Exporting Countries) has used monopoly power to force up the price of petroleum exports. See Chapter 25.

[19] The theory of the second-best first appeared in J. E. Meade, *Theory of International Economic Policy,* Volume II: *Trade and Welfare* (Oxford: Oxford University Press, 1955).

The theory of the second-best may justify selective import protection when price distortions make the private costs of particular domestic producers higher than the social costs to the country as a whole. Consider, for example, the cost effects of a selective excise tax imposed on a domestic producer. The tax makes private cost (which includes the tax) exceed social cost (which does not include the tax because it is an internal transfer from producers to the government of the same country). Hence, domestic production of the taxed product is less and imports of that product are greater than they would be in the absence of the tax. Since the country is obtaining additional imports at a higher social cost than it could obtain additional domestic output, the imposition of a "compensatory" import duty that would restrict imports and permit the expansion of domestic production would add to the nation's welfare up to the point where the marginal social costs of imports and domestic production became equal. Further restriction of imports beyond that point would lower the nation's welfare.

Probably the single most important application of second-best theory is to customs unions and free trade areas, such as the European Economic Community and the European Free Trade Area, which are examined in Chapter 16. To put the matter simply for the time being, it can be demonstrated that the elimination of import restrictions among members of a customs union or free trade area may cause a loss of welfare to the world as a whole. In other words, not every step toward free trade is necessarily a step toward greater economic efficiency and higher welfare.

It should be evident that the theory of second-best is not a general argument for protection. Under certain conditions, a selective import restriction may improve welfare; but under other circumstances (for example, when private cost is *less* than social cost), second-best policy may call for the elimination or reduction of a specific import restriction. In a sense all arguments for protection (aside from the purely fallacious) may be regarded as second-best since they all argue that certain constraints justify protection. Correctly interpreted, the theory of the second-best says that *any* policy that reduces divergences between marginal social costs and benefits will improve economic efficiency. This theory is not an argument for wholesale government intervention in the marketplace, especially when divergences are the result of previous intervention. Second-best theory focuses attention first on the possible removal of distortion-causing constraints; only when their removal is deemed unfeasible does a second-best policy become appropriate. The first-best policy remains free trade.

PERSISTENCE OF PROTECTION

Our examination of arguments for protection has revealed their vulnerability to economic analysis. Aside from the purely fallacious arguments, we have found that arguments for protection have only a conditional validity when they are evaluated from the perspective of economic efficiency. In most instances, protection is an inferior policy instrument because other policies can achieve the same (or better) result at a smaller cost. Even in those rare situations when protection brings a net gain to the protectionist country, it brings a net loss to the world economy. Because of their conditional validity at best, the arguments for protection are commonly abused in practice; the criterion of economic efficiency is overwhelmed by political factors. In the light of historical experience, protection once established tends to become a permanent institution under the relentless pressure of the vested interests it benefits, even when it outgrows any original usefulness for the nation.

If so little can be said in its favor, why is protection so persistent? Why do all nations of the world continue to implement this restrictive policy to one degree or another? The answers to these perplexing questions are not to be found in the realm of logic or economics. The answers, deeply embedded in human behavior, are found in the same forces of narrow self-interest, fear, ignorance, and prejudice that afflict international relations in general. So long as groups who gain from protection are able to persuade policy makers that their private interests coincide with the national interest, so long will protection continue to stultify the flow of trade among nations who are otherwise committed to competitive market economies. By the same token, the struggle for free or freer trade is a never-ending chronology of victories and defeats with no final outcome.

SUMMARY

1. The theory of international trade demonstrates that for the world as a whole free trade leads to a higher level of output and income than autarky. However, most contemporary economists are reluctant to support free trade without some reservations. Economic theory cannot demonstrate that *under all circumstances* free trade will improve economic efficiency or enhance economic welfare.

2. The essential difference between external and internal trade is political only; it is this difference that has nurtured protectionism through the ages. The long series of arguments for protection may be classified into four categories: (1) fallacious arguments, (2) questionable arguments, (3) qualified arguments, and (4) sophisticated arguments.

3. Fallacious arguments rely on plausibility or mass emotional appeal rather than economic logic: keep-money-at-home, home-market, equalization-of-costs-of-production, low-wage, and prevention-of-injury arguments.

4. Certain arguments for protection, although not entirely fallacious, represent an inferior policy or easily lend themselves to abuse: employment, anti-dumping, and bargaining-and-retaliation arguments.

5. Other arguments for protection find their justification either in noneconomic considerations or in expectation of long-term economic benefits that will more than compensate for the immediate costs of protection: national security, infant-industry, and diversification arguments.

6. Two arguments may justify import restrictions under certain conditions: the terms-of-trade argument (optimum tariff) and the theory of the second-best.

We call these arguments "sophisticated" because they appear in the literature of economic theory and have not been adopted by protectionist groups.

QUESTIONS AND APPLICATIONS

1. "Contemporary economists are reluctant to support the doctrine of free trade without some reservations, but remain firmly on the side of a policy of freer, if not free, trade." What is the explanation of this seemingly contradictory statement?

2. Which is the strongest argument for protection? Why?

3. "Governments spend a great deal of effort promoting exports while, at the same time, they impose all kinds of restrictions on imports." Discuss.

4. Define a truly infant industry. On the basis of your definition, are there any infant industries in the United States?

5. Why is fiscal policy preferable to import restrictions as a response to cyclical unemployment?

6. In presenting its case for protection (import quotas), the American Textile Manufacturers Institute has made the following statement: "With very few exceptions, foreign-made textiles do not sell in the United States because they are better, more stylish, or made more efficiently. The basic reason foreign textiles sell in such volumes in this country is that they are produced at wages far below the legal minimum here." Assuming its truth, does this situation justify protection?

7. A spokesman for the U.S. steel industry concluded his plea for import quotas as follows: "Does America want and need a strong steel industry? Does it want to maintain the maximum number of jobs at high wage standards? Does it believe in fair play in the competition for its own markets? Does our nation's security demand all the strength in steel we can possibly achieve? If so, something has to be done. I believe the proposed legislation represents a realistic solution of this problem—fair to all—and that it is worthy of your sympathetic support." What arguments for protection are implied in these questions? Justify your own response to each question.

SELECTED READINGS

Beveridge, Sir William. *Tariffs: The Case Examined*. London: Longmans, Green & Company, 1932.

Corden, W. M. *Recent Developments in the Theory of International Trade*. Special Papers in International Economics No. 7. Princeton: Princeton University Press, 1965. Chapter IV.

Ellsworth, P. T. *The International Economy*, revised edition. New York: Macmillan Co., 1964. Chapter 13.

Towle, Lawrence W. *International Trade and Commercial Policy*, second edition. New York: Harper Brothers, 1956. Chapters 19 and 20.

Yeager, Leland B. and David G. Tuerck. *Trade Policy and the Price System*. Scranton, Pennsylvania: International Textbook Company, 1966. Chapters 6-14.

CHAPTER 14

EXCHANGE CONTROL AND ITS EFFECTS

The direct interference of governments in the foreign exchange market is known as *exchange control* or *exchange restriction.* In effect, exchange control replaces the free operation of the market with official decisions that determine the uses and availabilities of foreign exchange for all or specific transactions. When exchange control covers all transactions, then the government becomes a pure monopsonist and monopolist of foreign exchange.[1]

THE ORIGINS OF EXCHANGE CONTROL

Exchange control was initially adopted by many governments during World War I when it became necessary to conserve scarce supplies of gold and foreign exchange for the financing of imports vital to the national economy. Following the war, however, exchange control was abandoned everywhere, and by the second half of the 1920's most nations had returned to the gold standard and the full convertibility that characterized the prewar system of international payments. At that time it was widely believed that only the exigencies of war justified the use of exchange control, and few observers expected to witness its revival in a period of peace. Yet, within a few years several governments had resurrected exchange control in the face of an event that was almost as convulsive as war in the suddenness of its impact on the international payments system—the international financial crisis of 1931.

The first peacetime use of exchange control by industrial countries arose as a response to the international financial crisis of 1931 that unloosed a panicky run on the gold and foreign exchange reserves of one country after another.[2] The crisis began inconspicuously when the Credit-Anstalt

---

[1] Controlled exchange rates are discussed in Chapter 7.

[2] In 1929 and 1930 a number of raw material exporting nations imposed exchange control to meet current account deficits brought on by the onset of depression in the industrial countries.

bank in Vienna was declared insolvent in the summer of 1931. This caused a loss of confidence in the ability of Austria to honor its international short-term obligations and there was an immediate large-scale withdrawal of funds from that country. Upon the failure of a large German bank in early July, the run by foreign creditors spread to Germany and to many eastern European countries that had borrowed heavily on short term during the 1920's. Fearful of an exhaustion of its reserves, the German government stopped the flight of capital funds by introducing exchange control in August. By the end of the year, most countries in eastern Europe, as well as Denmark and Iceland, had also applied exchange control to halt an outflow of capital. Foreign-owned balances in the exchange control countries were now "frozen" and could no longer be freely transferred into gold or convertible foreign exchange. Similarly, residents of the exchange control countries were no longer able to send capital abroad.

The institution of exchange control in Germany next started a run on the British pound sterling. The large short-term loans that the United Kingdom had made to Germany were now immobilized by exchange control, and this created a doubt as to the capacity of the United Kingdom to liquidate its own heavy short-term international indebtedness. The panic rapidly depleted British reserves; but, instead of following the example of Germany, the United Kingdom went off the gold standard in September, 1931, and allowed the pound sterling to depreciate. In June of the following year, the British government established the Exchange Equalization Fund to stabilize the pound at a level below its former gold parity. A number of other countries allowed their currencies to depreciate along with the pound sterling, and in this way gave birth to the Sterling Area.

By 1935 the international financial crisis and the global depression had split the international payments system into five groups: [3]

1. The *Sterling Area,* comprising principally the British Commonwealth and Scandanavian countries.
2. The *Dollar Area,* comprising the United States and most of the countries of Central America and northern South America.
3. The *Gold Bloc* countries of Western Europe.
4. The *Yen Area,* comprising Japan and her possessions.
5. The *Exchange Control Area* of central and southeastern Europe, dominated by Germany.

Some countries, such as Canada, Argentina, Brazil, and Chile, did not fall completely into any one currency area. The Canadian dollar was depreciated about 10 percent against the United States dollar but remained convertible. The other three countries also depreciated but adopted exchange control that rendered their currencies inconvertible.

---

[3] League of Nations, *International Currency Experience* (Geneva: League of Nations, 1944), p. 198.

Exchange control was practiced by Germany, the eastern European countries, and many countries in Latin America throughout the 1930's, long after the international financial crisis of 1931 had become history. Many new uses were found for exchange control and this served to perpetuate its existence. The currencies of the Dollar Area, the Sterling Area, the Yen Area, and the principal countries of Western Europe (excluding Germany and Italy) remained fully convertible, however, up to the outbreak of World War II. During the war, all countries exercised tight control over their economies and exchange control was only one of several instruments employed for that purpose.

After World War II most countries of the non-Communist world continued to restrict both current and capital transactions by means of exchange control.[4] In 1958 only eleven countries—all located in the Western Hemisphere—had *fully* convertible currencies that any holder could transfer freely into other currencies.[5] All other currencies were inconvertible to one degree or another. This widespread use of exchange control had profound effects upon international trade and payments. It sharply limited the scope of multilateral trade and divided the free world into distinct currency areas. To the individual trader, exchange control meant that he could no longer buy in the low-price market and sell in the high-price market without permission of the authorities. At times this permission was denied outright, and it was almost always limited in some way.

A massive liberalization of exchange restrictions started at the close of 1958 when ten countries in Western Europe established nonresident convertibility of their currencies on current account. In the early 1960's other industrial countries (including Japan) eliminated exchange restrictions on merchandise trade and, in most instances, on other current transactions as well. The industrial countries have also greatly moderated their restrictions on capital transactions and some have removed them entirely. At the start of the 1970's, therefore, exchange control was no longer a significant policy instrument for the countries of the industrial West.

The less-developed countries have not matched the liberalization of the developed countries. The great majority still retain exchange restrictions on trade and other transactions. For the developing countries, then, exchange control continues to be a major tool of foreign economic policy.

THE OBJECTIVES OF EXCHANGE CONTROL

The principal objectives of contemporary exchange control systems are listed at the top of page 328.

---

[4] Since all international transactions of Communist countries are channelled through state agencies, exchange control is an integral element of Communist trading systems.

[5] These countries were the United States, Canada, Mexico, Guatemala, El Salvador, Honduras, Panama, Venezuela, Haiti, the Dominican Republic, and Cuba.

1. The suppression of balance of payments disequilibrium (including the prevention of capital flight).
2. The facilitation of national planning.
3. The protection of domestic industries.
4. The creation of government revenue.

An exchange control system may be adopted to pursue two or more of these objectives and it is sometimes difficult to decide which objective is the dominant one. In addition to these basic objectives, exchange control may be used for a number of other purposes, such as strengthening the nation's bargaining position in trade negotiations and expanding exports to other exchange control countries.

THE SUPPRESSION OF BALANCE OF PAYMENTS DISEQUILIBRIUM

When a nation is unwilling or unable to adjust to a persistent deficit in its balance of payments by deflating the domestic economy or by depreciating its rate of exchange or by any other domestic measure of a fiscal or monetary nature, it must suppress the deficit by imposing direct controls over its international transactions. The most important direct control utilized by contemporary governments is exchange control that regulates the acquisition and disposition of foreign exchange. Other forms of direct control—import quotas and import licenses—usually supplement exchange control, although at times they may be used as substitutes.

Exchange control was first used in peacetime mainly for suppression of the unique sort of disequilibrium that is provoked by a flight of capital. When exchange control is used solely for this purpose, there is no reason to restrict imports of merchandise and services because the trouble is not in the current account. Moreover, exchange control need only be temporary, for once the panic has subsided, it may be lifted and most of the capital will return of its own accord. This last statement presupposes, however, a widespread belief that exchange control will not be reimposed. If there is doubt on this score, the cessation of exchange control will itself renew the capital flight. In this way, exchange control may perpetuate the loss of confidence and the speculative attitudes that engendered the original flight of capital. Fearing this consequence, governments tend to maintain exchange control long after the danger of capital flight is past.

There is another reason why exchange control that is imposed to restrain a capital flight may continue as a permanent feature of a nation's foreign economic policy. By maintaining an over-valued exchange rate, exchange control may itself create a current account deficit in the balance of payments and induce further disequilibrium in the balance of payments. This is why many nations, once they have adopted exchange control, dare not abandon it.

THE FACILITATION OF NATIONAL PLANNING

Exchange control may be used by governments as a policy instrument (along with others) to attain certain national economic goals, such as full employment and economic development. In the Communist countries the economy is directed toward specific goals by a comprehensive set of controls that decide the allocation of all productive factors as well as the allocation of the national product. Since private enterprise is forbidden, Communist governments carry on all production and thereby execute the national plans they have drawn up. All international transactions are conducted by state-trading agencies that behave in accordance with the dictates of the current national plans.

National planning in the market economies differs significantly from planning in the Communist economies. In the former, production rests largely in the hands of private entrepreneurs, and the price system is the main instrument in deciding the allocation of production and consumption. Consequently, non-Communist governments depend principally (although not exclusively) on fiscal and monetary policies instead of direct controls to implement their national economic programs. But since these programs are conceived in national terms, they sometimes demand an insulation of the national economy from the world economy. To achieve this insulation governments may impose exchange and trade controls that are supplemented, at times, by state trading in specific commodities.

Since World War II the governments of less-developed countries in Latin America, Asia, and Africa have made economic development their preeminent policy goal. The policies associated with that goal have tended to create inflationary pressures that have, in turn, induced deficits in the balance of payments. Lacking adequate reserves, many countries have been forced to make immediate adjustments to these external deficits. Because of the objectives of national planning, however, the choice of methods of adjustment has been narrowly circumscribed. Deflation has been avoided because it would slow down the rate of economic growth. Similarly, exchange depreciation has promised little help because any subsequent domestic inflation would offset its effects on international payments. Rather than moderate the goals of national planning, governments, therefore, have used exchange control and other direct measures to insulate the domestic economy from international repercussions. Apart from its insulation effect, the governments of less-developed countries have utilized exchange control to penalize imports of "nonessential goods" and favor imports of "essential goods" in accordance with criteria laid down by national development plans.

THE PROTECTION OF DOMESTIC INDUSTRIES

By restricting imports, exchange control inevitably protects domestic producers against foreign competition. Therefore, exchange control will be supported by protectionist groups, which will seek to enhance its protective features. When exchange control is not consciously oriented toward protection, but is set up simply to suppress an external deficit, it will not discriminate against those imports that have close domestic substitutes. All imports will be viewed indiscriminately as a drain on foreign exchange and they will be restricted only to stop that drain. When, however, exchange control also has a protectionist purpose, it will curtail imports of competitive products more stringently than imports of products not produced at home or in sufficient quantities. Once exchange control is established, it usually evolves in the direction of greater protection as a result of the lobbying activities of vested interests. This is also true of the import quotas and licenses that ordinarily accompany exchange control.

THE CREATION OF GOVERNMENT REVENUE

Exchange control is used in some countries to collect revenue for the government. In most instances this occurs where the exchange control authority sets the price at which it will buy foreign exchange below the price at which it will sell foreign exchange. For example, if the authority forces exporters to surrender dollar exchange at a rate of 10 pesos to the dollar and then sells dollar exchange to importers at a rate of 15 pesos to the dollar, it pockets 5 pesos for each dollar that it buys and sells.

Exchange control is used as a source of revenue mainly by developing countries. The reliance of nonindustrial countries on exchange control to provide government revenue is largely due to the difficulty of collecting income and other direct taxes. Most of these countries do not have the personnel and skills required to administer direct taxes, and often it is politically impossible to impose such taxes on wealthy individuals. By way of contrast, an exchange control system offers a ready-made apparatus for the collection of revenue with only slight additional administrative expense. Moreover, the tight regulations of exchange control make it difficult to avoid the tax whether in the form of a penalty exchange rate or an exchange tax.[6]

SINGLE-RATE SYSTEMS OF EXCHANGE CONTROL

No two nations have identical systems of exchange control. Some systems are lenient with almost fully convertible currencies, while others carefully police all uses of foreign exchange and may strongly discriminate against certain currencies. Many other variations in systems of exchange control are attributable to differences in objectives, differences in administrative competence, and differences in economic conditions. It is possible, however, to classify exchange control systems into two broad categories depending upon whether they employ one or several exchange rates.

---

[6] An exchange tax is a charge levied on transactions in foreign exchange.

Single-rate systems are administered by an exchange control authority that is the sole buyer and seller of foreign exchange. All foreign exchange transactions are carried on at one official rate of exchange. Exporters and others who receive foreign exchange from foreign residents are compelled to surrender it to the control authority at the official rate. Importers and others who must make payments to foreign residents must obtain permission to buy foreign exchange from the control authority at the official rate. The control authority also regulates the use of domestic currency (bank accounts) owned by foreign residents. Commercial banks are usually authorized to act as buying and selling agents of the exchange control authority. The key to the system of control is the requirement that all foreign exchange transactions involving domestic or foreign residents must pass through authorized banking channels.

THE SURRENDER OF FOREIGN EXCHANGE RECEIPTS

In order to regulate the expenditure of foreign exchange, the exchange control authority must make certain that all foreign exchange received by the nation's residents is actually surrendered to it. Otherwise foreign exchange that is not captured by the authorities may be used for illegal purposes, such as exporting capital, and thus it is not available to finance imports that the authorities consider desirable. Hence, surrender requirements must apply to all credit transactions in the balance of payments.

The surrender of foreign exchange to the control authority is usually accomplished in one of two ways. Under one method, all exports may be licensed by a trade control authority, and, before the merchandise is allowed to pass through customs, the export license must be validated by an authorized bank. To obtain a validation of his license the exporter is required to inform the bank of the destination of his export shipment as well as the amount of the payment and the currency in which it is to be made. The exporter also agrees to surrender to the bank his receipts of foreign exchange. When the exporter arranges for payment by drawing a bill of exchange against the foreign importer or against a bank, he must either discount the bill with the authorized bank or send it through that bank for collection. Thus, the authorized bank is certain to acquire the foreign exchange when payment is made on the bill.

In the second method, the surrender of foreign exchange receipts is insured by requiring the exporter to secure a sworn declaration from an authorized bank before his exports are allowed to pass customs. In obtaining the declaration, the exporter must inform the bank of the destination of his exports and the amount and kind of payment he is to receive for them. He also agrees to surrender to the bank his receipts of foreign exchange within a stipulated period.

These two methods of effecting the surrender of foreign exchange receipts apply to merchandise exports only. It is more difficult for the control authority to capture foreign exchange receipts arising out of exports of services, gifts, and capital movements. Close watch must be kept over all foreign-owned bank balances in the exchange control country, foreign securities owned by domestic residents must be registered with the control authority and sometimes held by an authorized bank, and the international mails must be screened for domestic and foreign banknotes.

Failure to surrender foreign exchange in accordance with the regulations of the control authority is a criminal act. The guilty party may be punished by the imposition of a fine or, in the case of an exporter, denied permission to export in the future. Violations of the exchange control laws of Nazi Germany carried the death penalty. Nevertheless, evasions of exchange control are widespread and the surrender procedures are never one hundred percent effective.

THE ALLOCATION OF FOREIGN EXCHANGE RECEIPTS

The exchange control authority is faced with several problems in the allocation of foreign exchange. First, it must decide how much foreign exchange to allot to the main categories of debit transactions of the balance of payments—merchandise imports, transportation services provided by foreigners, the servicing of foreign debts, travel expenditures of domestic residents, capital investment, etc.

After reaching a decision on the overall amount of foreign exchange to be distributed to each of these categories, the control authority must next decide on the allocation of foreign exchange to the individual items within each category. It must also determine the applicants who will receive foreign exchange and the amounts they will be granted.

Finally, the exchange control authority must often decide upon the allocation of foreign exchange by countries or by currency areas since it may have abundant supplies of some currencies and only scarce supplies of others. If all foreign currencies were convertible, this would not matter; but, when several other countries also employ exchange control, it is no longer possible to settle a deficit through multilateral transfers.

Ordinarily, the official rate of exchange overvalues the domestic currency. Regardless of the criteria used to allocate foreign exchange, therefore, it is not possible to satisfy the entire demand. The criteria of allocation will reflect the objectives of exchange control and current economic conditions. Imports that are considered vital to the nation's well-being will be afforded generous allotments of foreign exchange, while imports of "nonessential" items will receive only scanty allotments. Convertible currencies will be hoarded by the exchange control authority and released only for high priority imports. On the other hand, inconvertible currencies may be sufficiently abundant to permit their use for low-priority imports.

The individual importer is particularly concerned with the method used to allocate foreign exchange to the applicants within each category. Among the several methods employed are the following:

1. Individual allocation.
2. Exchange quotas.
3. Waiting list.
4. Prohibitions.
5. Tie-in import arrangement.

The method of *individual allocation* involves the examination of each individual request for foreign exchange and, upon approval, the issuance of a license that permits the holder to buy a stipulated amount of foreign exchange from an authorized bank. The virtue of this technique is its flexibility. However, it encourages the bribery and corruption of officials, and it places in their hands the powers of life and death over the business enterprises engaged in importing. Efforts are often made to limit the arbitrary nature of individual allocation by requiring the authorities to use the past imports, capital, taxes paid, etc., of the importing firm in deciding its exchange allotment. This procedure has the disadvantage of establishing fixed quotas for individual firms, and, unless safeguards are established, it may work an especial hardship on new or growing concerns.

Another method of allocation among applicants is the establishment of *exchange quotas* for each category of imports derived from estimates of the amount of foreign exchange that will be forthcoming over a specified period. Foreign exchange is then freely sold to all applicants on a first-come, first-served basis until the respective quotas are exhausted. Although this technique limits the exercise of discretion on the part of officials, it suffers from inflexibility.

The *waiting-list* method resembles the quota method. The exchange control authority places each application on a waiting list and takes care of it when the foreign exchange becomes available. Hence, no application is rejected, but the importer may have only a vague idea as to when he will obtain foreign exchange. Unless the priority of exchange allocation is strictly decided by the date of application, the waiting-list technique becomes as arbitrary as the individual allocation of exchange.

Prohibitions are often used to rule out any foreign exchange for certain import items from specific countries or from all countries. Prohibitions are actually zero exchange quotas, and the same effect may be obtained by not issuing licenses when the method of individual allocation is used by the control authority.

Finally, mention should be made of the *tie-in import arrangement* whereby foreign exchange is allocated for specified imports on condition that the importer buy complementary or similar domestic products in a certain proportion. The object here is to stimulate particular kinds of domestic production rather than to protect the balance of payments. This method of exchange allocation is very similar to the mixing quotas discussed in Chapter 12.

IMPORT QUOTAS AND LICENSES

Single exchange-rate systems are usually strengthened by a system of *import quotas* and/or *import licenses*.[7] The most common procedure is to require the importer to obtain first an import license from the trade control authority. Import licenses will be issued in accordance with import quotas for specified imports or on an individual ad hoc basis in the absence of import quotas. Ordinarily, the import license also serves as an exchange license permitting the importer to buy the foreign exchange necessary to finance his import shipment. In some countries, however, an exchange license is needed in addition to an import license; that is, the import license does not provide the importer with an automatic right to buy foreign exchange. The methods used to distribute import licenses among importers are similar to those used to allocate foreign exchange licenses.

As far as merchandise imports are concerned, import quotas or import licenses can do the same job as exchange control. In fact, they may do a better job. Import quotas and licenses allow only fixed quantities of merchandise to enter the country over a certain period, whereas exchange control simply limits the amounts of foreign exchange available for specified merchandise imports over a certain period. Under exchange control, therefore, variations in import prices or in the credit extended by foreign suppliers can lead to variations in the quantities of imports even though there is a fixed allotment of foreign exchange. This difficulty is avoided when exchange control is supplemented by import quotas and licenses. Of course, exchange control is more comprehensive than direct trade control since it covers service and capital transactions in addition to merchandise transactions. The importance of merchandise, however, as compared to other items in the balance of payments makes a widespread application of import quotas and licenses a very close substitute for exchange control with similar effects on international trade.

As we have noted, exchange control and quantitative import restrictions ordinarily are parts of the same overall system of direct control that is established by governments to suppress an external deficit. It follows, then, that international measures to remove or to reduce exchange control are likely to be ineffective unless steps are also taken to limit the use of import quotas and licenses.[8]

---

[7] The use of *export licenses* to compel surrender of foreign exchange receipts has already been mentioned. Export licenses may be used for several other purposes unrelated to exchange control, such as limiting exports of strategic military significance or conserving scarce commodities for use at home.

[8] The tariff is also an import restriction, but the uncertainty of its effects and the difficulties involved in changing it to meet new conditions make it a poor instrument of balance of payments adjustment. See Chapter 12.

THE CONTROL OF NONRESIDENT ACCOUNTS

When a country employs exchange control to suppress a deficit in its balance of payments, it must regulate not only the foreign exchange transactions of its residents but also the use of domestic bank accounts owned by foreign residents. This is especially the case when the exchange control country is an international financial center like the United Kingdom, for then a large proportion of its international receipts and expenditures are made by debiting and crediting accounts maintained in its banking system by foreign residents.

At the end of 1958 the United Kingdom and several other European countries took a long step toward full convertibility by making freely transferable all nonresident accounts arising out of current transactions. Previously the British government did not allow foreign residents of nondollar countries to transfer their sterling balances to residents of dollar countries, although they were free to transfer such balances to residents of a nondollar country other than their own to finance transactions on current account. This procedure was necessary to insure that all British exports to dollar countries were paid for in dollars. Otherwise, say, a French resident might have used his sterling account to finance imports from the United States, and this sterling could then have been used by an American resident to finance imports from the United Kingdom. Thus, the United Kingdom would have lost the opportunity to earn the dollars the American importer would have had to pay if sterling had not been acquired from the French resident.

MULTIPLE-RATE SYSTEMS OF EXCHANGE CONTROL

In a single-rate system of exchange control, the exchange rate itself plays no role in the allocation of foreign exchange among transactions, applicants, currencies, and countries. Indeed, the overvaluation of the exchange rate intensifies the task of allocation by diminishing the amount of foreign exchange in supply and, at the same time, increasing the amount of foreign exchange in demand.

In the multiple-rate systems of exchange control, however, two or more exchange rates are used to effect the allocation of foreign exchange, although they are usually used in conjunction with exchange licenses and direct trade controls. Because the task of allocation is at least partially carried out by differential exchange rates, multiple-rate systems rely far less upon administrative action than do single-rate systems. It is not surprising, therefore, that multiple-rate systems are associated with less-developed countries who may also find them attractive as devices to raise revenue.

Multiple-rate systems exhibit a bewildering variety. At one extreme are the systems that depend upon two or more "free" markets to allocate foreign exchange, with few direct controls of any kind. At the other extreme are the systems that use two or more fixed official rates that are supplemented by exchange licenses, import quotas, and other quantitative controls characteristic of single-rate systems. Our description is confined to remarks about those features peculiar to multiple-rate systems: penalty and preferential rates, fluctuating "free" market rates, mixing rates, and exchange taxes and subsidies.

When multiple-rate systems use fixed official rates of exchange, the simplest form occurs when the exchange authority sells foreign exchange at a single rate that differs from the single rate at which it buys foreign exchange. When the selling rate is higher than the buying rate in domestic currency (the usual case), the difference accrues to the government as revenue. More than two rates result when the exchange authorities buy exchange received for specific export goods at low *penalty* rates or at high *preferential* rates and/or sell exchange for "nonessential" imports at high penalty rates and for "essential" imports at low preferential rates. Ordinarily, penalty buying rates are applied only to exports that face an inelastic foreign demand that enables exporters to escape the incidence of the penalty rate by passing it on to foreign buyers. Sometimes mistakes are made, however, and then penalty rates depress the affected exports.

Many multiple-rate countries allow designated transactions in foreign exchange to be effected in a *fluctuating-rate* market. In such a market, a fluctuating rate of exchange adjusts the amount of foreign exchange in demand to the amount in supply. Since fluctuating rates are ordinarily considerably higher than the official rate, they favor sellers of foreign exchange and hence encourage those transactions whose exchange receipts may be sold at fluctuating rates. By the same token, buyers of foreign exchange at fluctuating rates are penalized and this tends to restrict transactions that must be financed in a fluctuating-rate market. Fluctuating-rate markets are used most frequently for invisible (service) and capital transactions and for high priority exports and low priority imports. At times, however, a country may use two or more fluctuating-rate markets for most, if not all, foreign exchange transactions, as was true of Chile at the end of 1969.

When a multiple-rate country wants to discriminate finely between different transactions by applying a large number of exchange rates, it may do so by *mixing* official rates with fluctuating rates in varying proportions. Exporters are allowed to sell different percentages of their foreign exchange receipts on the "free" market depending on their products. The higher the percentage, the greater the preferential treatment accorded to an exporter because the free rate of exchange is ordinarily much higher (when expressed in domestic currency) than the official rate. Conversely, importers are penalized by making them buy a high percentage of their foreign exchange in the free market. The device of mixing rates enormously heightens the power of the control authority to discriminate between narrow classes of exports or imports—minute variations in effective exchange rates become possible. It should be noted, however, that mixing rates also demand closer administrative supervision of specific export or import items than do rates that apply to a broad class of items.

Countries may *tax* or *subsidize* certain transactions in foreign exchange for revenue or control purposes. The effect is to alter the buying rates of exchange for the transactions in question, thereby creating multiple rates. At the end of 1969, for example, Colombia effected all foreign exchange transactions in a single fluctuating-rate market but exchange receipts from coffee exports were taxed at a rate equal to twenty percent of the market rate while receipts from many other exports were granted a fifteen percent tax credit.[9]

THE EFFECTS OF EXCHANGE CONTROL

We have investigated the origins, objectives, and nature of exchange control. What of its effects? The answer to this question is not simple. For one thing, the effects are manifold; for another, the effects vary greatly in intensity depending on the severity and comprehensiveness of exchange control. Here we can only briefly evaluate the principal effects of exchange control on international payments.

INCONVERTIBILITY AND BILATERALISM

By making a currency inconvertible, exchange control strikes at the heart of multilateral settlement, which permits a country to offset a deficit in one direction with a surplus in another direction. To illustrate, suppose that country A has traditionally run a deficit with country B that has been financed by a surplus with country C. But now country C imposes exchange control and no longer allows residents of country A to use its currency to buy the currency of country B. The effect is to force country A to balance its trade *bilaterally* with country B either by cutting its imports from, or raising its exports to, the latter. Usually the first alternative is adopted, and, as a result, country B suffers a loss of exports to country A that may force it to restrict imports from a third country. Thus, exchange control, by disrupting the pattern of multilateral settlement, may compel other countries, one after another, to restrict imports and even to adopt exchange control in turn. A lower volume of trade is not the only consequence of this train of events. The *quality* of trade is also worsened because it is no longer possible for the exporter to sell in the most profitable market or for the importer to buy in the least expensive market. The truth of this remark becomes clearer when we consider bilateral payments agreements.

BILATERAL PAYMENTS AGREEMENTS

When several countries employ exchange control, there is usually an accumulation of bank balances owned by nonresidents that cannot be freely

---

[9] For a detailed exposition of the Colombian system, see International Monetary Fund, *Twenty First Annual Report on Exchange Restrictions* (Washington: International Monetary Fund, 1970), pp. 111-118.

converted into other currencies. In order to liquidate these "blocked" balances and to avoid as much as possible the use of convertible currencies in the financing of trade, countries enter into bilateral payments agreements. In the 1950's the majority of trade between nondollar countries was financed in accordance with such agreements, which were often accompanied by trade agreements that specified the goods to be exchanged by the participating countries.

In the words of one authority, a bilateral payments agreement "provides a general method of financing current trade between two countries, giving rise to credits which are freely available for use by one country in making payments for goods and services imported from the other." [10] Bilateral payments agreements contain provisions relating to the unit or units of account that are to be used to record foreign exchange transactions, the amounts and the kinds of credit to be used to finance the net balances of either country, the settlement of balances not covered by credits and the settlement of final balances at the conclusion of the agreement, the tenure of the agreement, and the transferability of balances. The credit and transferability provisions are of particular importance.

Most bilateral payments agreements establish reciprocal credits known as *swing credits*. These credits permit each country to have a deficit in its trade with the partner country up to a specified limit before settlement must be made in gold, dollars, or in another agreed manner. At the conclusion of the agreement (which may run for several years), any outstanding balances must be settled in similar fashion. The presence of swing credits lessens the need of the partner countries to achieve an exact balance in their mutual trade, but it may expose the deficit country to a loss of gold or convertible currencies.

All bilateral payments agreements restrict in one way or another the transferability of domestic currency held by residents of the other partner country. This must be done if the agreement is to achieve its main function: the financing of trade with inconvertible currencies. The degree of transferability, however, may vary significantly in different agreements.

At one extreme are the restrictive *bilateral offset agreements* that allow no transferability to third currencies. Under this sort of agreement, usually found only between communist countries, any net balances are settled by an export of goods from the debtor country. Bilateral offset agreements, like barter, effectively prevent any multilateral settlement by destroying its very basis.

Exchange settlement agreements, as their name implies, allow for the settlement of final balances, and of balances beyond the swing credit, in gold, convertible currencies, or other agreed currencies. Although these agreements do not rigidly bilateralize trade, they do encourage bilateral

---

[10] Raymond F. Mikesell, *Foreign Exchange in the Postwar World* (New York: Twentieth Century Fund, 1954), p. 86.

settlement since each partner country seeks to avoid having to pay gold or third currencies to the other.

The restoration of current-account convertibility by the important trading nations of Europe at the close of 1958 led to the dissolution of many payments agreements. Although some 55 agreements were still in force at the end of 1969 between member countries of the International Monetary Fund, none involved a major trading country. Of some 240 agreements between member and nonmember countries, nearly 200 were with the Communist countries of Eastern Europe, 19 with Communist China, and 16 with other state-trading countries.[11] In conclusion, bilateral payments agreements are now extinct among major trading countries but are still common between the developing and Communist countries.[12]

THE REDISTRIBUTION OF MONEY INCOMES

The redistribution of money incomes that results from exchange control will vary depending upon the circumstances. Money income is diverted to the government by penalty selling rates of exchange, exchange taxes, exchange auctions, and the like. On the other hand, exporters and other sellers of foreign exchange may reap windfall profits when they are allowed to sell their exchange in fluctuating-rate markets. In contrast, importers are apt to enjoy windfall profits in a single-rate system because the restriction of imports will push up their domestic prices. When exchange control protects domestic industry, its redistribution effects are similar to those of protective tariffs and quotas as presented in Chapter 12. In the last analysis, the consumer is likely to bear the incidence of exchange control in the form of higher prices for the goods and services that he buys, both domestic and imported.

THE EVASION OF EXCHANGE CONTROL

Exchange control encourages widespread evasion on the part of residents and nonresidents alike. Evasion of exchange regulations by residents is criminal, since it flouts domestic law. The exchange control country, however, has no jurisdiction over nonresidents who are located outside its boundaries and who may also evade its exchange regulations.

Bilateral payments agreements are often designed to lessen evasion of the exchange control of one partner country by residents of the other partner country, but the success of payments agreements in this respect depends

---

[11] International Monetary Fund, *op.cit.,* pp. 5-6.

[12] Trade agreements are frequently combined with payments agreements. For example, since 1966 Ecuador and Poland have maintained a bilateral payments agreement to cover Ecuadoran exports of bananas, rice, cacao, and coffee to Poland and Polish exports of tools and agricultural machinery to Ecuador. Debit or credit balances on either account cannot exceed $2 million for more than six months. *International Financial News Survey* (May 15, 1970), p. 160.

upon the willingness and the ability of the government of the latter country to fulfill its obligations. The residents of free exchange countries, such as the United States, are able to evade the exchange regulations of other countries without violating domestic laws, since their governments are usually unwilling to enter into bilateral payments agreements with an evasion clause. Even if exchange control were fully effective in regulating all foreign exchange transactions within the exchange control country, it would not restrain much of the evasion practiced by nonresidents located abroad.

The number of evasion techniques is legion, including bribery and corruption of officials, false invoicing of exports and imports, and black market operations. False invoicing may involve the *underinvoicing* of exports so that part of the actual foreign exchange receipts is withheld from the control authority and placed by the importer or other agent in a foreign bank to the account of the exporter. The same thing may be accomplished through the *overinvoicing* of imports so that the importer obtains more foreign exchange than is needed to pay for his imports, the excess ending up in the importer's private bank account in a foreign country. Black market operations cover any illegal transactions in foreign exchange.

A SYNOPTIC VIEW OF CONTEMPORARY EXCHANGE CONTROL PRACTICES

Table 14-1 offers a synoptic view of the exchange control systems employed by members of the International Monetary Fund (IMF), which embraces almost all non-Communist countries. All the *highly industrialized developed* countries have now accepted Article VIII of the IMF agreement, which obligates them to refrain from restrictions on current payments.[13] However, six of the *less-advanced developed* countries and the vast majority of the developing countries remain under Article XIV, which allows them to retain current account restrictions. Actually nine developed countries (including three backsliding Article VIII countries—Austria, France, and the United Kingdom) and eighty-one developing countries had such restrictions at the end of 1969. No developed country, however, had more than one rate of exchange for current transactions while twenty developing countries had multiple-rate systems. Restrictions on capital transactions are prevalent throughout the world; only four developed countries and twenty developing countries did not have them. Also, only a small number of countries do not require their exporters to surrender foreign exchange receipts to the exchange authority (usually the central bank). To conclude, exchange controls of one sort or another remain very common in the contemporary world economy. Such controls generate constraints and risks for international business enterprise, which must somehow learn to cope with them.

---

[13] Article VIII and other features of the IMF Agreement are treated in Chapter 19.

Table 14-1

PRINCIPAL FEATURES OF EXCHANGE CONTROL SYSTEMS
OF IMF COUNTRIES AT THE END OF 1969

	Developed Countries [1]	Developing Countries [2]
Article VIII status	15	10
Article XIV status	6 [a]	107
Restrictions on current transactions [3]	9	81 [b]
Import rate(s) different from export rate(s) ...	0	20
More than one rate for imports	0	16
More than one rate for exports	0	14
Restrictions on capital transactions	17 [c]	97
Special rate(s) for some or all capital transactions and/or some or all services (invisibles) .	4 [d]	20
Surrender of export proceeds required	14 [e]	105
Bilateral payments arrangements with IMF countries	3 [f]	35
Bilateral payments arrangements with non-IMF countries	10	37

Source: Derived from International Monetary Fund, *Twenty-First Annual Report on Exchange Restrictions* (Washington: International Monetary Fund, 1970), pp. 568-572.
[1] Twenty-one countries: United States, Canada, Western Europe, Japan, Australia, New Zealand, and Union of South Africa.
[2] One hundred seventeen countries in Asia, Africa, and Latin America.
[3] Other than restrictions for security reasons.
[a] Finland, Greece, New Zealand, Portugal, South Africa, and Spain.
[b] Includes four countries whose practice is undetermined (Botswana, Equatorial Guinea, Lesotho, and Swaziland).
[c] Only Belgium-Luxembourg, Canada, West Germany, and the United States did not have capital restrictions.
[d] Belgium-Luxembourg, France, Ireland, and the United Kingdom.
[e] Only the United States, Sweden, the Netherlands, West Germany, Canada, Belgium-Luxembourg, and Austria did not require the surrender of export proceeds.
[f] Greece, Portugal, and Spain.

Is exchange control economically justified? The principal argument against exchange control is that its use raises obstacles to gainful international trade by restricting the convertibility of currencies, by distorting price and cost relationships, by discriminating between countries and currency areas, by perpetuating balance of payments disequilibrium, and by creating uncertainty and confusion. Hence, exchange control interferes with international specialization and trade in accordance with comparative advantage.

Despite this serious indictment, we have seen that exchange restrictions on current transactions have become a way of life for a good majority of the developing countries. The main explanation for the persistence of exchange control is that, although most nations pay lip service to the objective of free multilateral trade, they are unwilling to accept the monetary and fiscal disciplines necessary to sustain the convertibility of their currencies. Other objectives—full employment, economic development, national planning, etc. —are placed ahead of the attainment of international equilibrium. Exchange control then becomes a mechanism used to defend national policies against international repercussions, and under some circumstances exchange restrictions on current account may be justified as a second-best policy.

The achievement of a multilateral trading system does not require the abandonment of all forms of exchange control. Currencies used to finance current transactions in merchandise and services as well as in investment capital must be fully convertible. Exchange control, however, may be used to restrain an occasional capital flight without endangering multilateral trade. Another legitimate use of exchange control is its *temporary* employment to allow a nation enough time to make a fundamental adjustment to a persistent deficit in its balance of payments, assuming that its reserves are inadequate to perform the same task.

SUMMARY

1. The direct interference of governments in the foreign exchange market is known as exchange control. Exchange control restricts the right of holders of a currency to exchange it for other currencies. It thereby renders a currency inconvertible.

2. Aside from its use during World War I, the first peacetime application of exchange control by industrial countries occurred in response to the capital flight unloosed by the international financial crisis of 1931. During the 1930's, the exchange control area was centered in Germany and eastern Europe, although several countries in Latin America also adopted exchange restrictions in the face of balance of payments difficulties.

3. After World War II most countries continued to restrict both current and capital transactions by means of exchange control. However, a massive liberalization by the industrial countries began at the close of 1958 when ten European countries established nonresident convertibility of their currencies on current account. The great majority of developing countries still retain exchange control as a major tool of foreign economic policy.

4. There are many objectives of exchange control. Foremost among them are the suppression of balance of payments disequilibrium, the facilitation of national planning, the protection of domestic industries, and the creation of government revenue. The versatility of ends that may be served by exchange control is an important factor behind its continued use in contemporary international trade.

5. A useful distinction may be made between single-rate systems of exchange control and multiple-rate systems. In single-rate systems, all foreign exchange transactions are carried on at one official rate of exchange. All foreign exchange receipts are surrendered to an exchange control authority that allocates foreign exchange expenditures by types of import transactions, by countries and currency areas, and by applicants. Single-rate systems make use of import licenses and quotas in allocating foreign exchange.

6. In a multiple-rate system of exchange control, two or more legal exchange rates apply to different foreign exchange transactions. Because at least part of the task of allocating foreign exchange to different uses is carried out by

differential exchange rates, multiple-rate systems rely on administrative action far less than do single-rate systems. There is a bewildering variety of multiple-rate systems.

7. The most important effect of exchange control is its disruption of multilateral settlement and the forcing of international trade into bilateral channels. Exchange control thus limits the advantages to be gained from international specialization in a competitive world market. When several countries practice exchange control, blocked balances and the scarcity of convertible currencies raise formidable obstacles to trade. In order to liquidate blocked balances and to avoid the use of convertible currencies in the financing of mutual trade, exchange control countries negotiate bilateral payments agreements.

8. Exchange control also redistributes money incomes since exporters, importers, or the government are able to enjoy monopoly profits depending upon the nature of the system.

9. Exchange control is evaded by both residents and nonresidents in many ways, including bribery and corruption of officials, false invoicing of exports and imports, and black market operations.

10. The main indictment of exchange control is its interference with international trade based on comparative advantage. The achievement of a multilateral trading system, however, is compatible with the use of exchange control to stop a capital flight and with its temporary use to provide time for fundamental adjustment to an external payments deficit.

QUESTIONS AND APPLICATIONS

1. What is exchange control?
2. (a) Trace the origins of exchange control in the 1930's.
   (b) What is the present situation in the world economy with regard to exchange control?
3. (a) What are the principal objectives of contemporary exchange control systems?
   (b) How does exchange control serve these objectives?
4. (a) Describe the single-rate system of exchange control.
   (b) What is the key to this system of control?
   (c) How may the control authority insure the surrender of foreign exchange?
   (d) What allocation problems does the control authority face?
   (e) What methods may be used to allocate foreign exchange to applicants?
5. What is the role of import quotas and licenses in single-rate systems of exchange control?
6. Why does exchange control involve the control of nonresident accounts?
7. (a) How does the multiple-rate system of exchange control differ from the single-rate system?
   (b) What features are peculiar to multiple-rate systems?
8. Distinguish between preferential and penalty buying and selling rates of exchange.

9. In the multiple-rate system, what is the function of fluctuating market rates? Of mixing rates? Of exchange taxes?

10. Enumerate the principal effects of exchange control.

11. Describe the purpose and nature of bilateral payments agreements. Comment specifically on their credit and transferability provisions.

12. What is the proper use of exchange control?

SELECTED READINGS

de Vries, Margaret G. "Exchange Restrictions: Progress Toward Liberalization." *Finance and Development*, Vol. 6, No. 3 (September, 1969).

International Monetary Fund. *Exchange Restrictions*. Washington: International Monetary Fund, annual.

League of Nations. *International Currency Experience*. Geneva: League of Nations, 1944.

Trued, M. N. and R. F. Mikesell. *Postwar Bilateral Payments Agreements*. Princeton Studies in International Finance No. 4. Princeton: Princeton University Press, 1955.

CHAPTER **15**

U.S. COMMERCIAL POLICY AND THE GATT

As observed in Chapter 11, the rationale of government economic policies is that national economies, if left alone, would fail to achieve goals which are deemed to be in the national interest, such as full employment, price stability, a satisfactory rate of growth, an equitable distribution of income, and a strong balance of payments. Since economic activity is characterized by a high degree of interdependence among the different nations of the world, a policy in the best interests of a nation must take into account such interdependence since it affects and, in turn, is affected by the policies of other nations. Consequently, a wise national economic policy must be conceived within a broad international frame of reference, especially when the nation involved holds a dominant position in world affairs and when its conduct is apt to have important repercussions abroad.

Unfortunately most nations, large and small, are inclined to disregard this dual aspect of their economic policies and to ignore the fact that by building roadblocks of interference on one side of the international highway of commerce, they block the other side as well. Whether those artificial fences consist of tariffs, quantitative, or other restrictive measures, they tend to reduce trade in both directions to the detriment of everyone concerned. The United States, like other nations, has been guilty of this shortsighted approach to economic policy at various periods of its history, although in the past its action has been largely confined to tariff measures.

Although its earlier position of dominance has been eroded by the remarkable resurgence of Western Europe and Japan, the United States continues to exert a pervasive influence on the world economy. With only 6 percent of the world's population, this country produces about 30 percent of the world's goods and services and accounts for about 14 percent of all international trade.[1] Thus, the economic behavior of the United States can do much harm or good, depending upon the growth and stability of its economy as well as the direction of its foreign economic policy. A liberal U.S. trade policy enhances the gains from international specialization and helps promote world economic growth. Conversely, a protectionist trade policy runs the risk of widespread retaliation by other countries and a return to the "beggar-my-neighbor" policies of the 1930's.

United States commercial policy is a major component of a broader foreign economic policy that, in turn, is an integral part of the overall foreign policy of the nation. The success or failure of any of its constituent parts is reflected in the effectiveness of the whole. U.S. foreign policy has sought to promote economic strength at home and abroad, and to build and maintain cohesion in the non-Communist world. To accomplish these objectives, the United States has followed three basic economic policies:

1. A commercial policy for trade liberalization and trade expansion.
2. An investment policy for the promotion of U.S. private foreign investments, especially in developing countries.
3. A foreign assistance policy for the economic growth and development of friendly nations.

During the 1960's a growing concern over the persistent weakness of the U.S. balance of payments forced some modifications of these basic policies, such as the imposition of controls on private foreign investment. By the early 1970's, the measures undertaken by the U.S. Government to solve the balance of payments problem threatened to undermine its traditional policies in trade, investment, and foreign assistance.

This chapter considers only the trade or commercial policy of the United States, including the General Agreement on Tariffs and Trade (GATT). Subsequent chapters take up its balance of payments policy (Chapter 19), its foreign assistance policy (Chapter 18), and its foreign investment policy (Chapter 24).

EVOLUTION OF THE UNITED STATES TARIFF POLICY BEFORE 1934

The evolution of the United States tariff policy has been intimately related to the economic development of the country. The Constitution of the United States specifically vested in Congress the responsibility for regulating the foreign commerce of the nation. On March 4, 1789, a week before the inauguration of George Washington as President, a bill that was to become the Tariff Act of 1789 was introduced by James Madison. Since then, over 1,000 laws have been enacted to regulate American foreign trade. In the early years, customs duties provided from 80 to 90 percent of the federal

---

[1] For a more complete picture of the international trading position of the United States, see Chapter 2.

government's income. Subsequently this high ratio declined, but proceeds from customs duties continued to be an important source of federal revenue until World War I.

The history of the American tariff policy during this long period shows many swings reflecting the changing internal and external conditions of the time. After the War of 1812, however, there was a marked tendency for a high level of protectionism to dominate the picture, although there were short-lived periods of tariff reductions that temporarily interrupted the upward trend in protection.

After World War I, the United States emerged into a position of economic dominance, but the country was prevented from assuming effective world leadership because of the powerful forces of isolationism and protectionism at home. In the first half of the interwar period, the U.S. tariff resumed its upward climb to reach its highest level with the Tariff Act of 1930. It was not until the collapse of the world economy—including that of the United States—as a result of the Great Depression of the early 1930's that freer trade became the avowed policy of the United States as embodied in its Reciprocal Trade Agreements program of 1934.

After 1934, the United States gradually began to exercise its international responsibilities, but it was only after World War II that active world leadership was fully assumed and utilized to bring other nations along the road of more liberal trade.

TARIFF ACT OF 1789

The Tariff Act of 1789 was the first expression of United States commercial policy. This Act was inspired by Alexander Hamilton, then Secretary of the Treasury, who favored a mildly protective policy to encourage the development of infant industries that would create a greater domestic market for agricultural production and would achieve some degree of self-sufficiency for national security. A sharp cleavage occurred over this first tariff act between the North, which was anxious to grow industrially, and the South, which was unequipped for industrialization but was interested in maintaining its high exports of cotton. The overwhelmingly agricultural character of the American economy, however, and the wide popular interest in the traditional imports at the time did not encourage new domestic manufactures under the relatively mild protection afforded by the first tariff act. As a consequence, the tariff issue remained more or less in the background even though alterations and increases took place in succeeding years.

TARIFF OF 1816

In the early nineteenth century, the Napoleonic Wars, which caused England to blockade the European mainland, led to an American embargo in 1807 that was followed by the Nonintercourse Act of 1809 and a war with Britain in 1812. As a result, a large number of new industries were established in this country in order to supply the needs of the national economy. When peace with Britain was concluded in 1814, imports glutted the American market. Domestic producers were hard hit by the sudden inflow of cheaper imported goods that spelled disaster for many of them. Concern in Washington led to the enactment of the Tariff of 1816, the first protective measure of real consequence. Succeeding acts continued the upward trend in protection, and, by 1832, the situation had become so distasteful that it created a great deal of popular resentment and a threat of secession from the Union by South Carolina, whose legislature declared the tariff unconstitutional.

After 1832 the tariff issue was dominated by two contending schools of thought that became firmly established in the political affairs of the country. On the one side were the protectionists—identified with the Whigs and later with the Republican Party—and on the other side were the partisans of a tariff for revenue—represented by the Democratic Party. As a result, the tariff policy of the country vacillated with the political fortunes of either party, making the tariff issue a political football. Tariff revisions thus became the inevitable consequence of every change in administration in Washington.

EFFECTS OF WORLD WAR I UPON TARIFF POLICY

World War I stimulated the development of new industries in the United States and caused a vast expansion of industrial and agricultural activities. When peace came, the enlarged production facilities looked to markets abroad in addition to the domestic market. Nevertheless, trade liberalism was viewed as a threat to the economy. The forces of protectionism returned to power and remained in control of the government for twelve crucial years. During this period the world experienced unprecedented political and economic trials, culminating in a worldwide depression, the extent and intensity of which have never been equaled before or since. The new place of the United States in the concert of nations was not fully appreciated at home and the obligations of a leading nation were assumed either hesitantly or not at all.

In the commercial policy area, the United States was decidely reluctant to adjust to its new role of a creditor nation and to accept payment in goods and services for the vastly increased income from its foreign investments. Instead, it resorted to unprecedentedly high protectionism and isolationism. The Fordney-McCumber Act, enacted in 1922, marked a return to the high protectionist policy that had been temporarily interrupted in 1913. Some 2,400 changes in rates were made and the so-called "flexible provision" was added, authorizing the President to revise rates up or down by 50 percent when existing rates failed to equalize costs of production between domestic and foreign producers.

HAWLEY-SMOOT ACT OF 1930

Conceived at the beginning of an unprecedented world economic crisis, the Hawley-Smoot Act of 1930 was the crowning achievement of protectionism in this country. While the bill was still in the Senate, it brought protests from foreign nations and pleas from a group of American economists who opposed a policy fraught with disaster to the economy of this country and to the rest of the world. These economists pointed out that the contemplated action was unjustified either in principle or in practice and was bound to invite retaliation and to threaten world peace. In spite of these warnings, the Act was passed by Congress and signed by President Hoover, unleashing a worldwide movement of retaliatory measures.[2]

In the opinion of a noted scholar of U.S. trade policy:

> Few actions of the United States have been more detrimental to the foreign relations of this country than the Hawley-Smoot Tariff of 1930. Almost none of the rates could be justified in terms of the infant-industries argument or on grounds of national security. Many of the items on which tariffs were imposed or the rates raised were not in direct competition with any American product.[3]

Such inordinate action could not long endure without giving rise to countervailing forces for redress. After two years of the Hawley-Smoot tariff, the shrinkage of trade and the deterioration of the American economy were instrumental in convincing influential groups of the mutual relationship between imports and exports and of the effects of the American tariff policy upon the level of world trade. Their voices found more sympathetic ears in the new Administration that took the reins of the government in 1932. Under the stewardship of President Roosevelt and his Secretary of State, Cordell Hull, brighter horizons were in sight.

THE RECIPROCAL TRADE AGREEMENTS PROGRAM, 1934-1962

In 1934, Congress passed the Reciprocal Trade Agreements Act (RTA) —now superseded by the Trade Expansion Act of 1962, discussed later in this chapter—as an amendment to the Hawley-Smoot Tariff Act of 1930.

---

[2] According to the League of Nations Economic Survey of 1932-33, the Hawley-Smoot Tariff Act of 1930 was the signal for an outburst of tariff-making activity in other countries, partly, at least, by way of reprisals. Extensive increases in duties were made almost immediately by Canada, Cuba, Mexico, France, Italy, and Spain, followed by many other nations; and it was generally considered to be an unwarranted and unfriendly act of a creditor and powerful nation. See Asher Isaacs, *International Trade, Tariff and Commercial Policies* (Chicago: Richard D. Irwin, Inc., 1948), pp. 234-35.

[3] Raymond F. Mikesell, *United States Economic Policy and International Relations* (New York: McGraw-Hill Book Company, 1952), p. 62.

The RTA ushered in an era of commercial liberalism in this country and paved the way for similar trends abroad that culminated after World War II in the General Agreements on Tariffs and Trade (GATT)—an international organization for the promotion and practice of freer trade.

RECIPROCAL TRADE AGREEMENTS ACT OF 1934

The RTA Act of 1934 recognized the relationship between imports and exports and authorized the reduction of tariff rates up to 50 percent by means of bilateral trade agreements with foreign countries. The objectives of this program were clearly expressed in the preamble to the law itself which said that the Act was established:

> For the purpose of expanding foreign markets for the products of the United States (as a means of assisting in the present emergency in restoring the American standard of living, in overcoming domestic unemployment and the present economic depression, in increasing the purchasing power of the American public, and in establishing and maintaining a better relationship among various branches of American agriculture, industry, mining, and commerce) by regulating the admission of foreign goods into the United States in accordance with the characteristics and needs of various branches of American production so that foreign markets will be made available to those branches of American production which require and are capable of developing such outlets by affording corresponding market opportunities for foreign products in the United States. . . .[4]

To accomplish this purpose the Act authorized the President to negotiate bilateral agreements with other countries (not subject to Senate ratification) by offering tariff reductions in return for concessions. Each agreement was to contain an *unconditional most-favored-nation* clause so that all concessions made by either party to third countries would freely and automatically apply to the trade of the other party to an agreement. Thus, the United States would always receive most-favored-nation treatment of its exports from every agreement country. The United States would grant the concessions it gave to *all* countries, whether parties to the agreement or not.

Under this Act, the President was authorized to raise as well as to lower the basic rates of the Tariff Act of 1930 by not more than 50 percent. The prevailing rates were the highest in United States history and offered, therefore, the best bargaining position for obtaining concessions.

During the prosperous war years, the extension of the RTA Act evoked little concern or opposition. After World War II, however, Congressional attitude toward the program was mixed and, at times, uncertain. Periodic renewals met with increased opposition. While additional authority to reduce tariff rates was granted the President, other provisions were adopted to

---

[4] Public Law 316, 73d Congress, Sec. 350(a).

prevent contemplated reductions from inflicting harmful effects upon domestic industries, and to retract concessions already extended.

POSTWAR EXTENSIONS OF THE RTA ACT

The RTA Act was extended eleven times after its passage in 1934. The most significant changes occurred after World War II in the extensions of 1945, 1955, and 1958. These changes involved:

1. New authority for further reductions and increases in the rates of duties and, under certain conditions, the imposition of a duty on duty-free items.
2. The adoption of the so-called *peril-point provision,* which required the Tariff Commission to set minimum rates for contemplated concessions below which domestic industries might be harmed by imports.[5]
3. The adoption of an *escape-clause provision* to be included in every agreement to permit the withdrawal of extended concessions that subsequently might prove harmful to domestic industries.
4. The adoption of a *defense-essentiality amendment* to adjust imports of a product whenever such imports threaten to impair the national security.

Authority to Lower or Raise Duties. In 1945 the authority to reduce rates up to 50 percent was extended and was made to apply on rates existing as of January 1, 1945, which, in many instances, were already reduced under the original authority granted in 1934.

In 1955 the authority to reduce rates up to 50 percent was abolished, but new authority was granted to reduce rates existing as of January 1, 1955, by a maximum of 15 percent with the provision that no more than a 5 percent reduction each year for three years could be made. The President was also granted authority to cut existing rates that were above 50 percent ad valorem to 50 percent with no more than one-third of the cut to be made in any one year.

In 1958 the President was empowered to reduce the rates of duties existing as of July 1, 1958, by either 20 percent or 2 percentage points, with not more than half the reduction to be made in any one year. He was also granted the authority to raise duties as much as 50 percent above the 1930 Hawley-Smoot levels and, in escape-clause cases, to impose a duty up to 50 percent on duty-free items.

The Peril Point. The peril-point clause was first incorporated in the 1948 extension of the RTA Act. It was deleted in 1949, and reincorporated in 1951.

---

[5] The Tariff Commission is a nonpolitical agency of the government whose function is the investigation, study, and submission of recommendations to the President on tariffs and other matters pertaining to the foreign trade of the United States.

Before entering into negotiations with a foreign country, the President had to furnish a list of contemplated tariff concessions to the United States Tariff Commission for investigation, study, and recommendation. The findings of the Tariff Commission indicated what it considered to be the lowest rate of duty, or *peril point,* for each product below which tariff reduction would cause or threaten serious injury to the domestic industry producing similar or competitive goods. If the President subsequently permitted reduction beyond the peril points, his action remained valid.

The peril-point provision, therefore, was not binding upon the President and did not prohibit reductions beyond the limits set by the Tariff Commission, but it did constitute a restraining influence that was likely to carry weight during the negotiation of an agreement. Under the 1958 extension of the RTA Act, moreover, the Tariff Commission was directed to institute an escape-clause investigation whenever it found that a tariff concession had been granted that ignored the peril point so that an "increase in duty or additional import restriction was required to avoid serious injury to the domestic industry producing like or directly competitive articles." Thus, an unheeded peril point became an escape clause subjecting a concession to revision and possible reversal by Congress.

The Escape Clause. The escape clause was used occasionally in trade agreements as early as 1941, but more extensively after an executive order in 1947. In 1951 the escape clause became a statutory provision when it was incorporated into the extension of the RTA Act of that year. It provided that no concession in any trade agreement

> . . . shall be permitted to continue in effect when the product on which the concession has been granted is, as a result, in whole or in part, of the duty or other customs treatment reflecting such concession, being imported into the United States in such increased quantities . . . as to cause or threaten serious injury to the domestic industry producing like or directly competitive products.[6]

The escape clause could be invoked by request of the President, by resolution of either house of Congress or of the House Committee on Ways and Means, by motion of the Tariff Commission, or by application of any interested party. When an application was made, the Tariff Commission was required to make a prompt investigation and to report its findings, or to hold public hearings if so directed by the Senate Committee on Finance or by the House Committee on Ways and Means. The Commission was further required to recommend to the President the withdrawal, modification, or suspension of the concession in whole or in part, or the establishment of

---

[6] Public Law 50, 82nd Congress, 1st Session, and Public Law 85, 85th Congress, 2d Session.

import quotas necessary to remedy the situation. If the President rejected the Tariff Commission's recommendations, his action could be reversed by a two-thirds' majority vote in both houses of Congress under the 1958 extension of the RTA Act.

In arriving at a determination as to whether imports were causing or threatening injury, the Tariff Commission was directed to consider, among other factors, "a downward trend of production, employment, prices, profits, or wages in the domestic industry concerned, or a decline in sales, an increase in imports, either actual or relative to domestic production, a higher or growing inventory, or a decline in the proportion of the domestic market supplied by domestic producers."

It was rather incongruous for a law to provide for increased imports as a means for expanding exports and at the same time decree that the effectiveness of these means constituted proper criteria for their discard. Conceptually, therefore, the escape-clause and the peril-point provisions of the 1955 extension were in contradiction to the spirit and objectives of the RTA Act. They constituted a class legislation that championed the exclusive interests of producers to the detriment of consumers. Indirectly these provisions also discouraged development of imports since foreign producers, faced with the possible sudden alteration or withdrawal of a concession granted under a reciprocal agreement, were naturally fearful of making the necessary investments to develop products for the American market or for more suitable distribution facilities in this country.

Action on escape-clause applications rested essentially with the President. Fortunately the broader considerations of American foreign economic policy—also a Presidential function—prevailed in arriving at the final disposition of these cases. Of a total of 135 applications filed by industry before passage of the Trade Expansion Act in 1962, 41 reached the President for consideration, of which only 15 received favorable action. This relatively small percentage of successful applications had a retarding effect on the number of applications filed.

Defense-Essentiality Amendment. The extensions of the RTA Act in 1954, 1955, and in 1958, directed the President to use import restrictions to protect the industrial mobilization base of the country from injurious import competition whenever in his opinion, and upon the advice of the Office of Emergency Preparedness (OEP), such action was deemed necessary for national defense purposes. Subsequently the President requested the OEP to designate a representative to serve as an observer on the Trade Agreements Committee.

The role of the OEP opened another avenue through which domestic producers could seek relief from foreign competition in addition to the escape-clause and the peril-point provisions, which were under the jurisdiction of the United States Tariff Commission.

THE IMPACT OF THE RTA PROGRAM

The consequences of any specific aspect of a general policy upon an economy as complex as that of the United States are impossible of exact measurement. They are the result of the balance of many forces that, at times, work at cross-purposes. Some of these forces are known; others are hard to detect; and still others have roundabout effects that can only be conjectured. Because of this complexity, the results of the RTA program cannot be clearly isolated and appraised. Some indications of the results of this program after thirty years may be determined, however, by the comparison of available data, even though the data and their interpretation must be highly qualified.

The ad valorem equivalent of United States tariff rates fell under the RTA program from an average of 51.5 percent for dutiable imports in 1934 to 11.1 percent in 1962, as indicated in Table 15-1. Of course, such comparisons are statistically debatable because of the inherent limitations in their calculation. But the comparisons do point out the long distance traveled along the line of liberalization of the Hawley-Smoot Act of 1930.

Table 15-1

AVERAGE AD VALOREM RATES OF DUTY ON IMPORTS FOR CONSUMPTION UNDER UNITED STATES TARIFF ACT OF 1930, AS AMENDED

Period	Ratio of Dutiable to Total Imports	Ratio of Duties Collected to Value of Dutiable Imports
1931-1935	37.6	51.4
1936-1940	39.5	39.4
1941-1945	34.0	33.0
1946-1950	41.6	17.1
1951-1955	44.6	12.2
1956-1960	56.9	11.6
1961-1962	61.6	11.1 *

Source: Arranged from data in United States Department of the Treasury, *Annual Reports of the Treasury on the State of the Finances* (Washington: U.S. Government Printing Office, 1930-1964).
* Estimated.

DETERIORATION OF THE RTA PROGRAM

Developments in the 1950's indicated a strong tendency in favor of moderation and even of reversal of the liberal trade policy of the country under the RTA program as evidenced by (1) the stiffening attacks upon this program in general, (2) the opposition to specific rate reductions already effected, and (3) the implications of escape-clause and peril-point legislation.

In the 1950's, Congress curtailed the power of the President to reduce the tariff. The adoption of the peril-point, the escape-clause, the defense-essentiality amendments, and the new provision to reverse the President by Congressional action, demonstrated a growing difference in views between the Administration and the Congress as to whether the RTA program was to remain the vehicle for a liberal international trade policy or was to become a means for the protection of domestic producers, collectively and individually, against injury from foreign competition. Whenever consideration was given to a renewal of the RTA, vigorous opposition in Congress forced a further curtailment of the President's powers by means of restrictive amendments undermining the effectiveness as well as the very philosophy of the program.

Moreover, the item-by-item approach to bargaining under the RTA procedures, coupled with the principal-supplier concept as the basis for negotiation, resulted in a proliferation of tariff subclassifications for many products in order to confine the benefits of the lower duties to the negotiating parties. Otherwise these benefits would have accrued to third countries producing similar but not identical products without reciprocal concessions because of the *unconditional-most-favored-nation (MFN)* principle.[7]

Furthermore, after thirty years of tariff reductions under the RTA program, over 400 United States industrial products remained unaffected by negotiations and subject to the high rates of the Hawley-Smoot Tariff of 1930—an inherent weakness of the item-by-item bargaining system which tends to retain high protection whenever and wherever pressure by entrenched interests prevails.

In addition to these domestic protectionist policies that weakened the original intent of the RTA Act, international developments (most notably, the abandonment by the European Economic Community [EEC] in 1960-61 of the item-by-item approach to negotiations and the built-in preferential treatment within the EEC and the European Free Trade Association [EFTA]) were creating a new situation, putting the United States at a distinct disadvantage.

To meet the new international challenges, Congress, under the leadership of the late President Kennedy, passed the Trade Expansion Act of 1962 (TEA). Before turning to the TEA, however, it will be convenient to examine the nature of GATT, which has been the principal instrument in the liberalization of world trade since its creation in 1947.

---

[7] Under the MFN policy any reduction in the tariff of a nation is automatically extended to all nations, except, at times, to those considered politically or economically inimical. Item-by-item bargaining refers to tariff negotiations centered on specific products as opposed to across-the-board negotiations centered on linear, percentage reductions in the entire tariff schedule comprising all products. In following the principal-supplier concept, the United States offered concessions in negotiations with another country only on products for which that country was the major supplier to the United States.

THE GENERAL AGREEMENT ON TARIFFS AND TRADE (GATT)

After World War II, several international measures were undertaken to liberalize trade and payments between nations. Plans for the creation of a liberal, multilateral system of world trade were started while the war was still in progress. Initiated for the most part by the United States, these plans envisaged the close economic cooperation of all nations in the fields of international trade, payments, and investment. At the time, it was widely believed that such cooperation, formalized by agreements and implemented by international organizations, would avoid the mistakes of the past and lay the cornerstones for a progressive world economy. The two notable achievements of this wartime planning were the International Monetary Fund and the International Bank for Reconstruction and Development.[8] The first institution was to insure the free convertibility of currencies; the second was to supplement and stimulate the international flow of private capital.

Once the war had ended, it soon became apparent that the difficulties of postwar reconstruction in Europe and elsewhere had been greatly underestimated. The weakness of the United Kingdom was dramatically highlighted by its failure to restore the convertibility of the pound in the summer of 1947, despite the assistance of the Anglo-American loan negotiated the previous year. Attention shifted from the now distant goal of a global system of multilateral trade to the immediate threat posed by Western Europe's economic distress and by the spread of Communism. The end of ambitious international planning was symbolized by the refusal of the United States Congress in 1950 to ratify the treaty establishing an International Trade Organization (ITO). As we shall see, the failure of the ITO was offset somewhat by the existence of the General Agreement on Tariffs and Trade. In the 1950's and 1960's new arrangements to liberalize trade and payments have been regional in nature and have focused primarily on Europe.

THE BIRTH OF GATT

The effects of the failure of the ITO on international cooperation in commercial policy were considerably softened by the rise to prominence of the *General Agreement on Tariffs and Trade,* known as GATT.[9] GATT was an almost casual offshoot of the international conference held at Geneva

---

[8] The International Monetary Fund (IMF) is discussed in Chapter 19 and the International Bank for Reconstruction and Development in Chapter 18.

[9] The ITO Charter was signed by representatives of 54 countries at Havana, Cuba, on March 24, 1948. The Charter was an ambitious document covering not only commercial policy but also such topics as employment, economic development, state trading, cartels, and intergovernmental commodity agreements. The Charter has never been ratified by the signatory states; late in 1950, the United States Department of State announced that it would no longer press for Congressional approval.

in 1947 to consider a draft charter for the ITO. There the United States initiated six months of continual negotiations with twenty-two other countries that led to commitments to bind or lower 45,000 tariff rates within the framework of principles and rules of procedure laid down by GATT.

Technically, GATT was viewed by the United States Administration as a trade agreement that came under the provisions of the Reciprocal Trade Agreements Act and, hence, did not require the approval of Congress. It was considered a provisional agreement that would lapse when the ITO was established to take over its functions. In the interim, GATT was to serve as a token of America's willingness to implement a liberal trade policy and thereby gain the adherence of other countries to the projected ITO. GATT began its "provisional" existence on January 1, 1948, when eight of its contracting parties, including the United States, put into effect the tariff concessions negotiated at Geneva.[10]

MAJOR PROVISIONS OF GATT

The General Agreement is a document containing numerous articles and annexes. The tariff schedules listing the thousands of concessions that have been negotiated by the contracting parties are also part of the Agreement. Despite its complexity, GATT comprises four basic elements:

1. The rule of nondiscrimination in trade relations between the participating countries.
2. Commitments to observe the negotiated tariff concessions.
3. Prohibitions against the use of quantitative restrictions (quotas) on exports and imports.
4. Special provisions to promote the trade of developing countries.

The remaining provisions of GATT are concerned with exceptions to these general principles, trade measures other than tariffs and quotas, and sundry procedural matters.

Tariffs. GATT obligates each contracting party to accord nondiscriminatory, most-favored-nation treatment to all other contracting parties with respect to import and export duties (including allied charges), customs regulations, and internal taxes and regulations. An exception to the rule of nondiscrimination is made in the case of well-known tariff preferences, such as those between the countries of the British Commonwealth. No new preferences may be created, however, and existing preferences may not be increased. Frontier traffic, customs unions, and free trade areas are exempted from the general rule of nondiscrimination.

---

[10] A signatory of GATT is known as a *contracting party*. When the signatories act collectively in affairs of GATT, they are referred to as *contracting parties* since, legally, GATT is not an organization. For convenience of exposition, however, we shall frequently use the term "member" to refer to participation in GATT.

GATT legalizes the schedules of tariff concessions negotiated by the contracting parties and commits each contracting party to their observance. An escape clause, however, allows any contracting party to withdraw or modify a tariff concession (or other obligation) if, as a result of the tariff concession (or obligation), there is such an increase in imports as to cause, or threaten to cause, serious injury to domestic producers of like or directly competitive products. When a member country uses the escape clause, it must consult with other member countries as to remedies; if agreement is not reached, those countries may withdraw equivalent concessions.

Quantitative Restrictions. GATT sets forth a general rule prohibiting the use of quantitative import and export restrictions. There are, however, several exceptions to this rule. The four most important exceptions pertain to agriculture, the balance of payments, economic development, and national security.

The Agreement sanctions the use of import restrictions on any agricultural or fisheries product where restrictions are necessary for the enforcement of government programs in marketing, production control, or the removal of surpluses. This exception is important to the United States, which has placed import quotas on several agricultural products.

GATT also permits a member to apply import restrictions in order to safeguard its balance of payments when there is an imminent threat, or actual occurrence, of a serious decline in its monetary reserves or when its monetary reserves are very low. The member must consult with the contracting parties with respect to the continuation or intensification of such restrictions. Representatives of GATT must also consult with the International Monetary Fund when dealing with problems of monetary reserves, the balance of payments, and foreign exchange practices. Members of GATT are not to frustrate the intent of GATT by exchange action nor the intent of the Fund Agreement by trade restrictions. A country that adheres to GATT but is not a member of the Fund must conclude a special exchange agreement with the contracting parties.

GATT recognizes the special position of the developing countries and allows such countries to use nondiscriminatory import quotas to encourage infant industries. Prior approval, however, must be obtained from the collective GATT membership.

A member of GATT may use trade controls for purposes of national security. The strategic controls on United States exports come under this exception.

In addition to these four major exceptions, there are many of lesser importance. For example, members may use trade restrictions to protect public morals, to implement sanitary regulations, to prevent deceptive trade practices, and to protect patents and copyrights.

All quantitative restrictions permitted by GATT are to be applied in accordance with the most-favored-nation principle. Import licenses may not specify that goods be imported from a certain country.

Special Provisions to Promote the Trade of Developing Countries. In 1965 the contracting parties added a new Part IV—Trade and Development —to the General Agreement in recognition of the need for a rapid and sustained expansion of the export earnings of the less-developed member countries. Under the terms of the three articles comprising Part IV, the developed countries agree to undertake the following positive action "to the fullest extent possible": (1) give high priority to the reduction and elimination of barriers to products currently or potentially of particular export interest to less-developed contracting parties; (2) refrain from introducing or increasing customs duties or nontariff import barriers on such products; and (3) refrain from imposing new internal taxes that significantly hamper the consumption of primary products produced in the developing countries, and accord high priority to the reduction or elimination of such taxes. In addition, the developed countries agree not to expect reciprocity for commitments made by them in trade negotiations to reduce or remove tariffs or other barriers to the trade of less-developed contracting parties.

In return, the developing countries commit themselves to take "appropriate action" to implement the provisions of Part IV for the benefit of the trade of other less-developed contracting parties.

The concluding article, Article XXXVIII, pledges the contracting parties to collaborate jointly to take action in a number of ways to further the objectives of Part IV. A new Committee on Trade and Development is charged with keeping under review the implementation of the provisions of Part IV.

Other Provisions. Many other substantive matters are covered by the provisions of GATT: national treatment of internal taxation and regulation, motion picture films, antidumping and countervailing duties, customs valuation, customs formalities, marks of origin, subsidies, state trading, and the publication and administration of trade regulations. The intention of most of these provisions is to eliminate concealed protection and/or discrimination in international trade.

Several articles of GATT deal with procedural matters. In meetings, each member is entitled to one vote, and, unless otherwise specified, decisions are to be taken by majority vote. A two-thirds majority vote is required to waive any obligation imposed on a member by the General Agreement. Articles also cover consultation procedures and the settlement of disputes between members.

ACTIVITIES OF GATT

The members of GATT meet in regular annual sessions and special tariff conferences. A Council of Representatives deals with matters between sessions and prepares the agenda for each session. In addition, intersessional working groups have been appointed at regular sessions to report on specific topics at subsequent sessions.

Adding further to the continuous influence of GATT has been the practice of member governments to consult with each other before the regular sessions. The membership has obtained a secretariat from the United Nations that, among other things, publishes an annual report. In these and other ways, GATT has behaved like an international organization and, as a matter of fact, has been more effective than some legitimate organizations.

The main activities of GATT fall into three categories: (1) tariff bargaining, (2) quantitative restrictions, and (3) settlement of disputes.

Tariff Bargaining. The parties to GATT have participated in six tariff conferences to negotiate mutual tariff concessions. Most of these conferences have lasted about six months and have involved scores of bilateral agreements and thousands of tariff concessions.[11] The initial conference at Geneva negotiated 45,000 different tariff rates, and today the schedules of GATT include products that make up more than half the world's trade. All of these rates have been either reduced or bound against any increase in the future.

The magnitude of this accomplishment is unprecedented in tariff history; it represents a new approach to the task of lowering tariff barriers. Before World War II the most successful attempt to reduce tariffs by reciprocal bargaining was the trade agreements program of the United States. That program was limited, however, by its bilateral nature. GATT has overcome this disability by applying multilaterally the same principles and procedures that underlay the bilateral trade agreements of the 1930's.

Briefly, tariff negotiations at a GATT conference are conducted along the following lines. Each participating country prepares beforehand lists of products whose duties it is prepared to negotiate with other members of the conference.[12] Actual negotiations are carried on by *pairs* of countries in accordance with the "chief supplier" principle; that is, each country negotiates with another country on tariff rates for those products that are mainly supplied by the latter country. Thus, there is a great number of bilateral negotiations at each conference.

The results of the round of tariff negotiations at each conference are not finalized until all of them are gathered into a single master agreement signed by the participating countries. The concessions in the master agreement then apply to trade between all members of GATT. In this way, each member receives the benefits of every tariff concession and becomes a party to every tariff agreement.

---

[11] The sixth and most ambitious tariff conference (known familiarly as the "Kennedy Round") lasted more than three years. The Kennedy Round is evaluated later in this chapter.

[12] This procedure was reversed for the Kennedy Round: each country submitted an "exceptions list" containing a limited number of products on which it was *not* prepared to negotiate. In effect, the Kennedy Round substituted the traditional item-by-item bargaining for across-the-board bargaining.

GATT has brilliantly overcome the difficulties of a purely bilateral trade agreements program: (1) the reluctance of nations to lower or bind tariff duties unless a large number of their trading partners are taking similar action; and (2) the time-consuming negotiation of individual trade agreements, each containing its own code of conduct and other provisions.[13] While it is negotiating, each member knows that other members are also negotiating and that the results of those negotiations will accrue to its benefit. Countries are, therefore, apt to be more generous because the prospects of gain are greater. Moreover, one set of rules applies to every tariff concession and it is much more comprehensive in scope than would be possible in the case of individual bilateral agreements. GATT has also created an environment conducive to tariff bargaining, and it has often induced countries to bargain when they preferred to stand pat.

Quantitative Restrictions. Until 1959 GATT made only slow progress toward the elimination of import restrictions (quotas). The majority of GATT members took advantage of the balance of payments exception to the general prohibition of import quotas. The restoration of currency convertibility by Western European countries at the end of 1958 broke this logjam. At the Tokyo session of GATT in 1959, member governments reaffirmed their intention to abolish balance of payments restrictions as soon as possible. Since then, the major trading countries have abandoned quantitative import restrictions that were previously justified on grounds of a weak balance of payments or low monetary reserves. The problem has, therefore, shifted to the elimination of residual import restrictions no longer justified under the provisions of GATT, particularly those related to agricultural products.

Countries that continue to apply import restrictions for balance of payments reasons are required to hold periodical consultations with GATT. As a result, many countries have lowered or eliminated their restrictions or have removed objectionable features. Consultations are also mandatory when a member country introduces new restrictions or substantially modifies existing restrictions.

Perhaps the greatest contribution of GATT toward liberalizing import restrictions lies in its role as a forum for frank discussion between member countries. National measures in the field of commercial policy are now open to public scrutiny and criticism. Moreover, the close contact brought about by regular meetings, tariff conferences, and intersessional activities has helped to breed a common international viewpoint on trade policy. Hence, member

---

[13] The superior effectiveness of the multilateral approach of GATT to the bilateral approach of the 1930's is clearly observable in the experience of the United States. During 1934-45 this country negotiated trade agreements with twenty-nine countries; but, in a single GATT conference, that at Geneva in 1947, it completed negotiations with twenty-two other countries. The experience of the 1930's showed that the abandonment of protective import quotas through bilateral bargaining was virtually impossible.

governments take GATT into account when contemplating measures to protect their balance of payments and feel it necessary to explain and justify any action that is not in accord with the spirit of the Agreement.

Settlement of Disputes. One of the most striking but least publicized of GATT's accomplishments is the settlement of trade disputes between members. Historically trade disputes have been matters strictly between the disputants; there was no third party to which they might appeal for a just solution. As a consequence, trade disputes often went unresolved for years, all the while embittering international relations. When disputes were settled in the past, it was usually a case of the weaker country giving way to the stronger. GATT has improved matters tremendously by adopting complaint procedures and by affording through its periodic meetings a world stage on which an aggrieved nation may voice its complaint.

A large number of disputes have been resolved by bilateral consultations without ever coming before the collective membership. The mere presence of GATT was probably helpful in these instances. Thus, the British government repealed a requirement forbidding the manufacture of pure Virginia cigarettes when the United States protested the requirement as a violation of GATT.

When a dispute is not settled bilaterally, it may be taken by the complainant country to the collective membership at the next regular meeting on the basis that the treatment accorded to the commerce of the complainant country by the other disputant is impairing or nullifying benefits received under the Agreement. A panel on complaints hears the disputants, deliberates, and drafts a report. The report is then acted upon by the membership. In this way GATT resolved an extremely bitter disagreement between Pakistan and India.

In the event that the GATT recommendation is not observed, the aggrieved party may be authorized to suspend the application of certain of its obligations to the trade of the other party. Thus, the Netherlands was allowed to place a limitation on wheat flour from the United States because of the damage caused its exports by United States dairy quotas.

The most dramatic trade dispute erupted in 1963 between the United States and the European Economic Community. In the middle of 1962 the EEC countries sharply raised their duties on poultry imports, which came mostly from the United States. In Germany, the biggest United States poultry market, the duty was increased from 5 cents to 12.5 cents per pound. As a result, United States poultry exports to the EEC tumbled 64 percent in 1963. The charges and countercharges between this country and the EEC became known as the "chicken war." When bilateral negotiations between the two parties ended in a deadlock, a special panel of GATT experts was asked to arbitrate the question of damages to United States poultry exports. In October, 1963, the panel ruled that the United States had experienced a loss of $26 million (the United States had claimed damages of $46 million while the EEC put the figure at $19 million) and could withdraw concessions to the EEC of that amount if the parties could not reach a settlement. Both sides accepted the ruling but were unable to resolve the chicken war. In January, 1965, the United States imposed the high 1930 duties on imports of brandy, trucks, dextrine, and potato starch in retaliation for the EEC poultry import duties. This action affected EEC exports to the United States valued at $25.4 million in 1962. (Compensatory tariff concessions were later made to third countries which also exported these products to this country.) In this instance the GATT settlement machinery did not succeed in modifying the EEC duties on poultry, but it did limit the United States retaliation and prevented any counterretaliation by the EEC.

THE FUTURE OF GATT

GATT entered the 1970's with a membership of some eighty countries that together generated most of the world's trade. Nevertheless, the future role of GATT is clouded with uncertainty.

Despite its enormous success in liberalizing international trade in industrial products, GATT suffers from certain weaknesses that have become more prominent in recent years. GATT has failed to liberalize trade in agricultural products to any significant degree and, except for quantitative restrictions, it has not yet developed rules for the reduction or elimination of nontariff trade distortions. These two failures must be overcome if GATT is to spearhead the liberalization of trade in the 1970's.

Moreover, GATT has experienced only partial success in regulating trade measures adopted by member countries in response to balance of payments difficulties. As noted earlier, GATT has successfully limited the use of quantitative restrictions by the industrial countries for balance of payments purposes, but in recent years some of these countries have adopted import surcharges and export subsidies in violation of the rules. The most serious violation occurred in 1971 when the United States—the major trading country—imposed a 10 percent surcharge on its imports, thereby doubling its average level of duties.

Further, GATT has not been able to resist a steady erosion of the most-favored-nations principle, notably by the European Economic Community (EEC). Article XXIV of GATT permits member countries to form a customs union or free trade area (which are inherently discriminatory) only when they do not raise new barriers to trade with outside countries. Nevertheless, the EEC has created a highly protectionist system (variable import levies) to keep out agricultural products, and it has granted free entry or lower duties to many African and Mediterranean countries that are not extended to other GATT members.[14] By undercutting GATT's basic rule of nondiscrimination, these EEC policies threaten to supplant multilateral trading with a system of trade blocs practicing mutual discrimination.

---

[14] See Chapter 16.

Finally, GATT continues to exist as a mere executive agreement under the Protocol of Provisional Application which means, among other things, that member countries are not obligated to observe rules that are inconsistent with their domestic legislation existing at the time of their entry into GATT. GATT would be greatly strengthened as an instrument of trade liberalization if it were transformed into a permanent legal organization by the legislative approval of its member countries.

The future of GATT is dependent on the foreign economic policies of its members, particularly the United States and the European Economic Community. Only these two economic units have the capacity to lead GATT toward freer trade in the 1970's. GATT has been described as a "church with a congregation of sinners," but if the sinning gets out of hand, then the whole purpose of GATT is "cast into darkness." If the United States sincerely desires a liberal, multilateral trading system embracing the entire world, then it must take the initiative to overcome the weaknesses of GATT which, in the last analysis, flow from the protectionist policies of its members, including the United States.

THE TRADE EXPANSION ACT OF 1962 AND THE KENNEDY ROUND

The Trade Expansion Act of 1962 was a direct response to the progressive establishment of a customs union by the European Economic Community. The provisions of this Act gave the President sweeping authority to reduce or eliminate United States import duties in return for similar concessions from the EEC and third countries. The focus on prospective negotiations with the EEC inspired all of the President's tariff-cutting authority.

The EEC had become the most dynamic export market for the United States, taking about one-fifth of total United States exports in the first half of the 1960's. But this attractive picture was shadowed by fears of the future. United States-EEC trade prospects were threatened by several developments:

1. The degree of EEC discrimination on industrial products would increase sharply in the future: there would be zero duties on industrial trade among the Six while outsiders would pay the common tariff.

2. The common external tariff appeared to be more protective than the national tariffs it was displacing because in most instances it was higher than the former German tariff. This meant that German manufacturers— the major suppliers of most industrial products in the EEC—would enjoy greater protection than before, apart from the tariff advantages they were gaining within the EEC.

3. The common agricultural policy was very protectionist, limiting third countries to the role of residual suppliers and stimulating agricultural self-sufficiency in the EEC.

4. The economic growth of EEC countries had slackened in recent years, and it was expected that growth effects on imports would be less significant in the 1960's than in the 1950's.

This combination of factors pointed to a substantial diversion of trade, a substitution of intra-EEC trade for trade with third countries.

The key importance of EEC markets to the United States and the threat that these markets would become limited by protectionist policies convinced the new Kennedy Administration that the United States must make a strong effort to bargain down EEC trade barriers and prevent, or mitigate, the trade diversion that menaced the export interests of countries outside the Community. The persisting United States balance of payments deficit lent urgency to this decision.

NEGOTIATING AUTHORITY

During the five-year period from July 1, 1962, to June 30, 1967—the life of the new Act—the President was authorized to do any of the following:

1. To reduce by as much as 50 percent the rates of duties existing as of July 1, 1962.

2. To reduce up to 100 percent the tariff rates on the products of industries where the United States and the European Economic Community combined represented 80 percent or more of the free-world trade.[15]

3. To reduce to zero tariff duties of 5 percent or less existing as of July, 1962.

4. To eliminate tariffs on tropical products by agreement with the EEC subject to its extending comparable treatment and without discrimination as to source of supply of these products, but only if such products were not produced in the United States in significant quantities.

5. To eliminate tariffs on certain farm products if in the opinion of the President such action would tend to assure the maintenance or expansion of United States exports of like articles.

Except for the tropical products authority, which might be applied when proclaimed, the Act required that all other negotiable cuts be put into effect in at least five installments a year apart (the first when concessions are proclaimed) to allow domestic producers time to adjust to foreign competition.

ESCAPE CLAUSE

Unlike its predecessors, the new escape clause of the TEA required that injury or threat of injury to an industry be traceable to actual competitive imports caused by a concession and not by causes related to the dynamics of growth rather than to the granting of the concession itself.

The new law also drew the line between partial and total injury (by reason of a concession) to a company within an industry producing several products. For a company to qualify for redress, it was necessary to prove its case on the basis of its overall activities. Thus, a partial injury within an otherwise profitable whole operation was expected to be absorbed

---

[15] The 80-percent authority was rendered almost useless by the failure of Britain to enter the EEC.

by the company, even though the industry as a whole might qualify for redress.

In a case of a proven injury, the President could decide to maintain the concession for foreign policy considerations and certify the company and/or the displaced workers of that company for compensation under the *Adjustment Assistance* provision of the TEA—an important innovation in American tariff policy.

ADJUSTMENT ASSISTANCE

When injury was established but no escape-clause action taken, the President might initiate negotiations toward agreements with foreign countries to voluntarily limit exports to the United States, either individually or as a group, thus giving relief to injured United States industries. If only the less efficient firms within a given industry were affected by the increased imports, the law provided for governmental assistance to them in a variety of forms.

Assistance to Firms. An injured firm that was certified as such by the Tariff Commission might apply to the Secretary of Commerce for relief under the adjustment-assistance provision of the TEA. The various forms of assistance which could be extended singly or in combination are listed below:

1. Technological aid at governmental expense;
2. Financial assistance in the form of partial or outright loans or government guarantee for same; or
3. Tax relief in the form of a five-year carry-back loss privilege instead of the normal three-year provision of the general tax laws.

Assistance to Workers. Displaced workers, because of tariff concessions, were eligible under the law for various forms of assistance ranging from retraining, relocation, and hardship allowances to prolonged periods of unemployment compensation with additional benefits above the prevailing rates.

The adjustment assistance provisions of the TEA represent a path-breaking departure from the no-injury concept of the Reciprocal Trade Agreements Act, which deemed as permissible only tariff concessions that did not injure, or threaten to injure, American industry. Although the TEA recognized that tariff concessions were bound to increase imports and to cause hardship for industries and workers, such hardship was not to be remedied by an upward readjustment of duty rates (except in extreme instances). Instead, the Government was to extend financial and other assistance that enables injured firms to diversify into new lines of production and injured workers to train for new jobs. Adjustment assistance explicitly recognizes, therefore, that a policy of freer trade demands a policy of adaptation to the new conditions of import competition.[16]

THE KENNEDY ROUND

Backed by the Trade Expansion Act, the United States called for a new GATT Tariff Conference, and in May, 1963, the ministers of the GATT countries met in Geneva to decide on the basic principles that would guide negotiations scheduled to start in May, 1964. United States and EEC representatives clashed on several points, but compromises on both sides led finally to an apparent agreement on general principles:

> 1. Negotiations would cover all classes of products, including agricultural and other primary products. (The United States insisted on coverage of agricultural products which had been neglected in previous GATT negotiations.)
>
> 2. Negotiations would deal with nontariff trade barriers as well as tariffs.
>
> 3. Negotiations would be based on a plan of substantial and equal linear reductions with a bare minimum of exceptions which would be subject to confrontation and justification. However, in those cases where there were "significant disparities" in tariff levels, the tariff reductions would be based on special rules of general and automatic application. (This principle was a direct compromise between the United States and the EEC, the former fighting for substantial linear cuts, the latter holding out for special treatment of tariff disparities.)
>
> 4. Negotiations should provide for acceptable conditions of access to world markets for agricultural products.
>
> 5. Every effort should be made to reduce barriers to exports of the developing countries, and the developed countries should not expect to receive reciprocity from the developing countries.

Agreement on these principles did not resolve the differences between the United States and the EEC. As Ludwig Erhard remarked at the time: "We have agreed on the shell of the egg, but what the egg will contain we do not yet know." [17] The job of hammering out agreement on the contents of the "egg" was handed over to a newly created Trade Negotiations Committee. One issue bogged down the work of the Committee from the start— the question of tariff disparities. It so occupied the attention of negotiators that discussions on agriculture, nontariff trade barriers, and trade with developing countries had scarcely begun by May, 1964, when the Tariff Conference, popularly known as the Kennedy Round, opened officially.

---

[16] It is now widely agreed that the TEA rules for trade adjustment assistance are too stringent. Not a single firm or worker qualified for assistance during the 1960's.

[17] European Community Information (London), *European Community,* June, 1963, p. 2.

A brief description of the major issues in the Kennedy Round negotiations will help us understand why agreement was so difficult and why the grand objective of the Kennedy Round—an across-the-board 50 percent reduction in tariff duties—was not attained.

Tariff Disparities. Both the United States and the EEC agreed that the average height of their respective tariffs (as measured by the ratio of duties collected over the value of dutiable imports) was about the same, around 12 percent. But the EEC tariff was very homogeneous with most rates falling between 10 and 20 percent because the EEC tariff is an arithmetical average of its members' tariffs. In contrast, the United States tariff had some very high duties as well as some very low ones.

The United States wanted a 50 percent linear cut in tariff rates with a minimum of exceptions. In opposition, the EEC contended that a 50 percent cut would not be fair because it would still leave some United States duties at a high level. In the case of high U.S. rates and low EEC rates, the EEC wanted to cut its own duties by, say, 25 percent in return for 50 percent cuts by the United States. After more than a year of fierce argument, the GATT negotiators decided to circumvent the issue by permitting each country to place products subject to disparities on its exceptions lists. This did not solve the disparities problem but it did prevent an impasse in negotiations. In November, 1964, the United States, the EEC, and other industrial countries submitted lists of products that they wanted to be excepted from linear cuts.

The Agricultural Issue. The United States insisted that any tariff-and-trade package it negotiated in the Kennedy Round must provide an access to EEC markets for United States agricultural products. The United States negotiating plan contained these elements:

    1. Substantial reductions in any *fixed* import duties on agricultural products in line with reductions in industrial duties.

    2. The inclusion of variable import levies in negotiations in a meaningful way and, in particular, agreement on market-sharing arrangements in the EEC for both domestic and foreign producers involving nondiscriminatory global quotas.

    3. The removal of quantitative restrictions or state-trading activities that impeded trade in agricultural products.

The EEC steadfastly refused to negotiate on target prices and rejected any market-sharing arrangements. Instead, the Community proposed a "freeze" on the amount of domestic price support (the difference between the world price and the domestic price) in the Community, the United States, and other countries. The United States viewed this proposal as a binding of higher levels of protection in the EEC rather than as a reduction in trade barriers. The Community also proposed the negotiation of global commodity agreements.

Nontariff Trade Barriers. For the first time a GATT Tariff Conference addressed itself to the problem of nontariff trade barriers. These arise from a broad variety of national laws, regulation, and administrative procedures and they are often more restrictive than tariffs. Both the United States and the EEC have many nontariff barriers that frustrate traders on both sides of the Atlantic.

Europeans were (and are) particularly annoyed by the United States customs valuation based on the American selling price. Most United States imports are valued f.o.b. the foreign port of export; but organic chemicals and some other products are valued at the wholesale price in the United States of the competing American products, including distribution costs and profits. Europeans charged that the use of the American selling price can double or even triple the effective tariff rate, and they demanded its abolition. Strong criticism was also directed against the United States Antidumping Act and the "Buy-American" Act.

In turn, the United States charged the EEC with special taxes that discriminate against United States automobiles and other products, the practice of basing tariff rates and some taxes on high c.i.f. valuations, and many other barriers such as the French prohibition on advertising grain liquors.[18]

The Developing Countries. All the concessions made in trade negotiations among the industrial countries were to be extended to the forty-odd developing countries belonging to GATT without the need for reciprocal concessions on their part. The United States was also willing to completely eliminate tariffs on tropical products in return for similar action by the EEC. But the EEC was reluctant to move in that direction because it would destroy much of the preferential treatment now accorded the associated African states. Instead, the EEC favored the negotiation of global commodity agreements that would stabilize prices and insure orderly markets. The United Nations Conference on Trade and Development (UNCTAD) in 1964 highlighted the needs of developing countries for more generous treatment of their trade by the industrial countries.

RESULTS OF THE KENNEDY ROUND

The Kennedy Round officially ended on June 30, 1967, when fifty-three governments signed agreements to place into effect the results of four weary years of negotiation.[19]

The great achievement of the Kennedy Round was an average 35 percent reduction in duties on some $40 billion of trade in 60,000 industrial products. Table 15-2 (page 370) indicates the general character of reductions

---

[18] In 1963 the Italian road tax was $170 for a United States compact car, $44 for a Volkswagen, and only $17 for a Fiat. In France there is a surtax of $60 on a two-gallon container of grain spirits, a product not produced in France.

[19] To avert utter failure the Kennedy Round had to end when it did because the tariff-negotiating authority of the President expired at the same time.

by major industrial countries. Observe that these countries lowered duties on almost 70 percent of the value of their dutiable imports in 1964, the base year for Kennedy Round negotiations ($25.7 billion out of $37.0 billion), and that almost two-thirds of these dutiable imports experienced duty reductions of 50 percent or more ($16.9 billion).

Table 15-2

KENNEDY ROUND TARIFF REDUCTIONS ON IMPORTS OF SELECTED INDUSTRIAL COUNTRIES

(Billions of Dollars)

Total imports in 1964	59.7
Duty-free imports	22.7
Dutiable imports	37.0
Imports subject to tariff reductions	25.7
Size of reductions:	
Up to 20 percent	4.2
20 percent to 50 percent	4.6
50 percent	14.4
Over 50 percent	2.5
No tariff reductions	11.3

Source: Adapted from General Agreement on Tariffs and Trade, Press Release (Geneva: June 30, 1967).

Note: The industrial countries include the United States, the European Economic Community, the United Kingdom, Japan, Sweden, and Switzerland. All trade is covered except cereals, meat, and dairy products.

The 35 percent overall reduction far exceeded the tariff cuts of previous conferences. In 1956 the Geneva Conference achieved only a 4 percent average reduction and in 1962 the Dillon Round resulted in a 5 percent average reduction. Although the U.S. goal of a 50 percent linear tariff cut was not attained, the actual outcome of negotiations on industrial tariffs was extraordinarily successful in view of the many obstacles.

The Kennedy Round established an important precedent by including negotiations on agricultural products and nontariff trade barriers. However, the results were very disappointing, falling far short of U.S. negotiating objectives. In agriculture the Kennedy Round extended the International Wheat Agreement, agreed on a pact that would provide 4.5 million tons of cereal grains per year to needy countries, and lowered duties on some agricultural products making up less than $2 billion in trade. But the EEC refused to alter its variable-levy system for farm products and was not willing to move to free trade in tropical products because of its preferential arrangements with many African countries. Nevertheless, the intensive discussions between the United States and the EEC on agricultural problems did clarify many issues and in some instances pointed the way toward their resolution. In particular, it became evident to both sides that any substantial progress in the further liberalization of agricultural trade would depend on a willingness to negotiate on all aspects of agricultural programs, especially support levels.

The Kennedy Round reached two important agreements on nontariff trade barriers. One is an antidumping code that is intended to harmonize the administration of antidumping complaints in GATT countries.[20] The other is the special agreement on chemicals which provides that the United States may obtain additional tariff concessions (amounting to an overall tariff cut of 30 percent) on chemicals as well as concessions on some nontariff measures (especially the modification of European automobile taxes based on horsepower) in return for the elimination of its American Selling Price (ASP) system of valuation.[21] Although the actual results were modest, the Kennedy Round did spotlight the growing significance of nontariff trade distortions as tariff rates fell. There was a common agreement that the elimination of nontariff barriers would be a major task for the 1970's.

Although the developing countries received all of the Kennedy Round concessions without concessions on their part, their access to markets was only marginally enhanced because the concessions were mostly on industrial products that mainly benefited the industrial countries. The modest liberalization of trade in agricultural and tropical products denied them any major gains.

In conclusion, the Kennedy Round was highly effective in lowering duties on industrial products. Indeed, these duties are now so low that any further liberalization might well aim for their complete elimination. Although success was modest, the Kennedy Round was also the first tariff conference to open up negotiations on agricultural and nontariff trade barriers. History may well depict the Kennedy Round as the culmination of GATT's multilateral bargaining arrangements that were initiated in 1947. To free trade in agriculture and eliminate nontariff trade distortions in the 1970's and later decades, it may prove necessary to devise new strategies for international negotiations.

THE RESURGENCE OF PROTECTIONISM

Less than four months after the successful conclusion of the Kennedy Round, scores of bills were introduced in the U.S. Congress calling for the imposition of quotas on imports of steel, textiles, shoes, watches, meats, dairy products, lead, zinc, and a host of other products. In 1968 President

---

[20] See Chapter 12, pp. 295-297, for a discussion of antidumping.

[21] In the Kennedy Round the United States cut duties on most of its chemical tariffs by 50 percent or more while the Europeans made only a 20 percent cut with a 30 percent cut conditional upon the elimination of ASP. So far the U.S. Congress has refused to abolish the ASP. The ASP is treated in Chapter 12, p. 295.

Johnson asked Congress for a two-year extension of the tariff-cutting authority not used in the Kennedy Round, the abolition of ASP, and a liberalization of the criteria for trade adjustment assistance. However, faced with a rising tide of protectionist sentiment, this bill was never brought to a vote.

To redeem a 1968 campaign pledge to help the textile industry, President Nixon sought at the start of his new Administration to persuade Japan and other countries to apply "voluntary" quotas on their exports of woolens and synthetic textiles to the United States.[22] To place pressure on a reluctant Japanese government, the Administration encouraged the introduction of a bill in May, 1969, by the Chairman of the House Ways and Means Committee, that would limit textile imports to the average annual level in 1967-68.

In the expectation that textiles could be treated as a unique "exception," the President submitted to Congress later in 1969 a modest trade bill that asked for authority to make minor tariff adjustments when it became necessary to offer compensation to GATT members as a result of escape clause action, the elimination of ASP, and a liberalization of trade adjustment assistance. In May, 1970, the House Ways and Means Committee began six weeks of hearings on the President's trade proposals. Failing to obtain a voluntary textile quota from Japan, the Administration declared its support of a mandatory textile import quota on the last day of these hearings. This action proved to be an open invitation to all protectionists. Logrolling in the subsequent closed sessions of the Committee converted the President's bill into the most protectionist legislation since the Hawley-Smoot tariff of 1930. It provided for quotas on textiles, shoes, petroleum (the freezing of existing quotas), mink, glycerin, and contained a "basket" clause that would enable scores of industries to qualify for quota protection. In effect, any industry could ask for quota protection when it felt threatened by imports, and many of them would obtain such protection.

When the "Trade Act of 1970" was finally reported out by the Committee, over 4000 professional economists urged President Nixon to veto the bill if it passed the Congress.[23] Representatives of the EEC and European governments vigorously protested and spoke of retaliation if the bill became law. Although the spectre of a trade war stood in the wings, the House of Representatives passed the legislation in November and it appeared likely that the Senate would do the same. As fate would have it, however, the

---

[22] In 1961 the United States obtained quantitative limitations on cotton textile imports by negotiating the Long-Term International Cotton Textile Agreement. In 1968 steel producers in Japan and Europe agreed to "voluntary" limitations on exports to the United States. The United States also has its own quotas on a variety of agricultural products and petroleum.

[23] This action was reminiscent of the unsuccessful petition of over 1000 economists in 1930 asking President Hoover to veto the Hawley-Smoot bill.

Senate was compelled to adjourn by the Constitution before it could vote on the trade bill.

In 1970 the United States came close to reversing a commercial policy that had progressively liberalized world trade over almost two generations. Why did protectionism become so formidable? Two observations are pertinent. First, several factors combined to strengthen the appeals of protectionist interests: continuing domestic inflation coupled with growing unemployment; a chronic balance of payments deficit with a worsening trade balance; intense import competition; and isolationist tendencies generated by the Vietnam War. But equally important, the Administration, by trying to make textiles an exception to a liberal trade policy, gave the many protectionist interests a golden opportunity to claim exceptions for their own industries. In retrospect, one can see that the Administration's strategy to use the threat of Congressional action as a weapon of international negotiation acted to undermine its own leadership in the formulation of trade policy. The 1970 crisis reaffirmed the importance of Presidential initiative in the design of foreign economic policy.

U.S. COMMERCIAL POLICY FOR THE 1970'S

At the beginning of the 1970's, U.S. commercial policy appeared to be drifting with no clear direction. No new trade legislation had been passed by Congress since 1962, the President was without negotiating authority, and protectionist forces were threatening to negate the triumph of the Kennedy Round. At the same time, several developments in the world economy demanded a creative policy response on the part of the United States. At this time we give a brief mention of the more prominent of these developments.

The United States must resolve its balance of payments problem and help construct a viable international monetary system.[24] The imposition by the United States of a 10 percent surcharge in 1971 demonstrated in striking fashion that any further progress in trade liberalization was conditional on the restoration of equilibrium in its balance of payments.

The entry of the United Kingdom and other countries into the EEC in 1973 raises many questions about relations between the United States and this powerful economic group.[25]

Economic interdependence among nations (already high by historical standards) is likely to accelerate in the 1970's, bringing economic benefits but also constraints on national policy-making. Intense international competition will require more effective modes of national adaptation to shifts in comparative advantage.

---

[24] See Chapters 19 and 20.
[25] See Chapter 16.

Trade policy will have to recognize the special character of the multi-national corporation, which produces and markets throughout the world.[26] Much of the world's industrial trade (as well as investment and technology flows) is already determined by these corporations.

The drive by the developing countries to increase both traditional and manufactured exports to the industrial countries is a deep-seated phenomenon. One element of this drive is a demand for preferential access to the markets of the advanced nations.[27]

The breakdown of monolithic communism and the waning of the cold war is opening up new opportunities for trade and other economic relations with the socialist countries of the world, notably the Soviet Union and Mainland China.[28]

In responding to these forces, the United States can choose to continue a liberal commercial policy or regress to the protectionist policies it espoused before 1934. In the final analysis, it is a choice between a world of economic interdependence and a world of autarkic economic blocs.

SUMMARY

1. The history of the commercial policy of the United States is essentially the history of its tariff. Before 1934 tariff measures were relied upon for both revenue and protection. Tariff rates grew higher with the economic development and industrialization of the country.

2. The present basic tariff law is the Hawley-Smoot Tariff of 1930, the highest tariff in the history of the United States. However, the RTA program, introduced in 1934, permitted numerous reductions in rates by executive action; and today the United States tariff is among the lowest in the world.

3. From 1934 to 1962, the RTA program was the core of U.S. commercial policy, which is part of the broader foreign economic policy of the nation. In the 1950's, however, protectionist amendments caused a deterioration of the RTA program.

4. This drift toward protectionism was reversed by the Trade Expansion Act of 1962 (TEA) which gave unprecedented tariff-bargaining authority to the President.

5. The principal instrument in the liberalization of world trade since its creation in 1947 is the General Agreement on Tariffs and Trade (GATT). GATT comprises four basic elements: (1) the rule of nondiscrimination in trade relations between the participating countries; (2) commitments to observe negotiated tariff concessions; (3) prohibitions against the use of quantitative restrictions on exports and imports; and (4) special provisions to promote the trade of developing countries. GATT has fostered widespread tariff reductions

---

[26] See Chapter 21.
[27] See Chapter 18.
[28] See Chapter 24.

and has exerted steady pressure on member countries to abandon or relax quantitative restrictions. GATT has also developed machinery for the settlement of international trade disputes.

6. Backed by the TEA, the United States initiated a new GATT Tariff Conference that became known as the Kennedy Round. The Kennedy Round achieved a 35 percent overall reduction in the tariff rates of the industrial countries. It also included negotiations on agricultural trade and nontariff trade barriers with, however, only modest results.

7. After the triumph of the Kennedy Round the United States experienced a resurgence of protectionism that culminated in the "Trade Act of 1970" that providentially never came to a vote in the Senate.

8. At the beginning of the 1970's, U.S. commercial policy appeared to be drifting with no clear direction. No new trade legislation had been passed by Congress since 1962, the President was without negotiating authority, and protectionist forces were threatening to reverse the liberal policy of the last thirty-five years.

QUESTIONS AND APPLICATIONS

1. Why is the Reciprocal Trade Agreements Act a "watershed" in U.S. commercial policy?

2. Making reference to the peril point, the escape clause, and defense essentiality, describe the deterioration of the Reciprocal Trade Agreements Program in the 1950's.

3. What are the major provisions of GATT? Describe the mechanism for tariff negotiations under GATT.

4. On the basis of your own research, evaluate the role of GATT today.

5. Explain the purpose of the Trade Expansion Act of 1962. In what ways does the TEA differ from the Reciprocal Trade Agreements Act as extended in the 1950's?

6. What did the United States hope to get in the Kennedy Round? What were the actual results?

7. How do you explain the resurgence of protectionism in the United States?

8. Undertake research to identify and describe the major protectionist groups in the United States today.

9. What should U.S. commercial policy be in the 1970's? Be prepared to defend your answer.

SELECTED READINGS

Committee for Economic Development. *Trade Negotiations for a Better Free World Economy*. New York: 1964.

Congress of the United States. *A Foreign Economic Policy for the 1970's*. Hearings before the Subcommittee on Foreign Economic Policy of the Joint Economic Committee. Washington: U.S. Government Printing Office, 1970.

Future United States Foreign Trade Policy. Report to the President, submitted by the Special Representative for Trade Negotiations. Washington: U.S. Government Printing Office, 1969.

General Agreement on Tariffs and Trade. *The Activities of GATT.* Geneva: annual.

Taussig, Frank W. *The Tariff History of the United States,* 8th ed. New York: G. P. Putnam's Sons, 1931.

Weil, Gordon L. *Trade Policy in the 70's.* New York: The Twentieth Century Fund, 1969.

CHAPTER 16

ECONOMIC INTEGRATION IN WESTERN EUROPE

Postwar European economic cooperation began with the establishment of the Organization for European Economic Cooperation (OEEC) in 1948 to allocate Marshall Plan aid and accelerate the recovery of Western Europe. In the 1950's, quotas and payments restrictions on intra-OEEC trade were rapidly dismantled, and European countries grew accustomed to close cooperation on trade and other economic matters. However, many Europeans, as well as Americans, considered economic cooperation under the auspices of the OEEC inadequate to cope with Europe's problems. They argued that only economic integration that transcends national boundaries would enable Europe to match the continental economies of the United States and the Soviet Union. Economic integration would create the large competitive markets that are the necessary counterparts of mass production and economics of scale, and it would stimulate a more efficient allocation of labor, materials, and capital.

Supported by the United States, the drive toward European economic unity gained strength in the 1950's despite widespread doubts as to its ultimate success. Its first notable success was the establishment of the European Coal and Steel Community (ECSC) in 1952 to create a common market in coal, steel, and iron ore covering the six nations of France, Germany, Italy, Belgium, the Netherlands, and Luxembourg. The second big step toward economic unity was the negotiation and approval by these same countries of a treaty establishing the European Economic Community in 1957. The failure of negotiations for an OEEC-wide free trade area led to the formation of the European Free Trade Association (EFTA) in 1960 by the United Kingdom, the three Scandinavian countries, Switzerland, Austria, and Portugal. During the 1960's Western Europe remained at "sixes and sevens," but the split between the European Economic Community and the European Free Trade Association is now coming to an end. Great Britain, Denmark, and Ireland entered the Community at the beginning of 1973 and the other EFTA countries are making arrangements with the Community short of full membership.

The main feature of the European Economic Community (EEC) is the creation in planned stages of a customs union for both industrial and agricultural goods, involving the abolition of all restrictions on trade among member countries and the erection of a common external tariff. But EEC goes much further than this. A second objective is a full *economic union* with free movement of persons, services, and capital, and progressive harmonization of social, fiscal, and monetary policies. The ultimate objective is a *political union* of the member countries.

The formation of the EEC has introduced a new force to world trade and has provoked a major attempt by the United States to negotiate with the EEC to lower tariffs and other trade barriers. In this chapter we shall first describe the principal features of EEC and its progress toward the creation of a customs and economic union. Next, we shall consider some of the effects of European integration on international trade in the light of economic theory. Finally, we shall examine the policies of EEC toward the outside world, including the common external tariff, agricultural protection, the European Free Trade Association, the developing countries, and the United States.

Before moving on to a consideration of the EEC, it is instructive to outline the forms or stages of economic integration, as seen in Table 16-1.

Table 16-1

STAGES OF INTERNATIONAL ECONOMIC INTEGRATION

Stage of Integration	Abolition of tariffs and quotas among members	Common tariff and quota system	Abolition of restrictions on factor movements	Harmonization and unification of economic policies and institutions
1. Industrial free trade area	Yes*	No	No	No
2. Full free trade area	Yes	No	No	No
3. Customs union	Yes	Yes	No	No
4. Common market	Yes	Yes	Yes	No
5. Economic union	Yes	Yes	Yes	Yes

* Industrial goods only.

A *free trade area* is established when a group of countries abolishes restrictions on mutual trade but each member country retains its own tariff and quota system on trade with third countries. An *industrial* free trade area covers only trade in industrial products while a *full* free trade area includes all products. As an industrial free trade area, the European Free Trade Association (EFTA) represents only a modest form of economic integration.

A *customs union* is created when a group of countries removes all restrictions on mutual trade and also sets up a common system of tariffs and quotas with respect to third countries.

A customs union becomes a *common market* with the removal of all restrictions on the movement of productive factors—labor, capital, and enterprise. The EEC is now in this stage of evolution and is proceeding toward an economic union.

The completion of the final stage of *economic union* involves a full integration of the member economies with supranational authorities responsible for economic policy making. In particular, an economic union requires a single monetary system and central bank, a unified fiscal system, and a common foreign economic policy. The task of creating an economic union differs significantly from the steps necessary to establish the less ambitious forms of economic integration. A free trade area, a customs union, or a common market mainly result from the abolition of restrictions, whereas an economic union demands a positive agreement to transfer economic sovereignty to new supranational institutions.

THE CREATION OF A CUSTOMS UNION

The Treaty establishing the European Economic Community is a lengthy document comprising over 200 articles.[1] The Treaty lays down a timetable for the progressive development of a customs union but goes far beyond this goal—it contains numerous provisions relating to the free movement of persons, services, and capital, transportation, rules governing competition, the harmonization of laws, economic policies, social policies, and the organs of the Community.

INSTITUTIONS OF THE COMMUNITY

The basic institutions, or organs, of the Community are four in number: Commission, Council of Ministers, European Parliament, and Court of Justice.

The Commission is the executive body of the EEC and has two main functions. First, it administers the Treaty and other Community policies. Second, it initiates new policies by making proposals to the Council. The Commission represents the Community rather than the member states, and it is the driving force in the EEC.

Each Council of Ministers member represents his own national government. For the most part, the Council makes final policy decisions but can do so only on proposals by the Commission. During the first two stages of development, Council decisions required a unanimous vote, but then shifted to a majority vote basis.[2] It is through the Council that national governments

---

[1] The Treaty was signed in Rome on March 25, 1957, and was then ratified by the six countries. A separate treaty setting up a European Atomic Energy Community (Euratom) was signed and ratified at the same time. Both the EEC and Euratom treaties went into effect on January 1, 1958. Fusion of the three Communities (EEC, ECSC, and Euratom) into a single European Community was substantively accomplished in 1967.

[2] The third stage began in 1966.

influence and control the evolution of the EEC by approving, amending, or rejecting Commission proposals.

The European Parliament draws its members from the legislatures of the member countries. However, the Parliament does not pass laws and is not a true legislature since this function is performed jointly by the Commission and Council. The Commission must report to the Parliament annually and the latter must be consulted before certain specific decisions are taken. But the only important power of the Parliament is the right to remove the Commission by a motion of censure voted by a two-thirds majority.

The Court of Justice has the sole power to decide on the constitutionality of acts performed by the Commission and Council. The Court's judgments have the force of law throughout the Community and they are binding on all parties whether individuals, business firms, national governments, or other Community institutions.

FREE TRADE IN INDUSTRIAL PRODUCTS

The European Economic Community became a full customs union in July, 1968, when tariffs and quantitative restrictions were removed on all trade among its member countries and a common tariff system was established vis-à-vis nonmember countries. Behind this signal achievement lay a decade of commitment that was tested by a series of hard-fought negotiations, especially in agricultural policy.

Although trade in industrial products within the EEC is no longer obstructed by tariffs and quotas, it is not yet as free as trade within a single country. Many nontariff barriers continue to clog the arteries of commerce, such as differences in customs classification, varying taxation systems, border restrictions (for security, health, and technical reasons), and state monopolies. The Commission is working steadily on measures to harmonize customs legislation and eliminate licenses, visas, permits, and other export-import formalities so that the Common Market will have the same characteristics as a domestic market. However, certain barriers (for example, "tax frontiers" resulting from different tax systems) cannot be eliminated until the member countries agree to transfer more sovereignty to the Community.

FREE TRADE IN AGRICULTURAL PRODUCTS

Each of the six countries came into the EEC with its own domestic farm program involving price supports and import restrictions. This situation called for a different approach to free trade in agricultural products; namely, the establishment of a common agricultural policy that would not only free intra-Community trade but, at the same time, improve the economic position of Community farmers.

Negotiations for a Common Agricultural Policy. The EEC Treaty does not spell out the details of a common agricultural policy; they have had to be worked out in a series of laborious negotiations that at times threatened the very existence of the Community.

The EEC took its first big step toward a common agricultural policy in January, 1962, when the Council of Ministers (after a marathon session ending at 5 A.M.) agreed on the basic features of that policy and on regulations for grains, pork, eggs, poultry, fruit, vegetables, and wine. These regulations went into effect on July 30, 1962.[3] The second big step was taken at the end of 1963 (the "Christmas eve" marathon) when the Council agreed on a common policy for rice, beef, veal, dairy products, vegetable oil, and oilseeds. By November, 1964, when regulations covering these products went into effect, 85 percent of the agricultural output of the Community was under common organization.

These first two agreements did not extend to the common prices that would rule once a single agricultural market was fully established in the Community. This was the next order of business and it proved exceptionally arduous. The key factor was the common price of grain. Germany, the high-cost producer, tried to stall agreement on a common grain price while France, the low-cost producer, pressed hard for its early establishment. The issue was finally resolved in December, 1964 (in another marathon conference that ended at 5:15 A.M.), when the Council agreed on a common grain price—closer to the French than to the German price—applicable to member countries no later than mid-1967.

The adoption of a common grain price broke a logjam; it was then possible to start negotiations on other common agricultural prices. The EEC countries became full participants in a common agricultural policy when all remaining restrictions on their mutual trade in farm products were swept away at the end of June, 1968.

Structure of the Common Agricultural Policy. Americans should not find it difficult to understand the basic farm problem in the EEC because it is very much like the United States farm problem. A technical revolution is now sweeping European agriculture such as the one experienced by the United States during the 1940's. Productivity on farms in the EEC is increasing at a higher rate than industrial productivity; farmers are leaving the land; and per capita farm income is lagging behind that in other sectors of the economy. Production is almost equalling and, in some instances, surpassing the consumption of many commodities. The degree of self-sufficiency will most likely rise in the future—with or without a common agricultural policy.

Although the farm problems in the EEC and the United States have many common features, their impact on international trade is very different. The EEC is still the largest importer of farm products in the world while the U.S. is the world's largest exporter. Because it is a net exporter of

---

[3] At that time imports of all these products except fruit, vegetables, and wine became subject to variable levies. This precipitated the "chicken war" with the United States. See Chapter 15.

temperate farm products, agricultural policy in this country involves production controls, storage of surplus commodities, and the subsidization of exports, with import restrictions playing only a modest role except in dairy products. In contrast, agricultural policy in the EEC—a net importer of farm products—is based primarily on the restriction of imports. In this way the EEC hoped to avoid production controls and surpluses (so troublesome in this country) by placing the burden of adjustment on third country suppliers, notably the United States.

The structure of the common agricultural policy in the EEC is best illustrated by the common grain policy. First, there is a *target price*. This is the base price for grains to be established annually at the market of the region in the Community with the least adequate supplies. Farmers will receive subsidies in order to sell their crops at prices as close as possible to the target price.

Second, there is an *intervention price*. This is the price (between 5 and 10 percent below the target price) at which the Community will buy from producers. It is the guaranteed minimum selling price.

Third, there is a *threshold price*. This is the price used to calculate the variable levy on imported grains. The threshold price is fixed at a level that will bring the selling price of imported grains up to the level of the target price in the region of the Community with the least adequate supplies.

Fourth, the *variable import levy* is a tariff imposed on grain imports from countries outside the Community. It is determined daily and is equal to the difference between the world price for grain imports and the Community threshold price, taking any quality differences into account.

A hypothetical illustration may help to clarify the price structure of the common grain policy and the determination of the variable import levy:

		PER BUSHEL
1. Target price		$2.80
2. Intervention price		$2.60
3. Threshold price:		
Target price	$2.80	
Less transportation and marketing costs	.10	$2.70
4. Variable import levy:		
Threshold price	$2.70	
Less adjusted world price	$1.50	$1.20

In conclusion, two points need stressing. First, there are no production controls: the Community must buy any quantity of a commodity offered at the intervention price. Second, variable import levies make third countries residual suppliers of farm products; imports are allowed only when EEC producers fail to meet Community requirements. Consequently, the target prices are a key concern of the United States and other outside suppliers. High target prices encourage EEC production and cut down on imports; low target prices greatly mitigate this effect.

The Common Agricultural Policy in the 1970's. In the 1960's the EEC countries introduced a common agricultural policy that eliminated restrictions on mutual trade and established single target and intervention prices throughout the Community. But many problems remain to be resolved in the 1970's, notably food surpluses, inefficient farms, and a steady deterioration in farm income relative to other sectors. In the late sixties, high support prices caused mounting surpluses of butter, sugar, and grains that strained Community resources. (The 1971 Community budget allocated $2.35 billion to the Agricultural Fund out of total expenditures of $2.76 billion.) Furthermore, this policy encouraged inefficient farm production and exacerbated relations with third countries (especially the United States) as the EEC not only cut down on farm imports but also subsidized the export of food surpluses. Most importantly from the standpoint of political forces within the Community, this policy failed to halt the slippage of farm income.[4]

After a yearlong impasse between the Commission and the Council, the Council approved in March, 1971, a fundamental reorientation of the Common Agricultural Policy that will emphasize structural reform in the 1970's. During 1971-75, up to $1.5 billion is to be allocated to modernize farms and induce two million farmers (out of 10 million) to leave the land. By 1980 it is hoped that the number of EEC farmers will have fallen to 5 million. This major shift in emphasis from high support prices with no production controls to a program of structural reform should act to reduce overproduction, raise farm income, and ameliorate relations with third countries.

BUILDING A COMMON MARKET

To establish a common market that will match the freedom of national markets, the EEC must go far beyond the traditional dimensions of a customs union. To enhance the gains from a superior allocation of resources, factors of production must be free to move among the member countries and thereby equalize factor returns throughout the Community. Furthermore, as noted earlier, many nontariff measures that restrict trade or confer artificial competitive advantages on the producers of only one of the member countries must be eliminated if the pattern of EEC production and trade is to reflect fully the forces of competition, costs, and markets.

FREE MOVEMENT OF LABOR, CAPITAL, AND ENTERPRISE

Community workers and their dependents can now move freely among the member countries in response to employment opportunities. Information on such opportunities is coordinated by an EEC agency. When moving to a

---

[4] In February, 1971, disgruntled EEC farmers accompanied by three cows crashed the Council session in Brussels. A month later some 80,000 farmers staged a violent demonstration in the same city.

country, workers receive the same rights and benefits of social security as do nationals, and they also retain any rights and benefits they have earned through employment in another member country.

The EEC has achieved unconditional freedom of movement for direct investment, personal capital transfers, and short-term and medium-term commercial credits. However, some member countries still maintain discriminatory controls on new security issues and noncommercial loans and credits. Because capital restrictions are regarded as an important tool of balance of payments policy, the establishment of a common market for capital will depend upon the creation of a full economic union with a single monetary system.

The EEC has eliminated many restrictions on the right of member-country nationals to establish businesses and provide services throughout the Community. Council measures have been applied to manufacturing, trading, agriculture, forestry, mining and prospecting, insurance, and other fields. However, many complexities have slowed progress toward the mutual recognition of diplomas and the right of professional people, such as lawyers and physicians, to practice freely anywhere in the Community. Furthermore, national differences in company laws and public buying preferences accorded national firms continue to obstruct the freedom of establishment for Community enterprise.

RULES GOVERNING COMPETITION

The Rome Treaty gives to the Commission specific powers to prevent the formation of, or to break up, cartels and monopolies that lessen competition in the Common Market. The overriding purpose of this antitrust policy is to prevent private business agreements and industrial concentrations from nullifying Community-wide competition. Private restrictions are not to be allowed to replace the disappearing tariffs and other restrictions.

Although the EEC antitrust provisions (Articles 85 and 86) have been influenced by United States antitrust legislation, there is a fundamental difference in philosophy between the two. Under United States law *all* "unreasonable" restraints on trade are illegal, and agreements to fix prices, allocate markets, etc., are illegal per se regardless of their effects. In contrast, the EEC distinguishes between "good" and "bad" cartels and monopolies. Business agreements and concentrations that help improve the production or distribution of goods or promote technical and economic progress are legal in the EEC provided that they do not eliminate competition in a "substantial" part of the market.

The administration of antitrust policy in the EEC also differs from that in the United States. All cartels must register with the Commission, and to become legal they must be granted a dispensation. Failure to register makes a private agreement null and void and the Commission may impose retroactive penalties on the guilty parties. In this country there is no prior registration because all cartels are illegal by their very nature; instead, each case is decided on its merits and the parties involved are presumed innocent until proved guilty.

How effective is EEC antitrust policy likely to be? Certainly the Commission has ample authority to dismantle or regulate cartels and monopolies. The Commission has very sharp teeth: it may impose fines ranging up to $1 million, or 10 percent of annual sales, on companies that willfully violate or ignore its antitrust directives. The effectiveness of antitrust policy in the EEC depends, therefore, mainly on how the Commission uses its powers. The first important antitrust decision came in 1964, when the Commission forebade the German electronics firm, Grundig, to operate under an agreement giving a French firm, Consten, exclusive rights to Grundig sales in France. Since then the Commission has imposed heavy fines on firms participating in cartels and has clarified its interpretation of unfair business practices in a body of case law.

One can reasonably expect severe treatment of arrangements that nullify, or threaten to nullify, any liberalizing effects of the customs union, but there is little prospect of an antimonopoly drive in the EEC. The Commission is unlikely to prohibit mergers or to dissolve existing concentrations. Quite the contrary. There is a strong belief in the EEC that European firms are too small to compete effectively against United States firms.

Viewed broadly, the EEC's antitrust policy represents a radical break with the past. Although this policy is limited to trade among the member countries and does not apply to purely domestic trade or to trade with non-member countries, the Commission has already gone a long way toward establishing a common policy on competition in the EEC that is an indispensable part of a common market.[5]

HARMONIZATION OF INDIRECT TAXES

Indirect taxes on goods and services differ among the member countries. The consequence is a "tax frontier" that inhibits trade and distorts competition within the Community. The EEC is seeking to eliminate tax frontiers by harmonizing both the systems and rates of national indirect taxes.

The principal indirect tax is the *turnover* tax on sales. But some countries use the *cascade* system of taxation under which a tax is paid on the gross value of goods each time they are sold at the multiple stages of production ending in final consumption, while other countries use a *value-added* system that levies a tax only on the value added by each seller. The cascade system has two major disadvantages: (1) It is difficult to ascertain how much tax a particular good bears and consequently the size of border tax adjustments. Since the traditional treatment of indirect taxes in international trade involves a reimbursement of taxes to exporters by the exporting country and the imposition of taxes on importers (equal to domestic

---

[5] The broader subject of restrictive business practices in international business transactions is treated in Chapter 24.

indirect taxes) by the importing country, any uncertainty with regard to these taxes can lead to either excessive reimbursements or excessive border taxes with distorting effects on trade.[6] (2) Since the cascade tax is levied only on sales to *independent* buyers, it encourages vertical integration by companies with possible anticompetitive effects. In contrast, the value-added tax is the same whether collected at various stages or only once at the sale of the final product because the sum of the values added at intermediate stages is equal to the value of the final product.

In 1967 the Council required all member countries to adopt the value-added tax as the common turnover tax system. When this tax is used throughout the Community, then border tax adjustments will precisely reflect the turnover taxes borne by each product and there will no longer exist a tax incentive for vertical integration. However, tax frontiers will still remain because turnover tax *rates* will continue to differ among the member countries. Although the Commission has proposed the harmonization of rates, it is likely to take much more time because it raises questions of revenue and national sovereignty. Only when all EEC countries have the same rates of indirect taxes (excise taxes as well as turnover taxes) will tax frontiers become a thing of the past in the Community.

COMMON POLICIES FOR TRANSPORTATION AND ENERGY

To further enhance the effectiveness of the common market, the EEC is developing common policies in transportation and energy.

The common policy in transportation would create a market free of any national discriminations. This involves the elimination of double taxation on motor vehicles, common rules for international passenger traffic, coordination of investment in transportation facilities, the standardization of procedures for issuing trucking licenses, a common rate-bracket system, the application of rules of competition for road, rail, and inland waterway transportation, as well as many other matters in this very complex field. It is expected that air and sea transportation will also eventually come under a common policy. In 1968 agreement was reached on measures that prescribe competitive conditions for road, rail, and inland water transportation and also fix floor and ceiling rates for intermember truck traffic.

The first important step toward an integration of energy in the Community was taken in 1964 when the member governments agreed to carry out a common energy policy. This policy envisages equal access to energy supplies, supervision of mergers between energy companies, notification to the Commission of fuel and power price changes, and the harmonization of national pricing policies in fuel and power. However, actual progress toward

---

[6] The role of border tax adjustments as a nontariff barrier is discussed in Chapter 12.

a common energy policy has been slowed by the critical importance of energy to the member countries and the wide variety of their policies.

TOWARD AN ECONOMIC UNION

The EEC is much more than a customs union; it seeks to integrate all facets of the national member economies. The end result would be an economic union—a single economic system embracing the entire EEC. It was recognized from the start that a truly successful customs union would not be possible if each member country were free to choose its own policies without regard to the others.

"Harmonization" is a key word in the evolution of the economic union. Harmonization calls for the gradual elimination of differences in national legislation, administrative practices and policies, and their eventual integration to form a Community-wide policy carried out by common institutions. Since economic integration involves all aspects of the national economies, harmonization must proceed simultaneously on many fronts: antitrust policy, transportation and energy policy, trade policy, monetary and fiscal policy, wage and social policy, and so on. Actual progress toward economic union of the EEC countries has been very uneven—substantial in those areas where the Rome Treaty makes specific provision, but only modest in those areas where economic integration has to be negotiated in the Council of Ministers.[7]

THE PLAN FOR A FULL ECONOMIC UNION

In February, 1971, the Council of Ministers took a "historic" step by agreeing on the achievement of an economic and monetary union in ten years. In the words of the Council Resolution:

> In order to bring about a satisfactory growth-rate, full employment and stability within the Community, to correct structural and regional imbalances therein and to strengthen the contribution of the Community to international economic and monetary cooperation, thereby achieving a Community of stability and growth, the Council and the Representatives of the Governments of the Member States express their political will to introduce, in the course of the next ten years, an economic and monetary union, in accordance with a phased plan commencing on January 1, 1971.[8]

By 1980 the EEC would, according to the Resolution: (1) constitute a zone within which persons, goods, services, capital, and enterprise would move freely; (2) form an individual monetary unit within the international

---

[7] The Rome Treaty does not specifically call for economic union.

[8] Resolution of the Council and of the Representatives of the Governments of the Member States, European Community Information Service, Press Release (February 25, 1971).

system, characterized by the "total and irreversible" convertibility of currencies, the elimination of fluctuation margins of exchange rates, and the irrevocable fixing of parity rates, all of which are indispensable conditions for the creation of a single currency; and (3) hold the powers and responsibilities in the economic and monetary field enabling its institutions to administer the union.[9]

To move toward these goals, the Council initiated a three-year phase (1971-74) embracing a variety of measures to be undertaken by the Community and member countries:

1. Effective coordination of short-term economic policies, including compulsory prior consultation, quantitative guidelines for national budgets, and progressive harmonization of economic policy instruments.
2. Accelerated harmonization of indirect taxes.
3. Progressive liberalization of capital markets.
4. Stronger coordination in monetary and credit policies through compulsory prior consultation by central banks and the harmonization of monetary policy instruments.
5. Development of common external monetary policies.
6. Progressive narrowing of fluctuation margins among member currencies and possibly a de jure Community system for currency stabilization.

It is much too early to gauge the prospects for full economic union. A first step toward a common monetary policy (namely, the narrowing of rate variations among the currencies of the member countries) was postponed by the "collapse" of the international monetary system in August, 1971, when the United States abandoned the gold convertibility of the dollar. In the longer run, it remains an open question whether the member countries (notably France) will prove willing to transfer monetary and fiscal powers to the Community. Control over the monetary system and over government taxation and expenditures lies at the very heart of national sovereignty. Thus, the road to full economic union is still a long one, and a safe arrival is by no means inevitable. On the other hand, one is reminded of the ancient Chinese proverb: "Even a journey of a thousand miles begins with a single step."

TOWARD A POLITICAL UNION?

From the beginning the ultimate objective of the EEC has been political union—the establishment of a United States of Europe. Attempts in the early postwar years to move directly toward political union in Western Europe were frustrated by national jealousies and ambitions. It was then that men like Maurice Schuman and Jean Monnet turned toward economic integration as a means to achieve eventual political integration. The first concrete success in this direction was the creation of the European Coal

---

[9] *Ibid.*

and Steel Community in 1952 which pooled the coal and steel resources of the six countries. (Other countries, notably Great Britain, stayed out of the ECSC precisely because of its political implications.) In the early 1950's a new attempt to bring about political union by direct means was thwarted when in 1954 the French Assembly rejected the European Defense Community Treaty. Meanwhile, to the surprise of many, the ECSC got off to a strong start and progressively demonstrated that economic integration was not an illusion but a practical achievement. Its success led to the more ambitious EEC Treaty in 1957. The statesmen who drafted and negotiated the Rome Treaty firmly believed that they were building a new Europe, that gradual economic integration over the transitional period would be crowned by a political federation of the member countries.

It can be argued that the Community is already a political union in specific areas of economic and social policy. Certainly the member countries have given up much of their sovereignty in international trade and agriculture. On the other hand, it is also true that the national governments still retain control: the Commission proposes but the Council of Ministers disposes. The Community institutions are supranational only to a limited degree; real power remains with the national governments. As long as this situation prevails, political union is a distant goal and it is even doubtful whether full economic union can be brought about because it will demand enhanced powers for Community institutions to the detriment of national powers.

In any event, the EEC has already completed the formation of a common market and this achievement alone has had, and is continuing to have, profound effects on Europe's role in the world economy. The likelihood, then, is that the EEC (much enlarged by the entry of Great Britain, Denmark, and Ireland) will continue to be a powerful force in international trade and investment even if its higher goals of full economic and political union are not realized.

THE THEORY OF ECONOMIC INTEGRATION

Before reviewing the external economic relations of the Community, it will be instructive to delineate the theoretical benefits and costs of regional economic integration.

STATIC EFFECTS OF A CUSTOMS UNION

The theory of customs unions, a relatively new branch of economics, represents an extension of tariff theory to multinational discriminatory systems.[10] This theory analyzes the static, once-for-all changes in trade and welfare induced by the formation of a customs union or a free trade area.

---

[10] The pioneer work in this field is Viner's. See J. Viner, *The Customs Union Issue* (New York: Carnegie Endowment for International Peace, 1950). The theoretical effects of a tariff are discussed in Chapter 12.

Trade Effects. Because a customs union involves both free trade among its member countries (liberalization) and, at the same time, restrictions on imports from nonmember or third countries (protection), it has both positive and negative effects on trade. A positive effect occurs when the elimination of internal tariffs and other barriers stimulates *new* trade among the member countries that does not displace third-country imports. That is to say, the customs union induces a shift from a high-cost producer inside the union to a lower-cost producer also inside the union. This positive effect is called *trade creation*. On the other hand, a negative trade effect occurs when member countries now buy from each other what they formerly bought from third countries. Known as *trade diversion,* this negative effect results from a shift from a lower-cost producer outside the union to a higher-cost producer inside the union.

A simple model will clarify the meaning of trade creation and trade diversion. Let us assume three countries (A, B, and C) who are each capable of producing wheat and automobiles. Country A is the high-cost producer of both products, country B is the low-cost producer of automobiles, and country C is the low-cost producer of wheat. In the absence of restrictions, therefore, country A would import automobiles from country B and wheat from country C. Actually, however, country A keeps out automobile imports with a tariff and imports wheat despite a tariff. Now suppose country A and country B form a customs union, leaving country C outside the union as a third country. The trade effects on automobiles and wheat are shown in Tables 16-2 and 16-3, respectively.

After the formation of the customs union, buyers in country A shift from high-cost domestic automobiles to country B's automobiles, which can now be purchased at B's domestic cost because country A's 20 percent duty is abolished within the union. These imports represent trade creation because they do not displace automobile imports from country C, which are nonexistent. However, this is not true in the case of wheat. Buyers in country A shift from country C's wheat to country B's wheat, which they can obtain free of duty after the formation of the customs union. Although country C is the low-cost producer, it must pay a 20 percent duty in order to sell in country A, making its wheat noncompetitive with country B's.

Under what circumstances is a customs union likely to create trade rather than divert it? First, trade creation is enhanced when the economies of the member countries are very *competitive* with overlapping patterns of production. Then there are plenty of opportunities for specialization and trade among them. Conversely, when the pre-union economies are complementary, then the opportunities for new trade are limited because the economies are already specialized with respect to each other. Second, trade creation is positively related to the size of the customs union (as measured by its share of world trade and production) because the larger the size, the

Table 16-2

POSITIVE TRADE EFFECT OF A CUSTOMS UNION: TRADE CREATION

(Dollars)

	Country A	Country B	Country C
Unit cost (price) of automobile production ..	1500	1300	1400
Cost plus country A's duty (20%)	1500	1560	1680
Cost plus common duty (10%) after formation of customs union	1500	1300	1540

Table 16-3

NEGATIVE TRADE EFFECT OF A CUSTOMS UNION: TRADE DIVERSION

(Dollars)

	Country A	Country B	Country C
Unit cost (price) of wheat production	5.00	4.20	3.80
Cost plus country A's duty (25%)	5.00	5.25	4.75
Cost plus common duty (20%) after formation of customs union	5.00	4.20	4.56

greater the probability of the lowest-cost producers being located inside the union. Conversely, a customs union of small economic size is more likely to induce trade diversion. Third, the higher the pre-union duties of the member countries, the greater the likelihood of trade creation in products that were formerly protected against imports. Finally, the smaller the distances among member countries, the greater the scope for trade creation because of low physical transfer costs.

Welfare Effects. Customs union theory is concerned with the static effects of a customs union on world welfare rather than on the welfare of individual member or nonmember countries. From this perspective, the customs union "problem" is viewed as a special case of the theory of the second-best.[11] Starting from the premise that universal free trade would achieve the most efficient allocation of the world's resources and consumption (Paretian optimum), it does not follow that free trade among a limited number of countries would *necessarily* raise world welfare. Rather, the *net* welfare effect of a customs union would depend on the net balance of the production and

---

[11] See Chapter 13 for an explanation of the theory of the second-best.

consumption effects associated with trade creation and trade diversion, together with any changes in income distribution.

As to the production effects, trade creation improves the world's economic efficiency (and thereby raises its potential welfare) by substituting lower-cost production for higher-cost production. Conversely, trade diversion lowers the world's potential welfare by substituting higher-cost production within the union for lower-cost production outside the union.

As we have seen, trade restrictions also have *consumption* effects because they introduce discrepancies between the relative prices at which goods can be purchased (the marginal rate of substitution in trade) and their relative costs of production (the marginal rate of substitution in production).[12] By reducing this discrepancy, trade liberalization allows consumers to move to a higher level of satisfaction (higher indifference curve). It follows that trade creation has a positive consumption effect on welfare because it brings the production possibilities and the consumer preferences of the union into conformity. Conversely, trade diversion has a negative consumption effect because it widens the gap between the preferences of consumers in the union, on the one hand, and the world's production possibilities, on the other. Trade creation enhances consumer's choice; trade diversion constricts it.

To sum up, a customs union will improve world economic efficiency and potential welfare when trade creation outweighs trade diversion. However, *potential* welfare is not the same as *actual* welfare. Actual welfare depends not only on economic efficiency (the size of the pie) but also on income distribution (the sharing of the pie). In particular, income redistribution between the customs union and outsiders must be taken into account in any thorough evaluation of its welfare effects.

DYNAMIC EFFECTS OF A CUSTOMS UNION

The static theory of customs unions ignores the many dynamic effects of customs unions (and other forms of economic integration) on *economic growth*. A customs union can promote economic welfare not only by inducing higher efficiency (a movement *along* the production possibilities frontier) but also by stimulating growth (an *outward* movement of the production possibilities frontier). Indeed, the impact of its dynamic effects on world welfare may well overwhelm any negative static effects. Here only brief mention will be made of the many ways a customs union may promote economic growth.

The most obvious consequence of a customs union is *market extension*: producers (and consumers) enjoy free access to the national markets of all member countries whereas formerly their access was hindered or blocked

---

[12] For a review of these terms, see Chapter 3.

by import restrictions. Market extension sets in motion many forces. It makes possible *economies of scale* in many industries which could not be achieved in narrow national markets. A broader market also intensifies *competition,* forcing producers to cut costs, sell more aggressively, and look for new products. The combination of economies of scale and heightened competition is also apt to foster an increase in *enterprise size,* whether through internal growth, merger, or acquisition. Bigger firms, in turn, have more capacity to finance research and development, and thereby compete more effectively in *product innovation.*

To take advantage of new market opportunities and withstand the pressures of new competition, firms are compelled to make *investments* in plant and equipment that directly create new employment and income. Furthermore, the quality of investment will improve because investment decisions are made in the light of cost and market conditions throughout the union. By forcing the development of industrial centers that serve the enlarged market, a customs union also creates external economies; interactions among the many specialized firms in those centers bring costs down for all of them. Moreover, a bigger market induces new investment in infrastructure (such as transportation, power, and communications) that, in turn, promotes general economic efficiency and growth. Mention should also be made of the reduction in risk and uncertainty for entrepreneurs. With assured access to the markets of the member countries, a customs union's internal trade more closely resembles domestic, interregional trade than international trade. Faced with less uncertainty, therefore, entrepreneurs within the union are encouraged to make investments in plant and research in order to exploit the extended market over the long run.

It is to be expected that the greater the degree of economic integration, the greater the impact of these dynamic effects on growth. The liberalization of factor movements (common market) is especially noteworthy in this regard. It is not too much to say that the presence or absence of dynamic effects spell the success or failure of a customs union and more advanced forms of economic integration.

STATIC AND DYNAMIC EFFECTS OF THE EEC

This section offers a few empirical observations about the probable welfare effects of the European Economic Community. On general grounds, one would expect that trade creation resulting from the Common Market would outweigh any trade diversion; the member countries have competitive economies, the share of the EEC in world trade and production is high, the pre-union tariffs of the member countries were restrictive, and the member countries are geographically contiguous. Data on trade support this expectation as regards manufactures but point to substantial trade diversion in the case of agricultural products.

Table 16-4 shows EEC imports of manufactures in recent years. From 1963 to 1969, imports of manufactures by EEC countries from other EEC countries (intra-EEC imports) grew from 56.5 percent to 61.5 percent of total EEC imports of manufactures, with a corresponding decline in the import share of the rest of the world. However, this rather modest increase in the share of intra-EEC imports of manufactures was accompanied by a rapid growth in the *value* of manufactured imports from outside countries, from $8.7 billion in 1963 to $17.2 billion in 1969. These figures indicate that the dynamic effects of economic growth in the EEC have swamped any trade diversion effects. Actually the EEC has been a very expansive market for the manufactures of third countries.

Table 16-4

EEC IMPORTS OF MANUFACTURES IN 1963, 1967, AND 1969

Origin of Imports of EEC Countries	Value of Imports in Billions of Dollars (f.o.b.)			Percentage Distribution		
	1963	1967	1969	1963	1967	1969
Total imports	20.0	29.6	44.6	100.0	100.0	100.0
From EEC	11.3	17.9	27.4	56.5	62.9	61.5
From rest of world	8.7	11.7	17.2	43.5	37.1	38.5
North America	2.6	3.4	4.8	12.8	11.6	10.7

Source: Derived from General Agreement on Tariffs and Trade, *International Trade 1969* (Geneva: 1970), Appendix, Table C.

The story is different for food, as is shown in Table 16-5. The share of intra-EEC imports in total EEC food imports rose sharply from 1963, when variable levies were first imposed (at midyear), to 1969. At the same time, the share of rest-of-world food imports declined from 76.3 percent to 60.7 percent. This trade diversion effect was barely neutralized by the overall growth of EEC food imports, particularly in the case of North America (United States and Canada), which produces the same temperate-zone foodstuffs as the EEC. Observe that the value of food imports from North America actually dropped between 1967 and 1969 while intra-EEC imports rose from $3.2 billion to $5.1 billion. If North America had maintained its 1963 import share, then EEC food imports from that region would have reached $2 billion, or $0.5 billion more than the actual level.

Although our analysis is hardly definitive, the figures in Tables 16-4 and 16-5 support a tentative conclusion that the net welfare effect of the EEC has been positive, largely owing to the dynamic effects of economic growth. Between 1963 and 1969, the EEC's gross national product (at current prices) rose almost 50 percent, from $258.5 billion to $384.2 billion. In the same period, EEC imports of *all* products from outside countries increased from $24.5 billion to $39.3 billion, or 60 percent. Although the

Table 16-5

EEC IMPORTS OF FOOD IN 1963, 1967, AND 1969

Origin of Imports of EEC Countries	Value of Imports in Billions of Dollars (f.o.b.)			Percentage Distribution		
	1963	1967	1969	1963	1967	1969
Total imports	8.2	10.7	12.9	100.0	100.0	100.0
From EEC	2.0	3.2	5.1	23.7	30.2	39.3
From rest of world	6.2	7.5	7.8	76.3	69.8	60.7
North America	1.3	1.6	1.5	15.8	14.9	11.9

Source: Derived from General Agreement on Tariffs and Trade, *International Trade 1969* (Geneva, 1970), Appendix, Table C.

contribution of the EEC to the economic growth of its member countries cannot be empirically verified, nevertheless it is a fact that the EEC sustained a higher growth rate in the 1960's than either the United States or Great Britain. The positive dynamic effects on welfare were supplemented by trade creation in manufactures but partially offset by trade diversion in agriculture.

EXTERNAL ECONOMIC RELATIONS OF THE COMMUNITY

The European Economic Community and the United States are giants of world trade. Excluding trade among its members, the Community accounts for about 15 percent of the free world's exports, approximately the same as the United States. All the original six EEC countries (counting Belgium-Luxembourg as a single trading unit) belong to the ten principal trading countries shown in Table 2-2 in Chapter 2. Furthermore, with the exception of Japan, the EEC has been growing more rapidly than the other industrial areas. In the decade 1959-69 the average annual increase in the Community's real gross national product was 5.5 percent compared to 3.0 percent for the United Kingdom and 4.3 percent for the United States. Because of its economic size and dynamism, the external policies of the EEC have a pervasive influence on the composition, direction, and volume of international trade and investment.

The basic policy of the EEC toward third countries is expressed by the common external tariff and the variable import levies on agricultural products. The discrimination inherent in the common tariff and variable levies is a cause of concern to all third countries. This concern was behind the efforts to bargain down the EEC tariffs in the Kennedy Round.

This closing section briefly describes the relations of the Community with the European Free Trade Association (EFTA), with the countries that have been granted preferential status, with the developing countries, and with the United States.

THE COMMUNITY AND EFTA

EFTA is an industrial *free trade area* which was completed at the end of 1966 with the abolition of all restrictions on trade in manufactured goods among its member countries.[13] Unlike the EEC, each member country retains its own tariff and quota system and follows its own trade policies with respect to third countries. In its first decade (1960-1970), EFTA achieved a substantial economic success. Growing at an average annual rate of 11 percent (compared with 6.5 percent during the 1950's), intra-EFTA exports increased from $3.5 billion in 1959 to $10 billion in 1969.[14]

The principal motivation behind the formation of EFTA in 1960 was to set the stage for later negotiations with EEC to work toward a regional trading arrangement that would cover the whole of Western Europe. Because of the remarkable success of EEC, the United Kingdom opened negotiations in 1961 to enter EEC as a full member. By 1962 all EFTA members had expressed their willingness to join EEC or enter into an association with it. However, this was not to be—negotiations came to a sudden halt in January, 1963, when President Charles de Gaulle declared France's opposition to British entry. Although France also blocked a second attempt in 1967, Britain's third try for entry was crowned with success in June, 1971. Great Britain, Denmark, and Ireland became full members of the Community at the beginning of 1973. Great Britain will abolish all industrial tariffs on trade with the EEC by mid-1977 and will fully align its agricultural prices with those of the EEC by the end of 1977. The remaining EFTA members asked for arrangements short of full membership in the Community. In 1972, agreement was reached to establish a free trade area embracing these countries and the EEC that covers industrial products but not farm products.

The entry of Great Britain, Ireland, and Denmark has added greatly to the Community's size. Using data available in early 1973, population has expanded from 188 million to 253 million (United States: 205 million), and gross national product has risen from $427 billion to $695 billion (U.S.: $1,050 billion). Clearly an enlarged Community will have a profound influence on world trade and investment.

PREFERENTIAL ARRANGEMENTS

The Community has an *Association Convention* with eighteen independent African states that gives these developing countries free access to the Common Market under the same conditions as the EEC members.[15] In return,

---

[13] The original seven member countries of EFTA are Austria, Denmark, Norway, Sweden, Switzerland, Portugal, and the United Kingdom (Great Britain). Finland and Iceland subsequently joined the Association.

[14] European Free Trade Association, *EFTA Bulletin* (May, 1970), p. 23.

[15] When the Rome Treaty was signed in 1957 most of these African states were French colonies. Known as the Yaounde Convention, this preferential arrangement entered a new five-year term in 1971.

the eighteen countries are obligated to abolish quotas and lower tariffs on imports from the Community, but they retain the right to maintain old tariffs and quotas, or create new ones, in order to protect infant industries. In addition, the EEC's European Development Fund for Overseas extends development assistance to the associated states which is expected to reach $918 million in the period 1971-75.

In 1971, an association agreement came into force between the Community and the East African countries of Tanzania, Kenya, and Uganda. The EEC will eliminate restrictions on most imports from those countries in exchange for similar treatment by them, subject to their development and revenue requirements. This preferential arrangement (known as the Arusha Agreement) has no aid provisions.

The Community has also signed agreements with many Mediterranean countries. Association agreements intended to lead to full membership have been concluded with Greece (1961), Turkey (1963), and Malta (1970). In 1969, trade agreements were signed with Morocco and Tunisia; in 1970, with Spain and Israel. Future agreements with Egypt, Lebanon, Algeria, and Cyprus are in the planning stage. All of these arrangements contain preferential provisions. For example, the agreement with Spain provides for a mutual reduction in tariffs in several stages. In the agreement with Israel, the EEC is committed to lower duties on most imports of manufactures by 50 percent and on most agricultural products by 40 percent in return for a reduction in Israeli duties over a five-year period.

The EEC's preferential arrangements have been criticized by GATT, UNCTAD, and many third countries, notably the United States. They allege that the proliferation of these accords causes negative trade diversions (which particularly hurt tropical countries in Latin America and elsewhere which export the same products, such as coffee, cocoa, cotton, and bananas) and endangers the most-favored-nation principle (nondiscrimination). In reply, the Community points out that 90 percent of its trade is nondiscriminatory and that its preferential policy is limited to agreements with European countries which cannot become full members, developing African countries, and countries of the Mediterranean basin. It defends this policy as an instrument for economic development and political stability in the Mediterranean.

THE EEC AND THE DEVELOPING COUNTRIES

In 1971 the EEC became the first major trading power to grant generalized tariff preferences on imports of manufactures from developing countries.[16] Applying to ninety-one countries, the Community's offer fixes a progressive ceiling every year on each product and covers all manufactures and semimanufactures with no exceptions. These preferences should open up new export opportunities for many developing countries, but they do not lessen the negative trade diversion effects of the common agricultural policy

---

[16] For a discussion of preferential tariffs for developing countries, see Chapter 18.

and the preferential arrangements on agricultural products with African and Mediterranean countries.

THE UNITED STATES AND THE COMMUNITY

In the early 1970's, growing forces of protectionism, balance of payments difficulties, and the slow progress of the Community toward political unity have engendered in U.S. Government officials a "hard-headed" attitude toward trade relations with the EEC. We have already treated many of the issues between these two giants of world trade in our discussion of the Kennedy Round.[17] Some of these issues continue to bedevil trade relations, notably the common agricultural policy (during the late 1960's U.S. farm exports to the EEC began to decline in value) and nontariff trade barriers (the U.S. Congress has refused to abolish the American Selling Price). More recently, EEC preferential arrangements in the Mediterranean have hurt U.S. citrus exports, adding further complications to the problem of agricultural trade. Finally, the entry of Great Britain into the Community is raising concern in the United States about the possible negative effects for U.S. exports.

In the light of these troublesome relations between the United States and the Community, the words of President Kennedy have become more meaningful than when they were first uttered at the beginning of the 1960's:

> The two great Atlantic markets will either grow together or they will grow apart. . . . That decision either will mark the beginning of a new chapter—or a threat to the growth of Western unity.[18]

SUMMARY

1. The European Economic Community started its official existence at the beginning of 1958. The main feature of the EEC is the creation in planned stages of a *customs union* for both industrial and agricultural goods. A second objective is a full *economic union* with free movement of persons, services, and capital, and progressive harmonization of social, fiscal, and monetary policies. The ultimate objective is a *political union* of the member countries.

2. The basic institutions of the Community are four in number: Commission, Council of Ministers, European Parliament, and Court of Justice.

3. The EEC became a full customs union in 1968 when tariffs and quantitative restrictions were completely removed on all trade among its member countries and a common tariff system was fully established vis-à-vis nonmember countries.

---

[17] See Chapter 15.
[18] *Message to the U.S. Congress on Reciprocal Trade Agreements Program* (January 25, 1962).

4. Through a series of laborious negotiations the EEC has developed a common agricultural policy involving target, intervention, and threshold prices, and variable import levies. Two points need stressing: there are no production controls, and the variable import levies make third countries, such as the United States, residual suppliers of farm products.

5. The EEC has also built a common market with substantially free movements of productive factors among the member countries; namely, labor, capital, and enterprise. The EEC has rules governing competition, has adopted a value-added tax system, and is working on common policies in transportation and energy.

6. The Community hopes to achieve a full economic union by 1980 with an integration of all facets of the members' economies, notably a single monetary system.

7. It can be argued that the Community is already a political union in specific areas of economic and social policy. But it is also true that the Community institutions are supranational only to a limited degree and that real power remains with the national governments. As long as this situation prevails, political union is a distant goal. It is even doubtful whether full economic union can be brought about because it will demand enhanced powers for Community institutions at the expense of national powers.

8. The theory of customs unions analyzes the static, once-for-all changes in trade and welfare induced by the formation of a customs union or free trade area. The result of such changes culminates in either trade creation or trade diversion. A customs union will improve world economic efficiency and potential welfare when trade creation outweighs trade diversion. Aside from its static effects, a customs union may have many dynamic effects on economic growth and welfare: market extension, economies of scale, competition, enterprise size, and others. In the case of the EEC, positive dynamic effects have been supplemented by trade creation in manufactures but partially offset by trade diversion in agriculture.

9. The basic policy of the EEC toward third countries is expressed by the common external tariff and the variable import levies on agricultural products. But the EEC has departed from the most-favored-nation principle by entering into preferential arrangements with many African and Mediterranean countries.

10. In the early 1970's, Western Europe remained split between the EEC and EFTA. However, Great Britain, Ireland, and Denmark became full members of the EEC in 1973.

11. Despite the success of the Kennedy Round, trade relations between the EEC and the United States are troubled by the EEC's common agricultural policy and preferential arrangements.

QUESTIONS AND APPLICATIONS

1. Distinguish between the following forms of economic integration: free trade area, customs union, common market, and economic union.

2. Identify the institutions of the EEC and describe their functions.
3. What is the structure of the common agricultural policy? How does this structure affect EEC imports of farm products?
4. Evaluate the performance of the EEC in establishing a customs union and a common market.
5. What is a "tax frontier"? How is the EEC seeking to eliminate it?
6. Describe the EEC's plan for economic union by 1980. Do you think economic union is possible without political union?
7. (a) What is the meaning of trade diversion, trade creation, and dynamic effects?
   (b) Appraise the effects of the EEC on U.S. trade in terms of the above concepts. (This will require an analysis of relevant trade and other economic data.)
8. What is EFTA?
9. Be prepared to debate either side of the following question: Are the preferential arrangements of the EEC justified?

SELECTED READINGS

Balassa, Bela. *The Theory of Economic Integration*. Homewood, Ill.: Richard D. Irwin, Inc., 1961.

European Community Information Service. *Basic Statistics of the Community*. Washington: annual.

——————. *European Community,* monthly.

——————. *General Report on the Activities of the Community,* annual.

European Free Trade Association. *Building EFTA*. Geneva: 1968.

——————. *EFTA Bulletin*. Geneva: monthly and bimonthly.

Krause, Lawrence B. (ed.). *The Common Market, Progress and Controversy*. Englewood Cliffs, N. J.: Prentice-Hall, Inc., 1964.

Lipsey, R. "The Theory of Customs Unions: A General Survey." *Economic Journal,* Vol. 70 (1960), pp. 496-513. Reprinted in R. E. Caves and H. G. Johnson. *Readings in International Economics*. Homewood, Ill.: Richard D. Irwin, Inc., 1961.

Swann, D. *The Economics of the Common Market*. Harmondsworth, England: Penguin Books, Ltd., 1970.

CHAPTER 17

THE DEVELOPING COUNTRIES IN THE WORLD ECONOMY (1)

Two-thirds of the world's people live a daily round of grinding poverty. Occupying the vast stretches of Asia, Africa, and Latin America, these people belong to more than one hundred countries that are committed to programs of economic development intended to break the vicious circle of poverty. Industrialization has become the supreme national goal of these developing countries; it dominates their economic policies and will probably continue to do so for generations to come. In particular, the drive for economic development shapes the attitudes, policies, and expectations of the developing countries in the areas of international trade and external assistance.

In this and the following chapter we examine the role of international trade in economic development and the trade policies of the developing countries. We also look at the response that developed countries are making to the needs and demands of the developing countries. Regional integration schemes for economic development also merit our attention. But first we must comprehend the economic situation of the poor countries and the major obstacles to a betterment of their low standards of living, for it is this situation that generates the drive for development and the policies directed toward international trade and investment.

THE ECONOMIC SITUATION OF THE DEVELOPING COUNTRIES

Which are the developing countries? What is their stage of economic development? What are their major obstacles to further development? What is the record of two decades of development? These questions occupy our attention in the opening section.

WHICH ARE THE DEVELOPING COUNTRIES?

The most commonly used indicator to distinguish the developing from the developed countries is gross national product (GNP) per capita.[1] Table 17-1 classifies countries according to this indicator.

Table 17-1

COUNTRIES WITH A POPULATION OF ONE MILLION OR MORE CLASSIFIED BY THEIR PER CAPITA GROSS NATIONAL PRODUCTS IN 1968

GNP Per Capita (U.S. Dollars)	Countries (In Order of Income Rank)	
$2000 and over	1. United States 2. Sweden 3. Switzerland 4. Canada 5. France	6. Australia 7. Denmark 8. New Zealand 9. Norway
$1500–$1999	10. West Germany 11. Belgium 12. United Kingdom	13. Finland 14. Netherlands
$1000–$1499	15. East Germany 16. Israel 17. Puerto Rico 18. Austria 19. Czechoslovakia	20. Italy 21. Japan 22. USSR 23. Libya
$750–$999	24. Hungary 25. Ireland 26. Venezuela 27. Poland	28. Trinidad 29. Argentina 30. Rumania 31. Bulgaria
$500–$749	32. Greece 33. Spain 34. Hong Kong 35. Singapore 36. South Africa	37. Panama 38. Lebanon 39. Mexico 40. Uruguay 41. Yugoslavia
$350–$499	42. Chile 43. Jamaica 44. Portugal 45. Costa Rica 46. Mongolia	47. Albania 48. Peru 49. Nicaragua 50. Saudi Arabia

(Continued)

---

[1] Several terms are used to denote the developing countries: poor, underdeveloped, less-developed, nonindustrial, and emerging. These terms are used interchangeably in this and other chapters.

Table 17-1

COUNTRIES WITH A POPULATION OF ONE MILLION OR MORE CLASSIFIED BY THEIR PER CAPITA GROSS NATIONAL PRODUCTS IN 1968

(Continued)

GNP Per Capita (U.S. Dollars)	Countries (In Order of Income Rank)	
$250-$349	51. Malaysia 52. Guatemala 53. Colombia 54. Cuba 55. Iran 56. Turkey 57. Dominican Rep. 58. El Salvador	59. Taiwan 60. Honduras 61. Iraq 62. Ivory Coast 63. Jordan 64. Brazil 65. North Korea
$200-$249	66. Paraguay 67. Algeria 68. Ecuador 69. Southern Rhodesia 70. Tunisia	71. Zambia 72. Liberia 73. Papua + N. Guinea 74. Syria 75. Mozambique
$150-$199	76. Angola 77. Morocco 78. Ceylon 79. South Korea 80. Mauritania 81. Philippines	82. Ghana 83. Senegal 84. Egypt 85. Bolivia 86. Sierra Leone 87. Thailand
$100-$149	88. Cameroon 89. Kenya 90. South Vietnam 91. Cambodia 92. Central Africa Rep. 93. Southern Yemen 94. Uganda	95. India 96. Indonesia 97. Laos 98. Malagasy Rep. 99. Pakistan 100. Sudan 101. Togo
Less than $100	102. Mainland China 103. Congo Rep. 104. Guinea 105. Mali 106. North Vietnam 107. Afghanistan 108. Dahomey 109. Nepal 110. Tanzania 111. Burma 112. Ethiopia	113. Haiti 114. Niger 115. Nigeria 116. Rwanda 117. Yemen 118. Chad 119. Somalia 120. Burundi 121. Malawi 122. Upper Volta

Source: Adapted from International Bank for Reconstruction and Development, *World Bank. Atlas* (Washington: International Bank for Reconstruction and Development, 1970).

Most observers agree that countries with per capita GNP's below $500 are less developed without any qualification. At the same time, they also agree that certain countries with higher per capita GNP's belong to the developing-country group, such as Panama, Mexico, Uruguay, Venezuela, and Trinidad. Hence, it is not possible to draw a line in Table 17-1 separating developing from developed countries. Per capita GNP is only a partial indicator of economic development. More fundamentally, the *developed* countries have not only surpassed the "threshold" level of annual per capita GNP (say, $500), but have also demonstrated a capacity for sustained economic growth over a long period without concessional assistance (grants and/or low-interest, easy-payment loans) from external sources. However, the per capita GNP indicator offers certain advantages as a criterion of economic development: it distinguishes the least developed from the most highly developed countries, it is quantitative, and it rests upon the empirical truth that a threshold level of per capita income is a necessary, if not sufficient, condition for economic development.

Although the per capita GNP indicator places several Communist countries in the ranks of the developing countries, the conventional United Nations classification of developing countries excludes them. It also excludes the low-income countries in southern Europe (Portugal, Spain, Greece, and Turkey) that are badly in need of economic development. In most contexts, therefore, the term "developing countries" denotes the non-Communist countries of Africa (except South Africa), Asia (except Japan), and Latin America. Unless otherwise noted, the United Nations classification is used in this chapter.

The developing countries make up a highly heterogeneous group. In size of population they range from India with over 500 million inhabitants to the many developing countries, such as Barbados, with less than one million inhabitants. Some are highly endowed with minerals or fertile agricultural lands; others are mainly arid deserts or tropical rain forests. Some are much further advanced than others: Brazil possesses a major industrial center in its Sao Paulo region and Argentina has ten times the per capita GNP of the least developed countries. They also exhibit broad cultural, social, and political differences. Despite this diversity, the developing countries have common features relating to their poverty: low per capita incomes, high illiteracy rates, a predominance of agriculture and other primary production, and a dependence on commodity exports. These common features set them off from the economically advanced countries located mainly in Western Europe and North America.

The size of the income gap between the developed and less-developed world (including the Communist countries) is enormous. With only one-third the world's population, the developed world produces and consumes almost nine-tenths of the world's gross national product.[2]

---

[2] *Partners in Development,* Report of the Commission on International Development (New York: Praeger Publishers, 1969), p. 24.

The poverty of the developing nations is not new; it has been a way of life for untold generations. What is new is the bitter awareness of poverty, the knowledge that it is not inevitable, and the determination to raise living standards one way or another. Many of the countries of Asia and Africa have recently emerged from a colonial status to full political independence and others are moving in that direction. Independence has been accompanied by a virulent nationalism, high expectations, and, in many cases, antagonism toward the West.

What has been called "the revolution of rising expectations" is cause for both hope and fear. Of hope, for after centuries of stagnation the developing countries are now striving to create the conditions essential to economic and social progress. Of fear, for the frustration of their high expectations may turn these peoples toward undemocratic solutions (as it has already done in some instances) and against the West.

THE STAGES OF ECONOMIC GROWTH

How did the income gap arise? How do economies develop? In his highly influential book, W. W. Rostow identifies five stages of growth that characterize all societies.[3]

The Traditional Society. The traditional society is grounded on pre-Newtonian science and technology and pre-Newtonian conceptions of the physical world. Although some change must and does occur in such a society (ad hoc technical innovations, fluctuations in population, political and social movements, etc.), there is a ceiling on per capita output and income because of the absence of modern science and technology. The early civilizations of the Middle East and the Mediterranean, the dynasties of China, and Medieval Europe belonged to the traditional stage of economic growth.

The Preconditions for Takeoff. This is a transitional stage when societies develop the conditions necessary for the next stage. These preconditions were created first in Western Europe (led by Great Britain) in the late seventeenth and early eighteenth centuries when modern scientific discoveries were applied to agriculture and manufacturing.

Outside Western Europe the preconditions stage was initiated by the impact of another, more advanced society, notably the European. The spread of European political and economic power throughout the world in the eighteenth and nineteenth centuries disrupted traditional societies in Asia, Latin America, and Africa, introducing by actual demonstration the revolutionary idea that economic progress is both possible and desirable.

Because they are transitional, precondition societies are a mixture of the traditional and the new. A few enterprising persons take up the new

---

[3] W. W. Rostow, *The Stages of Economic Growth* (Cambridge, Massachusetts: Cambridge University Press, 1960).

ways, mobilizing capital and investing it in modern production facilities; but the masses of people remain peasants clinging to the traditional ways that spell low productivity and stagnation. A decisive factor in this stage is political—the building up of a centralized national state. The majority of poor nations now occupy this stage of economic development.

The Takeoff. This is the stage of the great watershed of economic growth: traditional resistances weaken and are finally overcome as the society enters upon a process of cumulative growth. Modern technology, modern organization, and modern attitudes come to dominate economic activity. The rate of net investment rises to 10 percent or more of national income; new industries are born, stimulating the birth of ancillary industries in widening ripples of influence. As agriculture becomes commercialized and more productive, peasants leave the land en masse to supply the expanding need for industrial labor. Over a decade or two, these new forces so transform the political, social, and economic structure of society that steady, sustainable growth becomes possible.

Rostow assigns the takeoff of Britain to the two decades after 1783; of France and the United States to the several decades preceding 1860; of Germany, the third quarter of the nineteenth century; of Japan, the fourth quarter of the nineteenth century; and of Russia and Canada, the quarter century preceding World War I.

Since World War II a number of developing countries appear to have reached the takeoff stage. Notable examples include Mexico and Brazil in Latin America, Egypt and Nigeria in Africa, Israel and Lebanon in the Middle East, and India and Taiwan in Asia.

The Drive to Maturity. In this stage of growth, the economy moves beyond the industries that originally gave impetus to its takeoff, such as textiles and steel. The society now has the capacity and technology to produce anything it chooses to produce, although it would be uneconomic to do so given the advantages of international specialization. Industrial processes become progressively more sophisticated; new industries, such as electronics and chemicals, come to the fore. The economy assumes a different role in world trade as shifts occur in its comparative cost structure: earlier import goods are now produced at home, new import requirements arise, and modern technology creates new export products.[4]

Historically, about sixty years were required for a society to move from the beginning of takeoff to maturity. Britain, the United States, Germany, and France had passed into this stage about the end of the nineteenth century. None of the developing countries has yet reached this stage.

---

[4] See the discussion of changes in the United States composition of trade in Chapter 2.

The Age of Mass Consumption. In this stage the society develops affluent standards of living and an emphasis on the production of durable consumer goods and services. The key symbol of this stage is the mass production and consumption of automobiles with their pervasive influence on life styles. The United States first entered this stage just before World War I; Western Europe and Japan did so in the 1950's.

Rostow acknowledges that his five-stage model of economic growth is necessarily an arbitrary and limited way of looking at the sequence of modern history. No historical model can take account of the many accidents and events that distinguish the evolution of one society from that of all the others, giving it a unique flavor. Another limitation of Rostow's model is its appearance of inevitability—each stage logically follows the preceding stage. We must recognize, however, that a society may stagnate indefinitely in the precondition stage or early phase of the takeoff stage, because of, say, a population explosion that prevents improvements in the standard of living. Indeed, it is this possibility (or even likelihood) of stagnation that haunts the spokesmen of many developing nations today. These qualifications in no way minimize the value of Rostow's contribution; his model illuminates a great deal of the history of economic development in the modern world. Rostow also offers us a broad understanding of how the income gap between the developed and developing nations arose and how it one day may be closed.

The majority of the developing nations is still building the preconditions for takeoff; a minority has entered takeoff; none has become a mature economy. Further progress requires a continuing modernization of economic, social, and political institutions. A key factor in this modernization is capital formation and its accompanying technology, which constitute the very heart of the development process.

OBSTACLES TO ECONOMIC DEVELOPMENT

The developing nations must overcome many obstacles to achieve a rate of investment that will provide a satisfactory rate of economic growth, especially in per capita terms. These obstacles comprise a complex set of both internal and external factors. Although it is widely agreed that the basic restraints on growth derive from the very structure of the poor societies, external conditions that hinder the exports of developing nations or limit the availability of financial assistance from abroad also can restrain growth. To become mature economies, the developing nations must undertake a massive transformation of their societies, and this can be accomplished only by their own peoples and national leaders. To do so, however, they need the capital goods and technology of the developed, industrial countries. This section looks at major obstacles to growth *within* the developing countries themselves; international trade and financial conditions that limit growth are taken up later in the chapter.

The situation of developing countries has been aptly described as interlocking sets of vicious circles that perpetuate economic stagnation and poverty. One of these vicious circles involves the savings-investment gap:

1. Productivity is low because investment is low;
2. Investment is low because saving is low;
3. Saving is low because income is low;
4. Income is low because productivity is low.

Thus, in a very real sense the poor nations are poor because they are poor.

Lack of Social Overhead Capital. Social overhead capital supplies the services—power, transportation, storage, communications, education, etc.—that are indispensable to modern industry and agriculture. The lack of this capital in the poor nations is a bottleneck to economic development. Inadequate transportation and communication facilities block the exploitation of attractive resources located in the interior regions of many countries in Latin America, Asia, and Africa. A food-deficit country like India may lose up to one-third of its agricultural output because it lacks storage facilities to protect against spoilage, rodents and other wastage. The absence of electrical power thwarts the establishment of the many industries dependent on it, as well as impeding community and urban development.

Educational facilities are a vital element of social overhead capital. The majority of the population of developing nations is illiterate. Lacking the basic skills and training necessary to industrial production or modern agriculture, these people can make little contribution to economic development. The developing countries must stamp out illiteracy mainly by educating the new generation of their peoples; unless this is done, there is little hope for the future.

Lack of Business Managers and Government Administrators. The efforts of countless, mostly private entrepreneurs gave Western Europe and North America the momentum to move into and beyond the takeoff stage of economic growth. Eagerly searching for new profit opportunities, these men combined factors of production in new ways and on a broader scale than ever before in history in order to produce new products for emerging markets. Later a large class of business managers arose to promote and administer the expanding private enterprise sectors of these economies. Today the professional preparation for careers in business is commonplace in the United States and is gaining recognition in Western Europe and Japan.

In contrast, the developing nations generally lack a business class that is willing to invest in new industrial enterprises and has the know-how to manage them. Their businessmen are likely to be traders and merchants engaging in foreign trade, wholesaling, and retailing rather than in manufacturing; they tend to be speculative, looking for quick profits in real estate or monopoly market situations. Frequently the upper class in the poor societies disapproves of business, preferring to invest in land and rearing their sons to be land-owning aristocrats, soldiers, lawyers, and diplomats instead of business executives. Partly owing to this class prejudice against business, foreigners dominate the commercial activity of many developing countries, such as the Chinese in Malaysia and the Philippines and the European Jews in Latin America.

Lacking private entrepreneurs, the governments of the developing nations must take the lead in formulating and implementing national development plans. Here another problem arises: the shortage of trained government administrators. The result is often incompetence, worsened by endemic bribery and favoritism. Ineffective systems of taxation fail to mobilize financial resources for capital formation; investment is allocated in ways that do not promote economic growth; public enterprises are operated inefficiently at a loss, draining off scarce capital rather than creating it.

Cultural Blocks to Economic Growth. Old ways and new ways live side by side in the developing societies, and in many, the old ways remain dominant. Preindustrial attitudes toward work and belief in traditional ways are very hard to change. And yet they must be changed if the economy is ever to achieve takeoff: workers must develop the motivations and discipline essential to industrial production; peasants must become commercial farmers, open to technological innovations in agriculture.

Poor motivation, high turnover, absenteeism, and a generally sloppy performance characterize the industrial workers of many developing nations. In the early stage of industrialization, an increase in wages may actually cause absenteeism because people work only to maintain a traditional standard of living, having no conception of a rising standard.[5] Undoubtedly, however, the peasant offers the most stubborn resistance to changing his ways. Getting him to use commercial fertilizers, improved seed strains, crop rotation schemes, etc., requires a time-consuming education process that is likely to be only partially successful, as witnessed by the community-development programs in India and Latin America.

Cultural blocks are often elusive and hard to identify. Once identified, they are hard to change. Nevertheless, they must be overcome because pre-scientific, traditional attitudes and beliefs act to reinforce the vicious circles of poverty that plague the developing nations.

The Population Explosion. It was not until 1800 that the world's population reached one billion persons. But if the present trends continue, the world's population (now 3.6 billion) will grow to 6.4 billion by the year 2000. Most of this huge increase will occur in the developing countries, whose

---

[5] This causes a "backward sloping supply schedule" for labor. This situation is not likely to last very long, particularly in urban areas where newly arrived workers are exposed to examples of higher standards of living.

current rate of population growth is 2.5 percent per year, about twice the rate of the developed countries.

The issue here is not whether this vast number of new persons in the developing countries will be able to survive, but rather how much faster economic development would proceed at a lower rate of population growth. In this sense, the population explosion is the single greatest obstacle to economic development. A representative sample of twenty-two developing countries shows that more than two-thirds of their total investment is devoted to just *maintaining* the level of per capita income, whereas the corresponding fraction for a sample of developed countries is less than one-fourth.[6] In other words, much of the increase in production of the poor countries is being consumed by the newly born.

Fundamentally, the population explosion is a consequence of the "public health" revolution in the poor countries. The introduction of modern medicine has cut death rates drastically (mainly in the early years of life), but has had no influence on birth rates, which remain at the traditional, high levels. Paradoxically, modern medicine by saving lives is making it more difficult to lift those lives out of poverty. In 1970, 22 percent of the population of the developing countries was under seven years of age, and 50 percent was under nineteen. Only recently have some governments of developing countries responded to this critical situation. Although twenty-two countries, with 70 percent of the population of developing areas, now have official population policies, only Hong Kong, Singapore, Korea, Taiwan, and Puerto Rico cut their birth rates sufficiently to reduce their rates of population growth in the 1960's.

TWO DECADES OF DEVELOPMENT

In the 1950's, the developing countries taken together recorded an average annual compound rate of growth in gross domestic product (GDP) of 4.6 percent.[7] This performance compares very favorably with the historical growth rates of 2 to 3 percent experienced by the developed countries over the last century. However, the effects of these high growth rates on per capita income were vitiated by a rapid rise in population averaging 2.2 percent annually. Thus, per capita GDP of the developing countries grew only 2.3 percent annually in the 1950's, less than the 2.8 percent of the developed countries.

At the beginning of the 1960's, the United Nations General Assembly announced the First Development Decade, setting as a minimum target for

---

[6] George C. Zaidin, "Population Growth and Economic Development," *Finance and Development* (March, 1969), p. 3.

[7] Gross domestic product at market prices is the market value of a country's output (before deductions for capital consumption) attributable to factors of production located in the territory of the given country. It differs from gross national product by the exclusion of *net* factor income payments (such as interest and dividends) received from the rest of the world.

the developing countries an annual growth rate of 5 percent. As Table 17-2 reveals, this goal was accomplished with a 5 percent growth rate for the

Table 17-2

REGIONAL GROWTH OF GROSS DOMESTIC PRODUCT IN CONSTANT PRICES, POPULATION, AND GROSS DOMESTIC PRODUCT PER CAPITA: 1950-67 AND 1970
(Percent per Year)

Area	1950-60	1960-67	1950-67	1970
Developing countries				
GDP	4.6	5.0	4.8	5.9
Population	2.2	2.5	2.3	2.6
GDP per capita	2.3	2.5	2.4	3.3
Africa				
GDP	4.0	4.0	4.0	5.1
Population	2.3	2.4	2.3	2.6
GDP per capita	1.7	1.6	1.7	2.4
South Asia				
GDP	3.6	4.1	3.8	4.8
Population	1.9	2.4	2.1	2.4
GDP per capita	1.7	1.7	1.7	2.3
East Asia				
GDP	4.7	5.6	5.1	7.1
Population	2.5	2.7	2.6	2.8
GDP per capita	2.1	2.8	2.4	4.2
Southern Europe				
GDP	5.2	7.1	6.0	5.9
Population	1.4	1.4	1.4	1.5
GDP per capita	3.7	5.6	4.5	4.3
Latin America				
GDP	5.0	4.5	4.8	6.6
Population	2.8	2.9	2.9	3.1
GDP per capita	2.1	1.6	1.8	3.4
Middle East				
GDP	6.0	7.2	6.5	5.1
Population	3.0	2.9	3.0	3.1
GDP per capita	2.9	4.2	3.4	2.0
Developed countries				
GDP	4.0	4.8	4.3	3.4
Population	1.2	1.2	1.2	1.0
GDP per capita	2.8	3.6	3.1	2.4

Sources: *Partners in Development*, Report of the Commission on International Development (New York: Praeger Publishers, 1969), Table 1, p. 358; and *World Bank* (Washington: Annual Report, 1971), Table 1, pp. 58-59.

Note: Developing countries—For 1950-67, the table covers eighty countries with approximately 97 percent of GDP of all developing countries with market economies; for 1970, seventy-four countries with 96 percent of GDP. Developed countries—Canada, United States, Western Europe (excluding Portugal, Spain, and Greece), Australia, Japan, New Zealand, and South Africa.

years 1960-67 and a 5.9 percent growth rate for 1970.[8] Over almost two decades of growth (1950-67) the developing countries as a whole sustained an average annual rate of growth of 4.8 percent in their GDP's. This impressive growth rate was cut in half on a per capita basis, however, because of the average annual growth in population of 2.5 percent during the same period.

The growth record of the past two decades demonstrates that the developing countries have made substantial progress. It does not support those who believe that these countries are permanently sunk in hopeless poverty, and offers encouragement to those who are committed to economic development. Nevertheless, it is sobering to recognize how distant is the achievement of a $500 per capita GDP for many developing countries. If the average annual per capita growth rate of the 1960's (2.5 percent) were to continue, it would take a generation (about twenty-eight years) to double the level of per capita income. This would leave many developing countries with a per capita GDP below $500 in the late 1980's. Even a quadrupling of per capita income (which would take fifty-six years) would not lift some countries to the $500 level.[9]

Moreover, the 2.5 percent growth rate is an aggregate rate for *all* developing countries. Table 17-2 indicates that Africa, South Asia, and Latin America have fallen far short of this figure in the last two decades. Actually 22 percent of the population of the developing world (excluding Mainland China) live in countries where per capita income has grown less than 1 percent since 1950, 48 percent in countries where per capita income has grown between 1 and 2 percent, and only 30 percent in countries where per capita income has grown at more than 2 percent.[10] In the 1960's, Indonesia, Argentina, Algeria, Ghana, and Uruguay experienced little or no increase in per capita incomes.

CAPITAL FORMATION, ECONOMIC GROWTH, AND CONSTRAINTS ON DOMESTIC INVESTMENT

Capital formation—the creation of transportation, communications, and power facilities; the construction of factories; the acquisition of machines, tools, and other instruments of production—is an essential condition of economic growth. The harnessing of mechanical energies, the organization of mass production, the utilization of modern technology, the education and training of workers—all of these are dependent on the formation of capital.

---

[8] The growth rates for 1966, 1967, 1968, and 1969 were 5.0, 4.9, 6.2, and 6.3 percent, respectively.

[9] See Table 17-1, pp. 402-403.

[10] *Partners in Development*, Report of the Commission on International Development (New York: Praeger Publishers, 1969), p. 29.

In the developed countries, capital resources per capita are high; in the developing countries, they are low.

INVESTMENT AND NATIONAL OUTPUT

To increase its stock of capital, a country must invest a part of its national product.[11] Investment reduces the resources available to satisfy immediate consumption, but it raises the level of consumption in the future by enhancing economic productivity. The relationship between new investment and a subsequent increase in real output depends on the marginal productivity of capital, which may be expressed as the *incremental capital-output ratio, or* k.

(1) $k = I_t / \triangle V_{t+1}$.

I_t is the investment in period t and $\triangle V_{t+1}$ is the resulting increment in real national output (gross domestic product) in the next period, which we shall take to be the following year. If, for example, $6 million of investment causes a $2 million increase in national output, then the capital-output ratio is 3.[12]

Given k, we can calculate the growth rate of a country's output once we know the annual rate of investment (r) expressed as a fraction (or percentage) of current national output.

(2) $r = I_t / V_t$.

Hence, the growth rate of gross domestic product is r/k. To illustrate, if a country is investing 15 percent of its gross domestic product on an annual basis and its incremental capital-output ratio is 3, then its rate of growth is 15%/3, or 5%.

In measuring the progress of the developing countries, we are particularly interested in the *per capita* growth rate (g). If p is the annual rate of growth in population, then

(3) $g = (r/k) - p$.

(Strictly speaking, we should calculate g by dividing the index of gross domestic product by the population index, but when the population growth rate is less than 5 percent, which is empirically true, equation (3) will render a close approximation of the true value and is much more simple to compute.)

---

[11] More precisely, a country must invest an amount beyond that needed to maintain its existing capital stock (capital consumption is measured by depreciation) if it is to add to its capital stock. In the subsequent discussion we shall ignore this distinction between gross and net investment.

[12] In both developed and developing countries, the incremental capital-output ratio generally falls between 2 and 4.

Returning to our previous example, if the annual rate of population growth is 2 percent, then the per capita growth rate in terms of equation (3) is

$$g = 15\%/3 - 2\% = 3\%.$$

Equation (3) tells us that a country can increase its rate of per capita growth by lowering its incremental capital-output ratio (k), by lowering its rate of population growth (p), and/or by raising its rate of investment (r). The incremental capital-output ratio is determined by many dynamic factors: as a country's capital stock increases relative to other productive agents, diminishing returns act to raise k, while a better allocation of investment, new technology, and improvements in human skills act to lower k by increasing the productivity of capital. Recent studies of long-term economic growth in the developed countries indicate that increases in productivity (decreases in k) account for a greater share of per capita income growth than the mere increase in capital utilized per worker at a constant level of technology.[13] It follows that the developing countries must continually work to lower k if they are to match the development experience of the advanced countries. As for population, we have already spoken about this growth constraint in the preceding section.

Given k and p, a country can increase its rate of growth by raising its rate of domestic investment (r). Negatively expressed, a country may fail to achieve a target rate of growth (say, 2 percent per capita per year) because r is too low. Suppose, for example, a country has an incremental capital-output ratio of 3, a rate of investment of 9 percent (rather than 15 percent as in our previous example), and an annual rate of population growth of 2 percent, then

$$g = 9\%/3 - 2\% = 1\%.$$

The relationship between domestic investment and economic growth has been emphasized by economists in growth models because it can be quantitatively defined, whereas the relationships between social and political factors and economic growth are both hard to quantify and fall outside the disciplinary boundaries of economics. Economists recognize, however, that investment is a *necessary* condition but not a *sufficient* condition for economic development. Investment must be accompanied by appropriate changes in attitudes,

---

[13] For the 1929-57 period in the United States, Denison attributes only 42 percent of the increase in output per worker to an increase in inputs (quality improvements in labor, more land, and more capital) and 58 percent to an increase in output per unit of input that mainly resulted from technological innovation and economies of scale. The increase in capital per worker (technology constant) explains only 9 percent of the growth rate. See Edward F. Denison, *The Sources of Economic Growth in the United States* (New York: Committee for Economic Development, 1962), Table 33, p. 270.

values, and institutions if an economy is to achieve a self-sustaining growth. Economic growth is only one element in the modernization of a traditional society. The foregoing remarks are not intended to dispute the importance of capital formation in the developing countries. Capital formation is the major instrument for the transformation of technical knowledge into technological innovation; infrastructure investment in transportation and communication makes possible economies of scale; social investment in education is necessary to improve human skills. It is correct, therefore, to view the rate of investment as a critical factor in economic development, although it is by no means the only critical factor. From this perspective, we now turn to a consideration of the constraints that may limit the growth of investment in the developing countries.

CONSTRAINTS ON DOMESTIC INVESTMENT FACED BY DEVELOPING COUNTRIES

The rate of domestic investment in a developing country may be constrained in three principal ways: (1) by the capacity of the country to absorb additional capital; (2) by the level of its domestic savings; or (3) by the availability of foreign exchange. With a given k, any one of these three constraints may impose a ceiling on the level of investment and, therefore, on the rate of growth in gross domestic product.

The *capital-absorption capacity* of a country depends on the availability of human factors (labor, managerial, and administrative) embodying skills that are necessary to transform investment funds (savings) into real investment. It also depends on the presence of an effective demand for the output resulting from investment. Suppose the target rate of growth is $\bar{t}$ and the rate of investment required to achieve this target rate is $\bar{r}$. Now let a be the country's current rate of capital absorption (expressed as a percentage of gross domestic product). Then if $\bar{r} > a$, absorptive capacity places a limitation on the rate of growth. Absorptive capacity is likely to be a critical constraint for an economy as a whole only when a country is in the early stages of growth.

In an open economy gross domestic product assumes this form:

(4) $GDP = C + I + G + (X - M)$.

This identity equation may be compared to that for gross national product, which is stated as equation (1) on p. 213 in Chapter 9. The only difference between the two is that exports (X) and imports (M) in the GDP identity are defined so as to exclude factor payments received from, or paid to, the rest of the world. Thus, GNP measures only the output resulting from factors of production owned by the country's residents, whereas GDP measures all output resulting from factors of production located on the country's territory regardless of their ownership.

Since gross domestic product equals gross domestic income (the sum of domestic consumption and domestic saving), it follows that domestic investment equals the sum of domestic saving and the import balance on current account which is financed by net borrowing from abroad:

$$(5)\ [14]\ I = S + (M - X).$$

In the absence of any net foreign borrowing $(M = X)$, then $I = S$, the rate of investment (r) equals the rate of domestic saving (s), and $r/k = s/k$. Now assume that a country's target rate of growth is $\bar{t}$ and the required rate of investment is $\bar{r}$ while the rate of domestic saving is s. Then if $s < \bar{r}$, there is a *domestic savings gap* that will prevent the attainment of the target rate of growth: $t = s/k = r/k < \bar{r}/k = \bar{t}$.

In the 1961-65 period, the savings rate of the developing countries as a group was 16 percent and the average capital-output ratio was 3.6. Thus, the domestic savings rate constrained their growth rate to $16\%/3.6$ or 4.4 percent, or about 1.8 percent per capita, given the 2.5 percent growth rate in population. Since the 5 percent target growth rate required an investment rate of 18 percent, the savings gap was 2 percent of gross domestic product.[15]

When its savings gap is financed by net borrowing from abroad that permits an excess of imports over exports, then a country is able to achieve its target rate of growth: $\bar{I} = S + (M - X)$, where $\bar{I}$ is the required level of investment. If b is $(M - X)$ expressed as a percentage of gross domestic product (the rate of foreign borrowing), then $\bar{t} = s/k + b/k = \bar{r}/k$. Thus, in the 1960's the developing countries were able to reach the 5 percent target rate of growth $(\bar{t})$ because external assistance (b) was about 2 percent of their combined gross domestic product.

In the absence of capital-absorption and savings gaps, the growth rate of a developing country may still be constrained by a *foreign exchange (trade) gap*. That is to say, domestic savings are a necessary condition but may not be a sufficient condition for raising investment in a developing country to a desired level. The explanation of this situation rests on the import requirements of real capital formation coupled with the structural inability of a developing economy to transform savings into foreign exchange through an increase in exports and/or a decrease in imports. In order to invest, a developing country must acquire from abroad the capital equipment and other investment goods (such as structural steel) that it is unable to produce at home. If the output released by domestic savings can be allocated to exports or import-substitution, then the foreign exchange necessary to purchase investment goods from abroad is forthcoming. In that event,

---

[14] The derivation of this identity is the same as the derivation of equation (7) on p. 214 in Chapter 9.

[15] These figures are derived from Table 1 in *World Bank* (Washington: Annual Report, 1971), p. 58.

there is no foreign exchange gap as distinct from a savings gap, a situation that is true of the advanced, developed economies. But in developing countries, the capacity to reallocate resources is commonly limited by internal structural obstacles as well as external obstacles that curb export growth.

Because of the foreign content of capital formation, a developing country will require a certain level of imports ($\overline{M}$) to sustain a desired level of investment ($\overline{I}$). In the absence of external borrowing, a country can only obtain $\overline{M}$ through exports (X). If, therefore, $\overline{M} > X$ there is a trade or foreign exchange gap that blocks the attainment of $\overline{I}$. The foreign exchange gap ($\overline{M} - X$) will place a ceiling on actual investment. As was true of the savings gap, the foreign exchange gap may be closed by external assistance (B). When it is fully closed ($B = \overline{M} - X$), then the foreign exchange gap no longer constrains the desired level of investment and growth.

Figure 17-1 offers a schematic representation of the three investment constraints.

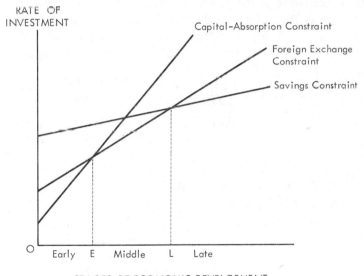

Figure 17-1

CAPITAL-ABSORPTION, FOREIGN EXCHANGE, AND SAVINGS CONSTRAINTS ON THE RATE OF INVESTMENT

It is reasonable to hypothesize that in the early stages of economic development the critical constraint is absorptive capacity. At *O-E,* however, the critical constraint becomes the availability of foreign exchange. In late stages of development, an economy exhibits diversified production and has the capacity to adjust its exports and imports to the desired gap between investment and domestic saving. In Figure 17-1, this capacity is realized at *O-L*; after *O-L* domestic saving becomes (and remains) the critical constraint on the rate of investment. The evidence suggests that the developing countries as a group are now in the middle stages of development and hence the foreign exchange (trade) gap is the critical constraint for most of them. At the 1964 UNCTAD Conference, United Nations experts estimated for the developing countries a savings gap of $12 billion in 1970 ($20 billion in 1975) and a trade gap of $20 billion ($32 billion in 1975). At the 1968 UNCTAD Conference, the experts projected for 1975 a trade gap of $17 billion to $26 billion, depending on different assumptions as to growth targets.[16]

Broadly speaking, two courses of action are open to the developing countries in the face of exchange gaps that will prevent the achievement of a target growth rate. The first course of action involves the use of policy instruments intended to reduce or eliminate the foreign exchange gap by expanding exports and/or contracting the level of required imports through import substitution. The remainder of this chapter and the first section of the next chapter look at the problems and policies of the developing countries with respect to export expansion and other trade policies. The second course of action is to obtain external financing of the foreign exchange gap from private and official sources, which will be discussed in the next chapter.

EXPORT PROBLEMS AND TRADE POLICIES OF THE DEVELOPING COUNTRIES

This section examines the key export problems faced by the developing countries, their general trade policies, and variations in their export performance.

SLOW GROWTH AND INSTABILITY OF COMMODITY EXPORTS

As was pointed out in Chapter 2, the share of world trade of the non-industrial areas has steadily fallen over the last two decades. In the early 1950's, this share was 27 percent; by the late 1960's, it was below 20 percent. Of deeper significance, the export growth of the developing countries has fallen behind their rising import requirements for economic growth.

Table 17-3 indicates the fundamental export problem of the developing countries: the composition of their exports has not adapted to the shift in world demand away from primary products and toward manufactures. The modest growth rate in total exports during the period 1953/55-1963/65 (4.3 percent) is mainly attributable to the very low growth rates of both food exports (2.6 percent) and exports of agricultural raw materials (1.1

---

[16] E. K. Hawkins, "Measuring Capital Requirements," *Finance and Development* (June, 1968), p. 5.

percent).[17] Together these two product groups accounted for more than half of total exports during most of these years. In contrast, the most dynamic export growth of the developing countries has occurred in manufactures, which remain, however, only about one-tenth of total exports.

Table 17-3

RATES OF GROWTH OF EXPORTS FROM THE DEVELOPING COUNTRIES BY MAIN COMMODITY GROUPS 1953/55 AND 1963/65

	Annual Average Value in Billions of U.S. Dollars		Annual Average Rate of Growth in Percent
	1953/55	1963/65	1953/55 to 1963/65
Food, beverages, and tobacco	8.8	11.3	2.6
Agricultural raw materials	4.3	4.7	1.1
Nonagricultural raw materials	2.2	3.6	5.2
Fuels	5.3	10.5	7.1
Total primary commodities ...	20.4	30.0	3.9
Manufactures	1.7	3.9	8.6
Total exports ...	22.3	34.1	4.3

Source: United Nations Conference on Trade and Development, *Recent Developments in Commodity Trade* (New York: United Nations, November, 1967).
Note: Figures may not add because of rounding.

Although petroleum exports are responsible for between one-fourth and one-third of the primary exports, they originate in only a few developing countries, which for the most part have relatively small populations, such as Libya, Saudi Arabia, and Kuwait. Hence, petroleum exports do not benefit the vast majority of poor nations, an unfortunate situation because unlike agricultural commodities they face a buoyant demand in the industrial areas. Nonagricultural raw materials, such as bauxite, copper, lead, and tin, also have better market prospects than agricultural commodities because of the exhaustion of these minerals in the industrial countries. But here again only a minority of the poor nations has significant mineral endowments.

To make matters worse, the primary exports of the developing nations have expanded more slowly than those of the developed nations: techno-logical innovations have greatly improved the productive capacities of primary industries (especially agriculture) in the latter while the population explosion

---

[17] During the same period, the total exports of the developed countries grew at a rate of 7.8 percent a year.

in the former has absorbed more of their primary output, leaving less for export. As a consequence, the industrial nations have increased their share of primary exports. Adding further to the troubles of the developing countries is the price instability of primary exports, accompanied at times by a longer-run deterioration in their prices relative to the prices of manufactures.

Why do commodity exports grow less rapidly than industrial exports? A full answer to this question would involve an examination of the specific supply and demand factors that influence the production and consumption of each of the many individual commodities. Such an examination is out of the question here. Instead we shall look at the main features of the demand for primary commodities in the industrial areas, and their effects on the primary exports of the developing areas. It is widely agreed that the slow, long-term growth of primary exports is traceable mainly to market conditions in the industrial areas rather than to supply conditions in the developing areas, although the latter should not be ignored.[18]

The *income elasticity of demand* for primary products tends to be low, taking on values below one.[19] This contrasts with the higher income elasticities for manufactured goods that seldom fall below unity. To illustrate, a 4 percent rise in national income may cause only a 2 percent rise in the consumption of agricultural products (income elasticity equal to 0.5), but a 6 percent rise in the consumption of manufactured goods (income elasticity equal to 1.5). The consumption of primary products in the industrial areas, therefore, does not keep pace with their general economic growth.

Low income elasticities for foodstuffs reflect family spending patterns. As far back as 1857 Ernst Engel observed that a poor family spends a higher proportion of its income on food than a family better off. Once a household has satisfied its needs for the basic necessities of food, shelter, and clothing, it spends additional income on durable consumer goods, personal services, travel, education, and the like.

The depressing effects of low income elasticities on the consumption of primary commodities in the developed nations have been reinforced by a continuing stream of synthetic, manufactured materials that replace natural materials. Starting before World War I with rayon and manufactured nitrates, the development of synthetics has now reached flood proportions in the industrial nations. After World War II synthetic fibers, artificial rubber, and detergents strongly challenged cotton, wool, jute, abaca, oils, fats, natural rubber, and other commodities. Today, for example, most of the rubber used in the manufacture of passenger automobile tires in the United States is

---

[18] Variations in supply conditions (such as crop yields) play a more important role in the short-run fluctuations of commodity exports.

[19] Income elasticity of demand measures the response in the amount demanded to a change in income, assuming the mathematical expression: $\dfrac{dQ/Q}{dY/Y}$. We can interpret this as the percentage change in amount demanded divided by the percentage change in income.

synthetic. As a result of this substitution in tires and other products, United States imports of natural rubber fell from 803 thousand long tons in 1952 to 413 thousand long tons in 1962. To conclude, synthetics have cut deeply into the consumption of agricultural raw materials and are partly responsible for the relatively slow growth of commodity exports from the developing to the industrial countries. This is not to say that natural materials are doomed to be entirely replaced by synthetics. It does mean that they must compete in quality and price with manufactured substitutes.

All of the industrial countries have agricultural programs that protect their farmers from competition in the open market. Most frequently, this involves the maintenance of domestic agricultural prices at levels higher than those prevailing in world markets. To prevent foreign producers from capitalizing on this situation, imports are restricted by tariffs or quotas. The variable import levies of the European Economic Community are an example of such restrictions.

In addition to import restrictions that are by-products of agricultural support programs, many European countries impose revenue duties or taxes on tropical agricultural products they do not produce at home. Mineral interests may also be protected against import competition; import quotas on petroleum in the United States and on coal in Western Europe fall into this category.

The primary exports of the developing nations have not even kept pace with the slow-growing consumption of primary commodities in the industrial areas. Increasingly the developed countries have been meeting their needs for foodstuffs and agricultural raw materials out of domestic production and imports from other industrial countries. They have been able to do so because the application of modern technology to agriculture has multiplied productivity to such an extent that production frequently outruns home consumption to generate export surpluses. As noted earlier, the developed countries have increased their share of world primary trade in recent years. Thus, agricultural imports from the developing areas are being displaced by the technologically advanced agricultural industries of North America and Western Europe. The displacement is greatest in temperate products, but the United States—the world's leading primary exporter—also exports large quantities of "tropical" products, notably cotton and rice.

To sum up, a variety of forces—low income elasticities, displacement by synthetics, import restrictions, and primary production in the industrial countries—have acted to curb the growth of primary exports from the developing countries.

Short-Run Price Instability of Commodity Exports. In addition to slow growth, the commodity exports of developing countries are subject to frequent and sudden price changes that cause unpredictable, short-run fluctuations in export earnings. This instability can be detrimental to economic growth since it disrupts development programs when the actual supply of foreign exchange falls short of the projected supply.

In the period 1950-65, the average annual price fluctuation of developing country exports was more than twice that of developed-country exports. Table 17-4 also shows that fluctuations in export quantities and earnings were about twice as great for the developing countries as for the developed countries. The price fluctuation indices of the five major commodities exported by the developing countries (accounting for about half their exports in the mid-1960's) reveal a considerable divergence in instability during the 1950-65 period: petroleum (4.0 percent), coffee (14.0 percent), sugar (11.1 percent), cotton, (7.0 percent), and natural rubber (13.1 percent).[20] Clearly the petroleum-exporting countries benefited from a high degree of price stability as well as a rising demand.

Table 17-4

AVERAGE FLUCTUATION INDICES OF EXPORTS FROM THE DEVELOPING AND DEVELOPED COUNTRIES, 1950-65
(Percent)

	Developing Countries	Developed Countries
Prices	8.8	3.7
Quantities	9.5	5.6
Earnings	11.8	6.2

Source: International Monetary Fund and International Bank for Reconstruction and Development, *The Problem of Stabilization of Prices of Primary Products* (Washington: 1969), Table 15, p. 41, and Table 19, p. 59.
Note: Each fluctuation index consists of an average over the period of annual percentage differences between the historically observed figure and the norm which is the calculated steady growth trend. The indices cover thirty-eight developing countries and fourteen developed countries.

The price volatility of commodities in world trade results from low *price* elasticities of supply and demand. Cyclical and random shifts in demand in the industrial countries cause sharp price responses because the supply of commodities is relatively fixed in the short run. Prices also react violently to shifts in supply, such as crop yield fluctuations, because the consumption of primary commodities in the industrial countries is relatively insensitive to price changes (price elasticity is below unity).

Deterioration in the Terms of Trade of Developing Countries. In some years the detrimental effect of stagnant commodity exports on the import capacity of the developing countries has been magnified by worsening terms of trade. The *net barter terms of trade* deteriorated 12 percent in the period 1950-62; that is to say, the same amount of exports paid for 12 percent less of imports in 1962 than in 1950. This deterioration in terms of trade offset

---

[20] International Monetary Fund and International Bank for Reconstruction and Development, *The Problem of Stabilization of Prices of Primary Products* (Washington: 1969), Table 16, p. 56.

a substantial part of the foreign aid and private investment received by the developing countries over these years. One estimate places the cumulative loss in external purchasing power resulting from changes in the terms of trade of the developing countries during the years 1951-62 at $16.7 billion or over one-third of the net inflow of long-term capital and grants recorded in that period ($45.9 billion).[21]

Some economists, notably those associated with the United Nations, believe there is a persistent, long-run tendency for the terms of trade of the developing countries to deteriorate. Raul Prebisch explains this alleged tendency along the following lines.[22] Because of the slow growth in demand for primary commodities, only a declining proportion of the labor force in the developing countries can be absorbed in their production. Improvements in the productivity of primary activities cause an even further drop in that proportion. Thus, the labor force has to be shifted to industrial production, but this takes a very long time and in the meantime the surplus labor exerts a downward pressure on the real level of wages in the developing countries. Higher productivity in the primary export industries, therefore, is reflected in lower prices rather than in higher wages. Thus, the fruits of technical advance in the developing countries are passed on to the industrial countries. In the latter, on the other hand, the relative shortage of labor and strong labor unions keep wages rising in step with rising productivity, preventing any fall in prices. Hence, a persistent deterioration of the terms of trade of the developing countries is the result of fundamental structural differences between the industrial centers and the peripheral, developing countries.[23]

The Prebisch model is hardly proof of a built-in, secular tendency for the terms of trade to turn against the developing countries. The historical record is ambiguous because of data inadequacies and the well-known difficulties of index number construction.[24] But the evidence indicates

---

[21] United Nations Conference on Trade and Development, *Financing for an Expansion of International Trade,* E/Conf. 46/9 (March, 1964), Table 15, p. 26.

[22] For a detailed presentation of his views see Raul Prebisch, "Commercial Policy in the Underdeveloped Countries," *American Economic Review* (May, 1959), pp. 251-73. Similar views are expressed by Gunnar Myrdal in *Rich Lands and Poor* (New York: Harper and Row, 1957).

[23] Although different, the Prebisch model brings to mind the notion of "immiserizing growth" introduced in Chapter 5 on p. 115. Immiserizing growth is possible only when export demand is inelastic *and* protrade growth actually reduces domestic production of import-competing goods. These and other stringent assumptions make immiserizing growth a theoretical curiosity that is not likely to be matched by real experience in the developing countries. See Jagdish Bhagwati, "Immiserizing Growth: A Geometrical Note," *Review of Economic Studies* (June, 1958), pp. 201-5.

[24] The concept of the net barter terms of trade is defined in footnote 12 in Chapter 3, p. 67, where it is referred to as the commodity terms of trade. In practice, the net barter terms of trade is calculated as an index: $\Sigma P_{x_1}/\Sigma P_{m_1} \div \Sigma P_{x_0}/\Sigma P_{m_0}$, where ΣP_x and ΣP_m are the weighted aggregates of export and import prices, respectively; 0 refers to the base period; and 1 refers to the year being compared with the base. The choice of the base period is important since a base period with highly favorable terms of trade is likely to show a subsequent deterioration and vice versa. In constructing index numbers, it is also difficult to allow for quality changes which occur more frequently in industrial than in primary products.

that periods of worsening terms of trade have alternated with periods of improving terms of trade. In the 1930's the terms of trade of the developing countries fell sharply; in the decade following World War II they improved beyond the level registered in 1913; in the last half of the 1950's (when Prebisch came forth with his model) they worsened; and in the mid-1960's they once again improved. Although the Prebisch model is weak on both theoretical and historical grounds, it is probably true that the developing countries were badly hurt by the deterioration of their terms of trade in the 1950's.[25] As we shall see, they are actively seeking ways to minimize the effects of any future deterioration.

TRADE POLICIES OF THE DEVELOPING COUNTRIES

The export problems of the developing countries are commonly aggravated by their own trade and general economic policies. The dominant goal of government policy makers in the developing countries is economic development, which is too often viewed as industrialization rather than self-sustaining economic growth. Since other goals are regarded as subordinate, the internal conflict of goals is resolved in favor of economic development except when events force policy makers to pay attention to matters such as inflation or the balance of payments. The policy tools chosen by many developing countries to advance their economic development have been economic controls, protection, and inflation; in so doing, they have rejected free markets, international specialization, and monetary stability. Unfortunately the neglect of internal and external balance and a disregard for the economics of comparative advantage have created problems that prevent the attainment of development targets. Two problems in particular deserve some comment: *inflation* and *import-substitution*.

When developing countries seek to close savings gaps through budgetary deficits (rather than surpluses), the resulting creation of new money breeds inflation and balance of payments deficits. Reluctant to correct these deficits by cutting domestic spending (and thereby falling short of development targets) or by exchange devaluation (in the belief it would not work, would cause more inflation, or for political reasons), governments respond with import and exchange restrictions. As the inflation proceeds, therefore, exchange rates become increasingly overvalued, hindering exports and encouraging the circumvention of import controls. Eventually controls break down and devaluation takes place. But unless devaluation is accompanied by an austerity policy (higher taxes and cutbacks in government spending), the vicious circle starts up once again. To sum up, inflation, overvalued exchange rates, and exchange restrictions all too frequently limit the exports of developing countries.

---

[25] Since the developing countries are most interested in changes in their capacity to import, the *income terms of trade* are more appropriate than the net barter terms of trade: $\Sigma P_x Q_x / \Sigma P_m$, where $\Sigma P_x Q_x$ is the aggregate value of exports and ΣP_m is the weighted aggregate import price.

During the 1930's, countries in Latin America progressively introduced regimes of high protection to restrict imports of consumer goods. Although initially provoked by the world depression, these protectionist policies were soon directed toward the promotion of internal industrialization. Isolated by import barriers, local enterprise was encouraged to manufacture consumer goods to replace imports. Because of a ready market and lack of foreign competition, import substitution proceeded quickly in shoes, clothing, household articles, and other nondurable consumer products. Furthermore, many European and U.S. companies were induced to set up plants in Latin American countries when their export markets were closed off by protection. During World War II, import substitution was intensified when many manufactured goods could not be imported from the industrial countries. After the war, import substitution was extended by some countries in Latin America (notably, Mexico, Brazil, and Argentina) to cover durable consumer goods, such as automobiles and capital equipment. With political independence, many developing countries in Asia and Africa followed the lead of Latin America.

When an economy develops, import-substitution occurs as a natural market phenomenon: economic growth involves a continual domestic substitution of imports and their replacement by new import goods. But when import-substitution is promoted through protectionist policies, then its national costs may exceed its national benefits. When protection is given to lines of production that do not have a potential comparative advantage, a country builds high-cost industries that are in fact a permanent drag on the economy. An indiscriminate policy of import-substitution becomes, then, a policy of economic self-sufficiency and a perversion of the infant-industry argument.[26]

After thirty years of high protection, the Latin American countries have run out of easy opportunities for import substitution. Furthermore, the costs of import-substitution are increasingly evident: diversified industrial plants that are entirely oriented toward the domestic market and whose level of costs, quality control, design, engineering, and product innovation is noncompetitive in export markets. The absurdity of extreme import-substitution in countries with small domestic markets that do not allow economies of scale is amply demonstrated by automobile production in several Latin American countries. In Colombia, Peru, and Chile the production costs of vehicles run two to three times higher than the cost of similar vehicles in the international market. Apart from the social costs of inefficient resource allocation, it is even doubtful that local automobile production saves foreign exchange for these countries because they must import most of the materials and components.[27] More generally, import-substitution policies

---

[26] See Chapter 13, p. 315 ff, for an evaluation of the infant-industry argument.

[27] See Bernard E. Munk, "The Colombian Automobile Industry: The Welfare Consequences of Import Substitution," *Economic and Business Bulletin* (Fall, 1970), pp. 6-22.

seldom decrease a country's dependence on imports but rather shift the composition of imports from consumer goods to industrial inputs and capital equipment.

Summing up, indiscriminate import-substitution policies are self-defeating; they do not foster self-sustaining growth over the longer run, they are seldom net savers of foreign exchange, and they discourage exports of manufactured products. Fortunately policy makers in the developing countries are becoming more aware of the dangers of blanket import-substitution. Raul Prebisch, an apostle of import-substitution policies in Latin America during the 1950's, now stresses the "absolute necessity of building up trade in industrial exports" and warns that "there are limits to import substitution in the developing countries which cannot be exceeded without a frequent and considerable waste of capital." [28]

Inward-oriented development policies involving inflation and import-substitution have been rejected by some developing countries in favor of outward-oriented policies dependent on monetary stability and export promotion. These differences in policy orientation go a long way toward explaining the striking variations in the export performance of individual developing countries. These variations are found even among countries that face similar external market conditions. On the basis of a statistical analysis of the export experience of developing countries, DeVries concludes that *supply* factors (such as the availability of export volumes for shipment, the variety and quality of goods, and price) were responsible for export performance "to a significant extent." He goes on to say: "Thus, there seems to be no justification for identifying the export problem of the developing countries as one created by sluggish external demand." [29] Although this statement would appear to be approximately true for *individual* developing countries, it is too strong for the developing countries as a *group*. Some countries can increase their share of a static export market, but it is impossible for all countries to do so. [30]

Our own conclusion is that the export problems of the developing countries are caused by both *external* market conditions (principally the slow growth and instability of commodity exports attributable to demand in the industrial countries) and *internal* conditions that are substantially influenced by the policies of developing countries. This conclusion points to another: changes in the trade policies of the industrial countries are a necessary but

---

[28] Raul Prebisch, *Towards a New Trade Policy for Development,* Report by the Secretary General of the United Nations Conference on Trade and Development (New York: United Nations, 1964), pp. 20 and 21.

[29] Barend A. DeVries, "The Export Performance of Developing Countries," *Finance and Development* (March, 1968), p. 7. See also Barend A. DeVries, *The Export Experience of Developing Countries,* Occasional Papers Number Three (Washington: International Bank for Reconstruction and Development, 1967).

[30] To assume that what is true of the part is necessarily true of the whole is to commit the fallacy of composition.

not a sufficient condition for a general alleviation of the export problems of the developing countries. As is true of economic development in general, the major effort must come from the developing countries themselves.

SUMMARY

1. The drive for economic development shapes the attitudes, policies, and expectations of the developing countries in the areas of international trade and external assistance.

2. Although the per capita GNP indicator places several Communist countries in the ranks of developing countries, the conventional classification excludes them. It also excludes the low-income countries in southern Europe. The term "developing countries" denotes, therefore, the non-Communist countries of Africa (except South Africa), Asia (except Japan), and Latin America. The size of the income gap between the developed and less-developed world is enormous.

3. Rostow identifies five stages of economic growth: the traditional society, preconditions for takeoff, takeoff, the drive to maturity, and the age of mass consumption. The majority of the developing nations is still building the preconditions for takeoff; a minority has entered takeoff; none has become a mature economy.

4. The developing countries must overcome many obstacles to achieve a satisfactory rate of economic growth, especially in per capita terms. The situation of the developing countries has been aptly described as interlocking sets of vicious circles that perpetuate economic stagnation and poverty. Major obstacles to economic development include lack of social overhead capital, lack of business managers and administrators, cultural blocks, and the population explosion.

5. At the beginning of the 1960's, the United Nations General Assembly announced the First Development Decade, setting as a minimum target for the developing countries an annual growth rate of 5 percent. Although this target was achieved for the developing countries as a whole, the high rate of population growth reduced the rate to 2.5 percent on a per capita basis. Despite grave obstacles, many developing countries have recorded substantial progress over the last two decades.

6. Capital formation is a necessary but not a sufficient condition for economic development. To increase its stock of capital, a country must invest a part of its national product. The relationship between new investment and a subsequent increase in real output may be expressed as the *incremental capital-output ratio*, or k. Hence, the growth rate of gross domestic product is r/k, where r is the annual rate of new investment. The per capita growth rate, therefore, is: $g = (r/k) - p$, where p is the annual rate of population growth.

7. The rate of domestic investment in a developing country may be constrained by the capacity of the country to absorb additional capital, by the level of its domestic savings, or by the availability of foreign exchange. In the absence of capital-absorption and savings gaps, the growth rate of a developing

country may be limited by a *foreign exchange gap*. Broadly speaking, two courses of action are open to the developing countries in the face of exchange gap that prevent the achievement of a target growth rate: (1) policies to expand exports and/or contract required imports, and/or (2) policies to obtain external financing from private and official sources.

8. The key export problems of the developing countries are traceable to the slow growth and instability of commodity exports on which they are so dependent for export earnings. Although the Prebisch model is weak on both theoretical and historical grounds, it is probably true that the developing countries were badly hurt by the deterioration of their terms of trade in the 1950's.

9. The export problems of the developing countries are commonly aggravated by their own trade and general economic policies which cause inflation and extreme import substitution.

QUESTIONS AND APPLICATIONS

1. What are Rostow's five stages of economic growth? Why is the takeoff stage so important? Choose five developing countries. At what stage of growth are they? Defend your answer.

2. What is meant by this statement: "The situation of developing countries has been aptly described as interlocking sets of vicious circles . . . ."?

3. Why do many development experts consider the population explosion as the single greatest obstacle to economic development? Do you agree with them? Why or why not?

4. Suppose a country is investing 20 percent of its gross domestic product on an annual basis and its incremental capital-output ratio is 4. What, then, is the annual rate of growth of its gross domestic product? Suppose further that the annual growth rate of its population is 2.5 percent. What is the per capita annual growth rate of its gross domestic product?

5. Define the three constraints on the rate of domestic investment in a developing country. In the absence of a savings gap, how can a developing country have a foreign exchange gap?

6. Why does the volume of commodity exports as a whole grow less rapidly than the volume of industrial exports in the world economy?

7. What factors cause the short-run price instability of commodity exports?

8. What are the commodity or net barter terms of trade? How does Prebisch explain the deterioration in the terms of trade of the developing countries? Do you agree with his explanation? Why or why not?

9. "Indiscriminate import-substitution policies are self-defeating . . . ." Discuss.

SELECTED READINGS

See the list of readings given at the end of Chapter 18.

CHAPTER 18

THE DEVELOPING COUNTRIES IN THE WORLD ECONOMY (2)

This chapter concludes our analysis of the developing countries by examining their demands for new trade policies, their efforts to achieve regional economic integration, and the availability of external assistance from the developed countries.

NEW TRADE POLICIES AND REFORMS ADVOCATED BY THE DEVELOPING COUNTRIES

A deepening recognition among the developing countries that the slow growth in their exports imposes a critical foreign exchange constraint on economic development has generated a series of demands addressed to the developed countries for new trade policies which would restructure the international trading system. These demands came to a dramatic focus at the first session of the United Nations Conference on Trade and Development (UNCTAD) held in Geneva in 1964. There the spokesman of over seventy developing countries called upon both the Western and Eastern developed countries for action on a broad front as laid down in a report by Raul Prebisch, then the Secretary-General of UNCTAD.[1]

As a permanent agency of the United Nations, UNCTAD has continued to press vigorously for new trade policies and its proposals have been incorporated in the action program of the Second United Nations Development Decade approved by the General Assembly in 1970.[2] The dominant

---

[1] United Nations, *Towards A New Trade Policy for Development,* Report by the Secretary-General of the United Nations Conference on Trade and Development (New York: United Nations, 1964).

[2] UNCTAD now comprises ninety-one developing countries as well as Western and Eastern developed countries. A second conference was held in New Delhi in 1968. Between conferences the work of UNCTAD is carried on by the United Nations Trade and Development Board.

goal of the action program is an average annual growth rate of 6 percent in the gross domestic product of the developing countries as a whole during the 1970's. To help achieve this goal, the developed countries are expected to undertake several policy measures in trade and financial assistance. Trade policy measures include:

1. The conclusion of new international commodity agreements.

2. Commitments not to raise current restrictions on imports of primary products and to give priority to their reduction or elimination.

3. Arrangements to establish generalized, nondiscriminatory, non-reciprocal preferential treatment for exports of the developing countries to the markets of the developed countries in manufactures and semimanufactures.

4. The progressive elimination of nontariff barriers affecting trade in manufactures and semimanufactures of interest to the developing countries.[3]

In this section we consider the key issues raised by international commodity agreements and preferential treatment, the two most controversial measures.

INTERNATIONAL COMMODITY AGREEMENTS

International commodity agreements are arrangements between producing countries or between producing and consuming countries that seek to stabilize the prices of specific primary commodities (such as wheat, coffee, rubber, and tin) through measures that involve buffer stocks, export controls, and export-import commitments.[4] Since 1945 four major international commodity agreements have been concluded under United Nations auspices. These four agreements covered wheat, tin, sugar, and coffee.[5] Excluding petroleum, these commodities account for about one-fifth of the commodity exports of the developing countries. The developing countries want a substantial increase in the number of commodities regulated by international agreement (cocoa, oilseeds, jute, bananas, tea, wine, iron ore, manganese, tobacco, and others) with provisions for promoting consumption as well as price stabilization.

Basically, three techniques may be used in international commodity agreements to achieve price stabilization. These are export controls, buffer stocks, and multilateral export-import contracts.

---

[3] See United Nations, *International Development Strategy*, Action Program of the General Assembly for the Second United Nations Development Decade (New York: United Nations, 1970), pp. 5-8.

[4] The control features of international commodity agreements resemble those of private cartels.

[5] Other arrangements exist in olive oil, whaling, and cotton textiles (under GATT). During the period 1950-55 there was an international agreement among producing countries in tea. Petroleum prices are fixed by agreements between the private oil companies and producing countries which belong to the Organization of Petroleum Exporting Countries (OPEC). (See Chapter 25.) In the 1930's, international commodity agreements in tin, wheat, sugar, tea, rubber, and copper were organized by producers through, or with the approval of, their governments.

The *International Coffee Agreement,* established in 1962 and now comprising about fifty exporting countries and twenty-five importing countries, relies on export restrictions to maintain and stabilize prices. Each exporting country is allotted a share of the global coffee market, known as its basic quota. This basic quota, together with estimates of global import requirements at a target price range, determines a country's quarterly and annual quotas for its coffee exports. Exporting countries are committed to adjust their coffee production to the levels required for domestic consumption and authorized exports and stocks. With modest exceptions, the importing countries are obligated to buy coffee only from member exporting countries. After ten years of success, the Agreement collapsed in 1972 when the member countries failed to agree on a new price and quotas.

The *International Sugar Agreement* (1954-1961 with a renewal in 1968) also utilizes export quotas, as well as maximum and minimum prices and commitments on national stocks. However, this agreement covers only the "free" sector of world trade in sugar. About half of the sugar trade comes under preferential import arrangements, notably U.S. quotas (about 25 percent of world trade) and U.K. quotas (about 10 percent of world trade). Any effort to raise the long-run price of sugar is doomed to failure because the major consuming areas can always increase their own production of beet sugar.

The *International Tin Agreement,* started in 1956 and comprising seven producing and twenty consuming countries, uses both a buffer stock and export controls. The buffer stock consists of supplies of tin held by the Agreement agency. If the market price is at or above the ceiling price, then the buffer stock manager must sell tin; if the price is at or below the floor price, he must buy tin. However, buffer stock operations have not been sufficient to control prices and they are frequently supplemented by export restrictions when market prices fall to the floor. For example, in September, 1968, export quotas were imposed on supplying countries and were not taken off until the beginning of 1970. In the face of buoyant demand, floor and ceiling prices were raised several times in the 1960's.

The first *International Wheat Agreement* in 1949 depended on a "multilateral contract" with no provisions for export restrictions or buffer stocks. Under the contract, exporting countries were obligated to sell a specified volume of wheat in the event wheat prices reached a stipulated minimum while importing countries were obligated to buy a specified volume in the event prices reached a stipulated maximum. Later the concept of guaranteed quantities was abandoned in favor of commitments by the exporting countries to meet all the commercial requirements of the importing member countries within an agreed price range and commitments by the importing countries to buy a specified percentage of their wheat imports from exporting member countries within an agreed price range. An International Grains Agreement, comprising five major exporting countries and about fifty importing countries, extended these provisions for the period

1968-1971.[6] However, it soon broke down under mounting wheat surpluses as exporting countries cut their prices below the agreed floor price of $2.17 per bushel. This marked the end of international efforts to stabilize the price of wheat. In 1971 a new International Wheat Agreement contained no price provisions and merely maintained consultative machinery.

International commodity agreements have been criticized on many grounds: their low probability of success in the face of dynamic market conditions; their negotiating and administrative complexities; their dependence on correct supply/demand forecasts; and the inherent conflict of interests between producing and consuming countries. Economists are particularly critical of export restrictions because they tend to promote a misallocation of resources both within and between countries by protecting inefficient producers. Our present interest in international commodity agreements is their actual and potential contribution to economic development. The actual contribution has been very modest. Only the International Coffee Agreement has benefited a large number of developing countries by maintaining prices above their equilibrium levels.[7] But even the potential contribution is surprisingly limited when compared to the expectations of the developing countries.

Only ten major commodities are exported primarily by the developing countries: cotton, sugar, coffee, bananas, rubber, rice, tea, cocoa, tin, and jute. In the face of competition from synthetics, any agreements to raise the prices of rubber and jute would be foolhardy. Cotton and rice are also poor candidates for commodity agreements because the United States is a major exporter of both, and rice is principally imported by developing countries. Of the remaining six commodities, coffee, tin, and sugar are already under agreements, while tea was in the 1950's. This leaves only bananas and cocoa. Bananas compete with other fruits and many years of negotiations have failed to reach an agreement on cocoa.

The number of suitable commodities would be greater if the purpose of international agreements were simply to smooth out year-to-year price fluctuations without disturbing the long-run trend of prices. Unfortunately, too, the contribution of such agreements to economic development is questionable. After an intensive study, Macbean found no correlation between export fluctuations and economic growth.[8] Hence, international agreements are not likely to help the developing countries unless they transfer resources to them via prices that are maintained above their long-run equilibrium

---

[6] This Agreement also included a Food Aid Convention (agreed to at the Kennedy Round) that committed developed member countries to specified contributions of wheat, coarse grains, or cash equivalents to the developing countries. This Convention was extended in 1971.

[7] All the major wheat producers except Argentina are developed countries; the tin producers represent only a few developing countries; and the International Sugar Agreement cannot maintain high sugar prices.

[8] Alasdair Macbean, *Export Fluctuations, Growth, and Policy* (Cambridge: Harvard University Press, 1967).

levels. But such agreements are the most difficult to negotiate because they oppose the interests of producers and consumers, and they are the most difficult to operate because they oppose long-run market forces. For one thing, demand must be price inelastic; otherwise higher prices will cause a decline in export earnings. This rules out commodities that have partial substitutes (synthetic or natural) or are producible in the importing countries. In addition, the exporting countries forming an agreement must have a monopoly over supply and they must agree to restrict exports and eventually production. The higher the price, the more unstable the agreement: exporting countries will have stronger incentives to export beyond their quotas and importing countries to look elsewhere for imports. All in all, then, the prospects of any substantial transfer of resources to the developing countries through international commodity agreements appear dim. Export diversification and external assistance offer far more promise to relieve the foreign exchange gap.

The intense interest of the developing countries in international commodity agreements stems as much from the commodity concentration of their exports as from their overall dependence on commodities in general. Many developing countries earn most of their foreign exchange from exports of one or two commodities, and some forty countries depend on three or fewer commodities for 80 percent or more of their exports. Diversification into other export commodities facing different market conditions would reduce dependence on a single commodity.[9] A more fundamental diversification calls for a shift toward processed foodstuffs and minerals and more sophisticated manufactures. This is the objective of preferential access to the markets of the industrial countries.

Another approach is the *compensatory financing* of export fluctuations. Spokesmen of the developing nations advocate a compensatory scheme that would automatically transfer financial resources to a developing country in order to offset a loss of foreign exchange resulting from worsening terms of trade. They argue that this would simply be an international extension of the compensatory programs that the industrial nations already offer their own agricultural producers.

Basically, a compensatory scheme would sustain the import capacity of a developing country by matching any decline in its external purchasing power due to worsening terms of trade with an equal amount of external financial assistance. Several technical problems would have to be overcome to set up such an arrangement. Initially from what base year should the terms of trade be calculated? That is, to what degree (if any) should compensation be granted for a past deterioration in the terms of trade? Once the scheme is in operation, should compensatory financing be based

---

[9] The International Coffee Agreement contains provisions to promote such diversification.

on yearly changes in the terms of trade, or on some other time period? Suppose the terms of trade of a developing nation improved. Should the scheme compensate industrial countries whose terms of trade have deteriorated? How would the financing be shared by the industrial countries? These and similar questions suggest the difficulties in designing a workable mechanism that would be acceptable to the participating governments.

A modest step in this direction was taken by the International Monetary Fund (IMF) in 1963 when it set up a facility which allows a member country to obtain financial assistance from the Fund up to 50 percent of its quota to compensate for temporary shortfalls in export receipts from the medium-term trend value of exports.[10] Since financial assistance must be repaid within three to five years, it offers little contribution to economic development.

PREFERENTIAL TREATMENT OF MANUFACTURES

The many difficulties encountered by primary exports (notably low income elasticities and synthetic substitutes) have convinced the developing nations that they must depend increasingly on industrial products to obtain a satisfactory, long-term growth in their exports. They are seeking a new pattern of international specialization whereby the industrial nations would export manufactures requiring advanced levels of technology while importing older and less complex manufactures from the developing nations.

Manufactures now account for about one-seventh of the exports of the developing countries, and only a few countries—Hong Kong, India, Mexico, Brazil, Argentina, Algeria, Taiwan, and South Korea—are responsible for the bulk of them. To improve this situation, the developing countries propose that *preferential treatment* be given to their exports of manufactures by the industrial countries, and that the developing countries accord preferential treatment to each other (but not to the industrial countries). Spokesmen of the developing countries assert that the most-favored-nation policy is suitable between economies on the same level, but not between rich and poor economies. They argue that preferential treatment for their industrial exports would be a logical extension of the infant-industry argument: if the infant industry needs protection in the domestic market, it needs even more protection in foreign markets in the form of preferences.

After several years of negotiations, eighteen developed countries agreed in 1970 to establish in the following year a generalized system of nonreciprocal and nondiscriminatory preferences on manufactured goods in favor of the developing countries. "Generalized" signifies that all the developed countries intend to participate, "nonreciprocal" means that the developed countries demand no concessions in return for preferential treatment, and "nondiscriminatory" means that all developing countries are to receive the same

---

[10] See Chapter 19 for a description of the IMF. The Fund also has a buffer stock financing facility, which has been used by the International Tin Agreement.

preferences. This agreement involves, therefore, a suspension with respect to the developing countries of the two traditional rules of international trade incorporated in GATT—most-favored-nation treatment and reciprocity.[11]

Although the industrial countries generally agreed to offer duty-free entry to most of the products granted preferences, they excluded from any preferential treatment many products of greatest interest to the developing countries, notably textiles, clothing, and processed agricultural products. Furthermore, the preference offers are limited either by an escape clause (United States and several other countries) or by import ceilings (EEC, Japan, and Austria). Finally, the preference schemes are intended to remain in force initially for ten years.

The European Economic Community was the first to implement its offer in July, 1971, and was shortly followed by Japan and Norway. The United States has yet to apply its preferential system (duty-free entry for most manufactures; no preferences for textiles, shoes, and petroleum products) and, given the resurgence of protectionism, the prospects for early action are not good. In particular, the United States is unwilling to extend preferences to those developing countries that give preferential treatment to the products of certain industrial countries, mainly the "reverse preferences" granted to the EEC by affiliated African countries and to the United Kingdom by Commonwealth developing countries.

Preferences to the developing countries may be viewed as a "second-best" solution. The first-best solution is free trade in manufactured products among all countries, developed and developing alike. The economic analysis of preferences runs along the same lines as that for customs unions and free trade areas: trade diversion, trade creation, and dynamic effects. No final verdict can be rendered because our empirical knowledge of these effects is inconclusive, and we offer here only a few closing observations.

First, the preference systems offered by the industrial countries are badly weakened by the general exclusion of products such as textiles and processed foodstuffs, in which many developing countries have a comparative advantage. Second, the actual preferences will benefit mainly the most advanced developing countries with substantial manufacturing sectors which are already exporting manufactures to the industrial countries. Third, developing countries cannot take advantage of whatever opportunities preferences offer their products unless they are willing to modify inward-oriented development policies that obstruct exports. Finally, the developing countries will not find it easy to expand their exports of manufactures to the industrial countries. Unlike commodities, manufactures require a comprehensive export marketing program based on up-to-date market research. Manufacturers in the developing countries must develop the capacity to compete in foreign markets not only in price but also in quality, promotion, channels of distribution, and in the other areas of export marketing.

---

[11] The industrial countries are also prepared to waive the most-favored-nation rule with respect to multilateral preference schemes among the developing countries.

ECONOMIC DEVELOPMENT THROUGH REGIONAL INTEGRATION

The great majority of the ninety-four non-Communist developing countries in Africa, Asia, and Latin America have small populations and national incomes. Sixty-six of these countries have populations of less than 10 million; fifty-three have gross national products of less than $1 billion.[12] Consequently, their domestic markets are also small. Furthermore, autarkic economic development relying on import substitution is not possible: small markets quickly limit growth, diversification, and economies of scale. In order to industrialize, therefore, small countries must find export outlets for their manufactures, a requirement that is amply met by small industrial countries such as the Netherlands and Switzerland. As the preceding section indicated, it will be difficult for the developing countries (especially for the least developed among them) to export manufactures to the highly competitive markets of the industrial countries. It is not surprising, therefore, that many developing countries are seeking to create institutional arrangements that will encourage a mutual trade in manufactured goods. The most notable efforts in this regard are the regional schemes for economic integration that have been inspired by the outstanding success of the European Economic Community. Table 18-1 (page 437) identifies the principal integration efforts.

ECONOMIC INTEGRATION IN LATIN AMERICA

The most ambitious schemes for regional economic integration have been launched in Latin America. Unfortunately we can offer here only a brief description of them.

The Central American Common Market. Five countries in Central America—Honduras, El Salvador, Nicaragua, Guatemala, and Costa Rica—have established the Central American Common Market (CACM). The weight of CACM in world trade is minimal; the member countries have a total population of 16 million, a per capita annual income of around $200, and an area about the size of France. Their economic problems are poverty, rapid population growth, overdependence on agriculture (about 75 percent of their exports consist of coffee, bananas, and cotton), and a dearth of development capital. CACM is intended to accelerate economic development by widening market opportunities, increasing specialization, making possible economies of scale in industry, and by attracting foreign capital.

The Treaty of Managua, which created CACM in 1961, provided for the immediate removal of restrictions on one-half the products in mutual trade and the progressive elimination of remaining restrictions by 1966. The Treaty also envisaged the promotion of regional industries, common finance

---

[12] F. Kahnert et al., Economic Integration Among Developing Countries (Paris: Organization for Economic Cooperation and Development, 1969), p. 51.

Table 18-1

REGIONAL INTEGRATION SCHEMES AMONG DEVELOPING COUNTRIES

Integration Scheme	Beginning Date	Country Membership	Degree of Integration	Planned Date of Achievement
Latin America:				
Latin American Free Trade Area	1960	Argentina, Bolivia, Brazil, Chile, Colombia, Ecuador, Mexico, Paraguay, Peru, Uruguay, Venezuela	Free Trade Area	1973
Andean Subregional Group	1969	Bolivia, Chile, Colombia, Ecuador, Peru	Common Market	1980
Central American Common Market	1961	Costa Rica, El Salvador, Guatemala, Honduras, Nicaragua	Common Market	1966
Caribbean Free Trade Association	1968	Antigua, Barbados, Guyana, Jamaica, Trinidad and Tobago, West Indies Associated States	Free Trade Area	1973-78
Africa:				
East African Economic Community	1967	Kenya, Uganda, Tanzania (excl. Zanzibar)	Common Market	1967
Central African Customs and Economic Union	1966	Central African Rep., Gabon, Congo (Brazzaville), Cameroon	Common Market	Indefinite

General Note: *Free trade area* and *common market* are defined in Table 16-1 on p. 378. A *common market* is associated with a *customs union* and also involves some harmonization of economic policies but falls short of an *economic union*. Compared to the other developing areas, regional economic cooperation has been very limited in Asia; in the Middle East, the Arab countries have agreed to establish a common market by 1974.

and payments agencies, and other steps leading to eventual economic union with a common monetary system.

CACM made very rapid progress in the early and middle 1960's. A customs union was virtually completed by 1966 along with freedom of capital movements. In the period 1960-65 intraregional exports reached a compound annual growth rate of 34 percent, and intraregional trade became more than 15 percent of total trade.[13] Furthermore, more than two-thirds of intraregional trade consisted of industrial products. But this striking success also spawned a rising discontent because not all the member countries shared equally in trade and industrial expansion. In particular, Honduras fell behind the others and especially behind El Salvador, whose value added in manufacturing grew the fastest. This discontent set the stage for a series of calamitous events. In 1969 a hotly disputed soccer match provoked a war between the two countries, and they have yet to restore political and commercial relations. Faced with a trade deficit of $50 million (of which three-fourths was intraregional), Honduras suspended its participation in the common market and imposed duties on regional imports at the beginning of 1971. The closure of the Honduran market led both El Salvador and Guatemala (the most advanced members) to greatly increase their exports of manufactures to Costa Rica and Nicaragua. Unwilling to let its trade deficit grow unchecked, Costa Rica in mid-1971 placed duties on several regional products. Guatemala and El Salvador immediately retaliated by closing their borders to Costa Rican goods. At the same time, Nicaragua was complaining that Guatemala and El Salvador were benefiting unfairly from the common market. Thus, at the beginning of the 1970's CACM was threatened with final dissolution by grievances over the distribution of the common market's benefits in an atmosphere of intense nationalism.

The Latin American Free Trade Association. In 1960 the Treaty of Montevideo gave birth to the Latin American Free Trade Association (LAFTA), which is by far the biggest integration scheme among developing countries. The eleven member countries cover a territory twice the size of the United States and have a population that is approaching 250 million. The average GNP per capita is about $450 (much higher than in other developing areas), but there are marked disparities among the members that range from Venezuela, with close to $1000, to Bolivia, with less than $200. Brazil, Argentina, and Mexico are much bigger than the other countries and are much more advanced in industrial development. Brazil alone has close to half the territory of LAFTA and 40 percent of its population.

As stated in the preamble of the Treaty, the objectives of LAFTA include ". . . the expansion of present national markets, through the gradual elimination of barriers to intraregional trade" and sustained ". . . efforts to achieve the progressive complementarity and integration of their national

---

[13] *Ibid.,* p. 73. In 1950 intraregional trade was only 3 percent of total trade.

economies on the basis of an effective reciprocity of benefits." [14] To achieve free trade by 1973, LAFTA depends on an annual negotiation of *national schedules* and a periodic negotiation of a *common schedule*. In negotiating its national schedule of tariff concessions to the others, each member country is obligated to cut import duties in an amount equal to 8 percent of the weighted average of its duties on imports from nonmember countries until they are entirely eliminated on intra-LAFTA trade.[15] Each member country chooses the products that enter its national schedule. In contrast, the common schedule lists the products for which *all* the member countries agree to eliminate import restrictions completely on intra-LAFTA trade by 1973. According to the Treaty, negotiations on the common schedule are to be conducted every three years (1964, 1967, 1970, and 1973) and each negotiation is to place on the common schedule products that account for not less than 25 percent of trade among the member countries.

These commitments to negotiate duty reductions are far less rigorous than the automatic reductions in the EEC and EFTA. In practice, moreover, trade liberalization has been interpreted to mean that members are required to lower restrictions only on products they were already importing from each other in substantial volume, a major loophole because most of the foreign trade of the LAFTA countries has been (and remains) with non-LAFTA countries. Another loophole is provided by escape clauses that allow members to withdraw concessions from the national or common schedules. The LAFTA countries have made full use of these loopholes, slowing down trade liberalization to a crawl in the late 1960's. Strong protectionist forces have prevented countries from extending concessions on products which they produce at home. It has become increasingly difficult, therefore, to keep to the 8 percent weighted average formula. The foundation of any eventual free trade area is the common schedule, but this mechanism is also in trouble. The first common list, agreed to in 1964, includes cotton, coffee, cocoa, and copper, but only a few manufactured goods. And so far, LAFTA has failed to reach agreement on a second common list that was due in 1967.

The LAFTA Treaty also provides for the integration of single industries through *complementarity* agreements. The first agreement established free trade in calculating and data processing machines (including materials and components) among Argentina, Brazil, Chile, and Uruguay. A second agreement on electron tubes among the same countries and Mexico became effective only in 1965. At the end of the 1960's, there were only four complementarity agreements, although several were under discussion. The small

---

[14] Edward G. Cale, *Latin American Free Trade Association: Progress, Problems, Prospects* (Washington: Department of State, U.S. Government Printing Office, 1969), p. 2.

[15] This obligation may be expressed as follows: $d = D(1 - .08n)$, where d is the weighted average of duties on intra-LAFTA trade; D is the weighted average of duties on extra-LAFTA trade; and n, the number of years since the Treaty entered into force.

number of these agreements has been a major disappointment to supporters of integration in Latin America.

So far LAFTA has made little real contribution to economic development in Latin America. Although intra-LAFTA trade has increased, non-LAFTA countries still took almost 90 percent of LAFTA country exports in the early 1970's. Furthermore, about 60 percent of total intra-LAFTA trade is trade between Brazil and Argentina. Some import substitution on a regional level has occurred, and complementarity agreements have fostered a modest degree of specialization. But LAFTA has not spurred investment in new industrial plants to serve the regional market because manufacturers (both local and foreign) are skeptical of the permanence of any trade liberalization in light of the escape clauses available to LAFTA members.

To revitalize the integration movement, the Presidents of the Latin American countries issued in 1967 at Punta del Este a Declaration that states ". . . beginning in 1970, [we resolve] to establish progressively the Latin American common market which should be substantially in operation within a period of not more than fifteen years." [16] The Declaration envisages a "convergence" of LAFTA and CACM and the incorporation of other Latin American countries into the new common market. Given the dubious experiences of LAFTA and CACM in recent years, the prospects for a Latin American Common Market (LACM) by 1985 do not appear to be good. More to the point, the obstacles that have stultified progress in LAFTA still remain: differences in levels of development and economic potential so great that some members gain far more from integration than others; deficiencies of transportation and communication that inhibit intraregional trade; divergent national economic, social, and development policies; heterogeneous production and cost structures that generate fierce opposition to trade liberalization; lack of market information, marketing channels, and financial facilities to support intra-LAFTA trade; uncertainty about the effects of trade liberalization; lack of a competitive spirit among local entrepreneurs; widely varying rates of inflation among member countries, coupled with unrealistic exchange rates; and others.[17] But the key obstacle is economic nationalism: an emotional reluctance to accept any obligations that limit the nation's right to determine its own economic policies. As long as the spirit of economic nationalism flourishes in Latin America, so long will any efforts toward economic integration (however grandiose in conception) prove illusory as an effective instrument to promote economic development.

The Andean Common Market. Fearful of becoming economic satellites of Brazil, Argentina, and Mexico, five small nations on the west coast of South America (known as the Andean Group) subscribed to the Andean Subregional Integration Agreement in Bogota in 1969. The overriding purpose

---

[16] "Recent Developments in the Latin American Integration Process," *Economic Bulletin for Latin America,* Vol. XIV, No. 2 (second half of 1969), p. 111.

[17] *Ibid.,* pp. 114-15.

of the Agreement is the development of a modern industrial economy on a regional scale through the creation of a common market within LAFTA by 1980. Free trade within the subregion and a common external tariff is to be achieved by linear, automatic adjustments in duties along the lines followed by the European Economic Community. However, the distinctive feature and central idea of the Andean Common Market is the regional allocation of investment in those industries, such as steel, automobiles, and petrochemicals, that require a large market to attain economies of scale.

Other mechanisms set up by the Agreement to carry out this regional investment obligate the member countries to sector industrial development programs that will promote the expansion and specialization of manufacturing production, make the best possible use of the subregion's resources, take advantage of economies of scale, and distribute fairly the benefits of integration. These programs are to be supported by common policies with respect to foreign investment and trade.[18] The member countries also intend to harmonize policies and coordinate development in agriculture. To solve problems of infrastructure, they are to adopt specific programs and projects in energy, transportation, and communications that are to be administered by multinational agencies owned by the governments (or nationals) in partnership. The members also plan to coordinate national financial and payments policies to mobilize public and private savings for regional investment. The Andean Development Corporation, set up in 1968, is the key institution in promoting and financing regional industrial development. Because of their low levels of development, Bolivia and Ecuador are to be given special treatment in the allocation of production and new industries.

It is manifest that the Andean Common Market contemplates a far higher degree of integration than LAFTA or even CACM. It is too early to judge whether the five member countries can overcome the forces of economic nationalism that have so weakened the other integration schemes. The real test will come with decisions on the allocation of regional investment and industry. Already political changes, notably in Peru and Chile, cast some doubt on the ultimate success of this bold venture.

The Caribbean Free Trade Association. Except for reserved commodities, all tariffs among the member countries were abolished when the Caribbean Free Trade Association (CARIFTA) came into existence in 1968. For items on the reserve list, customs duties are to be eliminated over a five-year period by the more developed countries and over a ten-year period by the less developed countries, namely, the West Indies Associated States (which form a common market), plus Montserrat and St. Vincent. Although the Agreement prohibits quantitative restrictions on intra-CARIFTA trade, exceptions are granted for agricultural products and balance of payments difficulties. CARIFTA has made very rapid progress, but it is much less ambitious than CACM or the Andean Common Market. Whether it can evolve toward

---

[18] The Andean Investment Code is described in Chapter 25 on pp. 637-640.

a more advanced stage of economic integration is a question for the future. With the establishment of CARIFTA, nearly all Latin American countries are now members of one or more regional integration schemes.

PROSPECTIVE BENEFITS OF REGIONAL ECONOMIC INTEGRATION

In Chapter 16 we discussed both the *static* effects of economic integration (trade creation and trade diversion) and the *dynamic* effects (economies of scale, competition, enterprise size, product innovation, and new investment).[19] The rationale for economic integration among the developing countries is based almost entirely on the dynamic effects; unlike economic integration among industrial countries, little attention is paid to trade effects. The immediate trade gains from economic integration among developing countries are expected to be small for several reasons. Their export sectors are oriented toward markets in North America, Europe, and Japan, rather than toward neighboring countries. In the 1960's trade among the developing countries as a whole amounted to about one-fifth of their total trade and was less for intraregional trade. Also, a trading infrastructure in transportation, communications, finance, and marketing is notably lacking for intraregional trade. Finally, the factor endowments of developing countries belonging to a region tend to be similar, thus reducing the opportunities for short-term gains from trade.

The special case for economic integration among the developing countries, then, is that the creation of large regional markets will allow the establishment of regional firms which can benefit from the dynamic effects, especially from economies of scale. Conversely, the size of most developing economies is too small to provide a market outlet for the full-capacity production of the most efficient, lowest-cost plants in many industries. To illustrate, Table 18-2 indicates the economies of scale in the rolling of flat products for a hypothetical steel mill in Latin America. Even after allowing for high transportation costs in the dispersed Latin American market, the advantage of a regional steel industry (as compared to numerous self-sufficient national industries) is evident when account is also taken of the import cost of flat products (about $182 a ton).

To reap the dynamic benefits of economic integration, the member countries must reach agreement on regional investment and compensation policies that will guide new investments in transportation, communications, industry, and agriculture. Agreement is necessary on the *location* of new industry (should a petrochemical plant be built in country A, B, or C?) and the necessary *regional allocation* of investment funds to that industry and location. It is abundantly clear that the member countries will not allow the marketplace to decide the location of regional industries. The less-developed countries fear the competitive strength of the more-developed

---

[19] See Chapter 16, pp. 389-395.

Table 18-2

COST OF ROLLING FLAT PRODUCTS IN HYPOTHETICAL PLANTS OF DIFFERENT SIZES

Cost Item	Annual Capacity of Plant in Thousands of Tons of Finished Products				Percentage Decrease in Cost from 100,000 Tons to 1,500,000 Tons
	100	400	800	1500	
	U.S. Dollars Per Ton				
Ferrous material	120.71	92.58	82.94	75.47	37.5
Salaries and wages ...	15.52	6.22	4.51	3.30	78.6
Other conversion cost .	12.30	10.67	8.60	7.30	40.7
Total direct cost	148.53	109.47	96.05	86.07	42.1
Capital charges	43.46	29.70	19.80	17.37	60.0
Total cost	191.99	139.17	115.85	103.44	46.1

Source: "The Iron and Steel Industry of Latin America, Plans and Perspectives," *Interregional Symposium on the Application of Modern Technical Practices in the Iron and Steel Industry to Developing Countries* (New York: United Nations, 1964), p. 107. Reproduced in G. Hung, "Economies of Scale and Economic Integration," *Finance and Development*, No. 2 (1968), p. 39.

countries; the poorest countries fear a widening of income gaps between them and other member countries. No country will enter (or remain in) a regional arrangement unless it expects to be better off as a member than as a nonmember. Hence, there must not only be a mechanism for the regional allocation of resources to new industries but also a compensatory mechanism (granting privileged treatment or otherwise transferring resources to member countries gaining the least) to assure a fair distribution of benefits.

At present no integration scheme has an operative regional investment policy, although there are provisions for one in CACM and the Andean Common Market. The obstacles to such a policy are many. In Latin America, where there are few "new" industries, vested interests and national pride greatly limit the scope of regional investment planning. Such a policy also requires a common policy toward foreign investors, something that is very difficult to achieve when countries compete for scarce investment capital in prestige industries. Another obstacle is the emphasis on reciprocity: the determination of each country not to give up more than it receives in return. But the gravest obstacle is economic nationalism that favors national planning over regional planning, national industries over regional industries, and nationals over foreigners. In conclusion, developing countries will be able to obtain economies of scale and other dynamic benefits from regional integration schemes only when and if they design mechanisms to achieve a regional allocation of new investment and, at the same time, a "fair" share in the benefits of integration for all member countries. Although the record of Latin America is somewhat discouraging, the prospective benefits of regional economic integration among the developing countries are so enormous that efforts to realize them are bound to continue into the foreseeable future.

EXTERNAL ASSISTANCE TO THE DEVELOPING COUNTRIES

The impressive economic performance of the developing countries in the past two decades would not have been possible without a substantial flow of resources from the advanced, industrial countries. Since 1950 this flow has equaled about 2 percent of the gross domestic product of the developing countries as a whole, and has financed about 20 percent of their imports and about 10 percent of their domestic investment. By providing compensatory financing of savings and foreign exchange gaps, external assistance has enabled the majority of developing countries to increase their rates of capital formation and economic growth. Indeed, the bulk of this assistance has paid for imports of equipment and other capital goods for investment in infrastructure, industry, and agriculture. Furthermore, technical assistance has directly enhanced productivity in the developing countries by transferring technology and human skills. At the end of the 1960's, over 100,000 technical experts were working in developing countries under official aid programs and over 80,000 students and trainees from the developing countries were studying in the industrial countries.[20]

It would be erroneous to view external assistance as the only, or most crucial, factor in the economic performance of the developing countries. Although the correlation between growth and import capacity is high (a finding consistent with the operation of foreign exchange constraints), the correlation between the amounts of external assistance received by a country and its rate of economic growth is low. The explanation is the presence of many other factors that influence economic growth, notably export behavior and general domestic policies. On the other hand, all the fast-growing developing countries have received large amounts of foreign assistance, excepting only a few petroleum countries that have experienced very rapid export growth. After studying the evidence, the Pearson Commission concluded: ". . . it is clear that aid, increasingly focused on the imperatives of long-term development, has helped to make possible a good record of development in the past two decades." [21]

EXTERNAL ASSISTANCE IN THE 1960'S

Table 18-3 indicates that *net* flows of financial resources to the developing countries rose from $7.8 billion in 1960 to $13.6 billion in 1969. About 90 percent of this external assistance is supplied bilaterally by the sixteen industrial countries that belong to the Development Assistance Committee (DAC) of the Organization for Economic Cooperation and Development (OECD). Most of the remaining assistance is supplied by these same

---

[20] Report of the Commission on International Development, *Partners in Development* (New York: Praeger Publishers, 1969), p. 51. This study is commonly referred to as the "Pearson Report" after the Commission chairman, Lester B. Pearson.

[21] *Ibid.,* p. 52.

countries through multilateral (international) agencies such as the World Bank Group. The Communist countries supply a comparatively small amount of assistance to the developing countries.

Table 18-3

NET FLOWS OF FINANCIAL RESOURCES TO DEVELOPING COUNTRIES FROM ALL SOURCES IN THE 1960'S
(Billions of U.S. Dollars)

	1960	1961	1962	1963	1964	1965	1966	1967	1968	1969
DAC member countries [1]	7.3	8.4	7.7	8.3	8.6	9.8	9.9	10.3	11.8	12.2
Multilateral agencies	0.3	0.3	0.4	0.7	0.8	0.9	0.9	1.0	0.8	1.2
Communist countries	0.2	0.3	0.4	0.4	0.4	0.3	0.3	0.3	0.3	0.3
Total net flows [2] ...	7.8	9.0	8.5	9.3	9.8	11.0	11.2	11.7	13.0	13.6

Source: *Development Assistance, 1970 Review* (Paris: Organization for Economic Cooperation and Development, December 1970), Table II-2, p. 31.
General Note: Net flows of financial resources are gross disbursements minus amortization receipts on earlier lending. These flows include both official and private sector resources.
[1] Countries that belong to the Development Assistance Committee of the Organization for Economic Cooperation and Development. DAC comprises all the non-Communist industrial countries except New Zealand. The only net flows not included in the table (New Zealand and Finland) rose from $5 million in 1960 to $23 million in 1969.
[2] May not add because of rounding.

Table 18-4 breaks down the flow of financial resources from the DAC countries to the developing countries by major types. *Official development assistance* involves the transfer of resources by the donor governments with the deliberate intent to promote economic development in the receiving countries. In 1969, about 85 percent of this assistance was transferred via bilateral, government-to-government programs, while the remainder was distributed via international institutions. Only official development assistance fully deserves the designation "foreign aid"; such as, grants and concessional loans for development. *Other official flows* consist mainly of official export credits which, although they provide resources to the developing countries, are primarily intended to promote DAC exports rather than economic development. Together the two official flows make up "official aid," which in 1969 accounted for 54 percent of the total flow of financial resources from the DAC countries to the developing countries.[22]

---

[22] In the period 1967-69, official aid for ninety-two developing countries averaged 13 percent of their imports of goods and services, 2.2 percent of their gross domestic product, and $3.56 on a per capita basis. See *Development Assistance, 1970 Review* (Paris: Organization for Economic Cooperation and Development, December, 1970), Table 24, pp. 204-205.

Table 18-4

COMPOSITION OF NET FLOW OF FINANCIAL RESOURCES TO DEVELOPING COUNTRIES FROM DAC COUNTRIES 1960, 1965, AND 1969
(Millions of U.S. Dollars)

	1960	1965	1969
I. Official development assistance	4,703	5,937	6,707
1. Bilateral grants and grant-like [1]	3,716	3,770	3,356
2. Bilateral development loans at concessional terms	452	1,802	2,343
3. Contributions to multilateral institutions ..	535	364	1,007
II. Other official flows [2]	262	302	585
1. Bilateral	195	297	594
2. Multilateral	67	5	−9
III. Private flows	3,150	4,182	6,280
1. Direct investment	1,767	2,496	2,566
2. Bilateral portfolio	633	687	1,260
3. Multilateral portfolio	204	248	414
4. Export credits [3]	546	751	2,040
Total official and private flows	8,115	10,420	13,571

Source: *Development Assistance, 1970 Review* (Paris: Organization for Economic Cooperation and Development, December, 1970), Table II-1, p. 30.

[1] Grant-like assistance comprises loans repayable in, and the transfer of resources through sales for, the currency of the recipient country.

[2] Official export credits and official multilateral portfolio investment.

[3] Includes only export credits guaranteed by donor country, including unguaranteed portions.

By their very nature, *private flows* cannot be directly manipulated by the governments of the DAC countries although they are commonly subject to regulations of one kind or another. Private flows are the net consequence of decisions by an untold number of entrepreneurs, investors, bankers, and traders. The dominant motivation behind these decisions is the prospect of economic gain (profit, interest, or capital appreciation) for the decision maker or his organization. Nor do private flows involve grants or concessional loans. Properly speaking, therefore, private flows should not be considered "foreign aid," even though they may provide developing countries with resources that are not obtainable from official assistance, such as technology and industrial management.

Direct investment occurs when business enterprises in the DAC countries acquire equity interests in affiliates in the developing countries. The conditions that promote or deter direct investment in the developing countries are explored at some length in Chapter 25. The *bilateral portfolio* flow represents the purchase by private investors in the DAC countries of bonds issued by borrowers in developing countries. Until the 1930's this was the main channel for private investment, but today only a few developing countries have the credit standing to borrow large amounts in international capital markets. In the 1960's, only Israel, Mexico, and Argentina were able to float more than $100 million in bonds. The *multilateral portfolio* flow is made up of private purchases of bonds issued by international development agencies, notably the World Bank. *Export credits* used to finance exports of the DAC countries to the developing countries ordinarily have a maturity of five years or more. Not only are they an expensive source of capital, but their easy availability can lead to overuse by developing countries. All in all, private flows accounted for 46 percent of the net flow of financial resources of the industrial countries to the developing countries in 1969.

As revealed in Table 18-5, the United States supplied slightly over one-third of the net flow of official and private resources and almost one-half of the net flow of official development assistance from the DAC countries to the developing countries in 1969. Although the United States remains by far the largest single source of external assistance, its relative importance declined markedly in the 1960's. In 1960, the U.S. share of the total resource flow was nearly one-half and its share of official development assistance was close to six-tenths.

How much external assistance *should* the industrial countries provide to the developing countries? Economic analysis cannot answer this question because it is essentially political in nature. However, the industrial countries have agreed to a target of 1 percent of their gross national products (at market prices) to be achieved sometime during the Second Development Decade. How close are they to this target? Table 18-5 indicates that seven countries, led by Portugal, exceeded the 1 percent target in 1969, while among the nine underachieving countries the United States ranked last with only 0.49 percent of its GNP. The majority of the DAC countries increased their GNP percentages during the 1960's, but the U.S. percentage dropped sharply after 1965 when it reached 0.78. Actually, the other fifteen DAC countries raised the share of their combined GNP to 1 percent in 1969.

The strategy of the Second Development Decade also includes a separate "mid-decade" target of 0.7 percent of GNP for official development assistance. However, the industrial countries have not been willing to accept this target, whose attainment would require a very considerable expansion of official aid. In 1969, official development assistance was only 0.36 percent of the DAC members' combined GNP. Here again the United States has moved in the other direction. As late as 1965, the U.S. percentage for official development assistance was 0.50, giving it fifth place among the DAC countries.

UNITED STATES FOREIGN AID POLICY

Foreign aid has been a dominant element in American foreign economic policy since World War II. During the early postwar years United States government assistance was directed mainly toward the rehabilitation and recovery of Western Europe—the Marshall Plan era. At the start of the 1950's United States foreign aid became oriented toward rearmament of

Table 18-5

RANKING OF DAC COUNTRIES BY NET FLOW OF TOTAL OFFICIAL AND PRIVATE FINANCIAL RESOURCES TO DEVELOPING COUNTRIES IN RELATION TO GROSS NATIONAL PRODUCT IN 1969

DAC Country	Official and Private Financial Resources [1]			Official Development Assistance [1]		
	Dollar Amount (Millions)	As Percentage of GNP	Rank	Dollar Amount (Millions)	As Percentage of GNP	Rank
Portugal	97.6	1.74	(1)	58.3	1.04	(1)
Netherlands	369.2	1.36	(2)	143.1	0.53	(4)
Germany	2,045.5	1.33	(3)	595.0	0.39	(8–9)
France	1,742.2	1.24	(4)	965.3	0.69	(2)
Denmark	151.0	1.13	(5)	54.3	0.41	(7)
Belgium	257.3	1.12	(6)	116.1	0.51	(5)
Italy	847.7	1.03	(7)	129.6	0.16	(14–15)
Target Percentage		**1.0**				
United Kingdom	1,068.7	0.97	(8)	431.3	0.39	(8–9)
Norway	75.2	0.78	(9)	29.5	0.31	(12)
Sweden	212.4	0.77	(10)	120.8	0.44	(6)
Japan	1,263.1	0.76	(11)	435.6	0.26	(13)
Australia	232.1	0.74	(12)	174.6	0.56	(3)
Austria	80.7	0.65	(13)	15.5	0.12	(16)
Switzerland	119.0	0.64	(14)	29.5	0.16	(14–15)
Canada	364.1	0.50	(15)	245.2	0.34	(10)
United States	4,645.4	0.49	(16)	3,163.0	0.33	(11)
Total	13,571.2	0.74 (of combined GNP)		6,706.7	0.36 (of combined GNP)	

Source: *Development Assistance, 1970 Review* (Paris: Organization for Economic Cooperation and Development, December, 1970), Tables 1, 2, 8, and 9, pp. 170, 171, 180, and 181, respectively.

[1] Includes flows to multilateral (international) agencies.

the free world, emphasizing military and defense support assistance. It was not until 1957 that United States foreign assistance turned definitely toward the developing countries. In that year Congress approved the creation of the Development Loan Fund to finance projects in the developing countries. Formal recognition of this turn in United States foreign aid occurred in 1961, when a new agency—the Agency for International Development (AID) —was set up to administer economic and technical assistance programs. That year also saw the birth of the Alliance for Progress—an ambitious program to accelerate economic growth in Latin America in close cooperation with the Latin American governments.

At present, AID administers three categories of foreign assistance: *security* programs that provide military and support assistance (52 percent of all assistance in 1969); *welfare and emergency relief* programs that take care of disaster victims, refugees, and the like (6 percent); and *development* programs that include development loans, technical assistance grants, the Peace Corps, agricultural credit sales, and multilateral assistance (42 percent). Some ninety countries participate in AID programs, but assistance is concentrated in about twenty. This multiplicity of programs has engendered confusion and doubt concerning the rationale of U.S. foreign aid. To obtain support from Congress, successive administrations have emphasized the political and economic advantages of foreign aid in the pursuit of national interests, advantages which have not been borne out in practice. Foreign aid cannot buy political allies and may even cause irritation between the giving and receiving countries. Nor can development assistance reap immediate economic dividends for the giving country unless its effectiveness is compromised by tying arrangements. The disenchantment with foreign aid in the United States proceeds, therefore, from its misuse as an instrument of foreign policy.

In his 1971 Message to Congress, President Nixon attempted to halt the deterioration of U.S. foreign aid by proposing a clear separation of security and development assistance and a major reorganization of foreign aid agencies.[23] In October of that year, however, the Senate, in an unprecedented action, rejected the Administration's foreign aid authorization bill, plunging U.S. foreign aid policy into crisis. This unexpected defeat, which formally ended more than twenty years of foreign aid, came from a coalition of conservatives (always opposed to foreign assistance) and liberals who had become unhappy with the military aspects of foreign aid. Hopefully a foreign aid policy will emerge for the 1970's that will disavow short-term national advantages and instead champion the long-term benefits of achieving self-sustaining growth in the developing two-thirds of the world community.

---

[23] *President Nixon's Message to Congress On Reorganization of U.S. Foreign Assistance Programs* (Washington: Agency for International Development, April 21, 1971).

INTERNATIONAL AGENCIES PROVIDING EXTERNAL ASSISTANCE

Although the bulk of external assistance to the developing countries has been supplied bilaterally by the industrial countries, substantial resources have also been channelled multilaterally through international agencies. We offer here thumbnail sketches of the most important agencies.

World Bank Group. The most prominent international lending agencies make up the World Bank Group, comprising the International Bank for Reconstruction and Development (IBRD or World Bank), the International Development Association (IDA), and the International Finance Corporation (IFC).[24] In fiscal 1971, the World Bank made seventy-eight loans totaling $1,896 million in forty-one countries; the IDA extended fifty-three credits to thirty-four countries amounting to $584 million; and the IFC assisted twenty-three enterprises in fifteen countries and made one regional investment for a total of $101 million.[25] Each of these agencies has its own resources, lending terms, and policies.

The World Bank finances development projects on long term (ranging up to thirty-five years) for which it charges a market rate of interest, currently 7¼ percent. All of its loans must be guaranteed by governments in the borrowing countries and must be repaid in hard, convertible currencies. The Bank obtains its loan funds from member-country subscriptions to its capital stock, by selling its own bonds on international capital markets, and by selling off its loan portfolios to private investors. Most Bank loans are used to finance infrastructure investments in transportation, electric power, agriculture, water supply, and education.

The inability of many developing countries to qualify for World Bank loans and their high interest costs led to the formation of the IDA. The IDA extends credits to developing countries for up to fifty years that are repayable in easy stages after a ten-year grace period and with no interest except a modest service charge. The IDA is frequently described as a "soft loan" agency while the World Bank is a "hard loan" agency. Unlike the Bank, IDA does not have its own capital; it is dependent on a continuing replenishment of its funds by the member countries.

The IFC does not make loans to governments as do the other agencies. Instead, it participates in industrial projects along with private investors, either as a lender or an investor in equity. In fiscal year 1971, for example, the IFC lent $4.5 million to Iran's only producer of nylon yarn to help finance a $17.1 million expansion in production, and it made both a loan

---

[24] The IBRD came into being as a sister organization of the International Monetary Fund and began operations in 1946. The IFC was set up in 1956 and the IDA, in 1961; both are affiliates of the IBRD. Almost all the non-Communist countries are members of the World Bank Group.

[25] World Bank, *Annual Report* (Washington: International Bank for Reconstruction and Development, 1971), p. 6.

and equity investment of $8 million in the Philippine Petroleum Corporation which is to build and operate a refinery. In the first fifteen years of its existence, the IFC made cumulative investments of $577.8 million in 172 business enterprises located in forty-seven developing countries. Other investors provided $2,465 million for those enterprises, making a total investment of $3,043 million.[26] As these figures indicate, the IFC has been able to function as a catalyst by bringing together private investors of the industrial and developing countries. The IFC obtains its investment funds from member-country subscriptions to its capital stock (now $107 million), from its right to borrow from the World Bank up to four times its own unimpaired capital and surplus, and from the sale of its own investment portfolio to private investors (thereby "recycling" its investment funds).

United Nations Development Program. The United Nations Development Program (UNDP) is the principal international agency in the field of technical assistance and preinvestment aid. In 1970, the UNDP spent $90 million on technical assistance and $235 million on preinvestment activities which are intended to identify, investigate, and present to financial agencies those projects in developing countries that merit investment. Most of the UNDP assistance is actually carried out by specialized agencies and other bodies of the United Nations. UNDP's resources, which come from the annual pledges of member countries, grew from $55 million in 1959 to nearly $200 million in 1969.

Regional Development Banks. Several development banks have been established in recent years to provide multilateral assistance to developing countries in different regions of the world. The *Inter-American Development Bank* was started in 1960 by the United States and all the Latin American countries except Cuba. The Bank has three categories of funds: ordinary capital used for loans at market rates ("hard-loan window"), special funds for loans on easy terms ("soft-currency window"), and a Social Program Trust Fund to finance low-income housing, education, and other social projects. Heavily dependent on continuing U.S. support, the Bank had outstanding loans of more than $4 billion at the end of 1970. The *African Development Bank* started operations in 1964 with a membership limited to independent African countries and an authorized capital of $250 million. The *Asian Development Bank* was established in 1966 with an authorized capital of $1.1 billion by nineteen Asian countries, eleven European countries, Canada, and the United States. Offering both hard and soft loans, the Bank had approved twenty-seven loans totalling $140 million for twenty-six projects in eleven developing countries by the end of 1969. Mention should also be made of the *Central American Bank for Economic Integration,* the *Caribbean Development Bank,* and the *European Development Fund.*

---

[26] *1971 Annual Report* (Washington: International Finance Corporation, 1971), p. 11.

THE DEBT SERVICE BURDEN OF THE DEVELOPING COUNTRIES

Less than one-third of net external assistance to developing countries takes the form of grants (Table 18-4). The remainder requires repayment and service payments of interest or dividends. As a consequence, many years of external assistance have saddled the developing countries with a mountain of external debt. By the end of 1969, eighty developing countries had accumulated an external *public* debt of almost $59 billion.[27] Half of this debt was owed by only eight countries—India, Pakistan, Brazil, Mexico, Indonesia, Iran, Argentina, and Chile. External public debt of the developing countries rose at an annual average rate of 13 percent in the 1960's, far higher than the 9 percent growth in their export earnings. Debt service payments reached $5 billion in 1969, about one-seventh of the total exports of the developing countries to the industrial countries. India, Pakistan, Argentina, and Mexico must use more than 20 percent of their foreign exchange earnings from exports of goods and services to make payments on their external public debt. In addition to the servicing of external public debt, the developing countries are also faced with income and amortization payments on private loans and foreign investment.

The growing debt service burden threatens to check the economic development of the developing countries by absorbing foreign exchange vitally needed to finance imports. It means that a substantial portion of their external assistance is being offset by interest, dividend, and amortization payments to the lending nations. Several steps can be taken to alleviate the burden of debt repayment. In the short run, credits can be consolidated to lengthen repayment periods. In the longer run, external assistance can be extended on more favorable terms such as grants instead of loans, longer loan maturities, longer grace periods, etc. Moreover, the developing countries can improve their investment planning so as to avoid unwise borrowing, bunching their borrowings at one time, relying excessively on short-term credits, and the like. Also, the cost of aid can be reduced by untying funds so that the developing countries can spend them in the most attractive markets. At present, it is commonplace for the industrial countries to tie aid in their bilateral programs so that funds must be spent in the aid-giving country.

SUMMARY

1. The dominant goal of the Second United Nations Development Decade is an average annual growth rate of 6 percent in the gross domestic product of the developing countries as a whole in the 1970's.

---

[27] *Annual Report, 1971* (Washington: International Bank for Reconstruction and Development, 1971), p. 50.

2. To help achieve this goal, the developed countries are expected to undertake several policy measures in trade and financial assistance. Trade policy measures include (1) the conclusion of new international commodity agreements, (2) commitments to liberalize imports of primary products, (3) arrangements to establish generalized, nondiscriminatory, nonreciprocal preferential treatment of the manufactured exports of developing countries, and (4) the progressive elimination of nontariff barriers.

3. International commodity agreements are arrangements between producing countries or between producing and consuming countries that seek to stabilize the prices of specific primary commodities through measures that involve buffer stocks, export controls, and import commitments or production controls. The prospects of any substantial transfer of resources to the developing countries through international commodity agreements appear dim.

4. Preferences for the developing countries may be viewed as a "second-best" solution. The first-best solution is free trade in manufactured products among all countries, developed and developing alike.

5. Developing countries are now participating in several schemes for regional economic integration. The most ambitious schemes have been launched in Latin America: the Central American Common Market, the Latin American Free Trade Association, the Andean Common Market, and the Caribbean Free Trade Association. To reap the dynamics benefits of economic integration, the member countries must reach agreement on regional investment and compensation policies that will guide new investments in transportation, communications, industry, and agriculture.

6. The impressive economic performance of the developing countries in the past two decades would not have been possible without a substantial flow of resources from the advanced, industrial countries. Since 1950 this flow has equaled about 2 percent of the gross domestic product of the developing countries as a whole, and has financed about 20 percent of their imports and about 10 percent of their domestic investment.

7. The industrial countries have agreed to a target of 1 percent of their gross national products (at market prices) to be achieved sometime during the Second Development Decade in assistance to the developing countries. The actual percentage in 1969 was 0.74, largely owing to a deterioration of the U.S. percentage in recent years.

8. At the beginning of the 1970's, U.S. foreign aid policy entered into crisis. The disenchantment with foreign aid in the United States proceeds from its misuse as an instrument of foreign policy.

9. Many international agencies provide external assistance to the developing countries: the World Bank Group, the United Nations Development Program, and regional development banks.

QUESTIONS AND APPLICATIONS

1. Describe the mechanisms for stabilizing prices under international commodity agreements. Are international commodity agreements likely to be effective

instruments for transferring resources from the rich to the poor countries? Why or why not?

2. Discuss the pros and cons of preferential treatment of the manufactured exports of the developing countries.

3. Why is the rationale for economic integration among the developing countries based almost entirely on the dynamic effects? Evaluate the current progress of a regional integration scheme among developing countries.

4. What is meant by "external assistance" to the developing countries? What are the major types of this assistance? What is "foreign aid"?

5. Undertake research to answer the following question: Why has U.S. foreign aid deteriorated in the last half of the 1960's?

6. Do the rich countries have an obligation to help the poor countries? Justify your answer.

7. Be prepared to discuss the advantages and/or disadvantages of (a) multilateral aid versus bilateral aid, (b) untied aid versus tied aid, and (c) soft loans versus hard loans.

SELECTED READINGS

Development Assistance. Paris: Organization for Economic Cooperation and Development, Annual Review.

International Development Strategy. New York: United Nations, 1970.

Johnson, Harry G. *Economic Policies Toward Less Developed Countries.* New York: Praeger Publishers, 1967.

Kahnert, F., *et al. Economic Integration Among Developing Countries.* Paris: Development Center of the Organization for Economic Cooperation and Development, 1969.

Lewis, W. Arthur. *The Development Process.* New York: United Nations Center for Economic and Social Information, 1970.

Millikan, Max F. *A Strategy for Development.* United Nations: Center for Economic and Social Information, 1970.

Partners in Development, Report of the Commission on International Development. New York: Praeger Publishers, 1969.

Rostow, W. W. *The Stages of Economic Growth.* New York: Cambridge University Press, 1960.

The Problem of Stabilization of Prices of Primary Products. Washington: International Monetary Fund, 1969.

U.S. Foreign Assistance in the 1970's: A New Approach, Report to the President from the Task Force on International Development. Washington: U.S. Government Printing Office, 1970.

Weintraub, Sidney. *The Foreign Exchange Gap of the Developing Countries,* Essays in International Finance No. 48. Princeton: Princeton University Press, September, 1965.

World Bank. Washington: International Bank for Reconstruction and Development, Annual Report.

THE INTERNATIONAL MONETARY SYSTEM AND THE U.S. DOLLAR, 1945-1971

The twin problems of the U.S. balance of payments deficit and international monetary reform have drawn enormous attention from international economists and central bankers since the beginning of the 1960's. And in 1971 they became matters of widespread public concern as mounting pressures on the international monetary system culminated in its collapse and a massive realignment of currencies ensued. Governments of the industrial countries must now undertake the formidable task of constructing a new system that will make possible a continuing expansion of world trade and investment in the coming decades. In this chapter and the next we examine the postwar international monetary system, the U.S. balance of payments problem, speculative short-term capital movements, the collapse of the Bretton Woods system, and the prospects for international monetary reform.

THE INTERNATIONAL MONETARY FUND (IMF)

While war still raged in Europe and Asia, representatives of the United States, Great Britain, and other Allied countries met at Bretton Woods, New Hampshire, in 1944 to reach final agreement on the postwar international monetary system. The delegates to the conference, who included the eminent British economist John Maynard Keynes, were mindful of the rise and fall of international monetary systems in the past and particularly of the monetary chaos that preceded the war. From 1870 to 1914, the international gold standard (centered in London) had reigned supreme, only to be abandoned at the outbreak of World War I.[1] Among the major countries only the United States maintained the gold convertibility of its currency during that conflict. After a period of freely fluctuating exchange rates, the gold standard was painfully restored in the 1920's, but only in the modified

---

[1] The mechanics of the international gold standard are discussed on pp. 163-165 in Chapter 7. See also pp. 150-153 in Chapter 6.

form of a gold exchange standard whereby central banks held some or all of their reserves in sterling, dollars, or francs rather than in gold. Global depression, heightened by massive flows of speculative capital, forced the collapse of this system in the early 1930's; Great Britain halted the gold convertibility of the pound in September, 1931, and the United States devalued the dollar by raising the price of gold from $20.67 to $35 an ounce in 1933. There followed a scramble by each country to protect its currency and trade vis-à-vis other countries. Competitive depreciations to promote exports and curb imports, inconvertible currencies, exchange control, currency blocs, and bilateral trade agreements became the order of the day.[2] Then came World War II.

The delegates at Bretton Woods were convinced that only an unprecedented degree of international monetary cooperation could hope to forestall a repetition of the 1930's. The outcome of their deliberations was the establishment of the International Monetary Fund, an international agency to administer a code of fair exchange practices and provide compensatory financial assistance to member countries in balance of payments trouble.[3]

The purposes of IMF are clearly set forth in Article I of its Articles of Agreement:

1. To promote international monetary cooperation through a permanent institution which provides the machinery for consultation and collaboration on international monetary problems.

2. To facilitate the expansion and balanced growth of international trade, and to contribute thereby to the promotion and maintenance of high levels of employment and real income and to the development of the productive resources of all members as primary objectives of economic policy.

3. To promote exchange stability, to maintain orderly exchange arrangements among members, and to avoid competitive exchange depreciation.

4. To assist in the establishment of a multilateral system of payments in respect of current transactions between members and in the elimination of foreign exchange restrictions which hamper the growth of world trade.

5. To give confidence to members by making the Fund's resources available to them under adequate safeguards, thus providing them with opportunity to correct maladjustments in their balances of payments without resorting to measures destructive of national or international balances of payments of members.

CODE OF FAIR EXCHANGE PRACTICES

Upon entering the Fund, a country must submit a *par value* of its currency expressed in terms of gold or in terms of the United States dollar of

---

[2] The collapse of the gold exchange standard in the 1930's is briefly treated on pp. 325-327 in Chapter 14.

[3] The Articles of Agreement of the Fund entered into force in December, 1945. A second Bretton Woods agreement established the International Bank for Reconstruction and Development.

the weight and fineness of gold in effect on July 1, 1944. All exchange transactions between member countries are to be effected at a rate that diverges not more than 1 percent from the par values of the respective currencies.

A member may change the par value of its currency only to correct a *fundamental* disequilibrium in its balance of payments and only after consultation with the Fund. If the Fund objects to the change but the member nevertheless goes ahead with it, the Fund may declare that member ineligible to use its resources.[4] Although the Fund may object to a proposed change in the par value of a currency, it cannot formally propose a change of its own accord. These provisions envisage, therefore, a system of stable exchange rates with an occasional devaluation (depreciation) or revaluation (appreciation) to remove a persistent disequilibrium in the balance of payments.[5]

Article VIII of the Agreement forbids members to restrict current (account) payments or to discriminate in their currency practices without the approval of the Fund. Members are also obligated to maintain the convertibility of foreign-held balances acquired or used in connection with current transactions. Thus, Article VIII clearly outlaws exchange control over international payments for merchandise and services. On the other hand, Article VI allows members to control capital movements as long as current transactions remain unaffected.

There are two exceptions to the provisions of Article VIII. One exception occurs when the Fund declares a currency to be scarce because the demand for the currency in question threatens the Fund's ability to supply it. A scarce currency declaration authorizes member countries to impose exchange control over all transactions in the scarce currency. The scarce currency provision explicitly recognizes that free convertibility cannot be sustained if most countries have persistent deficits with the same surplus country for, in that event, multilateral settlement of the deficits is out of the question. This provision also applies pressure on the surplus country to take remedial measures in order to avoid discrimination against its trade.

The most important exception to the provisions of Article VIII, however, is found in the provisions of Article XIV. This article allows a member country to retain exchange restrictions on current international transactions in effect when that country entered the Fund. Moreover, these restrictions may be adapted to changing circumstances in order to deal with balance of payments difficulties. The decision to abandon exchange restrictions permitted under Article XIV is left to the member country, but it is supposed to occur when such restrictions are no longer necessary to settle the balance of payments without undue dependence on the Fund's resources. Once a member abolishes its exchange control over current payments and accepts the

---

[4] If the proposed change, together with all previous changes, whether increases or decreases, does not exceed 10 percent of the initial par value of the member's currency, the Fund will raise no objection.

[5] This is the adjustable-peg system described on pp. 234-235 in Chapter 10.

obligations of Article VIII, it cannot reimpose similar exchange restrictions without the approval of the Fund.

Article XIV was conceived as a "transitional arrangement" that would not be necessary once the member countries had overcome the problems of readjustment which immediately followed World War II. Events proved otherwise, however, and it was not until 1961 that the major countries in Western Europe were able to accept the obligations of Article VIII. The last big trading country, Japan, came under Article VIII in 1964.[6] The remaining Article XIV countries are obliged to consult annually with the Fund on the continuance of exchange restrictions; but, as we noted earlier, the Fund has no power to decree their abolition. Nor do the Articles of Agreement specify the duration of the transitional period.

COMPENSATORY FINANCING BY THE FUND

In addition to administering a code of fair exchange practices, the Fund is also a source of compensatory financing for a member country experiencing a *temporary* disequilibrium in its balance of payments. The resources of the Fund come from the gold and currency subscriptions of its member countries.[7] Upon entering the Fund, each country is allotted a quota in accordance with its relative economic size. Twenty-five percent of a country's quota must be paid to the Fund in gold and the remainder in the country's own currency.[8] Since quotas are calculated in the 1944 U.S. dollar, the dollar equivalents of nondollar currencies are determined by their respective par values. The Fund started operations in 1947 with aggregate quotas of $8 billion, but successive quota increases had raised the total to $28.5 billion by 1971. The largest quota is subscribed by the United States ($6.7 billion); the next largest by Great Britain ($2.8 billion).

The size of a country's quota is significant in two respects. First, it determines, approximately, the voting power of a member's executive director. Thus, the executive director of the United States has 21.9 percent of the voting power of the Executive Directors; the executive director of the United Kingdom has 9.2 percent. This gives these two countries a dominant voice in the operation of the Fund. Second, the size of a country's quota determines the overall amount that it may draw from the resources of the Fund.

A member country is entitled to buy from the Fund, with its own currency, the currency of another member subject to the conditions listed at the top of page 459.

---

[6] By April, 1971, thirty-five countries had accepted Article VIII. The Fund has never invoked the scarce-currency provision.

[7] In 1971, 117 countries of the non-Communist world were members of the Fund.

[8] When a country's gold reserves are low, it is permitted to join the Fund without full payment of its gold subscription, using its own currency as a substitute. Full payment is expected, however, when the country's gold reserves become adequate.

1. The member desires to buy a currency in order to make currency payments consistent with the provisions of the Articles of Agreement.

2. The Fund has not given notice that its holdings of the desired currency are scarce.

3. The proposed purchase does not cause the Fund's holdings of the purchasing member's currency to increase by over 25 percent of its quota during the twelve-month period ending on the date of such purchase nor to exceed 200 percent of its basic quota.

4. The Fund has not previously declared that the member desiring to purchase is ineligible to use the resources of the Fund.

To illustrate, suppose that Norway wishes to buy dollars from the Fund against its own currency and has not yet utilized any of its drawing rights. Assuming the conditions outlined above are met, Norway will be permitted to buy dollars up to 25 percent of its quota, that is, 25 percent of $240 million, or $60 million. If Norway takes full advantage of this drawing right, the Fund will then hold Norwegian currency equal to 100 percent of Norway's quota—the original subscription equal to 75 percent of its quota plus the 25 percent now sold to the Fund for dollars. Providing the drawing conditions continue to be met, Norway will be able to purchase from the Fund an additional 240 million United States dollars (or the equivalent in other currencies) over the next four years. At that point Norway's drawing rights will be exhausted, since the Fund will hold Norwegian currency equal to 200 percent of Norway's quota.[9]

In practice, the Fund has freely allowed member countries to purchase other currencies up to the first 25 percent of their quotas (often called the *gold tranche*).[10] It has also waived the twelve-month requirement in many instances. The Fund will not permit a country to draw beyond 25 percent of its quota, however, unless convinced that the country in question is following policies directed toward the eventual achievement of convertibility or the avoidance of exchange restrictions. Convertibility is a principal objective of the Fund and it attempts to employ its resources accordingly.

The IMF also encourages liberal exchange policies by negotiating *standby agreements* with interested member countries. Through these agreements, member countries receive the Fund's guarantee that they will be allowed to draw on the Fund for the currency or currencies covered by

---

[9] This assumes that no other member country has purchased Norwegian currency from the Fund. If, for example, the Fund has sold Norwegian currency equal to 10 percent of Norway's quota, then Norway will be permitted to purchase additional dollars equal to 10 percent of its quota. Then the Fund will hold Norwegian currency equal to 200 percent of Norway's quota and drawing rights will be exhausted.

[10] A country's *reserve position in the Fund* equals its gold tranche *minus* any current utilization of its drawing rights *plus* the Fund's use of its currency to finance the drawings of other countries or to purchase gold. This reserve position is considered an unconditional asset that is part of a country's international reserves.

the agreement within a specified period of time. To qualify for a standby agreement, a country must satisfy the usual drawing conditions. By enabling a member to count definitely on aid from the Fund if it proves necessary at sometime in the future, standby agreements lend strength to national policies consistent with the Fund's purposes.

In addition to drawings under these general arrangements, a country may apply for a special drawing to obtain compensatory financing for a temporary decline in its export earnings. Intended to assist developing countries, such special drawings will not normally exceed 25 percent of a country's quota, but they may bring the Fund's holdings of a country's currency over the limit of twice its quota.

The resources of the Fund are intended to supplement the reserves of a country when it is faced with a temporary deficit in the balance of payments. Hence, the Fund is supposed to provide only *short-term* financial assistance that will be repaid by the borrowing country within the near future. Only if the Fund's resources revolve rapidly can they fulfill their function as an international reserve; if they become frozen through long-term arrangements between the Fund and member countries, they will not be available to meet new demands. The Fund is not a source of capital like the International Bank, and no member country should look to it for more than stopgap compensatory financing of an external deficit.

The IMF has adopted the rule that currency purchased from it by member countries should not remain outstanding for more than three to five years. A schedule of charges on the use of the Fund's resources puts teeth into this rule. The Fund also places pressure on a country to repurchase its currency with gold or an acceptable currency through a system of mandatory consultations.

In 1962 the Fund's resources were supplemented by the *General Arrangements to Borrow,* which were negotiated by ten industrial countries. Under this agreement the Fund may borrow up to $5.9 billion from the "Group of Ten" in order to provide compensatory financial assistance to one or more of the participating countries.[11] In 1970, the Fund activated an entirely new facility to supply reserve assets to its members, known as *Special Drawing Rights* or *SDR's.* SDR's are treated in the next chapter when we discuss the international liquidity problem.

ACTIVITIES OF THE FUND

From the start of operations in 1947 through April, 1971, the Fund sold $21.6 billion worth of currencies to its member countries. Most of this "lending" activity has occurred since 1956, when the Suez crisis compelled

---

[11] Participants in the General Arrangements, known as the "Group of Ten," are Belgium, Canada, France, Germany, Italy, Japan, Netherlands, Sweden, United Kingdom, and the United States. In 1964 Switzerland became an associate member.

many countries to come to the Fund for drawings and standby credits.[12] In the 1950's, almost all the drawings were made in U.S. dollars, but in the 1960's increasing use was made of other convertible currencies, such as the deutsche mark. These changes reflected, of course, the passing of the "dollar shortage" and the arrival of the "dollar glut" created by big United States payments deficits.

After a long period of relative quiescence, therefore, the Fund has become an important source of short-term compensatory financing for its member countries. The expansion of its resources has allowed the Fund to continue this active role in international finance.

In addition to acting as a secondary reserve, the Fund has also kept close watch over the exchange practices of its members. Since 1952 it has consulted annually with all Article XIV countries on the relaxation of exchange controls. It has sought to persuade countries to relax restrictions whenever conditions warranted, to abandon discriminatory currency practices, and to unify multiple exchange rates into a single rate. Toward these ends the Fund has given technical advice and assistance whenever requested, and its missions have visited many member countries. Through its publications and the speeches of its officials, the Fund has persistently warned against inflation and other sources of balance of payments disequilibrium and has urged member countries to adopt corrective policies consistent with the Fund's purposes.

EVALUATION OF THE FUND

The International Monetary Fund was originally intended to carry out its functions in a world economy enjoying a substantial degree of overall equilibrium and free of any persistent maladjustments, such as the dollar shortage or subsequent dollar glut. In such an economy, countries would adjust to temporary deficits in their balance of payments by resorting to their own reserves and, if necessary, to the resources of the Fund. Free convertibility would be maintained by all countries and exchange rates would be altered, after consultation with the Fund, only to correct a fundamental disequilibrium. In this way, the advantages of the gold standard—convertibility and stable exchange rates—would be gained while an occasional exchange devaluation would maintain equilibrium without the disadvantage of internal deflation. More specifically, the Fund was conceived as an antidote to the conditions of the 1930's. In those years convertibility was maintained between the dollar and the pound sterling (the key trading currencies), but its effects were compromised by disorderly exchange practices, including

---

[12] In 1947 eight European countries drew a total of $467 million from the Fund; then the Marshall Plan took over the job of compensatory financing. In the five years 1951-55, repurchases exceeded new drawings in every year, and at the end of 1955 the net amount of outstanding drawings was only $234 million.

competitive depreciation and the spread of exchange control to central and eastern Europe and to Latin America.

In the light of these observations, it is not surprising that the Fund could not fulfill its intended functions in the first decade of its existence. During those years nondollar countries showed persistent payments deficits and continued to restrict dollar payments. Moreover, unlike the 1930's, inflation rather than depression was the principal obstacle to external stability after World War II; and, with few exceptions, exchange rates were controlled to avert depreciation. During this period of restrictions and inconvertibility the Fund was mostly a bystander and little use was made of its resources. This passive role ended abruptly with the Suez crisis in 1956-57.

We can now see in retrospect that the Suez crisis coincided with the end of the dollar shortage—in 1958 the United States balance of payments suffered the first of a continuing series of big deficits which replaced the dollar shortage with a dollar glut. When called upon at the end of 1956, the Fund quickly responded with compensatory financial assistance that was needed to overcome the trade disruptions and fears of the time. The resumption of convertibility by Western European countries at the end of 1958 carried with it the widespread abandonment of exchange controls on current transactions and later, on capital transactions. With the accession of Japan to Article VIII in 1964, the Fund nearly achieved one of its basic purposes—the elimination of exchange controls for the bulk of world trade.

The return of convertibility, however, brought another problem in its wake—sudden, massive movements of speculative and flight capital among the financial centers of North America and Western Europe. As we shall see, this new source of instability, together with a progressive weakening of the dollar during the 1960's, ultimately forced a profound disruption of the Fund's par value system in 1971. We now turn to another aspect of the Bretton Woods monetary system as it evolved after World War II—the central reserve role of the U.S. dollar.

THE CENTRAL RESERVE ROLE OF THE U.S. DOLLAR

The Fund Agreement laid the basis for the international monetary system after World War II. But the system has evolved in a way that was not envisaged in that Agreement. During the 1950's the United States emerged as the prime reserve country with the dollar increasingly taking over the function of gold as an international reserve asset. No one planned this development; it arose as a response to the dominant postwar position of the United States in international trade and finance.[13] With well over

---

[13] As one writer put it, the dollar and the pound sterling ". . . became international currencies neither by Act of Congress (Parliament) nor by Act of God, but rather because they met various needs of foreign official institutions and foreign private parties more effectively than other financial assets could." See Robert Z. Aliber, *The Future of the Dollar as an International Currency* (New York: Praeger Publishers, 1966), p. 8.

half of all international money transactions being financed in terms of dollars, it became necessary for banks and business enterprises throughout the world to maintain dollar working balances. In the early fifties, as the European countries began to enjoy reserve surpluses, the most natural course of action for central banks was to convert those surpluses into dollar reserves rather than into gold. After all, interest could be earned on dollar assets and they could always be converted into gold at $35 per ounce if that ever became necessary.

The gold-exchange system that emerged in the 1950's is depicted in Figure 19-1. All of the non-Communist countries maintained a stable relationship between their currencies and the dollar either directly or through

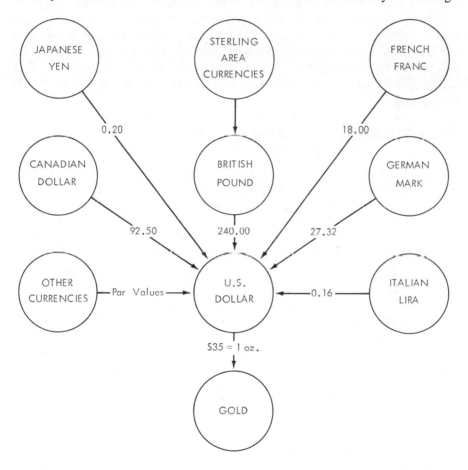

Note: Par values as of August 15, 1971, expressed as U.S. cents per currency unit.

Figure 19-1

THE CENTRAL RESERVE ROLE OF THE U.S. DOLLAR IN THE BRETTON WOODS INTERNATIONAL MONETARY SYSTEM

the British pound. For members of the Fund this relationship was expressed in the par values of their currencies; for nonmembers (the most important being Switzerland) it was a result of an autonomous stabilization policy. The U.S. dollar stood at the center of this system, and it was the only currency directly convertible into gold for official monetary purposes. Before World War I the pound sterling performed a similar function, but today the sterling area has shrunk to a small number of countries with mostly minor currencies.[14] In this limited fashion, the United Kingdom still operates as a central reserve country. As the Bretton Woods system evolved, however, the reserves of most countries became a mixture of gold and dollars, with a growing dominance of the latter.[15]

The extraordinary role of the dollar in the international monetary system has given the U.S. balance of payments a significance far transcending that of other countries' balances of payments. And it was the inability of the United States to restore equilibrium after more than a decade of deficits that proved the undoing of the Bretton Woods system. Before recounting that collapse, however, it is instructive to look at the U.S. balance of payments experience.

CONCEPTS OF SURPLUS AND DEFICIT IN THE U.S. BALANCE OF PAYMENTS

Since 1958 the United States has experienced a persistent deficit in its balance of payments. At first, the tendency was to regard these annual deficits as temporary in nature and not calling for any extraordinary measures by United States authorities. But by the fall of 1960 it had become obvious that the United States was facing a payments situation that was not self-corrective and showed signs of a disconcerting permanency.

The complexity of the United States balance of payments, the mutual interdependence of its individual items, the many factors—economic and political—that have a causal bearing on international transactions, and, in some instances, the lack of sound quantitative data—all of these circumstances have rendered impossible a precise determination of the cause or causes of the successive United States deficits. This is hardly surprising when we realize that a balance of payments is a summary of *all* the economic transactions between one country and the rest of the world over the year. It is also not surprising that economists should disagree—and sometimes sharply—as to the underlying cause or causes of the United States disequilibrium.

Analytical disagreements have inevitably engendered policy disagreements. All sorts of remedial measures have been urged upon the United

---

[14] The sterling area comprises members of the Commonwealth (excluding Canada), British possessions and trust territories, Iceland, the Irish Republic, Jordan, Kuwait, and Libya. These countries maintain all or part of their official reserves in the form of sterling balances.

[15] See Table 20-3 on p. 487.

States Government by American and European economists. These include the "classical medicine" of internal deflation, dollar depreciation, gold appreciation, floating exchange rates, capital issues control, orthodox measures to increase world liquidity, and a basic reform of the international monetary system. These policy recommendations have often been supported by cogent reasoning, but all of them have been controversial in one way or another. In the field of balance of payments analysis and policy, because of their extraordinary complexity, it is easy for highly trained economists to disagree among themselves—which they have done—over what is wrong with the United States balance of payments and what corrective action should be taken.

Surplus and deficit are economic concepts rather than accounting concepts, and there is disagreement as to the best way to measure disequilibrium in a balance of payments. Before looking at the United States payments situation, then, it will be instructive to describe briefly the three principal concepts of surplus and deficit.

We pointed out in Chapter 8 that the balance of payments always adds to zero because it is based on the principles of double-entry accounting. Thus, any concept of surplus and deficit involves a distinction between different items. In Chapter 8 we also discussed the theoretical distinction between autonomous and compensatory items, but in practice this distinction is not self-evident, depending in part on what the analyst is seeking to measure. The method of presenting a measure of surplus or deficit is to place some items "above the line" which are regarded as autonomous and the other items "below the line" which are viewed as financing the surplus or deficit (compensatory items).

Three concepts of surplus and deficit are currently used to measure the international payments position of the United States. Each concept has its advocates and critics. In appraising the balance of payments, it is important to know which concept is used and what it measures and does not measure. The three concepts are illustrated in Table 19-1 (page 466), which shows the U.S. balance of payments in 1970. Note the wide discrepancies among the basic, net liquidity, and official reserve deficits.

THE BASIC BALANCE

The *basic balance* is the sum of the balances on goods and services, unilateral transfers, and long-term private and government capital flows (items 1-5 in Table 19-1).[16] The key distinction of this concept is between long-term capital and short-term capital flows: all short-term capital flows (including official reserve transactions) are viewed as compensatory items. The basic balance comes closest to the theoretical concept of fundamental equilibrium introduced in Chapter 8. Except for military transactions and

---

[16] In the U.S. Department of Commerce presentation, the basic balance is designated as the "balance on current account and long-term capital."

Table 19-1

UNITED STATES BALANCE OF PAYMENTS IN 1970 SHOWING THE BASIC, NET LIQUIDITY, AND OFFICIAL RESERVE DEFICITS

(Billions of Dollars)

1. Net balance on goods and services [1]	3.6
2. Remittances, pensions, and other transfers	−1.4
3. U.S. Government grants [2]	−1.7
4. Long-term U.S. Government capital flows, net	−1.8
5. Long-term private capital flows, net	−1.5
6. *Basic balance* (1 + 2 + 3 + 4 + 5)	−3.0
7. Nonliquid short-term private capital flows, net [3]	−0.5
8. Allocations of Special Drawing Rights (SDR's)	0.9
9. Errors and omissions, net	−1.1
10. *Net liquidity balance* (Basic balance + 7 + 8 + 9)	−3.8
11. Liquid private capital flows: claims [4]	0.2
12. Liquid private capital flows: liabilities [5]	−6.2
13. *Official reserves transactions balance* (Net liquidity balance + 11 + 12)	−9.8
14. Nonliquid liabilities to foreign official agencies	−0.3
15. Liquid liabilities to foreign official agencies	7.6
16. U.S. official reserve assets	2.5
(a) Gold 0.8	
(b) SDR's −0.9	
(c) Convertible currencies 2.2	
(d) Gold tranche position in IMF 0.4	

Source: *Federal Reserve Bulletin* (Washington: U.S. Government Printing Office, December, 1971), Table 1, p. A74.

Note: Figures may not add because of rounding.

[1] Excludes military transfers under grants.
[2] Excludes military grants.
[3] Nonliquid short-term capital flows include changes in loans, collections, acceptance credits, and other credits to finance international trade.
[4] Changes in time and demand deposits and other negotiable instruments held abroad by U.S. residents.
[5] Changes in time and demand deposits and other negotiable instruments held in the United States by foreigners.

U.S. Government grants, the items that make up the basic balance are responsive primarily to economic conditions (prices, costs, consumer preferences, new products, etc.) and thereby reflect shifts in comparative advantage. Because it is not sensitive to short-run movements in interest rates, money market conditions, and foreign exchange speculation, the basic balance is intended to serve as an indicator of the long-term trends in the U.S. balance of payments.

THE NET LIQUIDITY BALANCE

The *net liquidity balance* is intended to measure changes in the liquidity position of the United States. To do so, it makes a distinction between *nonliquid* private short-term capital and *liquid* private short-term capital. The net liquidity balance is the sum of the basic balance plus net flows of nonliquid private short-term capital, allocations of Special Drawing Rights, and errors and omissions (items 7, 8, and 9 in Table 19-1). Another way to view the net liquidity balance is to look at the items below the net liquidity balance that finance it: net flows of U.S. and foreign liquid private short-term capital plus changes in liquid liabilities to central banks (foreign dollar reserves) and U.S. reserve assets.

THE OFFICIAL RESERVES TRANSACTION BALANCE

The *official reserves transactions balance* (also known as the official settlements balance) distinguishes between transactions of monetary authorities and all other transactions which are placed above this balance. Hence, it is the sum of the net liquidity balance and liquid private capital flows (items 11 and 12 in Table 19-1). It is intended to measure the net exchange market pressures on the dollar. The reserve balance is financed by changes in U.S. liquid liabilities to foreign central banks and U.S. official reserve assets (gold, SDR's, convertible currencies, and the gold tranche position in the IMF).

The main arguments favoring the use of the official reserves transactions balance are as follows:

1. Under the Bretton Woods international monetary system, national monetary authorities—central banks and Treasuries—are charged with the maintenance of stable exchange rates. As we learned in Chapter 7, they do this by providing the compensatory financing needed to equalize autonomous transactions in the foreign exchange market; that is, the amounts of foreign exchange supplied and demanded by persons, business firms, and nonmonetary government agencies.

2. In carrying out this stabilization, the monetary authorities gain or lose reserve assets (gold and foreign exchange) and experience a gain or loss in liabilities to foreign monetary authorities. Thus, the size of these reserve transactions is the best measure of the degree of intervention by monetary authorities in the foreign exchange market and hence of payments disequilibria.

3. Only monetary authorities have a responsibility to maintain stable exchange rates. The bulk of private international transactions is motivated by profit expectations which are not shared by monetary authorities. Thus, the distinction between monetary authorities, on the one hand, and all other participants in international transactions, on the other, is of great analytical significance.

4. Through the middle 1950's it was defensible to regard both private and official foreign liquid assets in the United States as foreign "reserves" without greatly distorting the facts. Thus, the liquidity concept was initially close to the official settlements concept. But today the principal currencies are freely convertible and there is a broad variety of financial transactions between private United States and foreign residents. The volume of liquid dollar assets held by foreign *nonmonetary* institutions has greatly increased primarily because of the need for higher levels of working capital to finance a growing volume of international trade and investment. To regard the increase in these liquid liabilities to foreign nonmonetary institutions as helping to finance a United States deficit is misleading.

Although conceding that the official reserves transactions balance is the best measure of changes in *actual* claims on U.S. reserve assets, some economists argue that the net liquidity balance is the best measure of the *potential* claims on U.S. reserve assets, since private foreign holders of dollars can sell them to their own monetary authorities. This point of view gained strength in 1969 and 1970 when substantial transfers were made between foreign private and official holders of dollars.

Furthermore, the official reserves balance is not a substitute for the basic balance. If our interest is not in the compensatory actions of monetary authorities but rather in the fundamental strength or weakness of the balance of payments, then the basic balance would appear to be superior to both the official reserves and net liquidity balances.

In closing, let us note that the controversy over the best way to measure disequilibrium in the United States balance of payments is not merely academic. The concept used will help shape attitudes toward the balance of payments and thereby influence United States payments policies.

U.S. PAYMENTS DEFICITS AND THEIR FINANCING

Table 19-2 indicates the net liquidity, official reserves, and basic deficits of the U.S. balance of payments in the 1960's and in 1970. Let us look first at the basic deficit.

THE BASIC BALANCE

During the period 1960-67, the *basic balance* was sustained by a merchandise trade surplus (ranging from $3.9 billion in 1967 to $6.8 billion in 1964) and a current account surplus inclusive of unilateral transfers (ranging from $1.8 billion in 1960 to $5.8 billion in 1964). The basic deficit in those years, therefore, is traceable to net outflows of long-term private and U.S. Government capital. The doubling of the basic deficit in 1967 is mainly attributable to sizeable increases in military expenditures and U.S. Government grants (current account items) and in U.S. Government capital outflows resulting from the step-up of the Vietnam war.

In 1968 the traditional merchandise export surplus nearly disappeared, dropping from $3.9 billion in 1967 to $0.6 billion. At the same time, the

Table 19-2

BASIC, NET LIQUIDITY, AND OFFICIAL RESERVE DEFICITS
IN THE U.S. BALANCE OF PAYMENTS, 1960-70
(Billions of Dollars)

Year	Net Liquidity Deficit	Official Reserves Deficit	Basic Deficit
1960	− 3.7	− 3.4	− 1.2
1961	− 2.2	− 1.3	0.0
1962	− 2.8	− 2.7	− 1.0
1963	− 2.6	− 1.9	− 1.3
1964	− 2.7	− 1.5	0.0
1965	− 2.5	− 1.3	− 1.8
1966	− 2.1	+ 0.2	− 1.6
1967	− 4.7	− 3.4	− 3.2
1968	− 1.6	+ 1.6	− 1.3
1969	− 6.1	+ 2.7	− 2.9
1970	− 3.8	− 9.8	− 3.0

Source: Federal Reserve Bank of St. Louis, *U.S. Balance of Payments Trends* (St. Louis: Federal Reserve Bank of St. Louis, 1972), p. 3.

current account balance became slightly negative (−$0.4 billion). But this deterioration was more than offset by an increase in foreign long-term capital inflows, much attracted by a buoyant stock market. Hence, the basic balance showed considerable improvement in 1968.

In 1969 the trade balance remained very weak (+$0.7 billion) while the current account deficit reached almost $1 billion. At the same time, the inflow of foreign long-term capital dropped by $2 billion. These developments brought about a sharp jump in the basic deficit. Although the trade surplus reached $2.1 billion in 1970 and the current account balance became positive (+$0.4 billion), this improvement was neutralized by deterioration in the long-term private capital account (item 5 in Table 19-1).

To sum up, the growth in the basic deficit in recent years is largely owing to a deterioration in the current account, especially in merchandise trade.[17] This experience has raised doubts about the competitive strength of the United States in the world economy.

THE NET LIQUIDITY AND OFFICIAL
RESERVES BALANCES

In the 1960's, the divergences between the basic balance and the *net liquidity balance* are attributable to changes in nonliquid short-term private capital flows and in errors and omissions, because Special Drawing Rights

---

[17] In 1971 the United States experienced its first trade deficit since 1888.

did not come into existence until 1970. In the period 1960-64, net flows of nonliquid private short-term capital ranged from −$0.7 billion (1962) to −$1.7 billion (1964), but they moderated in the period 1965-70, ranging from +$0.3 billion (1968) to −$0.6 billion (1969). In contrast, errors and omissions showed considerable variability throughout the 1960's, ranging from −$0.4 billion in 1966 to −$2.6 billion in 1969. Major shifts in errors and omissions were most likely induced by speculative capital movements.

Divergences between the net liquidity balance and the *official reserves balance* are mainly accounted for by shifts in liquid liabilities to private foreigners (item 12 in Table 19-1). In the period 1960-67, the two balances kept in fair agreement, changing in the same direction except in 1964 (when private liquid liabilities rose $1.0 billion). But in 1968 they recorded opposing balances, and in 1969 and 1970 they moved in the opposite directions. The big net liquidity deficit in 1969 (resulting from a $1.6 billion deterioration in the basic balance, a $2.1 billion deterioration in errors and omissions, and a $0.9 billion deterioration in nonliquid short-term capital) was more than offset by a massive inflow of foreign short-term capital (liquid liabilities to private foreigners rose from $3.8 billion in 1968 to $8.7 billion in 1969) to put the official reserves balance into surplus. In 1969, therefore, the divergence between the two balances was an enormous $8.8 billion. The very large inflows of foreign private short-term capital in 1968 and 1969 occurred when U.S. banks borrowed in the Eurodollar market in order to overcome stringent monetary conditions in the United States.[18] This borrowing drew not only on dollars generated by the net liquidity deficits in those years but also on foreign official reserves (item 15 in Table 19-1), which fell by $3.1 billion in 1968 and $0.5 billion in 1969. When monetary ease returned to the United States in 1970, however, this flow was reversed: U.S. banks paid back their Eurodollar loans (reducing liquid liabilities to private foreigners by $6.2 billion) while liquid liabilities to central banks (item 15 in Table 19-1) rose $7.6 billion.

This series of events demonstrates the extreme mobility of private short-term capital and the substitutive relationship between liquid liabilities to private foreigners and liquid liabilities to official foreigners. In 1968-70, therefore, the official reserves balance was remarkably volatilized by massive movements of interest-sensitive private short-term capital. In 1971 the official reserves balance continued to worsen as speculative capital outflows from the U.S. were added to the payback of Eurodollars, culminating in the August 15 declaration of inconvertibility by President Nixon.[19]

---

[18] For a description of the Eurodollar market, see pp. 492-494. U.S. banks borrowed Eurodollars mostly from their own branches in Europe.

[19] See p. 480 ff.

FINANCING THE U.S. DEFICITS

During the years 1958 through 1970, the United States experienced a cumulative reserve deficit of $26 billion. The United States financed this deficit by drawing on its gold reserves and by incurring liquid liabilities to foreign central banks. Table 19-3 records the changes in U.S. reserve assets during those years.

Table 19-3

RESERVE ASSETS OF THE UNITED STATES
(Billions of Dollars)

End of Period	Total Reserve Assets	Convertible Currencies	Reserve Position in IMF	SDR's	Gold Stock	Gold Stock as Fraction of Official Liquid Liabilities
1957	24.8		2.0		22.9	2.90
1960	19.4		1.6		17.8	1.75
1963	16.8	0.2	1.0		15.6	1.09
1966	14.9	1.3	0.3		13.2	0.96
1967	14.8	2.3	0.4		12.1	0.78
1968	15.7	3.5	1.3		10.9	0.88
1969	17.0	2.8	2.3		11.9	0.99
1970	14.5	0.6	1.9	0.9	11.1	0.59
1971 [a]	12.1	0.2	0.6	1.1	10.2	0.25

Source: *Federal Reserve Bulletin* (Washington: U.S. Government Printing Office, September, 1969), Table 4, p. A/5, and (December, 1971), Table 4, p. A77. Liquid liabilities to official institutions are shown in Table 19-4.
[a] August.

As a central reserve country, the international reserves of the United States consist mainly of gold. Gold reserves fell from $22.9 billion in 1957 to $11.1 billion at the end of 1970, or a total reduction of $11.8 billion. Exports of monetary gold, therefore, financed some 45 percent of the cumulative deficit. The other reserve assets provided only minimal compensatory financing for the period as a whole. The United States started using the currencies of other countries (mainly through bilateral swap agreements with foreign central banks) only in 1961, and SDR's were not activated until 1970.

The remaining cumulative deficit was financed primarily by an increase in liquid liabilities to official monetary institutions, as shown in Table 19-4. These liabilities rose from $7.9 billion in 1957 to $20.1 billion at the end of 1970, which is an increase of $12.2 billion.[20] This

---

[20] Additional compensatory financing was supplied by an increase in nonliquid liabilities to foreign official agencies (item 14 in Table 19-1) and by liabilities to the IMF arising out of gold transactions.

Table 19-4

U.S. LIQUID LIABILITIES TO FOREIGN COUNTRIES
(Billions of Dollars)

End of Period	Official Institutions	Banks and Other Private Foreigners	Total Liabilities
1957	7.9	5.7	13.6
1960	10.2	7.6	17.8
1963	14.4	9.2	23.6
1966	13.7	14.2	27.9
1967	15.6	15.8	31.4
1968	12.4	19.4	31.8
1969	12.0	28.2	40.2
1970	20.1	21.8	41.9
1971 a..............	40.7	17.2	57.9

Source: *Federal Reserve Bulletin* (Washington: U.S. Government Printing Office, December, 1971), Table 6, p. A78.
a August.

extraordinary rise in official liquid liabilities was possible only because of the central reserve role of the dollar. Dollars accumulated by foreign central banks were regarded as international reserve assets. A nonreserve country does not have this source of compensatory financing; it is compelled to rely on its own reserve assets and limited external assistance from the Fund and other agencies. Although foreign central banks became increasingly reluctant to add to their dollar reserves in the 1960's, as a group they had no alternative. By 1963 U.S. gold reserves barely covered liabilities to foreign central banks, and by the end of 1970 coverage had fallen to 59 percent. Any concerted attempt by central banks to convert their dollar holdings into gold, therefore, would have forced the United States to abandon gold convertibility, which was the foundation of the Bretton Woods system. As it turned out, a massive flight from the dollar in 1971 (financed by a truly fantastic increase in official liabilities from $20.1 billion at the end of 1970 to $40.7 billion by the end of August, 1971) persuaded the United States to halt gold convertibility on its own initiative on August 15, 1971.

REMEDIAL MEASURES TAKEN BY THE U.S. GOVERNMENT UP TO AUGUST 15, 1971

As we learned in Chapter 8, a country may adjust to a persistent deficit in its balance of payments in three broad ways: (1) through an internal deflation of prices and incomes relative to foreign prices and incomes; (2) through a devaluation of its exchange rate; or (3) through direct, nonmarket measures such as export promotion, exchange controls, and restrictions on trade and investment. In the 1960's the U.S. Government chose the third way by adopting an extraordinary variety of measures to directly influence all of the major classes of transactions making up the balance of payments.

MEASURES TO EXPAND EXPORTS

In 1960 the United States Government launched an Export Expansion Program to reinforce the marketing efforts of existing export enterprises and to induce domestic manufacturers to enter export markets for the first time. Run by the Department of Commerce, the program has many facets: regional export expansion councils composed of businessmen working closely with the regional Commerce offices, the establishment of permanent overseas trade centers for the exhibition of American products, trade mission programs involving trips abroad by businessmen and government officials to seek out new market opportunities, a program to encourage and assist American companies to participate in international trade fairs, as well as many supporting activities.

Adequate export financing at a reasonable cost is an important factor in making United States products competitive in foreign markets. In the 1960's the Export-Import Bank developed programs to provide various kinds of export credit, including long-term financing, medium-term guarantees against both commercial and political risks, and a short- and medium-term program operated by the Foreign Credit Insurance Association (FCIA) comprising seventy insurance companies. By insuring exports against nonpayment due to political risks and, in some instances, commercial risks as well, the Export-Import Bank and the FCIA make it easier for the exporter to obtain financing from his own bank and thereby sell his goods.[21]

In choosing export expansion over import restriction, the United States maintained its traditional policy favoring a liberal multilateral trading system. Indeed, the United States lowered its tariff after the Dillon and Kennedy Rounds.

MEASURES TO REDUCE U.S. GOVERNMENT OUTLAYS ABROAD

United States Government outlays abroad—military expenditures and foreign assistance to developing nations—are big debit items in the balance of payments. A sharp cutback in these outlays would go far toward eliminating the U.S. payments deficit, but only at the cost of sacrificing other key

---

[21] Established in 1934 by the U.S. Government, the Export-Import Bank makes long-term loans to foreign governments to finance the purchase of U.S. capital equipment in addition to providing financial assistance and guarantees to U.S. exporters. In 1972 the U.S. Government introduced a tax incentive to promote exports. Business firms are allowed to establish a Domestic International Sales Corporation (known popularly as DISC), whose activities are confined to export sales. Up to one-half of DISC income may be deferred from U.S. taxation when it is used for export development purposes.

objectives. This is a concrete illustration of what Chapter 11 calls the diversity and conflict of goals and the inadequacy of policy instruments.

The decision to station American troops in Western Europe and Japan was made by the United States Government in the late 1940's on military and political grounds. To call home these troops because they add to the payments deficit would entail the sacrifice of long-range political objectives, and the United States Government has clearly rejected this course of action. Nevertheless, in the early 1960's progress was made in reducing the *net* effect of military expenditures on the balance of payments. U.S. troops abroad were supplied to a greater extent with U.S. goods, cutting down on the foreign exchange cost of their maintenance. The United States also increased its military sales to foreign countries as offsets to its own military expenditures abroad. However, the effects of these measures were more than offset by rising military expenditures abroad after 1964 as the Vietnam war accelerated in tempo.

Nor did the United States abandon foreign assistance to the developing countries in the 1960's because of payments difficulties. But the net impact of each dollar of foreign assistance on the balance of payments was greatly reduced by tying government grants and credits to the procurement of U.S. goods and services. Most economists oppose tied grants and loans in principle because they distort the international allocation of goods and services. The tying of United States foreign aid, however, is a relatively mild form of restriction and its economic effects (as opposed to its payments effects) are probably minimal when account is taken of the quality and range of American production. This is not to say that tied assistance should become a permanent United States policy; it should be abandoned once the balance of payments deficit is overcome. Only by following an open policy itself can the United States hope to persuade other nations to stop tying their own foreign assistance.

MEASURES TO RESTRAIN U.S. PRIVATE CAPITAL EXPORTS

In the five years 1960-64 the outflow of United States private long-term capital jumped from $2.6 billion to $4.3 billion, and the outflow of short-term capital from $1.4 billion to $2.1 billion. This overall increase of $2.4 billion in United States capital outflows neutralized a good part of the improvement in the current account surplus recorded over the same period. U.S. officials had watched closely the size and growth of private capital exports, and the 1962 Revenue Act was intended to restrain direct investment in Western Europe and Japan. But *direct* action to curtail private capital outflows was not taken until 1963 (portfolio investment) and 1965 (direct investment and bank loans abroad).

The first direct action to lessen the outflow of private capital was the imposition in mid-1963 of an *interest equalization tax* on the value of foreign securities bought by U.S. residents. This tax, which was still in effect a decade later, has been effective in curbing the outflow of portfolio investment even though Canada, developing countries, and international financial agencies are granted exemptions. The tax has forced foreign borrowers to raise funds locally or in European capital markets.

The curtailment of United States portfolio investment after mid-1963 was more than offset in 1964 by a big jump in United States bank loans to foreign borrowers and a further growth in United States direct investments. This precipitated a series of measures called the voluntary restraint program.

In a special balance of payments message to Congress in February, 1965, President Johnson proposed a series of new steps to eliminate the payments deficit, including the application of the interest equalization tax to bank loans to foreigners of one year or more (except export credit), the voluntary cooperation of United States banks to limit their lending abroad, and the enlistment of United States business in a national campaign to limit direct investments abroad. Shortly thereafter, the Federal Reserve System and the Department of Commerce issued a set of guidelines to commercial banks and business corporations respectively, requesting them to achieve specified goals in restraining loans and investments abroad.

Although the voluntary program was successful in limiting the outflow of direct investment capital, it was replaced in 1968 by *mandatory investment controls* which still remain in existence. By compelling U.S. international enterprise to raise funds abroad to finance their foreign operations, these controls have greatly stimulated the development of the Eurodollar and Eurobond markets. The effects of the investment controls on the U.S. balance of payments are highly debatable, as is the role of direct investment in general. The controversy surrounding investment controls is taken up in Chapter 24.

MEASURES TAKEN BY U.S. MONETARY AUTHORITIES

Although compensatory financing is not an adjustment to a persistent deficit, the U.S. monetary authorities have sought to lessen the gold drain and forestall speculation by initiating measures that have been described as the "first line of defense" for the dollar.

Traditionally the United States has supported the dollar through a policy of passive stabilization. This policy shifted in May, 1961, when the United States Treasury actively intervened in the foreign exchange market for the first time since the early 1930's. Using its Exchange Stabilization Fund, the Treasury's first intervention was limited to sales of forward German marks to prevent excessive speculation in that currency which could lead to a flight from the dollar. Since then, it has extended its operations to other currencies in both spot and forward markets. Active stabilization of the dollar was massively reinforced in March, 1962, when the Federal Reserve System entered the foreign exchange market on its own account (for the first time since the late 1920's) rather than simply acting as an agent of the Treasury. In the ensuing years the United States monetary authorities have engaged in numerous transactions in all the leading currencies, mainly to prevent or moderate speculative capital movements in both the dollar and foreign currencies, especially the pound sterling.

As part of its new intervention activity, the Federal Reserve System entered into a series of reciprocal currency arrangements (commonly called *swap agreements*) with the central banks of Western Europe, Canada, and Japan. Under these bilateral arrangements a foreign central bank provides standby credits to the Federal Reserve System in return for an equal amount of standby credits. The credits are limited in size and must be liquidated (at the exchange rate prevailing at the time they were drawn) within three to twelve months, depending on the individual agreement. At the end of 1964 the total amount of swap standby credits was over $2.3 billion, but by 1971 it had climbed to $11.7 billion. The swap network has benefited foreign countries, such as Italy and Great Britain, by supplementing their reserves with an assured access to dollars, and, at the same time, has afforded the United States a buffer to absorb sudden speculative drives on the dollar and has thereby protected its gold reserves.

To reduce the "overhang" of United States liquid liabilities owing to foreign central banks, the United States Treasury has issued a series of medium-term bonds payable in dollars or in specified foreign currencies for sale to foreign governments and central banks. In effect, these sales of medium-term bonds relieved pressure on United States gold reserves by giving foreign central banks an opportunity to acquire an earning asset payable in their own currencies.

None of the foregoing measures introduced by the United States monetary authorities reduced the United States basic deficit. But they lessened the gold drain and dampened speculative capital outflows by influencing spot and forward rates of exchange (especially forward rates), by interposing a buffer of foreign central bank credits, and by converting a part of United States liquid liabilities to a less liquid, more stable form.

CONSTRAINTS IMPOSED ON U.S. PAYMENTS POLICY

In the 1960's, U.S. policy makers perceived many constraints that prevented them from making a fundamental adjustment to the balance of payments deficit. Conscious of U.S. leadership of the non-Communist world, they refused to cut back on military forces abroad or abandon foreign assistance to developing countries. Quite understandably, they also refused to deflate the economy in order to improve the balance of payments. In the first half of the 1960's, U.S. domestic policy was geared to expansion rather than contraction. Only in the late 1960's, when inflation got out of hand, did U.S. policy makers adopt anti-inflationary policies.

Why, then, did the United States not devalue the dollar in the 1960's? The answer to this question lies in the unique role of the dollar as a central reserve currency. This role conferred both benefits and costs on the United States. The clearest benefit was the willingness of foreign central banks to add dollars to their reserves, thus giving the United States a virtually unlimited and automatic access to compensatory finance and allowing it to postpone fundamental adjustment. The cost of this benefit was the commitment (as perceived by U.S. policy makers) to maintain a fixed link between the dollar and gold. Hence, the United States was not able to *initiate* a change in the external value of the dollar, which instead was dependent on the devaluations and revaluations of other currencies. It was also widely held that even if the United States did devalue the dollar by raising the price of gold, other countries would respond by devaluing their own currencies to the same extent and would thereby neutralize the effects of dollar devaluation on the balance of payments. There was also fear that a dollar devaluation would set off immense speculative activity endangering all countries. Only the monetary crisis of 1971 forced an abandonment of these perceptions and the undertaking of drastically new policies in August of that year. These new policies also underscored the weaknesses of the Bretton Woods system, which are examined in the next chapter.

SUMMARY

1. Agreement on the postwar international monetary system was reached at Bretton Woods, New Hampshire, in 1944. An international agency, the International Monetary Fund, was established to administer a code of fair exchange practices and provide compensatory financial assistance to member countries in balance of payments trouble.

2. In 1962, the Fund's resources ($28.5 billion in 1971) were supplemented by the *General Arrangements to Borrow,* which enable the Fund to borrow up to $5.9 billion from ten industrial countries (known as the "Group of Ten") to provide compensatory financial assistance to one or more of them. In 1970 the Fund activated an entirely new facility to supply reserve assets to its members, known as Special Drawing Rights or SDR's.

3. After World War II, the international monetary system evolved in a way that was not envisaged by the Bretton Woods Agreement. In the 1950's, the United States emerged as the prime reserve country, with the dollar increasingly taking over the function of gold as an international reserve asset.

4. Since 1958 the United States has experienced a persistent deficit in its balance of payments. Three concepts of surplus and deficit have been used by U.S. authorities in measuring disequilibrium in the balance of payments: the basic balance, the net liquidity balance, and the official reserves transactions balance. The United States has financed its reserve deficit by drawing down its gold reserves and by incurring liquid liabilities to foreign central banks.

5. The *basic balance* is the sum of the balances on goods and services, unilateral transfers, and long-term private and government capital flows. Hence, all short-term capital flows are viewed as compensatory items. The basic balance is intended to serve as an indicator of the long-term trends in the U.S. balance of payments.

6. The *net liquidity balance* is the sum of the basic balance plus net flows of nonliquid private short-term capital, allocations of Special Drawing Rights, and errors and omissions. It is financed by net flows of U.S. and foreign liquid private short-term capital and by changes in liquid liabilities to foreign central banks and U.S. reserve assets.

7. The *official reserves transactions balance* distinguishes between transactions of monetary authorities and all other transactions. As the sum of the net liquidity balance and liquid private capital flows, the reserve balance is intended to measure the net exchange market pressures on the dollar.

8. During the years 1958 through 1970, the United States experienced a cumulate reserve deficit of $26 billion, which was financed by drawing down its gold reserves and by incurring liquid liabilities to foreign central banks.

9. In the 1960's, the United States undertook a variety of measures to remedy its balance of payments deficit. These included efforts to expand exports, to reduce U.S. Government outlays abroad, to restrain U.S. private capital exports, to lessen the gold drain, and to discourage speculation. None of these measures involved a fundamental adjustment in the balance of payments. U.S. policy makers refused to cut back on military forces abroad, abandon foreign assistance to developing countries, deflate the economy, impose import restrictions, or devalue the dollar.

QUESTIONS AND APPLICATIONS

1. (a) What are the purposes of the International Monetary Fund?
   (b) What is the par value system of exchange rates?
   (c) What are the implications of the IMF rules on exchange rates?

2. Explain the compensatory financing system of the IMF.

3. "As the Bretton Woods system evolved, however, the reserves of most countries became a mixture of gold and dollars, with a growing dominance of the latter." Why did this development occur?

4. (a) Define the three concepts of deficit and surplus presented in this chapter. Which do you find most attractive? Why?
   (b) Trace the course of U.S. payments deficits since 1958.

5. (a) Describe the remedial measures undertaken by the U.S. Government before August 15, 1971, to overcome the deficit in the U.S. balance of payments.
   (b) Why did the United States not make a fundamental adjustment to its payments deficit in the 1960's by (1) deflating the domestic economy and/or (2) by devaluing the dollar?

SELECTED READINGS

See the list of readings given at the end of Chapter 20.

THE COLLAPSE AND REFORM OF THE BRETTON WOODS SYSTEM

In the 1960's the international monetary system was shaken by a series of crises in foreign exchange and gold markets. Although speculation against the dollar started as early as 1960, these crises became more frequent and more intense in the second half of the decade. Some of these crises were provoked by balance of payments disequilibria in non-dollar currencies accompanied by massive shifts of speculative funds among the major financial centers. But the most pervasive source of instability was the weakness of the dollar, which, given its role as the central reserve currency, raised doubts about the viability of the entire system.

MONETARY CRISES IN THE LATE 1960'S

In the middle 1960's, the continuing weakness of sterling (the second central reserve currency) was a major cause of disturbances in foreign exchange markets. Starting in June, 1967, tremendous speculative pressures built up against sterling, and in November it was officially devalued from $2.80 to $2.40. This action did not, however, restore stability in foreign exchange markets. Early in 1968, speculators turned to the London gold market in the expectation of a rise in the official price of gold. In order to maintain the London price at the official price of $35 an ounce, the United States and other members of the "gold pool" sold gold to the private market out of their own reserves.[1] During the first quarter of 1968, the United States lost $1.3 billion in gold, three-fourths of which went to support the London market.

This drain of official gold reserves to private speculators was stopped in March, 1968, when the gold pool members agreed to abstain from any further sales to the London market and also not to buy private gold in

---

[1] The gold pool was devised in 1961 by the United States, the United Kingdom, Belgium, Germany, Italy, the Netherlands, and Switzerland. The members of the pool agreed to share in the support of the London gold market.

the future. In this way there emerged the "two-tier" gold arrangement: an official price of $35 an ounce and a private price determined by private supply and demand. The decision to abandon all intervention in the London gold market served to freeze the amount of gold in official reserves—another step away from a gold-exchange standard and toward a dollar standard. Henceforth, central banks would engage in gold transactions only with other central banks.[2]

Scarcely had the gold crisis abated when France was racked by widespread student and worker protests in May and June, 1968. This political instability sparked a capital flight from the franc, especially into the German deutsche mark. Although French reserves fell drastically (France lost $2.8 billion in gold in 1968), the French government opted for exchange restrictions instead of devaluation. In 1969 there was a mounting expectation that the French deficit would force a devaluation of the franc while the German trade surplus would force a revaluation of the deutsche mark. Stability was eventually restored by a franc devaluation of 11.1 percent in August and the declaration of a higher par value for the deutsche mark in October.[3]

THE INTERNATIONAL MONETARY CRISIS OF 1971

Unlike the crises of the late 1960's, the crisis of 1971 was directly inspired by a loss of confidence in the dollar. In the third quarter of 1970, funds began to move at an enormous rate from the United States to financial centers in Europe and Japan. At first, these short-term capital flows were largely in response to interest-rate differentials, but in March, 1971 (when interest-rate differentials had narrowed), expectations of changes in exchange rates began to feed a growing speculation against the dollar. The ensuing sequence of events is presented in Table 20-1.

The actions taken by the United States on August 15 marked the end of the Bretton Woods system. On that day (a Sunday), President Nixon suspended "temporarily" the gold convertibility of the dollar and imposed a "temporary" surcharge on dutiable imports into the United States. He justified the suspension of convertibility as necessary to "defend the dollar against speculators" who "have been waging all-out war on the American dollar." But the more important purpose was to compel foreign governments to raise the value of their currencies against the dollar. In effect, foreign governments were offered a simple choice: continue to maintain existing exchange rates by accumulating more dollars without gold convertibility *or* revalue exchange rates. The import surcharge was intended to place further pressure on them; it would not be taken off until foreign governments altered their "unfair" exchange rates.

---

[2] Subsequently the IMF has purchased gold from South Africa under a bilateral agreement.

[3] The appreciation of the mark amounted to 9.29 percent. The mark was allowed to float freely for a month before the declaration altering its par value.

Table 20-1

COLLAPSE OF THE BRETTON WOODS SYSTEM:
A CHRONOLOGY OF EVENTS IN 1971

January February	Large movement of interest-sensitive funds from the United States to Europe, pushing European currencies against dollar ceilings.
March April	Overt speculation appears in foreign exchange markets. A strong trade surplus and restrictive credit policy intensify buying pressure on the deutsche mark. U.S. official reserve deficit for first quarter reaches $5.5 billion.
May 3-4 May 5	Bundesbank forced to absorb a capital inflow of $1 billion. Bundesbank suspends support of dollar after absorbing $1 billion in the first forty minutes of trading. Central banks of Netherlands, Switzerland, Belgium, and Austria also terminate support of the dollar.
May 10	When foreign exchange markets reopen, Swiss franc and Austrian schilling are devalued 7.07 percent and 5.05 percent, respectively, while German deutsche mark and Dutch guilder are allowed to float. Belgian market is split between official and financial markets.
June July	U.S. official reserves deficit soars to $11.3 billion for first half of year. U.S. trade deficit for second quarter is $1.0 billion. Outflow of speculative capital from United States continues. U.S. gold stock falls close to $10 billion.
August 1-14	U.S. Congressional subcommittee asserts dollar is overvalued; calls for general realignment of exchange rates. Abrupt acceleration of capital flight from dollar, which sells at its lowest level against the deutsche mark in twenty-two years.
August 15	President Nixon announces major new program: ninety-day freeze on wages and prices, new tax measures, 10 percent temporary surcharge on dutiable imports, and "temporary" suspension of the dollar's convertibility into gold.
August 16-20	West European governments keep their exchange markets closed. Fail to develop a coordinated response to U.S. measures.
August 23	European governments open foreign exchange markets on uncoordinated basis; each continues to adhere to pre-August 15 parity, but all except the French government cease to support the dollar. The French support commercial transactions market but not financial transactions market.
August 28	Japanese government suspends official intervention in the foreign exchange market. Yen immediately rises 4.7 percent.

(Continued)

Table 20-1

**COLLAPSE OF THE BRETTON WOODS SYSTEM:
A CHRONOLOGY OF EVENTS IN 1971
(Continued)**

September	Exchange rates of major trading currencies rise against the dollar except commercial rate for French franc. But it is not a "pure" float: many central banks continue to intervene on an ad hoc basis and some apply exchange restrictions.
September 15	Meeting of Finance Ministers of Group of Ten countries ends in total disagreement; U.S. demands—revaluation of other currencies, reduction in trade barriers, and more sharing of international defense burdens—shock foreign officials.
September 16	GATT urges the United States to end import surcharge.
October November	Pressure builds on the United States to end crisis; there is talk of retaliation in foreign countries. U.S. official reserves deficit reaches $12.1 billion for the first three quarters of year. Speculation intensifies.
December 1	U.S. Secretary of the Treasury surprises Group of Ten Finance Ministers at a meeting in Rome by suggesting a 10 percent dollar devaluation (rise in price of gold) as basis for negotiation.
December 14	At a meeting in the Azores, President Nixon and President Pompidou of France agree to work toward ". . . prompt realignment of currencies through devaluation of the dollar and revaluation of some other currencies."
December 17-18	Group of Ten Finance Ministers meet at Smithsonian Institution in Washington, D.C. United States agrees to 8.57 percent devaluation of the dollar (rise in price of gold per ounce from $35 to $38) and end of surcharge in return for revaluation of other currencies. President Nixon hails outcome as "the most significant monetary agreement in the history of the world."

The immediate response to the U.S. actions was a closing of foreign exchange markets in Europe and Japan. When they reopened, all of the major foreign currencies were left to float vis-à-vis the dollar with the exception of the French franc. Hence, the system depicted in Figure 19-1 no longer existed; the Bretton Woods system had died and a new system was waiting to be born.

THE SMITHSONIAN AGREEMENT

The weeks following August 15 were rife with uncertainty, rumor, and tension. Taking a hard line, the U.S. Government pressed the view that the dollar's troubles arose from the undervalued exchange rates, protectionist trade policies, and the inadequate defense-sharing expenditures of foreign governments. It demanded unilateral concessions in all three areas. Put on the defensive, the European and Japanese governments firmly resisted any change in the par values of their currencies, fearing the harmful consequences of revaluation on their exports and domestic economic situations. If the dollar is overvalued, they argued, then the United States should find a way to carry out a unilateral devaluation.

Meanwhile most of the leading currencies were floating at higher dollar values, but it was not a "clean" float as central banks intervened in the market to prevent a full appreciation. France refused to float its currency for commercial transactions although it permitted a floating rate for financial transactions. Foreign governments were reluctant to let their currencies float freely because they hoped to persuade the United States to devalue the dollar by raising the price of gold.

International monetary negotiations were undertaken within the framework of the Group of Ten. The first meeting in London on September 15-16 ended without an agreement. Sticking to its initial position, the United States demanded exchange rate adjustments that together with trade and defense-sharing concessions would produce a "turnaround" in the U.S. balance of payments of no less than $13 billion a year. A second meeting in Washington on September 26 also failed to resolve the crisis. It became evident that the United States was willing to let the crisis smoulder in order to attain its objectives. In October, when speculation against the dollar carried its "weighted" depreciation in foreign exchange markets to 7 percent, the American tactic of delay gained in strength.

At its third meeting in Rome on November 30, the Group of Ten started negotiations on a realignment of currencies for the first time. Although no agreement was forthcoming, the U.S. Secretary of the Treasury stated that those attending the meeting had discussed many hypothetical situations (including a 10 percent devaluation of the dollar) and the specific terms of a realignment of currencies. Retreating somewhat from its earlier position, the United States offered to accept a weighted depreciation of 11 percent, which would help the U.S. balance of payments by an estimated $9 billion. Continuing to insist on the need to increase the price of gold, the Europeans pointed to the problem of cross-rates among their own currencies. If the deutsche mark were to be revalued, say, 10 percent while the French franc remained unchanged, then France would obtain a 10 percent trading advantage against Germany. But if the dollar were devalued by 5 percent (through an appropriate increase in the price of gold), then the deutsche mark need be revalued only 5 percent and thereby confer only a 5 percent advantage on the franc. Free trade in the EEC and EFTA made cross-rates a prime concern to the Europeans, but the Japanese were also vitally interested in the value of the yen vis-à-vis European currencies.

The Rome meeting set the scene for the final act of the drama. At a meeting with President Georges Pompidou of France in the Azores on December 14, President Nixon agreed to include a dollar devaluation in a general realignment of currencies. The details of this realignment were worked out by the Group of Ten on December 17-18 in a meeting at the Smithsonian Institution in Washington. The Smithsonian Agreement was then formalized by the International Monetary Fund, which established a "temporary regime" allowing member countries to vary their exchange rates within margins of 2¼ percent on either side of the new "central rates" resulting from the currency realignment.[4] In return for the revaluation of other currencies, the United States agreed to raise the price of gold from $35 an ounce to $38 an ounce (a dollar devaluation of 8.57 percent), subject to the approval of Congress, and to immediately "suppress" its 10 percent import surcharge.

The new central rates of the currencies of the Group of Ten countries are shown in Table 20-2. The Japanese yen and the deutsche mark underwent the highest appreciations, followed by the Belgian franc and Dutch guilder. The French franc and British pound retained their old par values, and consequently their appreciation is entirely owing to the devaluation of the dollar. The Italian lira and the Swedish krona have central values lower than their old par values, thereby neutralizing some of the dollar devaluation.

The Smithsonian Agreement gave the United States the currency realignment it had requested in return for a modest rise in the price of gold, a

Table 20-2

CENTRAL RATES OF GROUP OF TEN CURRENCIES RESULTING FROM SMITHSONIAN AGREEMENT OF DECEMBER 18, 1971

Currency	Central Rates Expressed in Currency Units Per U.S. Dollar	Percentage Appreciation Vis-à-Vis U.S. Dollar
Belgian franc	44.81	+11.57
Canadian dollar [1]	—	—
French franc [2]	5.12	+ 8.57
German deutsche mark	3.22	+13.58
Italian lira	581.50	+ 7.48
Japanese yen	308.00	+16.88
Netherlands guilder	3.24	+11.57
Swedish krona	4.81	+ 7.49
British pound [2]	0.38	+ 8.57

Source: International Monetary Fund, *International Financial News Survey* (Washington: International Monetary Fund, December 22-30, 1971), p. 421.

[1] Floating rate established on June 1, 1970.
[2] Old par values.

---

[4] Those countries (notably France and the United Kingdom) which did not have new central values for their currencies were also free to choose the wider margins. Central rates could be converted into par values at the discretion of the individual member countries.

concession having no economic significance while the dollar remained inconvertible. More importantly, it was an achievement of international monetary cooperation, a triumph of enlightened self-interest over economic nationalism. It reflected the universal acceptance of the need for agreed rules to govern exchange rates and exchange practices. Hence, the collapse of the Bretton Woods system on August 15 did not degenerate into chaos as did the collapse of the international gold standard in the early 1930's. For all of its weaknesses, the Bretton Woods system had fostered intimate monetary cooperation on an unprecedented scale through the institutional machinery of the IMF and the Group of Ten. When the crunch came, this machinery proved equal to the challenge.

The Smithsonian Agreement resolved the immediate monetary crisis, but it did not tackle the problems of a durable monetary reform. The closing paragraph of the press communiqué announcing the Smithsonian Agreement outlines the dimensions of this grand task:

> The Ministers and Governors agreed that discussions should be promptly undertaken, particularly in the framework of the International Monetary Fund, to consider reform of the international monetary system over the longer term. It was agreed that attention should be directed to the appropriate monetary means and division of responsibilities for defending stable exchange rates and for insuring a proper degree of convertibility of the system; to the proper role of gold, of reserve currencies, and of special drawing rights in the operation of the system; to the appropriate volume of liquidity; to re-examination of the permissible margins of fluctuation around established exchange rates and other means of establishing a suitable degree of flexibility; and to other measures dealing with movements of liquid capital. It is recognized that decisions in each of these areas are closely linked.[5]

WEAKNESSES OF THE BRETTON WOODS SYSTEM

Successful international monetary reform demands a diagnosis of the ills of the Bretton Woods system as well as the prescription and implementation of the appropriate remedies. In this and the final section we sketch the weaknesses of the Bretton Woods system and the principal proposals for reform.

The poor performance of the Bretton Woods system in the 1960's is attributable mainly to three interrelated causes: (1) the problem of international liquidity formation centered on the dollar; (2) delays in balance

---

[5] International Monetary Fund, *International Financial News Survey* (Washington: International Monetary Fund, December 22-30, 1971), p. 417. The fragility of the Smithsonian currency realignment was forcefully demonstrated in February, 1973, (as this book was going to press) when the dollar was devalued a further 10 percent (raising the official price of gold from $38.00 to $42.22 an ounce) and the Japanese yen was left to float. This new crisis underscored the need for a fundamental reform of the international monetary system.

of payments adjustment; and (3) disequilibrating short-term capital movements.

THE PROBLEM OF INTERNATIONAL
LIQUIDITY FORMATION

International liquidity is the world's supply of gold, foreign exchange, and other assets ("owned" reserves) that are freely usable to finance payments deficits plus available facilities for borrowing them ("borrowed" reserves). Over the longer run, the growth of international liquidity is dependent on the growth of international reserve assets or owned reserves. Table 20-3 depicts the growth and composition of reserve assets between the end of 1959 and the end of September, 1971.

The most striking feature of Table 20-3 is the prominence of the U.S. dollar. During this period, nearly all the growth in total reserves ($59.9 billion) has come from an increase in the dollar holdings of foreign central banks—an increase of $35.6 billion in recorded U.S. liabilities and an increase of $17.1 billion in the "difference," which consists mostly of Eurodollar holdings.[6] The remaining growth ($7.2 billion) came from increases in reserve positions in the IMF and the creation of SDR's after 1969. Sterling reserves were stable over the period while gold reserves actually decreased by $1.7 billion. As noted earlier, no gold has been purchased by the major central banks from private sources since the agreement of March, 1968.

The Dependence of Reserve Formation on U.S. Deficits. As the Bretton Woods system has actually functioned, therefore, most of the growth in international reserves has come from an increase in U.S. liabilities to foreign central banks. This growth was not planned; it was the result of U.S. balance of payments deficits. In particular, the growth had nothing in common with the required level of international liquidity. If the U.S. deficit were to turn into a surplus, then dollar reserves would fall regardless of the need for international liquidity. More fundamentally, the dollar could not supply new reserves on a sustainable basis over the long run because of an inherent contradiction of the gold-exchange standard. A sustained increase in the official liabilities of the central reserve country would eventually reduce the gold cover below 100 percent (as happened to the dollar in the mid-1960's) and a continuing increase would cause a progressive loss of confidence in the gold convertibility of the reserve currency. At some point, foreign central banks would force a breakdown of the system by demanding gold from the central reserve country or the central reserve country itself would declare its currency no longer convertible into gold. As we have seen, the latter happened on August 15, 1971, and its effect was to transform the

---

[6] The Eurodollar market is discussed on pp. 492-494, in this chapter.

Table 20-3

GROWTH AND COMPOSITION OF INTERNATIONAL
RESERVES OF IMF MEMBER COUNTRIES
(End of Period—Billions of Dollars)

Reserve Asset	1959	1965	1968	1969	1970	1971 [a]	Increase (+) or Decrease (−) 1959-71
Gold	37.9	41.9	38.9	39.1	37.2	36.2	− 1.7
Foreign exchange.	16.2	23.8	31.9	32.3	44.5	68.9	+ 52.7
U.S. dollar	10.1	15.8	17.5	16.0	23.9	45.7	+ 35.6
U.K. pound	7.0	7.1	9.7	8.9	6.6	7.1	+ 0.1
Difference	−0.9	0.9	4.7	7.4	14.0	16.2	+ 17.1
Reserve positions in Fund	3.2	5.4	6.5	6.7	7.7	6.3	+ 3.1
Special Drawing Rights (SDR's) ...	—	—	—	—	3.1	5.9	+ 5.9
Total reserves ...	57.4	71.0	77.3	78.2	92.5	117.3	+ 59.9

Source: International Monetary Fund, *International Financial Statistics* (Washington: International Monetary Fund, February, 1970), pp. 13 and 15, and (February, 1972), pp. 18 and 23.
General Note: Totals may not add because of rounding. *Foreign exchange* mostly consists of U.S. liabilities to foreign official holders and, to a much lesser extent, U.K. liabilities to foreign official holders. From 1968, most of the *Difference* is attributable to official holdings of Eurodollars, which do not appear as U.S. liabilities to *official* holders. *Reserve positions in the Fund* equal member countries' gold tranches plus the Fund's use of their currencies for drawings or gold purchases. *SDR's* are unconditional reserve assets created by the Fund.
a End of September, 1971.

international monetary system from a gold-dollar standard into a pure dollar standard, a most fragile arrangement because of the reluctance of foreign central banks to add more dollars to their reserves.

The liquidity problem of the Bretton Woods system, therefore, is two-fold. In the short run, the amount of liquidity is dependent on erratic swings in the U.S. balance of payments, and in the long run, the dollar cannot be counted on to supply new liquidity.

How much international liquidity is needed? There is no simple answer to this question because it depends on the level of reserves each country *thinks* it should hold and the level it *actually* holds as a consequence of its policies. More generally, too much international liquidity is inflationary because countries are under little compulsion to make fundamental adjustments to deficits; too little liquidity, on the other hand, forces countries to respond quickly to deficits by imposing restrictions, deflating their economies, or devaluing their exchange rates. If the supply of international liquidity does not keep pace with demand, then countries will seek to obtain reserves from each other with the danger that they will slow down real economic growth in order to generate export surpluses or use restrictions to protect existing reserves.

In the 1960's there was widespread concern over the adequacy of international liquidity because of the expectation that the dollar would not continue to supply new reserves. Facilities for borrowed reserves were improved, notably by increasing the IMF quotas and strengthening the swap network among central banks. But borrowed reserves make no permanent contribution to the world's liquidity. Hence, attention was devoted to a scheme for the deliberate creation of a new reserve asset that came to be known as Special Drawing Rights.

Special Drawing Rights. SDR's constitute international reserve assets that may be used in the settlement of balance of payments deficits by countries participating in the Special Drawing Account administered by the International Monetary Fund. A decision to create SDR's requires the approval of a majority of the member countries holding 85 percent of the weighted voting power of the Fund. Once created, SDR's are distributed to participants in proportion to their Fund quotas. In 1969 it was agreed to allocate SDR's to the 104 participants in three annual stages: January 1, 1970 (SDR 3.4 billion); January 1, 1971 (SDR 2.95 billion); and January 1, 1972 (SDR 2.95 billion).[7]

Actually SDR's are merely bookkeeping entries punched out on a computer tape. What makes them a reserve asset is the commitment of the participating countries to accept SDR's in exchange for a convertible currency up to an amount equal to three times their own SDR allocations. Only one constraint is placed on a country's use of its SDR's for balance of payments settlements. It is expected to maintain over a five-year period average holdings of SDR's equal to 30 percent of its cumulative allocations. A country does not buy its SDR's, but all allocations of SDR's are subject to a charge of 1½ percent a year while member holdings of SDR's earn 1½ percent a year.[8] Once placed on the books of the IMF, SDR's remain in existence as a permanent addition to the world's reserve assets.

Ironically the first activation of SDR's coincided with a massive build-up of dollar reserves as short-term capital moved out of the United States in 1970 and 1971. As Table 20-3 indicates, total reserves rose from $78.2 billion to $117.3 billion between the end of 1969 and September, 1971. Instead of a liquidity shortage, there was a liquidity surplus. Although the SDR facility has not solved the liquidity problem, it opens up the possibility of a gradual replacement of dollars with SDR's in international reserves. In that event, the dollar would eventually lose its role as a reserve currency,

---

[7] One SDR unit is equal to one U.S. dollar of the 1944 gold content. As a result of the U.S. decision to raise the price of gold to $38 an ounce, the SDR unit now equals $1.08.

[8] Thus, a country that does not use its SDR's comes out even.

giving ground to an SDR-gold standard or an SDR standard.[9] Reserve creation would no longer be dependent on U.S. deficits but rather on the collective judgment of the IMF member countries.

INADEQUATE ADJUSTMENT MECHANISM

In accordance with the Bretton Woods Agreement, countries were expected to maintain stable exchange rates (within a band of 1 percent on either side of par values) and alter the par values of their currencies only to adjust to a fundamental disequilibrium in the balance of payments. In practice, the United States dollar emerged as the central reserve currency with a fixed parity while the other major currencies tended to maintain their parities even in the face of prolonged disequilibria. This almost rigid adherence to exchange parities encouraged speculation, provoked crises, and delayed adjustment.

Movements in the parities of the major currencies are depicted in Figure 20-1 (page 490) for January, 1947, to June, 1970. Note the small number of parity adjustments. Furthermore, when parity changes were made, they were usually in a downward direction that devalued the currencies vis-à-vis the dollar. For the period as a whole, all currencies lost value vis-à-vis the dollar except the Swiss franc and Japanese yen, which maintained the same parity. As a consequence, the dollar became substantially revalued in terms of other major currencies, and even when it became apparent in the 1960's that the dollar had become overvalued, upward adjustments in parities occurred only rarely in crisis situations. Ultimately, the United States was compelled to take unilateral action in order to achieve a currency realignment.

It is now widely accepted that exchange rates must become more flexible, given the unattractive alternative adjustment mechanisms of deflation and controls. Specific proposals to introduce more flexibility are cited in a subsequent section.

DISEQUILIBRATING SHORT-TERM CAPITAL MOVEMENTS

A third source of weakness in the Bretton Woods system as it functioned in the 1960's was the enormous flow of disequilibrating short-term capital between the major financial centers. The emergence of a truly integrated international capital market based on Eurodollars created a growing pool of liquid funds which could be rapidly switched from one center to another in response to interest-rate differentials (interest arbitrage)

---

[9] The dollar would still remain the major *intervention* currency (the currency used by central banks to maintain exchange stability) and the major *vehicle* currency (the currency used in the settlement of private international commercial and financial transactions).

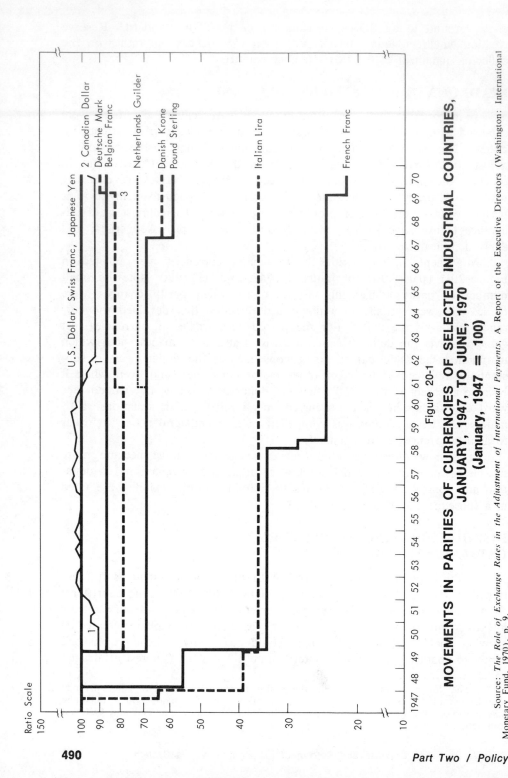

MOVEMENTS IN PARITIES OF CURRENCIES OF SELECTED INDUSTRIAL COUNTRIES, JANUARY, 1947, TO JUNE, 1970

(January, 1947 = 100)

Figure 20-1

Source: *The Role of Exchange Rates in the Adjustment of International Payments*, A Report of the Executive Directors (Washington: International Monetary Fund, 1970), p. 9.

1 The rates indicated are the par values agreed with the Fund except in the following cases: Swiss franc (nonmember currency); Japanese yen, to May, 1953; French franc, January, 1948, to March, 1960; Italian lira, to December, 1960; Canadian dollar, see footnote 2.

2 Fluctuating rate, September 30, 1950, to May 1, 1962; and June 1, 1970—.

or to expected adjustments in exchange rates.[10] Table 20-4 reveals the dramatic buildup of short-term capital movements between the major industrial countries in the period 1960-70. Observe that the massive outflow from the United States in 1970 was received mainly by West Germany.

Table 20-4

NET PRIVATE SHORT-TERM CAPITAL MOVEMENTS OF MAJOR INDUSTRIAL COUNTRIES, 1960-63, 1965, 1968-70
(Billions of Dollars)

Country	Average 1960-63	1965	1968	1969	1970
United States	−1.5	−0.7	3.0	5.6	−8.4
United Kingdom ..	0.4	0.5	−2.0	0.0	1.7
West Germany ...	0.4	0.7	1.9	1.5	6.5
France	0.0	−0.2	−1.6	0.7	1.4
Italy	−0.4	−1.6	−2.4	−1.9	−1.0
Japan	0.4	−0.4	0.1	−1.2	0.6
Canada	0.3	−0.3	−1.1	−1.3	−0.6
Switzerland	0.6 [a]	0.2 [a]	0.6	0.8	1.2
Gross movement [1] ...	4.0	4.6	12.7	13.0	21.4

Source: International Monetary Fund, *1967 Annual Report,* Tables 20 and 21, p. 34; and *1971 Annual Report,* Table 26, p. 86.
Note: Data include Errors and Omissions entries of respective balances of payments. Minus sign indicates capital outflow.
[a] Includes direct investment capital.
[1] Disregarding sign.

The quick transfer of billions of dollars from one center to another had (and still has) two broad consequences. First, it limits the freedom of national authorities to use monetary policy for domestic stabilization by intensifying the conflict between external and internal balance as depicted in Figure 11-2 on p. 263. When interest rates in one center rise above those in other centers, funds immediately leave the country with the lower rates, and vice versa. More often than not, these shifts of funds are disequilibrating for the domestic economy and/or the balance of payments. In 1969 high interest rates in the United States attracted billions of dollars from European centers. Although this inflow improved the official reserves balance, it also partly nullified the anti-inflationary policies of the U.S. Government by swelling the money supply. In 1971 high interest rates in West Germany (induced by a restrictive monetary policy to impede inflation) drew in billions of dollars from abroad, thereby inducing further inflation and adding to a huge balance of payments surplus. Indeed, liquid funds have become so

---

[10] Exchange speculation, capital flight, hedging, interest arbitrage, and forward exchange speculation are discussed in Chapter 7.

sensitive to money market conditions in major-currency countries that some economists advocate using monetary policy primarily for balance of payments purposes while domestic stabilization is left to fiscal policy.

A second consequence of the high international mobility of liquid capital was (and is) its disequilibrating impact on foreign exchange markets. In the 1960's speculation *against* currencies was demonstrably generated by delays in exchange rate adjustments. Deficit countries refused to devalue until it became obvious that they had to do so. Thus, speculators enjoyed a "no-lose" situation since the *direction* of any adjustment was certain (if not its precise timing) and it most probably would be substantial.

The term "speculator" has an invidious connotation, conjuring up the image of a shady character who is immoral, if not illegal, in his actions. President Nixon made use of this image when on August 15, 1971, he blamed speculators for waging an "all-out war on the American dollar." In truth, most of the speculators responsible for large-scale international transfers of funds are respectable bankers, traders, and financial executives of multinational corporations. The bulk of interest-induced transfers of capital is undertaken by large commercial banks and, to a much lesser extent, by managers seeking to maximize earnings on corporate cash assets. Capital flows in response to expected adjustments in parity exchange values are largely undertaken by traders and corporate managers to "cover" against the risk of exchange losses and, less commonly, to make a speculative gain. In addition to hedging in forward markets, exporters and importers try to speed up payments from a "weak-currency" country and, at the same time, delay payments to that country. Financial executives in multinational corporations strive to avert devaluation losses by moving funds from weak-currency countries to strong-currency countries, as well as by hedging. Since international corporations hold billions of dollars of liquid funds, the aggregate effect of their individual decisions can place tremendous pressure on an already weak currency. From the perspective of international traders and managers, however, the shifting of funds from one financial center to another is intended only to protect them against exchange losses, not to undermine a currency. A corporate treasurer would look very foolish (and possibly lose his job) if he were to hold a sizable quantity of a currency at the time of its devaluation.

The Eurodollar Market. The tremendous international flows of speculative short-term capital that began in the late 1960's were remarkably facilitated by the rapid growth of the Eurodollar market. Here we can only describe briefly the principal features of this novel international institution.[11]

---

[11] For a treatment of the theoretical aspects of the Eurodollar market, see Helmut W. Mayer, "Some Theoretical Problems Relating to the Euro-dollar Market," *Essays in International Finance No. 79* (Princeton: Princeton University Press, February, 1970); and Fritz Machlup, "Euro-dollar Creation: A Mystery Story," *Reprints in International Finance No. 16* (Princeton: Princeton University Press, December, 1970).

What are Eurodollars? Quite simply, Eurodollars are dollars that are deposited in foreign commercial banks (including the foreign branches of U.S. banks), for the most part in Europe. It is the foreign location of the banks that distinguishes Eurodollars from ordinary dollar deposits in U.S. banks. Eurodollars come into existence when someone transfers dollars from a U.S. bank to a foreign bank or when someone converts a foreign currency into dollars which are then deposited in a foreign bank. Actually the dollars underlying the Eurodollars resulting from such transfers never leave the U.S. banking system. A foreign bank accepting dollar deposits acquires a dollar balance in a U.S. bank, and when it lends Eurodollars, it draws down its U.S. dollar balance. Hence, transactions in the Eurodollar market involve shifts in the ownership of bank balances in the United States.

Some economists believe there is a third source of Eurodollars, namely, their creation through a fractional-reserve system in much the same way as occurs in domestic banking systems. In that event, the total quantity of Eurodollars can exceed the underlying dollar balances. As a corollary, the Eurodollar market then not only facilitates the international transfer of liquid funds, but also adds to their supply.[12]

Although centered in London, the Eurodollar market is dominated by the European branches of the leading American banks. Banks seek out Eurodollar deposits from individuals, banks, international traders, multinational corporations, and government agencies throughout the world by offering higher rates of interest than domestic banks.[13] In turn, banks lend out Eurodollars to the same groups at rates that are frequently lower than domestic rates. This is possible because the spread between borrowing and lending rates is smaller than in domestic markets as a consequence of the large size of most Eurodollar transactions and intense competition. Eurobanks, therefore, serve as intermediaries in a global money market whose size was estimated at $65 billion in 1971, of which the dollar component was about $51 billion.[14]

---

[12] For opposing views on the creation of Eurodollars through a multiple expansion of bank credit, see Fred H. Klopstock, "The Euro-dollar Market, Some Unresolved Issues," *Essays in International Finance No. 65* (Princeton: Princeton University Press, March, 1968); and Milton Friedman, "The Euro-dollar Market: Some First Principles," *Federal Reserve Bank of St. Louis Review* (July, 1971), pp. 16-24.

[13] Most Eurodollar deposits are demand or time deposits of less than thirty days. Many countries prohibit the payment of interest on domestic demand deposits, and in the United States the prohibition also covers time deposits of less than thirty days (Regulation Q).

[14] Any currency can assume "Euro" form when it is held as commercial bank deposits outside the home country. Deutsche marks and Swiss francs are the most common nondollar currencies used in this way. Hence, the Eurodollar market is more correctly described as a "Eurocurrency" market. But even this designation is somewhat misleading because some Eurocurrency deposits are held by banks located outside Europe, such as in Singapore. In brief, the Eurodollar market has become a market for borrowing and lending the world's major convertible currencies. The estimate of its size is taken from *International Financial News Survey* (December 22-30, 1971), pp. 422-423.

The development of the Eurodollar market was made possible by the establishment of free convertibility among the major currencies at the end of 1958, and by the broad acceptance of the dollar as an international transactions currency. But its explosive growth in the 1960's is mainly attributable to the U.S. balance of payments and the policies adopted to correct it. On the one hand, the persistent U.S. deficits continually added to the supply of dollars in foreign banks and, on the other hand, U.S. restrictions on capital exports (starting with the Interest Equalization Tax of 1963 and culminating with mandatory investment controls in 1968) stimulated the demand for Eurodollar funds by American companies operating abroad. The effect of these restrictions, therefore, was to move the international money market from New York, where it was subject to regulation, to Europe, where it is free of regulation.[15]

Today the Eurodollar market has become an indispensable element of the international financial system. Much of the growth in international trade and investment in the late 1960's was financed through this market. Because it mobilizes and allocates funds on a global basis free of government regulation, the Eurodollar market approaches the ideal allocating mechanism of economic theory. But, as already noted, the efficiency of this mechanism also enables banks, multinational enterprises, and speculators to transfer billions of dollars almost instantaneously from a weak-currency country to a strong-currency country. Certainly the architects of the Bretton Woods system did not foresee the grave threat to exchange stability that is posed by such a huge pool of liquid funds.

Curbing Disequilibrating Short-term Capital Movements. The large disruptive flows of short-term capital in recent years have drawn attention to measures to curb them. Many industrial countries (including the United States) have tried to influence or restrict such flows through a variety of special techniques: imposing selective taxation, limiting the foreign lending or borrowing of domestic commercial banks, prohibiting the payment of interest on foreign-held demand and time deposits, imposing reserve requirements on the foreign borrowings of domestic banks, intervening in forward markets, imposing selective exchange controls, and others. These techniques have often proved effective in influencing changes in the foreign assets and liabilities of domestic commercial banks, but they have had little or no effect on the short-term borrowing and lending by domestic nonbank business firms, to say nothing of leads and lags in international payments.[16]

---

[15] Since the Eurodollar market only supplies short- and medium-term financing, the need of American companies to raise investment capital abroad to finance their foreign operations gave a strong boost to the Eurobond market. Eurobonds are long-term debt securities denominated in dollars or in other convertible currencies which are offered outside the country of the borrower. Dollar Eurobonds are sold only outside the United States, mainly in Europe. Hence, the Eurobond market is foreign both to borrowers and to most investors.

[16] Arthur I. Bloomfield, "Controlling Private Short-Term Capital Outflows from the U.S.," *Wharton Quarterly* (Summer, 1971), p. 9.

By and large, the industrial countries have avoided comprehensive exchange controls over short-term capital movements even though they are permissible under the IMF Articles of Agreement. This reluctance stems from serious doubts about their feasibility and desirability. Short-term capital can move into and out of a country in so many ways that any attempt at full control requires a close regulation of all international transactions, current as well as capital. Hence, comprehensive exchange controls run the grave risk of "throwing the baby out with the bath water" by restricting legitimate international trade and investment and by curbing all short-term capital flows, not just speculative flows. Other consequences of exchange control are explored in Chapter 14. The feasibility of unilateral controls is also limited; no single country can hope to control or even greatly influence the Eurodollar market because of its size and international scope. Most fundamentally, controls attack only the symptoms of disequilibrium rather than the causes. After all, short-term capital movements can be equilibrating as well as disequilibrating.

Two approaches to curbing disequilibrating short-term capital movements go to their causes. The first approach is a better coordination of monetary policy (if not economic policy in general) among the industrial countries.[17] By moderating interest differentials among financial centers, policy coordination should greatly reduce yield-induced capital flows. The second approach is to introduce quicker international adjustment through flexible exchange rates and thereby prevent the prolonged speculative attacks on weak currencies. Whether these two approaches will be adopted by the major-currency countries remains a question for the future.

PROPOSALS FOR INTERNATIONAL MONETARY REFORM

Proposals for reform of the international monetary system may be grouped under two main headings: (1) the composition and control of international reserves, and (2) the mechanism of adjustment. Here we shall identify only the key proposals, making no attempt to discuss them in detail.

THE COMPOSITION AND CONTROL OF INTERNATIONAL RESERVES

Which shall be the major source of new international reserves in the decades ahead—gold, dollars, SDR's, or some other reserve asset? How

---

[17] One authority states flatly: "What is called the problem of short-term capital flows is actually a problem of the proper use of monetary policy; it is also a problem of the control instruments used to make monetary policy effective, as central banks must adapt themselves to the facts of the Eurodollar market and the multinational corporation." See Milton Gilbert, "The International System: Status and Prospects," *The Morgan Guaranty Survey* (December, 1971), p. 7.

shall the growth of reserves be managed so as to avoid too much or too little international liquidity?

The most conventional proposal is the *reconstruction of the gold-exchange standard* by restoring the convertibility of the dollar at a gold price high enough to build new confidence in that currency. This proposal does not solve the inherent contradiction of the gold-exchange standard with regard to reserve formation.

The most radical proposals would *make the IMF an international central bank.* Today all countries have central banks that provide the liquidity needed in the domestic economy. Why not set up an international central bank that would insure an adequate supply of international liquidity at all times? There are several proposals suggesting this solution to the liquidity problem, notably the *Triffin Plan.*[18] This plan would give the IMF the right to create (or destroy) international monetary reserves through open market transactions in member countries in the same way a national central bank creates or destroys commercial bank reserves by buying and selling securities in the open market. In addition, the IMF could create international reserves through advances or rediscounts requested by the central bank of a borrowing country. Each member country would be required to hold at least one-fifth (or some other fraction) of its monetary reserves in the form of deposits with the IMF which would be acquired initially by depositing gold and foreign exchange (mainly dollars and sterling). The IMF would convert its dollar and sterling holdings into long-term debts repayable in small annual installments by the United States and the United Kingdom. In this way dollar and sterling reserve assets would be gradually liquidated and as confidence in the new IMF grew, international reserves would come to consist entirely of IMF deposits.

Under the Triffin and similar plans the level of international reserves would be determined by the management of the Fund. It would require, therefore, a transfer of authority from national central banks to a supranational institution. This political factor is the single greatest obstacle to its adoption.

A proposal lying between these two extremes recommends that international reserves come from the creation of SDR's. All new reserves would be SDR's, and arrangements would be made to transfer dollars and other foreign-exchange reserves to the IMF in exchange for SDR's. Eventually all international reserves would consist of a mix of gold and SDR's, and at a later stage gold itself could be phased out as a reserve asset. Since the collapse of the Bretton Woods system, the proposal to use SDR's to supply reserve growth has gained wide acceptance, but the question of the future roles of the dollar and gold remain controversial.

---

[18] See Robert Triffin, *Gold and the Dollar Crisis* (New Haven: Yale University Press, 1961).

THE MECHANISM OF ADJUSTMENT

There is now a consensus among the Group of Ten countries that exchange rates should become more flexible so as to improve international payments adjustment. But how?

The most conventional proposal would maintain the Bretton Woods parity system, but would *strengthen the authority of the Fund* to obtain more frequent parity adjustments. At present, the Fund can only respond to a request for a parity change made by the member country in question. Nor can the Fund officially approve a floating rate even for a limited period of time. It is recommended, therefore, that the Articles of Agreement be amended to empower the Fund to *initiate* a request that a member country adjust the par value of its currency or even let its currency float for a time. Failure by a country to respond to such a request might be penalized by refusing it any further access to the Fund's resources. Although this proposal has merit, one may question whether it would be sufficient to introduce the necessary degree of flexibility in exchange rates.

The most extreme proposal is a system of *fluctuating exchange rates*. The characteristics of this system were examined in Chapter 10, and there is no need to go into them here. Let us note, however, that this system would also solve the liquidity problem by making international reserves unnecessary. Although theoretically attractive, fluctuating rates have little chance of adoption by governments. The experience with floating rates between the announcement of the dollar's inconvertibility and the Smithsonian Agreement demonstrated that governments are unwilling to let their currencies float without intervention by central banks.

A more modest proposal recommends *widening the band around parity* within which exchange rates are allowed to fluctuate. Under the Bretton Woods system the band was 1 percent on either side of par value. In theory, a wider band (say 3 percent) would let exchange rate variations play a limited adjustment role and would also moderate disequilibrating short-term capital movements by introducing some exchange risk. The desirability of a wider band is now accepted by the Group of Ten, and, as we have observed, the Smithsonian Agreement raised the band to 2¼ percent. However, wider bands alone would not achieve adjustment to a fundamental disequilibrium, nor would they stop speculative runs on a weak currency.

Another set of proposals would introduce frequent changes in par values in place of the abrupt changes of the "adjustable-peg" system of Bretton Woods. Known as *crawling (gliding or sliding) pegs (parities),* these arrangements call for automatic exchange rate adjustments in accordance with a formula. For example, one formula would require weekly changes in parity of $\frac{1}{26}$ of 1 percent (2 percent for the entire year) outside of a band of 5 percent on either side of parity. This formula would result in a "moving band." The great variety of these proposals makes them difficult to assess. Suffice it to say that these schemes for gradual changes in parities are much more appealing to academic economists than to central bankers, who are opposed to anything that robs them of their own discretion.

THE OUTLOOK FOR REFORM

International monetary reform remains an unfinished business. Debated by economists and government officials for many years, reform can no longer be postponed now that the Bretton Woods system has collapsed with the dollar's inconvertibility. The Smithsonian Agreement is only an interim arrangement that leaves unanswered the critical questions of liquidity and adjustment. How will these questions be answered in the international monetary negotiations that lie ahead? One can only speculate, but the probability is high that any new system will downgrade the reserve role of the dollar, upgrade the reserve role of SDR's, widen bands around parity, and create a mechanism for more frequent adjustments in currency parities. What does not seem to be in the offing is a fluctuating-rate system or a nondiscretionary system for frequent changes in parities. Finally, the design of the new system will depend in substantial degree on when and how the United States restores equilibrium in its balance of payments.

SUMMARY

1. In the 1960's, the international monetary system was shaken by a series of crises in foreign exchange and gold markets. Although other currencies were involved in these crises (notably the British pound and French franc), the pervasive source of instability was the weakness of the dollar.

2. The international monetary crisis of 1971 was directly inspired by a loss of confidence in the dollar. Confronted with an enormous speculative run on the dollar, the United States suspended the gold convertibility of the dollar on August 15 and thereby forced the collapse of the Bretton Woods system. The United States also imposed domestic wage and price controls, as well as a 10 percent surcharge on all dutiable imports.

3. The immediate response to the U.S. actions was a closing of foreign exchange markets in Europe and Japan. When they reopened, all of the major foreign currencies (with the exception of the French franc) were left to "float" vis-à-vis the dollar. However, foreign governments were reluctant to let their currencies float freely to higher dollar values because they hoped to persuade the United States to devalue the dollar by raising the price of gold. Hence, central banks continued to intervene in foreign exchange markets and, in some instances, further appreciation vis-à-vis the dollar was prevented by exchange restrictions.

4. After weeks of uncertainty, the Group of Ten countries negotiated the Smithsonian Agreement on December 18, 1971. In return for the revaluation of the other currencies, the United States agreed to raise the price of gold from $35 an ounce to $38 an ounce. However, this agreement did not tackle the problems of fundamental international monetary reform.

5. The poor performance and eventual collapse of the Bretton Woods system is attributable to three interrelated causes: (1) the problem of international liquidity formation centered on the dollar; (2) delays in balance of payments adjustment; and (3) disequilibrating short-term capital movements.

6. As the Bretton Woods system actually functioned, most of the growth in international reserves (liquidity formation) came from an increase in U.S. liabilities to foreign central banks. In other words, international liquidity formation was dependent on the continuation of a U.S. payments deficit which, in turn, undermined confidence in the dollar.

7. In response to widespread concern over the adequacy of international liquidity, agreement was reached in the late 1960's on facilities to create a new international reserve asset known as Special Drawing Rights (SDR's). SDR's were first activated at the beginning of 1970.

8. In accordance with the Bretton Woods Agreement, countries were expected to alter the par values of their currencies to adjust to persistent deficits and surpluses in their balances of payments. In practice, the dollar emerged as the central reserve currency with a fixed parity while other currencies tended to either maintain their parities or undergo devaluations. As a result, the dollar became overvalued. It is now widely accepted that exchange rates must become more flexible.

9. A third source of weakness in the Bretton Woods system was the massive flows of disequilibrating short-term capital between the major financial centers. The "speculators" responsible for large-scale international transfers of funds are, for the most part, respectable bankers, traders, and financial executives of multinational corporations seeking "cover" against the risk of exchange losses. These short-term capital movements were remarkably facilitated by the rapid growth of the Eurodollar market. As a free, global, money market, the Eurodollar market has become an indispensable element of the international financial system. But such a huge pool of liquid funds poses a grave threat to exchange stability.

10. Proposals for international monetary reform may be grouped under two main headings: (1) the composition and control of international reserves, and (2) the mechanism of adjustment. With regard to international reserves, the most conventional approach is the reconstruction of the gold-exchange standard, while the most radical approach is the creation of an international central bank. With regard to the adjustment mechanism, there is now a consensus that exchange rates must be made more flexible, but there is no agreement on the specific modality of higher flexibility.

11. International monetary reform in the 1970's is likely to downgrade the dollar as a reserve currency and upgrade SDR's. It is also likely to introduce more exchange-rate flexibility.

QUESTIONS AND APPLICATIONS

1. (a) Describe the actions of the United States on August 15, 1971.
   (b) Why did these actions bring about a collapse of the Bretton Woods system?

2. Be prepared to defend or criticize the U.S. decision to abandon the gold convertibility of the dollar on August 15, 1971.

3. (a) What is the Smithsonian Agreement?
   (b) Why is it only an "interim" agreement?
4. What is the problem of international liquidity formation? How is it related to the dollar? What is meant by the "inherent contradiction of the gold-exchange standard"?
5. What are SDR's? How are they created?
6. (a) When are short-term capital movements "disequilibrating"?
   (b) What are Eurodollars?
   (c) How does the Eurodollar market facilitate international capital movements?
7. With regard to international reserve formation, which reform proposal impresses you as the most desirable? Why?
8. International monetary reform is a continuing story. Prepare a report on what has happened in international monetary relations since the Smithsonian Agreement.

SELECTED READINGS

Board of Governors of Federal Reserve System. *Federal Reserve Bulletin*. Washington: U.S. Government Printing Office, monthly.

Fleming, J. Marcus. *The International Monetary Fund, Its Form and Functions*. Washington: International Monetary Fund, 1964.

Gold, Joseph. *Special Drawing Rights*. Washington: International Monetary Fund, 1970.

Grubel, Herbert G. *The International Monetary System*. Baltimore, Maryland: Penguin Books, Ltd., 1969.

International Monetary Fund. *Annual Report*. Washington: International Monetary Fund.

——————. *Articles of Agreement*.

——————. *International Financial Statistics*, monthly.

——————. *Summary Proceedings*, Annual Meetings.

——————. *The Role of Exchange Rates in the Adjustment of International Payments*, 1970.

Machlup, Fritz, and Burton G. Malkiel (eds.). *International Monetary Arrangements: The Problem of Choice*. Princeton: Princeton University Press, 1964.

Morris, Stephen. "The Bürgenstock Communiqué: A Critical Examination of the Case for Limited Flexibility of Exchange Rates." *Essays in International Finance No. 80*. Princeton: Princeton University Press, May, 1970.

Ossola, Rinaldo. "Towards New Monetary Relationships." *Essays in International Finance No. 87*. Princeton: Princeton University Press, July, 1971.

Triffin, Robert. *Gold and the Dollar Crisis*. New Haven: Yale University Press, 1961.

Triffin, Robert. *Our International Monetary System: Yesterday, Today, and Tomorrow*. New York: Random House, Inc., 1968.

PART THREE ENTERPRISE

Parts One and Two have assumed a macroscopic, national perspective in the description and analysis of international economic relations. Part One focused on the theory which has been developed to explain transactions among national economies; Part Two focused on the international economic policies of national governments. Although necessary, this perspective is no longer sufficient to explain the behavior of the world economy. Large multinational business enterprises now possess the financial and market power to make decisions that vitally affect the level, composition, and direction of international trade and investment. Multinational enterprises have become independent actors in the world economy, and there is no area of government policy that escapes their influence. The future evolution of the world economy will depend, therefore, not only on the behavior of national governments, but also on the behavior of multinational enterprises as they strive to achieve their goals on a transnational scale. Part Three investigates the nature, scope, and economic role of the multinational enterprise; the U.S. and other governments' policies toward the multinational enterprise; and the tensions that are generated by the complex relations between the multinational enterprise and the nation-state.

CHAPTER **21**

THE NATURE AND SCOPE OF MULTINATIONAL ENTERPRISE

In the 1960's, U.S. business firms went abroad on a massive scale unprecedented in the history of international enterprise. Today the production and sales of the foreign operations owned and managed by U.S. companies are some four times the value of U.S. exports, and they are growing at twice the rate. Increasingly, the prevailing response of big American companies to market opportunities abroad is the establishment of producing affiliates in foreign countries. The dominant agency in the surge of U.S. business abroad is the multinational enterprise—large industrial corporations that possess plants in many countries which produce for markets throughout the world. Many industrial firms in Western Europe have also become multinational enterprises, and they are beginning to emerge in Japan as well.

Because of their vast size, the worldwide operations of multinational companies are now a decisive force in shaping the patterns of trade, investment, and technology flows among nations. It has become impossible to understand the world economy without an appreciation of the many roles of multinational enterprises as producers, investors, traders, and innovators on a global scale. National governments must also reckon with this force because of its impact on domestic production, employment, trade, and the balance of payments. In so doing, they are commonly frustrated by the capability of multinational companies to far outrun the national jurisdiction in taxation, antitrust, and other policy areas. Moreover, many governments view the multinational enterprise as a *political* threat, representing, as it does, an intrusion into the national domain by a company whose control is exercised by a headquarters located in another country. Even in the United States, the multinational enterprise has come under growing attack by labor and protectionist groups who charge it with exporting jobs and technology to the detriment of the U.S. economy.

The many economic and political issues raised by the multinational enterprise are examined in later chapters. First, however, we need to learn something about the nature and scope of multinational enterprise and the dimensions of U.S. business abroad.

THE EVOLUTION OF A MULTINATIONAL ENTERPRISE

How have certain companies, for the most part headquartered in the United States and Western Europe, become multinational enterprises? This section throws some light on this question by using an explanatory model that traces the evolution of a manufacturing company from a domestic enterprise to a multinational enterprise.[1]

Most manufacturing enterprises prefer to remain wholly domestic, staying out of foreign operations. And as a matter of record, only a comparatively small number of manufacturers ever engage in international business. Businessmen grow up in the national market, where they gain confidence in their ability to judge market risks and meet local competition. In sharp contrast, international business appears complex, risky, and somewhat mysterious; it requires managers who know how to deal with foreign customers, foreign governments, and foreign peoples who may behave in bewildering ways. In brief, international businessmen must learn to cope with economic, social, political, and cultural barriers that have few, if any, counterparts at home. Is it any wonder, then, that most companies prefer to remain safely at home?

How, then, do some companies become international and even multinational? The actual historical experience of companies in the United States suggests that the process of internationalization is likely to be a gradual evolution that can be described in three stages: export, foreign production, and multinational enterprise.

THE EXPORT STAGE

This first stage starts with the initial inquiry about a company's products from a domestic export intermediary or directly from a foreign buyer. If the manufacturer responds positively to this inquiry, the result may be a foreign sale that he judges to be profitable. As a consequence, the manufacturer follows up subsequent inquiries and makes sales to other foreign buyers, probably via domestic export middlemen. At some point, however, the manufacturer decides that his export business should be actively developed rather than depend solely on unsolicited inquiries. To that end, he

---

[1] This section draws heavily on a paper prepared by the author in 1970 for the Economic Commission for Latin America, entitled "Reflections on the International Company and Its Role in the Development of Latin American Exports of Manufactured Products."

appoints an export manager with a small staff or, alternatively, he turns over this export business to an independent export agency in his own country.

If the manufacturer experiences a continuing expansion of export sales, the inadequacy of a small "built-in" export department or an outside export agency becomes progressively more evident. His next step, then, is the establishment of a full export department at the same level as his domestic sales department. He also decides to forego the use of domestic middle-men (such as manufacturers' export agents) for his sales to some, if not all, foreign markets. Further growth of export sales may justify the establish-ment of foreign sales branches and even assembly operations if his products are disassembled to obtain lower transportation costs to foreign markets.

The manufacturer has now evolved toward a systematic export pro-gram which is supported by market research, intensive advertising, and other forms of promotion. He may be selling full product lines in scores of foreign markets, and his export sales may be 10 percent or more of total company sales. But he still depends entirely on export operations (aside from modest foreign assembly operations in some instances) to penetrate foreign markets. This first stage in the international evolution of a manu-facturing company ends when, for reasons soon to be examined, the manu-facturer decides to enter foreign markets by means of foreign production under one or more arrangements.

THE FOREIGN PRODUCTION STAGE

Just as domestic manufacturers prefer to remain domestic, so do ex-porting manufacturers prefer to stay out of foreign production. Exports, however, are not always sufficient to achieve a manufacturer's objectives in foreign markets. He may be interested in foreign markets that cannot be penetrated, either absolutely or at an acceptable level of sales and profit, from a production base that lies outside those markets. The most common explanation of this situation, of course, is high tariffs or other import barriers imposed by governments, but it may also be that local competition within a foreign market becomes so intense that an outside manufacturer's products are effectively excluded. How, then, can the exporting manufacturer hope to penetrate such a market? Quite clearly, he must find a way to supply the foreign market from a production base located inside that market.

Basically, the exporting manufacturer may enter into foreign-base production in one of three ways: (1) licensing; (2) long-term contract arrangements with local producers; or (3) direct investment in manufactur-ing facilities. Which approach he chooses will depend on many factors, but generally U.S. manufacturers have started with *licensing* and have then progressively shifted to *direct investment,* avoiding contract supply arrange-ments with local producers for finished products (as distinguished from raw materials and components).

Licensing is ordinarily the first experience in foreign production for the exporting manufacturer because it appears so easy; it does not require any capital investment and does not offer any substantial risks. The manufacturer simply licenses the use of his patents, production know-how, or trademarks to an independent foreign producer in return for royalty payments, which are usually determined as a percentage of the licensee company's production or sales. In this way, the manufacturer is able to participate in the growth of a foreign market which he cannot exploit through exports. A pure licensing agreement means that the manufacturer has substituted an export of technology for the export of his own products.

The attractiveness of licensing as a mode of foreign market entry is likely to diminish for the manufacturer as a result of his actual licensing experience. Commonly, a licensee does not perform up to the expectations of the licensing manufacturer in sales and market development. When this happens, the manufacturer becomes frustrated because he has no managerial control over the licensee's operations. Even when the licensee performs well, however, the manufacturer may come to believe that he can do much better on his own. For the licensing manufacturer, then, direct investment becomes more and more appealing as the best way to enter certain foreign markets.

Ordinarily, the first direct investment by a manufacturing company in foreign production facilities marks a critical step in its evolution as an international enterprise. (However, this is not always the case. In particular, U.S. manufacturers are inclined to view their plants in Canada as "domestic" rather than "foreign." For such companies their first investment outside Canada becomes the critical step.) For the first time, the manufacturer commits substantial financial, managerial, and technical resources to an international venture. He now becomes exposed to risks (such as expropriation) that run far beyond the risks associated with exporting or licensing, and he has many more assets exposed to those risks. Foreign direct investment, therefore, involves the top management of a company in decisions relating to international business to a far greater extent than exporting or licensing.

The first investment abroad prepares the way for later investments. Eventually plants may be established in several countries to produce one or more of the manufacturer's product lines. At the same time, the manufacturer continues to export many products from his domestic plants to independent foreign buyers or (increasingly) to his own foreign affiliates. He also continues to engage in licensing, but many of his licensing agreements are now made with his own affiliates rather than with independent foreign producers.

Toward the end of the foreign production stage, the manufacturer will be penetrating markets throughout the world from several national production bases, supplemented by exports from the parent company as well as by licensing arrangements. At the level of the parent company, the management of these diverse operations becomes more and more arduous; painful episodes signal the necessity to integrate the company's far-flung operations within a single *enterprise system* in order to take full advantage of company resources and opportunities. This shift in management philosophy toward a global conception of the enterprise marks the beginning of the third stage of evolution—the multinational enterprise.

THE MULTINATIONAL ENTERPRISE STAGE

A company becomes a multinational enterprise when its management begins to plan, organize, and control its international production on a worldwide scale.[2] Such a company seeks answers to questions in global terms: Where in the world are our best markets? Where in the world should we manufacture our products for these markets? Where in the world should we undertake research and development to create new products for future markets? Where in the world should we obtain financing for our capital investments and current operations? Where in the world should we recruit people to staff our international organization?

The transformation of a foreign production company into a multinational enterprise does not happen quickly or painlessly. It is best thought of as a process that involves higher and higher degrees of multinationality. For example, this process requires a substantial (and oftentimes, drastic) reorganization of the company, including the replacement of top managers who cannot develop a global outlook. Although more than one form of organization is available to the multinational enterprise, one form in particular explicitly embodies a global orientation. It is depicted in Figure 21-1 (page 508).

The Board of Directors, the President, and the Vice-Presidents of the corporate staff all have worldwide responsibilities. For example, the Vice-President of Marketing has the responsibility to provide advice, technical assistance, and other staff support to marketing managers of the enterprise throughout the world. Other corporate staff vice-presidents (only some of whom are shown) have similar responsibilities in their own functional areas. Line management at the operations level is organized by geographical regions. The Regional Manager of Europe, for instance, holds the responsibility (and commensurate authority) for *all* the company's activities (production, finance, marketing, research and development, etc.) in Europe. In particular, he has direct authority over the company's affiliates located in the countries of that region. It is noteworthy that no distinction between foreign and domestic operations appears in this organizational form; for a

---

[2] We are offering here a *managerial* conception of the multinational enterprise. For other conceptions, see pp. 517-521.

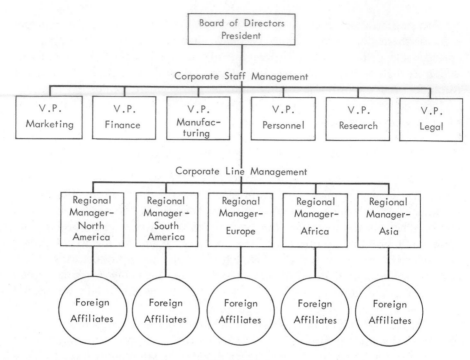

Figure 21-1

**WORLDWIDE ORGANIZATION OF A MULTINATIONAL
ENTERPRISE ON A GEOGRAPHICAL BASIS**

U.S. multinational enterprise, North America becomes just one of several world regions.

During the foreign production stage, a manufacturer is inclined to pursue a *binational strategy* with respect to foreign markets. That is to say, he perceives each foreign national market as unique and separate from other national markets, and thereby ignores potential relations among them and among his manufacturing affiliates located in different countries. By and large, the international production company invests in country X in order to supply a market in country X, not to supply markets in countries Y and Z or in the home country. Such a binational strategy is encouraged by government import restrictions that tend to isolate a national market from other national markets. Until the end of the 1950's, binational strategy was the dominant strategy of even the big international manufacturers.

At the multinational stage, the manufacturer abandons binational strategy for *multinational strategy*. National markets come to be viewed as segments of broader regional and world markets. As a result, managers focus their energies on building up *intraenterprise* transactions (flows of products, technology, capital, and personnel) among their many affiliates in order to capitalize on international specialization and economies of scale. It follows that multinational strategy can be a potent generator of international trade. Manufacturing facilities are established in country X not only (or even mainly) to supply the local market, but rather to supply other national markets through exports. Or facilities are established in country X to supply components to plants of the multinational enterprise located in third countries. We shall have more to say about these multinational logistical systems in Chapter 23 when we appraise the economic role of the multinational enterprise.

OBSERVATIONS ON THE EVOLUTIONARY SCHEME

Only a comparative handful of manufacturers (at most, 200 or so) in the United States and Europe have reached the multinational stage. All signs indicate, however, that many more manufacturers (including Japanese) will join the ranks of multinational enterprises in the decade ahead. Nevertheless, the majority of manufacturers engaged in international business will remain in the exporting stage, and some of them will not move beyond the foreign production stage. Most manufacturers in every country, of course, will remain wholly domestic in their orientation. There is, therefore, no inevitable progression to the multinational stage. Limitations of size and, more importantly, management philosophy will prevent many companies from becoming multinational, even among manufacturers who are presently exporting in substantial volume.

In would be a mistake, however, to judge the importance of multinational enterprises solely in terms of their small number. As we shall see, the representative multinational enterprise is very large, often dominating its home market as well as many foreign markets. IBM, as a prime example, has some 70 percent of the *world* market for computer equipment. Apart from size, multinational enterprises are concentrated in research-intensive, dynamic industries (such as pharmaceuticals, industrial chemicals, office and computing machines, petroleum refining, automobiles and other transportation equipment, and nuclear energy equipment) that will set the pace for economic growth and world trade in the years ahead.

EXPANSION OF U.S. BUSINESS ABROAD

The expansion of U.S. business into foreign production is not new. Today's multinational enterprises have roots that go deep into the American past. In the decades following the Civil War, the transformation of industrial corporations into national enterprises, together with notable improvements in transportation and communications, encouraged a number of American manufacturers with unique products to make investments in Canada and Europe. One of the pioneers, Singer, licensed a French company in 1855 to manufacture its new sewing machine (the first and last time Singer ever licensed a patent to an independent foreign concern), and in 1867 established its first plant abroad in Glasgow.[3] In 1879, Westinghouse started a shop in Paris to manufacture brakes; in 1882, Western Electric and International Bell Telephone Company jointly set up a manufacturing affiliate in Belgium; and by 1889, Eastman had incorporated a company in London to manufacture film for Kodak cameras imported from the United States.[4] In the 1870's and 1880's, then, many American companies with new products (screws, cash registers, elevators, steam pumps, locomotives, locks, and guns) were eagerly seeking export markets and, in some instances, entering into foreign production.[5]

It is noteworthy that this early movement of U.S. manufacturers abroad was based on new products, new methods of production, and new marketing methods which offered strong competitive advantages in foreign markets. From the very beginning, therefore, U.S. business investors appear primarily as exporters of technology and management rather than exporters of capital. By the turn of the century, the presence of U.S. companies in Europe was sufficient enough to alarm some observers, who spoke of "the American invasion" in much the same terms as J. J. Servan-Schreiber did some seventy years later.[6]

Although its historical roots are deep, nonetheless the multinational enterprise as we know it today is a recent phenomenon, emerging for the most part only since the mid-1950's. Before that time the inadequacies of the global infrastructure of communications and transportation, as well as the pervasive influence of restrictive government policies, rendered global business strategies nothing more than utopian dreams in the minds of a few entrepreneurs. The emergence of multinational enterprise systems directed and controlled by a single decision-center had to await the dramatic postwar improvements in communications and transportation and the massive liberalization of international trade and payments that gathered steam in the late 1950's.

The recency of the entry of many now prominent multinational enterprises into production abroad is a striking phenomenon. Table 21-1 (page 511), based on a study undertaken by the author, offers evidence in this regard.

---

[3] See Mira Wilkins, *The Emergence of Multinational Enterprise* (Cambridge: Harvard University Press, 1970), p. 38 ff. This book offers a detailed history of U.S. international business up to 1914.

[4] *Ibid.*, pp. 45, 51, and 59.

[5] *Ibid.*, p. 45.

[6] Three publications appeared in London in 1901-02, entitled *The American Invasion, The American Invaders,* and *The Americanization of the World.* See Mira Wilkins, *op. cit.,* p. 71. The full citation of the Servan-Schreiber book is J. J. Servan-Schreiber, *The American Challenge* (New York: Atheneum Publishers, 1968).

Table 21-1

PERIOD IN WHICH FIRST FOREIGN INVESTMENT WAS MADE BY EIGHTY-FOUR LARGE U.S. INDUSTRIAL COMPANIES

	Number of Companies	
Period	First Investment Outside U.S.	First Investment Outside U.S. and Canada
Before 1930	30	19
1930-1945	15	13
1946-1955	8	13
1956-1965	31	39

Source: Franklin R. Root, "Foreign Government Constraints on U.S. Business Abroad," *Economic and Business Bulletin* (September, 1967), p. 31.
Note: All of these companies appear in "The Fortune Directory of the 500 Largest Industrial Corporations," *Fortune* (May, 1971).

Over one-third of these companies made their *first* investment outside the United States only within the period 1956-1965. Almost half of the companies made their first investment outside the United States *and* Canada (which many managers view as more domestic than foreign) after 1955. The recency of foreign investment experience is particularly striking in regions other than the Western Hemisphere and Western Europe. For example, of the thirty companies reporting production units in Japan, twenty-six made their first investment there during the 1956-1965 decade. It is this dramatic upsurge of international production since the mid-1950's that has made the multinational enterprise such a dominant force in the world economy.

WHY COMPANIES GO ABROAD

Companies enter into foreign production for a variety of specific reasons that pertain to their own particular circumstances. In general, however, we can distinguish three broad categories of international business investors by their motivations.

Extractive Investors. The first category is extractive investors, who invest in mines, oil wells, forests, agriculture, and other primary operations designed to produce raw materials. Their motivation is readily apparent; namely, to obtain raw materials which are not available at home or available only at a higher cost. Mineral companies (such as Anaconda and Kennecott), petroleum companies in search of crude oil (such as Jersey Standard), and many metals manufacturers who have integrated backwards (such as U.S. Steel and Alcoa) fall into this category. Although the initial impulse of extractive investors is usually to obtain raw materials for transformation in the

United States, many investors subsequently market raw materials to other countries, either to independent buyers or to their own manufacturing affiliates.

Manufacturing Investors. The motivation of business investors who go abroad to manufacture is more complex and the subject of some controversy. Most probably the man in the street would say that American manufacturers go abroad because costs of production are lower there, a point of view shared by many union leaders. Marxists and other adherents of leftist philosophies would carry this a step further, charging that U.S. companies go abroad to exploit poorly paid foreign workers. However, numerous studies agree that lower production cost is seldom the major reason for a company's entry into foreign manufacturing. Table 21-2 offers the results of a recent inquiry into the investment motivations of seventy-four U.S. corporations representing a broad group of large multinational enterprises with aggregate sales of $113 billion and foreign investments of $14.4 billion (about 45 percent of *all* U.S. foreign manufacturing investment).

Table 21-2

MAJOR DETERMINANTS OF FOREIGN INVESTMENT DECISIONS AS RANKED BY RESPONDENTS IN SEVENTY-FOUR MULTINATIONAL ENTERPRISES IN MANUFACTURING

Major Determinant	Percentage of Respondents Indicating Determinant as "Most Important"
Market demands	57
Trade restrictions	20
Investment regulations	11
Labor cost advantages	5
Other	7

Source: Emergency Committee for American Trade, *The Role of the Multinational Corporation in the United States and World Economies* (Washington: 1972), p. 15.

Over half of the respondents stated that market demand was the most important determinant of their foreign investments. They cited the need to produce abroad because of major differences between U.S. and foreign product specifications, product perishability, and service and distribution requirements. One-fifth considered trade restrictions (tariffs, quotas, and other import barriers) as the dominant factor in their foreign investment decisions. These respondents stressed foreign investment as a means of circumventing trade restrictions that make their exports to a country noncompetitive. The third-ranked determinant, investment regulations, refers to the policies of some governments (notably those governments in the developing countries) that require the local affiliates of multinational companies to increase the domestic value added in their manufacturing operations as a condition for remaining in the host countries. These first three determining factors are all connected with the improvement or maintenance of the company's *market position* in foreign countries. Observe that only 5 percent of the responding companies regarded lower labor costs as the major determinant of their investment abroad.

This and other studies on investment motivations reach the same conclusion; namely, that considerations of *marketing strategy* dominate the vast majority of decisions to manufacture abroad.

Manufacturing investments are made for both defensive and aggressive reasons. The former include the necessity to invest to be able to meet competition or to overcome import barriers and other government restrictions. When the investment decision is purely defensive, the choice confronting managers is either to invest abroad or lose their markets. As one manager put it to this writer: "We went abroad because of the need to protect ourselves against the constant imposition of embargoes, tariffs, and so on. We were being priced out of the market by firms who were actually entering the market with manufacturing operations." [7] Manufacturers demonstrate an aggressive strategy when they invest in a foreign country in order to exploit present and anticipated market opportunities more effectively than is judged possible through exporting or licensing. Commonly, the motivation is to "beat out" the competition.

Studies of the investment motivations of managers are supported by statistical analyses. One analysis found a significant correlation between U.S. investment in the EEC and market size.[8] As we shall discover in the next chapter, statistics on U.S. investment abroad reveal that the bulk of manufacturing investment has gone into other industrial countries with expansive market opportunities rather than into developing countries where wage rates are low. To conclude, the evidence strongly supports the following statement which appears in a recent publication of the United States Department of Commerce: ". . . the fundamental forces impelling corporations to invest abroad is [*sic*] the quest for profit and the fear that their present or prospective market position will be lost to foreign or domestic competitors." [9]

---

[7] Franklin R. Root, "U.S. Business Abroad and the Political Risks," *MSU Business Topics* (Winter, 1968), p. 74.

[8] A. E. Scaperlanda and L. J. Mauer, "The Determinants of U.S. Direct Investment in the EEC," *The American Economic Review* (September, 1969), pp. 558-68. No significant correlation was found between U.S. investment in the EEC and economic growth or tariff discrimination.

[9] U.S. Department of Commerce, *Policy Aspects of Foreign Investment by U.S. Multinational Corporations* (Washington: U.S. Government Printing Office, January, 1972), p. 14.

Service Investors. The third category of international business investors embraces enterprises in transportation, banking, insurance, accounting, law, and advertising that provide services to multinational companies. When their customers move abroad, service enterprises must follow them if they are to maintain business relations. A U.S. bank is poorly prepared to service a multinational client if it does not have branches or agencies in foreign countries. The wave of foreign investment by service companies in the 1960's, therefore, is mainly a response to the appearance of multinational industrial enterprises which demand services on a world region or global scale.

PATTERNS OF EXPANSION ABROAD

The rapid expansion of U.S. business abroad is documented by statistical data on the new foreign activities (direct investment and licensing arrangements) of U.S. companies during the 1961-1970 decade. These data also reveal geographical patterns, ownership, and other patterns of U.S. business abroad.

New Establishments, Expansions, and Licensing. During the period 1961-1970, U.S. companies initiated over 10,000 separate activities relating to foreign production, as is shown in Table 21-3. About 63 percent of these activities consisted of direct investments in new establishments, with two-thirds being in manufacturing and one-third in nonmanufacturing. About 15 percent of the activities were direct investments in the expansion of already existing foreign production affiliates of U.S. companies, mostly in manufacturing. The remaining activities involved the licensing of patents, know-how, and trademarks by U.S. companies to foreign producers, some of whom were affiliates of the same U.S. companies.

Observe that over half of the new foreign activities were concentrated in Western Europe. The comparatively small number of activities in Japan was a consequence of policies that restricted direct investment. On the other hand, Japanese policy encouraged the licensing of local producers by U.S. companies, accounting for the fact that about half of all the new activities in Japan fell into that category.

All in all, the industrial areas attracted almost three-fourths of the new foreign activities of U.S. companies during the decade. Furthermore, almost 60 percent of the new activities in the developing areas were undertaken in Latin America.

Ownership Patterns. Table 21-4 reveals the ownership patterns of new foreign establishments started by U.S. companies from 1961 to 1970. In the first half of the period (1961-1965), 52.8 percent of the new establishments were wholly owned by U.S. companies. The remaining new establishments

Table 21-3

PATTERNS OF EXPANSION ABROAD BY U.S. COMPANIES FOR THE PERIOD 1961-1970

(Number of Activities)

Type of Activity	World Total	Western Europe	Canada	Japan	Total Industrial Areas *	Latin America	Other Developing Areas	Total Developing Areas **
New establishments:								
Manufacturing	4,401	2,203	478	307	3,200	690	511	1,201
Nonmanufacturing	2,229	1,257	166	118	1,673	267	289	556
Expansions:								
Manufacturing	1,268	630	240	24	969	215	84	299
Nonmanufacturing	304	178	28	10	234	42	28	70
Licensing agreements	2,184	948	145	472	1,677	290	217	507
All activities	10,386	5,216	1,057	931	7,753	1,504	1,129	2,633

Source: "American Investment Abroad: Who's Going, Where, How, and Why," *Business Abroad* (June, 1971), pp. 7 and 8. Data are compiled by Booz, Allen & Hamilton.
* Western Europe, Canada, Japan, Australia, and New Zealand.
** Latin America, Africa (including South Africa), and Asia (excluding Japan).

were *joint ventures* between U.S. companies and foreign companies (usually local) in which the participants (usually two in number) invest equity capital in varying amounts. The distinction between U.S. majority-owned joint ventures and U.S. minority-owned joint ventures is a real one because the former implies managerial control by the U.S. company.

Table 21-4

OWNERSHIP PATTERNS OF FOREIGN ESTABLISHMENTS OF U.S. COMPANIES STARTED IN THE PERIODS 1961-65 AND 1966-70 (Number of Establishments)

Ownership	1961-1965		1966-1970	
	Number	Percent	Number	Percent
Wholly U.S.-owned:				
Foreign branch	259		302	
Foreign subsidiary ...	1,448		1,710	
Subtotal	1,707	52.8	2,012	61.6
Joint ventures:				
U.S. majority-owned ..	381		416	
U.S. minority-owned ..	292		234	
Unknown interest	852		605	
Subtotal	1,525	47.2	1,255	38.4
All new establishments *.	3,232	100.0	3,267	100.0

Source: "American Investment Abroad: Who's Going, Where, How, and Why," *Business Abroad* (June, 1971), p. 9. Data are compiled by Booz, Allen & Hamilton.
* Excluding "indeterminable," which is 76 for 1961-65 and 55 for 1966-70.

These data show the strong and continuing preference of American companies for 100 percent ownership of their foreign affiliates. Despite the pressures exerted by many foreign governments to push U.S. companies into joint ventures, the percentage of wholly owned U.S. establishments rose sharply in the second half of the decade. As we shall discover in Chapter 25, the question of foreign ownership has become a sensitive political issue in industrial as well as in developing countries.

New Foreign Activities by Industry. Table 21-5 indicates that for the period 1961-1970, the chemicals and allied products industry accounted for more new foreign activities than any other industry. It was closely followed by the nonelectrical machinery and electrical machinery industries.

Observe also the high ranking of two service industries—transportation and business services, on the one hand, and finance and insurance, on the other. New activities in mining rank fairly low, with less than one-third the number reported for chemicals and allied products. It is evident that manufacturing industries provided the forward thrust of U.S. business abroad in the 1961-1970 decade.

Table 21-5

NEW FOREIGN ACTIVITIES OF U.S. COMPANIES RANKED BY INDUSTRY, 1961-1970
(Number of Activities)

Industry	Activities *
Chemicals and allied products	1,376
Nonelectrical machinery	1,317
Electrical machinery	1,006
Transport equipment	787
Transportation and business services	634
Finance and insurance	632
Food and kindred products	562
Fabricated metal products	529
Primary metal products	449
Scientific instruments	441
Mining	409
Wholesale retail trade	304
Paper and allied products	268
Rubber and plastic products	239
All other	1,433
All industries	10,386

Source: "American Investment Abroad: Who's Going, Where, How, and Why," *Business Abroad* (June, 1971), p. 8. Data are compiled by Booz, Allen & Hamilton.
* Number of new establishments, expansions, and licenses.

Size of Companies. About 250 very large companies with annual sales exceeding $450 million each were responsible for 27.6 percent of the new foreign activities of U.S. business in the period 1961-1970. (See Table 21-6, p. 518.) Large companies with sales ranging from $100 million to $449 million accounted for an additional 23.3 percent. Medium-sized and small companies initiated another 42.9 percent.

The small percentage of expansions (23.9) attributable to medium-sized and small companies is owing to the fact that they were more likely to be entering foreign production for the first time than were the larger companies. Furthermore, smaller companies favor licensing over direct investment to a much greater degree than larger companies, mainly owing to their lack of capital for direct investment and an unwillingness to assume the risks that go with such investment.

MULTINATIONAL ENTERPRISES

In this section we turn to the question of defining the multinational enterprise (MNE) and also identifying some actual MNE's.

SOME DEFINITIONS OF THE MNE

There is no single agreed definition of the multinational enterprise. This is hardly surprising in view of the fact that "multinationality" has many

Table 21-6

SIZE BY SALES VOLUME OF U.S. COMPANIES STARTING NEW FOREIGN ACTIVITIES, 1961-1970
(Number of Activities)

Sales Volume	Establishments		Expansions		Licenses		Total	
	Number	Percent	Number	Percent	Number	Percent	Number	Percent
$1 billion and up	962		448		268		1,678	
$450 million to $999 million	777		245		152		1,174	
Subtotal	1,739	26.2	693	44.1	420	19.2	2,852	27.6
$100 million to $449 million	1,537	23.2	438	27.9	446	20.4	2,421	23.3
Less than $100 million	2,801	42.2	376	23.9	1,287	58.9	4,464	42.9
Indeterminable	553	8.4	65	4.1	31	1.5	649	6.2

Source: "American Investment Abroad: Who's Going, Where, How, and Why," *Business Abroad* (June, 1971), p. 8. Data are compiled by Booz, Allen & Hamilton.

General Note: The *Fortune* 500 lists 120 industrial companies with 1970 sales of $1 billion or more; 122 companies with sales of $450 million to $999 million. In 1970, only 697 industrial companies had sales of $100 million or over. However, not all of these listed companies have foreign activities. On the other hand, this table also includes statistics for some companies in banking, insurance, transportation, and retailing not listed in the *Fortune* 500.

dimensions which may be viewed from any of several different perspectives, namely, economic, political, legal, managerial, and others.

Some observers regard *ownership* as the key criterion. In their view an enterprise becomes multinational only when the headquarters or parent company is effectively owned by nationals of at least two countries. Shell and Unilever, which are controlled by British and Dutch interests, are commonly cited as examples. By this ownership test, very few international companies may be called multinational. The dominant ownership interest in the overwhelming majority of big international companies is *uninational*; namely, American, British, French, or Swiss.[10] The ownership criterion has been rejected by most authorities who prefer to use the term "transnational enterprise" to designate a company with multinational ownership. Whether transnational enterprises will grow out of multinational enterprises in the decades ahead is an important question, but one that is more political than economic in its implications.

A second definition of the MNE relies on the criterion of the *nationality mix* of headquarters management. An international company is seen as multinational only when the managers of the parent company are nationals of several different countries. Here again, very few international companies would qualify as multinational enterprises because most have headquarters organizations which are entirely or mainly staffed with nationals of the home country. But uninational management may well prove to be a transitional phenomenon. Already it is commonplace for international companies to staff their foreign affiliates with local nationals all the way to the top levels, and some of these nationals are now being promoted to the parent headquarters. For instance, Jacques Maisonrouge, who heads the IBM World Trade Corporation in New York, is a French national who came up through the ranks in IBM-France. Multinational management, then, is more a consequence of the continuing evolution of the MNE than its distinguishing feature.

Most observers of large international companies have been concerned with their economic and business behavior. Accordingly, they have defined the MNE in terms of *organizational structure* and/or *business strategy*. Vernon sees the multinational enterprise as a "parent company that controls a large cluster of corporations of various nationalities."[11] Finding the essence of the multinational enterprise in its attempt "to treat the various national markets as though they were one," Behrman emphasizes the presence of a single management (strategy) center which guides the

---

[10] Of course, the shares of these companies may be held in comparatively small amounts by nationals of many countries. Indeed, several U.S. companies list their shares on stock exchanges in Europe and Japan. But the controlling ownership interest remains in the hands of nationals of the home country, where the parent company is located.

[11] Raymond Vernon, *Sovereignty at Bay* (New York: Basic Books, Inc., 1971), p. 4.

actions of foreign affiliates.[12] Perlmutter has distinguished three kinds of international companies by reference to the attitudes held by their top executives. *Ethnocentric* companies follow policies which are home-country oriented; *polycentric* companies follow policies which are host-country oriented; and *geocentric* companies follow policies which are world-oriented. To Perlmutter, a firm's multinationality may be judged by "the pervasiveness with which its executives think geocentrically."[13]

The foregoing conceptions may be combined in a single definition of the multinational enterprise that contains both structural and strategic (attitudinal) elements. A multinational enterprise denotes a headquarters or parent company that:

> 1. Engages in foreign production and other activities through its own affiliates located in several different countries.
> 2. Exercises direct control over the policies of those affiliates.
> 3. Strives to design and implement business strategies in production, marketing, finance, and other functions that transcend national boundaries, becoming thereby progressively more geocentric in outlook.

This is the definition that best describes the approach taken by this and later chapters.

Unfortunately organizational structure and business strategy do not lend themselves to direct quantitative measurement. Thus, the definition of the MNE for statistical data-gathering purposes must rely on "proxy variables," such as the percentages of a company's assets, sales, earnings, employment, or production abroad. A company whose foreign sales are 25 percent or more of total sales is certainly heavily involved in international business on both operational and strategic levels, and in most instances it probably qualifies as a multinational enterprise. But there is no magic percentage at which a company is transformed from a foreign production company into a multinational enterprise. The MNE is too complex a phenomenon to be captured by a single number. Any statistical definition of the MNE, however useful, is bound, therefore, to be arbitrary.

One investigation of 386 U.S. industrial corporations which are listed in the *Fortune* 500 has utilized percentages of foreign sales, earnings, assets, and employment to measure the degree of foreign content in their total operations. The overall results are depicted in Table 21-7, on the opposite page.

A similar investigation undertaken today would undoubtedly show substantially more companies in the first two brackets, reflecting the marked

---

[12] Jack N. Behrman, *Some Patterns in the Rise of the Multinational Enterprise* (Chapel Hill: University of North Carolina, 1969), p. 63.

[13] Howard V. Perlmutter, "The Tortuous Evolution of the Multinational Corporation," *Columbia Journal of World Business* (January-February, 1969), pp. 9-18.

Table 21-7

RELATIVE INVOLVEMENT IN FOREIGN OPERATIONS OF 386 U.S. CORPORATIONS IN 1964

Foreign Content	Number of Corporations	Percent of Corporations
Over 50 percent	7	2
25-50 percent	70	18
10-24 percent	122	32
Less than 10 percent	187	48
Totals	386	100

Source: Nicholas K. Bruck and Francis A. Lees, "Foreign Content of U.S. Corporate Activities," *Financial Analysts Journal* (September-October, 1966).

growth in international production since 1964. Even one year later, a follow-up study by the same researchers revealed an increase from seven to eleven companies with a foreign content over 50 percent.[14] IBM offers a specific instance of such growth. In 1964, it received only 29 percent of its total earnings from foreign sources; in 1970, however, the figure was over 50 percent.

SOME MULTINATIONAL ENTERPRISES CLASSIFIED BY INDUSTRY

To acquaint the reader with the names of some multinational enterprises, Table 21-8 (pages 522-523) lists the ten largest firms (U.S. and foreign) in seven industries which are prominent in international business. Not all of these companies are multinational in an organizational/strategic sense, but all of them look to foreign markets for sales and all of them face competition from both domestic and foreign rivals. Furthermore, the dynamics of the world marketplace are such that it is questionable whether any of these companies can survive without becoming increasingly multinational in their operations and strategy.

WHAT LIES AHEAD

This chapter has introduced the reader to a comparative newcomer to international business—the multinational enterprise. The following chapter offers a statistical overview of direct foreign investment, the bulk of which is undertaken by MNE's. Chapter 23 next investigates the role of the

---

[14] Nicholas K. Bruck and Francis A. Lees, "Foreign Investment, Capital Controls, and the Balance of Payments," *The Bulletin*, Nos. 48-49 (New York University, 1968), pp. 83-85.

Table 21-8

SOME MULTINATIONAL ENTERPRISES RANKED BY THEIR SALES IN 1970 ACCORDING TO INDUSTRY
(Billions of Dollars)

Company	Location of Headquarters	Sales
Automobiles:		
1. General Motors	U.S.	28.3[a]
2. Ford Motor	U.S.	15.0
3. Chrysler	U.S.	7.0
4. Volkswagenwerk	Germany	4.3
5. Daimler-Benz	Germany	3.0
6. Fiat	Italy	2.7
7. Toyota Motor	Japan	2.7
8. Renault	France	2.5
9. British Leyland Motor	U.K.	2.5
10. Citroën	France	1.4
Petroleum:		
1. Standard Oil (N.J.)	U.S.	16.6
2. Royal Dutch/Shell Group	Netherlands-U.K.	10.8
3. Mobil Oil	U.S.	7.3
4. Texaco	U.S.	6.3
5. Gulf Oil	U.S.	5.4
6. Standard Oil (Cal.)	U.S.	4.2
7. British Petroleum	U.K.	4.1
8. Standard Oil (Ind.)	U.S.	3.7
9. Atlantic Richfield	U.S.	2.7
10. Continental Oil	U.S.	2.7
Office and computing machines:		
1. I.B.M.	U.S.	7.5
2. Honeywell	U.S.	1.9
3. Sperry Rand	U.S.	1.8
4. Xerox	U.S.	1.7
5. National Cash Reg.	U.S.	1.4
6. Burroughs	U.S.	0.9
7. Olivetti	Italy	0.7
8. Control Data	U.S.	0.5
9. Addressograph Multigraph	U.S.	0.4
10. Digital Equipment	U.S.	0.1
Electrical equipment:		
1. General Electric	U.S.	8.7
2. I.T.T.	U.S.	6.4
3. Westinghouse Electric	U.S.	4.3
4. Philips' Gloeilampenfabrieken	Netherlands	4.2
5. Hitachi	Japan	3.3
6. RCA	U.S.	3.3

(Continued)

Table 21-8

SOME MULTINATIONAL ENTERPRISES RANKED BY THEIR SALES
IN 1970 ACCORDING TO INDUSTRY
(Billions of Dollars)
(Continued)

Company	Location of Headquarters	Sales
7. Siemens	Germany	3.2
8. Matsushita Electric Industrial	Japan	2.6
9. AEG Telefunken	Germany	2.3
10. Tokyo Shibaura Electric	Japan	2.3
Chemicals:		
1. Dupont	U.S.	3.6
2. Imperial Chemical Industries.	U.K.	3.5
3. Farbwerke Hoechst	Germany	3.0
4. Union Carbide	U.S.	3.0
5. BASF	Germany	2.9
6. Montecatini Edison	Italy	2.8
7. Farbenfabriken Bayer	Germany	2.5
8. Rhône-Poulenc	France	2.0
9. Monsanto	U.S.	2.0
10. Dow Chemical	U.S.	1.9
Pharmaceuticals:		
1. Ciba-Geigy	Switzerland	1.6
2. Warner-Lambert	U.S.	1.3
3. Hoffmann LaRoche	Switzerland	1.1
4. Mead	U.S.	1.0
5. Pfizer	U.S.	0.9
6. Sandoz	Switzerland	0.6
7. Sterling Drug	U.S.	0.6
8. Eli Lilly	U.S.	0.6
9. Takeda Chemical Industries .	Japan	0.5
10. Abbott Laboratories	U.S.	0.5
Food products:		
1. Unilever	U.K.-Netherlands	6.9
2. Swift	U.S.	3.1
3. Kraftco	U.S.	2.8
4. Nestlé	Switzerland	2.3
5. General Foods	U.S.	2.0
6. Borden	U.S.	1.8
7. Consolidated Foods	U.S.	1.7
8. Coca-Cola	U.S.	1.6
9. Beatrice Foods	U.S.	1.6
10. CPC International	U.S.	1.4

Sources: Compiled from "The Fortune Directory of the 500 Largest Industrial Corporations," *Fortune* (May, 1971); and also from "The 200 Largest Industrials Outside the U.S.," *Fortune* (August, 1971).
a 1971.

multinational enterprise from the perspective of economic theory. Together these three chapters lay the factual and theoretical groundwork for a consideration of U.S. public policy toward MNE's in Chapter 24, and the relations between the multinational enterprise and sovereign national governments in Chapter 25.

SUMMARY

1. In the 1960's, U.S. business firms went abroad on a massive scale unprecedented in the history of international enterprise. Because of their vast size, the worldwide operations of multinational companies are now a decisive force in shaping the patterns of trade, investment, and technology flows among nations.

2. The actual historical experience of companies in the United States suggests that the process of internationalization is likely to be a gradual evolution that can be described in three stages: export, foreign production, and multinational enterprise.

3. In the *export* stage, the manufacturer depends entirely on export operations to penetrate foreign markets. In the *foreign production* stage, he enters foreign markets through foreign production under one or more arrangements: (a) licensing, (b) long-term contract arrangements with local producers, or (c) direct investment. Generally U.S. manufacturers have started with licensing and have then progressively shifted to direct investment.

4. A company becomes a *multinational enterprise* when its management begins to plan, organize, and control its international production on a worldwide scale. At the multinational stage, the manufacturer abandons a binational strategy and replaces it with a multinational strategy; national markets come to be viewed merely as segments of broader regional and world markets.

5. Although its historical roots are deep, nonetheless the multinational enterprise as we know it today is a recent phenomenon, emerging for the most part only since the mid-1950's. The appearance of multinational enterprise systems directed and controlled by a single decision-center had to await the dramatic postwar improvements in communications and transportation and the massive liberalization of international trade and payments that gathered steam in the late 1950's.

6. We can distinguish three broad categories of international business investors by their motivations: extractive, manufacturing, and service investors. Extractive investors go abroad to obtain raw materials which are not available at home or available only at a higher cost. Although the motivation of manufacturing investors is complex, several studies agree that considerations of marketing strategy dominate the vast majority of decisions to manufacture abroad. Service investment is mainly a response to the appearance of multinational industrial enterprises which demand services on a world region or global scale.

7. Statistical data on the new foreign activities of U.S. companies during the 1961-1970 decade tell us much about the pattern of expansion abroad; namely, the kinds of activities and their location, ownership, industry, and company size.

8. There is no single agreed definition of the multinational enterprise. Some observers use the nationality mix of ownership or management as criteria to measure the degree of multinationality. Most observers, however, have been concerned with the economic and business behavior of MNE's. Accordingly, they have defined the multinational enterprise in terms of organizational structure and business strategy, including the attitudes of top managers. For our purposes, a multinational enterprise denotes a parent company that takes part in foreign production through its own affiliates, exercises direct control over the policies of its affiliates, and seeks to follow a worldwide strategy.

QUESTIONS AND APPLICATIONS

1. Why do most manufacturers prefer to remain wholly domestic, staying out of foreign operations?

2. (a) Describe the three stages in the evolution of a multinational enterprise.
   (b) Why is the first direct investment abroad by a manufacturing company usually a critical step in the evolution of the company as an international enterprise?

3. Distinguish between binational and multinational strategies of companies with respect to foreign markets.

4. Why is the multinational enterprise a "recent phenomenon" in view of the long history of international business?

5. (a) Explain the motivations of companies which enter into foreign production.
   (b) Check out your answer to (a) by asking executives in international companies located in your area why their companies have gone abroad.

6. (a) Identify the three elements of the definition of multinational enterprise used in this text.
   (b) Why is an international holding company which owns foreign affiliates but does not exercise active control over affiliate policies excluded from our conception of a multinational enterprise?

7. Prepare a research report on one of the industries listed in Table 21-8 (shown on pages 522-523) which describes the worldwide competitive structure of that particular industry and the recent international activities of some of its leading companies.

SELECTED READINGS

Behrman, Jack N. *Some Patterns in the Rise of the Multinational Enterprise.* Research Paper 18. Chapel Hill: University of North Carolina, 1969.

Donner, Frederic G. *The World-Wide Industrial Enterprise*. New York: McGraw-Hill Book Company, 1967.

Vernon, Raymond. *Sovereignty At Bay*. New York: Basic Books, Inc., 1967. Chapters 1-4.

Wilkins, Mira. *The Emergence of Multinational Enterprise*. Cambridge: Harvard University Press, 1970. Chapter X.

CHAPTER 22

A STATISTICAL OVERVIEW OF DIRECT FOREIGN INVESTMENT

There is a notable scarcity of statistical data on the multi-faceted role of the multinational enterprise in the world economy.[1] Conventional statistics are collected by governments and international organizations mainly to measure balance of payments transactions; that is, trade, service, capital, and monetary flows between the reporting country and the rest of the world. National income accounts do not distinguish foreign-owned production from locally owned production, and foreign trade statistics do not distinguish transactions between parent companies and their affiliates or between affiliates (intraenterprise transactions) from transactions between independent exporters and importers. As a consequence, we lack reliable data on the location, size, and composition of the foreign production carried on by MNE's, as well as the imports and exports associated with that production. On the financial side, we have only a sketchy knowledge of the aggregate current payments and receipts, sources and uses of capital financing, and size and distribution of earnings of multinational enterprises.[2]

Because of poor statistics, both home and host governments can only guess how the decisions of MNE's affect production, employment, money

---

[1] See Stefan H. Robock and Kenneth Simmonds, "International Business—How Big Is It?" *Columbia Journal of World Business* (May-June, 1970), pp. 6-19.

[2] U.S. Government statistics relating to the MNE are far superior to those of other governments. In 1960, the U.S. Department of Commerce published the most comprehensive survey to date of U.S. foreign business investments in 1957. (See U.S. Department of Commerce, *U.S. Business Investments in Foreign Countries* (Washington: U.S. Government Printing Office, 1960). In an attempt to evaluate the full effects of U.S. business investments both on the U.S. economy and the economies of host countries, this survey collected statistics on several aspects of U.S. foreign affiliates, including assets and financial structure, local and export sales, expenditures and tax payments in host countries, sources and uses of funds, and earnings. Although the Department of Commerce has made a similar survey for 1966, it has published so far only data relating to the U.S. balance of payments. Although these benchmark statistics are highly useful, they do not meet the need for information on the current operations of multinational companies.

supply, prices, exports, imports, the balance of payments, and other economic sectors. Thus, they are ill-prepared to devise rational policies toward multinational companies, running the risk that their actual policies are either ineffective or counterproductive. Better statistics would remove much of the confusion and debate about the economic role of MNE's, although they would hardly quiet debate about the MNE's political role.[3] Given the economic importance of MNE's, we can expect national governments to improve their statistical coverage. In the end, however, the task will have to be taken on by an international agency, because no single government can hope to cover all the worldwide activities of multinational enterprises.

The most common way to measure the economic activities of multinational companies is by using the statistical data that is available; namely, data on direct foreign investment by business firms. Here again, however, only a few governments (notably the United States) publish comprehensive data on direct foreign investment. This chapter relies, therefore, mainly on U.S. Government statistics that cover only the direct foreign investment of U.S. companies and the direct investment of foreign companies in the United States.

U.S. figures on direct foreign investment include investment by companies which are not multinational in the organizational/strategic sense discussed in Chapter 21. But as a matter of fact, most U.S. direct foreign investment is undertaken by a small number of big companies which can be fairly described as multinational. Although the U.S. Office of Foreign Direct Investment lists 3,350 American companies with direct investments abroad, the statistical data show that fewer than 140 companies account for nearly 60 percent of U.S. private direct investment in foreign countries.[4] The 187 U.S. parent companies studied by the Harvard Business School accounted for over 80 percent of all U.S. direct foreign investment in manufacturing.[5] Hence, we can reasonably regard the statistics on U.S. direct foreign investment as being a reliable measure of certain aspects of U.S. multinational enterprises.

Against this background, the present chapter offers statistical data on the overall international investment position of the United States; that is, the value, composition, and location of U.S. direct investment abroad; direct investment and the U.S. balance of payments; the sales of U.S. manufacturing and mining affiliates abroad; the exports of U.S. parent companies; and direct investment in the United States by foreign companies.

---

[3] See Chapter 25.
[4] U.S. Department of Commerce, *Policy Aspects of Foreign Investment by U.S. Multinational Corporations* (Washington: U.S. Government Printing Office, January, 1972), p. 41.
[5] James W. Vaupel and Joan P. Curhan, *The Making of Multinational Enterprise* (Boston: Harvard University, 1969), p. v.

INTERNATIONAL INVESTMENT POSITION OF THE UNITED STATES

Table 22-1 shows the overall international investment position of the United States in selected years over the period 1914-1970. An examination of this table reveals many features of the U.S. foreign investment experience and also depicts direct investment in relation to other forms of foreign investment.

Table 22-1

INTERNATIONAL INVESTMENT POSITION OF THE UNITED STATES IN SELECTED YEARS, 1914-1970
(Billions of Dollars at Year End)

	1914*	1919	1930	1939	1946	1957	1965	1970
U.S. investments abroad	3.5	7.0	17.2	11.4	18.7	54.2	106.6	155.5
Private	3.5	7.0	17.2	11.4	13.5	36.8	81.6	119.9
Long-term ..	3.5	6.5	15.2	10.8	12.3	33.6	71.4	104.7
Direct ...	2.6	3.9	8.0	7.0	7.2	25.3	49.5	78.1
Portfolio .	0.9	2.6	7.2	3.8	5.1	8.3	21.9	26.6
Short-term .	na	0.5	2.0	0.6	1.3	3.2	10.2	15.2
U.S. Government [1]	—	—	—	—	5.2	17.4	25.0	35.6
Foreign investments in the U.S.	7.2	4.0	8.4	9.6	15.9	31.4	58.8	97.5
Long-term	6.7	3.2	5.7	6.3	7.0	12.8	28.3	46.7
Direct	1.3	0.9	1.4	2.0	2.5	4.8	8.8	13.2
Portfolio ...	5.4	2.3	4.3	4.3	4.5	8.0	19.5	33.5
Short-term [2] ..	0.5	0.8	2.7	3.3	8.9	18.5	30.6	50.7
U.S. net creditor position	−3.7	3.0	8.8	1.8	2.8	22.8	47.7	58.1
Net long-term .	−3.2	3.3	9.5	4.5	10.3	36.3	63.3	87.7
Net short-term [3]	−0.5	−0.3	−0.7	−2.7	−7.4	−13.5	−15.6	−29.6

Source: U.S. Department of Commerce, *Survey of Current Business* (Washington: U.S. Government Printing Office), various issues.

* At June 30.

[1] Excludes World War I loans and monetary gold stock; includes some short-term assets ($5.9 billion in 1970).

[2] Includes nonliquid liabilities to foreign official agencies.

[3] Includes short-term assets of U.S. Government (excluding gold) and nonliquid liabilities to official agencies.

na Not available.

General Note: Data for early years are not wholly comparable to data for later years because of different sources and methods. Figures may not add because of rounding.

U.S. INVESTMENT ABROAD

The value of all U.S. investment abroad (private and government, short-term and long-term) rose from $3.5 billion in 1914 to $155.5 billion in 1970. This impressive growth, however, has not been steady. After reaching a peak of $17.2 billion in 1930, foreign investment declined during the global depression of the 1930's as Americans stopped making new investments and liquidated old investments. Many portfolio investments were defaulted on by countries which lacked the foreign exchange to service them. The Depression also caused a precipitous drop in earnings on direct investments and thus discouraged new foreign ventures by American companies. Aside from foreign loans made by the U.S. Government, foreign investment remained fairly stagnant during World War II. In the years 1946-1957, however, foreign investment increased by over $35 billion, with government loans accounting for about one-third of the increase, and private investment (mostly direct) accounting for the rest.

During the years 1957-1970, U.S. investment abroad jumped over $100 billion to reach $155.5 billion by 1970. Over four-fifths of this growth came from private investment, notably direct investment, which more than tripled in value from $25.3 billion in 1957 to $78.1 billion in 1970. The years 1957-1970, therefore, may be aptly labeled the period of direct investment which reflected the emergence of the multinational enterprise.

The relative shares of private portfolio and direct long-term investment abroad have varied greatly over the period 1914-1970. *Portfolio* investment is long-term investment in which the private investor does not exercise any managerial control. The investor either holds foreign bonds or other non-equity securities which do not confer ownership rights or he holds stock shares (or other equities) in a foreign company in an amount too small to give him managerial control. In contrast, *direct* investment is a long-term equity investment in a foreign firm that gives the investor managerial control over that firm. Direct investment is *par excellence* business investment because direct investors are almost exclusively corporations or individuals representing a business enterprise.[6] After a remarkable expansion in the 1920's, portfolio investments substantially declined in the 1930's and regained the level of 1930 only in 1955. However, the resumption of European convertibility at the end of 1958 generated a wave of new portfolio investment in the early 1960's as European, Japanese, and Canadian borrowers floated bond issues in New York. After 1963, portfolio investment was restricted by the interest equalization tax, and by 1970 it was only about one-third the value of U.S. direct investment abroad.[7]

FOREIGN INVESTMENT IN THE UNITED STATES

The character of foreign investment in the United States differs in many respects from U.S. investment abroad. Since the 1930's, short-term investments (including bank balances, Treasury bills, and the like) have represented a significant share of total foreign investment in this country. In

---

[6] A more precise definition of direct investment is given on p. 531.

[7] See Chapter 19, pp. 474-475. The resumption of European convertibility in 1958 is referred to in Chapter 14 on p. 327.

1970, short-term investments were more than half of total investments, reflecting both the role of the United States dollar as a central reserve currency and the U.S. balance of payments deficit.

Foreign investors have also shown a decided preference for portfolio investments as opposed to direct investments. In 1970, the former were two and one-half times larger than the latter. Nevertheless, direct investments in the United States by foreign companies have not been stagnant in recent years, rising by 50 percent from 1965 to 1970. As we shall observe later in the chapter, there are now signs that foreign companies will greatly increase their direct investments in the United States during the 1970's.

U.S. NET CREDITOR POSITION

In light of the large, persistent deficit in the U.S. balance of payments since 1957, it may surprise some readers that the United States continued to increase its net international creditor position in the 1960's. The main explanation of this seeming contradiction is that the growth of U.S. long-term investment abroad has exceeded the growth of its short-term foreign liabilities resulting from the payments deficit. By 1970 the United States had become both an enormous net international creditor on long-term account ($87.7 billion) and an enormous (but smaller) net international short-term borrower ($29.6 billion). The rapid expansion of direct investments abroad by American multinational companies has been the key factor in sustaining the net international creditor position of the United States.

U.S. DIRECT INVESTMENT ABROAD

Where are U.S. direct foreign investments located? What is their distribution by industry? How are the plant and equipment expenditures of U.S. foreign affiliates financed? What is the rate of return on U.S. direct investment abroad?

Before taking up these questions, it is desirable to define more precisely the meaning of "direct investment" and "book value." The U.S. Department of Commerce defines *direct foreign investment* to include "all foreign business organizations in which a U.S. person, organization, or affiliated group owns an interest of 10 percent or more." [8] In addition, the Department counts as direct foreign investment "a foreign business organization in which 50 percent or more of voting stock is owned by U.S. residents even though no single U.S. group owns as much as 10 percent." [9]

---

[8] U.S. Department of Commerce, *U.S. Direct Investments Abroad 1966, Part I: Balance of Payments Data* (Washington: U.S. Government Printing Office, 1970), p. 2.

[9] *Ibid.* Foreign affiliates of U.S. companies which are organized as foreign corporations are commonly called *subsidiaries;* foreign affiliates may also be organized as *branches* through which U.S. parent companies conduct business in their own names and always have full ownership. Unless there are special tax advantages of a branch, U.S. companies generally organize their affiliates as separate corporations. For this reason we shall at times use "subsidiary" as a substitute for "affiliate."

The dollar values of direct foreign investments are the values carried on the books of the U.S. parent companies. The *book value* of an investment is its value at the time the investment was made; thus, it is a "historical" value which is not adjusted to changes in price levels. Since worldwide inflation has been a chronic condition since World War II, the book values of U.S. direct investments made some years ago badly understate their current replacement values. The market value of U.S. direct investment abroad is almost certainly substantially higher than the reported book value.

Year-to-year increases in the book value of U.S. direct foreign investment are the net resultant of (1) the outflow of new capital from the United States, (2) new issues of securities sold abroad by U.S. companies to finance capital expenditures abroad (but not securities issued by their foreign affiliates or short-term borrowing abroad), (3) reinvested earnings of foreign affiliates, and (4) valuation adjustments, mostly associated with liquidations of existing holdings. The third and fourth sources of yearly changes in the book value of direct investment are not recorded in the U.S. balance of payments.

U.S. DIRECT FOREIGN INVESTMENT BY AREA

Table 22-2 presents data on the area distribution of U.S. direct foreign investment for the years 1950, 1959, and 1970.

Table 22-2

U.S. DIRECT INVESTMENT ABROAD BY AREA, 1950, 1959, and 1970
(Millions of Dollars)

Area	1950	1959	1970
All areas	11,788	29,735	78,090
Canada	3,579	10,171	22,801
Europe	1,733	5,300	24,471
Australia, New Zealand, and South Africa	366	1,116	4,348
Japan	19	210	1,491
All industrial areas	5,697	16,797	53,111
Latin America	4,576	8,990	14,683
Middle East	692	1,208	1,645
Africa [1]	147	520	2,612
Asia [2]	320	901	2,477
All developing areas	5,735	11,619	21,416
International [3]	356	1,320	3,563

Sources: U.S. Department of Commerce, *U.S. Business Investments in Foreign Countries* (Washington: U.S. Government Printing Office, 1960), Table 3, p. 91, and Table 1, p. 89, for 1950 and 1959, respectively. U.S. Department of Commerce, *Survey of Current Business* (Washington: U.S. Government Printing Office, October, 1971), Table 6A, p. 32, for 1970.
[1] Excluding South Africa.
[2] Excluding Japan.
[3] Mainly investment in foreign-flag shipping.
Note: Figures may not add because of rounding.

Part Three / Enterprise

In 1970, about two-thirds of all direct investment was concentrated in the industrial areas. This distribution contrasts sharply with the distribution in 1950 when the amount of direct investment in the industrial areas was slightly *below* that in the developing areas. Demonstrably, U.S. direct investment in the 1950's and (especially) the 1960's has flowed mainly to the advanced countries. Canada and Western Europe account for most of the direct investment in the industrial areas. Direct investment in Japan is far lower than would be expected from the size of that country's gross national product. This "underinvestment" in Japan is a direct consequence of severe restrictions on the entry of American companies.

Over two-thirds of U.S. direct investment in the developing areas is centered in Latin America. The other developing areas have attracted relatively small amounts of investment, mainly in petroleum and other extractive operations. This tendency of U.S. companies to invest in the industrial areas is likely to continue in the 1970's in view of the high political risks and limited market opportunities in the majority of developing countries. In particular, we can expect a sharp jump in U.S. direct investment in Japan as that country progressively liberalizes its foreign investment policy.

U.S. DIRECT INVESTMENT BY INDUSTRY

As shown in Table 22-3, manufacturing has been the most dynamic form of direct investment in the 1960's. In 1959, manufacturing investment was

Table 22-3

U.S. DIRECT INVESTMENT ABROAD BY INDUSTRY IN INDUSTRIAL AND DEVELOPING AREAS, 1959 AND 1970
(Billions of Dollars)

Area	All Industries	Mining and Smelting	Petroleum	Manu-facturing	Other Industries[1]
All areas					
1959	29.7	2.9	10.4	9.7	6.8
1970	78.1	6.1	21.8	32.2	17.9
Industrial areas					
1959	16.8	1.3	4.3	8.1	3.1
1970	53.1	3.7	11.7	26.7	11.0
Developing areas					
1959	11.6	1.6	5.3	1.6	3.1
1970	21.4	2.5	8.4	5.5	5.1
International					
1959	1.3		0.8		0.5
1970	3.6		1.7		1.9

Sources: U.S. Department of Commerce, *U.S. Business Investments in Foreign Countries* (Washington: U.S. Government Printing Office, 1960), Table 1, p. 89, for 1959. U.S. Department of Commerce, *Survey of Current Business* (Washington: U.S. Government Printing Office, October, 1971), Table 6A, p. 32, for 1970.
1 Includes agriculture, transportation, public utilities, trade, and finance.
Note: Figures may not add because of rounding.

32.6 percent of all direct investment; in 1970, it was 41.2 percent. Manufacturing accounted for $22.5 billion of the $48.4 billion increase in U.S. direct investment during the period 1959-1970.

Only a small share of direct investment in the industrial areas is extractive (mining and crude petroleum). Much of the petroleum investment in the industrial areas should be regarded as "manufacturing" because it consists of investment in refineries. This investment (plus investment in marketing facilities) explains why petroleum investment in the industrial areas is higher than in the developing areas, which account for the bulk of direct investment in petroleum extraction.

In the developing areas, extractive investment was responsible for about one-half of all direct investment in 1970. However, manufacturing investment was by far the most dynamic form of investment in the 1960's, rising from $1.6 billion in 1959 to $5.5 billion in 1970, or more than tripling in value. This shift toward manufacturing investment in the developing countries will probably accelerate in the 1970's as expropriations of foreign extractive investments discourage new extractive investment while, at the same time, new opportunities for foreign manufacturing investments are opened up by continuing industrialization.

"International" investment refers to investment by American companies in foreign-flag shipping. About half of this investment has been undertaken by petroleum companies which own large fleets of tankers.

The 133 largest U.S. direct investors abroad are classified by industry in Table 22-4. As mentioned earlier, this small number of companies is responsible for nearly 60 percent of all U.S. direct foreign investment.

PLANT AND EQUIPMENT EXPENDITURES BY FOREIGN AFFILIATES OF U.S. COMPANIES

Table 22-5 reveals that the foreign affiliates of U.S. companies spent $13.1 billion in 1970 on plant and equipment, spending $6.0 billion to maintain their physical assets (depreciation) and $7.1 billion to acquire new assets (net investment).[10]

In 1970, less than one-third of the funds to finance plant and equipment expenditures came from the United States; the remaining funds came from reinvested earnings (22.1 percent) and foreign borrowing (46.6 percent). The decline of the United States as a source of funds since 1965 (when it was 46.0 percent) was forced on American companies by official restraints on U.S. capital outflows. It is apparent, however, that the ability of large multinational enterprises to obtain funds from outside the United States (mainly in the Eurodollar and Eurobond markets) has enabled them to

---

[10] Hence, the book value of U.S. foreign direct investment increased by $7.1 billion in 1970.

Table 22-4

DISTRIBUTION OF THE 133 LARGEST U.S. DIRECT INVESTORS ABROAD IN 1970 BY STANDARD INDUSTRIAL CLASSIFICATION (SIC) GROUPS

SIC Number	Description	Number of Companies
291	Petroleum refining	15
283	Drugs	13
281	Industrial chemicals	11
333	Nonferrous metals	9
352	Farm machinery	6
357	Office and computing machines	6
371	Motor vehicles and equipment	5
203	Canned, cured, and frozen foods	5
284	Soaps, cleaners, and toilet goods	5
301	Tires and inner tubes	4
366	Communication equipment	4
331	Blast furnace and basic steel products	3
363	Household appliances	3
262	Paper and pulp mills	3
Other	Twenty-nine SIC groups with one or two large investors in each group	41
Total		133

Source: U.S. Department of Commerce, *Policy Aspects of Foreign Investment by U.S. Multinational Corporations* (Washington: U.S. Government Printing Office, January, 1972), p. 26.

Table 22-5

PLANT AND EQUIPMENT EXPENDITURES BY THE FOREIGN AFFILIATES OF U.S. COMPANIES AND THEIR FINANCING 1965-1970
(Billions of Dollars)

Year	Plant and Equipment Expenditures (1)	Sources of Funds		
		Reinvested Earnings	Outside United States	United States (2)	(2) as % of (1)
1965	7.4	1.5	2.5	3.4	46.0
1966	8.6	1.7	3.7	3.2	37.2
1967	9.3	1.6	4.8	2.9	31.2
1968	9.4	2.2	4.8	2.4	25.5
1969	10.8	2.6	5.6	2.6	24.1
1970	13.1	2.9	6.1	4.1	31.3

Sources: U.S. Department of Commerce, *Policy Aspects of Foreign Investment by U.S. Multinational Corporations* (Washington: U.S. Government Printing Office, January, 1972), Table 9, p. 64; *Survey of Current Business* (Washington: U.S. Government Printing Office, September, 1971), Table 1, p. 28, and (October, 1971), Table 3, p. 28.

continue their expansion abroad. Indeed, it is doubtful that U.S. capital restraints have slowed down the pace of that expansion.[11]

RATE OF RETURN ON U.S. DIRECT INVESTMENT ABROAD

Table 22-6 indicates the rates of return on U.S. direct investment in all geographical areas and in the three areas that account for four-fifths of that investment.

Table 22-6

RATE OF RETURN ON U.S. DIRECT INVESTMENT IN MANUFACTURING BY AREA, 1959, 1963, 1967, and 1970
(Percent)

Year	All Areas	Western Europe	Canada	Latin America
1959	13.0	17.9	10.5	9.1
1963	11.6	12.8	9.9	8.9
1967	9.3	9.5	8.0	8.1
1970	11.2	13.5	6.9	11.4

Source: U.S. Department of Commerce, *U.S. Business Investments in Foreign Countries* (Washington: U.S. Government Printing Office, 1960), Table 1, p. 89, and Table 37, p. 126; *Survey of Current Business* (Washington: U.S. Government Printing Office), various issues.
General Note: The rate of return on direct investment represents earnings divided by the book value of investment at the beginning of the year.

For all geographical areas the rate of return in 1970 was lower than in 1959, although the rate of return in Latin America was higher in 1970 than in 1959. In recent years the rate of return on manufacturing investment abroad has been about the same as the rate of return *within* the United States. Generally speaking, therefore, it is not true that direct foreign investments in manufacturing offer returns that substantially exceed returns in the United States. During the 1960's, the rate of return in Western Europe was notably higher than the rates of return in Canada and Latin America, reflecting the rapid economic growth of that area.

DIRECT INVESTMENT, THE U.S. BALANCE OF PAYMENTS, AND MULTINATIONAL ENTERPRISE

In recent years much controversy has swirled around direct foreign investment as a result of disagreement concerning its effects on the U.S. balance of payments. Disagreement proceeds from the many short- and long-term effects of direct investment on the items comprising the balance

---

[11] See Chapter 24, pp. 574-576, for a discussion of the effects of U.S. capital restraints on direct investment.

of payments, not all of which can be quantified in a straight-forward fashion. Chapter 24 will examine this and other controversies in U.S. foreign investment policy. Our present purpose is simply to offer data that relates to some of the effects of direct investment, and more generally of multinational enterprise, on the U.S. balance of payments and trade.

DIRECT INVESTMENT OUTFLOW AND INCOME RECEIPTS

Table 22-7 compares the outflow of funds leaving the United States for direct investment abroad with the receipts of income from direct foreign investment made in previous years. In every year from 1960 through 1970, income receipts have exceeded the outflow of funds for direct investment. Furthermore, the net credit balance has followed a generally rising trend. With regard to these two items, then, the figures show conclusively that U.S. direct foreign investment has been a major source of strength for the U.S. balance of payments.

Table 22-7

DIRECT INVESTMENT AND THE U.S. BALANCE OF PAYMENTS: U.S. DIRECT INVESTMENT FLOWS AND INVESTMENT INCOME RECEIPTS, 1960-1970
(Millions of Dollars)

| Year | Long-term Private Capital Flows | | Funds Leaving U.S. for Direct Investment | Receipts of Income From U.S. Investment Abroad ** | Net Credit Balance |
	Direct Investment Flows (Net)	Funds Raised Abroad *			
	(1)	(2)	(1)–(2)	(3)	(3)–[(1)–(2)]
1960	1674		1674	2954	1280
1961	1598		1598	3430	1832
1962	1654		1654	3844	2190
1963	1976		1976	4019	2043
1964	2328		2328	4687	2359
1965	3468	52	3416	5162	1746
1966	3661	445	3216	5374	2158
1967	3137	278	2859	5956	3097
1968	3209	785	2424	6519	4095
1969	3254	631	2623	7340	4717
1970	4445	378	4067	7906	3839

Source: U.S. Department of Commerce, *Policy Aspects of Foreign Investment by U.S. Multinational Corporations* (Washington: U.S. Government Printing Office, January, 1972), Table 9, p. 64, and Table 10, p. 65. See also *Survey of Current Business* (Washington: U.S. Government Printing Office, June, 1971) and (October, 1970).
* New issues of securities sold abroad by U.S. corporations. Excludes most securities issued by subsidiaries incorporated abroad, as well as bank borrowings and other credits.
** Interest, dividends, branch earnings, fees, and royalties.

EXPORTS OF U.S. PARENT COMPANIES

Table 22-8 reveals the 1965 export performance of 320 U.S. multinational enterprises that together controlled almost 3600 foreign affiliates and were responsible for well over one-half of all U.S. direct investment abroad.

Table 22-8

DISTRIBUTION OF EXPORTS OF 320 U.S. PARENT COMPANIES BY SIZE IN 1965
(Millions of Dollars)

	Number of Companies	Value	Percent
Total worldwide exports	297 [a]	8,518	100.0
$100 million and over	19	4,153	48.7
$50 million to $99.9 million	23	1,566	18.4
$10 million to $49.9 million	94	2,162	25.4
Less than $10 million	161	637	7.5

Source: U.S. Department of Commerce, *Survey of Current Business* (Washington: U.S. Government Printing Office, May, 1969), Table 2, p. 38.
Note: Figures may not add because of rounding.
[a] Twenty-three companies reported no exports from the United States.

Only 23 of these companies did not export from the United States in 1965; the remaining companies exported over $8.5 billion of merchandise. Truly striking is the fact that a mere 19 companies (with individual export sales of $100 million or more) accounted for almost half of these exports. Only 42 companies were responsible for over two-thirds of the exports of all 320 companies. The $8.5 billion of exports constituted nearly 45 percent of *total* U.S. nonagricultural exports in 1965. It is evident, therefore, that *the same multinational enterprises that are the major direct investors abroad are, at the same time, the major exporters of industrial products from the United States.* The data in Table 22-8 offer no support to those who argue that U.S. direct foreign investments act to displace U.S. exports.

Table 22-9 throws further light on the exports of these same companies by showing the role of foreign affiliates as buyers of U.S. goods.

For all industries, 51.8 percent of company exports were channeled through their foreign affiliates. Only thirty-nine companies did not export to their affiliates. These *intraenterprise* exports, involving "sellers" and "buyers" belonging to the same multinational company, were directly dependent on the existence of foreign affiliates, demonstrating a stimulating effect of direct foreign investment on U.S. exports. Affiliates purchased export goods from their parent companies for a variety of purposes: for further processing and assembly, for resale without further manufacture, for capital equipment, and for other miscellaneous purposes. In addition to their purchases of $4.4 billion from parent companies, foreign affiliates also purchased $618 million from independent suppliers in the United States.

Table 22-9

EXPORTS OF 320 U.S. PARENT COMPANIES IN 1965: TOTAL WORLDWIDE VERSUS THOSE CHANNELED THROUGH THEIR FOREIGN AFFILIATES

(Millions of Dollars)

	All Industries		All Manufacturing		All Non-manufacturing[1]	
	$	%	$	%	$	%
Total worldwide exports of 320 companies *	8,518	100.0	7,866	100.0	652	100.0
Exports to unaffiliated foreign purchasers	4,102	48.2	3,809	48.4	294	45.1
Exports channeled through their foreign affiliates **	4,416	51.8	4,057	51.6	358	54.9
Purchased by affiliates	4,142	48.6	3,788	48.2	354	54.3
For further processing or assembly	1,496	17.6	1,468	18.7	28	4.3
For resale without further manufacture	2,199	25.8	2,003	25.5	197	30.2
Capital equipment	263	3.1	203	2.6	60	9.2
Other and unallocated	184	2.2	115	1.5	70	10.7
Sold on commission basis by affiliates	273	3.2	269	3.4	4	0.6
Purchases by their affiliates from independent U.S. suppliers other than parents	618		468		150	

Source: U.S. Department of Commerce, *Survey of Current Business* (Washington: U.S. Government Printing Office, May, 1969), Table 1, p. 37, and Table 6, p. 40.

* Twenty-three companies reported no exports from the United States.
** Thirty-nine companies reported that no U.S. exports were channeled through their affiliates.
[1] Mining, petroleum, trade, and other. The petroleum industry alone accounted for $564 million of worldwide exports and $290 million of exports channeled through affiliates.
Note: Figures may not add because of rounding.

SALES OF U.S. MANUFACTURING AND MINING AFFILIATES

Table 22-10 reveals that the sales of U.S. manufacturing affiliates reached almost $60 billion in 1968, far exceeding export sales of manufactures made in the United States.[12] For all areas, almost four-fifths of these sales were local, taking place in the country of manufacture. Of the remaining sales, $4.7 billion were exported to the United States, while $8.5 billion were exported to third countries. However, some 80 percent of the U.S. imports from manufacturing affiliates came from Canada, mainly in products covered by the U.S.-Canadian Automotive Agreement of 1965.[13] Excluding the exports of Canadian affiliates manufacturing transportation equipment, total exports of foreign affiliates to the United States were only $2.5 billion in 1968, or 4.2 percent of their overall sales.

Table 22-10

SALES OF U.S. FOREIGN MANUFACTURING AFFILIATES BY AREA AND DESTINATION IN 1968
(Millions of Dollars)

Area	Total Sales (1)	Local Sales (2)	(2) as a % of (1)	Exported to U.S.	Exported to Other Countries
All areas	59,676	46,465	77.9	4,741	8,470
Canada	18,548	13,369	72.1	3,787 a	1,392
Europe	25,835	19,195	74.3	549 b	6,091
Latin America	7,966	7,213	90.5	212	541
Other areas	7,327	6,688	91.3	193	446

Source: U.S. Department of Commerce, *Survey of Current Business* (Washington: U.S. Government Printing Office, October, 1970), Table 3, p. 20.
a Of which transportation equipment is $2,247 million.
b Of which transportation equipment is $230 million.
Note: This data covers approximately 500 major U.S. parent companies.

In contrast to this pattern of manufacturing affiliates' sales, sales of mining affiliates are substantially exports to the United States and third countries (Table 22-11). In 1968, 35.4 percent of their sales were exports to the United States. The figures in Tables 22-10 and 22-11 support the distinction drawn in Chapter 21 between foreign manufacturing investments that are made primarily to penetrate foreign markets and foreign extractive investments that are made primarily to obtain raw materials for the home and other industrial countries.

---

[12] See Chapter 2, p. 49.

[13] This Agreement, which established free trade in new automobiles and parts between the United States and Canada, has greatly encouraged American automobile companies to produce in Canada for sale in the United States.

Table 22-11

SALES OF U.S. FOREIGN MINING AFFILIATES BY AREA AND DESTINATION IN 1968
(Millions of Dollars)

Area	Total Sales (1)	Local Sales (2)	(2) as a % of (1)	Exported to U.S.	Exported to Other Countries
All areas	5,269	1,119	21.2	1,864	2,286
Canada	2,058	542	26.3	912	604
Europe	105	47	44.7	3	55
Latin America	1,814	317	17.5	696	801
Other areas	1,292	213	16.5	253	826

Source: U.S. Department of Commerce, *Survey of Current Business* (Washington: U.S. Government Printing Office, October, 1970), Table 4, p. 20.

DIRECT INVESTMENT BY NON-U.S. MULTINATIONAL ENTERPRISES

This section takes a brief look at the direct foreign investment activities of companies which are headquartered outside the United States.

DIRECT FOREIGN INVESTMENT BY MAJOR COUNTRIES

Because of the relative abundance of statistics on U.S. direct foreign investment, it is commonly assumed that almost all multinational enterprises are American. Table 22-12 (page 542) offers data that disproves this assumption by comparing U.S. direct foreign investment with that of other countries.

In 1966, direct foreign investment by all countries was almost $90 billion, with the United States responsible for about three-fifths of this world total and foreign countries (mainly European) responsible for the remainder. This distribution of direct foreign investment roughly agrees with the distribution of gross national product between the United States and the other industrial countries. Hence, the emergence of multinational enterprise is a phenomenon which is associated with all industrial countries, not just with the United States.

DIRECT FOREIGN INVESTMENT IN THE UNITED STATES

Earlier in this chapter we observed that foreign investors have shown a decided preference for portfolio investment in the United States as opposed to direct investment. But, at the same time, it is evident from Table 22-1

Table 22-12

DIRECT FOREIGN INVESTMENTS BY MAJOR COUNTRIES AT THE END OF 1966
(Millions of Dollars)

Country	Petroleum	Mining and Smelting	Manu-facturing	Other	Total
World	25,942	5,923	36,246	21,472	89,583
United States	16,264	4,135	22,050	12,113	54,462
United Kingdom	4,200	759	6,028	5,015	16,002
France	na	na	na	na	4,000 a
Germany	200	100	1,800	400	2,500
Sweden	na	na	na	na	793
Canada	na	250 a	2,988 a	na	3,238
Japan	na	na	na	na	1,000

Source: U.S. Department of Commerce, *Policy Aspects of Foreign Investment by U.S. Multinational Corporations* (Washington: U.S. Government Printing Office, January, 1972), Table 1, p. 9. Based on OECD statistics.
na Not available.
a Estimated.

that direct investment by foreign companies in the United States has been growing rapidly in recent years, jumping from $8.8 billion in 1965 to $13.2 billion in 1970. Table 22-13 supplies further information on direct foreign investment in the United States at the end of 1970.

The United Kingdom is the single most important direct investor in the United States, followed rather closely by Canada. The Netherlands and

Table 22-13

DIRECT FOREIGN INVESTMENTS IN THE UNITED STATES AT THE END OF 1970
(Millions of Dollars)

Country	Total	Manu-facturing	Finance and Insurance	Petroleum	Other
All countries	13,209	6,105	2,250	2,981	1,873
Canada	3,112	1,831	324	189	768
Europe	9,515	4,061	1,800	2,766	888
United Kingdom	4,110	1,391	1,135	1,209	375
Netherlands ...	2,121	652	58	1,311	100
Switzerland	1,550	1,152	351	—	47
Other	1,734	866	256	246	366
Other areas	582	213	126	26	217

Source: U.S. Department of Commerce, *Survey of Current Business* (Washington: U.S. Government Printing Office, October, 1971), Table 10, p. 38.

Switzerland are next in importance. Toward the end of the 1960's, however, both Germany and Japan stepped up the pace of their direct investment in this country. From 1967 through 1970, the value of Germany's direct investment in the United States (led by three chemical companies: Hoechst, BASF, and Bayer) almost doubled to $617 million.[14] During the same years, Japan increased its direct investments in the United States by more than 60 percent, mostly in sales and service facilities to develop markets for Japanese-made products.[15]

At the end of 1970, 766 manufacturing enterprises in the United States were owned wholly or in part by 491 foreign corporations. The United Kingdom's Imperial Chemical Industries is making chemicals in the United States; Italy's Olivetti is making typewriters; Switzerland's Nestlé, chocolate; Canada's Massey-Ferguson, agricultural machinery; Germany's BASF, plastics; and Switzerland's Hoffmann-LaRoche, drugs.[16] Well-known companies in the United States which are affiliates of European multinational enterprises include Shell, Facit, SKF, U.S. Potash, Brown and Williamson, Beecham Products, Brown Boveri, Buitoni Foods, Carling Brewery, CIBA Pharmaceutical, Decca Gramaphone, Seagram, Electrolux, Lever Brothers, and Lipton.

Direct investment in the United States is stimulated by a variety of factors. The major attraction is the sheer size and growth potential of the American market. Direct investment in manufacturing also enables European companies to eliminate transportation costs and to circumvent U.S. tariffs and import quotas. Power costs are also lower in this country, and American labor is highly productive. U.S. corporate income taxes are lower than similar taxes in many European countries, and capital can be raised easily in the United States and often at a lower cost than in foreign countries. Although European companies protest the stringency of U.S. antitrust laws, the Justice Department has approved the tie-up between British Petroleum and Standard Oil of Ohio and the merger of the Netherlands' KZO with International Salt.[17] Furthermore, the devaluation of the dollar and rising wage levels in Europe and Japan have brought down the relative cost of

---

[14] "A Big Foreign Stake in U.S. Industry," *Fortune* (August, 1971), p. 118.

[15] *Ibid.* However, Mitsui has announced plans to build a petrochemical plant in the United States. See "Foreigners Up the Ante," *Business Week* (August 16, 1969), p. 56.

[16] *Ibid.* These companies are all big multinational enterprises. For instance, the operating affiliates of Hoffmann-LaRoche are grouped under two holding companies, one based in Basel and the other a Canadian corporation with its headquarters in Montevideo, Uruguay. The Basel company embraces all operations in continental Europe, North Africa, and the Middle East. The Canadian company covers the English-speaking world, South America, and Asia. The American affiliate in New Jersey has sales of nearly $500 million, accounting for 40 percent of Hoffmann-LaRoche's worldwide sales. See "The Secret Life of Hoffmann-LaRoche," *Fortune* (August, 1971), p. 132.

[17] See Chapter 24, pp. 591-595.

investment in this country. All signs point to an upsurge of direct foreign investment in the United States during the 1970's.

SUMMARY

1. There is a notable scarcity of statistical data on the multifaceted role of the multinational enterprise in the world economy. As a consequence, we lack reliable data on the location, size, and composition of the foreign production carried on by MNE's, as well as the imports and exports associated with that production. The most common way to measure the economic activities of MNE's is by using the statistical data which are available; namely, data on direct foreign investment by business firms.

2. The relationship between direct foreign investment and multinational companies is intimate: fewer than 140 companies account for nearly 60 percent of U.S. direct investment abroad.

3. The United States continued to increase its net international creditor position in the 1960's because the growth of long-term investment abroad (mainly direct) exceeded the growth in short-term liabilities owed to foreign countries. By 1970, the United States had become both an enormous net international creditor on long-term account ($87.7 billion) and an enormous (but smaller) net international short-term borrower ($29.6 billion).

4. In contrast to *portfolio* investment, *direct* investment involves managerial control by the investor. The dollar values of direct foreign investments are the values carried on the books of U.S. parent companies (*book values*). About two-thirds of all U.S. direct investment is concentrated in the industrial areas. During the period 1959-1970, manufacturing accounted for $22.5 billion of the $48.4 billion increase in U.S. direct foreign investment. The shift toward manufacturing investment will probably accelerate in the 1970's. The three industries that lead in direct investment abroad are petroleum refining, drugs, and industrial chemicals. In 1970, less than one-third of the funds to finance plant and equipment expenditures of U.S. foreign affiliates came from the United States. In general, the rate of return on U.S. direct foreign investment in manufacturing has been about the same as the rate of return on similar investments in the United States in recent years.

5. In every year of the period 1960-1970, income receipts from direct foreign investment have substantially exceeded the outflow of funds for direct investment in the U.S. balance of payments. With respect to these two items, direct foreign investment is a major source of strength for the U.S. balance of payments.

6. In 1965, 297 U.S. parent companies accounted for nearly 45 percent of total U.S. nonagricultural exports. A mere 19 companies accounted for almost half of those exports. Thus, the same multinational enterprises which are the major direct investors abroad are also the major exporters of industrial products from the United States. Figures for 320 U.S. parent companies reveal that over half of their exports are channeled through their foreign affiliates.

7. The sales of U.S. manufacturing affiliates far exceed U.S. exports of manufactured products. For all areas, almost four-fifths of the sales of U.S. manufacturing affiliates occurred in the country of manufacture. Four-fifths of the $4.7 billion exported by these affiliates to the United States came from Canada, mainly in products covered by the U.S.-Canadian Automotive Agreement. In contrast, sales of U.S. mining affiliates were substantially to the United States and third countries.

8. The emergence of multinational enterprise is a phenomenon which is associated with all industrial countries, not just with the United States. At the end of 1970, 766 manufacturing enterprises in the United States were owned in whole or in part by 491 foreign corporations.

QUESTIONS AND APPLICATIONS

1. Comment on the principal features of the international investment position of the United States over the period 1914-1970.
2. (a) Distinguish between *portfolio* and *direct* foreign investment.
   (b) To what extent are American multinational companies responsible for U.S. direct foreign investment?
3. (a) What is the *book value* of a direct foreign investment?
   (b) Why does book value understate the market value of U.S. direct investment abroad?
4. (a) How do you explain the area distribution of U.S. direct investment abroad?
   (b) How do you explain its distribution by economic sector? By specific industry?
5. "In 1970, less than one-third of the funds to finance the plant and equipment expenditures of U.S. foreign affiliates came from the United States." Explain.
6. What is meant by *intraenterprise exports*? How do they differ from "traditional" exports?
7. "The same multinational enterprises that are the major direct investors abroad are, at the same time, the major exporters of industrial products from the United States." Why is this so?
8. Why are the sales of United States manufacturing affiliates abroad mostly *local*? Is this also true of the sales of U.S. mining affiliates abroad? Why or why not?
9. Undertake research on the U.S.-Canadian Automotive Agreement to answer this question: Why has the Agreement stimulated General Motors, Ford, and other U.S. companies to produce more automobiles and parts in Canada for sale in the United States?

SELECTED READINGS

U.S. Department of Commerce. *Policy Aspects of Foreign Investment by U.S. Multinational Corporations.* Washington: U.S. Government Printing Office, January, 1972.

—————. *Survey of Current Business*. Washington: U.S. Government Printing Office, monthly.

—————. *U. S. Business Investments in Foreign Countries*. Washington: U.S. Government Printing Office, 1960.

—————. *U.S. Direct Investments Abroad 1966, Part I: Balance of Payments Data*. Washington: U.S. Government Printing Office, 1970.

Vaupel, James W., and Joan P. Curhan. *The Making of Multinational Enterprise*. Cambridge: Harvard University Press, 1969.

CHAPTER **23**

THE MULTINATIONAL ENTERPRISE AS AN INTERNATIONAL TRANSFER AGENT

In Chapter 21 we defined the multinational enterprise as a headquarters or parent company that:

1. Engages in foreign production and other economic activities through its own affiliates located in several different countries;
2. Exercises direct control over the policies of those affiliates; and
3. Strives to design and implement business strategies in production, marketing, finance, research and development, and other areas that transcend national boundaries, thereby becoming progressively more global in its orientation.

We now examine the role of the multinational enterprise as an *international transfer agent* in the world economy. The multinational enterprise becomes an international transfer agent when it moves products and factor services (capital, technology, and management) among national economies.

THE MULTINATIONAL ENTERPRISE SYSTEM

The multinational enterprise performs its role as an international transfer agent through institutional/organizational arrangements that collectively make up the *multinational enterprise system*. This system, as depicted in Figure 23-1 (page 548), comprises the parent company and its foreign affiliates.

The parent company (denoted by the *P* circle) is the enterprise decision center which determines the goals and controls the operations of the entire system. The key decisions of the parent company relate to the establishment (or acquisition), country location, size, and "product mix" of its production affiliates; the direction, volume, and composition of transfers among the affiliates; and the national markets to be served by the affiliates. These strategy decisions generate a pattern of factor and product flows among the members of the system. The parent company and its affiliates (denoted by the *A*

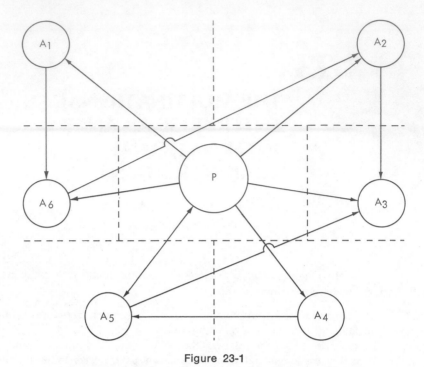

Figure 23-1

THE MULTINATIONAL ENTERPRISE SYSTEM

circles) are located in different countries, as indicated by the dashed lines. Most of the affiliates perform both production and marketing functions, but some perform only a marketing or financial function.

The affiliates are connected to the parent company and, in some instances, to other affiliates by a variety of cross-national flows of products, capital, technology, and management.[1] Flows of factor services, usually accompanied by product flows, generally move from the parent company to the affiliates. Any of these kinds of flows may also link pairs of affiliates. To illustrate, A_1 may transfer parts or components (which it manufactures) to A_6, which uses them to manufacture other products. A_4 may transfer certain finished products to A_5, which then resells them in the local market. Idle funds accumulating in A_2 may be transferred to A_3 to finance a capital expansion. A_5 may develop new technology which is transferred to A_3. A manager in A_6 may be transferred to a new position in A_2. Some products and factor services may also be transferred from an affiliate to the parent company, such as A_5 to P.

---

[1] They are also connected by financial flows that represent the financing and payment of the real flows. These include product payments, capital funds, interest and dividend payments, royalties, and management fees. Our interest in this chapter is focused on the real flows of products and factor services rather than on the associated financial flows.

One of the distinctive features of the multinational enterprise system is the rapid growth of interaffiliate transfers as managers in the parent company try to improve the performance of the entire system. During the foreign production stage, as described in Chapter 21, the parent company follows a *binational* strategy. That is to say, its managers perceive foreign countries as constituting insulated markets, insulated production bases, and insulated capital markets. In this stage, the parent company invests in country X to supply a market in country X, not to supply markets in country Y, country Z, or the world in general. The consequence of a binational strategy is to confine flows of products and factor services mostly to transfers between the parent company and individual affiliates and thereby minimize interaffiliate transfers. However, in the multinational stage the parent company abandons a binational strategy for a *multinational* strategy. As already observed, managers now perceive a worldwide market for the company's products, and they work to build up interaffiliate transfers on regional or global levels to take advantage of similarities among national markets, economies of scale, and international specialization. Hence, the multinational enterprise system becomes progressively more integrated in production, marketing, finance, research and development, and management.

Several *external* constraints may limit the integration of a multinational enterprise system, and a parent company also encounters *internal* constraints, such as the domestic orientation of many managers. External constraints include all the obstacles to international trade which were examined in Parts One and Two. Most prominent are the restrictions imposed by governments on the flows of factor services, products, and current payments. When trade restrictions are severe, they inhibit interaffiliate product transfers. Furthermore, uncertainty about future government actions and unstable political conditions in some host countries may greatly enhance the risks of interdependence among affiliates. In Figure 23-1, for instance, an interruption in the production or shipments of A_1 will halt the production of A_6 unless the latter has access to another supplier. Or again, the host government may prevent A_5 from importing products from A_4 to fill out its product line.

As a result of external and internal constraints, the parent company will seldom push the integration of its system to a logical extreme. Instead, integration is most likely to be partial, applying to some regions but not to the entire world or to some products but not to all products. In particular, many parent companies have been reluctant to integrate the operations of affiliates in the industrial countries with the operations of affiliates in the developing countries because of restrictions and political instability prevalent in the latter.

To conclude, the multinational enterprise system functions as an international transfer agent for both products and factor services. Although the pattern of these transfers will depend on the parent company's strategy and various constraints, the parent company is the only source of certain factor services (notably, system-wide management) and is usually the principal source of capital and technology. However, as we have seen, the parent company may also initiate factor flows (as well as product flows) among its affiliates in different countries and from them back to itself. Hence, the multinational enterprise system recapitulates in microcosm the international economic system of trade and factor movements among national economies.[2] We shall now take a closer look at product and factor transfers within the multinational enterprise system.

TRANSFERS OF PRODUCT IN THE MULTINATIONAL ENTERPRISE SYSTEM

As noted above, the multinational enterprise system generates many cross-national product transfers within the system itself.[3] These intraenterprise product transfers are the direct consequence of the decisions made by the parent company managers relating to three strategy questions:

1. Where in the world are the markets for our final products?
2. Where should we locate our production facilities to supply those markets?
3. Where and from whom should we source the product inputs (raw materials, parts, components, capital equipment) necessary to the manufacture of our final products?

For each country market of the multinational enterprise's final products, parent company managers must decide whether to produce within the market or export into it from a production base located in another country. For each manufacturing affiliate, parent company managers must decide whether to make or buy the necessary product inputs and, if the decision is to make them, then the managers must decide whether to make them in the same country as the affiliate in question or to source them from an affiliate in another country. When the parent company is following a multinational strategy, these decisions will create some degree of system integration in marketing, in production, or in both.

INTEGRATION IN MARKETING

Figure 23-2 depicts a pattern of intraenterprise product transfers resulting from a high degree of integration in marketing. Instead of having

---

[2] For an elaboration of this conception, see Franklin R. Root, "A Conceptual Approach to International Business," *Journal of Business Administration* (Summer, 1969), pp. 18-28.

[3] The system also generates cross-national sales to nonsystem customers and cross-national purchases from nonsystem suppliers. Both of these extraenterprise transactions and the cross-national transfers within the system (intraenterprise transfers) constitute the international trade created by the system. The relative importance of extraenterprise transactions and intraenterprise transfers is suggested by Table 22-9 on p. 539, which indicates that 320 U.S. parent companies in 1965 channeled over half of their exports through foreign affiliates. Unfortunately data is not available on the product transfers among the foreign affiliates of these U.S. parent companies.

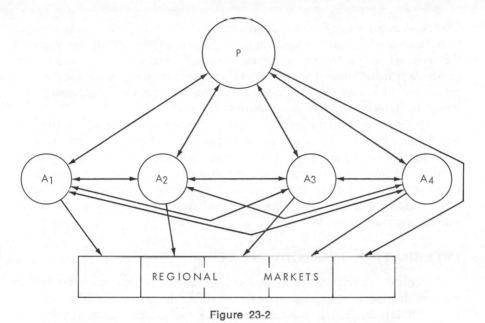

Figure 23-2

PRODUCT TRANSFERS WITHIN THE MULTINATIONAL ENTERPRISE SYSTEM: INTEGRATION IN MARKETING

the parent company (P) and each foreign affiliate (the A's) produce full product lines, the parent company managers achieve a pattern of specialization among them, taking into account the scale of operations and the mix of factor services available at each of the country locations (including the home country), the logistical costs of storage, handling, and transportation, and the constraints imposed by import duties, quotas, and other trade restrictions. The transfer of finished products among affiliates and between affiliates and the parent company enables the multinational enterprise system to offer full product lines in each country market at lower costs and/or higher quality levels than would be possible if those lines were entirely produced by each affiliate.

Furthermore, the parent company and each affiliate is assigned a *regional* market which it is best prepared to serve. For example, the French affiliate (A_1) serves all markets in the EEC, the Mexican affiliate (A_2) serves all markets in Latin America, and so on. Hence, the parent company and the affiliates are exporting products to multicountry regional markets as well as participating in intraenterprise trade. This multimarket approach can be the source of advantages separate from economies of specialization and scale derived from production. On the cost side, an international standardization of products in the multinational enterprise system makes possible the application of the same marketing policies to multicountry markets. For instance, the costs of designing an advertising program, such as Jersey Standard's "Tiger in Your Tank," may now be spread over a hundred country markets.

On the demand side, product standardization (involving the same product lines, trademarks, brand names, and packaging offered by all members of the system) helps to create a multinational product image which can stimulate demand throughout the world. In this way, the multinational enterprise can take advantage of communication links among consumers and industrial buyers in different countries.

Multinational enterprises offer many examples of integration in marketing. Suffice it to observe at this point that General Motors and Ford supplement their product lines in the United States with automobiles manufactured by their affiliates in Europe; Singer and National Cash Register make their older products in foreign affiliates and their newer products in the United States; and Cummins Engine makes a diesel engine in its British affiliate for sale throughout the world.

INTEGRATION IN PRODUCTION

Vertical integration in production also creates product transfers within the multinational enterprise system. Vertical integration occurs when a manufacturer decides to produce at least some of the inputs required to manufacture his finished products. At the extreme, vertical integration can extend backward into raw material extraction, but for most manufacturers (except for heavy industries, such as steel and other metals, chemicals, and oil refining), it is likely to go no further than the production of certain components and parts that are assembled into final products. Vertical integration becomes international in scope when a multinational enterprise system produces raw materials, components, or other inputs in one or more of its member companies (including the parent company) for use in production by member companies in other countries.

Figure 23-3 depicts one pattern of intraenterprise product transfers that results from vertical integration in production. The parent company (P) transfers product inputs to affiliates A_2, A_3, and A_4 for use in their production. At the same time, A_1 manufactures a component which is transferred to A_4, while A_2 and A_3 also manufacture inputs for A_4. Subsequently A_4 uses all these inputs to manufacture the final product, which is then sold to worldwide markets.

Vertical integration enables the multinational enterprise system to reap the advantages of international specialization and economies of scale, as was also true of integration in marketing. The classic example of vertical integration on a global scale is provided by the major petroleum companies, whose production affiliates (mostly located in developing countries) ship crude oil to refinery affiliates (mostly located in industrial countries), which in turn ship refined products to marketing affiliates for sale throughout the world. Massey-Ferguson, a Canadian multinational enterprise, combines a transmission made in its French affiliate, an engine made in its British affiliate, and an axle made in its Mexican affiliate to produce in the United States a tractor

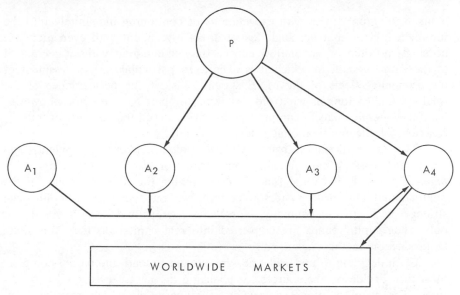

Figure 23-3

**PRODUCT TRANSFERS WITHIN THE MULTINATIONAL
ENTERPRISE SYSTEM: INTEGRATION IN PRODUCTION**

for sale in world markets.[4] Another illustration of international vertical integration is Ford's sourcing of the engine for the Pinto, which is manufactured in the United States, from its German affiliate. Another multinational enterprise manufactures refrigerators in Europe by producing the mechanical elements in its German affiliate and the structural elements in its French affiliate, while final assembly is done by its Italian affiliate.

TRANSFERS OF CAPITAL IN THE MULTINATIONAL ENTERPRISE SYSTEM

As was shown in the previous chapter, the MNE is the dominant vehicle for direct foreign investment. For the most part, decisions to invest directly abroad are made by managers in multinational parent companies. Unlike portfolio investment, which is a pure transfer of capital, direct foreign investment is the transfer of a bundle of factor services that represent in their totality an extension of a business enterprise across national boundaries. In a behavioral sense, therefore, direct foreign investment encompasses everything that MNE's do when they establish and manage their affiliates in different countries.

We have observed that the direct investment activities of MNE's initiate a complex set of product and factor flows within a multinational system, which

---

[4] "The Rewarding Strategies of Multinationalism," *Fortune* (September 15, 1968), p. 104.

is an ongoing enterprise with expectations of continuing indefinitely into the future. It follows that no single act of direct investment and, even more so, no single product or factor flow can be fully understood without relating it to the entire system of which it is a part. In particular, any assessment of the economic effects of the MNE should consider the performance of the total system. As long as we avoid mistaking the part for the whole, however, fruitful economic analysis can proceed by investigating the constituent transfer functions of the multinational enterprise system.

The international transfer of *real* capital (plant, equipment, and permanent working capital) commonly (but not always) occurs first as a *financial* transfer of capital funds.[5] In examining the flow of capital in the multinational enterprise system, therefore, we must consider the financial strategy of the parent company. Nonetheless, we should keep in mind that only when capital funds are converted into real capital do they contribute to production in the system.

Upon deciding to undertake new investment abroad, the parent company must then decide on the sources for financing the necessary capital expenditures. For a multinational enterprise pursuing a global strategy, the appropriate question is: Where in the world should we obtain financing for our affiliate in country Y? The answer to this question (and others like it) will determine the pattern of capital flows within the enterprise system and between the enterprise system and outside financial sources located in different countries.

SOURCES OF CAPITAL FINANCING

In deciding on the sources of financing for investment abroad, two questions are prominent in the deliberations of managers in most parent companies: (1) Should funds be obtained at home (the country of the parent) or abroad? (2) Should funds be obtained from sources *within* the system (parent company and affiliates) or from sources *outside* the system (investment banks, security markets, and other financial institutions)? Thus, the enterprise has four basic sourcing options, as depicted in Figure 23-4.[6]

A choice of either option 1 or 2 results in the transfer of capital from the home country to a host country. The transfer may initially take the form of funds (financial transfer) or the form of capital equipment and inventory (real transfer).[7] Again, the transfer may represent an equity contribution, a

---

[5] For a discussion of the distinction between real and financial capital transfers at the *national* level, see Chapter 24, pp. 576-578. For a discussion of capital as a factor of production, see Chapter 5, pp. 111-112.

[6] A truly global company would not draw a distinction between home and foreign countries, but only a handful of multinational enterprises are truly global in their financial strategies.

[7] Intangibles, such as patent rights, management services, and goodwill may also be capitalized. This practice is more common when the affiliate is a joint venture than when it is wholly owned by the parent company.

	INTERNAL SOURCES	EXTERNAL SOURCES
HOME COUNTRY	1	2
FOREIGN COUNTRIES	3	4

Figure 23-4

BASIC CAPITAL-SOURCING OPTIONS
FOR THE MULTINATIONAL ENTERPRISE

formal loan, or an informal advance. Under option 1 in Figure 23-4, financing comes from the retained earnings of the parent company. Under option 2, the parent company obtains financing from financial institutions in the home country.

Under options 3 and 4, no net transfer of capital occurs between the home and foreign countries because the funds are both raised abroad and invested abroad. Alternative 3 is available to the parent company only when it has affiliates with retained earnings.[8] When capital expansion in a given affiliate is financed by the affiliate's own earnings, no international transfer of capital takes place.[9] When, however, a given affiliate obtains capital funds (or real capital) from another affiliate located in a different country, there does occur an international transfer of capital. If, for example, the parent company directs a transfer of capital from its affiliate in Cologne to its affiliate in Paris, then capital moves from Germany to France.

Under option 4, the affiliate may obtain capital from local financial institutions with or without the guarantee of the parent company. Or the parent company may raise capital funds under its own name from external sources in the host country of the affiliate. In both instances, the resulting capital flow is domestic, not international.[10] When, however, the parent company (or more rarely, an affiliate) obtains external capital funds from a third country or from an international market (Eurodollars or Eurobonds, for example), then capital flows to the host country from one or more third countries.[11]

---

[8] The entire cash flow of affiliates (earnings plus depreciation allowances) may be used for capital financing, but we are concerned here only with a *net* expansion of capital.

[9] Since the retained earnings *could* be repatriated to the parent company, one can argue that the use of retained earnings should be considered a capital flow from the parent to the affiliate. However, in their financial decisions most multinational enterprises draw a distinction between repatriated earnings and earnings retained abroad. Furthermore, the United States does not enter the retained earnings of U.S. affiliates abroad in its balance of payments.

[10] However, the sale of securities abroad by the U.S. parent company is entered in the U.S. balance of payments as a long-term capital inflow, but when the funds are spent on investment abroad an offsetting entry of a long-term capital outflow (direct investment) is also recorded. Hence, the transaction is merely a bookkeeping entry with no net effect on the balance of payments.

[11] Eurodollars and Eurobonds are described in Chapter 20, pp. 492-494.

CAPITAL-SOURCING PREFERENCES

The final choice of a capital-sourcing option depends on the strategy preferences of the parent company and on a variety of constraints. As to the choice between home country versus foreign country sources, apparently the majority of U.S. parent companies strongly favor the use of capital funds generated abroad by their affiliates, including their retained earnings and local loans obtained without the parent's guarantee. Although new affiliates depend much more on parent company funds, established affiliates are almost always compelled to obtain much of their financing from local sources.[12] However, in those enterprises whose operations involve a large volume of exports shipped to affiliates from the United States, the parent companies frequently extend long-term inventory loans on open account.

When capital funds are sourced in the United States, parent companies show a preference for internal as opposed to external sources. One survey of over 100 U.S. international companies found that 45 percent of the companies had never borrowed in the United States to finance foreign projects (although such borrowing was not considered a deterrent to foreign investment); 13 percent indicated that they did not want to borrow at home to finance investment abroad; 5 percent indicated a willingness to borrow at home only for investment in Canada; and the remaining 37 percent did borrow in the United States to finance foreign investment, although most of these companies did not borrow for *specific* foreign projects, financing them instead out of general borrowings for total corporate requirements. This last group consisted of large multinational companies with global interests who pooled all their capital funds for effective operation and control of the entire enterprise system.[13]

CONSTRAINTS ON CAPITAL-SOURCING POLICIES

Numerous factors both at home and abroad act to constrain the capital-sourcing choices of parent companies. Here we mention only the more prominent ones without going into detail.

Exchange restrictions in the home country may limit the capital a parent company can invest abroad, as do controls in the United States.[14] Generally controls in the home country compel a parent company to rely more on foreign-source capital than it would otherwise care to do. Exchange restrictions in a *host* country may cause a parent company to rely more on local financing of an affiliate's capital needs because of a reluctance to transfer funds into an inconvertible currency. High rates of *inflation,* high *exchange risks,* or high *political risks* (such as a threat of expropriation) also favor local financing, other things being equal. All too often, however, a

---

[12] Judd Polk, Irene Meister, and Lawrence Veit, *U.S. Production Abroad and the Balance of Payments* (New York: The Conference Board, 1966), p. 78 ff.

[13] *Ibid.,* p. 80.

[14] For a discussion of U.S. investment controls, see Chapter 24, pp. 574-583.

parent company encounters these conditions in developing countries which, at the same time, cannot provide local financing to meet all of the affiliate's capital requirements. In that event, the parent company has no choice but to transfer capital into the host country unless it is willing to limit the growth (and perhaps endanger the survival) of its affiliate.[15]

Some countries also limit the foreign-owned affiliate in its *access to local capital sources*. Somewhat paradoxically, the same countries may also limit the parent company's *ownership interests* in the local affiliate to a given percentage (commonly 49 percent). This ownership constraint can raise a serious financing problem for the joint-venture affiliate because the parent company may be unwilling to lend to the affiliate as opposed to making an equity investment.

Taxation in home and host countries may also influence the source of capital financing in a multinational enterprise system, as well as the kind of financing used (equity versus loan). To illustrate, the United States does not ordinarily tax foreign earnings until they are repatriated to the parent company, but it may tax capital transfers among foreign affiliates by regarding them as "constructive" loans or investments of the parent company. This tax policy encourages the retention of earnings in the affiliate and thereby encourages local financing. Probably the most important single effect of taxation in host countries on capital-sourcing decisions lies in the differential impact of the diverse tax systems on affiliate earnings and therefore the amounts available for new investment, either in the host country or elsewhere.[16]

Varying *costs of capital* in different countries will also influence the choice of *external* capital sources. As the multinational enterprise becomes more global in its operations, it establishes intimate links with financial institutions in many countries and with international financial centers. Thus, it is in a position to raise capital in low-cost locations for transfer to high-cost locations. As regards *internal* capital sources, the logical cost to the enterprise is the highest marginal opportunity cost of capital funds anywhere in the entire multinational enterprise system. Nonetheless, parent companies commonly make a decision to invest in a particular country without comparing investment opportunities in other countries (including the home country).[17] Most parent companies do, however, have a desired rate of return on capital which, in effect, is their internal cost of capital.

In closing, it should be evident that a U.S. parent company may undertake direct investment abroad without using its own capital resources or even without any transfer of capital from the home country to the host country. An inescapable conclusion is that *international capital transfers are not a*

---

[15] Hedging in forward exchange, swap arrangements, and investment guarantees provided by the home government may be used by the parent company to offset some of the risks. For a treatment of the U.S. investment insurance program, see Chapter 24, pp. 583-586.

[16] See Chapter 24, pp. 586-591, for a further treatment of taxation.

[17] Judd Polk, Irene Meister, and Lawrence Veit, *U.S. Production Abroad and the Balance of Payments* (New York: The Conference Board, 1966), p. 73.

necessary element of direct foreign investment.[18] Rather, the necessary element is an international transfer of entrepreneurial management.

Although not strictly necessary, direct foreign investment almost always involves at least *some* capital transfer from a parent company to its affiliate, especially when the affiliate is new. And, as we have observed, capital-sourcing decisions in the multinational enterprise system may generate many capital transfers between second and third countries.

SOME REMARKS ON THE THEORY OF INTERNATIONAL CAPITAL TRANSFERS

Conventional economic theory has relied on a model of portfolio investment to explain the international movement of capital as a factor of production. This theory postulates interest-rate differences among countries as the cause of international capital movements. Capital moves from country A to country B because the long-term interest rate (return on capital) is higher in country B than in country A, reflecting the comparative abundance of capital in the latter. Capital continues to move from country A to country B until interest rates are equal and the marginal product of capital in the two countries is the same.

This theory may be depicted in terms of the simple formula for capitalizing a stream of earnings, $C = Y/i$, where C is the value of a capital asset, Y is the stream of income produced by the asset, and i is the rate of interest.[19] Then capital moves from country A to country B when the value of an asset is higher in country A than in country B for the *same* income stream. Investors in country A will purchase the lower-priced asset in country B. This theory offers a good explanation of international movements of portfolio capital and short-term capital when account is taken of foreign exchange and other risks.[20]

But is a difference in i between two countries a good explanation of *direct* foreign investment? Do multinational enterprises establish foreign affiliates because they expect to earn higher rates of return on the same assets than at home? Or do they invest abroad because they expect to earn a higher income on the same assets than do local companies in the host country, the cost of capital (i) to both being the same?

Statistical data does not support the hypothesis that rates of return on direct foreign investment are higher than rates of return on home investment.

---

[18] In 1970, less than one-third of the capital expenditures of U.S. affiliates abroad were financed by funds from the United States. See Table 22-5, p. 535.

[19] The more elaborate formula discounts the stream of earnings for futurity to obtain its present value. The simple formula indicates that if an asset permanently generates an annual income of, say, $100, then it is worth $2,000 when capitalized at an interest rate of 5 percent.

[20] See the discussion of forward rates of exchange in Chapter 7. For an attempt to explain direct foreign investment with portfolio theory, see Robert Z. Aliber, "A Theory of Direct Foreign Investment," in Charles P. Kindleberger (ed.), *The International Corporation* (Cambridge, Massachusetts: The M.I.T. Press, 1970).

Sometimes they are; sometimes they are not. Nor can the country distribution of U.S. direct foreign investment be explained by yield differences between host countries and the United States. For instance, the book value of U.S. manufacturing investments in Canada rose more than $4 billion between 1963 and 1970, even though the rate of return was below that in the United States and in most other areas during those years.[21]

The second hypothesis, that multinational enterprises expect to earn a higher income (Y) than local competitors, appears to be a superior explanation. It is consistent with the observed fact that multinational enterprises must assume many costs of international business that are not assumed by local companies. They must overcome barriers imposed by distance, time, information gaps, nationality, culture, and other aspects of a foreign environment that are not experienced by uninational firms. These higher costs must be offset by higher incomes than are earned by local competitors.[22] To earn a higher income, the multinational enterprise must possess advantages over local competitors that derive from its superior technology, its entrepreneurial and other management skills, and its worldwide organization.[23]

The hypothesis that direct foreign investment occurs because of differences in Y rather than differences in i is also consistent with the acquisition of local companies by multinational enterprises. Why should the MNE be willing to pay more for a company than local investors? The most plausible answer is that the MNE expects to earn higher profits (a higher Y) from the acquired company than do local investors. Furthermore, this hypothesis is consistent with the observed fact that European MNE's invest in the United States at the same time that American MNE's in the same industry are investing in Europe. Both sets of companies believe that they can compete effectively in each other's territory.

To conclude, international differences in the cost of capital (i) cannot explain direct investment flows among countries, although they may influence such flows. Far more important is the expectation of MNE managers that they can earn higher profits (Y's) on their assets than can local competitors. This expectation rests on the superior technology and entrepreneurial skills of the multinational enterprise, subjects to which we now turn.

TRANSFERS OF TECHNOLOGY IN THE MULTINATIONAL ENTERPRISE SYSTEM

The multinational enterprise functions as an *international innovation system* that goes far beyond the traditional mode of international technological

---

[21] See Table 22-6, p. 536.

[22] For a schematic treatment of these costs, see John Fayerweather, *International Business Management* (New York: McGraw-Hill Book Company, 1969), Figure 6.1, p. 170.

[23] This is not to deny that large multinational enterprises may have better credit ratings than local companies, enabling them to raise capital funds more inexpensively. But local companies do not *necessarily* have lower credit ratings than multinational enterprises.

diffusion through imitation.[24] Indeed, the comparative advantage of the MNE in world markets centers on its mastery of the innovation process far more than its mere size or financial strength. Multinational enterprises are research-intensive, and their remarkable growth proceeds from their capacity to create and market new products on a global scale.

TECHNOLOGY AND TECHNOLOGICAL INNOVATION

Technology needs to be distinguished from *technological innovation*. Technology, as such, is a body of knowledge that is applicable to the production of goods and the creation of new goods. Technology, therefore, consists of ideas about products and how to make them rather than the products themselves or production facilities.[25] Today—with only modest exceptions—the source of new technology is scientific research and invention in industrial, government, and university laboratories.

Technological innovation, on the other hand, is the entire process whereby research and invention are converted into technology that is then applied to the production of "new" products or improvements in the production of "older" products.[26] Innovation involves many activities performed by different groups of people: technical research; development (the conversion of research into industrial technology through process and product designs, engineering specifications, "scaling-up," etc.); production start-up (all activities necessary to begin actual production); marketing start-up (all activities necessary to launch a marketing program); and market research (the identification and measurement of market opportunities for new products). Taken together, these activities and their linkages comprise the innovation system. Because of its complexity, the process of innovation is subject to numerous failures. Many research discoveries are not developed into technology; available technology may not be used to transform production functions or create new products; and new products may not succeed in the marketplace for one or more reasons.

INTERNATIONAL TRANSFER OF TECHNOLOGICAL INNOVATION

Technological innovation may spread from one country to another either (1) through the transfer of technical knowledge (via licensing, trade,

---

[24] This section draws on Franklin R. Root, "The Role of International Business in the Diffusion of Technological Innovation," *Economic and Business Bulletin* (Summer, 1968).

[25] Like all words that refer to a wide variety of phenomena, technology has no standard definition. In particular, the distinction between technology as knowledge and its embodiment in capital equipment, industrial processes, and products is commonly obscured by writers. The derivation of the word indicates that its essential meaning is that of a kind of knowledge.

[26] The influence of technological innovation on international trade is examined in Chapter 5, pp. 116-123.

technical publications, official technical assistance programs, and other forms of communication) that is then "imitated" in new production functions and new goods by local business enterprises, or (2) through the transfer of innovation by multinational enterprises that establish operations in the recipient country via direct investment.

The first mode of innovation diffusion is critically dependent on the willingness and capacity of nationals to utilize the imported technology. Nations differ widely in this regard. Japanese entrepreneurs are able to turn imported technology quickly into new products which may even be exported to the original country source of the technology. A well-known example is their use of transistor technology to create the transistor radio, which found its biggest market in the United States, the source of the original technology. The United States itself has used European technology to produce new products in advance of the originators. Evidence indicates that imitation works less quickly in Europe than in Japan or the United States. In the developing countries, however, imitation works slowly or not at all because they lack the industrial and entrepreneurial skills that are necessary for innovation. As the pace of innovation quickens, lags in innovation (to say nothing of complete failure) place a nation at an increasing disadvantage in international competition. The consequences of the failure of a country's nationals to imitate foreign technology (or generate their own) may be alleviated, however, by the transfer of innovation within the multinational enterprise system.

A unique contribution of the multinational enterprise is the *internationalization of the entire innovation process*. The MNE undertakes technical research, development, production start-up, marketing start-up, and market research on a global scale. In this way the MNE overcomes the entrepreneurial gaps that constrain the spread of innovation through imitation alone.[27]

As we noted in Chapter 21, multinational manufacturers set up production abroad to gain new markets or to hold on to markets that were first developed through direct exports. International investment strategy, then, is firmly market-oriented; the dominant consideration is the foreign market potential of products in which the company believes it has an advantage. If the investment region is highly developed, such as Western Europe or North America, most opportunities for multinational enterprises are found in new products that have not been imitated by local producers. This is why research-intensive industries are responsible for most of the U.S. direct investment in Western Europe.

When a multinational enterprise establishes operations in a new country, it does not simply duplicate its operations as they exist in the home or third countries. Adaptations to local conditions are usually necessary in production, marketing, or in the product itself. As a company becomes more international,

---

[27] In contrast to entrepreneurial gaps among countries, the international mobility of technical knowledge is usually quite high.

all the elements of its innovation system are affected by its foreign operations. At the multinational stage, when a company views itself as a single, global entity, a multinational innovation system emerges that ties together research centers, production, and markets located throughout the world. Flows of information relating to market research, technical research, production programs, and marketing programs connect the parent company with its affiliates and connect the affiliates with each other to form one system guided by a dominant management center. In this way, each affiliate has access to both the inputs (scientific discoveries, manufacturing engineering specifications, etc.) and the outputs (new products) of the entire multinational enterprise system.

Some specific examples will serve to illustrate the innovation process in a multinational company.

> 1. IBM has six research and development laboratories in Europe. In the beginning IBM used these labs primarily to support the local markets. As time went on, IBM discovered that it could not make full use of its technical manpower when R and D missions were limited to the needs of a single country or even a single region. In 1961, when IBM undertook the development of its System 360, it was decided to bring the European laboratories into the worldwide development program. Once the several units in the new line were agreed upon, each lab, whether in the United States or in Europe, was given a specific mission. The smaller machine came from Germany; the medium-sized machine was designed in England; and the larger computers were designed in U.S. laboratories. The French, Dutch, and Swedish labs, as well as U.S. labs, produced a variety of input-output equipment necessary to apply the computers to the many applications for which they were designed.[28]

> 2. A Ford team of U.S. and West German engineers developed the Taunus 12M automobile with the Western European market in mind. Ford of England's engineers designed the U.S.-built Falcon's transmission. A Ford executive declared, "We're at a point where any design may be the result of a multinational exchange of ideas."[29]

Not all multinational enterprises have internationalized their innovation systems to the extent of IBM or Ford. Many American multinationals still try out new products in the United States before producing them abroad, and they concentrate R and D in U.S. laboratories. But as multinational enterprises become more and more global, the innovation function is expanded as managers perceive the advantages of tapping research brains in several countries and quickly introducing new products in many national markets. We can reasonably expect, therefore, more dispersal of corporate R and D facilities; in effect, laboratories will be taken to the research workers rather

---

[28] Elmer S. Groo, Vice-President of IBM World Trade Corporation, in U.S. Department of Commerce, *Technology and World Trade* (Washington: U.S. Government Printing Office, 1967), pp. 123-124.
[29] "Multinational Companies," *Business Week* (April 20, 1963), p. 70.

than the other way around.[30] Some multinational enterprises have already begun to economize on research expense by using the small and medium-sized production facilities of their affiliates for trial runs of new products.[31]

THE TRANSFER OF INNOVATION TO DEVELOPING COUNTRIES

Attracted by big, dynamic markets, U.S. industry has moved mainly into Western Europe and other economically advanced areas. Nonetheless, it would be erroneous to infer that the multinational enterprise has contributed little to technological innovation in the developing countries.

As indicated earlier, the capacity of local enterprise in developing countries to imitate imported technology is generally very limited, and in some instances, virtually nonexistent. Thus, the transfer of technology to these countries is a necessary but insufficient condition for innovation. Unfortunately the direct transfer of innovation by multinational enterprises is also subject to many constraints in the developing countries. Aside from restrictive government policies, which are taken up in Chapter 25, two factors especially inhibit innovation transfer: (1) small, stagnant, domestic markets, and (2) the absence of an industrial "infrastructure" consisting of people with technical and management skills, supporting industries, transportation, power, communications, and other services. Apart from their obvious limitation on sales potentials, small markets often require major and costly adaptations in product line and design, manufacturing, and marketing. The absence of an industrial infrastructure makes it very difficult to staff new affiliates with nationals at the technical and management levels. Furthermore, the scarcity of local suppliers of components and other production inputs forces the affiliate either to make many of its required inputs, to buy them from abroad (when permitted by the host government), or to develop local sources of supply through technical and financial assistance.[32]

To begin production in a developing country, therefore, multinational enterprises are usually compelled to staff the new affiliate with expatriate technical and management personnel drawn from the parent company or

---

[30] The principal arguments for the centralization of R and D in the home country are the ease of coordination and the avoidance of duplication. In view of the remarkable improvements taking place in long-distance communication, these arguments are not convincing when set against the advantages of decentralization.

[31] Howe Martyn, "Manufacturing Abroad: Opportunities and Problems," *Michigan Business Review* (May, 1968), p. 12.

[32] It is easy to underestimate the technical knowledge needed to produce even a comparatively simple industrial product. A diesel engine for commercial trucks has 750 parts that require as many as 300 different, narrowly specified materials. All in all, some 10,000 separate manufacturing steps are necessary to convert materials and castings into the finished parts for a single engine model. In the United States some 200 plants supply parts and components to the diesel engine manufacturer. See Jack Baranson, "Transfer of Technical Knowledge by International Corporations to Developing Economies," *American Economic Review, Papers and Proceedings* (May, 1966), pp. 260-261.

affiliates in other countries. This arrangement is not only costly, but may run counter to the nationalistic policies of the host government. Hence, multinationals strive to "nationalize" the affiliate staff as quickly as possible through training programs at the worker, technical, and management levels. The magnitude of this effort is seldom appreciated by host governments or critics of multinational enterprise.

Official technical assistance to developing countries via bilateral programs and international agencies tends to emphasize training grants for study in the donor country, whereas many training programs of multinational companies take place in the affiliate. And yet, an OECD study concluded:

> The evidence collected strongly suggests that the number of people trained in Member countries [Western Europe, Japan, Canada, and the United States] by private enterprise at its own expense probably exceeds substantially the number of officially financed trainees in industry and trade. The number of persons trained by foreign private enterprise in developing countries is most probably considerably superior to the number trained in the Member countries surveyed.[33]

It would appear, then, that multinational enterprise transfers more technology (and far more innovation) to the industry of developing countries than all the technical assistance and other aid programs of governments and international agencies. It is perhaps a comment on our times to observe that this vital contribution has received little publicity and almost no official recognition by the United Nations Conference on Trade and Development (UNCTAD) or the representatives of most developing countries.

To sum up, the multinational enterprise takes advantage of international technology and entrepreneurial gaps in producing and marketing new products on a global scale. Although international production is the principal vehicle used by the MNE to transfer technology to host countries, it is by no means the only vehicle. The establishment of local research and development facilities, the training and education of local nationals, the use of local subcontractors and suppliers, and the introduction of advanced management practices also serve to spread technology. Furthermore, the intraenterprise product transfers (trade) of multinational enterprises, and their licensing and cross-licensing arrangements with independent foreign companies, transfers technology among countries. Multinational enterprises may also indirectly stimulate innovation in host countries by creating new primary markets (for example, the market for integrated circuits in Europe), by encouraging local companies to emulate them (positive demonstration effect), and by forcing local companies to innovate to withstand competition.[34] The pace of innovation in Western Europe during the 1960's would have been much

---

[33] "Technical Assistance and Private Enterprise," *The OECD Observer* (Paris: Organization for Economic Cooperation and Development, December, 1967), p. 36.

[34] James Brian Quinn, "Technology Transfer by Multinational Companies," *Harvard Business Review* (November-December, 1969), pp. 152-154.

slower in computers, specialized plastics, electronic test and measuring instruments, numerically controlled machine tools, and in many other new products if American companies had not invested there. Because Western Europe has an advanced industrial society, local companies would have eventually imitated these products on their own, but more slowly than that which actually took place because of the direct innovation of U.S. companies in Europe.[35] As stated by an OECD report on technology gaps: "The efficient exploitation of advanced technologies calls for both technological resources beyond national boundaries and access to markets that are international in scope."[36] The multinational enterprise has responded to these requirements to a far higher degree than has any other institution in the world economy.

TRANSFERS OF ENTREPRENEURIAL SKILLS IN THE MULTINATIONAL ENTERPRISE SYSTEM

The international transfer of entrepreneurial skills is the distinctive (and unique) function of the multinational enterprise system.[37] Entrepreneurial managers centered in the parent company take the initiative in combining natural resources (land), capital, labor, and technology in different countries in order to produce goods and services for sale in local and external markets. Ordinarily, much of the capital and all of the technology are brought into a host country by the multinational enterprise, but it is the transfer of entrepreneurial skills that truly distinguishes the MNE from other modes of capital or technology transfer, such as portfolio investment or licensing. In brief, the multinational enterprise, as its name implies, transfers *enterprise* from one country to another.

We have already anticipated the transfer of entrepreneurial skills in our discussion of technology transfer because of our emphasis on technological *innovation*. We noted that the transfer of technical knowledge (technology *per se*) is a communicative process, but that the transfer of technological innovation by the MNE requires not only the transfer of technical knowledge but also the transfer of management skills to overcome entrepreneurial gaps.

The international transfer of entrepreneurial skills by the multinational enterprise is not limited to technological innovation; it serves to mobilize all the factors of production for new tasks in new markets. The key decisions which result from the exercise of entrepreneurial skills by the parent company include answers to the strategic questions presented in Chapter 21: Where in the world are our best markets? Where in the world should we manufacture

---

[35] It is not fortuitous that the Soviet Union and the Eastern European countries, which have kept out the MNE, have also fallen behind in several areas of industrial technology and innovation.

[36] Organization for Economic Cooperation and Development, *Gaps in Technology*, General Report (Paris: Organization for Economic Cooperation and Development, 1968), p. 41.

[37] We distinguish entrepreneurial skills (which innovate) from *administrative* skills, which direct and otherwise support the routine activities of a program or organizational unit.

our products to supply these markets? Where in the world should we undertake research and development to create new products for future markets? Where in the world should we obtain financing for our capital investments? Where in the world should we recruit the technical and managerial staff for our parent company and affiliates? In short, entrepreneurial decisions determine the structure and evolution of the entire multinational enterprise system.

Two aspects of entrepreneurial management in the multinational enterprise deserve additional comment: (1) the perception of economic opportunity, and (2) the deliberate assumption of risk.

THE PERCEPTION OF ECONOMIC OPPORTUNITY

Strongly oriented toward corporate growth through innovation, the managers of multinational enterprises continually search for new economic opportunities. Their "opportunity horizons" are far broader than the horizons of domestic managers; they extend into many countries and world regions. What is a dazzling opportunity to a multinational manager may not even be noticed by a domestic manager in the same industry. In general, the managers of a multinational enterprise perceive far more opportunities than managers of uninational enterprises, if only because so many of their opportunities are generated by differences among national economies. For example, a given product is seldom in the same phase of its life cycle in all countries. A product which is experiencing market saturation in the United States may be in a growth stage in, say, Western Europe or not even on the market in some developing countries.[38] Again, local competition may be very strong in one country but moderate in another. Aside from market differences, multinational managers can take advantage of international cost differences; they can alter the patterns of specialization and exchange among affiliate companies and, in the longer run, shift the country locations of production, R and D, and other activities.

The perception of economic opportunity depends not only on the horizons of managers, but also on their access to information about markets, competitors, new technology, government policies, and general economic and political conditions. Hence, multinational enterprises organize "intelligence" systems to gather information from sources both within and outside the enterprise. The intelligence systems of some firms (for example, the large petroleum companies) are superior to those of most national governments. Continuous scanning of the international horizon for new opportunities is a vital entrepreneurial activity of the MNE.

---

[38] A conventional nomenclature of product life cycle stages is introduction, growth, maturity, saturation, and decline. In Chapter 5, p. 121, we discussed the product life cycle in reference to international technology gaps, noting the transition of a product from a specialty product to a standardized product and even to an undifferentiated commodity.

THE DELIBERATE ASSUMPTION OF RISK

The perception of economic opportunity alone does not make an entrepreneur. He must also act to exploit the opportunity in an appropriate way. In so doing, he must also assume the risks that accompany innovation. Multinational enterprises have demonstrated both a willingness and a capacity to assume risks in countries throughout the world.[39]

Although the opportunities perceived by multinational managers are ordinarily far greater than those perceived by uninational managers, so also are the risks of multinational enterprises. These risks may be broadly classified as *economic* and *political*. Economic risks proceed from uncertainty about demand, competition, costs, and other market conditions. They are the same in kind, if not in degree, for the multinational enterprise as for the domestic enterprise. The same, however, cannot be said of political risks. For the multinational enterprise, political risks emanate from uncertainty about political events of many kinds, such as war, revolution, coup d'etat, expropriation, taxation, devaluation or revaluation, exchange controls, and import restrictions. These events are political (as opposed to economic) because they result from government actions or bear on the political authority of a nation, although they may be influenced (or even caused) by economic conditions. In addition to the economic risks of innovation, therefore, multinational enterprises must deliberately assume extraordinary political risks in performing their entrepreneurial role in the world economy.[40] The capacity of multinational enterprises to bear such risks is enormously enhanced by their great size and financial strength, their dispersal of operations in many countries, and the sophistication of their management.

THE CONTRIBUTION OF THE MULTINATIONAL ENTERPRISE TO THE WORLD ECONOMY

In closing, it is instructive to repeat some statements about international trade and factor movements which were made in Chapter 5.[41]

Both trade and factor movements bring about a superior allocation of resources among nations. Trade enables a country to take advantage of international specialization in production by exporting products with low opportunity costs and importing products with high opportunity costs. International factor movements achieve a better allocation of productive agents by transferring relatively abundant factors (such as technology and entrepreneurial skills) in one country to a second country where they are relatively scarce and where they may be combined with relatively abundant

---

[39] In Chapter 4 we treated the subject of ignorance, uncertainty, and risk in international trade. What we said then is also pertinent to investment and the multinational enterprise.

[40] Some political risks assumed by the multinational enterprise are treated in Chapter 25.

[41] See pp. 126-128.

factors (such as natural resources and labor) in the production of goods and services. Under conditions of perfect competition, the flow of factors would continue until their marginal productivities (and prices) were the same everywhere. Then the international allocation of factors would be optimal because any further factor movement would lower production and consumer satisfactions for the world as a whole. Although such an optimal allocation can hardly be achieved in the world as we know it, it follows that the greater the mobility of factors among countries, the better their international allocation and the higher the efficiency of the world economy.

In light of these theoretical considerations, it is evident that the multinational enterprise system is making a major contribution to the allocative efficiency of the world economy in carrying out its role as an international transfer agent. The contribution of the MNE has been compared with the earlier role of the national corporation in building a single, national economy by moving capital, technology, and entrepreneurial skills from regions of factor abundance to regions of factor scarcity. In the same way that the activities of national corporations helped to integrate regional economies into national economies, so the activities of multinational enterprises are helping to integrate national economies into a world economy.[42]

But the MNE's contribution to the static, allocative efficiency of the world economy is far less important than its contribution to the rate of innovation within that economy. The multinational enterprise is first and foremost an innovator. Through international production and trade, the MNE quickly spreads new ideas, new products, new production functions, new methods of management and organization, and other innovations on a global scale. *International innovation* defines the special contribution of the multinational enterprise; no other institution or group of institutions can match this contribution. And so, the multinational enterprise has become the preeminent agent of change in the world economy.

The positive contribution of the MNE to the world economy does not *necessarily* imply a positive economic contribution to each and every country, although the presumption is strong that all countries can share in the benefits of a more efficient and more dynamic world economy. The economic benefits and costs of direct foreign investment for both home and host countries are explored in the next two chapters. Chapter 25 also takes up the controversial question of the *political* costs of the multinational enterprise, which may be perceived by some host countries as outweighing any net economic benefits.

---

[42] Some economists challenge the conclusion that multinational enterprises improve the allocative efficiency of the world economy on grounds that they are oligopolistic rather than purely competitive firms. See, for example, Stephen Hymer, "The Efficiency (Contradictions) of Multinational Corporations," *The American Economic Review* (May, 1970), pp. 441-448. Although the possible anticompetitive effects of the multinational enterprise should not be ignored (see Chapter 24), this position surely overstates the case. The national corporations which integrated regional economies into national economies were also, in essence, oligopolists.

SUMMARY

1. The manifold activities of the multinational enterprise may be usefully conceptualized as the performance of international transfer functions. The multinational enterprise becomes an international transfer agent when it moves products and factor services (capital, technology, and management) among national economies.

2. The multinational enterprise performs its role as an international transfer agent through institutional/organizational arrangements that collectively make up the multinational enterprise system. This system comprises the parent company, its foreign affiliates, and the relationships among them. The strategy decisions of the parent company generate a pattern of factor and product flows among the members of the system.

3. Intraenterprise product transfers are the direct consequence of the strategy of the parent company. When the parent company is following a multinational strategy, its decisions will create some degree of system integration in marketing, in production, or in both.

4. Direct foreign investment is the transfer of a bundle of factor services that represent in their totality an extension of a business enterprise across national boundaries.

5. The international transfer of *real* capital by the MNE commonly (but not always) occurs first as a *financial* transfer of capital funds. The parent company must decide whether to obtain funds at home or abroad and whether to obtain funds from within the enterprise or outside it. The final choice of the capital-sourcing option depends on the strategy preferences of the parent company and on a variety of constraints: exchange restrictions, political risks, access to local capital sources, taxation, and capital costs. International capital transfers are not a necessary element of direct foreign investment, although they usually accompany it.

6. International differences in the cost of capital (i) cannot explain direct investment flows among countries, although they may influence such flows. Of far greater importance is the expectation of managers in multinational enterprises that they can earn a higher income (Y) on their assets than can local competitors.

7. The multinational enterprise functions as an *international innovation system* that goes far beyond the traditional mode of international technological diffusion through local imitation. The MNE undertakes technical research, development, production start-up, marketing start-up, and market research on a global scale. It would appear that the multinational enterprise transfers more technology (and far more innovation) to the industry of developing countries than all the technical assistance and aid programs of governments and international agencies.

8. The international transfer of entrepreneurial skills is the distinctive (and unique) function of the multinational enterprise. Managers centered in the parent company take the initiative in combining natural resources (land), capital, labor, and technology in different countries in order to produce goods and services for sale in local and external markets.

9. The multinational enterprise makes a major contribution to the allocative efficiency of the world economy, but its key contribution is innovation.

QUESTIONS AND APPLICATIONS

1. (a) What are the constituent elements of the multinational enterprise system?
   (b) "The strategy decisions of the parent company generate a pattern of factor and product flows among the members of the system." Explain.
2. Describe five external constraints that may limit the integration of a multinational enterprise system.
3. (a) What is integration in marketing? Integration in production?
   (b) Explain the possible advantages of each form of integration to the multinational enterprise. Are there any possible disadvantages?
4. What is direct foreign investment?
5. "International capital transfers are *not* a necessary element of direct foreign investment." Explain.
6. Defend the hypothesis that international differences in the cost of capital (i) cannot explain direct investment flows among countries.
7. (a) Distinguish between technology and technological innovation.
   (b) How does technological innovation spread from one country to another?
8. "A unique contribution of the multinational enterprise is the internationalization of the entire innovation process." Explain.
9. (a) What are entrepreneurial skills?
   (b) Why are the political risks assumed by multinational enterprises described as "extraordinary" in the text?

SELECTED READINGS

Kindleberger, Charles P. *American Business Abroad*. New Haven: Yale University Press, 1969. Lectures 1 and 6.

Kindleberger, Charles P. (ed.). *The International Corporation*. Cambridge, Mass.: The M.I.T. Press, 1970. Chapters 1, 2, and 6.

Organization for Economic Cooperation and Development. *Gaps in Technology, General Report*. Paris: Organization for Economic Cooperation and Development, 1968.

Polk, Judd, Irene Meister, and Lawrence Veit. *U.S. Production Abroad and the Balance of Payments*. New York: The Conference Board, 1966. Chapter 4.

"The International Firm and Efficient Economic Allocation." *The American Economic Review* (May, 1970), pp. 430-453.

"The Rewarding Strategies of Multinationalism." *Fortune* (September 15, 1968).

U.S. Department of Commerce. *Technology and World Trade*. Washington: U.S. Government Printing Office, 1967.

CHAPTER 24

U.S. POLICY TOWARD
THE MULTINATIONAL
ENTERPRISE

In order to effectively perform its role as an international transfer agent, the multinational enterprise must be able to move capital, technology, entrepreneurial skills, products, and funds freely throughout the world in response to market opportunity, costs, and competition. The contribution of the MNE to the efficiency and growth of the world economy is dependent, therefore, on the willingness of national governments to refrain from restricting its activities in ways that force it to suboptimize international production and trade for the world as a whole. But as we frequently observed in Part Two, national governments are concerned only indirectly, if at all, with the maximization of the world's economic efficiency and growth. Rather, their concern is the protection and advancement of the national interest as they perceive it in any given situation. National governments, therefore, regard the multinational enterprise from the perspective of its political-economic benefits and costs to the nation—not to the world at large.

The activities of multinational enterprises bear directly on the balance of payments, production, trade, employment, growth, and international competitive position of both host and home economies. Furthermore, they raise fundamental political questions relating to external control over the domestic economy, extraterritoriality, and national sovereignty. Consequently, national governments seek to influence, regulate, and otherwise control the behavior of the multinational enterprise so as to promote their own perceived national interests, paying only scant attention to the effects of their policies on the world economy. Although the United States is the home country of the majority of contemporary multinational corporations, the U.S. Government is no exception to the preceding statement. In this chapter we look at U.S. policy toward the multinational enterprise, and in Chapter 25 we take up the policies of other countries and the overriding political question of national sovereignty and the multinational enterprise.

What, then, is the policy of the U.S. Government toward the MNE? As we shall discover, the answer to this question is not a simple one.

Actually the United States does not have a policy toward the multinational enterprise. The rapid emergence of the multinational enterprise has caught the U.S. Government unprepared to deal with it as a distinctive institution. Instead, the United States applies a variety of policies to different facets of the MNE, policies that were formulated at a time when the multinational enterprise was not yet a policy issue, with the result that many of them are based on considerations unrelated to the multinational enterprise as a unique economic organization. These policies cover direct investment, the balance of payments, taxation, antitrust action, diplomatic protection of U.S. companies abroad, and other matters. Before examining specific U.S. policies that affect the multinational enterprise, however, a brief review of traditional U.S. policy toward direct investment abroad by U.S. companies is in order.

TRADITIONAL U.S. POLICY TOWARD DIRECT FOREIGN INVESTMENT

The fundamental thrust of U.S. foreign economic policy since 1934 has been to extend the freedom of international trade and investment. Before World War II, U.S. foreign investment policy was a mixture of laissez-faire (letting U.S. companies invest abroad when and where they chose to do so) and strong diplomatic protection of U.S. companies in foreign countries. After World War II, U.S. policy shifted to active encouragement of direct foreign investment by American companies, at first as an instrument to help European reconstruction, and somewhat later as a means (along with "transitional" foreign aid) to transfer resources to the developing countries. It was also recognized that U.S. foreign investment creates export markets for U.S. products and develops foreign sources of raw materials and fuels needed by U.S. industry, as well as affording a profitable employment of U.S. capital. In the 1950's, the Government also supported the foreign investment of U.S. companies as a way of alleviating the "dollar shortage" of foreign countries. Finally, direct foreign investment was viewed as a positive element in the struggle with the Communist powers to keep the developing countries in the free world.

The onset of the persistent U.S. balance of payments deficit in 1958 marked the beginning of the end of this supportive investment policy. Once promoted as a means of relieving the "dollar shortage," private foreign investment was accused in the 1960's of intensifying the "dollar glut." Capital outflows to Western Europe drew special criticism from Government authorities who asserted that Western Europe was no longer in need of U.S. foreign investment, and, indeed, should step up its own foreign assistance and private investment in the developing countries. In 1962 the United States revised its tax code to strike down the use of "tax havens" by U.S. companies abroad and thereby accelerate the repatriation of their foreign earnings to the United

States.[1] And in 1965 the Government initiated a "voluntary" restraint program (succeeded by a mandatory program in 1968) to curb the outflow of private direct investment to other industrial countries. At the same time, the United States continued to actively support direct investment in the developing countries. Steps taken to alleviate balance of payments deficits, therefore, have split U.S. investment policy into two parts; that is, active discouragement of private direct investment by U.S. companies in other industrial countries (when such investment involves the use of U.S. capital funds) and active encouragement of private direct investment in the developing countries. This switch in investment policy did not represent any disavowal of the traditional arguments favoring American investment anywhere in the world; rather, the switch was considered a temporary aberration which would be abandoned when the balance of payments recovered its strength. Only in the late 1960's did labor and protectionist groups rise to challenge the traditional arguments by asserting that direct foreign investment by American companies had detrimental effects on the U.S. economy.

The traditional policy of the United States with respect to private foreign investment has involved treaties of Friendship, Commerce, and Navigation with many countries; diplomatic assistance to American investors abroad; insistence on most-favored-nation treatment of American investments; and, at times in the past, the military protection of American-owned property abroad, notably in Central American and Caribbean countries.

In recent years the U.S. Government has attempted to negotiate treaties that deal more specifically with the conditions that affect investment abroad. These treaties have included provisions that protect the right of American investors to engage freely in business activities in a foreign country, including freedom from restrictions on the ownership or management of business enterprise. Other provisions may guarantee national or most-favored-nation treatment in taxation and other matters; reasonable requirements regarding the employment of local workers; the unrestricted remittance of earnings and repatriation of capital; and freedom from expropriation, or prompt, adequate compensation in the event of expropriation.

The negotiation and ratification of investment treaties is a very slow process; treaties are noticeably lacking with countries in which the investment climate is most unfavorable. It has proved extremely difficult, for example, to reach agreement with developing nations on the free transfer of earnings and capital. Investment treaties, therefore, have had only a limited success in lowering obstacles to U.S. companies abroad. There have been frequent suggestions for the negotiation of an international investment code that would enunciate principles of international law applicable to private foreign investment. However, the gap between the capital-exporting nations

---

[1] See pp. 586-591 for a discussion of tax havens and other aspects of U.S. taxation of foreign-source income.

and the developing nations in this regard makes the negotiation of an agreement satisfactory to all parties very doubtful.[2]

BALANCE OF PAYMENTS CONTROLS ON
U.S. DIRECT INVESTMENT

The U.S. Government introduced mandatory controls on direct foreign investment by U.S. companies in January, 1968, as a "temporary" measure to allow time for more fundamental measures to improve the balance of payments. In 1965, "voluntary" controls had also been introduced as a temporary remedial action, only to have the mandatory controls introduced three years later. Mandatory controls were still in effect in 1972, bringing to mind the French aphorism, "Only the temporary endures."

THE REGULATIONS

Investment controls are administered by the Office of Foreign Direct Investments (OFDI) of the U.S. Department of Commerce.[3] The OFDI defines U.S. direct investment as the sum of capital outflows for direct investment from the United States plus reinvested earnings from existing U.S. direct investments abroad. The rules that determine how much an individual firm is allowed to invest abroad in the current year are much too complex to go into here. Generally an enterprise may invest in the developing countries (Schedule A) up to 110 percent of its base period average (1965-1966) in those countries; in the industrial countries of continental Western Europe (Schedule C) up to 35 percent of its base period average in those countries; and in the other industrial countries, which make up Schedule B (notably the United Kingdom, Japan, and Australia), up to 65 percent of its base period average in those countries. In response to strong protests, Canada was exempted from U.S. controls in March, 1968.

Since 1968 the OFDI has made many changes in its regulations, all in the direction of liberalization. The minimum investment quota which is not subject to controls has been raised from $100,000 to $2 million for the industrial countries and from $4 million to $6 million for the developing countries, effectively removing from control all but the large, multinational enterprises. Firms are also permitted to hold at the end of each month as much as $100,000 in liquid foreign balances compared to a previous maximum of $25,000, provided they do not exceed their average foreign balances held in the base period 1965-1966. Most importantly, the OFDI has adopted an "earnings allowable" formula as an alternative to the base period formula in determining how much a company may invest abroad in the current year. Companies may now invest on a worldwide basis up to 40 percent of the

---

[2] See Chapter 25, pp. 647-648.

[3] The Government also restrains the foreign lending of U.S. banks and other financial institutions under the Voluntary Credit Restraint Program administered by the Federal Reserve Board.

increase in earnings over the 1966-1967 average of their foreign affiliates. Hence, the more profitable its foreign operations, the more a company can invest abroad.[4]

EXPERIENCE UNDER INVESTMENT CONTROLS

As a balance of payments measure, the investment controls are not intended to restrain U.S. direct foreign investment per se, but rather to limit the financing of that investment with U.S. funds and retained foreign earnings. Hence, the controls do not restrict foreign borrowing by U.S. companies. What, then, has been the experience under the control program?

The data does *not* indicate that U.S. multinational enterprises have cut back on their investment expenditures to any substantial degree as a result of the investment controls. Table 22-5 on p. 535 indicates that the plant and equipment expenditures by the foreign affiliates of U.S. companies rose from $9.4 billion in 1968 (the first year of the mandatory controls) to $13.1 billion in 1970. Similarly, Table 22-7 on p. 537 reveals that U.S. direct investment flows (including funds raised abroad) continued to increase after 1967.

The most dramatic impact of the controls has been on the capital-sourcing policies of multinational enterprises. These companies have been able to expand their investments in Europe and other industrial areas in the face of stringent U.S. controls by borrowing capital funds abroad, especially in the Eurodollar and Eurobond markets. Largely in response to these controls, U.S. multinational enterprises have developed intimate contacts with foreign banks and the foreign branches of U.S. banks so as to markedly strengthen their ability to obtain capital financing outside the United States. In terms of Figure 23-4 on p. 555, U.S. investment controls have forced MNE's to make much greater use of capital-sourcing option 4 and much less use of option 1. In brief, U.S. multinational enterprises have countered U.S. controls by making their financial policies more multinational, a shift that is likely to endure after the controls have ceased to exist.

The controls have also strengthened the Eurodollar and Eurobond markets and accelerated the movement abroad of U.S. banks and other financial institutions. Although companies have complained that foreign borrowing is more costly than borrowing in the United States, it does not appear that higher interest costs have been an important inhibiting factor in making new foreign investments. This conclusion is consistent with the theory which was advanced to explain direct foreign investment in Chapter 23.

To conclude, U.S. investment controls have probably had a net positive *short-run* effect on the U.S. balance of payments by restraining the outflow of investment dollars. Because of them, U.S. companies have transferred fewer dollars abroad, increased the repatriation of their foreign earnings

---

[4] "U.S. Firms Have Learned to Live with the OFDI," *Business Abroad* (July, 1971), p. 10.

and liquid balances, and remarkably expanded their foreign borrowing. But this immediate liquidity effect on the balance of payments may well have been obtained only at the cost of a greater negative effect on the balance of payments over the long run. In view of the fact that U.S. investment controls have been in existence in one form or another since 1965, it is arguable that the long-run effect now outweighs the short-run effect, making the controls a detriment to the balance of payments. To understand this point, we must consider the theory of balance of payments adjustment to flows of investment capital and, on a less abstract level, the overall impact of the MNE on the balance of payments.

THE THEORY OF BALANCE OF PAYMENTS ADJUSTMENT TO EXPORTS OF INVESTMENT CAPITAL

A net export of investment capital (portfolio or direct) from one nation to the rest of the world involves both a financial transfer and a real transfer. The *financial transfer* occurs when residents of the lending country transfer purchasing power (usually in the form of bank balances) to residents of the borrowing country. This financial transfer does not make the lending country a *net* exporter of capital because its export of long-term capital (the original loan or investment) is exactly offset in the balance of payments by an import of short-term capital; namely, the funds acquired and not yet spent by the foreign borrowers.[5]

A *net* export of long-term capital occurs only when the borrowed (invested) funds are spent, directly or indirectly, on goods and services of the lending country. Then the export of long-term capital is no longer offset in the balance of payments by an import of short-term capital but, instead, by exports on current account. These exports of merchandise and services that are financed by the export of long-term capital represent the *real transfer* of capital from the lending country to the borrowing country.

Thus, a nation can be a net exporter of capital only when it has a net surplus on current account. Similarly, a nation can be a net importer of capital only when it experiences a net deficit on current account. Hence, to invest abroad a nation must develop a net export balance on current account (inclusive of unilateral transfers) while the borrowing nation must have a net import balance. This necessity for adjustments in the current account in order to effect a net movement of capital between nations comprises the transfer problem.

When a long-term foreign investment is "tied," the transfer problem is easily solved. The proceeds of a tied loan must be spent in the lending

---

[5] Residents of the borrowing country acquire from residents of the lending country bank balances that are located in the lending country, the borrowing country, or elsewhere. In the first instance, the short-term international liabilities of the lending country are increased while, in the second and third instances, its short-term international assets are decreased. Hence, in all instances the lending country experiences a short-term capital inflow (credit) that offsets its autonomous long-term capital outflow (debit). See Chapter 8.

country; and, when the spending occurs, it shows up as exports on current account from the lending to the borrowing country. But suppose the loan is not tied and, further, that the loan funds are not spent in the lending country. How then is the real transfer of the loan brought about? The answer is found in the processes of adjustment to disequilibrium that were examined in Chapters 9 and 10.

Briefly, an export of long-term capital creates a deficit in the balance of payments of the lending country and a surplus in the balance of payments of the borrowing country. When exchange rates are free to vary, this disequilibrium causes a depreciation in the investing country's currency and an appreciation in the borrowing country's currency. These adjustments in the exchange rate cease when the lending country develops a surplus on current account that exactly offsets its export of long-term capital, and the converse occurs in the borrowing country.

When exchange rates are held stable, the real transfer of a long-term capital movement is mainly effected by an inflation of incomes and prices in the country or countries in which the borrowed funds are spent; that is, in our example, in the borrowing country and/or a third country. Some deflation of incomes and prices may also occur in the lending country if the outflow of purchasing power brought about by the capital export leads to a decline in domestic spending.[6] These income and price effects would then restore equilibrium along the lines discussed in Chapter 9. The end result would be a surplus on current account in the lending country equal to its long-term capital export and an equivalent deficit on current account in the borrowing country that stems directly from trade with the lending country or multilaterally from trade with other countries.

From the perspective of adjustment theory, then, the balance of payments argument for investment controls is as fallacious as the balance of payments argument for import restrictions. As we learned in Chapters 9 and 10, market adjustment to a payments deficit involves either a deflation of prices and incomes relative to foreign prices and incomes (stable-rate system) or a devaluation of the exchange rate (variable-rate system). Government restrictions on investment capital outflows (or on any other autonomous debit item in the balance of payments) act to suppress the deficit but do not correct the underlying market forces that cause it. The only argument for investment controls that is compatible with the theory of adjustment is their use as a stop-gap measure to allow a government time to initiate fundamental market adjustments through deflationary monetary and fiscal policies or exchange devaluation. But this argument is particularly weak with respect to controls on direct investment because direct investment (unlike untied portfolio investment) commonly involves shipments of capital equipment, parts, and supplies from the investing country to the foreign affiliates of the direct

---

[6] This would occur, for example, if foreign investment diverted funds from domestic investment or if the decline in the domestic money supply caused a decline in spending.

investor rather than a movement of funds. Hence, real adjustment to a net export of direct investment capital is likely to occur more quickly than adjustment to an outflow of portfolio capital or to a deficit in merchandise trade. For the same reason, direct investment controls can have only a short-run positive effect on the balance of payments because lower investment outflows will soon bring about lower merchandise exports and, somewhat later, lower investment income. As a matter of fact, investment controls did not eliminate the U.S. balance of payments deficit, and in 1971 the United States was finally compelled to make a fundamental adjustment by devaluing the dollar.

THE IMPACT OF U.S. DIRECT FOREIGN INVESTMENT ON THE U.S. BALANCE OF PAYMENTS

The multiple effects of foreign investment by U.S. multinational enterprises on the U.S. balance of payments may be usefully grouped into two categories: (1) financial flow effects, and (2) trade flow effects. The individual effects, so grouped, are depicted in Table 24-1.

Table 24-1

EFFECTS OF U.S. DIRECT FOREIGN INVESTMENT ON THE U.S. BALANCE OF PAYMENTS

Effect	Debit	Credit
A. Financial flows		
1. Direct investment outflow from U.S.	X	
2. Foreign borrowing by U.S. direct investors		X
3. Interest payments on foreign borrowings	X	
4. Income received from direct foreign investment ..		X
5. Receipts from royalties and fees		X
B. Trade flows		
1. Associated exports		X
2. Displaced exports	X	
3. Imports	X	

Financial Flow Effects. Increases in the book value of U.S. direct investment abroad result either from an outflow of capital from the United States or from reinvestment of the earnings of the foreign affiliates of U.S. companies. The first mode of financing involves a debit entry in the U.S. balance of payments (A.1) whereas the second mode of financing does not enter the balance of payments at all.[7] As noted earlier, U.S. multinational enterprises have responded to investment controls by borrowing heavily abroad to finance new investments. These foreign borrowings appear in the U.S. balance

---

[7] Only the foreign earnings of U.S. companies actually repatriated to the United States are recorded in the U.S. balance of payments.

of payments as an inflow of long-term capital (A.2). This positive effect is somewhat offset by the interest paid to the foreign lenders (A.3).

Increments to U.S. investment abroad generate a flow of income to the United States in subsequent periods, a credit entry in the U.S. balance of payments (A.4). This income flow depends both on the rate of return on investment and the share of earnings that is repatriated to the United States. U.S. direct investment abroad also generates income in the form of royalties, as well as fees for management and other services provided by the parent company to its affiliates (A.5).

What has been the net effect of these financial flows on the U.S. balance of payments? Table 22-7 on p. 537 shows there has been a net credit balance in every year over the period 1960 through 1970. But this credit balance is badly understated after 1967 because Table 22-7 does not include foreign bank borrowings by U.S. direct investors. When account is taken of such borrowings, the cumulative net effect of the financial flows associated with the direct investment of U.S. multinational enterprises over the period 1961-1970 is a net credit balance of $35.3 billion.[8] As far as financial flows are concerned, then, U.S. direct foreign investment has been a major source of strength for the U.S. balance of payments.

Trade Flow Effects. Depending on the circumstances, direct foreign investment by U.S. multinational enterprises may have a positive or negative effect on U.S. merchandise exports. On the one hand, direct investment may increase exports by generating *associated exports* that involve flows of capital equipment, parts, raw materials, and finished goods from U.S. parent companies to their own foreign affiliates. The presumption is strong that these associated exports would not have occurred in the absence of foreign investment. On the other hand, U.S. direct investment may decrease U.S. exports by causing (1) the manufacture of products in foreign countries which would not have been manufactured by foreign companies, and (2) the sale of these manufactured products in foreign markets heretofore supplied by exports from the United States. This is the *displaced-exports* effect.

Given these two possible effects, has the *net* export effect of U.S. direct foreign investment been positive or negative? Unfortunately we cannot give a straightforward answer to this question. Part of the difficulty is attributable to the inadequacy of empirical data concerning the relationships between the direct investment (international production) activities of U.S. multinational enterprises and their U.S. exports. But the fundamental problem is the impossibility of *conclusively* demonstrating what would have happened to U.S. exports in the absence of all U.S. direct foreign investment. Specifically, does the foreign production of U.S. multinational enterprises replace U.S. exports, or does it rather replace *potential* foreign-owned production in the host

---

[8] Susan B. Foster, "Impact of Direct Investment Abroad by United States Multinational Companies on the Balance of Payments," *Monthly Review* (New York: Federal Reserve Bank of New York, July, 1972), Table 1, p. 172.

countries? If U.S. production abroad simply replaces U.S. exports, then the net export effect of U.S. direct investment is clearly negative. At the other extreme, if U.S. production abroad simply replaces *potential* foreign-owned production (which would become *actual* production in the absence of U.S. investment), then the net export effect is positive, because in that case U.S. direct foreign investment generates associated exports while it does not displace any exports.

The net export effect depends, therefore, on the motivation and behavior of U.S. investing companies and on the willingness and capability of foreign companies to take advantage of investment opportunities in their own or in third countries. What are the most reasonable judgments in this regard?

First, it should be established that in evaluating the trade effects of U.S. direct foreign investment we are speaking almost entirely about investments in manufacturing. Extractive investments abroad by U.S. companies do not displace U.S. exports because the motivation of extractive investors is to obtain raw materials which are not available in the United States or available only at a higher cost. By the same token, extractive investments are not likely to give rise to imports which would otherwise not have occurred because in the absence of those investments, the United States would import the same raw materials from foreign firms.

In Chapter 21 we discussed the motivation of U.S. direct foreign investment in manufacturing, concluding that considerations of marketing strategy dominate the vast majority of decisions by U.S. companies to manufacture abroad. When the investment decision is purely defensive, then the choice confronting U.S. companies is either to invest abroad or lose their export markets. Even when the investment decision is aggressive, the motivation is commonly to "beat out" the competition. In general, therefore, U.S. manufacturers invest abroad either to hold on to markets that they can no longer supply competitively with U.S. exports or to prevent the loss of markets to foreign competitors in the foreseeable future.[9] This motivation is a reflection of the competitive international economy; U.S. companies must respond to market forces in order to survive in foreign markets as well as in their home markets.[10]

Evidence relating to the motivations and behavior of multinational enterprises, therefore, supports the contention that U.S. exports to foreign affiliates are mostly exports that would not have occurred in the absence of those affiliates and that export displacement is modest. The size of associated exports is indicated by the fact that 320 U.S. parent companies shipped over

---

[9] The testimony of U.S. business executives is overwhelming on this point. See, for example, the company cases presented in National Foreign Trade Council, Inc., *The Impact of U.S. Foreign Direct Investment on U.S. Employment and Trade* (New York: National Foreign Trade Council, Inc., November, 1971), pp. 12-28.

[10] They must also respond to foreign government policies that restrain U.S. exports to foreign markets.

half their exports (the total of which accounted for nearly 45 percent of total U.S. nonagricultural exports in 1965) to their own foreign affiliates.[11]

Has U.S. manufacturing investment abroad generated U.S. imports that would not have occurred in its absence? If such investment is mainly a response to lower foreign costs of production or other market factors, then the answer is clearly negative. For in that event, independent foreign companies would have supplied similar products to the United States instead of U.S.-owned affiliate companies. Most investments by U.S. manufacturers to "source" components, assemblies, and finished products from their affiliates for use in the United States appear to fit this case. For example, U.S. manufacturers of television sets (and many other electrical consumer products) can only compete with Japanese-made sets in the U.S. market by exporting U.S.-made components to their foreign affiliates in Taiwan and elsewhere for assembly into sets which are then shipped to the United States. In the absence of those affiliates, far more television sets would be imported from independent Japanese companies. Furthermore, the statistical data show that only a small fraction of the production of U.S. foreign affiliates is shipped to this country. As mentioned in Chapter 22, excluding the special case of automotive imports from Canada, these shipments amounted to only $2.5 billion in 1968.

In light of the foregoing discussion, we arrive at a judgment that the *net* trade effect on the U.S. balance of payments of U.S. direct foreign investment has been positive. A more cautious conclusion is reached in a recent study of this question:

> . . . while there may be some net export gain or loss or import creation in the short run, over a longer time horizon the portions of the observed changes in export and import patterns which can reasonably be ascribed to the direct investment process itself probably tend approximately to balance out or perhaps be a net positive item. Rather, most of the observed alterations in trade patterns should more appropriately be viewed as market responses to shifts in worldwide relative competitive conditions, and would have occurred whether or not the foreign facilities were owned by United States investors.[12]

When account is taken of the effects of financial flows as well as trade flows, U.S. direct foreign investment emerges as a critical source of strength for the U.S. balance of payments.

The Recoupment Period Controversy. Given that direct foreign investment is a positive factor in the U.S. balance of payments, it does not necessarily

---

[11] See Tables 22-8 on p. 538 and 22-9 on p. 539.

[12] Susan B. Foster, "Impact of Direct Investment Abroad by United States Multinational Companies on the Balance of Payments," *Monthly Review* (New York: Federal Reserve Bank of New York, July, 1972), p. 177.

follow that such investment is a positive factor in the short run. After all, a specific investment abroad does not *immediately* generate a return flow of earnings. The financial and trade effects which we explored in the previous sections are the cumulative consequences of all previous capital outflows that have added to the asset value of U.S. direct investment abroad. How long, then, is the short run? How many years does it take for a dollar of *new* U.S. direct foreign investment to generate a return flow of earnings, service income, and net export receipts which are equal to that dollar? In other words, what is the *recoupment period* of U.S. direct foreign investment?

The length of the recoupment period is a controversial issue which has obvious implications for public policy. If the recoupment period is very short, then government controls that restrict investment cannot be justified on balance of payments grounds. However, if the recoupment period is long, then investment controls can help the balance of payments for several years. Elaborate studies employing sophisticated econometric models have served only to fuel the recoupment period controversy rather than resolve it. The output of these models is crucially dependent on assumptions regarding the rate of return, the repatriation ratio, and (particularly) the net trade effect of direct foreign investment. When it is assumed that foreign investment largely *displaces* U.S. exports, then the models indicate lengthy or even infinite recoupment periods.[13] When, conversely, it is assumed that foreign investment does not displace exports but does generate associated exports, then the models indicate short recoupment periods.[14]

In our own judgment, the recoupment period of U.S. direct foreign investment for the world as a whole is most probably on the order of five or six years. Given such a recoupment period, U.S. investment controls (first imposed in 1965) are no longer aiding the balance of payments but instead are hurting it. Our objection to these controls, however, has nothing to do with recoupment periods. It is erroneous to use balance of payments criteria to evaluate the desirability of direct foreign investment. The basic economic rationale of international investment is its contribution to the productive efficiency and growth of the entire world economy. Even at the national level, the economic benefits and costs of foreign investment should be

---

[13] See G. C. Hufbauer and F. M. Adler, *Overseas Manufacturing Investment and the Balance of Payments,* U.S. Treasury Department, Tax Policy Research Study Number One (Washington: U.S. Government Printing Office, 1968). Employing a variety of assumptions, the models used in this study result in estimates of recoupment periods for the world (weighted averages of regional recoupment periods) that range from 9.2 years to infinity, when the original investment is *never* matched by return flows. (See *ibid.,* Table 5-13, p. 67.) In a subsequent article one of the coauthors rejected the policy implications of these estimates which favor investment controls. See F. Michael Adler, "The High Cost of Foreign Investment Restraints," *Columbia Journal of World Business* (May-June, 1968), pp. 73-81.

[14] In a rebuttal of the Hufbauer-Adler study, Behrman obtained recoupment periods that range from less than one year for Canada to one year for Latin America and to two years for Europe. See Jack N. Behrman, *Direct Manufacturing Investment, Exports and the Balance of Payments* (New York: National Foreign Trade Council, Inc., 1968), p. 16.

measured in terms of its contribution to allocative efficiency, growth, and development.[15] The economic benefits of foreign investment should not be sacrificed to the expediencies of the balance of payments, especially when more suitable policy instruments are available to governments to restore balance of payments equilibrium.

OTHER U.S. POLICIES TOWARD THE MULTINATIONAL ENTERPRISE

Aside from investment controls, several other policies of the U.S. Government influence the behavior of multinational enterprises. We now turn to a brief treatment of these policies and the issues raised by them.

PROMOTION OF DIRECT INVESTMENT IN DEVELOPING COUNTRIES

Since the Second World War, the United States has actively promoted private foreign investment in the developing countries, introducing investment insurance (guarantees) in 1948. Until 1971 most investment incentive measures were administered by the Agency for International Development (AID), but now these functions have been transferred to a new institution known as the Overseas Private Investment Corporation (OPIC), which has also been given new authority and resources to promote investment.

OPIC. OPIC was created by the Foreign Assistance Act of 1969 "to mobilize and facilitate the participation of United States private capital and skills in the economic and social progress of less developed friendly countries and areas, thereby complementing the development assistance objectives of the United States." [16] With a joint public-private board of directors, OPIC is expected to aggressively seek out qualified prospective investors in contrast to AID's passive approach, which mainly focused on making facilities available to investors who wanted them.

OPIC inherited from AID the following major incentive programs:

1. The *investment insurance program,* under which U.S. investors are provided coverage against the political risks of (a) expropriation and confiscation, (b) war, revolution, and insurrection, and (c) inconvertibility of profits and capital.

2. The *investment guaranty program,* under which coverage against both political and commercial risks is provided for financial loans (mostly portfolio investments) by U.S. institutional investors, such as insurance companies.

3. The *investment survey program,* under which OPIC pays half the cost of an investment survey undertaken by a prospective U.S. investor if subsequently the investor decides not to go ahead with the project.

---

[15] See Chapter 25, pp. 611-623, for a treatment of the economic benefits and costs of direct foreign investment to host countries.

[16] *Foreign Assistance Act of 1969* (PL 91-175), Part I, Title IV.

In addition to these programs, OPIC was given a major new authority in the form of the Direct Investment Fund (initially capitalized at $40 million), which it can use to make dollar loans to investors and to purchase convertible debentures and other debt instruments issued by them.

The incentive of most importance to multinational enterprises is the investment insurance program. To be eligible for such insurance:

> 1. The investor must be a U.S. citizen, a U.S. corporation at least 51 percent owned by U.S. interests, or a wholly owned affiliate (foreign or domestic) of such a corporation.
>
> 2. The investment must be a new project, including the expansion of an existing foreign operation.
>
> 3. The investment must be in a developing country that has signed an Investment Guarantee Agreement with the U.S. Government.
>
> 4. The application for risk coverage must be specifically approved by the foreign host government in writing.
>
> 5. OPIC must approve the investment as serving the host country's social and economic needs.[17]

Investment insurance is available to U.S. foreign investors up to a maximum of twenty years. The fee schedule for this insurance, expressed as a percentage of the risk coverage, is three-tenths of 1 percent on convertibility policies and six-tenths of 1 percent on both expropriation and war-revolution-insurrection policies. In addition to this current coverage, the investor may also obtain standby coverage (which allows him to increase his coverage at a later time) at a cost of one-fourth of 1 percent for each policy. From 1948 through 1969, over 4,000 policies with a total risk coverage of $9 billion were issued to investors.[18] Given the fact that investments in petroleum exploration and extraction are not eligible for investment insurance, it is estimated that about two-thirds of eligible new U.S. investments in developing countries are being insured at the present time.

Has the investment insurance program stimulated U.S. direct investment in the developing countries? No conclusive answer is possible, but the following points are pertinent. First, like other incentives, investment insurance cannot turn an unprofitable investment into a profitable one. A multinational enterprise will not invest in a developing country simply because it can obtain insurance against political risks. If an investment project is judged to be unpromising on economic grounds, the enterprise will not go

---

[17] Investment Guarantee Agreements have been signed with over ninety developing countries, although some agreements do not cover all three risk categories. The host government agrees to recognize the transfer of the rights and claims of the private investor to the U.S. Government in the event of payment under his insurance contract, but the host government is not obligated to provide special treatment for the insured investment.

[18] Organization for Economic Cooperation and Development, *Investing in Developing Countries* (Paris: Organization for Economic Cooperation and Development, 1970), p. 100.

ahead with it even if investment insurance is available at no cost. Second, there may be situations where a multinational enterprise will not proceed with an economically attractive project in a developing country because political risks are deemed to be too high. Here the availability of insurance may tip the balance in favor of investment, although it is unlikely to do so if political risks are viewed as severe. After all, investment insurance covers only actual asset loss; it does not cover the investor's loss of prospective profits which made the investment desirable in the first place. In light of these considerations, investment insurance has probably encouraged a marginal increase in U.S. direct investment in the developing countries. But investment insurance has not been able to alter the regional pattern of U.S. direct investment, which, as we saw in Table 22-2, p. 532, continues to favor the industrial areas.

Multilateral Investment Insurance. Proposals for the creation of a multilateral investment insurance scheme, involving both the industrial and developing countries, have been under active consideration for more than a decade. The International Bank for Reconstruction and Development (IBRD) has prepared a draft of "Articles of Agreement of the International Investment Insurance Agency" which is now under review by national governments. This Agency would insure international investors against political risks (especially for projects involving investors from several countries), would settle claims by arbitration, and would finance compensation payments from the contributions of the participating nations. The Agency would supplement rather than replace the bilateral insurance schemes which now exist in a majority of the industrial countries, but it could function as a reinsurance agent for national investment insurance.

Interest in multilateral investment insurance has been renewed in the United States by the rash of expropriations experienced by U.S. companies in Latin America in recent years.[19] Fears have been raised about the capacity of OPIC to meet claims on expropriation policies. In 1971 OPIC, with only $85 million in reserves, faced potential claims of $216 million by U.S. companies whose assets were seized by the Chilean government.[20] If OPIC were forced to ask Congress for a special appropriation to pay claims on expropriation insurance (which is backed by the credit of the U.S. Government), the political consequences would probably damage the investment insurance program. Almost certainly, OPIC would become much more selective as to the countries and kinds of investment for which it would be willing to issue insurance. Many businessmen also believe that a multilateral agency would be more able and willing than the U.S. Government to exert "leverage"

---

[19] "International Accord to Underwrite Business Abroad Is Sought," *Journal of Commerce* (July 21, 1971), p. 1. See also p. 631 ff. in Chapter 25.

[20] "U.S. Insuring Agency May Face Claims of $216 Million in Chile," *The New York Times,* March 6, 1972, p. 5.

on host governments to prevent expropriation or to insure adequate compensation.

Two major issues prevent the establishment of a multilateral insurance agency: (1) the question of compulsory arbitration, and (2) the question of financial contributions. The United States and other industrial countries want compulsory arbitration; the developing countries reject such arbitration as an infringement on their national sovereignty. The United States also wants all participating countries to contribute funds for compensation payments to investors. Here again, the developing countries are generally opposed to the idea of helping to finance payments to private investors whose claims against host countries are upheld by an arbitration commission.

U.S. TAX POLICY TOWARD MULTINATIONAL ENTERPRISE

Operating in many countries, multinational enterprises are subject to multiple tax jurisdictions. National tax systems are exceedingly complex, with many differences among them with respect to forms of taxation (for example, direct and indirect taxes), statutory rates, effective rates (what taxpayers actually pay), and the taxation of foreign-source income. Our interest in this section is the national taxation of foreign-source income, and in particular, the taxation of the income of multinational enterprises by the U.S. Government.

Differences among national income tax systems influence several kinds of decisions made by the managers of multinational parent companies, notably the choice of country in which to locate operations, the legal form (branch or corporation) for the establishment of those operations, the method of financing operations (loan or equity, domestic or foreign), and the determination of the prices of products and other assets which are transferred among the many national units of the multinational enterprise system.[21] Because of its potency to influence business decisions, both home and host governments frequently employ tax policy to promote or deter the investment and other activities of multinational enterprises.

Multiple Tax Jurisdictions. Multiple tax jurisdictions create two sets of problems: (1) "overlapping" jurisdictions, and (2) "underlapping" jurisdictions. When overlapping occurs, two or more governments claim tax jurisdiction over the same income of the same multinational enterprise. Hence, overlapping jurisdictions raise the problem of *double taxation*, a problem of

---

[21] Differences among national *indirect* tax systems also affect decision making in the multinational enterprise because of their effects on production costs, prices, and the cost of transferring products among countries. See Chapter 16, pp. 385-386, for a discussion of the "tax frontier" in the European Economic Community. The role of indirect taxes as nontariff trade barriers is treated in Chapter 12, pp. 298-299.

immediate concern to enterprise managers. Conversely, underlapping occurs when some or all of the income of a multinational enterprise falls between tax jurisdictions and thereby escapes any taxation. The result is *tax avoidance*, which is a problem for governments. To understand how overlapping and underlapping can happen, we need to know something about the tax jurisdictions of national governments.

National governments may choose to exercise a *territorial* tax jurisdiction, a *national* tax jurisdiction, or both. Under a territorial tax jurisdiction, a government taxes only business income that is generated by operations located on the national territory. A government following this jurisdictional principle taxes both domestic and foreign-owned business operations taking place *within* its borders, but exempts from taxation all foreign-source income which is earned by national companies *outside* its borders. This approach is generally used by France, Italy, the Netherlands, and some twenty-five other countries.[22] When, however, a government exercises national tax jurisdiction, both the domestic *and* foreign-source incomes of national companies are liable for taxation by that government. Thus, the U.S. Government (which follows the national principle as do the majority of governments) taxes U.S. multinational enterprises on their worldwide incomes. If a government exercised *only* a national tax jurisdiction, it would exempt from taxation the income earned on its territory by nonnational companies owned by foreigners. But this does not happen because governments which claim a national tax jurisdiction also claim a territorial jurisdiction.

If all national governments were to adopt only a territorial tax jurisdiction, then the problem of double taxation would largely disappear for the multinational enterprise. Its affiliates would pay income taxes to their respective host governments, and dividends paid to the parent company by the affiliates would be exempt from taxation by the home government. Still remaining, however, would be the thorny problem of deciding where the income of a multinational enterprise was "rightfully" earned, a problem which is intensified by the ability of the enterprise to alter the national source of its income through adjustments in transfer prices. Given territorial tax jurisdiction only, a multinational enterprise could minimize its tax liabilities by arranging transfer prices so as to concentrate income in low-tax countries. Hence, governments would have to agree on the proper allocation among countries of the income of multinational enterprises in order to fully resolve the twin problems of double taxation and tax avoidance.

U.S. Taxation of Foreign-Source Income. In general, the U.S. Government does not distinguish between income earned at home and income earned

---

[22] National Foreign Trade Council, Inc., *Economic Implications of Proposed Changes in the Taxation of U.S. Investments Abroad* (New York: National Foreign Trade Council, Inc., 1972), pp. 11 and 13.

abroad. However, to minimize double taxation the Government does allow multinational enterprises headquartered in the United States to credit their U.S. income tax liabilities with income taxes paid to foreign governments.[23]

Until the 1962 Revenue Act, the tax treatment of the foreign branches of U.S. multinational enterprises was basically different from the treatment of their subsidiaries which were incorporated in host countries. Considered a part of the U.S. parent company, the foreign branch was (and is) taxed by the U.S. Government on its current income in the same way as domestic income, with credit granted for foreign taxes paid by the branch. However, the foreign subsidiaries of U.S. multinational enterprises were viewed as legally distinct from the parent company, and as foreign corporations doing business on foreign soil they were not subject to the tax jurisdiction of the U.S. Government. Hence, the income of foreign subsidiaries was taxable by the U.S. Government only when it was received by the U.S. parent company as dividends, royalties, management fees, or other forms of income. This tax treatment made possible the *deferral* of U.S. taxes on the foreign-source income earned by subsidiaries when that income was retained abroad rather than sent home to the parent company. To increase their tax deferrals, U.S. multinational enterprises frequently established nonoperating subsidiaries in "tax haven" countries, such as Panama and Switzerland, where taxes on foreign-source income were low or nonexistent. U.S. parent companies then channelled the earnings of their operating subsidiaries outside the United States to their tax-haven subsidiaries, where they became available for reinvestment in foreign countries throughout the world without payment of the U.S. corporate income tax.

In 1962 the Kennedy Administration asked Congress to eliminate the tax deferral "privilege" for U.S.-owned subsidiaries located in industrial countries and also to eliminate all tax-haven subsidiaries, regardless of their locations. Congress rejected the first request but gave the President his second request. The Revenue Act of 1962 struck hard at tax-haven subsidiaries by making their incomes subject to U.S. taxation when it was earned, regardless of whether or not it was repatriated to the United States. Specifically, when 30 percent or more of the income of a U.S.-controlled foreign subsidiary (more than 50 percent of the voting stock is held by the U.S. parent) takes the form of nonoperating, passive income (mainly dividends and royalties) received from other foreign subsidiaries controlled by the same U.S. parent,

---

[23] A major tax concession is granted to U.S. companies that qualify as a Western Hemisphere Corporation. Such companies must do all their business in the Western Hemisphere, receive 95 percent of their income from sources outside the United States, and earn 90 percent of their income from the active conduct of a trade or business. Western Hemisphere Corporations are granted a reduction of 14 percentage points from the normal U.S. corporate income tax rate. However, the effects of this exemption on direct foreign investment have been minimal because these corporations are involved predominantly in exporting from the United States. Investment income earned in U.S. possessions also qualifies for certain tax exemptions.

then that passive income is subject to immediate U.S. taxation with no deferral. If more than 70 percent of the income of a controlled foreign subsidiary is this sort of passive income, then *all* the income of the subsidiary is subject to immediate U.S. taxation.[24] However, if less than 30 percent of a U.S.-controlled foreign subsidiary's income is nonoperating income received from subsidiaries of the same parent company, then the U.S. government taxes that subsidiary's income only when it is repatriated to the United States. The 1962 Act forced U.S. multinational enterprises to dissolve their tax-haven subsidiaries or convert them into operating companies in accordance with the 30-70 percent rule.[25] It has also saddled multinational enterprises with onerous reporting requirements, and has made U.S. taxation a more critical factor in international business decisions.

To get its "fair share" of the income earned by U.S. multinational enterprises, the U.S. Treasury insists that a U.S. parent company use "arm's length" prices in all transactions with its foreign affiliates. Arm's length prices are the prices of the same or similar products and services which are paid or charged by the parent company in transactions with independent sellers and buyers. In the absence of such transactions (a common occurrence), arm's length prices are prices that represent full standard costs and appropriate markups. Section 482 of the Internal Revenue Code gives the Treasury the authority to reallocate the income between a U.S. parent company and its foreign affiliates in accordance with the arm's length standards.[26] The Treasury's interpretation of arm's length pricing has aroused much criticism from managers of multinational enterprises who consider the Treasury's reallocations as frequently unrealistic and arbitrary. Nonetheless, the Treasury authority to reallocate income is clearly necessary if U.S. parent companies are to be prevented from shifting income to foreign affiliates at the expense of U.S. tax revenue. It is rational for U.S. parent companies to establish transfer prices which will maximize the post-tax consolidated profits of the entire multinational enterprise system, and this behavior could very well involve shifting income from the United States (a high-tax country) to affiliates in low-tax countries either by charging low prices for the products and services it "sells" to its affiliates or by paying high prices for the products and services it "buys" from them.[27]

Each national government insists that the units of a multinational enterprise operating on its territory make some taxable profits, although no other

---

[24] This is known as the 30-70 percent rule.

[25] The 30-70 percent rule still allows multinational enterprises to reap some tax-haven benefits. See, for example, "Sophistication Comes to the Tax Havens," *Fortune* (February, 1969), p. 95 ff.

[26] See Warren J. Keegan, "Multinational Pricing: How Far is Arm's Length?" *Columbia Journal of World Business* (May-June, 1969).

[27] For a survey of the transfer pricing policies of U.S. multinational enterprises, see The Conference Board, *Intercompany Transactions in the Multinational Firm* (New York: The Conference Board, 1970).

government has gone as far as the United States in reallocating profits. When the U.S. Government reallocates the profits of a multinational enterprise in a way which is unacceptable to a foreign government, then the enterprise may experience double taxation. The U.S. Government tries to overcome this problem by negotiating bilateral tax treaties with foreign governments whereby both signatories recognize the same allocation of income between related taxpayers. Bilateral tax treaties also contain provisions designed to eliminate other forms of double taxation and to prevent tax avoidance by nationals of the two countries.

The U.S. Controversy over Foreign-Source Income Taxation. The attempt by the Kennedy Administration in 1962 to eliminate all tax deferral for U.S.-controlled subsidiaries in the industrial countries and tax-haven subsidiaries in all countries was motivated by a belief that such changes in the taxation of foreign-source income would help the balance of payments by restraining U.S. investment in Europe and by immediately increasing tax receipts from U.S. parent companies. But in arguing its position, the Treasury also appealed to the principle of tax equity; namely, that U.S. multinational corporations should bear the same tax burden as U.S. domestic corporations. The tax deferral for foreign-source income was portrayed as an unfair advantage (an "interest-free loan" from the Treasury to the U.S. parent company) because it was not available to U.S. companies whose income was made entirely within the United States. It was also alleged that tax deferral violated the principle of tax neutrality by encouraging U.S. companies to invest abroad rather than at home. Thus, the Treasury raised the fundamental issues of any system of taxation: *equity* and *neutrality*.[28]

In making its argument, the Treasury looked at the taxation of foreign-source income from the perspective of *domestic* tax equity and *domestic* tax neutrality. Domestic equity demanded that all U.S. companies in similar situations pay the same tax (with credit allowed for foreign taxes) regardless of the national source of their income. Domestic neutrality demanded that U.S. domestic and U.S. foreign investors pay the same taxes so that their choice of investment location would not be affected by tax considerations.

In rebutting the Treasury's position, the spokesmen for U.S. multinational enterprises argued that it was correct to view the taxation of foreign-source income only from the perspective of *foreign* tax equity and *foreign* tax neutrality. For them, tax equity and tax neutrality were achieved only when U.S.-controlled foreign affiliates bore the same tax burden as their foreign competitors in the host countries. If the tax burden of their affiliates were higher than that of local competitors, then U.S. parent companies

---

[28] A tax system is *equitable* when it imposes the same burden on all companies (or citizens) in similar situations who are located in the same tax jurisdiction. A tax system is *neutral* when it does not alter the relative post-tax profitability of different lines of economic activity and, therefore, does not distort the allocation of resources.

would be placed at a competitive disadvantage, which would force a cutback in their foreign investments and have detrimental effects on the balance of payments and the international economic position of the United States.[29]

The heart of this controversy was a fundamental disagreement over the proper tax jurisdiction of the United States. In effect, the Treasury argued for the nationality principle while multinational enterprises upheld the territorial principle. The Treasury wanted to treat U.S. multinational enterprises in the same way as U.S. domestic enterprises, with allowances for taxes paid to foreign governments. In opposition, U.S. multinational enterprises wanted to be treated as multinational enterprise systems comprising many separate units which operated on the territories of different nations and which were subject to different tax jurisdictions. The 1962 Tax Act did not resolve this controversy; as we shall see, it has been renewed in the 1970's by attacks on U.S. multinational enterprises which have been spearheaded by U.S. labor unions. As a consequence, the tax controversy has now become part of a much broader controversy: Are multinational enterprises good or bad for the United States?

U.S. ANTITRUST POLICY AND THE MULTINATIONAL ENTERPRISE

As business firms incorporated in the United States, the U.S. parent companies of multinational enterprises are clearly subject to the antitrust laws of the United States.[30] But what may surprise many readers is the extent to which these laws also apply to their foreign affiliates, to their licensing arrangements with foreign companies, and to their acquisitions of foreign companies. Even foreign companies operating abroad come under the jurisdictional sweep of U.S. antitrust policy when their behavior has actual or potential anticompetitive effects in the United States.

U.S. antitrust policy toward multinational enterprises can only be assessed in terms of court decisions, whose general implications are usually

---

[29] For the extensive testimony of both sides of the tax controversy, see U.S., Congress, House, Committee on Ways and Means, *The Tax Recommendations of the President Contained in His Message Transmitted to the Congress, April 20, 1961,* 87th Cong., 1st sess., 1961, volumes 1-4.

[30] The most important antitrust provisions are Sections 1 and 2 of the Sherman Act and Section 7 of the Clayton Act. Section 1 forbids contracts, combinations, or conspiracies "in restraint of trade or commerce among the several states, or with foreign nations." Section 2 makes illegal the monopolization of or attempt to monopolize "any part of the trade or commerce among the several states or with foreign nations." Section 7 prohibits a corporation from acquiring another corporation "where in any line of commerce in any section of the country, the effect of such acquisition may be substantially to lessen competition, or tend to create a monopoly." In brief, Section 1 is an anticartel provision; Section 2 is an antimonopoly provision; and Section 7 is an antimerger provision. For the full text of U.S. antitrust laws, see U.S., Congress, House, Committee on the Judiciary, *The Antitrust Laws,* 85th Cong., 2d sess., 1959.

uncertain because they deal with specific cases. Antitrust lawyers frequently disagree on the significance of a particular case. All too often, questions of law supersede questions of economics. In this section we can do no more than indicate the potential antitrust constraints on multinational enterprises as suggested by court decisions, and then identify the key issues raised by U.S. antitrust policy.

Extraterritorial Jurisdiction. The U.S. Government claims antitrust jurisdiction over the behavior of U.S. companies and their foreign affiliates regardless of where that behavior may take place. That is to say, the Government exercises jurisdiction over the *entire* multinational enterprise system when the parent company is incorporated in the United States. The rationale for this extraterritorial jurisdiction is that business behavior anywhere in the world may restrain U.S. exports or imports or have anticompetitive effects in the United States. After a review of almost fifty years of court cases, a committee of experts concluded:

> We feel that the Sherman Act applies only to those arrangements between Americans alone, or in concert with foreign firms, which have such substantial anticompetitive effects on this country's "trade or commerce . . . with foreign nations" as to constitute unreasonable restraints. . . . We believe that conspiracies between foreign competitors alone should come within the Sherman Act only where they are intended to, and actually do, result in substantial anticompetitive effects on our foreign commerce.[31]

What, then, are the antitrust implications of extraterritorial jurisdiction for U.S. multinational enterprises?

Antitrust Guidelines. Until the 1960's only the Sherman Act was applied to business behavior outside the United States. The many court decisions appear to point to the following guidelines for admissible behavior by multinational enterprises.

Because it takes two or more parties to make a conspiracy, a U.S. parent company may allocate markets and fix prices among its foreign branches (which are legally parts of the parent company) without violating the antitrust laws. It is also generally considered safe for a U.S. parent company to do the same with its 100-percent-owned foreign subsidiaries. However, when a foreign subsidiary is only partly owned by a U.S. parent company, then any *formal* anticompetitive agreements entered into between the majority and minority interests run the risk of antitrust violation, as indicated by the

---

[31] *Report of the Attorney General's National Committee to Study the Antitrust Laws* (Washington: U.S. Government Printing Office, 1955), p. 76.

Timken Case.[32] (Actually with majority control there should be no need for a U.S. parent company to enter into formal agreements with minority interests.) Foreign joint ventures involving a U.S. company and other companies (foreign or U.S.) as coowners of the same foreign firm are particularly open to antitrust action. In general, agreements between the joint venture and its parents that limit competition among them are illegal unless they are necessary to the licensing of a patent or trademark. Agreements between a U.S. company and an independent foreign company which have anticompetitive effects on U.S. trade are illegal under the Sherman Act.

It follows from this last statement that licensing arrangements between U.S. and foreign companies must not contain any restrictions on prices, production, or market territories. However, because a legal monopoly is conferred on holders of patents and trademarks, a U.S. company may set restrictive conditions in licensing a foreign company to use its patents or trademarks. Even then, the restrictions can only be those necessary to protect the patent and trademark rights. In 1970 the Justice Department filed a suit charging Westinghouse and two Japanese companies (Mitsubishi Electric and Mitsubishi Heavy Industries) with illegally conspiring to *not* sell certain products (including transformers and television sets) in each other's countries. According to the suit, the agreement not to compete was part of an agreement under which the companies exchanged patents and other technical information. The Justice Department asked the Court to require action by Westinghouse and the Japanese companies that would restore competition between them and to permanently enjoin Westinghouse from entering into similar agreements with any foreign companies. In a statement Westinghouse pointed out that if the Department won the case, then the Japanese companies would be able to "manufacture Westinghouse-designed products in Japan with low-wage labor and then sell those products in the United States in direct competition with similar products manufactured in the United States by American labor." [33] This statement raises one of the many issues of U.S. antitrust policy; namely, does that policy help or hurt the international competitive position of the United States?

---

[32] *Timken Roller Bearing Co.* v. *United States, 341 U.S. 593 (1951).* The United States charged U.S. Timken, British Timken, and French Timken with violation of Section 1 of the Sherman Act because of mutual agreements to fix prices, allocate markets, and restrain U.S. exports and imports. At the time of the suit, U.S. Timken owned 30 percent of British Timken (a U.K. corporation), while an Englishman named Dewar owned 24 percent; U.S. Timken and Dewar each owned 50 percent of French Timken (a French corporation). The Court prohibited further enforcement of the agreements, stating that common ownership did not exempt them from the antitrust laws. This decision raised the question of "intraenterprise conspiracy," especially with respect to minority foreign affiliates of U.S. companies.

[33] "U.S. Concern Sued with Two in Japan," *The New York Times,* April 23, 1970, p. 1. See also, "Should License Cut Out Competition?" *Business Week* (May 2, 1970), p. 20.

In recent years the United States has used Section 7 of the Clayton Act to stop the acquisition of foreign companies by U.S. companies. In 1964 the Court ordered the Jos. Schlitz Brewing Company to divest itself of its part ownership of Labatt, the third largest Canadian brewer, which, in turn, owned the General Brewing Corporation of California. In its decision, the Court concluded that this indirect control of General Brewing by Schlitz "would substantially lessen competition in the sale of beer in the United States." [34] In 1968 the United States attacked the acquisition of Braun, a German corporation, by Gillette. With this acquisition, Gillette gained entry into the European electric shaver market. Although Braun did not sell shavers in the United States (where it had a licensing agreement with Ronson) and Gillette did not manufacture or sell electric shavers anywhere, the Justice Department contended that all shaving instruments were competitive and that after the expiration of the Braun-Ronson agreement, Braun might enter the U.S. market with its own electric shaver. Therefore, if allowed to stand, Gillette's acquisition of Braun would rule out future *potential* competition between Braun and Gillette in the U.S. market. [35] These and other recent Section 7 cases indicate that U.S. multinational enterprises must pursue their foreign acquisition strategies under severe antitrust constraints.

The application of U.S. antitrust laws to business behavior outside the United States is sure to engender conflicts with the laws and policies of other countries. [36] Indeed, the United States has been accused of "judicial imperialism" in seeking to apply its antitrust laws to the foreign operations of U.S. companies and even to the operations of foreign companies. The probability of conflicts is heightened by the wide diversity of national policies toward anticompetitive business behavior. Most developing countries have no antitrust laws, and the United States is sharply divergent from the other industrial countries in its antitrust philosophy and practice. EEC policy, for instance, distinguishes between "good" and "bad" cartels and "good" and "bad" mergers. [37] Actually European governments strongly support mergers between national companies so that they may compete more effectively with the "American giants." [38]

European countries are also inclined to view U.S. antitrust policy as an intended barrier to investment in the United States by European multinational

---

[34] Carl H. Fulda and Warren F. Schwartz, *Regulation of International Trade and Investment* (Mineola, New York: The Foundation Press, 1970), pp. 635-639.

[35] *Ibid.*, pp. 640-642.

[36] A treatment of conflicts arising out of the extraterritorial jurisdiction of U.S. antitrust laws may be found in Jack N. Behrman, *National Interests and the Multinational Enterprise* (Englewood Cliffs, N. J.: Prentice-Hall, Inc., 1970), Chapter 8.

[37] See Chapter 16, pp. 384-385, for EEC rules governing competition.

[38] James Leontiades, "Transatlantic Split over Business Bigness," *MSU Business Topics* (Summer, 1970), pp. 21-27. See also Philip Siekman, "Europe's Love Affair with Bigness," *Fortune* (March, 1970), p. 95 ff. Somewhat ironically, the first (and so far only) antimerger suit of the EEC Commission has been brought against Europemballage, the European holding company of Continental Can of the United States.

enterprises. When, in 1969, the Justice Department moved to stop the proposed merger between British Petroleum (BP) and Standard Oil of Ohio (Sohio), it provoked an angry response in Europe. *The London Times* said, "It is felt in London that if such a merger were rendered impossible, it would be a serious matter, not only for British Petroleum but for the United Kingdom." [39] Denying any attempt to bar foreign firms from the United States, the Justice Department subsequently agreed to a settlement which allowed the merger to go ahead.

Issues of U.S. Antitrust Policy Relating to the Multinational Enterprise. Few subjects are as complex, contradictory, and uncertain as U.S. antitrust policy at home and abroad. It is a delight to lawyers, a challenge to economists, a brooding presence to businessmen, and a profound mystery to laymen. It raises many political, economic, and social questions that, for lack of space, cannot be treated here.[40] In closing, therefore, we shall simply list the key issues that will make U.S. antitrust policy a subject of growing controversy in the years ahead.

1. Does U.S. antitrust policy help or hurt the international economic position of the United States?[41] Does it promote or deter the attainment of other goals of U.S. foreign economic policy?

2. Does U.S. antitrust policy weaken the competitive strength of U.S. multinational enterprises vis-à-vis foreign companies which are subject to milder forms of antitrust regulation or to none at all? If so, is this result congruent with the national interest of the United States?

3. Should the United States seek to apply U.S. antitrust standards to the foreign operations of U.S. multinational enterprises? Or should the United States adopt a territorial jurisdiction, leaving the regulation of anticompetitive business behavior to each national government on its own territory?

4. Is U.S. antitrust policy naive, given the oligopolistic character of U.S. and foreign multinational enterprises? To what extent is U.S. antitrust policy an ideological commitment rather than a realistic policy for the world economy of the 1970's and beyond?

5. Is U.S. antitrust policy alone sufficient to regulate the anticompetitive behavior of U.S. multinational enterprises? Can the United States achieve its antitrust goals by acting unilaterally?

6. What are the prospects for international antitrust regulation? How might it be achieved?

---

[39] "U.S. Move to Block Tie of British Petroleum and Sohio Irks Europeans," *Wall Street Journal,* October 7, 1969, p. 30.

[40] Some of these questions are taken up in U.S., Congress, Senate, Committee on the Judiciary, Subcommittee on Antitrust and Monopoly, *International Aspects of Antitrust,* 89th Cong., 2d sess., 1966.

[41] As far back as 1918, the U.S. Congress recognized that antitrust policy might hurt U.S. exports when it passed the Webb-Pomerene Act, which allows American companies to form export cartels.

U.S. STRATEGIC EXPORT CONTROLS ON TRADE AND INVESTMENT

In the 1960's, private enterprise in the West entered into many ad hoc arrangements with state enterprises in the Communist countries of Eastern Europe that went far beyond traditional export-import trade. These arrangements extended from pure licensing agreements (involving the transfer of technology from a Western enterprise to an Eastern enterprise, or vice versa) to equity participation by Western enterprises in joint ventures with Yugoslavian state enterprises. However, because of the ideological opposition of Communist countries to the concept of private ownership, most East-West business arrangements fell short of equity investment by Western enterprises, although in some instances the agreements were close substitutes for such investment.[42]

Consider, for example, technical and industrial cooperation agreements which have many variants. In a joint manufacturing or coproduction project, the Western enterprise supplies a mix of capital equipment, technology, and/or components while the Communist enterprise constructs the plant and undertakes production of the product in question. As payment, the Western enterprise gets a share of production, which it sells in Western markets; the Eastern enterprise sells its share of production in Eastern markets. To illustrate, a U.S. company through its Dutch subsidiary has entered a coproduction agreement with a Polish enterprise to manufacture and sell chemical equipment. The U.S. subsidiary provides technology and supervision while the Polish enterprise provides equipment, labor, and materials. The U.S. subsidiary sells its share of the finished product in the West, and the Polish enterprise sells its share to the Soviet Union.[43] One of the few U.S. parent companies directly involved in a coproduction agreement is Simmons Machine Tool. Skoda in Czechoslovakia makes large machine tools to Simmons' specifications and Simmons then sells them in the United States under the Simmons-Skoda name.[44] In yet another variant of industrial cooperation agreements, the Western enterprise provides technology and, at times, some equipment to an Eastern enterprise to manufacture a component that is then exported to the Western partner for use in the production of its finished product.

Western enterprises have also sold entire industrial plants to Eastern European countries or have contracted to build plants in the East under "turnkey" arrangements. Under the latter arrangement, the Western enterprise constructs and equips the plant and trains local technicians and workers so that production can start immediately when the Eastern managers assume

---

[42] At present, only Yugoslavia and Rumania allow equity investments by Western enterprises in joint ventures of up to 49 percent, but Hungary allows foreign companies to participate in the profits of joint undertakings.

[43] William A. Dymsza, "East-West Trade: Types of Business Arrangements," *MSU Business Topics* (Winter, 1971), p. 26.

[44] "Going 50-50 in East Europe," *Business Week* (January 16, 1971), p. 41.

control. In 1971, for example, Swindell-Dressler of the United States won a contract to design the foundry for the Kama River truck plant in the Soviet Union.[45] Another U.S. company has contracted to build a manufacturing line in the same project for diesel truck cylinder blocks.[46] Rheinstahl, a West German firm, has contracted to plan a new radiator factory in Hungary involving the delivery of machines on credit and the training of Hungarian technicians and workers. In return, Rheinstahl is guaranteed over a five-year period either a fixed percentage of the product or industrial goods of an equivalent value.[47]

A more recent type of industrial cooperation avoids the ownership problem by establishing a 50-50 East-West joint venture in a third (non-Communist) country. For instance, Tower International, based in Canada, plans to set up a joint tire venture with an Eastern European enterprise in Switzerland. The Eastern partner will own and operate the tire plant in its country, but the Swiss company will have the right to buy tires at cost from the plant and market them anywhere outside the Communist bloc countries.[48] This and similar third-country joint ventures enable the Eastern enterprise to obtain technology and the Western enterprise to obtain low-cost products. Western and Eastern enterprises are also collaborating to do business together in third countries. Simmering-Graz-Pauker of Austria and a Polish company, for instance, are building a sugar factory in Greece.[49]

Eager to promote their tourist business, Eastern European countries have contracted with Hilton International and Intercontinental Hotels, a Pan American subsidiary, to supply know-how and to even manage hotels.[50] To make Western tourists feel at home, Eastern enterprises have signed franchise contracts with Coca-Cola and Pepsi-Cola. As elsewhere in the world, these U.S. multinational beverage enterprises sell their concentrates to the franchise bottlers and provide them with assistance in production and marketing.[51]

So far most of the industrial cooperation agreements have been negotiated between Western European and Eastern European companies. In the 1960's, U.S. companies were kept out of many East-West business arrangements by U.S. strategic controls on the export of products and the transfer of technology to Communist countries.[52] The basic restrictive legislation was

---

45 "U.S. Trade with Eastern Europe—Status and Prospects," *The Morgan Guaranty Survey* (September, 1972), p. 6. Swindell-Dressler is a division of Pullman.

46 "The Russians Open Wider to Business," *Business Week* (July 22, 1972), p. 20.

47 James A. Ramsey, "East-West Business Cooperation: The Twain Meets," *Columbia Journal of World Business* (July-August, 1970), p. 18.

48 "Going 50-50 in East Europe," *Business Week* (January 16, 1971), p. 41.

49 *Ibid.*

50 *Ibid.*, pp. 41-42.

51 "The Real Thing, East European Nations Discover That Things Go Better With Coke," *Wall Street Journal,* June 21, 1972, p. 1.

52 These controls were applied extraterritorially to the affiliates of U.S. multinational enterprises. For information on other U.S. measures that have restricted East-West trade, see Chapter 2, pp. 31-32.

(and is) the Export Control Act of 1949, as amended in subsequent years. Export restrictions were embodied in a list of some 1,300 product categories (including their associated technology) that could not be exported without prior approval from the U.S. Department of Commerce in the form of validated licenses. In all but 200 categories, equivalent products and technology became freely available in the 1960's to Communist buyers from the other industrial countries of the West. As a direct consequence of controls, therefore, U.S. companies failed to profit from East-West business to the detriment of U.S. exports and the balance of payments.

Owing largely to the political frictions resulting from the Vietnam war, efforts by American businessmen and others to lessen the severity of U.S. export controls were fruitless during the 1960's. Only at the end of the decade did the passage of the Export Administration Act of 1969 signal a distinct turn toward liberalization. The Export Control Act of 1949, as amended, had required the denial of export licenses to items that contributed significantly to the military *or* economic potential of a Communist bloc country. The 1969 Act eliminated the criterion of "economic potential" by stating, "It is the policy of the United States . . . to restrict the export of goods and technology which would make a significant contribution to the military potential of any other nation or nations which would prove detrimental to the national security of the United States." [53] Under this legislation, the Department of Commerce has removed some 2,000 individual items from the export control list, bringing it into closer agreement with the export control lists of Western European countries and Japan.[54] Furthermore, the Department is now likely to approve for export any listed item that is freely available from other Western countries.

The liberalization of U.S. export controls is now proceeding rapidly as part of a massive liberalization of economic relations between the United States and the Communist countries. In 1971 the United States lifted its embargo on trade with Mainland China, and Congress gave the President the discretion to extend Export-Import Bank credits on exports to Eastern Europe. In 1972 the United States entered into a three-year agreement with the Soviet Union that involved U.S. credits of $500 million to finance the purchase of U.S. grains by the Soviet Union. More significantly, in 1972 the United States started negotiations with the Soviet Union to work out a comprehensive trade agreement, covering most-favored-nation treatment for Soviet exports to the United States, the provision of business facilities for U.S. firms in the Soviet Union, the handling of commercial arbitration, the reciprocal granting of credits, the settlement of World War II Lend-Lease

---

[53] Public Law 91-184, 91st Congress, H.R. 4293, December 30, 1969.

[54] "U.S. Trade with Eastern Europe—Status and Prospects," *The Morgan Guaranty Survey* (September, 1972), p. 8. Export controls are determined multilaterally by the NATO countries and Japan through the Coordinating Committee (COCOM). The COCOM list has been much smaller than the U.S. list.

obligations of the Soviet Union, maritime agreements, joint projects, and the treatment of patents, copyrights, licenses, and taxes.[55]

All of these recent developments point to the opening of a new era in U.S. economic relations with the East. In that event, U.S. multinational enterprises will be able to compete for East-West business opportunities on an equal basis with European and Japanese enterprises. One sign of the times is a wide-ranging agreement between Occidental Petroleum Corporation and the Soviet government under which Occidental will provide patents and technological know-how in five fields (the exploration, production, and use of oil and gas; metal treating and plating; the design and building of hotels; agricultural fertilizers and chemicals; and the conversion of garbage into fuels and other useful products) in exchange for Soviet oil, natural gas, metals, and other raw materials. Under the provisions of the agreement, joint teams of American and Soviet technicians will meet both in the United States and the Soviet Union to carry out projects and programs.[56]

From a broader perspective, the liberalization of East-West economic relations will encourage the progressive spread of multinational enterprises to encompass the Communist countries. Both Western and Eastern enterprise have demonstrated a remarkable versatility in creating new forms of industrial cooperation to their mutual benefit. East-West business ventures, which have been called "transideological enterprise," may well mark the emergence of truly global multinational enterprise systems in the 1970's and beyond.[57]

DOMESTIC ATTACKS ON THE MULTINATIONAL ENTERPRISE

The resurgence of protectionism in the United States threatens not only international trade (its traditional victim) but also direct foreign investment by U.S. multinational enterprises. Domestic attacks on direct foreign investment are now raising the key issue of U.S. policy toward the multinational enterprise: Is the multinational enterprise good or bad for the U.S. economy?

LABOR'S OPPOSITION TO THE MULTINATIONAL ENTERPRISE

Opposition to the multinational enterprise in the United States is spearheaded by organized labor. The principal charges leveled against the multinational enterprise by organized labor are set forth in the following discussion.

---

[55] "Trade Talks with the USSR a 'Continuing Process'—New Round Is Readied," *Commerce Today* (September 4, 1972), p. 16.

[56] "Soviet Trade Set by Occidental Oil," *The New York Times,* July 19, 1972, p. 1.

[57] See Howard V. Perlmutter, "Emerging East-West Ventures: The Transideological Enterprise," *Columbia Journal of World Business* (September-October, 1969).

U.S. Multinational Enterprise Exports Jobs by Investing in Foreign Production. This argument maintains that foreign production substitutes for production in the United States by displacing exports from the United States and by creating competitive U.S. imports. Both of these effects cause unemployment in the United States. Between 1966 and 1969, the American Federation of Labor and the Congress of Industrial Organizations (AFL-CIO) estimates a net loss of 500,000 job opportunities in the United States attributable to shifts in U.S. trade. This figure does not include job losses caused by foreign trade barriers or by markets lost to United States multinational enterprises in foreign countries.[58] One American labor leader stated the problem in these words:

> There seems to be a kind of speedup on the part of multinational firms to transfer plants, production, products, and technology—and jobs—outside the borders of the United States. Entire industries, growth industries, in fact, badly needed here, and many thousands of urgently needed jobs are exported. To many of us in the labor movement it portends a mass exodus.[59]

Of particular concern to U.S. labor is the establishment of U.S.-owned plants in Taiwan, Singapore, Mexico, and elsewhere to assemble U.S.-made components into products for export back to U.S. parent companies, a practice that is most common in consumer electronic products. Labor accuses these "runaway" plants not only of exporting U.S. jobs but also of exploiting low-paid foreign workers.

U.S. Multinational Enterprise Exports Jobs by Transferring Technology Abroad. This transfer makes possible the quick duplication in foreign countries of sophisticated manufactures based on U.S. technology, much of which was developed at the expense of United States taxpayers in government-sponsored research projects. If the multinational enterprise did not license technology to independent foreign producers or to their own foreign affiliates, then it would take much longer for foreign countries to manufacture competitive products which might either displace U.S. exports or displace home-made products in the U.S. market. "This is the technology upon which Americans depend for their jobs and upon which our national defense must rely."[60]

---

[58] *A Trade Policy for America, An AFL-CIO Program* (Washington: AFL-CIO, undated), p. 11. This pamphlet is based on testimony by AFL-CIO President George Meany before the Subcommittee on International Trade of the Senate Finance Committee on May 18, 1971.

[59] Statement of Paul Jennings, President, International Union of Electrical, Radio, and Machine Workers in U.S., Congress, Joint Economic Committee, Subcommittee on Foreign Economic Policy, *A Foreign Economic Policy for the 1970's*, 91st Cong., 2d sess., 1970, part 4, p. 814.

[60] *A Trade Policy for America, op. cit.*, p. 8.

U.S. Multinational Enterprise Enjoys "Unfair Advantages" Which Are Not Available to U.S. National Companies. Many foreign governments offer inducements to attract investment by multinational enterprises, such as tax exemptions, duty-free imports, low-cost government loans, and accelerated depreciation. More to the point, multinational enterprises also receive extraordinary benefits from U.S. policy.

> The U.S. Government must stop helping and subsidizing U.S. companies in setting up and operating foreign subsidiaries. Sections 806.30 and 807 of the Tariff Schedules should be repealed; these sections of the Tariff Code provide especially low tariffs on imported goods assembled abroad from U.S.-made parts. Moreover, the U.S. tax deferral on profits from foreign subsidiaries should be eliminated, so that the profits of these subsidiaries will be subject to the U.S. corporate income tax for the year they are earned.[61]

U.S. Multinational Enterprise Can Circumvent U.S. National Policies. "The multinational is not simply an American company moving to a new locality where the same laws apply and where it is still within the jurisdiction of Congress and the government of the United States. This is a runaway corporation, going far beyond our borders." [62]

A traditional supporter of freer trade, the AFL-CIO has now adopted a program calling for legislation that would curb both U.S. imports and U.S. direct foreign investment "for the protection of American workers and for the preservation of our industrial society." [63] In 1971 this program was introduced in the U.S. Congress as *The Foreign Trade and Investment Act of 1972*, popularly labelled the "Burke-Hartke Bill" after its original cosponsors.

MAJOR PROVISIONS OF THE BURKE-HARTKE BILL

The Burke-Hartke Bill is a mix of traditional protectionism (restrictions on imports) and "new" protectionism (restrictions on U.S. direct foreign investment).[64] We present below a brief description of its major provisions.

Taxation of Income of U.S.-Controlled Foreign Subsidiaries. As indicated earlier in this chapter, the United States does not presently tax the operating income of U.S.-controlled foreign subsidiaries until that income is repatriated to the parent company in the United States. The Burke-Hartke Bill would eliminate tax deferral by having the United States tax all foreign-source income when it was earned, regardless of whether or not it was repatriated to the U.S. parent company. This provision would obligate a U.S. parent

---

[61] *Ibid.,* pp. 14-15.
[62] *Ibid.,* p. 9.
[63] *Ibid.,* p. 14.
[64] The Foreign Trade and Investment Act of 1972 was introduced in September, 1971, in the Senate by Senator Vance Hartke (S.2592) and in the House by Congressman Joseph Burke (H.R. 10914).

company to pay taxes on dividends it has not received or to repatriate dividends it might otherwise wish to retain for reinvestment abroad.

Foreign Tax Credits. Under present law, U.S. parent companies are allowed to credit the foreign taxes paid by their foreign affiliates against their U.S. tax liabilities. The Burke-Hartke Bill would repeal this law by allowing no credit for foreign taxes. This change would dramatically reduce the after-U.S.-tax returns on direct foreign investment of U.S. parent companies, as indicated in Table 24-2. By imposing double taxation on U.S. multinational enterprises, the abolition of foreign tax credits would also violate the principle of domestic tax neutrality, to say nothing of foreign tax neutrality. It would act as a powerful *dis*incentive to U.S. direct foreign investment. The rate of the combined foreign and U.S. taxation on foreign-source income would jump from the present 48 percent to 70 percent or higher for those U.S. multinational enterprises which receive most of their foreign-source income from operations in other industrial countries where income tax rates approximate the U.S. rate.

Table 24-2

HYPOTHETICAL ILLUSTRATION OF THE EFFECTS OF THE BURKE-HARTKE REPEAL OF THE FOREIGN TAX CREDIT

	Present Law	Burke-Hartke
Net income of foreign subsidiary	$100	$100
Less foreign income tax	(40)	(40)
Less foreign withholding tax on repatriated income	(5)	(5)
Net income (dividend) to U.S. parent	$ 55	$ 55
Taxable dividend to U.S. parent	$100	$ 55
U.S. corporate income tax (48%)	$ 48	$ 26.40
Less foreign income tax credit	(40)	—
Less foreign withholding tax credit	(5)	—
Net U.S. corporate income tax	$ 3	$ 26.40
Net dividend to U.S. parent	$ 55	$ 55
Net income from foreign subsidiary after U.S. taxes	$ 52	$ 28.60
Combined foreign and U.S. taxes as a percentage of foreign-source income	48	71.4

Foreign Investment Controls. The Burke-Hartke Bill would give to the President the authority to prohibit any person within the jurisdiction of the United States from making a direct or indirect transfer of capital "to or within any foreign country . . . when in the judgment of the President the transfer would result in a net decrease in employment in the United States." [65]

---

[65] Title VI, Sec. 601(a).

The penalty for violating any regulation issued under this provision would be a fine of not more than $100,000 and imprisonment of not more than one year for each violation.

Transfers of Patents and Other Industrial Property to Foreigners. The Burke-Hartke Bill would authorize the President to prohibit the holder of a U.S. patent from manufacturing the patented product, using the patented process, or licensing others to do so outside the United States when the President deemed such action would contribute to increased unemployment in the United States. The penalty for violating this provision would be the withdrawal of patent protection in U.S. courts. Another provision of the Bill would tax any gain realized on the transfer of a patent, an invention, a copyright, or any similar property right from a U.S. parent company to its foreign subsidiary. Under present law such transfers are tax-free if the intent is not the avoidance of U.S. taxes.

Quantitative Restrictions on Imports. The Burke-Hartke Bill would set a ceiling for individual categories of imported goods at the average annual quantity imported into the United States during the years 1965-1969. The application of this comprehensive quota system would cause a massive roll-back of current U.S. imports. For subsequent years, the limits would be increased or decreased by the amounts necessary to maintain the same ratio of imports to domestic U.S. production as existed in the 1965-1969 base period. In brief, this provision would forsake the advantages of international specialization by freezing the composition and historical level of U.S. imports. It would replace market forces with an administrative bureaucracy to determine the flow of goods into the United States.[66]

EVALUATION OF THE BURKE-HARTKE BILL

The adoption of the Burke-Hartke Bill into law would have profound effects on the entire range of U.S. foreign economic policy. Most likely, it would trigger massive retaliation by the EEC, Japan, and other countries. It would also strongly deter U.S. direct foreign investment because of double taxation and would cripple the operations of U.S. multinational enterprises with actual and potential restrictions on intraenterprise transfers of products, capital, technology, and management. All of this would be done in the name of promoting U.S. employment.

We do not have the space to offer a detailed critique of the Burke-Hartke Bill. However, much of what we would say has already been said in Chapters 12, 13, and 15 and in the discussions of balance of payments

---

[66] The Burke-Hartke Bill also contains provisions to strengthen the Antidumping Act and the countervailing duty law, as well as a provision to facilitate escape clause action and adjustment assistance. Another provision repeals the duty-free reentry of U.S.-made goods.

controls and tax policies in this chapter. One question, however, deserves specific comment: Do U.S. multinational enterprises reduce *overall* employment in the United States? Fundamentally, the answer to this question depends on whether U.S. direct foreign investment has negative or positive trade flow effects, a subject that was taken up earlier in this chapter. We now supplement that analysis with references to studies of the domestic employment experience of U.S. multinational enterprises.

As noted earlier, the AFL-CIO alleges a loss of 500,000 job opportunities over the period 1966-1969 attributable to shifts in U.S. trade. This figure was arrived at by estimating that in 1966 about 1.8 million jobs would have been required to produce the 74 percent of U.S. imports assumed to be "competitive" with U.S.-made products. For 1969 the comparable estimate was 2.5 million jobs, an increase of 700,000 "lost" job opportunities. Since higher U.S. exports created 200,000 new jobs over the same years, the net loss in job opportunities, therefore, was 500,000. This estimating method is dubious on several grounds. First, it defines competitive imports to include all foreign products that *could* have been produced in the United States, thereby ignoring competitive market conditions. More to the point, there is nothing in this analysis that reveals a causal connection between U.S. direct foreign investment and the alleged employment effect. Actually the imports which have probably been responsible for most of the displacement of American workers (textiles, shoes, steel, and automobiles) are mainly produced by independent foreign companies, not U.S.-owned foreign affiliates.

Empirical studies of the employment effects of U.S. direct foreign investment contradict the view of labor that U.S. multinational enterprises export jobs. A study of the 1965-1970 employment levels in fourteen U.S. industries which included the largest U.S. direct foreign investors revealed that in eleven industries domestic employment rose at a composite rate of 16 percent (close to the overall U.S. rate of 16.9 percent), while in the remaining three industries, employment fell an average of 5 percent.[67]

In light of these findings, the Department of Commerce study concludes:

> What seems clear from these data is that the effects on employment due to cyclical and other factors present in the domestic economy tend to swamp the adverse effects—if any—that might result from the foreign trade side. The argument that overseas investment is causing job losses in the United States does not appear to be borne out. Rather, the basic employment trend for these investment-oriented industries has been upward.[68]

---

[67] U.S. Department of Commerce, "Policy Aspects of Foreign Investment by U.S. Multinational Corporations," *The Multinational Corporation, Studies on U.S. Foreign Investment,* Volume 1 (Washington: U.S. Government Printing Office, 1972), pp. 26-29.

[68] *Ibid.,* p. 28.

Other studies reinforce this conclusion. In an investigation of nine industries, Stobaugh estimated the net employment effects of U.S. direct foreign investment to be positive in six industries and zero in the other three industries.[69] In a third study, which used rank correlation statistical techniques, Hawkins concluded that industries with a relatively high foreign investment exhibited faster *domestic* growth, faster export growth, and a relatively strong trade balance position, all of this implying that foreign investment rarely displaces U.S. workers in absolute terms.[70]

Empirical research indicates, therefore, that restrictions on U.S. multinational enterprises would *not* increase U.S. employment and indeed might decrease it. When account is taken of all the damaging consequences of the Burke-Hartke provisions for U.S. economic relations with the rest of the world, the conclusion that it would not achieve its employment goal is a most damning indictment. In terms of both its exclusive preoccupation with a single goal to the exclusion of all others and its ineffectiveness to reach even that single goal, the Burke-Hartke Bill fails the test of rational policy formation. It is a flagrant example of blind protectionism that can only harm the U.S. and world economies.

THE NEED FOR A COMPREHENSIVE U.S. POLICY

This chapter began by stating that the United States does not have a policy toward the multinational enterprise, but instead pursues several policies that were formed at a time when the multinational enterprise was not a policy issue or were formulated for reasons unrelated to its unique characteristics. An examination of traditional policies toward direct foreign investment, balance of payments controls, the promotion of direct foreign investment in developing countries, tax policy, antitrust policy, and strategic export controls substantiates that contention. Contemporary U.S. policy toward the multinational enterprise calls to mind the fable of the blind men and the elephant. What is the multinational enterprise? Is it an international trader? An exporter of capital? An exporter of technology? An exporter of management? A possessor of considerable oligopolistic market power? A source of tax revenue? A major source of short-term capital movements? An institution subject to many national jurisdictions but not completely subject to any single jurisdiction? The answer, of course, is that the multinational enterprise is all of these things—and more.

U.S. policy makers must transcend the traditional distinctions between trade, investment, and balance of payments policies if they are to develop

---

[69] *Ibid.,* "U.S. Multinational Enterprises and the U.S. Economy," Exhibit 3, pp. 8-14.

[70] Robert G. Hawkins, *U.S. Multinational Investment in Manufacturing and Domestic Economic Performance* (Washington: Center for Multinational Studies, February, 1972), p. 22.

a comprehensive policy toward the multinational enterprise. Failure to do so will insure the continuation of "suboptimizing" policies such as those described in this chapter, a situation rife with internal and external conflicts of goals. To design and implement a rational policy, U.S. policy makers must obtain the answers to two fundamental questions: (1) What is the national interest of the United States in the multinational enterprise over the long run? (2) What comprehensive policy toward the multinational enterprise will enhance that interest?

The answer to the first question is dependent on the overall goals of U.S. foreign economic policy. As stated at the end of Chapter 15, the United States can choose to continue a liberal commercial policy or regress to the protectionist policy it espoused before 1934. In the final analysis, it is a choice between a world of economic interdependence and a world of autarkic economic blocs. The multinational enterprise can promote the national interest of the United States only if that interest is defined in terms of an open, competitive, world economy. A world of protectionist blocs would doom the multinational enterprise to eventual extinction.

Given a clear perception of the national interest in the multinational enterprise, U.S. policy makers should design a policy that optimizes the value of that institution to the United States. To a very substantial degree, the instruments of contemporary U.S. foreign economic policy are multinational enterprise systems headquartered in the United States. The success or failure of U.S. policies relating to export promotion, assistance to developing countries, East-West trade, taxation of foreign-source income, and the maintenance of competitive markets depends critically on the behavior of multinational enterprise systems. U.S. policy makers must learn much more about that behavior and how it can be influenced to serve the national interest. The development of an effective policy, therefore, will require more cooperation than heretofore experienced between the U.S. Government and the representatives of multinational enterprises, what one writer calls in a global context the "emerging partnership of governments and international business." [71] But it will also require closer cooperation between the U.S. Government and foreign governments, extending even to the harmonization of specific policy areas such as taxation and antitrust. No single government can reasonably expect to regulate the conduct of multinational enterprise systems that operate in multiple national jurisdictions.

U.S. policy makers must comprehend the rapid evolution of the multinational enterprise. In the years ahead many more firms will evolve from U.S. companies that happen to have extensive foreign operations to multinational enterprises that happen to have their headquarters in the United States. The question of U.S. policy toward the multinational enterprise

---

[71] Jack N. Behrman, *U.S. International Business and Governments* (New York: McGraw-Hill Book Company, 1971), Chapter One.

becomes, therefore, part of the larger question of public policy toward the multinational enterprise by the community of nations. In particular, the national interests of foreign countries that host the affiliates of U.S. parent companies should not be ignored in the formation of U.S. policy. The next chapter considers the national interests of host countries in the multinational enterprise and, more broadly, the conflict between the multinational enterprise and national sovereignty.

SUMMARY

1. Before World War II, U.S. foreign investment policy was a mix of laissez-faire (letting U.S. companies invest abroad when and where they chose to do so) and strong diplomatic protection of U.S. companies in foreign countries. The onset of the persistent U.S. balance of payments deficit in 1958 marked the beginning of the end of this supportive investment policy.

2. The U.S. Government introduced mandatory controls on direct foreign investment by U.S. companies in January, 1968, after three years of "voluntary" controls. The most dramatic impact of the controls has been on the capital-sourcing policies of multinational enterprises. From the perspective of adjustment theory, the balance of payments argument for investment controls is as fallacious as the balance of payments argument for import restrictions. The multiple effects of foreign investment by U.S. multinational enterprises on the U.S. balance of payments may be grouped into financial flow effects and trade flow effects. The evidence supports the judgment that both effects have been positive. The economic benefits of foreign investment should not be sacrificed to the expediencies of the balance of payments, especially when more suitable policy instruments are available to restore balance of payments equilibrium.

3. Since World War II, the United States has actively promoted private foreign investment in the developing countries through an investment insurance program that provides coverage against political risks.

4. Operating in many countries, multinational enterprises are subject to multiple tax jurisdictions. This situation creates two sets of problems: double taxation and tax avoidance. Following the national rather than the territorial principle of tax jurisdiction, the United States taxes U.S. multinational enterprises on their worldwide income. To limit double taxation, the United States allows credits against foreign taxes; to limit tax avoidance, the United States insists that a U.S. parent company use "arm's length" prices in all transactions with its foreign affiliates. The controversy over the equity and neutrality of U.S. taxation of foreign-source income reflects a fundamental disagreement over the proper tax jurisdiction of the United States.

5. The United States claims antitrust jurisdiction over the behavior of U.S. companies and their foreign affiliates regardless of where that behavior may take place. The rationale for this claim is that business behavior anywhere in the world may restrain U.S. exports or imports or have anticompetitive effects in the United States. In seeking to apply the U.S. antitrust laws to the foreign

operations of U.S. companies (and even to the operations of foreign companies), the United States has been accused of "judicial imperialism." This and several other key issues will make U.S. antitrust policy a subject of growing controversy in the years ahead.

6. In the 1960's, private enterprise in the West entered into many ad hoc arrangements with state enterprises in the Communist countries of Eastern Europe that went far beyond traditional export-import trade. But many U.S. companies have been kept out of East-West business arrangements by U.S. strategic controls on the export of products and the transfer of technology to Communist countries. The current liberalization of these controls should enable U.S. multinational enterprises to compete for East-West business opportunities on an equal basis with European and Japanese enterprises in the 1970's.

7. The resurgence of protectionism in the United States threatens not only international trade (its traditional victim) but also direct foreign investment by U.S. multinational enterprises. Supported by the AFL-CIO, the Burke-Hartke Bill would abolish foreign tax credits and tax deferral, restrict the export of direct investment capital and technology, and roll back U.S. imports with a comprehensive quota system. Empirical research indicates that restrictions on U.S. multinational enterprises would *not* increase U.S. employment and, as a matter of fact, might decrease it. All in all, the Burke-Hartke Bill is a flagrant example of blind protectionism that can only harm the U.S. and world economies.

8. U.S. policy makers must transcend the traditional distinctions between trade, investment, and balance of payments policies if they are to develop a comprehensive policy toward the multinational enterprise, and thereby avoid the continuation of "suboptimizing" policies such as those described in this chapter.

QUESTIONS AND APPLICATIONS

1. (a) What is the rationale for balance of payments controls on U.S. direct foreign investment?
   (b) Why have these controls not forced U.S. multinational enterprises to cut back on their foreign investment expenditures?

2. According to the theory of payments adjustment, how does a country's balance of payments adjust to an export of capital (a) when the exchange rate is free to vary, and (b) when the exchange rate is held stable?

3. (a) Identify the financial flow effects and the trade flow effects of U.S. direct foreign investment.
   (b) Why is it impossible to ascertain conclusively the net export effect of U.S. direct foreign investment?

4. (a) What is the recoupment period controversy?
   (b) What are the implications of this controversy for U.S. direct investment controls?

5. Has the U.S. investment insurance program stimulated U.S. direct investment in the developing countries? Be prepared to defend your answer.

6. (a) "Multiple tax jurisdictions create two sets of problems." What are they? How do they occur?
   (b) Describe the main features of U.S. tax policy toward foreign-source income.
   (c) How do the U.S. tax authorities seek to minimize both double taxation and tax avoidance?
   (d) Be prepared to argue either side of the controversy over the taxation of foreign-source income, employing the concepts of tax equity and tax neutrality.
7. (a) What is implied by the extraterritorial jurisdiction of U.S. antitrust policy?
   (b) Do the lenient antitrust policies of foreign governments place U.S. multinational enterprises at a disadvantage in competing against foreign multinational enterprises in world markets? Why or why not?
8. (a) What are the main features of East-West coproduction agreements?
   (b) Why does the United States maintain strategic export controls?
   (c) What have been the effects of strategic export controls on U.S. multinational enterprises?
   (d) Discuss: "East-West business ventures may well mark the emergence of truly global multinational enterprise systems in the 1970's and beyond."
9. (a) Undertake research to ascertain the views of U.S. organized labor toward the multinational enterprise.
   (b) What are the major provisions of the Burke-Hartke Bill?
   (c) Prepare to debate either side of the question: Are multinational enterprises good or bad for the United States?

SELECTED READINGS

Behrman, Jack N. *Direct Manufacturing Investment, Exports and the Balance of Payments.* New York: National Foreign Trade Council, Inc., 1968.

Brewster, Kingman, Jr. *Antitrust and American Business Abroad.* New York: McGraw-Hill Book Company, 1958.

Emergency Committee for American Trade. *The Role of the Multinational Corporation in the United States and World Economies.* Washington: 1972.

Fulda, Carl H., and Warren F. Schwartz. *Regulation of International Trade and Investment.* Mineola, New York: The Foundation Press, 1970. Chapter VI, Section 3.

Hufbauer, G. C., and F. M. Adler. *Overseas Manufacturing Investment and the Balance of Payments.* Washington: U.S. Treasury Department, 1968.

National Association of Manufacturers. *U.S. Stake in World Trade and Investment.* Undated.

National Foreign Trade Council, Inc. *Economic Implications of Proposed Changes in the Taxation of U.S. Investments Abroad.* New York: National Foreign Trade Council, Inc., 1972.

——————. *The Impact of U.S. Foreign Direct Investment on U.S. Employment and Trade,* 1971.

Ruttenberg, Stanley H., and Associates. *Needed: A Constructive Foreign Trade Policy*. Washington: The Industrial Union Department, AFL-CIO, 1971.

U.S. Congress. *A Foreign Economic Policy for the 1970's*. Hearings before the Subcommittee on Foreign Economic Policy of the Joint Economic Committee. Washington: U.S. Government Printing Office, 1970. Part 4.

U.S. Department of Commerce. *The Multinational Corporation*. Washington: U.S. Government Printing Office, 1972. Volume 1, Parts I and II.

U.S. Senate. *International Aspects of Antitrust*. Hearings before the Subcommittee on Antitrust and Monopoly of the Committee on the Judiciary. Washington: U.S. Government Printing Office, 1967. Part 1.

CHAPTER 25

THE MULTINATIONAL ENTERPRISE AND NATIONAL SOVEREIGNTY

The multinational enterprise is perceived by policy makers in host countries as both an economic institution which creates benefits for and costs to the local economy and as a quasi-political institution which threatens the power and even the sovereignty of the nation. A lengthy examination of the policy issues generated by this twin role of the multinational enterprise would carry us far beyond the scope of this book and into the realm of political science and international law.[1] Our purpose here is the more modest one of identifying the principal issues and, when possible, offering conceptual approaches to their objective analysis. All of these issues relate in one way or another to the mutuality and conflict of interests between national governments and the multinational enterprise. The crucial question, then, is whether both parties will learn how to expand the mutuality and contract the conflict of their respective interests. Upon the answer to this question will depend the evolution of the world economy in the remainder of this century.

We shall begin by exploring the economic and political benefits and costs of direct foreign investment to host countries. Next we shall look at the constraints and risks that confront the multinational enterprise in host countries. We shall conclude the chapter by evaluating the need for international regulation of the multinational enterprise.

THE ECONOMIC BENEFITS AND COSTS OF DIRECT FOREIGN INVESTMENT TO HOST COUNTRIES

Direct foreign investment has multiple effects on the economy of a host country in terms of production, employment, income, prices, exports, imports,

---

[1] Two recent publications explore the present and prospective relations between nation-states and the multinational enterprise: Richard Eells, *Global Corporations, The Emerging System of World Economic Power* (New York: Interbook, Inc., 1972); and "The Multinational Corporation," *The Annals* (Philadelphia: The American Academy of Political and Social Science, September, 1972).

the balance of payments, economic growth, and general welfare. Some of these effects confer benefits on the host country; some of them incur costs. Some effects occur almost immediately, and some may take a generation. In this section we offer a conceptual approach to the measurement of the net benefit/cost ratio of direct foreign investment, which takes into account its many effects and their impact over time.

The fundamental effect of direct foreign investment (representing the sum total of the many individual effects) is its contribution to the national income (net national product) of the host country over time. Closely related to this national income effect but deserving special treatment is the effect of direct foreign investment on the balance of payments of the host country over time.

THE NATIONAL INCOME EFFECT

What is the contribution to a host country's net national product of, say, the manufacturing affiliate of a multinational enterprise? Clearly it is less than the value of the affiliate's output because some of the inputs used to manufacture that output (raw materials, parts, supplies, etc.) were produced by other firms. Our first approximation of the affiliate's contribution, therefore, is to subtract from the value of its output the value of all inputs purchased from other firms (including, of course, the parent company). Algebraically, if O represents the output of the affiliate and I represents the inputs purchased from local and foreign firms, then:

$$(1) \text{ Benefits} = O - I.$$

This is the conventional expression of the net value added by a firm to national product. When all outside inputs are subtracted from the firm's output, we are left with the contribution of the factors of production directly employed by the firm as measured by the sum total of its factor payments (wages, salaries, interest, rent, and profits). Thus:

$$(2) \text{ Benefits} = O - I = F + R,$$

where F represents the affiliate's total factor payments to labor, capital, and land, and R represents the return (profit) to entrepreneurial management.

Conventional net value added, however, is not an adequate measure of the contribution of a *new* foreign-owned affiliate to the national product of the host country. It does not take account of the *opportunity cost* of the local factors of production employed by the affiliate, namely, the national product which those factors would have produced if they were *not* employed by the affiliate. Only to the extent that these local factors are used more productively by the affiliate than they would have been in its absence does their employment by the affiliate make a net contribution to national product. When the affiliate uses workers or resources that would otherwise be idle, then the opportunity cost is zero. At the other extreme, if the affiliate takes workers or resources away from other equally productive firms, then the opportunity cost is equal to the payments for their services by the affiliate. Our second approximation of the benefits of the affiliate, therefore, is to deduct the opportunity cost of the *local* factors of production used by the affiliate. Thus:

$$(3) \quad \text{Benefits} = (F + R) - N,$$

where N represents the opportunity cost of local factors.

So far we have considered only the direct benefits of the affiliate. To be complete, we must also include its *indirect* benefits, the net sum of its external economies and external diseconomies. The external economies of the affiliate act to raise the productivity of other firms in the host country and thereby increase the national product. To illustrate, the affiliate may enable its local customers to cut costs or enter into more productive lines of activity by selling them established products at lower prices, by assuring them a reliable and adequate supply of products, by selling them new products, by offering technical assistance, and so on. The affiliate may also benefit local suppliers by providing a demand that enables them to achieve economies of scale and by offering them technical assistance to meet the affiliate's requirements. Competitive pressures exerted by the affiliate may force local firms to become more efficient. Training programs of the affiliate to upgrade the skills of its workers benefit other firms when workers leave the affiliate to enter their employ. More generally, the example of a modern, progressive enterprise may stimulate innovation by local entrepreneurs (positive demonstration effect). Against these and other external economies must be set any external *dis*economies that decrease the productivity of local firms, such as losses in efficiency because of higher demands placed on them by the affiliate, structural unemployment caused by the competition of the affiliate, and the discouragement of local entrepreneurs (negative demonstration effect). Our third approximation of the affiliate's contribution to the national product of the host country takes account of its net external economies. Thus:

$$(4) \quad \text{Benefits} = (F + R) - N + L,$$

where L represents *net* external economies (external economies *minus* external diseconomies).

Our final approximation of benefits explicitly recognizes that the affiliate pays taxes on its net income (R) to the host government. R, therefore, is the sum of the after-tax income of the affiliate (R^*) and the income taxes paid by the affiliate to the host government (T). Thus:

$$(5) \quad \text{Benefits} = (F + R^* + T) - N + L.$$

The *costs* of direct foreign investment to the host economy are the sum total of all payments to the *foreign* factors of production (including technology) used by the affiliate (profits or dividends, interest, royalties, management fees, etc.) which are transferred out of the country. Thus:

(6) Costs $= E$,

where E represents payments to foreign factors of production.

The net benefit/cost ratio of direct foreign investment to the host economy, therefore, is $\dfrac{(F + R^* + T) - N + L}{E}$. If the ratio is greater than 1, then benefits exceed costs to the host economy, and vice versa. Is this ratio likely to be greater than 1 for direct foreign investment in general? Both theoretical and empirical considerations support the assertion that direct foreign investment is generally beneficial to host economies.

Theoretically, it has been shown that under competitive conditions the net addition to the output of the host economy from direct foreign investment must *always* exceed the return to the investor because of the diminishing marginal product of capital. An inflow of foreign investment lowers the marginal product of *all* capital in the host economy and therefore reduces the net income on all previous foreign investments.[2] Even when one drops the assumption of a diminishing marginal product of capital, host-government taxation would appear sufficient in most instances to insure that the net earnings of foreign investors are less than their contribution to national product, aside from any net external economies.

Empirical verification of the economic benefit/cost ratio of direct foreign investment is difficult to attain. Statistics on the foreign operations of U.S. multinational enterprises offer some basis for estimating factor payments (F), after-tax profits (R^*), and local taxes (T), but none at all for estimating the opportunity cost of local factors (N) or net external economies (L), which would be difficult to quantify in any event. Estimates of F, R^*, T, and external factor payments (E) for U.S. direct manufacturing investment in Latin America in 1966 are shown in Table 25-1.

Table 25-1 indicates that U.S. manufacturing investment in Latin America made a sizeable net contribution to the national product of that region in 1966.[3] However, by ignoring opportunity cost this estimate implicitly assumes that the opportunity cost of the local factors used by U.S. affiliates in Latin America was zero. Nonetheless, even if we were to

---

[2] G. D. A. MacDougall, "The Benefits and Costs of Private Investment from Abroad: A Theoretical Approach," in Richard E. Caves and Harry G. Johnson (eds.), *Readings in International Economics* (Homewood, Ill.: Richard D. Irwin, Inc., 1968), pp. 172-196.

[3] Actually the total cost of U.S. manufacturing investment in Latin America for 1966 was *less* than that shown in Table 25-1 because only $112 million of net after-tax income was repatriated to the United States. Over the longer run, however, the entire net after-tax income ($316 million) represents a cost of U.S. investment to Latin America.

Table 25-1

ECONOMIC BENEFITS AND COSTS OF U.S. DIRECT MANUFACTURING INVESTMENT IN LATIN AMERICA IN 1966
(Millions of Dollars)

Factor payments by U.S. manufacturing affiliates (F)		$1,377
Wages and salaries	$1,147	
Interest	$ 149	
Royalties, service charges, etc., to foreign factors	$ 81	
Net after-tax income (R*)		$ 316
Taxes paid to host government (T)		$ 464
Total benefit to national product (F + R* + T)		$2,157
Payments to foreign factors (E): royalties, etc.		$ 81
Payments to foreign factors (E): net after-tax income		$ 316
Total cost to national product (E)		$ 397
Benefit/cost ratio before allowance for opportunity cost and net external economies [(F + R* + T)/E]		5.4

Sources: Figures for wages, salaries, interest, and taxes are taken from Table 19, p. 51, in Herbert K. May, *The Effects of United States and Other Foreign Investment in Latin America* (New York: The Council for Latin America, Inc., 1971). Figures for royalties, etc., and for net after-tax income are taken from U.S. Department of Commerce, *U.S. Direct Investments Abroad 1966, Part I: Balance of Payments Data* (Washington: U.S. Government Printing Office, 1970). All figures in Table 25-1 are from statistics compiled by the U.S. Department of Commerce.

assume that the opportunity costs of those factors were equal to the payments they received from the U.S. affiliates, the contribution would remain positive: $T - E = \$464$ million $- \$397$ million $= \$67$ million. Most probably opportunity costs are on the low side in Latin American countries because of high unemployment, the presence of large endowments of unexploited resources, the low level of worker skills, and the frequently unproductive use of local savings. Thus, U.S. manufacturing affiliates have added to national products by increasing the demand for unemployed, underemployed, or unutilized factors and by improving the allocation of factors. Most observers also conclude that U.S. manufacturing affiliates have created net external economies that encourage economic growth in Latin America.[4] Certainly the statistical evidence places the burden of proof on those who allege that Latin America's national product would have been larger in the absence of direct foreign investment.

Several studies point to the net benefits of direct foreign investment to host economies. Donald T. Brash, a New Zealand economist, states in his study of U.S. investment in Australia: ". . . it seems likely that in most circumstances foreign investment results in a rise in domestic real income."[5] John H. Dunning, a British economist, estimates that the presence of American companies in the United Kingdom has a total measurable benefit

[4] For a contrary view, see p. 639.

[5] Donald T. Brash, *American Investment in Australian Industry* (Cambridge: Harvard University Press, 1966), p. 273.

of between 2 and 2½ percent of the gross national product, a range he considers less than the full benefit.[6] A study of foreign investment in Canada by a task force of Canadian economists asserts: "In sum, the host country typically benefits, and often substantially, from foreign direct investment." [7] In his highly popular book, J. J. Servan-Schreiber warned his fellow Europeans about the costs of restricting the entry of U.S. companies: ". . . we would be double losers—denying ourselves both the manufactured products we need and the capital funds that would then be invested in other countries." [8]

Our general conclusion that direct foreign investment offers net benefits to host economies should not be taken to mean that *every* foreign-owned affiliate necessarily makes a net contribution. When, for example, a host government exempts an affiliate from taxation, it may be questioned whether the benefits outrun the costs. Also, the foregoing analysis assumes that factor and goods prices in the host economy reflect their true scarcities and that the exchange rate does not seriously depart from the equilibrium rate. If such is not the case, the social contribution of foreign investment may be less than its social costs, although the same is also true of domestic investment. Finally, the benefit/cost ratio may shift over time, a subject we shall explore in a later section.

THE BALANCE OF PAYMENTS EFFECT

Direct foreign investment has numerous individual effects on the balance of payments of a host country that change significantly over time. The initial transfer of capital to the host country to establish, say, a manufacturing affiliate contributes a once-for-all benefit to the balance of payments. Once the affiliate starts operations, it may provide continuing benefits to the balance of payments by using some or all of its output for export or for import substitution. On the other hand, the affiliate may import raw materials or other inputs to sustain its operations at a continuing cost to the balance of payments. Profit repatriation and payments to foreign factors of production by the affiliate also constitute continuing drains on the host country's foreign exchange. Again, higher local income generated by the affiliate may induce more host country imports via the marginal propensity to import. Finally, if the affiliate is liquidated, any capital repatriation is a once-for-all cost to the balance of payments.

[6] Congress of the United States, *A Foreign Economic Policy for the 1970's,* Hearings before the Subcommittee on Foreign Economic Policy, Joint Economic Committee, Part 4—The Multinational Corporation and International Investment (Washington: U.S. Government Printing Office, 1970), p. 798.

[7] *Foreign Ownership and the Structure of Canadian Industry,* Report of the Task Force on the Structure of Canadian Industry (Ottawa: Queen's Printer, January, 1968), p. 38.

[8] J. J. Servan-Schreiber, *The American Challenge* (New York: Atheneum Publishers, 1969), p. 26.

We can represent these benefits and costs algebraically as follows:

(7) Balance of Payments Benefits $= K + X + S,$

where K is the initial inflow of investment capital; $X,$ the exports of the affiliate; and $S,$ the replacement of imports by the affiliate's output (import substitution).

(8) Balance of Payments Costs $=$
$$(R^{**} + F^*) + (M + M^*) + D,$$

where R^{**} is repatriated earnings; $F^*,$ payments to other foreign factors of production; $M,$ imports by the affiliate; $M^*,$ imports induced by higher local income via the marginal propensity to import; and $D,$ any disinvestment (liquidation) of the affiliate. The net benefit/cost ratio of direct foreign investment for the balance of payments of the host economy, therefore, is

$$\frac{K + X + S}{(R^{**} + F^*) + (M + M^*) + D}.$$

Over the long run, the balance of payments effect of direct foreign investment cannot be distinguished from its national income effect. We can understand why this is so by returning to equation (13) on p. 221 in Chapter 9, namely, $X - M = GNP - (C + I_d + G).$ This equation indicates that direct foreign investment will *improve* the balance of payments when its national income effect (increase in GNP) is not offset by an equal or greater increase in domestic absorption ($C + I_d + G$). The most probable outcome over the long run is for domestic absorption to match an increase in gross national product so that the balance of payments effect of direct foreign investment becomes neutral.

Over the shorter run, however, direct foreign investment may cause a balance of payments deficit because factors of production in the host country are not fully mobile. Hence, the economy may not be able to shift quickly out of the production of "home" goods into the production of export or import-substitution goods so as to achieve the net export balance necessary to finance any net foreign-exchange expenditures associated with an affiliate. This condition of lagged adjustment is particularly representative of developing countries that have a structural inability to transform savings into foreign exchange through an increase in exports or a decrease in imports. As a consequence, developing countries commonly experience a foreign exchange constraint on their economic growth that is distinguishable from a savings constraint.[9] Over the shorter run, therefore, a net increase in imports of goods and factor services which are directly or indirectly attributable to the operations of a foreign-owned affiliate may cause a persistent deficit (a

---

[9] For a discussion of these constraints, see Chapter 17, pp. 416-418.

decrease in $X - M$) because of structural rigidities in the host economy that prevent an adjustment to the balance of payments. In other words, over the shorter run an affiliate may bring about an increase in domestic absorption that exceeds its own contribution to the national product.

Faced with foreign exchange constraints and heavy debt-service burdens, policy makers in host developing countries are highly sensitive to the balance of payments effect of direct foreign investment. They regard with favor those foreign investment projects that will quickly replace imports or create exports so as to provide the foreign exchange necessary to finance the external transfer of earnings and factor payments. Conversely, foreign investment projects that are not import-saving or export-creating are likely to be discouraged by policy makers even though the projects in question will contribute significantly to economic growth. Thus, the foreign investment policies of many developing countries seek to maximize short-run balance of payments gains at the cost of sacrificing long-run gains in national income and economic growth.

Ideally a host country should maintain balance of payments equilibrium by resort to monetary, fiscal, and exchange rate policies, together with measures to speed up the reallocation of resources. But the existential fact is that policy makers in the developing countries must deal with immediate, pressing demands for scarce foreign exchange. In that situation, the short-run balance of payments effect of direct foreign investment tends to overwhelm the long-run national income effect in the formulation of policy. It is all the more necessary, therefore, to stress that the fundamental contribution of direct foreign investment to the host economy lies in the growth of national product through a superior allocation of resources, new technology, and improvements in local factor skills.

THE COINCIDENCE AND CONFLICT OF ECONOMIC INTERESTS

Our analysis of the benefits and costs of direct foreign investment points to a coincidence of economic interests between the multinational enterprise and the host country. As is true of other forms of economic specialization and exchange, direct foreign investment is a "positive sum game" which benefits both players. Within this fundamental harmony of interests, however, there is likely to be a continuing conflict of interests as both the multinational enterprise and the host country strive to maximize their respective shares of the net economic benefits of foreign investment. This conflict may be exacerbated by different perceptions of the benefit/cost ratio of an affiliate held respectively by the parent company and the host government, perceptions that may change radically over time. The resolution of this continuing conflict depends essentially on the current power positions of the two parties. Ordinarily, both sides are constrained in their negotiations and bargaining by the recognition of their own self-interests in the activation and sustained performance of the affiliate in question. By pressing their own interests too hard, both risk the loss of actual or prospective economic gains. Hence, the conflict of economic interests between the foreign investor and the host government tends to be resolved to the satisfaction of both parties by a process of give and take which may be repeated many times over during the life of the affiliate.[10]

DISAGREEMENT ON THE PRESENT VALUE OF BENEFITS AND COSTS

So far our conceptual approach to the measurement of the national income and balance of payments effects of direct foreign investment is a static analysis which implicitly assumes that there is time for all the benefits and costs to occur. Since benefits and costs follow different time paths, a more useful approach views benefits as a future stream of annual increments to national income and costs as a future stream of external income and factor payments. To obtain the *present values* of these streams, it is necessary to discount future benefits and costs at an appropriate rate. The present value of benefits (costs), therefore, is the sum of the discounted annual benefits (costs) in the future. We can restate equations (5) and (6) in present value form as follows:

(9) Net Present Value of Benefits $=$

$$\sum_{t=1}^{t=n} \left(\frac{[F_t + R^*_t + T_t] - N_t + L_t}{[1 + d]^t} \right).$$

(10) Net Present Value of Costs $= \sum_{t=1}^{t=n} \left(\frac{E_t}{[1 + d]^t} \right).$

In these equations, t is the number of years and d is the rate of discount. The higher the value of d, the greater the weight given to benefits and costs in the near future, and vice versa.[11]

When direct investors implicitly or explicitly discount future benefits and costs at a rate that differs from the rate used by the host government, then the two parties will disagree on the present value of those benefits and costs to the host country. Since it is rational for the multinational enterprise to use the marginal opportunity cost of its capital (the next best alternative use for it elsewhere in the world) to discount its own future benefits and

---

[10] This statement assumes the absence of any serious *political* conflict between the multinational enterprise and the host government.

[11] The net present value of balance of payments benefits is $\sum_{t=1}^{t=n} \left(\frac{K_t + X_t + S_t}{[1 + d]^t} \right),$

and balance of payments costs, $\sum_{t=1}^{t=n} \left(\frac{[R^{**}_t + F^*_t] + [M_t + M^*_t] + D_t}{[1 + d]^t} \right).$

costs, it tends to apply the same rate to discount future benefits and costs to the host country. When the host government seeks to maximize the income effects of foreign investment, the proper discount rate is the marginal productivity of capital in the host economy, a rate which should agree rather closely with the discount rate of the multinational enterprise. In that event, the investor and the host government will reach an easy agreement on the present value of the benefits and costs of a prospective investment. When, however, the multinational enterprise considers *political* risks to be high in the host country, it may add a risk premium to its discount rate so that the combined rate of the multinational enterprise exceeds the host government's rate. Then the enterprise will place a higher value on short-run benefits and costs than the host government.

However, apart from situations of high political risk, it is more common for the host governments of developing countries to discount the future more heavily than the multinational enterprise. Pressed by the need for immediate action to relieve foreign exchange shortages, to slow down inflation, to raise tax revenues, and to curb unemployment, host government officials generally place a much higher value on the early benefits and costs of foreign investment than on its more distant benefits and costs. As we have already noted, this concern with the shorter run frequently makes the balance of payments effects of a prospective foreign investment more critical in the eyes of government officials than its longer-run national income effects. The ensuing disagreement between the multinational enterprise and the host government on the present value of a proposed investment is most prominent in negotiations on entry. Once the investment is approved by the host government and the affiliate starts production, then disagreement is more likely to proceed from shifting perceptions of benefits and costs in the *current* period rather than the present value of benefits and costs over the indefinite life of the investment.

SHIFTING PERCEPTIONS OF BENEFIT/COST RATIOS OVER TIME

As perceived by host country policy makers, the benefit/cost ratio of a foreign-owned affiliate is likely to shift over time and, more often than not, in a negative direction. In the early years of an affiliate's operations, perceived benefits usually substantially exceed perceived costs. On the benefit side, the multinational enterprise brings new capital, technology, and entrepreneurial management to the host economy, and external economies are high as the affiliate trains workers, establishes connections with local suppliers and customers, and begins to compete in local markets. At the same time, perceived costs are usually low in the early years as the affiliate makes only modest profits (or incurs losses) which are mostly reinvested to build up its competitive position. As time goes on, however, host government officials frequently perceive a decline in benefits and a rise in costs. The multinational enterprise may no longer be transferring new capital and technology to the affiliate and the affiliate may generate fewer external economies as its operations become routine. On the other hand, profit repatriation may become ever larger as the affiliate achieves market success and has only modest needs for new capital. At some point, host government officials may even come to believe that the affiliate's operations could be performed entirely by local managers and workers, and that external income and factor payments constitute a continuing cost with no offsetting benefits. Alternatively, they may believe they can negotiate more satisfactory arrangements with another multinational enterprise.

While the host government's perception of the benefit/cost ratio of an affiliate is shifting downward, the parent company's perception may be shifting upward. Managers in the parent company are inclined to interpret the rising production, sales, and local tax payments of the affiliate as evidence of its growing contribution to the host economy. Furthermore, they view repatriated profits as a reward for entrepreneurial efforts that go back to the birth of the affiliate. In effect, the multinational enterprise tells the host government, "Look at all we have done for you since we came to your country!" And the host government replies, "Yes, we appreciate that, but what have you done for us lately?" Figure 25-1 depicts this widening divergence between the benefit/cost perceptions of host government officials and multinational enterprise managers.

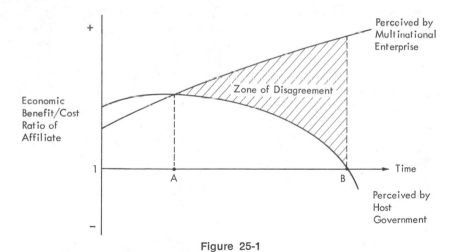

Figure 25-1

DIVERGENCE OF PERCEIVED ECONOMIC BENEFIT/COST RATIOS OF AN AFFILIATE BETWEEN THE HOST GOVERNMENT AND THE MULTINATIONAL ENTERPRISE

Up to point A, the host government is satisfied with the benefit/cost ratio of the affiliate and it may even believe it has the better of the arrangement with the multinational enterprise. As the zone of disagreement widens beyond point A, however, the host government will undertake measures to reverse the deterioration in its perceived benefit/cost ratio by demanding, for example, that the affiliate establish an R and D center, increase its exports, obtain more materials and components from local suppliers and less from abroad, promote nationals to top management positions, pay more taxes, and cease paying royalties to its parent company. If the host government's perception shifts beyond point B, where costs exceed benefits, then it may press the multinational enterprise to sell the affiliate to local investors. The ultimate action of the host government is a unilateral expropriation of the affiliate. Seldom, however, will the host government's perception of the *economic* benefit/cost ratio of an affiliate move beyond point B unless that perception is distorted by negative political factors which are unrelated to the economic performance of the affiliate.

These shifting perceptions of economic benefits and costs are closely associated with shifts in the relative power positions of the host country and the multinational enterprise. Before the initial investment is made, the host government is often in a weak bargaining position because the multinational enterprise usually has several options to invest in other countries. To obtain the investment, therefore, the host government may have to offer concessions, such as a tax exemption for the first five years of the affiliate's operations. Once the investment is made, however, the power balance tends to shift in favor of the host government. The multinational enterprise has now committed resources which may be lost if the affiliate does not maintain its viability. As the host country becomes less dependent on the affiliate for capital, technology, management, access to export markets, or external economies, it is in a better position to insist on new conditions to maintain (or increase) its share of economic benefits. As long as the multinational enterprise considers disinvestment more costly than accommodation to the host government's conditions, it will keep its affiliate in operation. On the other hand, it is in the economic interest of the host government to practice some restraint so as not to "kill the golden goose" by forcing the multinational enterprise to abandon local operations. The history of relations between the international petroleum companies and host developing countries is a classic example of this reversal of power positions over time.[12]

The reversal of power positions need not be true of every direct investment; it may be slowed down or even halted when the multinational enterprise is able to keep the host country continually dependent on it for new technology, new products, or access to export markets. The power positions of IBM and other high-technology multinational enterprises have suffered little, if any, erosion in host countries for this reason. In closing, we should recall that these conflicts of interest do not negate the fundamental mutuality of economic interests between host governments and the multinational enterprise. Both parties are likely to reach an accommodation of

---

[12] See pp. 640-643.

their mutual interests unless host government policy makers turn against an affiliate for political reasons.

THE CHALLENGE OF THE MULTINATIONAL ENTERPRISE TO THE NATIONAL SOVEREIGNTY OF HOST COUNTRIES

Although there is a fundamental harmony of *economic* interests between host countries and the multinational enterprise, there is also a fundamental conflict of *political* interests that poses a challenge to the national sovereignty of host countries. Government officials, intellectuals, labor leaders, businessmen, and other groups in host countries regard the multinational enterprise as far more than a business institution that raises questions of only economic benefits and costs. From their perspective, the multinational enterprise contributes economic benefits, but at the cost of imposing actual or potential constraints on the policy decisions of national authorities as well as threatening the "integrity" of the national community. They see the multinational enterprise as a political institution that can exercise decision-making power over key segments of the national economy from a headquarters located outside the national territory and beyond the jurisdictional reach of their government. They allege, therefore, that the multinational enterprise limits or thwarts the capacity of the host government to achieve economic, social, and other goals in pursuit of the national interest. Furthermore, representatives of host countries perceive the multinational enterprise as an actual or potential instrument for the extraterritorial application of the laws and policies of the parent company's home government. They view a multinational enterprise which is headquartered in the United States as an American enterprise that espouses the interests of the United States and, in any event, is fully subject to the authority of the U.S. Government. Finally, host country nationals see the multinational enterprise as an outsider, an intruder into the national community whose loyalty to the host country is questionable at best.

These perceptions of the political role of the multinational enterprise give rise to fears and allegations that are best described as *issues* which are subject to continuing disagreement, debate, and controversy within host countries (internal conflict of goals), between host countries and the multinational enterprise, and between host and home countries. Moreover, these fears and allegations will remain issues in the future unless direct foreign investment and the multinational enterprise can be "depoliticized" by multilateral international agreements that spell out the rights and responsibilities of the multinational enterprise vis-à-vis national governments, together with limitations on the territorial jurisdiction of those governments. In this section we shall briefly treat the political issues of the multinational enterprise as three major issues: the issue of national interest, the issue of extraterritoriality, and the issue of nationalism.

THE ISSUE OF NATIONAL INTEREST

The issue of national interest arises on two levels: (1) the divergent policy goals of host governments and the multinational enterprise, and (2) the constraints placed on government policy making by the independent power of the multinational enterprise to make decisions affecting the host country. It is alleged that the multinational enterprise ignores or opposes national policy goals and renders national policy instruments ineffective.[13]

Apart from the fact that a host government pursues social and national security goals that have no counterparts in the goals of the private multinational enterprise, goal conflicts between the two parties are almost certain to occur because of the profound difference in the perspectives of the respective decision makers. The host government conceives its economic and other goals in *national* terms; it tries to maximize *national* values in its policies. In contrast, the multinational enterprise conceives its goals in *geocentric* terms; it tries to maximize *enterprise system* values on a global scale. Host government officials ask, "Is this policy good for our country?" Multinational enterprise managers ask, "Is this policy good for our worldwide company?" Clearly the answers to these two questions need not be the same.

The issue of national interest, however, is not a conflict of goals as such; rather, it is the power of the multinational enterprise to act independently of national policies. Even if country and enterprise goals were always harmonious, no government would want to turn its power over to the multinational enterprise. On the other hand, if the multinational enterprise lacked power, then a host government could take measures to insure that the multinational enterprise always acted in the national interest. The power of the multinational enterprise comes from its possession of scarce capital, technology, and management, and the capability to deploy these resources throughout the world. Thus, the multinational enterprise is able to award or deny economic benefits to host countries. This brings us to the second dimension of the national interest issue, namely, the constraints placed on national policy making by the multinational enterprise with a consequent loss of "national independence."

Many specific allegations have been made against the multinational enterprise with regard to its power to circumvent national policies. From the perspective of the host government, the multinational enterprise can manipulate intraenterprise transfer prices to avoid local taxes, minimize import duties, circumvent exchange controls on capital outflows, and accomplish other purposes that are detrimental to the national interest. Other allegations relate to the investment and operating policies of the multinational enterprise. To illustrate, a multinational enterprise may decide

---

[13] For a discussion of national economic goals and policy instruments, see Chapter 11.

that its global logistical system will benefit by shifting production from country A to country B or by lowering exports from country A in favor of more exports from country B. Or again, the multinational enterprise may decide to undertake R and D only in the home country, a policy that makes the affiliates "branch plants" dependent on the parent's technology. Whether or not the multinational enterprise *actually* follows policies that are detrimental to the national interest is not the point; it is the capability of the multinational enterprise to do so that is at issue. No government, jealous sovereign that it is, cares to have a substantial or key element of the national economy controlled by decision centers located in another country.

THE ISSUE OF EXTRATERRITORIALITY

Host countries may also perceive the multinational enterprise as a threat to national sovereignty because of its identification with the policies of the home government. Multinational enterprises headquartered in the United States are particularly suspect because of the extraterritorial claims of the powerful U.S. Government. As we observed in Chapter 24, the U.S. Government exercises jurisdiction not only over the U.S. parent company, but over the entire multinational enterprise system as well. Moreover, the U.S. Government has actually constrained the foreign operations of U.S. parent companies in order to carry out its policies regarding antitrust laws, East-West trade, and foreign investment. A Canadian Task Force report on direct foreign investment in Canada (investment which is predominantly owned by U.S. companies) states flatly:

> The most serious and intractable of tensions results to the extent that the home country, in which the parent is resident, regards the entire multinational enterprise as subject to its jurisdiction and policies.[14]

Whereas the issue of national interest arises because the host country perceives the multinational enterprise as being too independent, the issue of extraterritoriality arises because the host country perceives the multinational enterprise as being too dependent on the home country.

In several specific instances, the U.S. Government has compelled the foreign affiliates of U.S. parent companies to behave in ways that were considered detrimental by host governments. To illustrate, in 1964 the U.S. Government forbade a French company wholly owned by IBM to sell computers to the French government. In 1966, the Government denied a license to a U.S.-owned British company to sell electrical connectors for use in the British manufacture of airplanes intended for Communist China. In 1968, it also refused a license to the Belgian affiliate of a U.S. company

---

[14] *Foreign Ownership and the Structure of Canadian Industry,* Report of the Task Force on the Structure of Canadian Industry (Ottawa: Queen's Printer, January, 1968), p. 48.

to export farm equipment to Cuba.[15] In 1972, the U.S. Government denied General Electric a license to transfer jet engine technology to SNECMA, France's state-owned aircraft engine manufacturer, as part of a joint agreement to develop a new engine. Although the Government justified the refusal on national security grounds, the real reason may well have been the fear that France would benefit commercially from U.S. technology.[16]

In matters of jurisdictional dispute between two sovereign states, the multinational enterprise is caught in the middle. To avoid this unhappy situation, U.S. parent companies have undoubtedly prevented their foreign affiliates from taking action that would get the parents in trouble with the U.S. Government, whether it concern export controls, antitrust, or foreign investment controls. To host governments, the subjection of U.S.-owned local companies to U.S. Government policies constitutes a direct violation of their territorial sovereignty. For that reason, efforts by the United States or any other home country to use parent companies to extend their laws and policies beyond the national domain act to endanger the viability of the multinational enterprise.

Host countries may also be fearful that multinational enterprises will call upon their home governments to support them in disputes with host governments. Particularly sensitive to this possibility, Latin American countries uphold the Calvo Doctrine, which denies the foreign investor any right to obtain support from his home government in a dispute with the host government. The attempt by the International Telephone and Telegraph Company (ITT) to get the U.S. Government to exert economic pressure on the Allende government of Chile reinforced allegations throughout Latin America that U.S. multinational enterprises pose a threat to national economic independence. The fact that the U.S. Government refused to support ITT and that ITT was not able to stop the expropriations of its telephone and hotel subsidiaries in Chile did not quell the wave of anti-American sentiment which damaged the image of all U.S. multinational enterprises in Latin America.[17]

THE ISSUE OF NATIONALISM

In Chapter 1, we pointed out that nationalism injects an emotional energy into international relations, often inciting governments to behavior that undermines the achievement of their own political and economic goals.

---

[15] These and other cases are examined in Jack N. Behrman, *National Interests and the Multinational Enterprise* (Englewood Cliffs, N. J.: Prentice-Hall, Inc., 1970), Chapter 7.

[16] "A Stalled Engine Angers the French," *Business Week* (October 21, 1972), pp. 22-23.

[17] "Papers Show I.T.T. Urged U.S. to Help Oust Allende," *The New York Times,* July 3, 1972, p. 3. "I.T.T. Dispute Helps Allende Politically," *The New York Times,* March 24, 1972, p. 6.

In no other realm of external economic relations is nationalism more prominent than in direct foreign investment and the multinational enterprise. Economic nationalists are apostles of the closed economy; they regard the multinational enterprise as an enemy that preaches the seditious doctrine of an interdependent world economy. To nationalists, it is essential that the government maintain absolute sovereignty over all business firms within the national domain. Hence, they reject the foreign ownership of local firms that serves as a channel for foreign influence on the economy, the society, and the national culture. The multinational enterprise is the unwelcome guest which establishes permanent residence in "our" country.

Practically all people experience nationalism to one degree or another. However, the most intense expression of economic nationalism today is found in the developing countries. Nationalists in these countries label direct foreign investment as "neocolonialism" or "economic imperialism," arguing that its purpose is to perpetuate economic and political dependence on the industrial countries. Governments in some developing countries consciously exploit nationalism to build loyalty to the state; political parties try to ride to power on the horse of antiforeign nationalism that pits "us" against "them." Frustrated by widening gaps between economic expectations and economic performance, governments are eager to use multinational enterprises as scapegoats for their own policy failures.

Nationalism in the developing countries has struck particularly hard at foreign investment in extractive industries. Natural resources are regarded as a national heritage that belongs to all the people. A common allegation against the foreign extractive investor is, "You take away our resources and leave us with an empty hole!" But the real grievance of nationalists is not the economic cost of direct foreign investment but rather the fact of foreign ownership, which sets the local affiliates of multinational enterprises outside the national society and national loyalties. Two incidents affirm this point. After the expropriation of the U.S.-owned International Petroleum Company by the Peruvian government in 1968, the following slogan of the new Peruvian petroleum company, Petroperu, appeared on billboards and posters throughout the country: "It's better . . . and it's ours." [18] Shortly after the expropriation of U.S.-owned copper companies by the Chilean government in 1971, the author witnessed in Santiago banners strung across streets and hung from office windows which bore the slogan: "Copper is now Chilean!" Economic nationalists reject, therefore, the legitimacy of foreign ownership, regardless of the economic benefits it may bring to their country.

Economic nationalism is by no means absent in the industrial countries, but it seldom dominates policies toward direct foreign investment. As a

---

[18] "Life with Peru's Junta: Can Business Patience Outlast Exasperation?" *Business Abroad* (October, 1969), p. 22.

chastening thought, however, the reader might ask himself what the reaction of many Americans would be to the takeover of a big, well-known U.S. company by, say, a Japanese multinational enterprise.

AMBIVALENCE AND TENSIONS IN HOST COUNTRIES

The coexistence of economic benefits and political costs associated with direct foreign investment makes the attitudes and policies of host countries toward the multinational enterprise highly ambivalent and creates tensions that accompany any "love-hate" relationship. Unfortunately host countries are unable to resolve this ambivalence and relieve their tensions through an objective evaluation of economic benefits and political costs because there is no way to measure political costs and thereby establish trade-offs between the two. What, after all, is the political cost of foreign ownership? How much is a feeling of national pride that comes from the expropriation of a foreign-owned petroleum or copper company worth to a people? One might answer, it is worth as much as a people are willing to forego in economic benefits. However, a people can know the economic consequences of these actions only if an objective appraisal of economic benefits and costs is made in advance by responsible authorities.

The most one can reasonably expect, then, is that increasingly host governments will evaluate the full economic benefits and costs of direct foreign investment in formulating their policies toward the multinational enterprise. This will minimize erratic shifts in policy that harm both foreign investors and host countries. But objective economic analysis will not remove ambivalence or cure tensions. These will persist as governments everywhere struggle to maintain national sovereignty in a world economy that is reaching toward ever higher levels of global interdependence.

POLICIES AND ACTIONS OF HOST GOVERNMENTS TO MINIMIZE THE POLITICAL COSTS OF DIRECT FOREIGN INVESTMENT

The concerns in host countries over the political costs of direct foreign investment center on the actual or potential exercise of control over the national economy by foreign companies and by the home governments of those companies. The legal basis of control by a foreign parent company is its ownership of local affiliates. Hence, attempts to prevent, reduce, or eliminate *foreign ownership* constitute many policies and actions of host governments that are taken to minimize the political costs of direct foreign investment. In this section we examine restrictions on foreign ownership, expropriation, the Andean Investment Code (which introduces the concept of "limited maturity" investments by foreigners), and recent negotiations relating to ownership between host governments and multinational enterprises in the petroleum industry.

RESTRICTIONS ON FOREIGN OWNERSHIP

All countries discriminate against the foreign ownership of local companies in at least some industries. In general, these restrictions are most severe in the developing countries, but they are by no means insignificant in the industrial countries.

Exclusion of Foreigners from Key Industries. Both industrial and developing countries exclude foreigners from direct investment in certain "key" industries that are regarded as essential to national security or as having a pervasive influence on the national economy and society. Key industries commonly include public utilities, airlines, shipping lines, communications media (television, radio, and publications), banks, and insurance companies. In developing countries, excluded industries may also encompass agriculture, forestry, fisheries, extraction (mining and petroleum), and basic industries (iron and steel, petrochemicals, etc.), which may also be reserved for state enterprise.

Requirements for Local Participation in Ownership. In addition to excluding foreign ownership from certain sectors of the economy, host governments may also require local ownership participation in some industries. Among the industrial countries, only Japan prevents 100 percent foreign ownership in certain industries open to foreign investment by requiring majority ownership by Japanese interests. In other words, Japan permits the entry of foreign companies into many of its industries *only* as minority joint venture partners with Japanese companies. Under pressure from the other industrial countries, Japan first moved to liberalize its ownership policies in 1967 when it established two classes of "liberalized industries" in which foreign companies were allowed up to 50 percent ownership (33 industries) and up to 100 percent ownership (17 industries).[19] In 1971 Japan completed a fourth round of liberalization that increased the number of industries open to 100 percent foreign ownership to 228, and reduced to 7 the number of industries in which case-by-case screening is imposed on foreign investment proposals.[20] However, the bulk of Japanese industry still remains closed to 100 percent foreign ownership.[21] Japan's basic policy appears to be that of the joint venture in which foreign participation is limited to 50 percent of equity.

Although Japan is unique among the industrial countries in requiring joint ventures, many developing countries follow that policy. Mexico, for

---

[19] "Foreign Investment in Japan, A Change of Policy?" *The OECD Observer* (Paris: Organization for Economic Cooperation and Development, April, 1968), p. 46.

[20] Japan Trade Center, "Government Implements Eight-Point Program on International Economic Policy," *Information Service* (undated).

[21] Yusaku Furuhashi, "New Policy Toward Foreign Investment? Issues in the Japanese Capital Liberalization," *MSU Business Topics* (Spring, 1972), p. 35.

example, requires at least 51 percent Mexican ownership in a broad range of industries. For many years, Mexico has pursued a policy of progressive "Mexicanization" of foreign-owned companies by converting them into joint ventures with local business interests. In 1971, Anaconda, a major U.S. copper producer, sold 51 percent of its Mexican mining affiliate to Mexicans; in 1965, American Smelting and Refining Company (another U.S. copper producer) had done the same with its Mexican affiliate.[22] The government of India insists that the "majority interest, ownership, and effective control of an undertaking should be in Indian hands." [23] In developing countries where there is no legal requirement for local ownership participation, the host government nonetheless may "persuade" foreign investors to enter into joint ventures with local entrepreneurs. Investors report, for example, that the Iranian government refuses to allow 100 percent foreign-owned investments.[24]

Prohibition of Acquisitions by Foreign Companies. Even the governments of industrial countries that follow liberal policies toward new foreign investment may refuse to approve the acquisition (takeover) of a locally owned company by a foreign investor. In Western Europe, France has been the most restrictive on acquisitions. It has, for example, prohibited the takeover by Westinghouse Electric Corporation of the French company, Jeumont-Schneider, an action that has frustrated Westinghouse's strategy to control a sizeable share of Europe's heavy electrical equipment industry. However, when the economic benefits appear great the French government may alter this policy as it did in 1972, when it gave the Ford Motor Company permission to acquire majority control of Richier, a big manufacturer of heavy construction equipment.[25]

In Canada, where foreign ownership of the manufacturing sector is over 50 percent and is even higher in some extractive sectors, the government has abandoned its traditional policy of laissez-faire toward foreign investment. In 1972 it moved to set up machinery for Cabinet-level screening of all future foreign acquisitions of Canadian-owned companies with gross assets of at least $250,000 or annual revenues of at least $3 million.[26] Canadian Prime Minister Trudeau stated that Canada "has reached a trade-off situation where it can pick and choose" among prospective foreign investments and "become more economically independent without becoming poor." [27]

---

[22] "Anaconda to Sell Mexico 51 Percent of Its Cananea Mine," *The New York Times,* August 28, 1971, p. 31.

[23] Indian Investment Centre, "The Climate for Foreign Investment in India," *Monthly Newsletter* (July 20, 1972), p. 49.

[24] *Obstacles and Incentives to Private Foreign Investment 1967-1968* (New York: National Industrial Conference Board, Inc., 1969), I, 11.

[25] "Ford Finds French Favor," *France Actuelle* (September, 1972), p. 8.

[26] "Canada's Adroit Move," *The New York Times,* May 7, 1972, p. 2.

[27] "Nationalism Spreads in Canada," *The New York Times,* January 28, 1972, p. 47.

In Australia, where foreign ownership equals 35 percent of the equity of domestic companies, the concern over foreign investment also focuses on takeovers. In 1972, International Telephone and Telegraph Company was forced to postpone a bid for Frozen Food Industries, a Melbourne-based company, by a public outcry spawned by fears that Australia was "becoming a second Canada." [28]

In spite of its recent liberalization, Japan generally limits foreign ownership in an existing Japanese company to less than 25 percent because the Japanese Commercial Code gives any stockholder holding 25 percent or more of a company's outstanding stock the right to appoint representatives on the board of directors.[29] In 1971, General Motors Corporation was able to acquire 34.2 percent of Isuzu Motors, Ltd. of Japan, but only by agreeing not to increase its capital participation beyond 34.2 percent for the next five years, not to hold more than four seats of a twenty-seven-member board of directors, and not to have its board members serve as chairman or president of Isuzu.[30]

Many developing countries also oppose foreign acquisitions. When he took office in 1970, President Echeverría of Mexico publicly censured local businessmen who sold their companies to foreign investors.[31]

EXPROPRIATION

The expropriation of foreign-owned companies is the most dramatic action a host government can take to minimize the political costs of direct foreign investment. Broadly defined, *expropriation* includes any seizure of foreign-owned property by a host government. When foreign owners are not compensated for their seized properties, expropriation becomes *confiscation*. Most expropriation is also *nationalization* because the host government assumes permanent ownership of the expropriated property. At a single stroke, then, expropriation deprives the foreign parent company of all ownership rights in its affiliate, including the right to control the affiliate's operations. The economic costs of expropriation to the host country may be extraordinarily severe. Apart from costs associated with the disruption of the affiliate's operations, expropriation commonly deters new foreign investment (which may be desired by the host government) and it invites retaliation by the investor's home government.[32] Nevertheless, the forces of

---

[28] "Australia: It Fears Becoming a Second Canada," *Business Week* (May 20, 1972), p. 46.

[29] Furuhashi, *op. cit.,* p. 36.

[30] "G.M.-Isuzu Accord Praised by Roche," *The New York Times,* July 17, 1971, p. 29. Several countries require that certain officers of a corporation or a certain percentage of its board of directors be nationals.

[31] "Chrysler to the Rescue," *Fortune* (March, 1972), p. 33.

[32] Expropriation may also hurt the foreign investment climate in other host countries. As a result of the Cuban expropriations in 1960, new U.S. investment in other Latin American countries fell sharply. The Cuban expropriations probably cost the rest of Latin America at least $500 million of new U.S. investment during the years 1960-62.

economic nationalism are now so strong in the developing countries that expropriations in extractive and public utility industries have become almost commonplace.

Expropriation is a direct exercise of national sovereignty. Traditional international law has recognized the right of sovereign states to expropriate the property of foreigners, but it has also upheld an "international standard" which requires "prompt, adequate, and effective" compensation.[33] Since World War I, this international standard has been repeatedly challenged by Communist and developing countries. In 1962 a resolution of the General Assembly of the United Nations incorporated the position of the developing countries by stating: "The owner shall be paid appropriate compensation, in accordance with the rules in force in the State taking such measures in the exercise of its sovereignty and in accordance with international law." [34] This statement amounts to a substitution of a national standard for the international standard. Because of the split between the West and the South (supported by the East), therefore, there is no generally accepted rule for compensation in cases of expropriation. Furthermore, the developing countries (where most expropriations occur) have been loath to enter into bilateral or multilateral treaties that commit them to "just compensation" in the event of expropriation.

A Brief History of Expropriation. U.S. companies have experienced many expropriations of their foreign investments since World War I. The first significant expropriations occurred during the years 1917-1920 when the new Soviet government seized all business properties belonging to foreigners and nationals alike while proclaiming its right to expropriate without compensation. This *universal* expropriation set the precedent for expropriations by Communist governments in Eastern Europe and Mainland China after World War II and by the revolutionary Cuban government which came to power at the end of 1958. The Soviet expropriations also paved the way for nationalist expropriations in the developing countries of Asia, Africa, and Latin America.

The first important non-Communist expropriation occurred in Mexico in 1938 when the government took over the affiliates of U.S. and British petroleum companies. Prolonged negotiations finally led to a settlement of compensation claims in the 1940's. Unlike the Soviet expropriations, the Mexican expropriation was *selective,* involving only foreign petroleum properties. It was this Mexican action, then, that established the precedent for the many expropriations of foreign investments in mining, petroleum,

---

[33] "Adequate" compensation is payment of the full market value of the property. "Effective" compensation is payment in a convertible currency.

[34] United Nations, General Assembly Resolution 1803 (XVII), 14 December 1962.

agriculture, and public utilities which have taken place in the developing countries since World War II.

The most traumatic expropriation experience of U.S. companies occurred in Cuba in 1960. For over half a century, U.S. companies considered Cuba a safe (and profitable) place for investment; not a single American investor bothered to take out U.S. investment insurance against the risk of expropriation. In 1960 the Cuban government seized the assets of scores of U.S. companies (valued at $1.4 billion) without the payment of any compensation.

In reviewing the U.S. expropriation experience, one study identified 187 U.S. companies which had suffered expropriations over the period 1917-1965. These companies were involved in 240 separate acts of expropriation, 171 in Communist countries (including Cuba) and 69 in non-Communist, developing countries.[35] Since 1965, several more U.S. firms have experienced expropriations of their foreign investments in developing countries.

Two Recent Cases of Expropriation. The seizure of the properties of the International Petroleum Company by the Peruvian government in 1968 and the seizure of the copper-mining subsidiaries of Anaconda Company and Kennecott Copper Corporation by the Chilean government in 1971 are the most prominent expropriations of U.S. foreign investments in recent years. Each of these cases is very complex, reaching far back into history. All we can do here is indicate the major events leading to expropriation and the ensuing disputes over compensation.

On October 9, 1968, six days after a coup d'etat that brought it to power, the New Revolutionary government of Peru seized and occupied the oil fields of La Brea y Parinas, a refinery, and related properties belonging to the International Petroleum Company (IPC), a fully owned Canadian subsidiary of the Standard Oil Company of New Jersey.[36] Within a few months the government had taken over all IPC assets in Peru, including a retail distribution network which held a dominant position in the domestic petroleum market. The dispute between IPC and Peru dates back to 1924, when IPC acquired La Brea y Parinas, whose title derived from an unusual grant to the Quintana family in 1826. While other petroleum companies operated in Peru only under concessions, IPC held both surface and sub-surface rights to La Brea y Parinas as a full owner. Consequently, IPC was not subjected to the same taxation on crude oil production as other companies. From the beginning Peruvians regarded IPC's special situation as an infringement on national sovereignty because Peruvian law (following

---

[35] Franklin R. Root, "The Expropriation Experience of American Companies," *Business Horizons* (April, 1968), p. 71.

[36] Thereafter, October 9 was called the "Day of National Dignity" and postage stamps were issued to commemorate it.

Spanish precedent) confers on the state the exclusive ownership of all subsurface wealth. In opposition, IPC insisted on a strict interpretation of its ownership title. The expropriation in 1968, therefore, was the culmination of a long, bitter dispute between IPC and successive Peruvian governments.[37]

Offering to compensate IPC, the Peruvian government actually deposited a $70 million check payable to IPC. But there was a catch: the check would be released only after IPC paid $690 million to the Peruvian government. The government claimed this enormous sum (three times the book value of IPC's assets!) on the basis that IPC had operated illegally in Peru since it started operations in 1924. Apparently the $690 million was calculated by multiplying the quantity of oil exported by IPC over forty-four years by the current crude oil price less an allowance for freight and operating costs.[38] Thus, the government sought to turn back the clock to the initial investment of IPC in Peru, an approach which one writer has called "retroactive expropriation." [39]

The prospects for any early settlement of this compensation issue are poor. Although the IPC case is unique in many respects, the new Peruvian government has espoused a policy of economic nationalism which has led to the expropriation of other U.S. investments, including the sugar properties of W. R. Grace and Company. The government has also promulgated a new industrial law requiring joint ventures and their eventual ownership by workers. These policies have greatly discouraged new foreign investment in Peru.

In July, 1971, the new government of Chile, under President Salvador Allende, expropriated the huge copper mining affiliates of Anaconda Company and Kennecott Copper Corporation. For over fifty years these two U.S. companies had produced most of Chile's copper. As a consequence of their massive operations, Chile became dependent on copper for 80 percent of its exports and for 75 percent of its government revenue. The move to nationalize the copper industry in Chile started under the government of President Eduardo Frei, who pursued a strategy of "Chileanization" which made the Chilean government a joint venture partner of the U.S. companies. In 1967, Kennecott sold 51 percent of its El Teniente mine to the government for $80 million (which was then lent back to the government), and Anaconda sold a 25 percent interest to the government in its new Exótica mining venture. In 1969, under government pressure, Anaconda agreed to a gradual nationalization of its two largest operating units,

---

[37] This dispute and other events surrounding the expropriation are examined in some detail in Richard N. Goodwin, "Letter from Peru," *The New Yorker* (May 17, 1969), pp. 41-109.

[38] David K. Eiteman, "A Model for Expropriation Settlement, The Peruvian-I.P.C. Controversy," *Business Horizons* (April, 1970), pp. 87-88.

[39] *Ibid.*, p. 88. The idea of retroactive expropriation was not a new one in Peru. The previous government, under Belaúnde, had made a claim of $144 million against IPC on grounds of "unjust enrichment." This amount was the government's estimate of IPC's entire profits for the preceding fifteen years.

Chuquicamata (the world's largest open-pit copper mine) and El Salvador. It sold an immediate 51 percent interest to the Chilean government for $197 million, to be paid over a period of twelve years, and, more important, it gave the government an option to acquire the remaining interest between January, 1973, and December, 1981. Also in 1969, both companies agreed that their income from Chilean operations would be limited on the basis of a copper sales price of 40 cents per pound, with all extra income going to Chile. It was estimated at the time that this agreement would boost Chile's share of the revenue from the El Teniente mine alone from 72.6 percent to 91.8 percent.[40] The mines continued to be managed under contract by the U.S. companies. By 1970, then, the prospect was for a full nationalization of the copper mines through a process of negotiation between the Chilean government and the U.S. companies. Despite this prospect, both companies were continuing to invest in Chile, with Kennecott planning to put $230 million into El Teniente, while Anaconda was planning to put $150 million into Exótica.

The election of Salvador Allende as President of Chile in September, 1970, changed everything. Supported by a coalition of Marxist Socialists and Communists, Allende set out to redeem his campaign pledge to expropriate the remaining U.S. copper interests. After securing a constitutional amendment which allowed the government to gain full control of the copper mines without paying the sums required under contracts signed by the Frei Administration, Allende seized the copper mines in July, 1971. Although Allende declared his intention to pay "fair compensation" for the U.S. investments, which had a book value of $400 million, he announced in September, 1971, that Anaconda and Kennecott "owed" the Chilean government $774 million for "excess profits" over the preceding fifteen years. In so doing, Allende borrowed the concept of retroactive expropriation first used by Peru, Chile's neighbor to the north. Furthermore, the Chilean Copper Corporation claimed a $1 billion deduction from the compensation owed the U.S. companies for alleged deficiencies in property, equipment, and plans at the mines and mills.[41] The expropriation became, then, confiscation with no compensation to be paid the U.S. owners.

The reader may well wonder why Chile chose to expropriate when nationalization was already under way. The explanation is the Marxist ideology of the new government, intensified by nationalism, that rejected any foreign ownership in the copper industry. Allende's ideological victory, however, was purchased at a heavy economic cost: it disrupted copper production, stopped the planned investment of the U.S. copper companies, scared prospective foreign investors away from Chile, and provoked retaliation by the U.S. Government. In October, 1972, Kennecott sought

---

[40] "Kennecott Gives Chile New Profit from El Teniente," *The New York Times,* October 6, 1969, p. 9.

[41] "Allende's Copper Challenge to the U.S.," *The New York Times,* October 3, 1971, p. E-3.

court orders to block payments by European customers to the Chilean Copper Corporation, and it had already won such an order in Paris.[42] The settlement of this case is very unlikely as long as a Socialist-Communist government remains in power in Chile.

These two cases of expropriation are representative of other recent expropriations in developing countries that have also involved takeovers of natural resource, extractive companies. The nationalization of extractive industries has become a pervasive policy in the developing world. On the other hand, except in developing countries dominated by Marxist Socialist or Communist governments, which are ideologically opposed to all private ownership of industry, foreign investors have seldom experienced expropriation in manufacturing sectors of the host economy. Whether foreign investments in manufacturing in the developing countries will remain comparatively safe from expropriation is a question for the future. As observed earlier, foreign investors in manufacturing are already subject to restrictions on ownership in many host countries.

U.S. Policy toward Expropriation. When a host country confiscates a foreign investment, it can reasonably expect diplomatic protests and even retaliation from the investor's home country. In particular, the U.S. Government staunchly defends the international standard of prompt, adequate, and effective compensation for U.S. investments expropriated by host governments. The United States enforces this policy through international treaties, diplomatic pressures, the cessation of bilateral aid and credits to the expropriating country, and through efforts to block similar aid and credits by international agencies such as the World Bank.

In 1961 the U.S. Congress passed the Hickenlooper Amendment to the Foreign Assistance Act, requiring the President to suspend all foreign aid to the government of any country which expropriates U.S. property without taking "appropriate steps" within six months of the expropriation to compensate U.S. owners in accordance with the international standard. Successive U.S. Presidents have opposed this amendment because it restricts their flexibility in dealing with expropriations. Consequently, the Amendment has been applied to only one country, Ceylon, in 1963. Fearful of the reaction of other Latin American countries to application of the Amendment to Peru after its seizure of IPC's properties in 1968, the Nixon Administration has taken a lenient view of "appropriate steps" taken by Peru to settle the issue of compensation.

Confronted by a rash of expropriations of U.S. business investments, the U.S. Government announced a stronger policy at the beginning of 1972. The key passage in its statement reads as follows:

---

[42] "Chile Assailed by Kennecott, Seeks Support," *The New York Times,* October 17, 1972, p. 55.

. . . when a country expropriates a significant United States interest without making reasonable provision for [prompt, adequate, and effective] compensation to United States citizens, we will presume that the United States will not extend new bilateral economic benefits to the expropriating country unless and until it is determined that the country is taking reasonable steps to provide adequate compensation or that there are major factors affecting United States interests which require continuance of all or part of these benefits.[43]

The statement goes on to say that the United States could be expected to "withhold its support of loans under consideration in multilateral development banks." However, the new policy would not apply to humanitarian assistance, such as earthquake and famine relief.

The policy statement replaced an ad hoc policy of treating expropriations on a case by case basis without general guidelines. The United States had actually placed this new policy into effect even before its formal announcement. After Peru seized IPC's assets, U.S. aid fell from $60 million to $9 million in 1969. In 1971, the Export-Import Bank refused to finance the purchase by Chile of jet airliners because of its failure to compensate Kennecott and Anaconda. Also in 1971, the United States abstained as a sign of disapproval on loans by the World Bank to Bolivia and Guyana because of unsettled questions of compensation for expropriated U.S. property.[44] More recently, the United States voted against a loan by the World Bank to Iraq, which expropriated the Iraq Petroleum Company, involving the interests of two U.S. oil companies.[45]

Summing up, the United States has responded to a wave of expropriations that started in the late 1960's (notably in Latin America) by adopting a policy of retaliation in aid and credit cutoffs when the expropriating government does not offer compensation according to the international standard. It is too early to say whether this policy will slow down confiscations in the developing countries. Conceivably, this policy could provoke more expropriations (confiscations) by stimulating fears of outside interference in the host countries.

THE ANDEAN INVESTMENT CODE

In December, 1970, representatives of the five countries belonging to the Andean Common Market approved a statute (known as Decision No. 24) for a common policy on the treatment of foreign capital and imported

---

[43] "Nixon Announces Tough U.S. Stand on Expropriation," *The New York Times,* January 20, 1972, p. 1.

[44] "World Bank Used for U.S. Protest," *The New York Times,* June 28, 1971, p. 47.

[45] "Vote 'No' in the World Bank," *The Wall Street Journal,* June 30, 1972, editorial page.

technology.[46] This common policy distinguishes three types of enterprise: *national,* where 80 percent or more of the capital investment is domestic, that is, held by nationals of the member countries; *mixed,* where 51 percent to 80 percent of the capital investment is domestic; and *foreign,* where less than 51 percent of the capital investment is domestic.

The most controversial provisions of the Andean Investment Code relate to the transformation of foreign enterprises into mixed enterprises according to a fixed schedule. A foreign enterprise *already existing in a member country* must agree to become a mixed enterprise in order to enjoy the trade liberalization benefits of the Andean Common Market. If it so agrees, then the participation of domestic investors in its capital investment must reach 15 percent within three years and it must reach at least 51 percent within fifteen years in Colombia, Chile, and Peru, and within twenty years in Bolivia and Ecuador. Domestic participation must reach 45 percent before two-thirds of the total period is completed. *New foreign enterprises* established in a member country after mid-1971 must agree to become mixed enterprises within a time period not exceeding the same number of years that apply to existing foreign enterprises. Unlike the latter, however, new enterprises are *compelled* to become mixed enterprises, whereas existing foreign enterprises must become mixed enterprises only if they wish to enjoy the trade liberalization benefits of the Common Market. Under these provisions, therefore, new foreign investors must eventually turn over a majority of their capital shares (and presumably control) to local investors, a process that has been called "investment fade-out." The state or state enterprises are to have first refusal on the shares of foreign capital offered to domestic investors.

The Code has several exceptions. No new foreign investments are allowed in public utilities, financial institutions, domestic transportation, communications, or domestic wholesale/retail trade. Generally, existing foreign enterprises in these sectors must offer within three years at least 80 percent of their share capital to local investors. Another exception is the extractive industries. During the first ten years of the common investment policy, member countries may grant concessions of up to twenty years' duration to foreign enterprises for the exploration and exploitation of minerals, oil, gas, or forestry products. These extractive foreign enterprises are not required to become mixed enterprises although they are encouraged to do so.

Several general rules apply to all foreign investment. Before authorizing its use, the appropriate national agency will determine the effective contribution of imported technology. Generally, foreign enterprises will have no access to local credit, and the interest paid to a foreign parent company is limited to three percentage points above the prime rate in the lender's country. Reinvestment of profits by a foreign enterprise will require a

---

[46] For a description of the Andean Common Market, see Ch. 18, pp. 440-441.

permit from the appropriate national authority, as is true of all new investments. Foreign investors will have the right to repatriate profits up to 14 percent of the book value of the investment. Finally, disputes between foreign investors and member governments will be settled only in a way that fully recognizes the sovereignty and legal authority of the host country.

The Andean Investment Code is an important landmark in the evolution of foreign investment policies because of its novel fade-out provisions. For the first time, foreign investors will be required to transfer majority ownership to local investors according to a fixed timetable. The *idea* of planned foreign divestment (fade-out) was first proposed by scholars in the United States, most notably by Albert Hirschman in a publication which drew wide attention.[47] Hirschman argues that foreign direct investment can be at its "creative best" when supplying missing factors of production in the early stages of a country's development, but later on it may stunt that development by displacing local factors and discouraging local entrepreneurs. Hence, foreign investment is a "mixed blessing." Hirschman concludes that a policy of "selective liquidation and withdrawal of foreign private investment is in the best mutual interests of Latin America and the United States." [48] He then goes on to examine possible arrangements for the transfer of foreign investments to local ownership and control, including an Inter-American Divestment Corporation (which would acquire foreign-owned assets and hold them until they could be sold to local investors in Latin America) and "built-in divestment" involving a gradual transfer of all or the majority of a foreign investment to local ownership in planned stages.

Jack Behrman has strongly criticized Hirschman's divestment proposal.[49] Viewing the proposal as serving only political or psychological objectives, Behrman argues that divestment may discourage economic development by transferring ownership to less enterprising local groups. He concludes that host countries have ways other than compulsory divestment to take advantage of foreign investment while minimizing concerns arising from foreign control.

The real test of the Andean Investment Code lies in the future. The Andean countries want foreign investment, but only on terms that include the controversial fade-out requirements. Given the limited economic dimensions of the Andean Common Market and the high level of political risks in the subregion, it is doubtful that the member countries can attract the foreign investment and technology they want for the manufacturing sectors of their economies. Their bargaining power vis-à-vis multinational manufacturers does not look strong. Regardless of the failure or success of the

---

[47] Albert O. Hirschman, *How to Divest in Latin America and Why,* Essays in International Finance No. 76 (Princeton: Princeton University Press, November, 1969).

[48] *Ibid.,* p. 9.

[49] Jack N. Behrman, "International Divestment: Panacea or Pitfall?" *Looking Ahead* (Washington: National Planning Association, 1970).

Andean Investment Code, however, the idea of divestment has gained legitimacy, and it will probably be translated into policy in other developing countries during the 1970's, possibly under more favorable circumstances. It would appear, then, that multinational enterprises will have to learn to adapt to host government policies that set time limits on ownership and control.

THE ORGANIZATION OF PETROLEUM EXPORTING COUNTRIES

The Organization of Petroleum Exporting Countries (OPEC) was formed in 1961 by Iran, Iraq, Kuwait, Saudi Arabia, and Venezuela in response to a unilateral reduction in the posted price of crude oil in August, 1960, by the major multinational petroleum companies, a reduction which cut the oil revenues of these countries.[50] During the 1960's, the OPEC (grown to ten members with the entry of Abu Dhabi, Algeria, Indonesia, Libya, and Qatar) followed a defensive strategy that prevented any further decline in posted prices.[51] It was unable, however, to force a rise in posted prices, which were $1.79 per barrel in 1970 compared to $2.18 per barrel in 1948. A surplus of oil in the 1960's weakened the bargaining power of the OPEC countries vis-à-vis the petroleum companies, which possessed the only worldwide marketing networks. Efforts by the OPEC to control the supply of oil by allocating production among its member countries (prorationing) were frustrated by a reluctance to accept national export quotas. In 1970, therefore, the multinational petroleum companies still maintained control over the price and volume of oil produced in the OPEC countries. Within a year, however, the balance of power shifted radically against the petroleum companies as the worldwide buyers' market turned into a sellers' market which promised to endure into the foreseeable future. Holding 80 percent of the world's known oil reserves and providing 90 percent of the world's oil exports, the OPEC quickly took advantage of this power shift in a series of historic confrontations with the petroleum companies that have transformed the international petroleum industry.[52] The first set of confrontations focused on the distribution of economic benefits; the second set focused on the ownership of crude oil production in the OPEC countries.

Negotiations on the Distribution of Economic Benefits. At its twenty-first conference in December, 1970, the OPEC adopted Resolution No. 120, which demanded a general increase in posted prices, a standard tax rate of

---

[50] The tax collections of the oil-producing countries are based on the official posted price of petroleum, which may differ from the actual market price.

[51] Nigeria became the eleventh member of OPEC only in mid-1971.

[52] Gurney Breckenfeld, "How the Arabs Changed the Oil Business," *Fortune* (August, 1971), p. 113 ff.

55 percent on oil revenues, and compensation for inflation in the industrial countries.[53] The OPEC gave the companies thirty-one days to make an acceptable offer to the Arabian Gulf countries; otherwise, the OPEC member countries would take "concerted and simultaneous action." In response, the companies announced their willingness to negotiate with all ten members of the OPEC to conclude a single common agreement. Rejecting this proposal, the OPEC insisted on separate negotiations on a regional basis. In this way, the OPEC for the first time became an effective cartel, forcing the companies into two major negotiations at Tehran and Tripoli in 1971. The OPEC's objective was purely economic, namely, to increase the producing countries' share of total oil revenues.

The Tehran negotiations were held between the OPEC's six Arabian Gulf countries (Iran, Iraq, Saudi Arabia, Abu Dhabi, Kuwait, and Qatar) and the seven major multinational petroleum companies (Standard Oil of New Jersey, Royal Dutch/Shell, Texaco, Mobil, Gulf, Standard Oil of California, and British Petroleum), plus several smaller companies. To counteract the group bargaining of the OPEC, the oil companies negotiated as a team for the first time.[54] But the winning cards were all in the OPEC's hands. By threatening a unilateral increase in posted prices and taxes and a shutdown in production, and by hinting at nationalization, the Arabian Gulf countries were able to increase their oil revenues by an extraordinary amount in a five-year agreement reached on February 14, 1971.

The Tehran Agreement raised the posted price to $2.15 per barrel, plus an annual increase of 5 cents a barrel to match company profits from higher market prices, and an annual increase of 2.5 percent to compensate for inflation in the industrial countries. It also set the tax rate at 55 percent. This settlement is expected to increase the oil income of the Gulf countries by 25 percent a year.[55] In return, the oil companies obtained security of supply and guaranties against any unscheduled increases in the posted price over the five-year life of the Agreement.

Although the Tehran negotiations involved hard bargaining, they were conducted in a businesslike fashion by well-informed negotiators. (One of the first acts of the OPEC in 1961 was to hire European consultants to make detailed studies of all aspects of the petroleum industry.) In contrast, the Tripoli negotiations between the revolutionary government of Libya and twenty-five oil companies, which started ten days after the signing of the

---

[53] Libya had paved the way for these demands by gaining a 40 cent per barrel increase in the posted price and an increase in the tax rate from 50 to 55 percent in September. Also, earlier in 1970 Venezuela unilaterally raised its tax rate from 52 percent to 60 percent.

[54] To do so, the U.S. companies received an antitrust waiver from the U.S. Government.

[55] "5-Year Oil Accord is Reached in Iran by 23 Companies," *The New York Times,* February 15, 1971, p. 1. Before the Tehran Agreement, the Gulf countries collected a 50 percent tax on a posted price of $1.79.

Tehran Agreement, were filled with threats and recriminations by Libyan officials. The Libyan leader, Col. Mumammar el-Qaddafi, threatened to halt all oil exports if his demands were not met, a threat taken seriously by the oil companies because Libya at the time held $1.4 billion in idle foreign exchange. The outcome of these embittered negotiations in April of 1971 was a jump in the posted price of Libyan crude oil from $2.55 to $3.45 a barrel (more than twice the Tehran increase) along with tax and other provisions similar to the Tehran Agreement.[56] All in all, the Tehran and Tripoli Agreements will add an estimated $25 billion to the oil income of the OPEC countries over a five-year period.[57]

Negotiations over Ownership. The multinational petroleum companies (and ultimately the consuming, industrial countries) paid dearly for what they hoped would be five years of stability. This hope was soon dashed by subsequent events. After the devaluation of the dollar in December, 1971, the OPEC demanded and quickly obtained a further increase in posted prices to offset the decline in the dollar's value. But of far greater importance, the OPEC summoned the oil companies to Geneva in January, 1972, to negotiate the participation of its member countries in the ownership of the local crude oil affiliates of those companies. The OPEC thereby sounded a new note. Whereas the Tehran and Tripoli Agreements were concerned only with the *economic* issues of prices, taxes, and revenues, the new negotiations were to deal with the *political* issues of ownership. Setting the end of February, 1972, as a deadline, the Gulf countries demanded the right to buy 20 percent of the twelve production affiliates operating on their territories. The crucial issue in the ensuing negotiations was the compensation for the assets to be transferred to the Gulf countries. The latter were willing to pay only the book value of the assets with no compensation for oil reserves in the ground; the companies argued that they should receive some compensation for the loss of future profits from those reserves. An accord (the New York Agreement) was finally reached in October, 1972, between the Gulf countries (excluding Iran) and twenty-three oil companies that granted the governments the right to acquire an immediate 25 percent share of the crude oil affiliates. This share will rise in stages to a 51 percent controlling interest by 1983, where it will remain until the expirations of the concession agreements, which range from 1993 to 2018. In turn, the governments will compensate the companies at a price somewhat above book value, but not for oil reserves in the ground. The companies are committed to buy back the governments' share of crude oil production until the latter can market the oil on their own.[58]

---

[56] After the Tehran Agreement, Indonesia obtained an increase of 51 cents per barrel. In April, 1971, Algeria unilaterally raised the posted price to $3.60 a barrel.

[57] "Iran to Extend Western Oil Pact to 1994," *The Wall Street Journal,* June 27, 1972, p. 14.

[58] "Oil Concerns Set Accord with Five Arab Countries," *The New York Times,* October 6, 1972, p. 1.

The New York Agreement offers the oil companies little assurance of stability in the Gulf countries, to say nothing of the other OPEC countries. Agreements have frequently been broken by the sovereign OPEC countries. The most likely prospect is full nationalization of crude oil production by the OPEC countries before the end of this decade. Algeria, Iraq, Libya, and Venezuela are already closer to full nationalization than ownership participation in crude oil affiliates. The primary motivation behind nationalization is political; nationalization is unlikely to increase the economic benefits of the OPEC countries and may well decrease them. Once the international petroleum companies no longer hold assets in the OPEC countries, those assets can no longer be used as hostages in negotiations. And when the national oil companies of the OPEC countries venture into the world petroleum market on their own, they will encounter the stiff competition of the multinational oil companies in the marketing of petroleum products to end users. Conceivably, nationalization could even destroy the OPEC, as the national companies compete against each other for shares in the petroleum market. On the other hand, nationalization will not eliminate the multinational petroleum companies, such as Standard Oil of New Jersey or Royal Dutch/Shell. Although these companies will no longer hold massive reserves in the OPEC countries, they will continue to refine and market much of the OPEC's oil. Moreover, their scarce technology and management skills will continue to be demanded by the OPEC and other developing countries, and they will be provided under service contracts if concessions are not available. Finally, the multinational companies will continue to explore for, and exploit, new oil fields under the oceans and elsewhere in the world. Nonetheless, the preponderant influence of the multinational oil companies is now a thing of the past, for they must share their market power with the OPEC countries who will operate their petroleum industries as competitors as well as suppliers. Whether the dramatic power reversal that has taken place in the international petroleum industry will be matched in other extractive industries, such as the copper industry, is a question for the future.

TOWARD AN ACCOMMODATION BETWEEN NATION-STATES AND THE MULTINATIONAL ENTERPRISE

Our analysis of the benefits and costs of direct foreign investment earlier in this chapter demonstrated a coincidence of economic interests between the multinational enterprise and host countries. Within this fundamental harmony of interests, there is, of course, a continuing conflict of interests, as both the multinational enterprise and host countries strive to maximize their respective shares of net economic benefits. But in the absence of political conflict, this conflict over the division of gains can be resolved to the satisfaction of both parties who recognize that their mutual benefits are dependent on the viability of the foreign investment in question. By pressing their own interests too hard, both risk the loss of actual or prospective economic gains. In principle, therefore, conflicts of economic interests are resolvable because international economic transactions constitute a positive-sum game in which both participants can gain from its continuation and both can lose from its cessation. The coincidence of economic interests rests on the contributions that the multinational enterprise makes to the host economy as an international transfer agent of products, capital, technology, and entrepreneurial skills.

In spite of this fundamental harmony of economic interests, the multinational enterprise is coming under mounting attacks in host countries on political grounds. This political conflict centers on control of the multinational enterprise's behavior within the host country. Host governments want control in order to maximize national socio-political values on a national scale; the multinational enterprise wants control in order to maximize enterprise economic values on a global scale. Unlike the conflict of economic interests, the political conflict is a power contest or zero-sum game in which one party gains at the expense of the other.

Can governments slay the dragons of the multinational enterprise? [59] Certainly no government, acting individually, can do so because it has jurisdiction over only one national element of the multinational enterprise system.[60] And it is difficult to imagine governments acting collectively to that end. But if many governments were to apply unilateral restrictions on the operations of multinational enterprises within their territories, then they would seriously cripple the economic efficiency of multinational enterprise systems. Can multinational enterprises slay the dragons of national sovereignty? Some scholars, viewing the nation-state as obsolescent, foresee political power passing to the multinational enterprise and other transnational functional institutions.[61] But surely this is a fanciful notion in a world of intense nationalism. If, then, neither party is capable of destroying the other to achieve complete control over its own behavior, it can choose either to reach an accommodation with the other or else exacerbate the political conflict in pursuit of selfish interests.

BILATERAL ACCOMMODATION AT THE NATIONAL LEVEL

At the bilateral, national level, the range of accommodation between a national sovereignty and the multinational enterprise is defined by two

---

[59] Jack N. Behrman, "Can Governments Slay the Dragons of Multinational Enterprise?" *European Business* (Winter, 1971), pp. 53-62.

[60] The U.S. Government has the power to destroy *U.S.-based* multinational enterprises but not enterprises headquartered in other countries. In any event, U.S. policy makers do not perceive U.S. multinational enterprises as posing a threat to the national sovereignty of this country. The controversy in the United States over the multinational enterprise is a dispute concerning its economic benefits and costs, as was shown in Chapter 24.

[61] See, for example, Frank Tannenbaum, "The Survival of the Fittest," *The Columbia Journal of World Business* (March-April, 1968), pp. 13-20.

extreme postures. For the national sovereignty, the extreme posture is the adoption of a policy of laissez-faire that allows the multinational enterprise to pursue freely its own interests regardless of the benefits and costs to that sovereignty. Laissez-faire policy, therefore, represents a full accommodation by the nation to the multinational enterprise. For the multinational enterprise, the extreme posture is the transfer of all ownership and managerial control of its local operations to the national sovereignty or its representatives while, at the same time, continuing to sustain those operations with loan capital, technology, and management skills. By substituting contractual arrangements for ownership and control, the multinational enterprise becomes a service company that fully accommodates the political interests and nationalism of the host country.

Neither of these extreme postures is probable in the foreseeable future, although they may be assumed by individual nations and multinational enterprises in particular circumstances. The intellectual argument for a laissez-faire market economy has been decisively rejected by nations in the twentieth century for the doctrine of the welfare state, which takes on responsibilities for economic growth, employment, and social justice. Furthermore, even during the heyday of laissez-faire policies in the last quarter of the nineteenth century, economic nationalism never disappeared as nations commonly used tariffs to discriminate against foreign business enterprise. Even on purely economic grounds, nations reject a laissez-faire policy that would allow concentrations of private economic power, institutionalized in multinational enterprises and international cartels, to determine the world's pattern of industry and trade and the distribution of the world's income.

As we have discovered, the actual responses of national governments to the political costs of the multinational enterprise range from comparatively mild restrictions on foreign ownership to confiscatory expropriations. By impairing the capacity of the multinational enterprise to function as an international transfer agent, these responses lower the contribution of the multinational enterprise to the world economy and, more often than not, to the host economy, regardless of their political justification. Given the national perspective and nationalistic attitudes of host governments, bilateral policies to minimize the political costs of the multinational enterprise are inevitably restrictive, as they are motivated by an intent to prevent, reduce, or eliminate foreign ownership and control. Bilateral accommodation by the nation-state, then, is a question of the degree of restriction on foreign ownership and control; the lower the degree of restriction, the higher the accommodation, but restriction is never entirely absent.

Will the multinational enterprise accommodate the political interests and nationalism of host countries by voluntarily abandoning ownership and control over its affiliates? In Chapter 21 we defined the multinational enterprise as a parent company that engages in foreign production through its own affiliates located in several different countries, exercises direct control over the policies of those affiliates, and strives to design and implement business strategies that transcend national boundaries. Hence, a general substitution of contractual service arrangements for the ownership and control of production affiliates would transform the multinational enterprise into an entirely different institution. Some observers, sensitive to attitudes in many developing countries, believe that the multinational enterprise will evolve in that direction in order to eliminate political conflicts with host nations.[62] But what is more probable is that the multinational enterprise will enter into contractual arrangements (minority joint ventures, service contracts, coproduction schemes) as a *second-best* strategy only in those countries that prevent a *first-best* strategy of ownership and control. We can expect to see, therefore, a proliferation of contractual arrangements in the 1970's as the multinational enterprise extends its activities into the Communist countries. And as we have already noted, the multinational enterprise is being forced to abandon direct investment for contractual arrangements in the exploitation of extractive resources in the developing countries. Furthermore, policies exemplified by the Andean Investment Code will compel the substitution of fade-out direct investment for traditional direct investment in at least some of the developing countries. Notwithstanding these constraints imposed in the East and the South, the multinational enterprise will in all likelihood continue to have the freedom to pursue a first-best strategy in the West, which remains its major arena of operations. The broad picture which emerges from this analysis, then, is the multinational enterprise that follows a first-best strategy of ownership and control in the industrial world and, at the same time, follows a second-best strategy of contractual arrangements in the Communist and developing worlds. This second-best strategy is second-best not only for the multinational enterprise but for the world economy as well. Lacking any firm control, the multinational enterprise will generally refrain from integrating operations in the Communist and developing countries with its logistical system in the industrial world. The resulting fragmentation of its operations will make the multinational enterprise a far less efficient institution as suboptimization in individual host countries replaces optimization across national boundaries.

To conclude, bilateral accommodation offers no promise of any general resolution of the political conflict between the multinational enterprise and host nations. Moreover, when individual nations force an accommodation in ownership and control by the multinational enterprise, they limit its economic efficiency to the detriment of both the host and world economies. Is there, then, any way to broaden the range of accommodation so as to reduce the political costs of the multinational enterprise as perceived by host

---

[62] See, for example, Peter F. Gabriel, "Adaptation: The Name of the MNC's Game," *The Columbia Journal of World Business* (November-December, 1972), pp. 7-14.

nations and, at the same time, preserve the economic efficiency of the multinational enterprise system?

MULTILATERAL ACCOMMODATION AT THE INTERNATIONAL LEVEL

The range of accommodation between the nation-state and the multinational enterprise would be enormously broadened by multilateral agreements and institutions that conferred both rights and responsibilities on the multinational enterprise vis-à-vis national governments. Indeed, only through international agreements among governments can disputes between multinational enterprises and host countries be transformed from political issues into legal issues to be resolved by impartial international tribunals in accordance with agreed principles of equity.

Today the multinational enterprise has economic power without legitimacy, while many nations have legitimacy without economic power. The multinational enterprise has no transnational legal identity; it is an aggregation of *national* companies. It is dependent on a convention that obligates host governments to extend to foreign enterprise the national treatment they accord to domestic enterprise. Functioning as it does in a legal vacuum, the multinational enterprise has no legal rights or legitimacy as a multinational system and, accordingly, it has no legal responsibilities toward the world community. George Ball proposes to fill that legal vacuum by an international treaty that would enable a parent company to be incorporated under an international companies law. This law would be administered by a supranational body composed of representatives from various countries which would exercise not only the ordinary domiciliary supervision but would also enforce antitrust laws and administer guarantees with regard to confiscatory expropriation.[63] Under this law, the parent company would trade its national legal identity for legal recognition in all countries. Although this proposal may strike readers as utopian, it is only fair to point out that the EEC is working on a European Companies Law along similar lines.

The multinational enterprise also operates in a policy vacuum at the international level. To regulate international trade, governments have created GATT; to regulate international monetary relations, they have established the IMF. But where is the international machinery to regulate and supervise direct foreign investment and the multinational enterprise? So far only a single, small step has been taken in that direction. In 1969, the International Center for the Settlement of Investment Disputes was set up under the auspices of the IBRD. Under the Convention ratified by the participating governments, the private investor is granted the right for the first time to

---

[63] George W. Ball, "Cosmocorp: The Importance of Being Stateless," *The Columbia Journal of World Business* (November-December, 1967), p. 29.

take direct international legal action against a national state. Once the private investor and the host country have consented to submit a dispute to the Center, they come under the conciliation and arbitration provisions of the Convention.

To fill the policy vacuum, a much broader approach has been suggested that would be directed toward the formation of a General Agreement for the International Corporation, along the lines of GATT.[64] Apart from a single master agreement, specific international treaties for cooperation, coordination, and harmonization in taxation, antitrust laws, property rights, investment insurance, securities registration, patents, rights of establishment, repatriation of earnings and capital, and other policies would go a long way toward depoliticizing issues between the multinational enterprise and host countries.

The international regulation of the multinational enterprise will not come quickly or all at once. But as governments come to recognize that uninational efforts to regulate the multinational enterprise are ineffective and carry a heavy national cost that is likely to prove unbearable in the long run, we can reasonably look forward to international agreements that will spell out the rights and responsibilities of the multinational enterprise in different areas of conduct. Multinational businessmen should welcome international regulation and they should work with governments to that end. The multinational enterprise can hope to gain legitimacy only through a multilateral accommodation of its own interests with national interests at the international and supranational levels.

In conclusion, nation-states can choose to restrict the multinational enterprise with unilateral policies at high economic costs, or they can choose to adapt to a new world economy of international production by entering into multilateral agreements that will regulate the multinational enterprise in the interest of all countries while preserving its economic viability. In turn, the multinational enterprise cannot escape its social role. As a key architect in the organization and direction of international trade and investment, the multinational enterprise will exert a profound influence on the welfare of nations in the decades ahead. What is demanded of the multinational enterprise is a positive affirmation of its social responsibility in all countries and a continuing search for ways to harness its unique capabilities to serve all the world's peoples.

SUMMARY

1. The multinational enterprise is perceived by policy makers in host countries as both an economic institution which creates benefits and costs to the local

---

[64] Paul M. Goldberg and Charles P. Kindleberger, "Toward a GATT for Investment: A Proposal for Supervision of the International Corporation," *Law and Policy in International Business*, Vol. II (1970), pp. 295-325.

economy and a quasi-political institution which threatens the power and even the sovereignty of the nation.

2. The fundamental economic effect of direct foreign investment (representing the sum total of many individual effects) is its contribution to the national income (net national product) of the host country over time. Closely related to this national income effect but deserving special treatment is the effect of direct foreign investment on the balance of payments of the host country over time.

3. The net benefit/cost ratio of direct foreign investment for the national income of the host economy is $\dfrac{(F + R^* + T) - N + L}{E}$. On both theoretical and empirical grounds, direct foreign investment generally offers net benefits to the host economy.

4. The net benefit/cost ratio of direct foreign investment for the balance of payments of the host economy is $\dfrac{K + X + S}{(R^{**} + F^*) + (M + M^*) + D}$. Ideally a host country should maintain balance of payments equilibrium by resorting to monetary, fiscal, and exchange rate policies, together with measures to speed up the reallocation of resources.

5. As is true of other forms of economic specialization and exchange, direct foreign investment is a "positive sum game" which benefits both players. Within this fundamental harmony of interests, however, there is likely to be a continuing conflict of interests as both the multinational enterprise and the host country strive to maximize their respective shares of the net economic benefits of foreign investment. The resolution of this conflict depends essentially on the current power positions of the two parties. An accommodation of their mutual economic interests is highly probable unless host government policy makers turn against the multinational enterprise for political reasons.

6. Although there is a fundamental harmony of *economic* interests between host countries and the multinational enterprise, there is also a fundamental conflict of *political* interests that poses a challenge to the national sovereignty of host countries. This political conflict may be treated in terms of three major issues: national interest, extraterritoriality, and nationalism.

7. The coexistence of economic benefits and political costs associated with direct foreign investment makes the attitudes and policies of host countries toward the multinational enterprise highly ambivalent and creates tensions that accompany any "love-hate" relationship. Unfortunately host countries are unable to resolve this ambivalence and relieve their tensions through an objective evaluation of economic benefits and political costs because there is no way to measure political costs and thereby establish trade-offs between the two.

8. Attempts to prevent, reduce, or eliminate *foreign ownership* constitute many policies and actions of host governments that are taken to minimize the political costs of direct foreign investment. Restrictions on foreign ownership include the exclusion of foreigners from key industries, requirements for

local participation in ownership, and prohibitions against acquisitions by foreign companies.

9. The expropriation of foreign-owned companies is the most dramatic action a host government can take to minimize the political costs of direct foreign investment. Since World War I, U.S. companies have experienced many expropriations of their foreign investments in both Communist and developing countries. Two recent cases are the seizure of the properties of the International Petroleum Company by the Peruvian government in 1968 and the seizure of the copper-mining subsidiaries of Anaconda Company and Kennecott Copper Corporation by the Chilean government in 1971. The U.S. Government insists on prompt, adequate, and effective compensation for U.S. investments expropriated by host governments. The U.S. Government has responded to a wave of expropriations that started in the late 1960's by cutting off aid and credits to the expropriating government when compensation is not offered in accordance with the international standard.

10. The Andean Investment Code is an important landmark in the evolution of foreign investment policies because of its novel "fade-out" provisions. For the first time, foreign investors will be required to transfer majority ownership to local investors according to a fixed timetable. It would appear that multinational enterprises will have to learn to adapt to host government policies that set time limits on ownership and control.

11. The Organization of Petroleum Exporting Countries (OPEC) has transformed the international petroleum industry by compelling the multinational oil companies to redistribute economic benefits in favor of its member countries and to transfer partial ownership in crude-production affiliates to the host governments. Whether this dramatic power reversal between host governments and the multinational enterprise will be matched in other extractive industries is a question for the future.

12. Bilateral accommodation offers no promise of any general resolution of the political conflict between the multinational enterprise and host nations. But the range of accommodation would be enormously broadened by multilateral agreements and institutions that conferred both rights and responsibilities on the multinational enterprise vis-à-vis national governments.

QUESTIONS AND APPLICATIONS

1. Why is the conventional concept of net value added inadequate to measure the contribution of a *new* direct foreign investment to the national product (income) of a host country?

2. Does every foreign-owned affiliate necessarily make a net contribution to the economy of the host country? Be prepared to explain your answer.

3. "Over the long run, the balance of payments effect of direct foreign investment cannot be distinguished from its national income effect." Explain the reasoning behind this statement.

4. What is the coincidence and conflict of economic interests between host countries and the multinational enterprise (direct foreign investment)?

5. Explain the dynamics of shifting perceptions of economic benefit/cost ratios over time.

6. Distinguish among the issues of national interest, extraterritoriality, and nationalism with respect to the political costs of direct foreign investment to the host country. Have any actual examples of these issues appeared recently in the press? If so, briefly explain.

7. Why are host countries ambivalent toward direct foreign investment and the multinational enterprise?

8. Undertake research to ascertain any restrictions on foreign ownership imposed by an industrial country of your choice (for example, France) and by a developing country of your choice (for example, Brazil).

9. Should the United States Government take *any* action with respect to host governments that expropriate the investments of U.S. companies? Why or why not?

10. Why was the OPEC so successful in its negotiations with the multinational oil companies in 1971 and 1972?

11. "A second-best strategy of contractual arrangements as substitutes for ownership and control is second-best not only for the multinational enterprise but for the world economy as well." Explain the reasoning behind this statement. Do you agree with it? Why or why not?

12. Write a short essay entitled "Prospects for the International Regulation of the Multinational Enterprise."

SELECTED READINGS

Behrman, Jack N. *National Interests and the Multinational Enterprise.* Englewood Cliffs, N. J.: Prentice-Hall, Inc., 1970.

Bernstein, Marvin D. (ed.). *Foreign Investment in Latin America.* New York: Alfred A. Knopf, 1966.

Blake, David H. (ed.). "The Multinational Corporation." *The Annals.* Vol. CDIII. Philadelphia: The American Academy of Political and Social Science, September, 1972.

Brash, Donald T. *American Investment in Australian Industry.* Cambridge: Harvard University Press, 1966.

Eells, Richard. *Global Corporations, The Emerging System of World Economic Power.* New York: Interbook, Inc., 1972.

Foreign Ownership and the Structure of Canadian Industry. Report of the Task Force on the Structure of Canadian Industry. Ottawa: Queen's Printer, 1968.

Gabriel, Peter P. *The International Transfer of Corporate Skills.* Boston: Division of Research, Harvard Business School, 1967.

Levitt, Kari. *Silent Surrender.* New York: St. Martin's Press, 1970.

Litvak, I. A., *et al. Dual Loyalty, Canadian-U.S. Business Arrangements.* Toronto: McGraw-Hill Company of Canada, Limited, 1971.

May, Herbert K. *The Effects of United States and Other Foreign Investment in Latin America.* New York: Council of the Americas, 1970.

Pisar, Samuel. *Coexistence and Commerce.* New York: McGraw-Hill Book Company, 1970.

Robinson, Richard D. *International Business Policy.* New York: Holt, Rinehart, and Winston, 1964.

United Nations. *Foreign Investment in Developing Countries.* New York: United Nations, 1968.

United Nations. *Panel on Foreign Investment in Developing Countries.* New York: United Nations, 1969.

INDEX

Customs Cooperative Council, 274
Customs nomenclature, 274
Customs union, 272; as related to the theory of the second-best, 322; consumption effects of, 392; creation of a, 379-383; defined, 378; dynamic effects of, 392-393; economies of scale as an effect of, 393; increases in enterprise size as an effect of, 393; intensified competition as an effect of, 393; liberalization of factor movements as an effect of, 393; market extension as an effect of, 392-393; product innovation as an effect of, 393; static effects of, 389-392; trade creation effects of, 390-391; trade diversion effects of, 390-391; welfare effects of, 391-392
Cyclical disequilibrium, 198-199
Cyclical unemployment, 312

D

Debit transactions, international, 182-184
Debt service burden of developing countries, 452
Defense-Essentiality Amendment, as an extension of the RTA Act of 1934, 353
Deficit, concepts of, 465-466
Deficit disequilibrium, balance of payments, 201-202
Demand, income elasticity of, defined, 420; internal, as the basis for manufactured exports and imports, 129-130; reciprocal, in determining equilibrium rate of exchange, 66-68
Demand ratios, dissimilar factor, 62-63
Destabilizing speculation and capital flight, 200
Developing countries, 7-8, 401, 429; and use of national planning, 329; as related to the stages of economic growth, 405-407; association agreements of, with EEC, 396-398; as treated by the Kennedy Round, 369, 371; bilateral portfolio flows to, 446-447; capital-absorption capacity of, 415; commodity agreements of, 430-434; compensatory financing of, 433-434; constraints on domestic investment faced by, 415-418; debt service burden of, 452; deterioration in terms of trade of, 422-424; direct investment in, 446; domestic savings gap of, 416; economic development through regional integration in, 436-443; economic situation of, 401-412; effect of synthetics on trade of, 420-421; export credits extended to, 446-447; export problems of, 418-424; exports of manufactures of, 434; expropriation in, 632-633; external assistance to, 444-452; foreign exchange gap of, 416-417; future MNE relations with, 646; identified, 402-405; import-substitution in, 424-426; inflation in, 424; international transactions of, 7-8; major commodity exports of, 432; multilateral portfolio flows to, 446-447; new trade policies and reforms advocated by, 429-435; obstacles to economic growth in, 407-410; preferential treatment of export manufactures of, 434-435; promotion of direct investment in, 583-586; relations of EEC with, 396-398; restrictions on foreign ownership of certain industries in, 629-630; short-run price instability of commodity exports of, 421-422; slow growth and instability of commodity exports of, 418-424; special GATT provisions to promote the trade of, 359; trade of industrial countries with, 27-29, 129, 131-132; trade policies of, 424-427; transfer of technological innovation to, 563-565; two decades of development in, 410-412
Development Assistance Committee, Organization for Economic Cooperation and Development, 444-448
DeVries, Barend A., 426
Direct investment, as a step toward MNE, 505-506; balance of payments effect of, 616-618; by non-U.S. MNE's, 541-544; challenge of, to national sovereignty of host countries, 623-628; classified by major countries, 541-542; defined, 189, 530-531; disagreement on present value of benefits and costs to host countries, 619-620; economic benefits and costs to host countries, 611-623; in developing countries, 446, 583-586; in the U.S., 530-531, 541-544; national income effect of, 612-616; net benefit/cost ratio of, 612-616; policies and actions of host governments to minimize political costs of, 628-643; reasons for, in manufacturing, 512-513; shifting percep-

tions of benefit/cost ratios of, 620-623; statistical overview of, 527; *see also* Multinational enterprise and U.S. direct investment
Disequilibrium system of trade, 307
Displaced-exports effect, 579
Diversification argument for protection, 318-319
Divestment, 639-640
Dollar Area, 326-327
Domestic absorption, 221
Domestic expenditure, as related to stable-rate system adjustment, 221-222
Domestic goods, 91
Domestic income multiplier, 219-220, 226-227
Domestic International Sales Corporation, 473
Domestic investment, constraints on, faced by developing countries, 415-418
Domestic savings gap, 416
Domestic specialization and interregional trade, 15-16
Double-column tariff schedule, 275-276
Double taxation, 586-587
Drawbacks, a tariff mitigation, 276
Dumping, 295-296
Dunning, John H., 615-616

E

Eastern Trading Area, 29
East-West business arrangements, 596-599; third-country joint ventures, 597; turnkey arrangements, 596-597
East-West trade, 29-32
Economic development, as a goal of foreign economic policy, 258; through regional integration, 436-443
Economic efficiency, as an objective of international trade, 304-305
Economic growth, capital formation as the basis of, 412-418; obstacles to, in developing countries, 407-410; stages of, 405-407
Economic integration, 128-129, 133-134; common market, 379, 383-387; complementarity agreements of, 439-440; customs union, 378-383; economic union, 379, 387-388; free trade area, 378; full free trade area, 378; industrial free trade area, 378; in Africa, 437; in Latin America, 436-442; in Western Europe, 377; of developing countries, 436-443; stages of, 378-379; theory of, 389-395
Economic opportunity, 566
Economic planning, instability and, 20
Economic policies, national, 10
Economic self-sufficiency, 14-15
Economics of location, 94
Economic union, building an, 387-388; defined, 379
Economic warfare, 258-259
Economic welfare, 257; as an objective of international trade, 304-305
Economies of scale, 96-100; as a dynamic effect of customs unions, 393; as induced by nonprice competition and mass consumption, 102; external, 98; internal, 98; role of, in decreasing costs, 98-100
Employment argument for protection, 311-313
Energy, common policies for, within the EEC, 386-387
Engel, Ernst, 420
Enterprise, free movement of, within the EEC, 383-384; multinational, *see* Multinational enterprise; state, 8
Enterprise size, increase in, a dynamic effect of customs unions, 393
Enterprise system, *see* Multinational enterprise
Entrepreneurial skills, as distinguished from administrative skills, 565; deliberate assumption of risk in, 103-104, 567; perception of economic opportunity in, 566; transfer of, in MNE, 565-567
Equalization-of-costs-of-production argument for protection, 308-309
Equilibrium rate of exchange, 77, 236-237
Equity of a tax system, 590
Escape clause, 310; as an extension of the RTA Act of 1934, 352-353; of the TEA of 1962, 365-366
Ethnocentric companies, 520
Eurobond market, 494, 575

Eurodollar market, 492-494, 575
European Coal and Steel Community, 377, 388-389
European Defense Community Treaty, 389
European Development Fund, 451
European Economic Community (EEC), 272, 377-378; and preferential treatment of manufactures of developing countries, 435; and the Kennedy Round, 367-371; as related to the theory of the second-best, 322; as related to the TEA of 1962, 364-365; association agreements with developing countries, 396-397; building a common market, 383-387; cascade system of taxation, 385-386; Commission of, 379; common agricultural policy in the 1970's, 383; common policies for transportation and energy, 386-387; Council of Ministers of, 379-380; Council Resolution for full economic union, 387-388; Court of Justice of, 380; creation of, 379-383; erosion of most-favored-nation principle, 363; European Parliament of, 380; external economic relations of, 395-398; free movement of labor, capital, and enterprise within, 383-384; free trade in agricultural products within, 380-383; free trade in industrial products within, 380; harmonization of indirect taxes within, 385-386; institutions of, 379-380; negotiations for common agricultural policy, 380-381; 1963 trade dispute with U.S., 362-363; objectives of, 378; plans for economic union, 387-389; preferential arrangements, 396-397; relations with developing countries, 397-398; relations with the European Free Trade Area, 396; relations with the U.S., 398; role of, in GATT, 364; rules governing competition within, 384-385; static and dynamic effects of, 393-395; structure of common agricultural policy, 381-382; tax frontiers within, 385; toward a political union, 388-389; treaty establishing, 379; turnover tax on sales, 385; use of border tax adjustments, 298-299; value-added system of taxation, 385-386
European Free Trade Association, 377-378; as related to the theory of the second-best, 322; relations with the EEC, 396
European Parliament of the EEC, 380
Exchange, forward, 173
Exchange control, 12, 167-169; and its effects, 325; as a constraint on capital-sourcing policies of MNE, 556-557; a synoptic view of contemporary, 340-342; defined, 325; effects of, 337-340; evasion of, 339-340; multiple-rate systems of, 335-337; objectives of, 327-330; origins of, 325-327; single-rate systems of, 330-335
Exchange Control Area, 326-327
Exchange control authority, defined, 331
Exchange depreciation, 234-247; as an influence on terms of trade, 246-247; competitive, and overvaluation, 237; deciding on the equilibrium rate, 236-237; effects of, 237-247; income and price effects of, 244-246; purchasing-power parity doctrine theory of, 235-236
Exchange Equalization Fund, 326
Exchange rate, see Rate of exchange
Exchange restriction, see Exchange control
Exchange settlement agreements, 338-339
Exchange speculation and capital flight, 171-173
Exchange Stabilization Fund, 475-476
Exchange subsidies, 337
Exchange taxes, 337
Excise tax, 298
Export Administration Act of 1969, 598
Export balance, fallacies of maintaining for its own sake, 38
Export Control Act of 1949, 598
Export controls, as used in commodity agreements, 430-431; GATT policy on, 358; liberalization of U.S., toward Communist countries, 598-599
Export credits extended to developing countries, 446-447
Export duties, 272; effects of, 288-289
Export Expansion Program, 473
Export-Import Bank, 473
Export-import contracts, multilateral, as used in commodity agreements, 430-431
Export problems of developing countries, 418-424
Export quotas, 291-292
Exports, capital, long- and short-term, 184-185, 191; commodity, of developing countries, 418-424; displacement

of, 122-123; financing of, 140-142; manufactured, as determined by internal demand, 129-130; measures to expand exports to correct U.S. balance of payments deficits, 473; measures to restrain U.S. private capital to correct U.S. deficits, 474-475; of industrial and developing areas, 29; of market economies, 26-27; preferential treatment of export manufactures of developing countries, 434-435; short-run price instability of commodity exports of developing countries, 421-422; specialization in, 35; underinvoicing of, 340
Exports and imports, influence of elasticity of demand of, 239-242; influence of elasticity of supply of, 242-243
Export stage of evolution toward MNE, 504-505
Expropriation, 631-637; as related to investment insurance, 585; defined, 631; retroactive, 634; U.S. policy toward, 636-637; universal, 632
External diseconomies, defined, 304
External economies, as an argument for infant-industry protection, 317; defined, 304
Extractive investors, as international business investors, 511-512
Extraterritorial jurisdiction, 592

F

Factor change, antitrade effects of, 113-115; consumption effects of, on trade, 115; neutral effects of, 113-114; pro-trade effects of, 113-115; supply effects of, on trade, 115
Factor demand ratios, dissimilar, 62-63
Factor endowments, capital, 111-112; commonalities in, 108; heterogeneity and change in, 107-115; human, 109-111; land, 107-109; natural resources, 107-109; rarities in, 108; theory of, see Comparative advantage; ubiquities in, 108; uniquities in, 109
Factor movements, as a complement of international trade, 128-129; as a substitute for international trade, 126-128; liberalization of, a dynamic effect of customs union, 393
Factor price ratios, dissimilar, 59-61
Factor prices, as equalized through factor mobility and international trade, 126
Factor productivity, as affected by technological innovation, 116-117
Factor reversal, 77, 119
Factors of production, heterogeneity and change in, 107-115; international mobility of, 12-13, 123-129; labor-intensive, 61; land-intensive, 61; unemployed, as an influence on comparative advantage, 104; see also Factor endowments
Factor supply ratios, dissimilar, 61-62
Federal Reserve System, 475-476
Financial capital, 112
Financial flow effects of U.S. direct investment on U.S. balance of payments, 578-579
Financial transactions, 186
Financial transfer of capital, 576
First Development Decade, United Nations, 410-412
Floating-rate systems, 233
Fluctuating exchange rates, 497; argument for, 247-249
Fluctuating-rate market rates, 336
Fluctuating-rate system, 204, 233-234; argument for, 247-249
Food Aid Convention, 432
Fordney-McCumber Act, 348
Foreign aid, defined, 445
Foreign aid policy, defined, 261
Foreign Assistance Act of 1969, 583; Hickenlooper Amendment to, 636
Foreign Credit Insurance Association, 473
Foreign economic policy, as an influence on private interests, 255-256; autarky as a goal of, 256; balance of payments equilibrium as a goal of, 258; balance of payments policy area of, 261-262; commercial policy area of, 260; contemporary issues of, 269; defined, 254-255; diversity and conflict of goals of, 262-265; economic development as a goal of, 258; economic warfare as a goal of, 258-259; economic welfare as a goal of, 257; foreign aid policy area of, 261; full employment as a goal of, 257; goals

London financial center, 150
Long-term contract arrangements, 505
Long-term financial transactions, 186
Losses, entrepreneurial, as a result of the deliberate assumption of risk, 103-104; windfall, 103
Low-wage argument for protection, 309-310

M

Macroscopic perspective of international economic relations, 8-9
Management, mobility of, 125
Mandatory investment controls, 475
Manufacturing investors, reasons for investment abroad, 512-513
Marginal productivity, principle of diminishing, 71-72, 79
Marginal propensity to consume, 219
Marginal propensity to import, 219
Marginal propensity to save, 219
Marginal rate of substitution in consumption, 79
Marginal rate of substitution in production, 75
Marginal rate of substitution in trade, 75
Market demand, as the major reason why manufacturers invest abroad, 512-513
Market economies, and use of national planning, 329; exports of, 26-27; international trade of, 24, 27-30; principal trading countries of, 25-27; trade of, with centrally planned economies, 30; trade of, with industrial and nonindustrial areas, 27-29
Market extension, as a dynamic effect of customs unions, 392-393
Marketing, integration of, in MNE, 550-552
Marketing costs, as an inhibition of trade between industrial and nonindustrial countries, 131-132
Marketing theory of trade, 129-132
Market separations, 131-132
Market transactions, 7
Marshall-Lerner condition, 244
Merchandise and services transactions, 184
Mexico, expropriation in, 632-633; restrictions on foreign ownership of certain industries in, 629-631
Mint parity, 164-165
Mixed enterprise, as defined in Andean Investment Code, 638
Mixing quotas, 299
Mixing rates of exchange control, 336
Mobility, of capital, 125-126; of factors of production, 123-129; of labor, 124-125; of land factors, 124; of management, 125
Monetary effects, of international payments, illustrated, 147-149
Monetary gold transactions, 185
Money incomes, redistribution of, as an effect of exchange control, 339
Monopolistic competition, 96
Monopoly, 96; and its use of nonprice competition, 101-103; EEC policy toward, 384-385; net effect of, on international trade, 100-101; prices, 97; profits, 96-97
Monopsony, 96
Most-favored-nation principle, as applied in the RTA Act, 350; defined, 355; treatment of foreigners, 259
Multilateral export-import contracts, as used in commodity agreements, 430-431
Multilateral pattern of international trade, 33-36
Multilateral portfolio flows to developing countries, 446-447
Multilateral quota, 290
Multilateral settlement of trade balances, 35
Multinational enterprise (MNE), 8-9, 507-509, 517-524; Andean Investment Code, 637-640; and national sovereignty, 611; as an international transfer agent, 547; bilateral accommodations with host countries, 644-647; challenge of, to the national sovereignty of host countries, 623-628; classified by industry, 521-523; coincidence and conflict of interests of, and host country, 618-619; constraints on capital-sourcing policies of, 556-558; contractual arrangements of, with host countries, 646; contribution of, to the world economy, 567-568; deliberate assumption of risk by, 567; direct investment by non-U.S. MNE's, 541-544; direct investment in the U.S. by non-U.S. MNE's, 541-544; direct investment of, classified by major countries, 514-542; effect of, on U.S. balance of payments, 536-541, 578-583; evolution of a, 504-509; experience of, under investment controls, 575-576; exports of U.S. parent companies, 538-539; expropriation effects on, 631-637; extractive investors, 511-512; history of U.S. business expansion abroad, 509-517; integration of marketing as a part of, 550-552; integration of production as a part of, 552-553; interest of, in international trade, 17-18; internal and external constraints on, 549; internationalization of innovation of, with host countries, 647-648; multilateral accommodations of, with host countries, 647-648; nature and scope of, 503; new foreign activities of, by industry, 516-517; Organization of Petroleum Exporting Countries, 640-643; ownership patterns of, 514-516; patterns of expansion of, 514-517; perception of economic opportunity by, 566; plant and equipment expenditures by foreign affiliates of U.S. companies, 534-536; policies and actions of host governments to minimize political costs of, 628-643; proposals for accommodation between nation-state and, 643-648; proposed international regulation of, 647-648; recoupment period controversy of, 581-583; restrictions by host countries of, on ownership of certain industries, 629-631; sales of U.S. manufacturing and mining affiliates, 540-541; service investors, 514; size of, 517; sources of capital financing of, 554-556; system of, 547-550; transfers of capital in, 553-559; transfers of entrepreneurial skills in, 565-567; transfer of innovation to developing countries by, 563-565; transfers of product in, 550-553; transfers of technology in, 559-565; why companies go abroad, 511-514; why manufacturers invest abroad, 512-513; see also Direct investment and U.S. policy toward MNE
Multinational enterprise system, see Multinational enterprise
Multinational strategy, 508, 549
Multiple-rate systems of exchange control, 335-337; exchange taxes and subsidies, 337; fluctuating-rate market rates, 336; mixing rates, 336; penalty rates, 336; preferential rates, 336
Multiple tax jurisdictions, 586-587; overlapping jurisdictions, 586-587; underlapping jurisdictions, 586-587

N

National defense argument against international trade, 19-20
National economic policies, 10
National enterprise, as defined in Andean Investment Code, 638
National income, determination of, in a stable-rate system, 214-218
National income and foreign trade, equation relating, in a stable-rate system, 214; relationships between, in a stable-rate system, 212-221
National income effect of direct investment, 612-616
Nationalism, 5-7; as a threat to the MNE, 626-628
Nationalization, defined, 631
National output, as related to investment, 413-415
National planning, as employed by Communist countries, 329; facilitation of, as an objective of exchange control, 329
National schedule of tariff reductions, 439
National security argument for protection, 314-315
National sovereignty, 4, 9; challenge of MNE to the national sovereignty of host countries, 611, 623-628; proposals for accommodation between nation-state and MNE, 643-648
National tax jurisdiction, 587
National treatment of foreigners, 259
Nation-state, 5-6
Natural resources, as a factor endowment, 107-109
Negotiated bilateral quota, 290

Net barter terms of trade, 422-423
Net benefit/cost ratio of direct investment, 612-616
Net creditor position of the U.S., 531
Net errors and omissions account of IMF Standard Presentation, 193-194
Net liquidity balance in U.S. balance of payments, 467, 469-470
Neutrality of a tax system, 590
New products, as affected by technological innovation, 116-123
New York Agreement, 642-643
New York financial center, 143-144, 152
Nonindustrial countries, *see* Developing countries
Nonliquid financial transactions, 186
Nonprice competition, 96; as used by monopolies, 101-103; as used by oligopolies, 100-103; effect of, on trade, 101-103; style factors of, 101-102
Nontariff trade barriers, 289-300, 369-371; and the Kennedy Round, 367-371; antidumping regulations, 295-297; customs classification and valuation, 295; economic effects of quotas, 292-294; export quotas, 291-292; GATT policy on quantitative restrictions, 361-362; import quotas, 289-291; linked-usage regulations, 299; local-content regulations, 299-300; mixing quotas, 299; procurement policies, 299; subsidies, 297-298; taxes, 298-299; technical and health regulations, 299; within the EEC, 380

O

Official reserves account of IMF Standard Presentation, 193
Official reserves transactions balance in U.S. balance of payments, 467-470
Office of Direct Foreign Investments, 574-575
Oligopoly, 96; and its use of nonprice competition, 100-103; net effect of, on international trade, 100-101; prices, 97
Opportunity cost, 57-58; as influenced by transportation costs, 94-95; constant, in relation to production possibilities, 74-77; increasing, in relation to production possibilities, 77-82
Optimum tariff, 320-321
Organization for Economic Cooperation and Development (OECD), Development Assistance Committee, 444-448
Organization for European Economic Cooperation (OEEC), 377
Organization of Petroleum Exporting Countries (OPEC), 640-643; negotiations over distribution of economic benefits, 640-642; negotiations over ownership, 642-643; New York Agreement, 642-643; Tehran negotiations, 641; Tripoli negotiations, 641-642
Overinvoicing of imports, 340
Overlapping tax jurisdictions, 586-587
Overseas Private Investment Corporation (OPIC), 583-585
Overvaluation of exchange, 237

P

Payment at a distance, as a function of the foreign exchange market, 143
Penalty rates of exchange, 336
Per capita income, as an influence on demand, 130-131
Peril point, 310; as an extension of the RTA Act of 1934, 351-353
Perlmutter, Howard V., 520
Peru, expropriation in, 627, 633-634
Polycentric companies, 520
Population explosion, as an obstacle to economic development in developing countries, 409-410
Portfolio investment, as preferred by foreign investors in the U.S., 531; defined, 189, 530
Power, as the essence of international political relations, 5
Prebisch, Raul, 423-424, 426, 429
Predatory dumping, 314

Preferential arrangements of the EEC, 396-397; criticism of, 397
Preferential rates of exchange, 336
Preferential treatment agreements, 434-435
Prevention-of-injury argument for protection, 310
Price adjustment, as affected by price elasticities, 229-230; obstacles to, 230-231; role of, in balance of payments adjustment in a stable-rate system, 227-231
Price effect of tariffs, 284
Price elasticity of demand, 239
Price ratios, dissimilar factor, 59-61
Prices, absolute international differences in, as a cause for international trade, 55-56; determination of, in a closed economy, 63-64; determination of, in an open economy, 64-65; elasticities of, 229-230; monopoly, 97; mutual interdependence theory of, 64; oligopoly, 97
Price-specie flow mechanism, 210-212
Principal-supplier concept, defined, 355
Principal trading countries, 25-27
Principle of diminishing marginal productivity, 71-72, 79
Processing tax, 298
Procurement policies of governments, as a nontariff trade barrier, 299
Product, transfers of, in MNE, 550-553
Product innovation, a dynamic effect of customs unions, 393
Production, integration of, in MNE, 552-553; vertical integration in, 552-553
Production functions, 60; defined, 117; dissimilar, as affected by technological innovation, 116-120
Production possibilities, and indifference curves, as related to comparative advantage, 73-84; constant opportunity costs, 74-77; curve, 74-79; identical, with dissimilar tastes, 82-84; increasing opportunity costs, 77-82
Productivity, principle of diminishing marginal, 71-72, 79
Product life cycle, 121-122, 566
Profits, entrepreneurial, as a reward for the deliberate assumption of risk, 103-104; monopoly, 96-97; windfall, 103
Protection function of tariffs, 279-280, 284
Protectionism, 20, 257, 263-264; after World War I, 348; arguments for, 303, 306-322; as employed by Latin American countries, 425-426; Burke-Hartke Bill, 601-605; fallacious arguments for, 307-310; fallacy of composition of arguments for, 307; Hawley-Smoot Act of 1930, 349; opposition of U.S. labor to MNE, 599-601; persistence of, 322-323; qualified arguments for, 314-319; questionable arguments for, 311-314; resurgence of, 371-373; sophisticated arguments for, 319-322; summary of arguments for, 306-307
Provision of credit, as a function of the foreign exchange market, 142-143
Purchasing power, transfer of, 209-210
Purchasing-power parity doctrine, 235-236

Q

Quantitative restrictions, *see* Nontariff trade barriers
Quotas, as compared with tariffs, 294; economic effects of, 292-294; effects of import, on the balance of payments, 293-294; export, 291-292; import, 289-291, 334; mixing, 299; trade and protection effects of, 292-293

R

Random and seasonal disequilibrium, 198
Rarities, as factor endowments, 108
Rate of exchange, 155-157; active stabilization of, by monetary authorities, 165-167; adjustment of, 497-498; argument for flexible, 247-249; base, 157; competitive depreciation and overvaluation of, 237; controlled, 167-169; defined, 11; depreciation of, 234-247; determination of, 65-68, 155, 160-162; domestic barter, 79-82; equilibrium, 66-68, 77, 236-237; fluctuating, 497; forward, 155, 173-178; forward, determination of, through interest arbitrage, 174-177; forward, speculation in, 177-178; freely fluctuating, 157-162; international barter, 75-77;

passive stabilization of, through the gold standard, 163-165; penalty, 336; role of, in distribution of gains from trade, 65-68; speculation in, and capital flight, 171-173; spot, 155-157; stable, 162-167; *see also* Stabilization of exchange rates

Real capital, 112

Real transactions, 186

Real transfer of capital, 576

Reciprocal demand, 75-77; role of, in determining exports and imports, 68-70

Reciprocal Trade Agreements (RTA) Act of 1934, 350-353; authority to lower or raise duties as a postwar extension of, 351; defense-essentiality amendment, 353; escape clause, 352-353; peril point, 351-353; postwar extensions of, 351-353; unconditional most-favored-nation clause, 350

Reciprocal Trade Agreements Program, 349-355; deterioration of, 354-355; impact of, 354

Recoupment period controversy, 581-583

Regional development banks, 451

Regional integration, *see* Economic integration

Residence, concept of, 182

Retroactive expropriation, 634

Revenue Act of 1962, 588-589

Risk, as a key factor in international trade, 103-104; economic and political, 567

Road taxes, 298

Rostow, W. W., 405-407

S

Savings leakage, 225

Seasonal and random disequilibrium, 198

Second Development Decade, United Nations, 447

Secular disequilibrium, 200

Servan-Schreiber, J. J., 616

Service investors, as international business investors, 514

Sherman Act, 591

Short-run adjustment in a stable-rate system, 207-210

Short-term financial transactions, 186

Sight bill of exchange, 140

Single-column tariff schedule, 275

Single-rate system of exchange control, 330-335; allocation of foreign exchange receipts in, 332-334; control of non-resident accounts in, 335; import quotas and licenses in, 334; surrender of foreign exchange receipts in, 331-332

Smithsonian Agreement, 482-485

Soviet Union, expropriation in, 632

Special Drawing Rights, 460, 488-489; proposed use in international reform, 496

Specialty, defined, 121

Specific duties, 273

Speculation, 171-172; as a cause of the international monetary crisis of 1971, 492; destabilizing, and capital flight, 200; destabilizing and stabilizing, 172

Speculative capital movements, destabilizing, 196-197

Spot rate of exchange, 155-157

Stabilization of exchange rates, 162-167; active, by monetary authorities, 163-165; arguments for, 162-163; passive, through the gold standard, 163-165; techniques of, 163-167

Stable-rate system adjustment to balance of payments disequilibrium, 204, 207; as related to domestic expenditure, 221-222; classical theory of, 210-212; compensatory financing in, 207-208; obstacles to price adjustment in, 230-231; price elasticities in, 229-230; price-specie flow mechanism in, 210-212; role of price adjustment in, 227-231; short-run, 207-210; short-term capital flows in, 208-209; transfer of purchasing power in, 209-210; via foreign trade multiplier, 221-227

Standard International Trade Classification, 274

Standard product, defined, 121

Standby agreements, IMF, 459-560

State enterprises, 8

State trading, 96; as employed by Communist countries, 96

Sterling Area, 326-327

Structural disequilibrium, 199-200

Structural unemployment, 312

Style factors of nonprice competition, 101-102

Subsidiary, defined, 531

Subsidies, 297-298; exchange, 337

Supply effects, of factor change on trade, 115

Supply ratios, dissimilar factor, 61-62

Suppressed disequilibrium, 203

Surplus, concepts of, 465-466; in U.S. balance of payments, 464-468

Surplus disequilibrium, 201-202

Swap agreements, 476; as used by MNE, 557

Swapping, in forward exchange, 173

Swing credits, 338

Synthetics, effects of, on trade of developing countries, 420-421

T

Target price of agricultural products in the EEC, 382

Tariff quota, 290-291

Tariffs, ad valorem, specific, and compound duties, 273; and nontariff trade barriers, 271; and tariff systems, 271-277; as compared with quotas, 294; balance of payments function of, 280-281; bargaining activities of GATT in, 360-361; classification of products, 273-274; common schedule of reductions, 439; customs area, 271-272; disparities in, as treated by the Kennedy Round, 368-371; economic effects of, 281-289; functions of, 278-281; GATT policy on, 357-358; Kennedy Round, 367-371; making of, 278; mitigation of, 276-277; national schedule of reductions, 439; optimum, 320-321; protection function of, 279-280; revenue function of, 279, 284; TEA of 1962, 364-367; transit, export, and import duties, 272-273; variable import levy on agricultural products in the EEC, 382; *see also* U.S. tariff policy

Tariff systems, double-column tariff schedule, 275-276; measurement of, 285-288; single-column tariff schedule, 275; triple-column tariff schedule, 276

Taussig, Frank W., 211-212

Tax avoidance, 587

Tax deferral, 588-591

Taxes, 298-299; as a constraint on capital sourcing policies of MNE, 557; avoidance of, 587; border tax adjustments, 298-299; cascade system of taxation within the EEC, 385-386; domestic direct, 298; domestic indirect, 298; double taxation, 586-587; equity, 590; exchange, 337; excise, 298; harmonization of, within the EEC, 385-386; indirect, 385-386; multiple tax jurisdictions, 586-587; national tax jurisdiction, 587; neutrality, 590; processing, 298; road, 298; territorial tax jurisdiction, 587; turnover tax on sales within the EEC, 385; U.S. taxation of foreign-source income, 587-591; U.S. tax policy toward MNE, 586-591; value-added system of taxation within the EEC, 385-386

Tax frontiers, within the EEC, 385

Tax havens, 588-589

Technical and health regulations as a nontariff trade barrier, 299

Technical coefficients of production, 60-61

Technological innovation, 96; defined, 116, 560; effects of, 116-123; international transfer of, 560-563; role of, in decreasing costs, 98; transfer of, to developing countries, 563-565

Technology, as an aid to capital growth, 112; defined, 116, 560; gaps, 118-123; transfers of, in MNE, 559-565

Terms of trade, as affected by exchange depreciation, 246-247; commodity, 67, 423; deterioration in, of developing countries, 422-424; net barter, 422-423

Terms-of-trade argument for protection, 319-321

Territorial tax jurisdiction, 587

Theory of economic policy, 265-269; policy instruments and targets, 266-269

Theory of the second-best, 321-322; as related to customs unions effects on world trade, 391-392

Theory of trade, *see* Comparative Advantage, theory of 30-70 percent rule, 589

Threshold price, of agricultural products, in the EEC, 382

Tied grants and loans, 576-577; in U.S. foreign aid, 474
Time bill of exchange, 140
Trade acceptance, a, 140
Trade Act of 1970, proposed, 372-373
Trade balance, *see* Balance of payments
Trade creation, a static effect of customs unions, 390-391
Trade diversion, a static effect of customs unions, 390-391
Trade Expansion Act (TEA) of 1962, 355, 364-367; adjustment assistance, 366-367; adjustment assistance to firms, 366; adjustment assistance to workers, 366-367; and the Kennedy Round, 364-371; escape clause, 365-366; negotiating authority of the President, 365
Transfer, a, 138-139
Transfer costs, *see* Transportation costs
Transideological enterprise, 599
Transit duties, 272
Transportation, common policies for, within the EEC, 386-387
Transportation costs, and other transfer costs, 87-95; effects of, on international trade, 88-92; effects of, on location of industry, 92-95; rate discrimination in, 89-91; third country discrimination in, 90-91; weight-gaining products and, 93-94; weight-losing products and, 92-93
Treaty of Managua, 436-438
Treaty of Montevideo, 438-439
Triffin Plan, 496
Trilateral arbitrage, 170-171
Triple-column tariff schedule, 276
Turnkey arrangements, 596-597
Turnover tax on sales, within the EEC, 385
Two-point arbitrage, 170
Two-tier gold arrangement, 480

U

Ubiquities, as factor endowments, 108
Uncertainty, as a market imperfection of international trade, 103
Unconditional most-favored-nation clause of the RTA Act, 350
Underinvoicing of exports, 340
Underlapping tax jurisdictions, 586-587
Unemployment, and comparative advantage, 104; cyclical, 312; structural, 312
Unilateral quota, 289
Unilateral transfers, 185
Unilateral transfers account of IMF Standard Presentation, 190-191
Uniquities, as factor endowments, 109
United Nations, Conference on Trade and Development (UNCTAD), 369, 429-430; Development Program, 451; First Development Decade, 410-412; Second Development Decade, 429-430, 447
U.S. antidumping rules, 296
U.S. antipollution standards, as a restriction on imports, 300
U.S. antitrust policy, and the MNE, 591-595; compared with that of EEC, 384-385; extraterritorial jurisdiction, 592; guidelines of, 592-595; issues of, 595
U.S. balance of payments, 38; as affected by U.S. direct investment, 536-541, 578-583; basic balance, 465-466, 468-469; controls on direct investment, 574-583; IMF Standard Presentation, 187; net liquidity balance, 467, 469-470; official reserves transactions balance, 467-470; surplus and deficit in, 464-468; theory of balance of payments adjustment to exports of investment capital, 576-578
U.S. balance of payments deficits, 38, 47-50, 464-468; constraints imposed on U.S. payments policy, 476-477; corrective measures taken by U.S. monetary authorities, 475-476; dependence of reserve formation on, in the Bretton Woods system, 486-488; financing of, 468-472; interest equalization tax, 474-475; mandatory investment controls, 475; measures taken to correct, 472-477; measures taken to expand exports, 473; measures taken to reduce foreign aid, 473-474; measures taken to restrain private capital exports, 474-475; outlook for correction of, 49-50

U.S.—Canadian Automotive Products Trade Act of 1965, 39-40, 47, 540
U.S. commercial policy, 345; contemporary, 373-374
U.S. dependence on international trade, 43-47
U.S. direct investment, 529-536; as affected by the Burke-Hartke Bill, 603-605; balance of payments controls on, 574-583; by area, 532-533; by industry, 533-534; effect of, on U.S. balance of payments, 536-541, 578-583; expansion of, 509-517; experience under investment controls, 575-576; exports of U.S. parent companies, 538-539; international position of, 529-531; net creditor position of, 531; outflow and income receipts, 537; plant and equipment expenditures by foreign affiliates of U.S. companies, 534-536; rate of return on, 536; recoupment period controversy, 581-583; sales of U.S. manufacturing and mining affiliates, 540-541; theory of balance of payments adjustment to exports of investment capital, 576-578; traditional policy toward, 572-574; *see also* U.S. trade
U.S. dollar, 455; central reserve role of, 462-464; *see also* Bretton Woods system, International monetary reform, *and* Smithsonian Agreement
U.S. foreign policy, basic principles of, 346; foreign aid, 447-449, 473-474; liberalization of trade with Communist countries, 598-599; role of, in GATT, 364; toward expropriation, 636-637
U.S. labor, opposition of, to MNE, 599-601
U.S. policy toward MNE, 583-599; Agency for International Development, 583; antitrust policy, 591-595; Burke-Hartke Bill, 601-605; domestic attacks on MNE, 599-605; liberalization of trade with Communist countries, 598-599; multilateral investment insurance, 585-586; need for a comprehensive policy, 605-607; opposition of labor to MNE, 599-601; OPIC, 583-585; promotion of direct investment in developing countries, 583-586; strategic export controls on trade and investment, 596-599; taxes, 586-591
U.S. standard of living, basis of, 309-310
U.S. tariff policy, effects of World War I upon, 348; evolution of, before 1934, 346-349; U.S. Tariff Act of 1816, 347-348; U.S. Tariff Act of 1930, 309; U.S. Tariff Act of 1922, 309; U.S. Tariff Act of 1789, 347; U.S. Tariff Commission, 351
U.S. trade, 36-50; composition of, 39-42; composition of exports and imports by end-use categories, 39-40; direct foreign investment in the U.S., 541-544; direction of, 42-43; distribution of exports and imports by geographical areas, 42-43; exports of U.S. parent companies, 538-539; Kennedy Round, 367-371; leading exports and imports, 41-42; levels of technology, 48-49; 1963 dispute with EEC, 362-363; principal exports and imports of, 44-46; relations with EEC, 398; role of technological innovation in, 121-122; share of, in world exports of manufactures, 48; TEA of 1962, 364-367; transportation rate discrimination against exports, 89-91; U.S. dependence on, 43-47; value and volume of, 37-38; with Communist countries, 31-32; *see also* U.S. direct investment
U.S. trade balance, *see* U.S. balance of payments
Unrequited transfers account of IMF Standard Presentation, 190-191

V

Value-added system of taxation, within the EEC, 385-386
Variable import levy, on agricultural products in the EEC, 382
Variable-rate system adjustment to disequilibrium, 233-237; adjustable-peg system, 233-235; argument for, 247-249; competitive depreciation and overvaluation, 237; deciding on equilibrium rate, 236-237; exchange depreciation (devaluation), 234-247; floating-rate systems, 233; fluctuating-rate system, 233-234; purchasing-power parity doctrine, 235-236; types of, 233
Vernon, Raymond, 121-122, 519
Vertical integration in production, 552-553
Voluntary Credit Restraint Program, 574
Voluntary export quota, 290

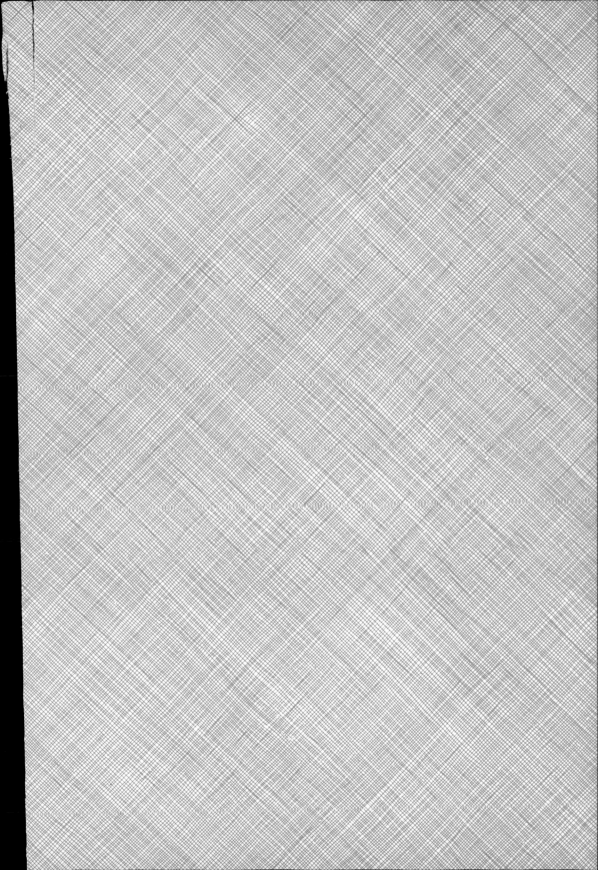